MW01054705

The Landscape Lighting Book

Second Edition

The Landscape Lighting Book

Second Edition

Janet Lennox Moyer, I.A.L.D.

JOHN WILEY & SONS, INC.

This book is printed on acid-free paper. ♾

Published by John Wiley & Sons, Inc., Hoboken, New Jersey
Published simultaneously in Canada

For general information on our other products and services or for technical support, please contact our Customer Care Department within the United States at (800) 762-2974, outside the United States at (317) 572-3993 or fax (317) 572-4002.

Wiley also publishes its books in a variety of electronic formats. Some content that appears in print may not be available in electronic books.

Library of Congress Cataloging-in-Publication Data:

Moyer, Janet Lennox, 1954–
The landscape lighting book / /Janet Lennox Moyer.—2nd ed.
p. cm.
Includes bibliographical references and index.
ISBN 0-471-45136-3 (cloth : alk. paper)
1. Garden lighting. 2. Landscape architecture. I. Title.

SB473.4.M69 2003
621.32′29—dc22

2004059335

Printed in the United States of America

10 9 8 7 6 5 4

This book is dedicated to
Michael Stewart Hooker,
the man with whom I shared my
passions about life and lighting.
Michael's genius sparked and guided
the giant leap forward that is
this second edition. I love him always.

And to
Fran Kellogg Smith,
who has been a guiding star for me
throughout my career.

2004 Preface

The overall intention expressed in the original preface is timeless and remains valid for this revision. Whether centuries ago, a decade, or just yesterday, the moments we take to surround ourselves with a garden or landscape provides us with transcendent experiences. The ability to extend a landscape's magic into the night offers us more beauty, mystery, serenity, and space. Light makes this extension possible.

In the ten years since producing the initial edition of this book, technology and computerization have transformed the way we document lighting projects. At the time of the first edition, hand drawings served as the predominant documentation format. Today, practically all representational information—conceptual drawings through record documents and maintenance procedures—is produced using computers.

This allows the transferral of a great deal more information, the ability to track unending changes on projects, and the opportunity for thorough, continually up-to-date project detail. Numerous examples of drawing and specification techniques and format are discussed and exhibited in the completely revised Chapter 4, "The Design Process—Documenting and Installing Landscape Lighting"; the new Chapter 5, "Follow-up Work—Record Documents and Project Maintenance"; and the 29 pages of the new Documents Appendix. All this new information will help designers and installers better create, implement, and maintain landscape lighting systems.

To help designers visually explain lighting possibilities for their clients, I have completely replaced the color plates (now expanded by eight pages) with new imagery. I have added numerous photograph and drawing examples throughout the book.

Finally, the concept of "garden evolution" has been added in a new chapter. This explains the impact of lighting on all the changes that occur to individual plants and the overall garden throughout the seasons of one year and over the years that gardens mature, along with the penchant of all gardeners to keep developing their landscapes. My last seven years in New York have allowed my students and me to study these changes and become enamored with the incredible nature of winter lighting.

JANET LENNOX MOYER

Brunswick, New York
June 2004

Preface

Landscape lighting offers an incredible expansion of the enjoyment of both residential and commercial properties. It makes outdoor spaces usable at night and adds a magical view into the landscape from interior spaces. However, to produce effective lighting requires skill and thorough planning. After practicing landscape lighting for many years and finding no accessible guidelines to use in learning the problems and process of landscape lighting, I realized that sharing my knowledge in the form of a book would help the lighting industry, including designers of all kinds—landscape architects, architects, interior designers, and lighting designers—as well as contractors and property owners.

Any design project starts by analyzing the needs of a project, so this book starts with a discussion of how to evaluate a project and by familiarizing the reader with both the way people see light and how we, as designers, can introduce light in an organized fashion to create or sculpt a night scene from a dark landscape. The first part of the book ends by examining the process of designing and building a lighting system.

The second part of the book presents enough technical information to allow inexperienced designers, as well as designers familiar with interior lighting, to approach designing a landscape lighting system. Designers need to understand how light sources work and which ones to choose, the important aspects of fixtures and what will allow them to function and last in the harsh outdoor environment, the types of available controls and how to approach planning a control system, and the basics of the wiring system that feeds the fixtures and lamps.

The last two parts of the book examine specific design issues. Part III presents the needs of the three basic types of applications: residential spaces, public spaces, and atriums. Part IV focuses on elements of design that will make up the parts of a landscape: plants, sculptures and structures, paths and stairs, buildings or facades, and water features. Knowing the characteristics and special considerations of these applications and elements helps designers to organize their design concepts and develop a cohesive lighting design.

Some lighting books provide information on lighting basically from a technical viewpoint. I have tried to balance the importance of design and technical information in this book. There are other books that delve more deeply into how light is produced, the nuances of light sources, the chemistry of corrosion and materials or finishes, and lighting calculations. For people who want more information after reading this book, the bibliography at the end of the book lists sources of further information.

Light has the ability to transform a space, creating emotional responses or simply making an environment comfortable. While I love what light does throughout the day and inside buildings at night, the effect that it has on a landscape is special. For me, it is like a gift of additional time to enjoy our surroundings. I hope this book allows you, too, to benefit from this gift.

JANET LENNOX MOYER

Berkeley, California
May 1992

Acknowledgments

This revision unfolded during a difficult time, one in which I suffered the loss of my closest friend, true love, and most potent collaborator, Michael Stewart Hooker. Friends and colleagues supported the effort with more love than imaginable. Dr. David Brearey continued his support from the first edition and cheered me on during many difficult occasions. Naomi Miller and Tom Williams continually fed me physically and spiritually. Ken Rice followed me to the East Coast and acquiesced to photographing in rain and snow! Both Dan Dyer and Kevin Simonson also came out night after night—rain or snow—to photograph Lighting Research Center students mock-ups.

Numerous Rensselaer Polytechnic Institute LRC master's candidates and architecture students, enrolled in my design courses, spent hours setting up mock-ups and then coming back to learn about photographing their efforts. Thanks to each one: C. Brooke Carter, David Cyr, Peping Dee, Richard DePalma, Dan Dyer, Brain Fuller, Francisco Garza, Sumi Han, Lara Jacobson, Carole Lindstrom, Michael Meyer, Kelly Miller, Jason Neches, Rohini Pendyala, Jamie Perry, Eve Quelleman, Insiya Shakir, Javier Ten, John Tokarczyk, Allan Tweed, and Kami Wilwol. The fruits of their efforts add to the breadth of good design illustrated in this book.

Thea Chassin, Naomi Miller, and Tom Williams offered images of their work to illustrate how far we have come in these past ten years to create beautiful night scenes. I appreciate all my clients who allowed me to photograph their landscapes and support my efforts to advance this design field.

There are always special people behind the scenes who make a significant contribution to a task this large. I would like to offer special thanks to Patricia Rizzo and Chris Forget, who attempted to keep some semblance of normalcy and sanity in our office during this arduous task; to Richard DePalma, Dan Dyer, Peping Dee, John Tokarczyk, and Insiya Shakir, who helped organize and prepare many initial illustrations; to my always supportive sister, Mary Lennox, and my wonderful parents, Betty and Dick Lennox; to my patient editor, Margaret Cummins, and to Diana Cisek and her production staff.

N.J. Smith came into the fray of preparing the new art in the last few months. His tireless efforts made the difference of finishing this work. Eric Herman offered his graceful editorial skill, guidance, and inspiration whenever I felt lost or unsure.

At the heart of this revision, though, is the incredible design, technical, business, and theoretical genius of my life and business partner, the late Michael Stewart Hooker. I lost him at the beginning of this revision and didn't know how I could possibly get through it without him by my side. In the end, his life's body of work—best illustrated by the new information and collection of documentation included in Chapters 4 and 5, and the Documents Appendix—was at my fingertips. His unending love was with me throughout the work on each of those new contributions. Thank you, Michael.

Contents

I

PROJECT DEVELOPMENT

1

Assessing Project Needs

As with all architectural design processes, lighting design is based on creativity and responding to project needs. The development of a responsive design concept results from collecting information about the project. Some information will be gained during the initial interview for the job, but the bulk of it is gathered once a contract has been signed and the project has begun. This chapter addresses the information-gathering stage of the project, which includes:

- Interviewing the client(s) and other design team members to establish the scope and design direction of the project
- Reviewing the plans to gain an understanding of the landscape design concepts
- Visiting the site to gain a visual understanding of the project
- Synthesizing the information to create a base from which design ideas will develop

INTERVIEWING CLIENTS AND THE DESIGN TEAM

Interviews present an opportunity to start collecting valuable information about the project and develop a working communication channel between members of the design team. The lighting designer can learn how various team members feel about light and their desires for the lighting approach or its effects on the project. Interviewing other consultants, such as the irrigation or soils engineers, provides the link to valuable technical information.

Clients

Many clients have limited understanding of the design process involved in lighting or what can be done with light to create an atmosphere. They often have preferences about the atmosphere, but no idea how to achieve it. Interviewing the client or end user builds the foundation for successful landscape lighting. The interview can open a strong communication channel between client and designer, which will help throughout the project. It can develop a trust between the client and the designer that encourages the client to rely on the designer for guidance throughout all phases of the project.

In interviewing clients, ask questions that allow clients to provide information regarding their design needs and desires. Then, listen carefully to the information they provide. Discuss the client's personal feelings about light, the anticipated use(s) of the landscape at night, the anticipated maintenance of both the garden and the lighting, budget constraints, and deadlines. Break the discussion into three distinct categories: information retrieval, information dissemination, and client commitment.[1] During each area of discussion, ask questions to retrieve needed information, then provide the client with choices or guidance, and finalize the discussion with an understanding between client and designer.

Consider showing a portfolio. This presents the designer's experience and introduces lighting ideas to a client. The designer can lead the client through past projects, discussing how the lighting effects and techniques shown in the photographs relate to this project. It provides a time for client feedback and discussion of their lighting goals. This is the time for the designer to show strengths that relate to this client's project. The strengths can be creativity, technical knowledge, construction experience, or simply a history of quick project completion.

Offer to take the client and other design team members on a tour of local projects. This experience clearly shows clients what lighting can do for a landscape and showcases the designer's skills and abilities. These visits often stimulate clients' thinking about lighting, triggering new feelings or ideas about lighting their property.

Clients' Expectations

Ask clients their feelings about light and their expectations of lighting in their landscape. People want landscape lighting for various reasons: view out from inside a room, use of the space for one or more activities, identification of the property, safety of people in the landscape, and security of people and property on the site or inside buildings. They often do not even have a clear idea of what they want. The designer must have a clear idea of the client's expectations before embarking on a design concept. When interviewing a client, be sure to cover the following points:

- Understand the client's basic likes and dislikes about landscape lighting. Some clients want to see beautiful fixtures; others may want fixtures totally hidden. The client may want a dramatic scene with high contrast (see Figure 1.1) and limited areas lit, or the client may be sensitive to glare and prefer less contrast (see Figure 3.2).
- Determine what the client dislikes about the existing lighting (or other landscape lighting that the client has seen). Ask about lighting the client has seen and likes, including specifically what attracted the client's attention to that lighting. It may be a neighbor's lighting or something the client saw in a magazine. Understand the client's light level requirements. What does the client mean by "a little" or "soft" lighting? How much light is "a lot" of light?

Figure 1.1. *Lighting can transform a landscape into a dramatic scene. Successful landscape lighting stems from knowing how to create effects and understanding how to balance light levels between areas of the visual composition (see Color Plate 2). Lighting Design: Janet Lennox Moyer, MSH Visual Planners; Photograph: Michael McKinley; Landscape Design: Magrane Latker Landscape Design.*

- Discuss what impelled the client to install landscape lighting. This will give the designer information about the client's perspective on landscape lighting. Often, a specific event or issue sparked the client's interest. It may be safety, the need to see the way from a door to a parking garage, or a desire to see the landscape at night.
- Talk about the atmosphere or appearance the client would like to create. Encourage the client to use adjectives to describe the scene. Words such as "dramatic" and "theatrical" present a different image than "simple" and "subtle."
- Inquire about the impression the client would like visitors to experience. Answers will vary from drawing attention to the site to impressing visitors to welcoming guests.

Next, discuss *space use* issues. Often clients will not know how they will use their outdoor spaces once they have lighting. Ask specific questions about the kind of entertaining or daily/family use the client might envision. Ask about the type, size, and frequency of events the client might want to plan. This starts to define a client's goals for the project.

- Discuss what activities will take place in the landscape after dark. In many areas, there may not be any activities outside at night (due to climate) during certain times of the year.
- Consider activities that occur inside buildings and the importance of view out to the landscape.
- Determine specific lighting needs or expectations. When several needs surface, this may indicate that flexibility will be required in the lighting system controls.
- Explore safety and security issues.
- Discuss who will be using the space(s). Older people or people with any visual disabilities have special lighting needs that must be considered in planning the lighting.

Maintenance

Two kinds of maintenance issues should be discussed: landscape maintenance and lighting maintenance.

Landscape Maintenance

- Consider changes that could occur to the landscape over time—decks, pathways, patios, structures, or sculptures that may be modified, added, moved, or removed.
- Inquire who provides normal maintenance.
- Ask what services are included in normal maintenance.
- Ask about the maintenance schedule.
- Discuss whether the basic planting design will develop further over time.
- Determine if seasonal planting occurs in certain areas. This may mean not installing lighting fixtures in that planting area. Working around fixtures while maintaining the planting can be cumbersome and fixtures can be knocked out of adjustment.
- Ask who makes the planting decisions. This decision maker might be the landscape architect or designer together with the owner or the head gardener. This person(s) should be included in the discussion of the lighting design and briefed on the required maintenance of the lighting.
- Inquire about fertilization, including both schedule and materials used. Due to corrosion implications, this fertilizer information may affect the lighting equipment selection.

All these issues indicate how careful the designer will need to be in the selection and placement of fixtures. Unless the owner maintains the grounds, few people working at the site understand the necessity of not moving the fixtures and coordinating the maintenance of the landscape with the lighting to preserve the lighting effects.

Lighting Maintenance

Prompt the client to think about the future. Successful lighting depends on long-term functionality of the system. This requires proper maintenance and the ability of the lighting system to grow and change with the landscape.

Any discussion of lighting maintenance requires educating the client. As with the landscape, maintenance of the lighting system requires continuous design input. Landscapes continually change due to hardscape revisions or use changes, as well as plant growth and death. Changes require lighting adjustments to maintain desired effects, such as adding or deleting fixtures, moving fixtures to retain effects as plants grow, and changing lamps to different wattages or beamspreads as plants mature. Also, lamps burn out and must be replaced over time. Identify who will be the appropriate person to provide the lighting maintenance. After the design has been installed, familiarize this person and the owner with the operation of the fixtures.

Maintenance of lighting can be part of the lighting designer's contract with the owner. An effective approach includes an annual site review by the designer. After surveying the existing conditions, the designer can recommend what maintenance, if any, should be done.

The timing for this site review will vary based on the garden maturity when the lighting is installed. A newly planted garden will need lighting maintenance sooner and more frequently than will a mature garden. This concept must be discussed with the client at the beginning of the project for the client to understand fully the implications of landscape lighting.

Budget

One of the most critical factors to an owner is budget. Clients unfamiliar with lighting costs may have no idea what to expect or have an unrealistic expenditure in mind. Bringing up this issue during the initial interview prevents wasted design time, avoids introducing the client to ideas or equipment inappropriate for the project, and maintains good relations throughout the project.

- Determine the anticipated life cycle for commercial landscapes or how long an owner plans to live at a residence.
- Ask what budget, if any, has been planned.
- Provide the owner with basic cost information to help develop a preliminary budget.

When the budget is limited but the owner wants thorough lighting, consider planning the project in phases. This stretches the budget over a longer time frame and eliminates inconveniences at a later date. For example, plan a complete lighting design, install conduit throughout the landscape for future power distribution, but limit the initial fixture installation to areas directly around the building. In this case, always budget the total installation and plan a schedule for installing the remainder of the design to ensure that it happens.

Deadlines

The last area to cover, in questioning the client, involves time. Whether the project is a large public commercial project or a small private residential project, involving only lighting installation, deadlines exist. One or more of the following six deadlines may be involved:

- Design
- Installation bids
- General construction
- Preliminary wiring
- Installation completion
- Aiming/adjusting the lighting system

The lighting designer should be brought in to start planning the landscape lighting after the landscape design has been substantially completed but before final construction documents are completed. Lighting ideas may affect other areas of design, such as structural details or planting layout, and need to be addressed while changes can still be made. A schedule needs to be agreed upon by all parties (including the owner, other design team members, and the lighting designer), allowing the lighting designer time to evaluate and plan the lighting while still fitting into the overall project schedule. Take care not to let unrealistic deadlines push the lighting design too quickly. The time required for conceptual design, design development, and construction drawings will vary from project to project, based on the project size, complexity, number of people involved in the design process, and the lighting designer's workload.

The most crucial deadline is completion date. Bank loans for construction may be involved, as may scheduled use of the landscape. Commercial projects may be working toward the opening of a public park or a major public appearance of a political, religious, or entertainment figure. Residential projects often need to function for a special party.

In collecting all this information about the project, conflicts may arise between scope and budget. Possible solutions include phasing the project, using less expensive equipment to retain the overall design intent, simplifying the design intent to retain high-quality fixtures, or discussing increasing the budget with a client who has the means. In some cases, a chunk of the budget can be saved by having the client tackle the installation. This requires experience in electrical installation. Discussing all these issues at the start may avoid potential conflicts from occurring during the planning stage of the project.

Other Design Team Members

Most projects consist of a group of design professionals—landscape architects, interior designers, engineers (including structural, mechanical, electrical, and soils), fountain designers, and other specialists (including geologists and lighting designers). Consider how each member affects the lighting design and coordinate with them.

Start with the landscape architects, as it is their design that the lighting complements. Discuss the atmosphere envisioned for the night appearance of the garden. Listen carefully for clues about their approach to the project and solutions to the design issues. The landscape architects may have in mind a clear view of the lighting but not know how to achieve it. Or they may not have developed any concept and want to discuss all the options. Discuss how the site relates to neighboring properties. Should the lighting relate to them visually or remain visually separate?

Ask the landscape architects to walk through the project, either on plan or at the site, and discuss their design concepts for the landscape. Together, identify any special lighting needs. For example:

- Traffic patterns for new sites
- Changes of traffic patterns on an existing site
- Areas with specific uses requiring specific lighting, such as sports areas, gathering places for parties, or other functions

- A particular vista or focal area requiring special attention
- A specimen plant, sculpture, or architectural feature meant as a prime focal point
- Grade changes such as stairs or berms that lighting should address for safety

The client may also supply some of this information. In case of conflict between the client's vision of the landscape and the landscape architects' vision, be sure to clarify the design direction in the most diplomatic way as quickly as possible.

REVIEWING ARCHITECTURAL AND LANDSCAPE PLANS

Thoroughly understanding a landscape design helps the designer plan lighting that responds to all the project needs. Drawings build a picture of the competed landscape in the designer's mind. Before starting to develop a lighting concept, gather and study all the available drawings on the project.

With new construction, procure both architectural and interior design drawings of the buildings on the site, including building layouts and furniture layouts, along with sections, elevations (see Fig. 1.2), lighting plans, and details. The architectural drawings show how the building(s) fit into the landscape and the views from the interior to the exterior, and vice versa. The physical appearance of the building itself is an element to consider in the landscape lighting. Locations of windows identify view areas within buildings. Furniture arrangements further clarify how people will view the landscape through the windows. Elevations show window size and positioning in a space that helps direct fixture location and aiming to accommodate night views.

The drawings to procure from the landscape architect include:

- Site plan
- Demolition plan
- Grading plan
- Hardscape plan
- Irrigation/plumbing plan
- Electrical plan
- Planting plan
- Construction details
- Elevations
- Sections
- Perspective drawings

Each of these drawings helps build the lighting designer's understanding of the project and represents a strong communication tool between the two designers. Sometimes the landscape architect does not realize how these drawings help the lighting designer. The following list identifies the importance of each for the lighting designer:

- The *site plan* provides orientation to the landscape on the site and an overview of all areas comprising the project.
- The *demolition plans* identify what is being removed from the existing layout of the landscape.
- The *hardscape plan* introduces the organization of the garden as well as traffic paths, stairs, decks, patios, pergolas, and other structures, such as retaining walls. It shows the juxtaposition of living areas, work areas, view areas, focal points, parking areas, equipment rooms, and other visual or activity areas included in the landscape design (see Figure 1.3).
- The *irrigation plan* shows where new ditches will be dug and water conduit installed, as well as the location of irrigation heads and other irrigation equipment.
- The *electrical plan,* done early in the project development, locates the main electrical service for the landscape, locates the equipment room(s), and ensures that sleeves for electrical distribution are installed under hardscape in the early phases of construction. This plan may be produced before the lighting designer gets involved in the project. It may be done by the electrical engineer on large projects. At other times the landscape architect includes the information provided by the lighting designer on an electrical sheet.
- The *planting plan* adds a new layer of information about the landscape design. It is part of the "decoration" of the space. Planting plans may be simple or complex. Landscape architects vary in the way they present planting plans. Often, they use a symbol for each plant type with an identification line leading from the symbol to the margin of the drawing where the plant name is listed. For typical trees and ground covers, a symbols list may be provided on the drawing. Sometimes a separate list of plant identification is produced and not printed on the drawing. In this case, be sure to procure that list (see Figures 1.4 & 1.5).
- *Construction and/or structural details* give added information about the seating, stairs, trellises, pergolas, sculpture bases, tree wells, stages, and buildings. These details further clarify the design and provide information regarding potential fixture mounting locations.
- *Elevations and sections* provide details not evident on any plan. They show the effect of natural or

modified grading on elements within the landscape (see Figures 1.2 & 1.3). These often provide information as to how and where to mount lighting equipment.

- *Perspectives* provide a realistic view of the completed project. Look at the before and after landscape photographs, along with perspective drawings, of a residential project in northern California in Figures 1.6 to 1.9. This series of views show how much a garden can change during landscape development. They also show how clearly the perspective drawings show the final design. This information completes the picture of the landscape, helping the lighting designer fully understand the landscape design.

Sometimes no landscape drawings exist, limited drawings exist, or the drawings are under development. The type of available drawings influences the way a lighting project develops. When no drawings exist on completed, mature landscapes, the lighting designer has three options:

- To develop landscape drawings
- To draw rough sketches of the landscape
- To work without producing lighting drawings

Each of these approaches has drawbacks.

Developing landscape drawings adds significantly to the project cost and requires hiring a landscape architect. Working with rough sketches requires close coordination between the lighting designer and the electrical contractor. Small projects can be done without producing lighting plans, but again increases the designer's on-site involvement and coordination effort with the electrical contractor. All fixtures, wiring trenches, and transformers must be field-located and staked for future reference.

Models help in visualizing complex structures and understanding the landscape construction opportunities. Borrow the model (when possible) while developing the lighting concepts and photograph the model for future reference. If the landscape architects are seriously debating whether or not to build a model, your explaining how it could help on the project may be all the impetus they need to produce one.

VISITING THE SITE

Visiting the site is imperative. It helps the designer understand how the property fits into the neighbor-

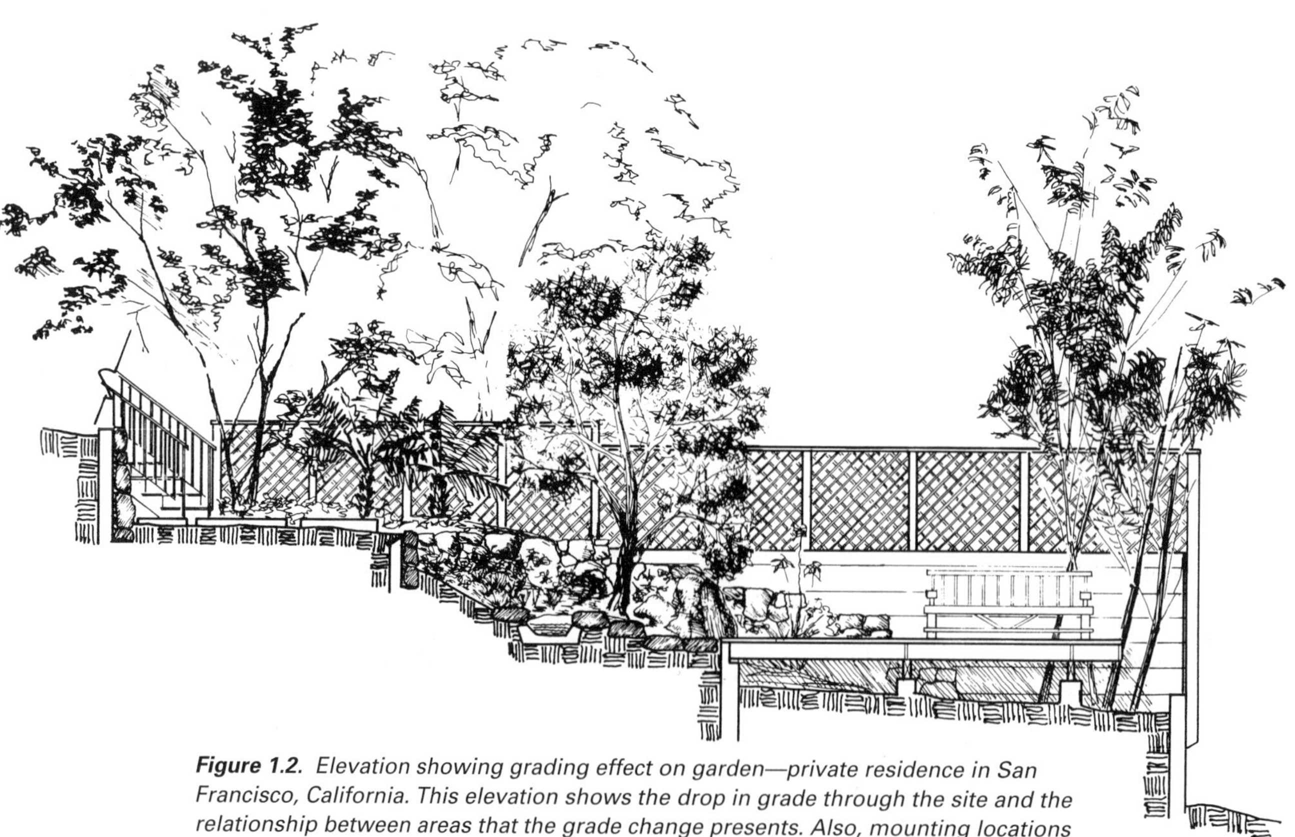

Figure 1.2. *Elevation showing grading effect on garden—private residence in San Francisco, California. This elevation shows the drop in grade through the site and the relationship between areas that the grade change presents. Also, mounting locations for light fixtures or auxiliary electrical equipment can be identified. Design & Drawing: Gary Millar.*

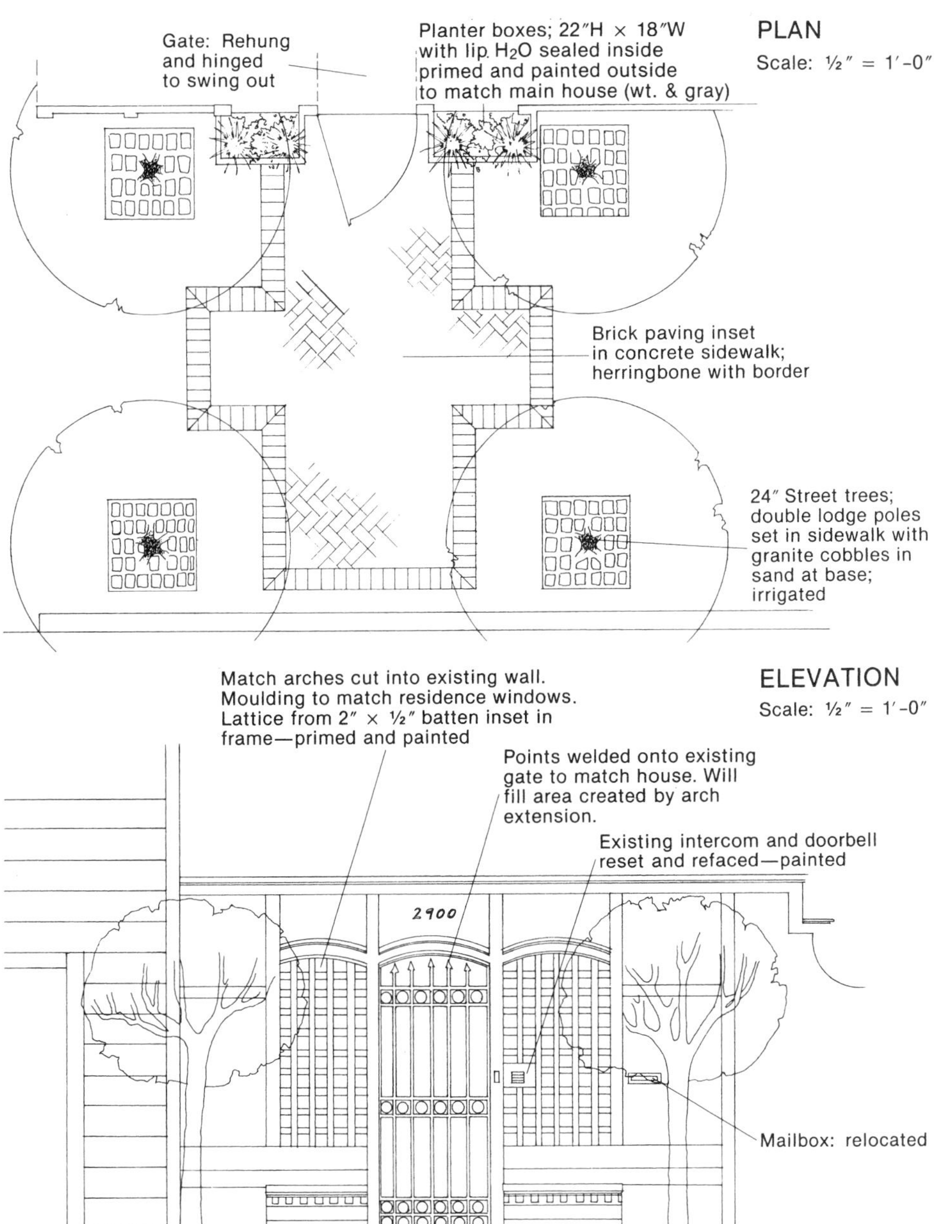

Figure 1.3. Hardscape plan and elevation at garden entry—Thornton residence in San Francisco, California. The hardscape plan shows the changes to the street access and the new planting and entrance structure. Elevations and sections show style and detailing. This decorative information never shows on plans. Landscape Design: Magrane Latker Landscape Design; Drawing: Lezlie Johannessen.

hood. It shows existing elements (plants, structures, etc.) important to the final design. Vistas will become apparent, including views:

- Within the landscape (from one area to another)
- From the garden to other properties
- From the landscape into buildings on the site
- From buildings out into the landscape

Look at all these views to help build a mental image of the scene. Include glimpses around corners or from one area to another. Take care to light juxtaposing areas, as this will be important to the success of the lighting. Provide a "visual destination" at the end of a walkway or a view and outside windows. Study views of the landscape from streets or adjacent properties. This helps determine how the initial view of the garden should appear and how to avoid light pollution or glare going into neighboring properties. Also, make note of any lighting on adjacent properties that may affect the project.

Documenting Site Conditions

Note any existing conditions that may affect design decisions for the lighting:

- Roof overhangs for potential recessed or surface-mounted fixtures.

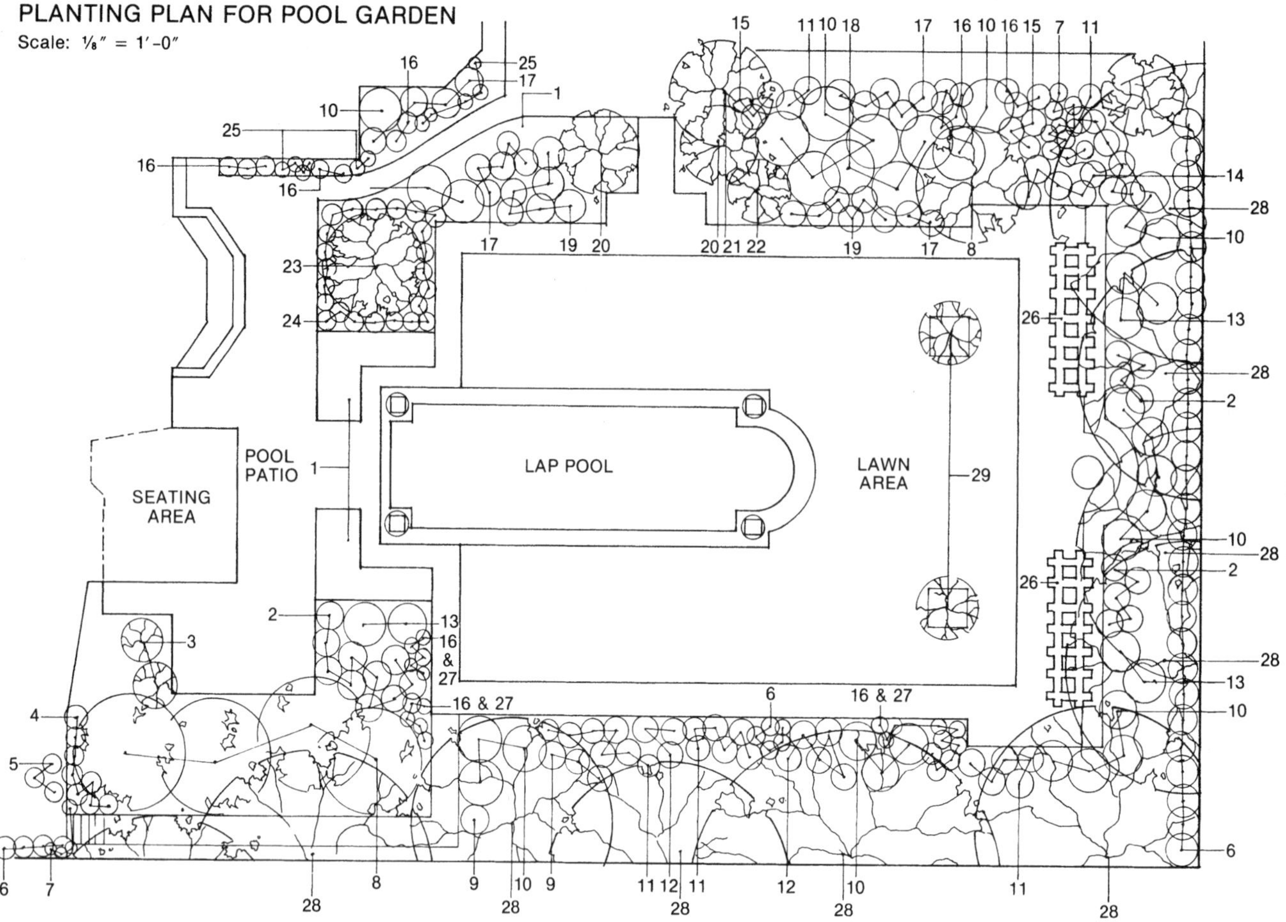

Figure 1.4. *Planting plan. The planting plan provides information about plant types and locations in the landscape. Understanding each plant's characteristics as well as the integration of each individual into the overall landscape design helps the lighting designer develop a lighting concept. Landscape Design: Magrane Latker Landscape Design; Drawing: Lezlie Johannessen.*

Figure 1.5. *Plant list. The plant list can take several forms. It may simply be a list with the Latin or botanical name and the common name or the Latin name only (as shown here). It may list the names and have symbols for easy recognition of each plant on the plan. Sometimes there will be a combination of lists and symbols or just an identification arrow pointing to the plant with the name printed outside the drawing boundary. Landscape Design: Magrane Latker Landscape Design.*

PLANT LIST FOR POOL GARDEN

1. Perennials to be selected
2. Azalea—*Belgiam indica* hybrid
3. *Cornus finbriata*
4. *Sarcococca hookerana humilis*
5. Annuals, rotational
6. *Syzygium paniculatum*
7. Zantedeschia hybrid
8. *Camelia japonica* (existing)
9. *Woodwardia fimbriata*
10. Rhododendron species
11. Azalea—Kurume hybrid
12. *Hydrangea quercifolia*
13. *Viburnum plicatum tomentosum 'Mariesii'*
14. *Camelia sasanqua* hybrid
15. *Viburnum davidii*
16. *Liriope muscari*
17. Azalea—Southern indica hybrid
18. *Camelia japonica* (existing)
19. *Camilia sasanqua 'Apple Blossom'*
20. *Acer palmatum 'Bonfire'*
21. *Acer palmatum* species
22. *Acer palmatum 'Roseo-Marginatum'*
23. Citrus (existing)
24. Hemerocallis hybrid
25. *Berginia crassifolia*
26. *Wisteria sinensis*
27. *Bergenia ciliata*
28. *Quercus agrifolia*
29. *Cornus florida*

Figure 1.6. *"Before" view of landscape. Visiting the site provides an understanding of the scale of the project and the relationship between one area and another. It identifies or reinforces an understanding of dominant views within the landscape, from interior spaces out into the landscape, and from adjacent properties into the landscape. Photograph: Janet Lennox Moyer.*

Figure 1.7. *Perspective sketch of pool garden. Three-dimensional views of the landscape provide information that may not be evident by studying two-dimensional drawings. It clarifies relationships between areas and design elements, as well as the composition of the landscape. Note how similar this sketch is to the photograph of the garden after construction has been completed (see Fig. 1.9). Landscape Design & Drawing: Magrane Latker Landscape Design.*

Figure 1.8. *Perspective of the trellis structure. This second perspective of the pool area helps to understand the construction idea for the trellis structure. Mounting locations for fixtures can be identified with this much information. Landscape Design & Drawing: Magrane Latker Landscape Design.*

Figure 1.9. *Photo of pool garden after construction—view of the completed pool garden. Note how closely the perspective sketch resembles the completed garden. Landscape Design: Magrane Latker Landscape Design; Photograph: Janet Lennox Moyer.*

- Existing hardscape that will remain.
- Location(s) of existing power in the landscape.
- Location of the existing power supply panel. When a panel does exist, inspect it for overall capacity, capacity currently used, and total spare capacity. Be sure to assess how much of the currently used capacity will remain used and the amount that will be freed up for new lighting use. Early evaluation of potential total wattage will show whether the electrical service is large enough or needs to be upgraded.
- Any existing or potential safety hazards that will or might need lighting attention. This would include the edges of pools, fountains, streams, or other waterways; changes in elevation and stairways; and paths or walkways through the site.
- The relationship of adjacent properties. Surrounding properties should be included in the designer's thinking to ensure that no light trespass or annoying glare affects these neighbors or inadvertently lights their building. Learn about the owner's relationship with neighbors. Neighbors may be able to help during the project, such as providing access for equipment to the site or other unforeseen issues. Understanding their sensitivities may allow the lighting designer to allay any client/neighbor tensions that could develop over the new lighting.

Make notes and sketches about impressions of the site and lighting ideas. Try to visualize the proposed landscape improvements as well as absorbing existing conditions.

Photograph every view and every detail of the site. The photographs help recall the site while working on the design. A project that is close by allows the designer to revisit the site. If the site is not near enough to revisit easily, take more photographs than seems necessary. The one view critical to finalize a detail always seems to be missing. Again, make notes about impressions or lighting ideas. These can easily be forgotten by the time when design actually starts.

Soil Considerations

Soil information can prove to be critical. Soil penetration and soil stability varies radically from one soil type to another. The mounting detail for light poles will therefore vary from one soil type to another. Clay soils may be difficult to penetrate and will affect construction cost due to additional trenching time required for conduit and additional time required to mount fixtures. Clay soils do not drain well, potentially discouraging ground-recessed equipment or light fixtures. Sandy soils may not support electrical equipment or light fixtures properly, requiring special mounting details. The inherent moisture content of a soil layer or the added content due to irrigation affects potential fixture corrosion. This in turn affects the selection of fixtures based on construction materials, methods, and finishes.

The arrangement of soil layers provides important information. Movement can occur at the juncture of two soil layers. This movement can nick the fixture surface allowing moisture or dirt to contact the metal. This may cause pitting on the fixture surface. Movement also causes soil instability, which may affect fixture selection or installation methods. (See Chapter 8 for more information on the corrosion potential of fixtures.)

Evaluate the soil on the project. Soils are graded based on three types of materials: clay, silt, and sand (see Figure 1.10).[2,3] The percentage of each determines the makeup of that particular soil. Soil makeup will affect the ease of installation for wiring, lighting poles, junction boxes, and stake-mounted and recessed fixtures.

Soils are identified by different types of characteristics and existing conditions:[4]

- Amount of clay, silt, and sand
- Types and quantities of minerals
- Presence or absence of salts
- Amount of organic material

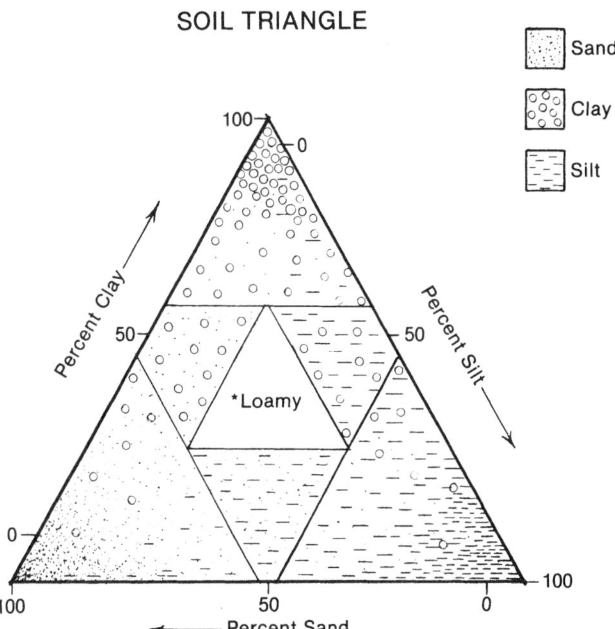

Figure 1.10. *Soil structure triangle. Soil classification is based on the amount of three particle types that occur in the soil: clay, silt, and sand. Other factors influence the classification: the number and kinds of layers, the kinds and amounts of minerals, the presence or absence of salts, the amount of organic matter, and the drainage characteristics. From Kermit Berger,* Introductory Soils *(New York: Macmillan, 1968). Drawing: Lezlie Johannessen.*

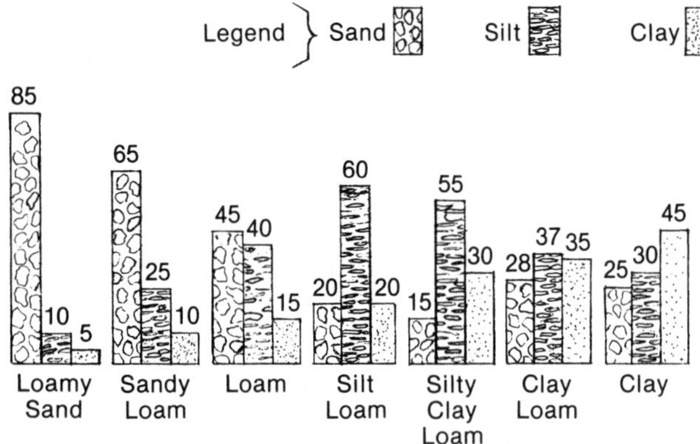

***Figure 1.11.** Soil classification chart. The height of the bar shows various percentages of sand, silt, and clay materials in the various textural classes of soil. Clay particles are extremely fine and are the active portion of the soil. In addition to these mineral components, soils will have varying amounts of organic material. From Kermit Berger,* Introductory Soils *(New York: Macmillan, 1968); Drawing: Lezlie Johannessen.*

- Drainage characteristics
- Inherent moisture content
- Number and types of layers (see Figure 1.11)

A site survey may have been done on a large project by a soils engineer. The report may not be readily interpreted by a lighting designer, but a discussion with the soils engineer will explain the soil conditions. Sometimes the landscape architect may be familiar with the soil condition and can provide this information. Soils survey maps are available from the Department of Agriculture (USDA) or local Soils Conservation Services. These have limited use, as they cover large areas and do not offer detailed information. They do provide clues about the overall site soil type. Be aware that the soil makeup may vary throughout a site.

Perhaps the most useful information for the lighting designer can be gained by digging holes and checking the conditions at several areas in the site. A handheld auger or sampling tube shows the soil consistency and texture. This does not provide information about the chemical makeup of the soil. The landscape architect may have contracted a soils engineer to perform a soils test. If not, contact a soils analysis lab. Ask them to test for soil pH (see Chapter 8) and identify any salts or other corrosive elements in the soil.

SYNTHESIZING THE INFORMATION

After all this initial information has been gathered, allow time to think about it. Study the plans and try to visualize the landscape design. This may be the most critical time of the project. Conscious and subconscious analysis of this information leads to the core direction for the lighting design.

Look again at traffic patterns, views, and vistas, and identify all focal areas or points. Keep in mind the use of the space. One of the most important aspects of this study phase is to become familiar with the plant materials. Refer to the plant list supplied on or with the planting plan. (See Chapter 14 for information on plant material.) Research each plant listed. Recognize that this list will be revised up to the day that all plants are installed in the ground.

Many factors influence these planting changes. The landscape architect may determine at some point in the project that another plant is more appropriate. In procuring the plant material, some of the desired plants may not be available, requiring a change in plant type. In other cases, the plant material may exist, but not be of acceptable quality or the right size. Many times the landscape architect, while locating plants on the site, determines that plant locations need to be shifted to create the desired massing effects. Also, the quantity of a specific plant may change due to site relationships. Sometimes more plants are installed, sometimes fewer. This means that the lighting plan needs to stay flexible until all the plant material has been installed.

Other elements of the project can also change. Deck or patio sizes and shapes can change or they may be moved to another location. Structures may be added, deleted, or moved. Keep in contact with the landscape architects and other designers working on the project. Impress upon them the importance of communicating changes and developments as they occur.

As the lighting designer assimilates this information, the lighting concept starts to formulate. The daytime view can be retained, reinforcing the fundamental landscape design, or changed to sculpt a new view at night (see Figures 1.9 & 1.1). The most complete information regarding the lighting desires of the owner, the physical layout of the site, the juxtaposition of buildings with the landscape, and the landscape design concept provides the best opportunity to develop a successful lighting system.

REFERENCES

1. Robert B. Miller and Stephen E. Heiman, *Conceptual Selling,* Miller-Heiman, Inc., Walnut Creek, California, 1987, pp. 63–104.
2. S. W. Boul, F. S. Hole, and R. J. McCracken, *Soil Genesis and Classification,* Iowa State University Press, Ames, Iowa, 1973, p. 27.
3. Kermit C. Berger, *Introductory Soils,* Macmillan, New York, 1968, p. 106.
4. Ibid., p. 105.

2

Vision and the Perception of Light

The human mind continually tries to create meaning or order out of the external stimuli received through the eye. To design with light, the designer needs to understand how the two organs (eye and brain) work and the interaction between them. The process of seeing starts with the eye receiving stimuli and culminates with the brain interpreting information, translating it into shape, size, texture, depth, motion, and position.

Light functions as a stimulus. The light pattern in a space creates a response from a viewer. If the light changes in the space, a person's feeling or reaction to the space will change. Human beings are dynamic—continually responding. This applies to the sensitivity of both the eye and the brain to light. Under differing lighting circumstances, the human interpretation of a space will change.

The brain organizes the information continuously arriving through the eye in an attempt to produce order and meaning from the jumble of sensory data received. During the interpretation process, the brain constructs a view for the person. While the actual functioning of the brain is not clearly understood, scientists know that the brain has a memory capability that provides both expectations and a storehouse of previous experiences that allow people to interpret familiar objects in low light levels.

At times, the brain corrects information to fit a best or simplest interpretation. For example, in the dark, the eye cannot distinguish color easily, but the brain remembers that the brick in a wall is red. This phenomenon is called *color constancy*. Phenomena of this type occurring in the brain help people cope with their surrounds. The seeing process provides valuable information to the designer that helps guide what could or should be done with landscape lighting.

Human vision is selective due to the physical structure of the eye. Designers need to be aware of how the eye deals with stimuli, which is called brightness, and, equally important, how the mind steps in when the eye cannot cope with the stimuli presented. This chapter will look at both the physical and psychological aspects of the seeing process. Since landscape lighting involves primarily low light levels, this discussion will emphasize the way the eye functions in dark environments and how light cues can direct people. For further information about the functioning of the eye or the seeing process, see the list of reference books in the Bibliography.

HOW THE EYE WORKS

The eye sees images of brightness. Light enters the eye and strikes the *retina*, a layer of light-sensitive cells along the back wall of the eye (see Figure 2.1). The retina has two types of photo receptors: *cones*, high-light-level receptors, and *rods*, low-light-level receptors. These receptors generate photochemical reactions that travel along the optic nerve to the brain. The brain collects these signals and translates them into pictures.

The eye reacts to light levels by involuntary action of the *iris*, a kind of shutter mechanism. In bright light, the iris protects the eye by closing over the *pupil*, the black, circular opening that allows light to pass to the retina (see Figure 2.1). In dim light, the iris opens to expose more pupil and allow more light into the eye. Adjusting to bright light is called *photopic vision*, and to dim light, *scotopic vision* (see Figure 2.2).

In light levels approximately equal to or greater than 1 footcandle, images of brightness impinge primarily on the *fovea*, a spot on the retina directly behind the pupil containing the highest concentration of cones. The fovea, due to acute light sensitivity, allows us to discern variations of color, details, and shape. Natural lighting levels drop significantly from day to night. Moonlight produces only a fraction of the level produced by the sun (see Figure 2.3). As the light level drops below 1 footcandle,[1] perception switches to the rod receptors. They provide peripheral vision, consisting of the perception of brightness contrast and movement. This occurs because they line the retinal wall with greatest concentration at the side of the eye, gradually decreasing in number as they approach the fovea.

The eye perceives an object based on the amount of light reflecting off it. Three factors influence the amount of light that will reflect off the object to the eye: color, texture, and finish. Light colors reflect more than dark colors (see Figure 2.4). Smooth textures reflect more than rough surfaces (see Figure 3.4). Shiny surfaces reflect more than matte surfaces. The apparent brightness of an object also depends on the brightness of the surrounding area or brightness contrast from one to the other.

Changes in brightness level within the field of view trigger two involuntary adaptation responses in the eye: expansion or contraction of the iris and a photochemical change. Although the eye adapts to a wide range of levels, it does not respond as well to large changes of brightness in the field of view. The iris opens and closes as the eye moves from one brightness to another controlling the amount of light allowed to enter into the eye. This causes no long-term effect on the eye, but during extended viewing muscle fatigue can cause eye discomfort when several brightly lit focal points have no fill light between them to act as a "brightness bridge." Refer

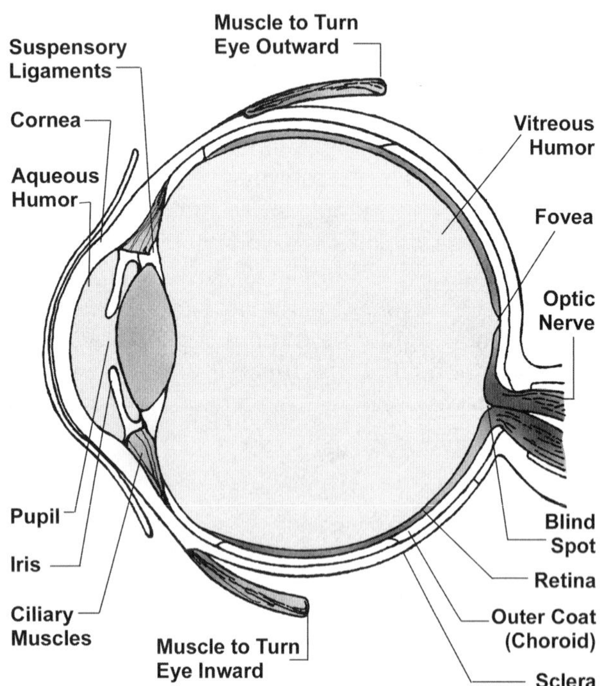

Figure 2.1. Parts of the eye. Drawing: Lezlie Johannessen.

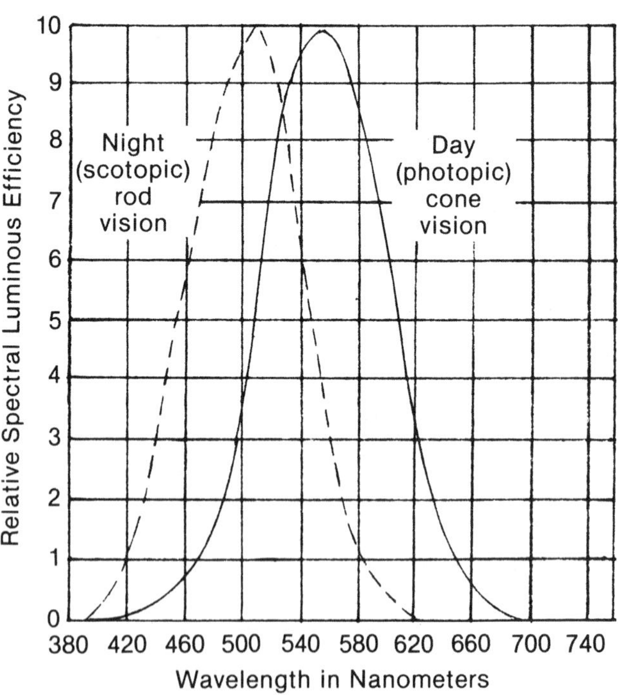

Figure 2.2. *As the light level varies, the eye's response to color shifts. In high light levels, the eye sees color according to the solid line on the graph. As the light level drops, the way the eye sees color shifts to the dashed line on the graph. This tells designers that the eye has less sensitivity in the warm end of the visible spectrum. Cool colors are more easily discernible. Based on material from* The IES Fundamentals Course Manual, *1976, Illumination Engineering Society of North America, New York.*

to Figure 2.5 for recommended brightness relationships (luminance ratios) for various lighting situations.

Both cones and rods have compounds that respond to light and send signals to the brain. *Rhodopsin* or *visual purple,* located in rods, permits dark *adaptation.* Exposure to high light levels bleaches rhodopsin, impeding the rods' ability to respond. Darkness starts the regeneration of rhodopsin, permitting the eye to begin responding as a person moves from a brightly lit space to a dark space. However, it takes several minutes for a view to start appearing. Complete adaptation takes 20 to 30 minutes. The eye adapts more quickly when shifting from low to high light levels. Initial response occurs within a minute, and full adaptation between 7 and 12 minutes.[2,3]

The dark-adapted eye can recover quickly when exposed to a flash of light (10 seconds' exposure to a dim light requires roughly 60 seconds' recovery time).[1] However, extreme shifts in brightness level cause momentary disorientation.[4] Minimize this problem by providing a transition level of light between areas with a sharp contrast in brightness level.

Current research suggests that the eye continually adjusts to changes in spectrum of light, quantity of light, location of response in the retina, and length of exposure. Due to this dynamic response, scientists have difficulty in clearly identifying how vision works. Sensitivity to light includes functions in the eye, in pathways to the brain, and in the brain. Research into brain functions, including memory and expectations, may change our understanding of vision in the near future.

LIGHT LEVELS*

CONTRIBUTION FROM FULL MOON	0.01–0.02	fc
DAYLIGHT		
At North Window	50–200	fc
Outdoor Shade	100–1000	fc
Direct Sunlight	5000–10000	fc
Office Lighting	30–100	fc
STREET LIGHTING		
Commercial	0.5–1**	fc
Residential	0.25–0.75**	fc
SIDEWALKS		
Commercial	1–5***	fc
Residential	0.25	fc

* Light levels in landscapes at night contrast dramatically with daylight levels and typical average interior night light levels.
** Calculated to be average maintained levels.
*** Municipalities often require minimum levels. The level varies throughout the U.S. Procure local regulations.

Figure 2.3.

REFLECTANCES OF BUILDING MATERIALS AND OUTSIDE SURFACES

Materials		*Reflectance (percent)*
Brick	light buff	48
	dark buff	40
	dark red glazed	30
Cement		27
Marble	(white)	45
Paint	(white)	
	new	75
	old	55
Glass	clear	7
	reflective	20–30
	tinted	7
Asphalt	(free from dirt)	7
Earth	(moist cultivated)	7
Granolite pavement		17
Grass	(dark green)	6
Macadam		18
Slate	(dark clay)	18
Snow	new	74
	old	64
Vegetation	(mean)	25
Bluestone, sandstone		18

Figure 2.4. *Based on material from the* IES Lighting Handbook, Reference Volume, *Illuminating Engineering Society of North America, New York, 1984.*

LUMINANCE RATIOS: *Brightness Difference Between Two Objects or Areas in Exterior Environments*

2:l	Edge of perceptible contrast; not enough difference to attract attention to a focal point
3:1 – 5:1	Range of acceptable contrast between primary and secondary focal points
Up to 10:1	Range of acceptable contrast between primary focal point and fill or surround light for exterior areas with low ambient lighting
Up to 100:1	Range of acceptable contrast between primary focal point and fill or surround light for interiors or areas with high ambient lighting
100:1 – 1000:1	Range of contrast between street and surround

LUMINANCE OF SKY

Overcast with moon	0.001	Footlamberts
Clear moonlight	0.01	Footlamberts
Deep twilight	0.1	Footlamberts

Figure 2.5.

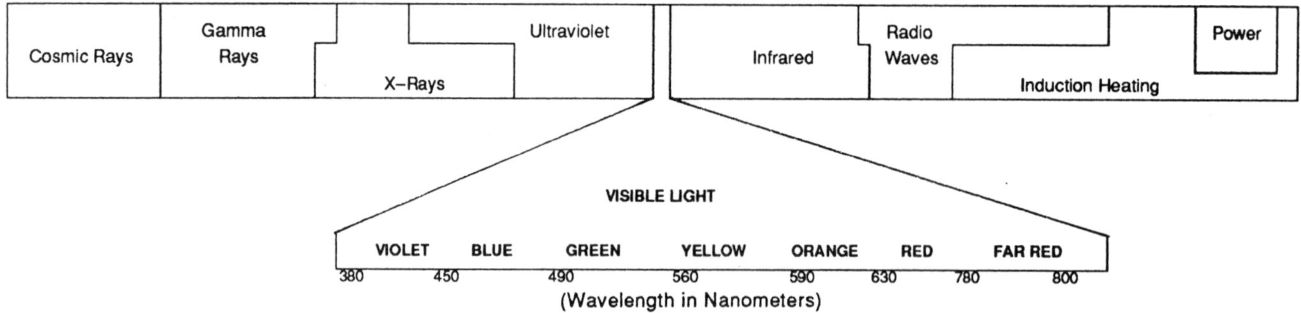

Figure 2.6. The electromagnetic spectrum shows the continuum of all electric and magnetic radiation. The portion visible to the human eye is the small portion roughly in the middle, called the visible spectrum. The expanded portion showing the visible spectrum shows how it encompasses all colors of the rainbow, from violet to red. Drawing: Lezlie Johannessen.

DESIGNING FOR THE EYE

Plan for eye response in dark environments. Since brightness attracts the eye, a contrast between dark and light causes the eye to attempt to adapt to both brightnesses. When a viewer focuses on the light object for several seconds to several minutes, dark adaptation may be broken. Then, when shifting view to a dark area, the eye will have to start adapting again. Understanding how the eye works helps direct landscape lighting decisions:

- Use dramatic changes in brightness level cautiously to minimize or eliminate eye discomfort.
- Provide transition light levels in border areas between interior and exterior spaces to soften brightness contrast.
- Layer light into the landscape to provide a brightness-level balance, which allows the eye to move through the space without a continual shift of the iris opening.
- Provide even light level along walkways to aid in human comfort and minimize fatigue. Pools of light confuse the eye and cause shifts of the iris opening size.
- Control the brightness of light-fixture lenses or openings. This minimizes uncomfortable contrast and directs attention to the intended lighting effects rather than to the fixture.

Eye defects and physical deterioration of the eye due to aging affect the eyesight of many people. These disorders include the inability of the eye to accommodate. *Accommodation* refers to the ability of the eye to locate and focus on an object in the visual field. *Ciliary muscles* and *suspensory ligaments* change the shape of the lens from flattened for long distances to spherical for short distances. The pupil size changes, becoming larger for distant objects and smaller for near objects.

As people age, the lens becomes less elastic, preventing it from changing shape to focus on objects at differing distances from the eye. This aging process begins at approximately 30 and accelerates past 40.[5] Other aging problems include:

- Yellowing of the lens and other eye components, which affects color perception, primarily in the blue end of the visual spectrum.
- Clouding of the lens, which obscures detail and affects perception of brightness. To compensate, raise the light levels and reduce brightness contrast.
- Shrinkage of many eye components, due to reduced fluids in the eye, which limits the range of pupil opening size and therefore the amount of light entering the eye. This causes exaggerated brightness contrast to the eye, requiring careful brightness control.
- Hardening of the lens, which limits its ability to change size. This affects focusing on close objects.
- Reduced coordination and loss of elasticity of muscles and ligaments, which control many eye functions. This restricts adaptation, requiring more careful brightness contrast control.

Color perception also plays a part in night vision, but to a lesser extent than during day vision. The color response of the eye shifts in low light levels toward the blue end of the *visible spectrum* (see Figure 2.6). Although this suggests that cool light sources may be seen more easily, a balanced or white light offers the best approach. The eye, familiar with the relatively balanced white light from the sun and the warm color of incandescent light in

TERMINOLOGY	
FOOTCANDLE:	Measurement of illumination or quantity of light falling on a subject. Symbol: fc. (Note: The European measurement is lux. The approximate conversion of fc to lux is 1 fc = 10.76 lux. The scientific conversion multiplies fc × 0.09 to determine lux or 1 lux = 10.76 fc.)
FOOTLAMBERT:	Measurement of luminance or quantity of light reflected off the surface of an object. The eye sees luminance or footlamberts, rather than footcandles, making this measurement more important than footcandles. Symbol: fl.
LUMINANCE:	The amount of light reflecting off the surface of an object. This term takes into account the scattering of light as it reflects off a surface.
LUMINANCE CONTRAST:	The relationship between luminances of an object and its background or between two areas in a landscape.
BRIGHTNESS:	The amount of light, seen by the eye, reflecting from the surface of an object. This term takes into account the state of adaption of the eye.
ELECTROMAGNETIC SPECTRUM:	A continuum of radiation, including all wavelengths of electric and magnetic radiation. Much of this radiation is not seen by the human eye. The portion that can be seen is called the "visible spectrum" (see Figure 2.6).

Figure 2.7.

residences at night, favors white light sources. While inconclusive, preliminary research shows a better visual response to light from a continuous wide band across the visible spectrum.[6] Light sources with discontinuous spectral output may make focusing difficult.

PERCEPTION

The combination of the eye admitting light and the brain interpreting this visual information provides cues and direction to people at night. One phenomenon of light is that the human eye is always attracted to the brightest light in the field of view. Designers can use this to build a composition by planning which area or object in a landscape should be brightest. This can work against a design when the brightness of a fixture lens is not controlled, distracting the eye from a more important element in the composition.

Designers can direct how people see a space by controlling the brightnesses introduced into the space. A soft light level in the front of a space with a more brightly lit object or area farther into the space draws the eye through the space to the distant object. Controlling brightnesses can also direct people's movement through a space. Walking through a dimly lit area will feel comfortable as long as the person is heading toward an area with a higher light level visible to the viewer from the outset.

When a designer plans to vary the level of light from one area to another or one object to another, care must be taken not to create too high a brightness contrast. A large difference in light level from one object to another introduces confusion to a space. Many landscapes will have multiple areas of interest, requiring several areas with high light levels and areas of less interest that do not require accent lighting. Uneven numbers will produce a more stable effect in a lighting composition. Three represents the most stable number of objects lit to the same level. This creates a triangle of interest, allowing the eye to move from one area to another in a continuous motion. When two objects are lit as focal objects the eye bounces from one to another. To avoid a spotty effect when highlighting multiple objects, introduce a lower fill light level between the objects, providing a bridge from one object to the next.

People feel comfortable when they can see the boundaries of a space. It does not matter whether the light is soft or strong (this is directed by design intent), just that the edges of the space are identified. In large landscapes, the designer or owner does not always want to treat the entire property with light. A decision should be made as to what should be the visual boundary.

When planning the lighting for a project, the designer can direct the viewer's eye through a space. Introduce light that creates a path through the darkness, taking the eye to an area intended for use or viewing (see Figures 17.17 & Color Plate 60). The manipulation of light to make a statement in a space becomes a composition of light. Basic composition techniques and tools apply to landscape lighting as they do to all art forms. The following chapter will discuss these ideas to help the designer learn how to approach the lighting of any type of project.

REFERENCES

1. Bill Jones, "The Influence of Spectral Energy Distribution of Light Sources on Visual Performance," unpublished paper presented at the 1989 IES South Pacific Coast/Pacific Northwest Bi-Regional Conference, pp. 1, 4.
2. James L. Nuckolls, *Interior Lighting for Environmental Designers,* Wiley, New York, 1976, p. 14.
3. The Committee on Colorimetry of the Optical Society of America, *The Science of Color,* Optical Society of America, Washington, D.C., 1953, pp. 110–113.
4. Ibid., p. 112.
5. James L. Nuckolls, *Interior Lighting for Environmental Designers,* Wiley, New York, 1976, pp. 323–327.
6. Bill Jones, "The Influence of Spectral Energy Distribution of Light Sources on Visual Performance," unpublished paper presented at the 1989 IES South Pacific Coast/Pacific Northwest Bi-Regional Conference, pp. 4–6.

3

Luminous Composition

Light has the capability to create shape, emotional response, even a new reality in a familiar space through the use of composition. Composition consists of the organization of elements using one or more design principles. Luminous composition asks designers to answer the questions "What do I want to show with light?" and "How should these elements appear?"

Light can shape how a space is viewed. It visually expands or limits depth and directs the eye through the space according to the relationship of brightness between one object or area and another. Light introduces emotional qualities to the space such as romance, mystery, drama, and excitement. Light sculpts the focal object(s), emphasizing specific aspects or altering the daytime appearance. In developing a composition, think about how light imparts a quality that creates mood. Consider how light affects spatial perception.

Evaluate the daytime composition. How does the organization of elements—walls or other boundaries, paving, stairs, plants, architectural structure—influence the way the space should appear at night? Should a sequence of elements be lit to enhance the repetition? Consider whether the lighting should follow the natural appearance or use its capabilities to create a new scene. One of the strengths of lighting design is its ability to create an illusion either by withholding light or by shifting emphasis from the expected. See Figures 3.19 & 3.20.

In developing a composition, be as specific as possible in answering these questions and considering these issues. Start by identifying all the elements in the landscape that should appear at night. It also helps to identify those elements that should fade into the background (see Figure 3.1). The absence of light can emphasize part of a composition (see Figure 3.12) or disrupt the scene. Then plan how to organize the elements using brightness levels and lighting techniques.

DEFINING OBJECTIVES

Landscape lighting has three basic objectives: providing *safety, security,* and *aesthetics.* These three objectives address specific issues about night environments:

SAFETY — *Avoid injury.* Landscape lighting should provide a clear view of any potential obstacles in the environment, such as steps, intersection of land and water, and children's toys left out on the patio.

SECURITY — *Avoid intrusion by trespasser.* Light can be a deterrent to an intruder and it adds psychologically to an inhabitant's feeling of protection. Security lighting can be a separate system, one layer of the overall composition controlled separately (for use when other layers are not needed), or an integral part of the overall system.

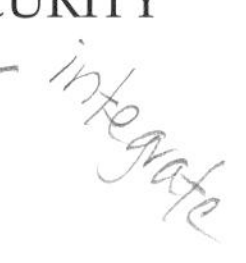

AESTHETICS — *Allow enjoyment of the environment.* Lighting the exterior can provide a view from the interior out into the landscape, psychologically enlarge the interior space by visually fusing it with the landscape, and provide for activities such as entertaining and sports.

Consider all three objectives when starting the lighting design for a landscape project. One objective may be more important for a particular client and therefore dominate the design needs. However, whenever possible, have aesthetics dictate by integrating safety and security elements into a visually pleasing night scene.

EXPRESSING IDEAS

Creating a pleasing luminous composition from the darkness requires effective expression of visual design. Good visual design depends on careful observation, imagination, and the proper use of composition elements.

Observation

Careful observation trains the eye to evaluate a scene. What should be perceived in the site? In some settings one object or area may be visually most important. In others, several objects or areas may have equal visual importance. Consider how each element relates to the scene and to the other elements in the scene. Plan the order in which each element should be viewed (see Figures 3.2, 3.3, & Color Plate 3).

Imagination

Simple compositions make clear statements. Compare lighting a space with photographing the same space. The camera records scenes, objectively limiting the photographer's ability to control the view. The photographer can select the viewing location but cannot enhance or diminish the importance of objects in the scene. Lighting provides the opportunity to *create* the scene *subjectively* by selecting areas to emphasize and deemphasize. This control of what will be seen provides the lighting designer with unlimited ability to shape the composition.

Night provides a black hole from which a designer can create a scene. Once the scene has been evaluated, start to make decisions about how to introduce light. Emphasize strong points and hide weak points. Use light to sculpt the darkness and move the viewer's eye through the space. Keep in mind basic design bal-

Figure 3.1. *A view to this tree with a sense of ground plane provides a view from a dining room window. The trees and shoreline beyond are left dark. Lighting Design: Janet Lennox Moyer, MSH Visual Planners; Photograph: Kenneth Rice Photography, www.kenricephoto.com.*

ance—for example, using uneven numbers of focal points creates a stable image. This may mean introducing a higher amount of light onto an area in the composition that intrinsically does not warrant being considered a focal point (see Color Plate 6).

Composition Elements

Light creates form out of darkness and then influences that form by the quality and direction of light. Contrast of tones affects the apparent depth of a space. Objects that have different reflectances but are lit with the same amount of light will appear different in brightness (see Figure 3.4).

Depth

Varying the amount of brightness introduced into areas of a scene determines the appearance of depth in the space. To manipulate depth, identify three zones in the scene: foreground, midground, and background. The general rule in creating depth calls for providing the brightest light in the background, with the foreground second in brightness, and the midground darkest (see Figures 3.5 & 3.6). The foreground zone provides the visual transportation from the higher light levels of the interior space to the darker environment of the exterior. Many circumstances call for breaking this general rule:

- Limiting depth to hide an ugly feature in the background such as a power pole. In this case, the background may not be lit at all.
- Limiting depth to add mystery or drama to the scene. Again, light may be withheld from the background (see Color Plate 2).
- Calling attention to a focal point in the middle area while hinting at depth by providing a layer of soft light in the background (see Figure 3.7).

Knowing whether to use this rule, use a modified version of it, or break the rule completely depends on the statement the designer wants to make in the landscape. The effectiveness of the statement will depend on careful introduction of light onto focal areas and then balancing brightnesses throughout the scene.

Quality and Direction of Light

Quality of light consists of two types: harsh light and soft light. *Harsh light,* produced by a point source of light—the sun, incandescent, and high-intensity discharge (HID) electrical light sources—accentuates contrast; defines shape, line, and texture; and directs view. Harsh light provides sparkle. It can also produce glare.

Soft light reduces contrast. Shapes, lines, and textures will be less clearly defined. Generally, soft light is created by a diffuse or linear light source such as an overcast sky or fluorescent lamps. However, careful use of point sources can create soft lighting in night environments.

Direction of light affects the ability to increase or decrease texture, as well as to influence depth in a scene. Quality and direction work together in their effects on design. Analyzing basic lighting approaches shows the influence of quality and direction of light.

- *Frontlighting* shows the detail of an object and tends toward dramatic effect. It flattens the object's appearance by eliminating shadows that show form (see Figure 14.64).
- *Backlighting* produces extreme contrast, showing the shape of an object while decreasing texture and eliminating detail (see Figures 14.42 & 14.43).
- *Sidelighting* increases texture and creates strong shadows (see Figures 14.61 & 14.62).

Employing a combination of these three directions provides the advantages of each and tends to make objects or whole scenes look more natural. In lighting a tree, for example, frontlighting will show detail; backlighting will emphasize the form and provide three dimensions to the view; sidelighting will show interesting trunk characteristics by emphasizing texture (see Figure 14.64). This issue of direction of light can be provided interchangeably by up- or downlighting.

View

View influences landscape lighting in many ways. A landscape may be viewed but not used at night. An area may have one viewing direction or multiple viewing directions. The views may be from the inside to the outside, from the outside to the inside, from one area of the landscape to another, or in several of these directions.

Some views will be from outside the property. The landscape may be seen from a road, from a hill above the property, or from an adjacent property. Always consider these external viewing points as well. Two issues are involved. Viewing the landscape from the street relates to composition, whereas viewing from someone else's property addresses light trespass and glare. Always ensure that the intended lighting will not disturb someone on another property in any way.

Always identify all viewing locations to understand how people will be approaching the landscape. Then prioritize the views. The view from an executive conference room in an office complex may seldom be used at night, while the dining room may be used exten-

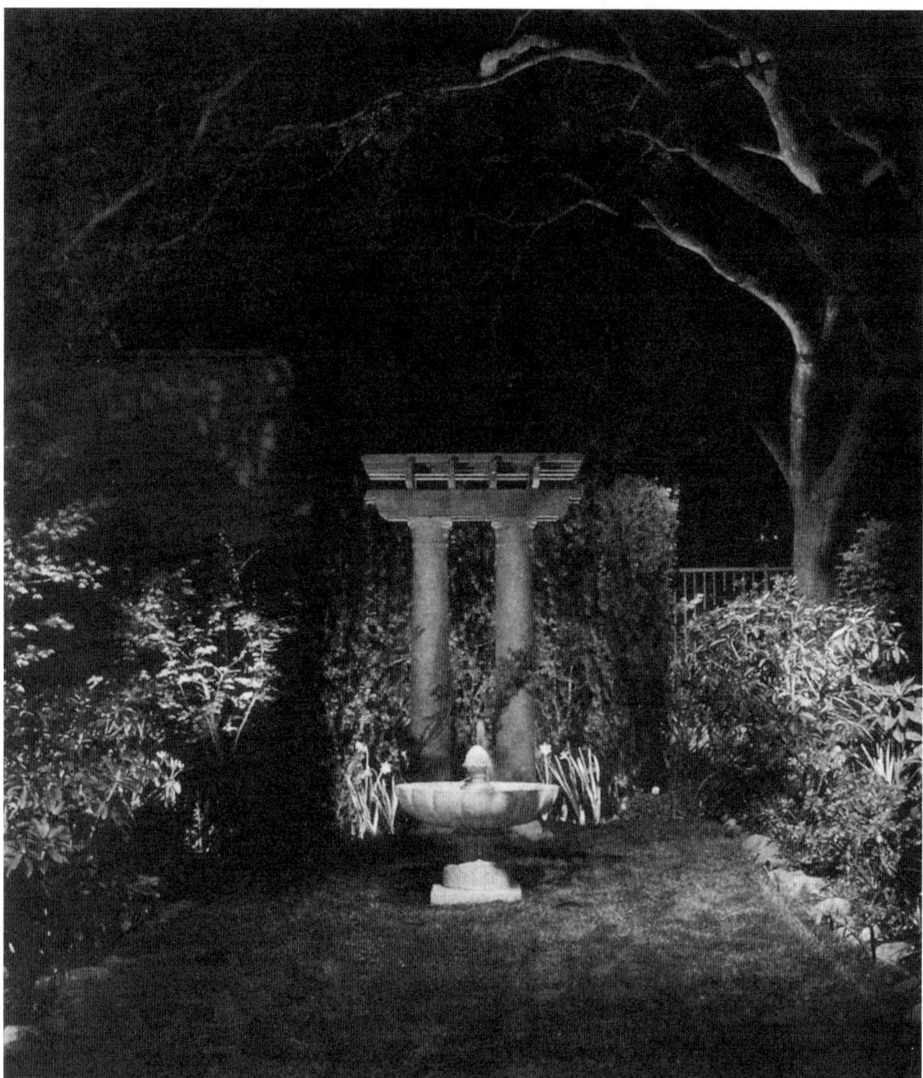

Figure 3.2. *This Piedmont, California, garden has a formal, symmetrical design. The fountain serves as the main focal point, with the columns and Yew hedge creating a backdrop. The borders frame the composition. Downlighting introduces the highest light level on top and to the front of the fountain, making it the main focal point. Downlighting creates a natural appearance on the Rhododendrons in the right-side planting bed. The Rhododendron in the left planting bed appears more dramatic due to uplighting. Downlighting in front of the columns and from the side provides separation for the fountain from the background. Uplighting the hedge adds to the separation. A soft wash in front of the fountain introduces the lawn (see Figure 3.3). Lighting Design: Janet Lennox Moyer, MSH Visual Planners; Landscape Design: Magrane Latker Landscape Design; Photograph: Michael McKinley.*

sively. This would make the view out from the dining room more important than that from the conference room.

Additionally, the view may be straight across a landscape or from one level to another. The viewer may be situated below the garden looking up at it or above the garden looking down into it. When viewing down into a garden, use care in aiming and shielding of uplights to eliminate glare. Viewing up into a garden requires careful aiming of downlights. In situations with multiple viewing angles or changes in site grade, the location, aiming, and shielding of a fixture become critical. The placement must be reviewed from all viewing locations at night to ensure obscuring the brightness of the lamp and the inside of the fixture. It helps to use a lamp deeply recessed into the fixture body and then to add a matte black louver providing at least 45° off-axis shielding. The last accessory useful to minimizing or eliminating glare is an angled hood that is adjustable vertically on the fixture body and rotates horizontally (see Figures 4.18 & 7.4).

When a window comes between the viewer and the view, the lighting must address the reflective quality of the window. If the level of light introduced to the landscape is not properly balanced with the interior lighting, the window becomes a black mirror obscuring all or part of the view. Use the following guidelines:

- View from inside to the outside (see Figures 3.8 & 3.12)—the lighting levels of all surfaces outside windows (vertical and horizontal) need to be higher than the inside levels. Vertical interior surfaces opposite the window cause the greatest negative effect on view. Provide separate control (either a separate switch or dimming capability) of the lighting for this surface to minimize or eliminate this problem.

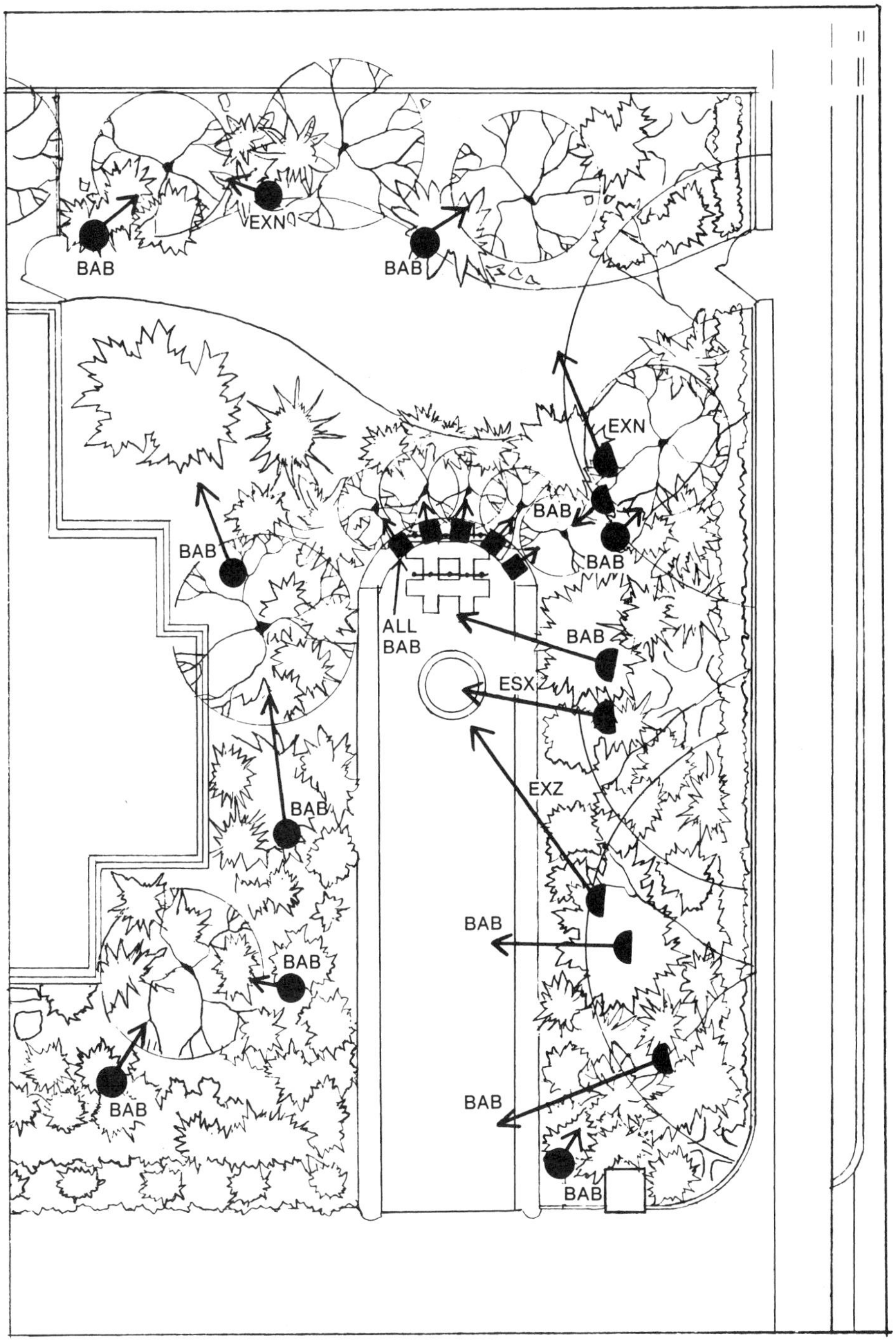

LAMP LEGEND			
ESX	20 WATT	13°	MR16
BAB	20 WATT	38°	MR16
EXZ	50 WATT	24°	MR16
EXN	50 WATT	40°	MR16

FIXTURE LEGEND	
←■	Below grade adjustable 12 volt incandescent luminaire
←◖	Tree mount adjustable 12 volt incandescent luminaire
←●	Stake mount adjustable 12 volt incandescent luminaire
•—•—•	12 volt incandescent strip light

Figure 3.3. Alley garden plan. This plan shows the location, lamping, and aiming of all the fixtures used. Drawing: Lezlie Johannessen & Richard DePalma.

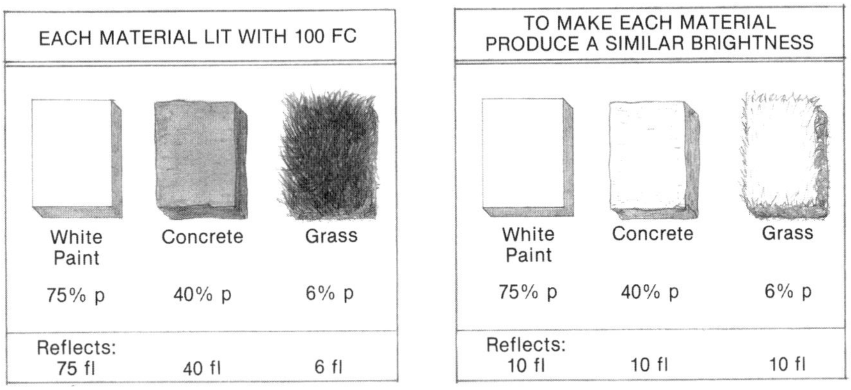

EACH MATERIAL LIT WITH 100 FC		
White Paint	Concrete	Grass
75% p	40% p	6% p
Reflects: 75 fl	40 fl	6 fl

TO MAKE EACH MATERIAL PRODUCE A SIMILAR BRIGHTNESS		
White Paint	Concrete	Grass
75% p	40% p	6% p
Reflects: 10 fl	10 fl	10 fl

*p = Reflectance

Figure 3.4. The left chart shows how different 100 footcandles will appear on objects with differing reflectances. To make them appear to be of the same brightness, the right chart shows the difference required in quantity of light. Drawing: Lezlie Johannessen.

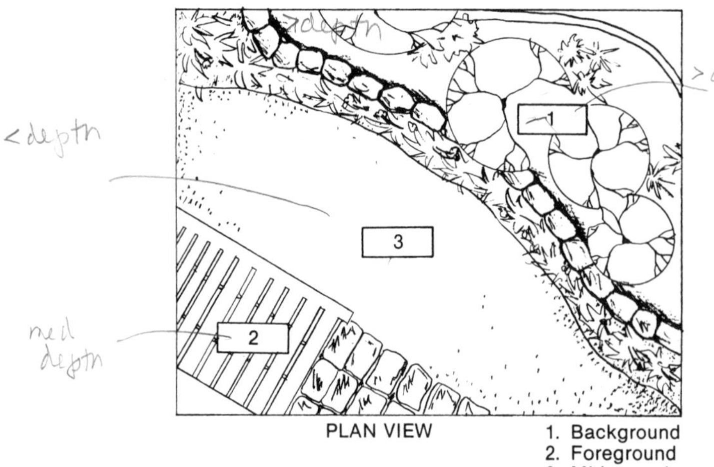

A.

B.

C.

Figure 3.5. *Landscape zones. Divide all areas into three zones: foreground, midground, and background. The amount of light used in each zone either increases or decreases depth in the composition. Highest level of light in the front diminishes depth. Highest level in back emphasizes depth, making the space feel larger. The drawing shows ranking the zones to increase depth. Drawing: Lezlie Johannessen.*

Figure 3.6. *This series of sketches shows how the visual composition changes as the treatment of the midzone varies. A. In this first sketch, the midzone is left dark. This visually separates the foreground from the background, which emphasizes the background and decreases the sense of depth. B. In this sketch, moonlighting introduces a soft pattern of light and shadow in the midground that softly ties the foreground to the background. C. This last sketch shows floodlighting the midground, visually integrating all three zones, and increasing apparent depth. Drawing: Lezlie Johannessen.*

- View from the outside to the inside—the same issue with the window exists as above. In this case, vertical and horizontal surface lighting on the inside needs to be higher than the levels outside.
- View in both directions equally important—the lighting on both sides of the window needs to be closely balanced when the views are adjacent (see Figures 3.8 & 3.9). When the views look in different directions, follow the one-way-view rule (see Figures 3.10 to 3.12).

This issue consists of controlling offending brightness (from the viewing side) and providing high-enough light levels to show the scene. Evaluate the surfaces that comprise the view and plan enough lighting on those surfaces. For example, if lawn represents 75 percent of the view through the window, the lawn becomes the primary surface determining the minimum lighting level required. This issue does not change the composition but determines required light level.

With multiple viewing directions, the control of fixture brightness becomes paramount. This means selecting fixtures that shield the light source or providing shielding louvers or shrouds. Aiming angles of both uplights and downlights need to be controlled carefully to avoid glare. This also increases the need for carefully balancing the composition from one area to another.

City views further complicate the situation. Typically, they become the focal point and therefore set the lighting levels. All areas surrounding the city view should be balanced to create a pleasing composition (see Color Plate 21).

Mood or Atmosphere
Lighting can evoke excitement, drama, mystery, romance, or any number of moods. It defines how a person should feel in a space. This power of light provides the capability to affect substantially how a space appears. For example, to create a sense of quietness, use soft, sweeping strokes of downlight (see Color Plates 40 & 41).

High brightness contrast creates *drama* (see Figure 3.14). Exciting to look at, high contrast does not produce comfort for people in a space. Many situations exist where people will tend not to be in the landscape at night, and therefore looking at the landscape is more important than use. For example:

- Lack of access to the landscape (upper-floor apartments or steep slopes)
- Inclement weather discouraging use of the landscape
- Landscape intended primarily for daytime use (office park landscapes)
- Residential landscapes to expand the interior space visually
- Large landscapes where not all areas can or should be lit for use

Use dramatic lighting with care when people will be in the landscape. Confine it to restricted areas at boundaries or where people will not go. Provide a less severe contrast in areas where people will spend time at night.

Another mood, *mystery*, relies on uneven light, similar to drama, but with less contrast (see Figure 3.1). The contrast occurs primarily due to parts of the landscape remaining undefined. All mood lighting relies on uneven lighting and contrast. The type of mood produced relies on how contrast is used.

Balance
Several types of balance can be utilized in landscape design: *symmetry*, *asymmetry*, and *rhythm*. When balance makes a strong statement in a landscape, the lighting should maintain that balance at night.

Figure 3.7. *This mature Crape Myrtle (*Lagerstroemia indica*) has a higher, wider canopy opening a view to the trunk. Six low-voltage fixtures (with 20- to 50-watt MR16 flood lamps) located around the outer edge of the canopy produce the full shape of the tree. Using several fixtures with low-wattage lamps produces a natural appearance and a soft effect appropriate to a residential neighborhood without street lighting. Lighting Design: Janet Lennox Moyer, Luminae Souter Lighting Design; Landscape Design: Judith Peterson & Sally Slavin; Photograph: ©1990 Douglas A. Salin, www.dougsalin.com.*

A *symmetrical* layout offers visual stability and formality, while *asymmetry* presents tension or movement in a space and informality. When lighting a symmetrical layout, introduce equal brightness from one side of the composition to the other in order to retain the balance (see Figures 3.2 & 3.3). With asymmetrical landscape layouts, the lighting designer has more options to change the appearance (see Color Plates 2 & 3).

Repetition of a plant or shape in a landscape creates *rhythm*. This makes a strong daytime statement that can be useful to carry through to the landscape lighting.

Figure 3.8. *View out into the garden was imperative in this Kensington, California, garden due to the expanse of glass. Providing a higher level of light on the plants outside allows the viewer to see through the windows. Where the interior light level is higher, a reflection shows in the window (note the decorative fixture reflecting in the window behind the piano). A 120-volt incandescent or HID source works better than low-voltage incandescent for this technique. Lighting Design: Janet Lennox Moyer, Luminae Souter Lighting Design; Photograph: Mary E. Nichols.*

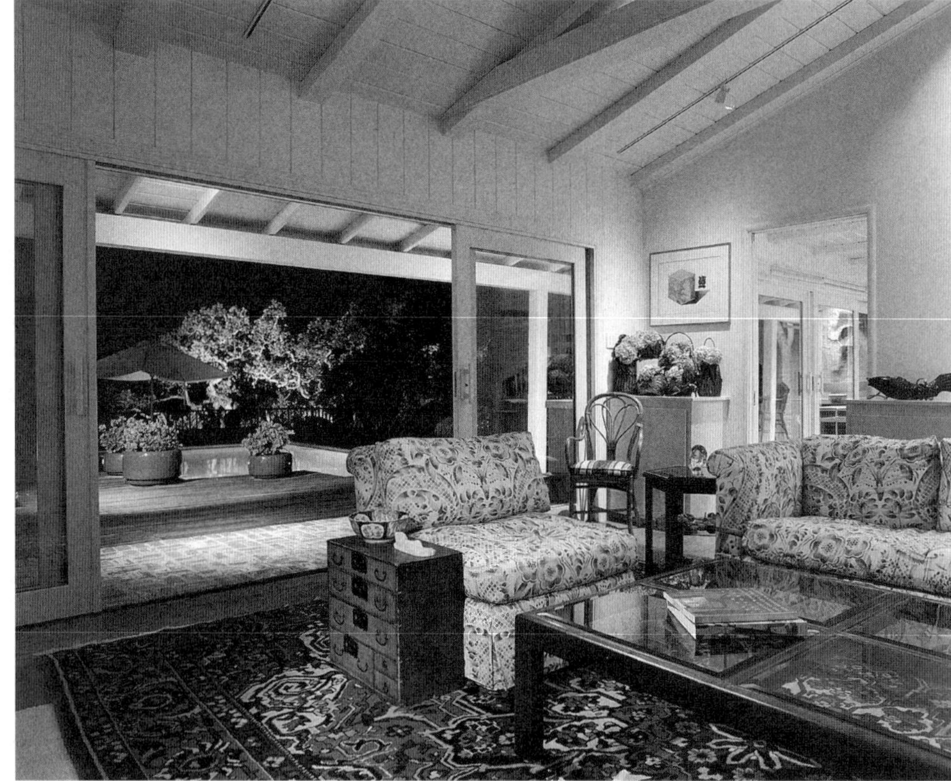

Figure 3.9. *Connecting the interior to the exterior allows a flow of function and enjoyment. The light level just outside the doors is high to allow for food and beverage tables during entertainment. Uplight on one Oak in the background provides some depth/boundary, and yet retains a sense of privacy. Lighting Design: Janet Lennox Moyer, MSH Visual Planners; Photograph: Kenneth Rice Photography, www.kenricephoto.com.*

__Figure 3.10.__ This Tiburon, California, home lit with 120-volt incandescent sources illustrates using a high light level inside to allow a view to the interior. It also shows using light to direct guests through the property to the front door by lighting only plants on the left side and bringing up the light level at the covered porch. Lighting Design: Janet Lennox Moyer, Luminae Souter Lighting Design; Photograph: ©1987, Douglas A. Salin—www.dougsalin.com.

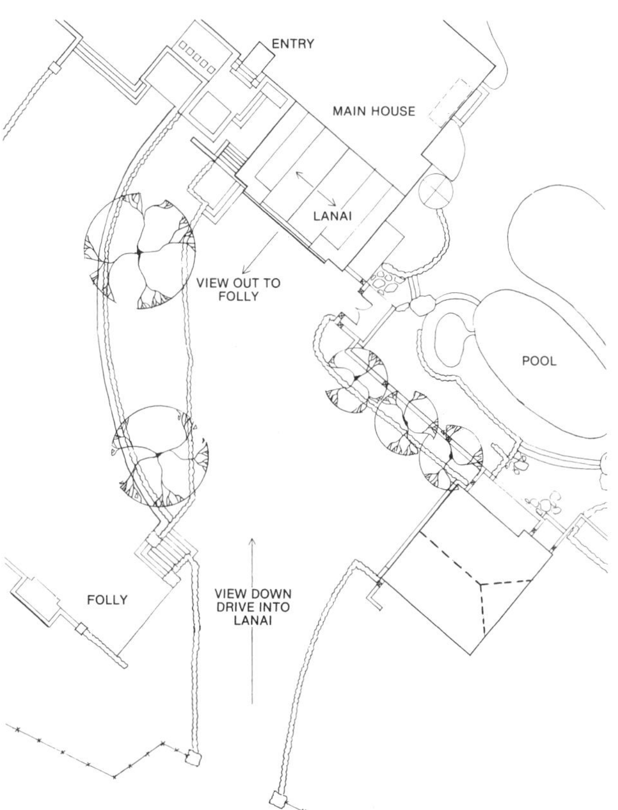

__Figure 3.11.__ This Tiburon, California, home plan illustrates the need for viewing both into a building from the landscape and out to the landscape from inside. Drawing: Lezlie Johannessen.

__Figure 3.12.__ Looking out through the lanai windows to the garden illustrates balancing light levels. Since all the walls are glass the light level outside can be lower than inside. Note the dark areas behind and to the side of the brick folly. Keeping these areas dark increased contrast, emphasizing the structure. Then, bringing up the levels seen through the left and right doors completes the composition. Lighting Design: Janet Lennox Moyer, Luminae Souter Lighting Design; Photograph: ©1987, Douglas A. Salin—www.dougsalin.com.

Figure 3.13. *Up- and downlighting creates a mini-composition within the larger composition shown in Figure 3.15. Uplight and downlight fixtures carefully placed to disappear during the day and at night in all seasons. The uplighting reveals the form of the Cherry trees, while the downlighting provides the owner with a sense of place by connecting the trees with the ground plane and spilling light onto the path connecting to the dock. Lighting Design: Janet Lennox Moyer, MSH Visual Planners; Photograph: Kenneth Rice Photography, www.kenricephoto.com.*

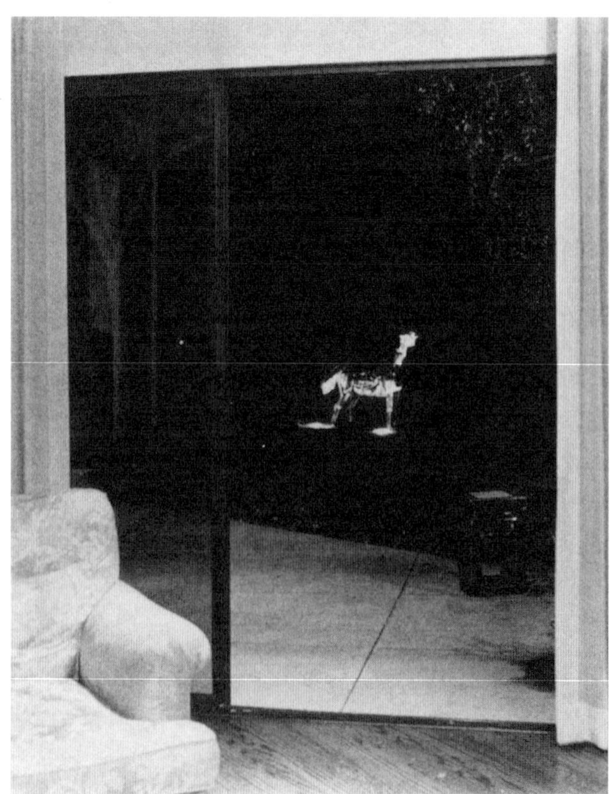

Figure 3.14. *View of a steel horse in a Woodside, California, backyard. Below-grade fixtures at the horse's front and back legs emphasize form. One above-grade fixture located 10 feet away throws a wash to fill in the rest of the body. The rest of the yard remaining in darkness creates high contrast and drama. Lighting Design: Lee Boyack; Photograph: Kenneth Rice Photography—www.kenricephoto.com.*

Figure 3.15. Driving a long driveway, this vista at the far end of the upper pond creates a visual destination vista to welcome people. As they near the pond, lighting at the lower pond visually directs guests to turn left and cross over the bridge on the way to the house. Lighting Design: Michael Stewart Hooker, Janet Lennox Moyer, & Paul Schreer, MSH Visual Planners; Photograph: Kenneth Rice Photography, www.kenricephoto.com.

Lighting these repeating shapes directs the viewer's eye through the space to a focal point or provides a visual link between two focal points.

Focal Points

Focal points direct how to structure a visual composition. There may be one or more focal points. Consider the interaction between focal points when developing a composition. With three elements of interest in a scene, one may be most important, a second next, and the third last. One may be more important than the other two, which are equal in importance, or they may all be equally important (see Color Plates 14 & 21).

An uneven number of focal points provides stability in the scene (when using multiples to create a rhythm effect, the odd versus even number issue becomes less important). In some cases, this may suggest leaving an object dark that is a daytime focal point in order to create visual stability.

One focal point permits the design to take on either a formal, symmetrical format (see Color Plates 45 & 46) or an informal, asymmetrical format (see Color Plate 59). The interaction of three focal points or elements in the scene creates a strong, stable image. Two focal points create instability, as the eye jumps continually from one to the other.

Cohesion

Cohesion is one of the most important tools of luminous composition. It is the element that determines how well the combination of elements work together in the scene. Lighting focal points alone will produce a spotty appearance. After identifying and determining the order of importance for the focal points, think about how the viewer's eye will move from one element to another. High contrast causes the eye to jump from one area to another because the shift from light to dark causes a visual break that is difficult for the eye. Providing a soft layer of light or light pattern(s) between focal points visually connects or ties the focal points together. This makes the composition comfortable for long-term viewing.

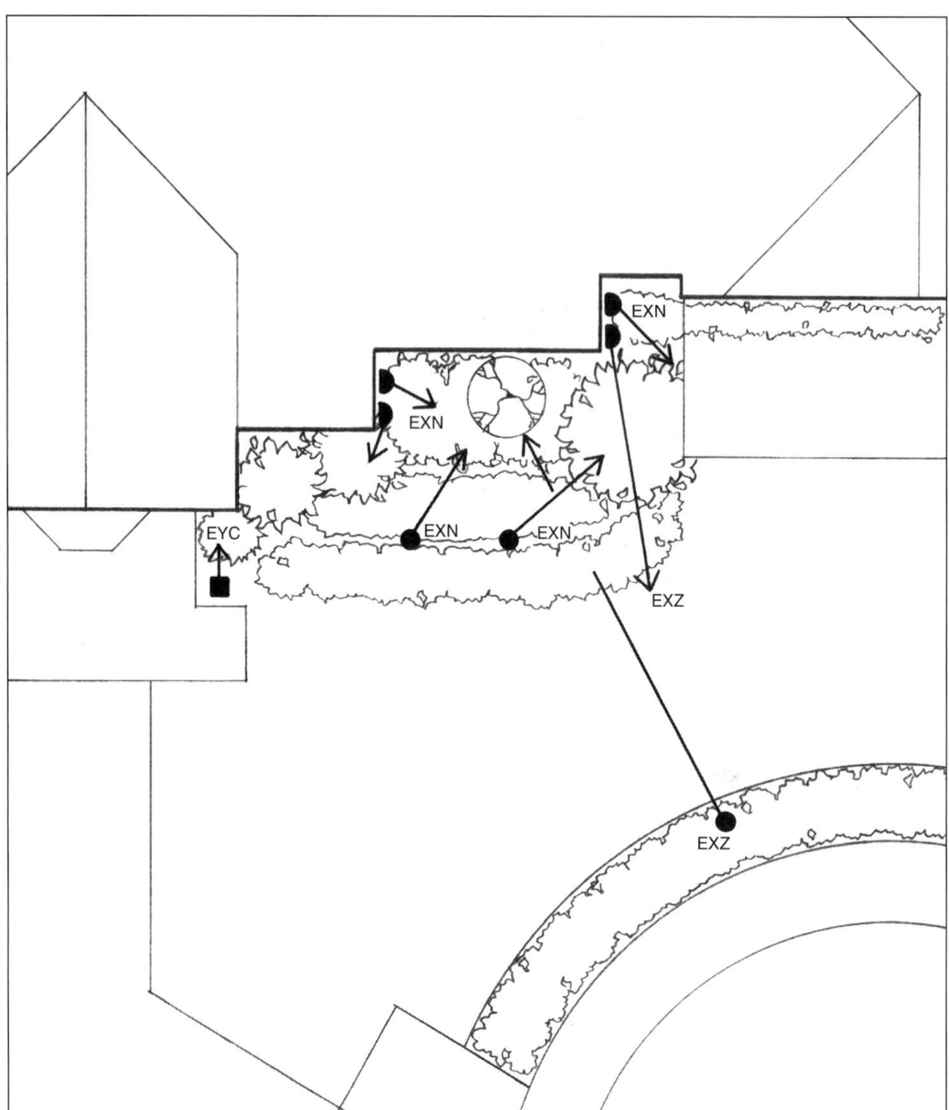

Figure 3.16. *This plan shows the space illustrated in the following sketches and the final lighting plan for it. Four fixtures mounted under the roof eaves downlight the planting and surrounding grass. Drawing: Lezlie Johannessen & Richard DePalma.*

LAMP LEGEND			
EXN	50 WATT	40°	MR16
EXZ	50 WATT	24°	MR16
EYC	75 WATT	42°	MR16

FIXTURE LEGEND	
←■	BELOW GRADE ADJUSTABLE 12 VOLT INCANDESCENT LUMINAIRE
←◖	EAVE MOUNTED ADJUSTABLE 12 VOLT INCANDESCENT LUMINAIRE
←●	STAKE MOUNTED ADJUSTABLE 12 VOLT INCANDESCENT LUMINAIRE

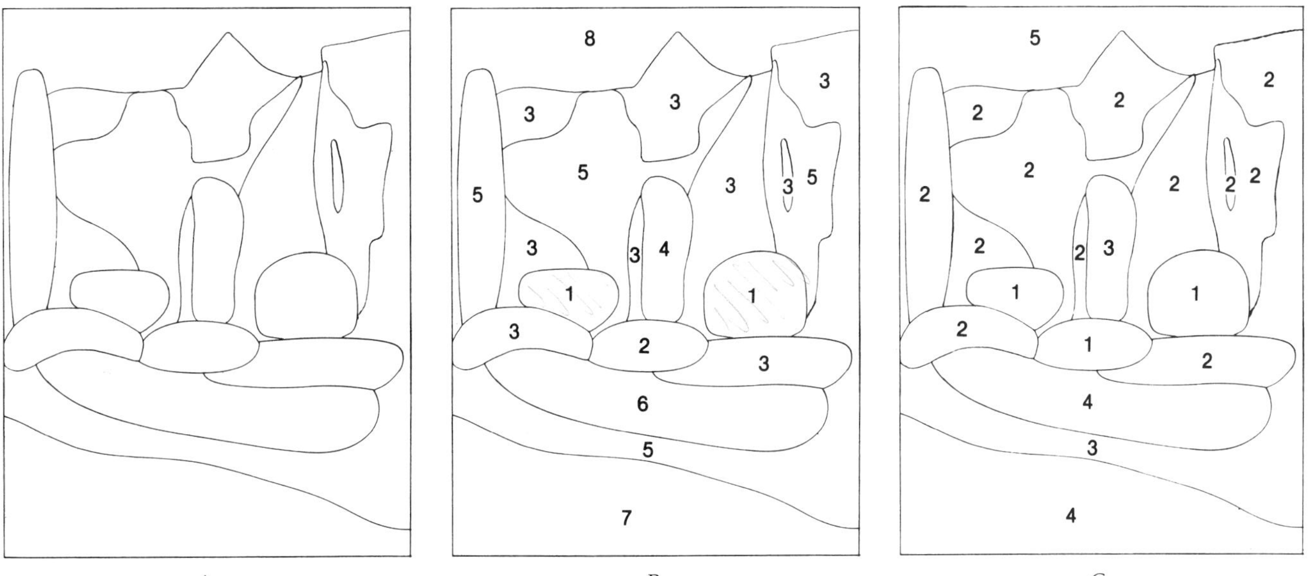

Figure 3.17. *A. Outline areas of the photograph or drawing that should be considered separately in the luminous composition. B & C. Assign the numeral 1 to areas that should be brightest. Use increasing numbers to represent areas of decreasing brightness. Make several numbered sketches to consider different approaches. Drawing: Lezlie Johannessen.*

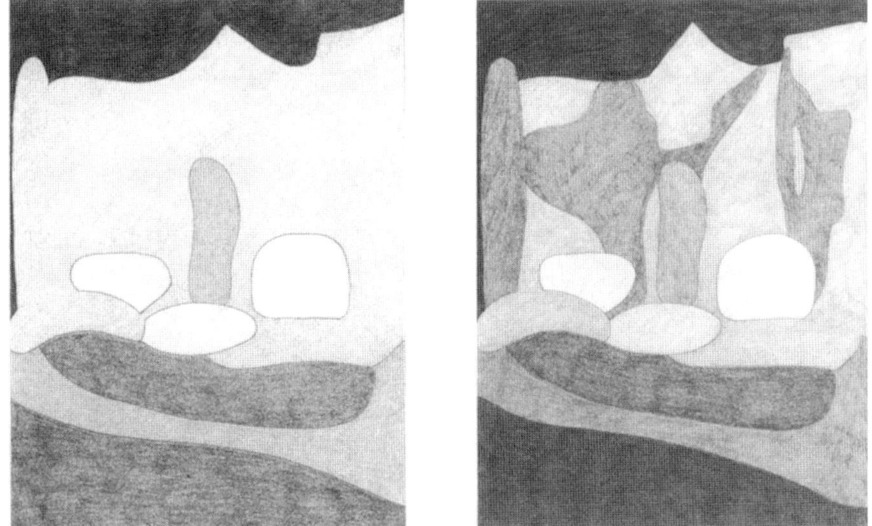

Figure 3.18. *Shading in the areas develops a rough idea of how the light affects the space. Areas with a numeral 1 in Figure 3.17 are not shaded. Areas with a numeral 2 are softly shaded. The darkness of the shading increases as the numbers increase. Drawing: Lezlie Johannessen.*

Figures 3.19 & 3.20. *Selecting areas of a garden to leave in darkness creates a private space in this northern California backyard. Lighting Design: Janet Lennox Moyer; Photograph: Kenneth Rice Photography, www.kenricephoto.com.*

Use cohesion when the landscape will be used for entertaining, sports, or any type of public access. In large commercial areas, provide cohesion in some areas (the pathways, for example) while introducing mood lighting in other areas.

To preview the effect of design ideas, sketch potential luminous compositions from a drawing or photograph of the landscape. Using a tissue overlay over a photograph, elevation, or perspective drawing, identify areas that should be visually separated in the scene. Next, plan a hierarchy of brightnesses by assigning a number to each area. Depending on the complexity of the landscape, the quantity of numbers used may vary. Each number represents a conceptual quantity of light or one layer in the visual composition. More than one area or element can use the same number whenever their visual impact in the scene should be equal. These numbers can also be used to identify layers or effects that should be controlled separately (see Figures 3.16, 3.16A, 3.17, & 3.18).

With all areas identified by number, shade each area to show a rough view of the brightness composition for the scene. This technique guides the designer's eye to create visual compositions using light as the artistic medium. By trying several variations of light layers on the scene, the most appropriate design approach will emerge. It may not be any one of the sketches, but a combination of parts from several sketches (see Figures 3.16 & 3.18).

Careful planning and the utilization of composition elements help lighting respond to project needs and present a pleasing night appearance. Too much existing landscape lighting today was installed with little or no thought to either day or night appearance. In any community, many examples of fixture glare and a blast of indiscriminate light from a fixture degrade the appearance of the surroundings. No matter how simple the lighting system, thinking about the lighting from this compositional approach will create an effect that enhances the environment.

4

The Design Process: Documenting and Installing Landscape Lighting

Once the lighting designer and the client have met to discuss the project and a project agreement has been signed, work begins on the project. The process of turning initial design ideas into a completed, installed lighting system involves several steps. First, the owner needs to understand the design, which requires the designer to produce *presentation documentation* to convey the design intent, to express the quality/performance of the system, and to show an example(s) of the proposed lighting equipment. After receiving approval of the conceptual design from the owner, the designer then proceeds to produce working drawings, typically called *contract documents,* that provide the directions for the electrical contractor to install the lighting system.

After contract documents have been issued and bids have been reviewed, a contractor will be selected to carry out the installation. The designer and contractor will then walk the site, marking the locations of all equipment and accessories. Once the equipment has been installed, the designer will direct the aiming of the system to provide the desired lighting effects. During this phase of project work, the design team and the installing contractor need to note locations of all equipment, any changes in types or quantities of equipment, and any other information important for future project maintenance.

The last step in documentation includes providing the owner with as-built documentation, typically called *record documents.* This documentation includes drawings and specifications of all installed equipment, a description of all maintenance tasks that need to be done to keep the system functioning properly, and a schedule for ongoing design and maintenance.

The design and construction process for lighting projects varies with the size of the project, other construction (architectural or landscape) occurring simultaneously on the site, and the state of the site. On large projects that involve developing a new site, the lighting design will be just one part of the project, which may include architectural and landscape architectural design and construction. In this case, presentations to the owner are often integrated with other landscape design issues, and lighting drawings and specifications are integrated into a package of documentation for the entire project.

Alternatively, when lighting a relatively small and/or previously developed site, the documentation and process may be simplified. In some cases, it may make fiscal sense; in others, the owners may request that no drawings be produced, preferring that the entire design be developed through a combination of written requirements and on-site directions from the designer to the contractor. The major drawbacks to this approach include a greater risk of the contractor misunderstanding the design intent and the absence of any final documentation provided to the owner for ongoing system maintenance. In all cases, the designer should at least produce a sketch of the lighting layout on the site for the contractor and a sketch of the locations of fix-

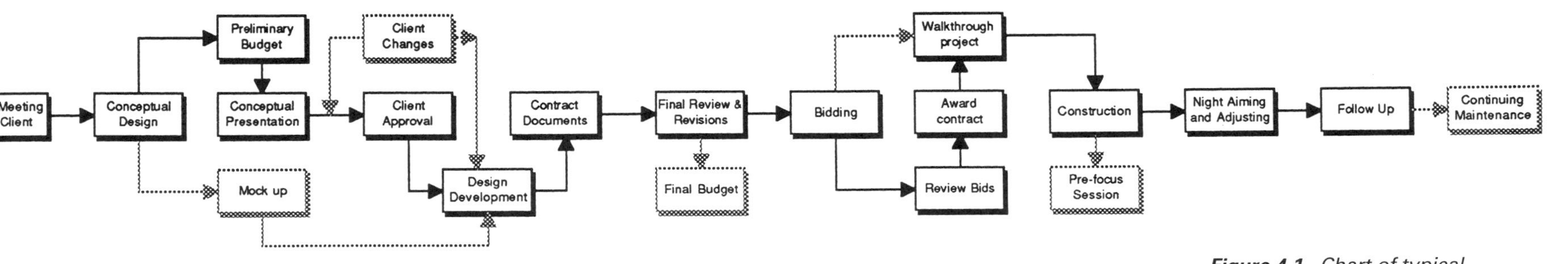

Figure 4.1. *Chart of typical project flow.*

Maple Tree 13
Edge of maze garden
Trunk
Pot
up FMW
up FMW
up FMW
Branch
Pot
Plan of maple branch coming towards patio. As viewed while standing at water feature and facing maple.
sketch #3
No Scale 3/02
MSH Visual Planners
Limited Liability Company
Holms Landscape Lighting
Lafayette, CA
Brunswick, New York
518.235.4756
Oakland California
510.595.4360

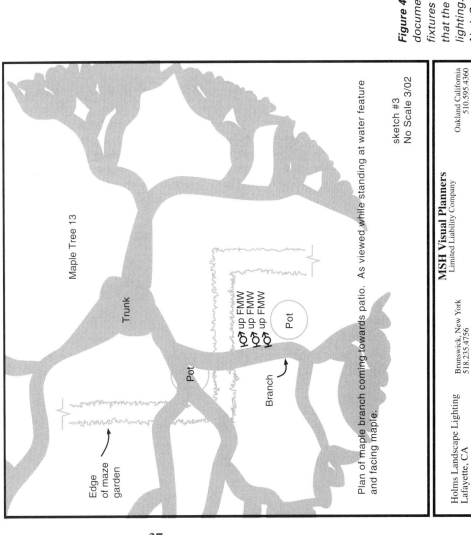

Figure 4.2. *This sketch documents the location of fixtures in Maple Tree 13 so that the client can maintain the lighting. Drawing: Jim Gross & N. J. Smith.*

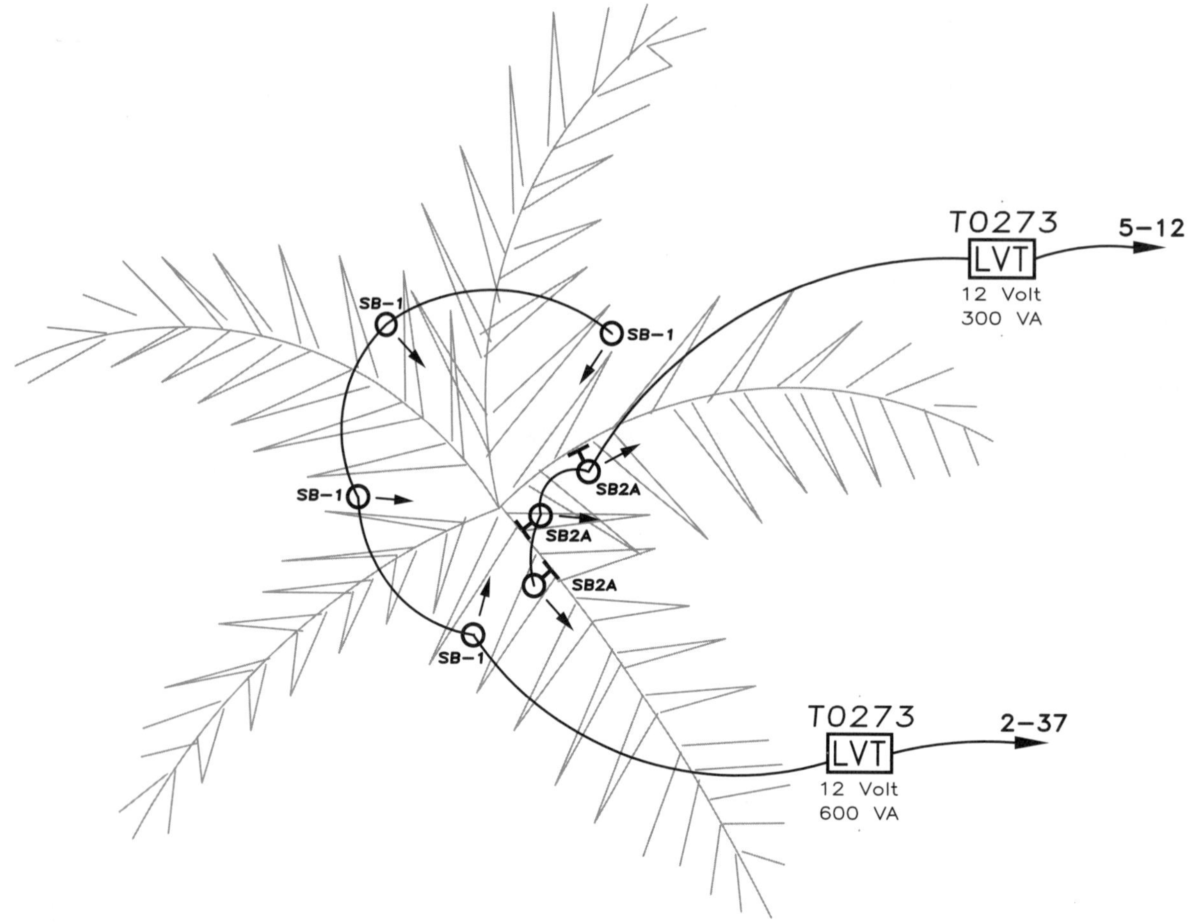

Figure 4.3. *Show all lighting information with dark, thick lines. All background information should show but be softened or lightened to allow the lighting to be easily identifiable. Having plant materials, hardscape, and structures on the plan provides a sense of context for future maintenance. Drawing: N. J. Smith.*

tures, lamps utilized, and aiming intent for the owner to use in maintaining the system (see Figures 4.2 & 4.4).

Regardless of the complexity or formality of the process and the type of documentation produced, the basic flow of steps to produce a finished lighting installation follows the same path (see Figure 4.1). This chapter discusses the work involved from conceptual design documentation through contract documents and construction. The next chapter will cover the process of converting contract documents into record documents and the maintenance documentation necessary to keep the lighting system functioning properly.

PROJECT COMMUNICATIONS

On any construction project, success requires clear communication between the team members—owner(s), designer(s), and installing contractor(s). Decisions made and directions taken at each stage must be clearly understood and supported by all people involved in the design and installation of the project work. Information can be disseminated verbally or visually, through photographic, written, or drawn documentation.

The results of successful communication, using any or all of these means of communication, will include:

- Execution of the design as conceived
- Maintenance of the design intent over the planned project life span
- Control of project costs
- Adherence to project schedules
- Owner satisfaction with the quality of the design and the construction process, the design concept, the project installation, and the performance of the design

At the time of the first edition of this book, most project drawings were done by hand. Today, computer technology allows the landscape designer to electroni-

Figure 4.4. A marked-up photograph clearly documents information that the owner and/or installer needs to understand. This can accompany drawings or be used when no site drawings exist. Drawing: Jim Gross & N. J. Smith.

cally transfer project information and drawings over the Internet, via a CD, or through a Web-based project management site. Having access to project information on a computer offers the lighting designer the ability to provide more information to the client than previously affordable, to easily show the client multiple options, to quickly change ideas/direction as the project progresses, and to keep lighting documents current as the project evolves (landscape design, civil engineering, architecture, etc.). Because of these benefits, hand drawings are no longer widely produced.

COMPUTER-AIDED DESIGN (CAD)

Lighting designers typically work from landscape drawings provided by the landscape designer. Using the landscape designer's AutoCAD (or other software program) project files as a base, lighting designers can create a wide range of drawing options from simple graphic representations of fixture quantity and location to elaborate renderings of proposed techniques.

As the project starts, the lighting designer needs to understand the documentation standards to be followed. The landscape team's CAD manager provides the lighting team with the document and CAD standards, including:

Document Standards

- Sheet size
- Drawings scales
- Title block layout
- Sheet name and numbering system
- Document issuing procedures: ID, name, and date

Figure 4.5A–C. *This series shows a daytime view of Evening Island at the Chicago Botanic Garden along with a rendering of the lighting concept and a photograph of the mockup. The complexity of plant material does not lend itself to realistic rendering. Lighting Design: Janet Lennox Moyer & Dan Dyer, MSH Visual Planners; Rendering: Dan Dyer; Photographs: Dan Dyer.*

CAD Standards

- Layer names
- Line weights
- Text and fonts
- Pen colors
- Pen widths
- Pen numbers
- XREF (external reference) files: overlay or attachment
- Adding new layers

Once the lighting designer has received a finished background plan from the landscape designer, the process of adding the layers with lighting information into the project drawing can begin. The lighting documentation should be produced on new lighting layers that no other team members modify in any way. This allows lighting updates to be done without affecting other work in other disciplines.

Often the computer files received by the lighting designer have more information than needed for understanding the lighting. Removing information unnecessary to the lighting by turning off layers simplifies the lighting background and allows the lighting information to show more easily and clearly. All landscape information should be softened to allow the lighting information to show most boldly (see Figure 4.3). Since the landscape background is likely to keep changing until well into or after construction completion, the lighting designer needs to stay in contact with the landscape designer to ensure that the background utilized for the lighting design documentation is current and accurate.

Often complete or accurate site drawings do not exist. The lighting designer may have to either produce the background or update the files provided with tree locations, new patios, pools, walkways, and so on. This coordination can take significant time and needs to be considered in the fee structure for the project.

The number of lighting layers and how the project is organized will depend on the scale and complexity of the project. Large-scale projects often require multiple sheets for the lighting layout. Trying to put the entire site onto one sheet would make the scale too small to read. Complicated projects might require a separate layer for fixture location, transformer, and/or controls information. Some projects require multiple sheets of schematic wiring and installation details.

Figure 4.6A–C. *Looking at this individual tree in the Chicago Botanic Garden shows even more clearly how rendering on plant materials is not as effective at showing lighting as a mock-up. Lighting Design: Janet Lennox Moyer & Dan Dyer, MSH Visual Planners; Rendering: Dan Dyer; Photographs: Dan Dyer.*

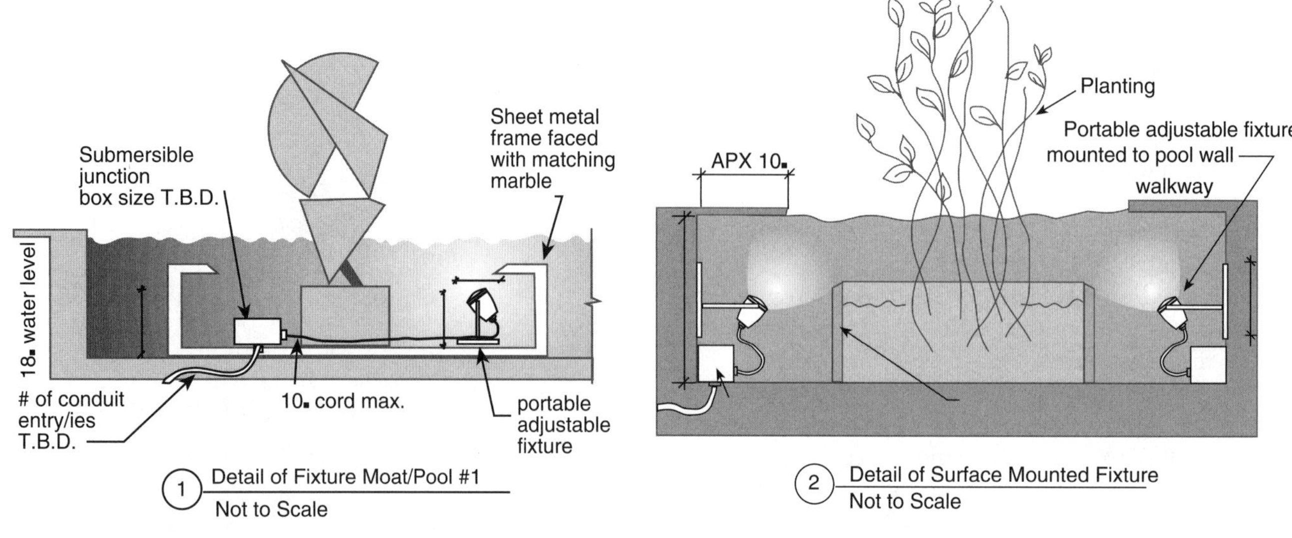

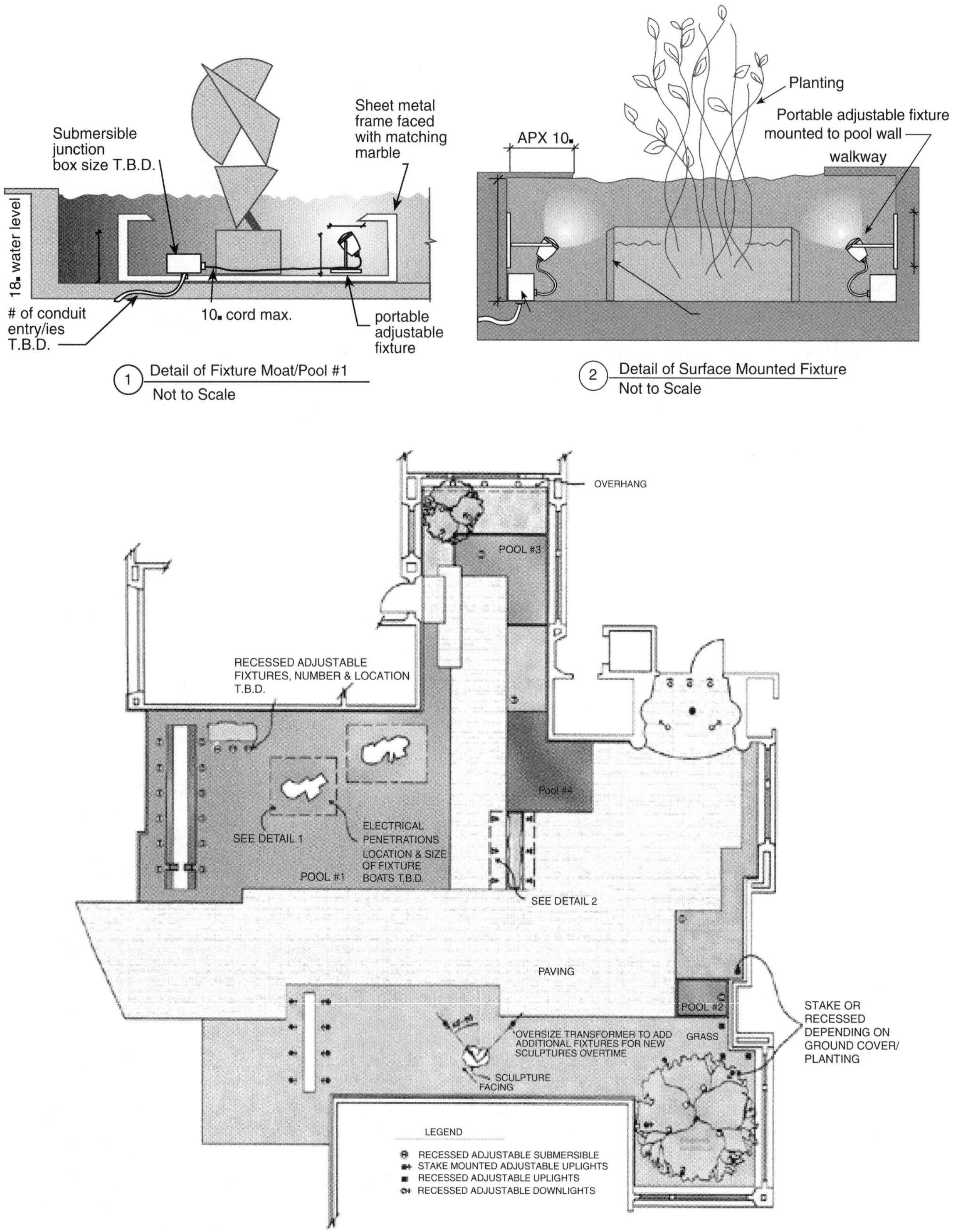

Figure 4.7A–C. *Preparing conceptual sketches using computer capabilities conveys ideas easily (color adds to the clarification—the water areas would be blue, for example). Drawings: Insiya Shakir, Jim Gross, & N. J. Smith.*

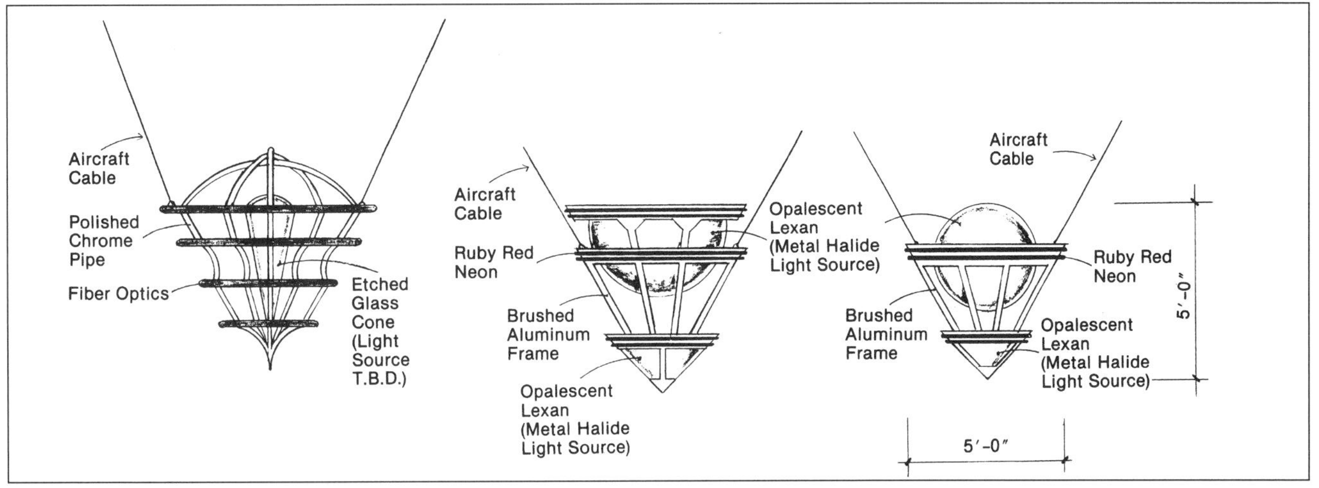

A.

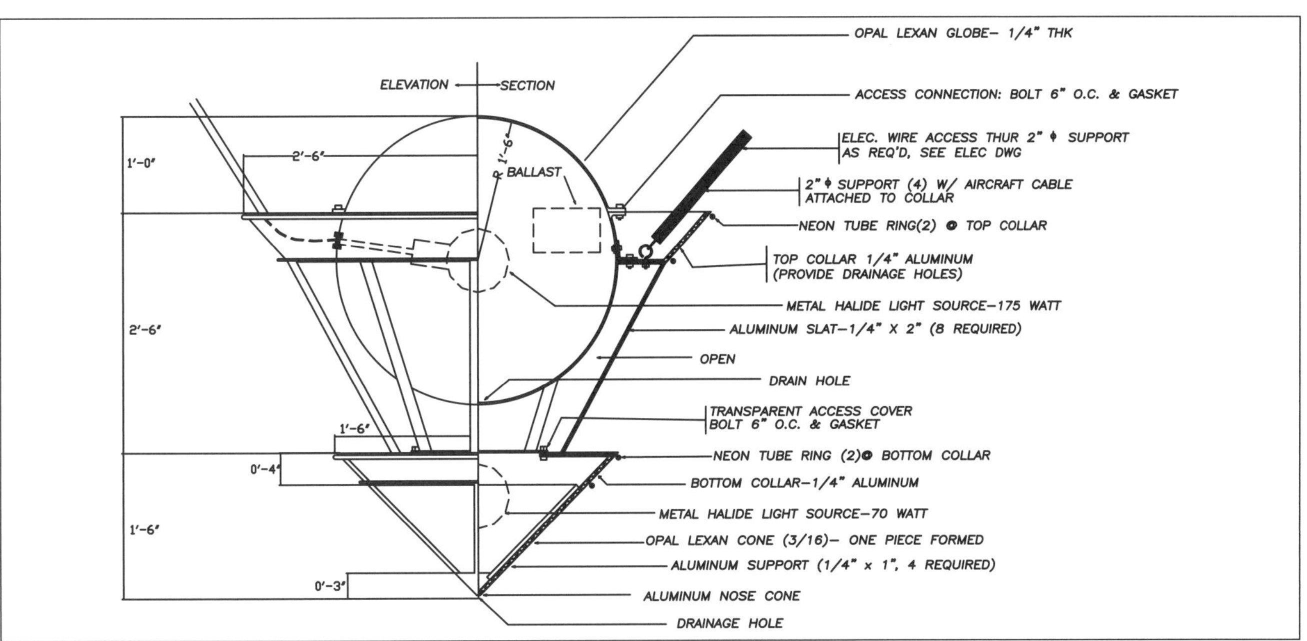

B.

C.

Figure 4.8A–C. *Ten years ago, the right-hand fixture had just been selected from this trio of sketches for the Pierce Transit Commerce Street Improvements custom pendant. Winona Lighting then produced the construction submittal drawing (B). The transition from conceptual design to construction, while dramatic in the technical requirements and detailing, ends up producing a fixture exactly as the design team imagined it. Conceptual Fixture Design & Drawings: Lezlie Johannessen, Jan Moyer Design; Submittal Drawing: Winona Lighting; Photograph: Amphion Environmental.*

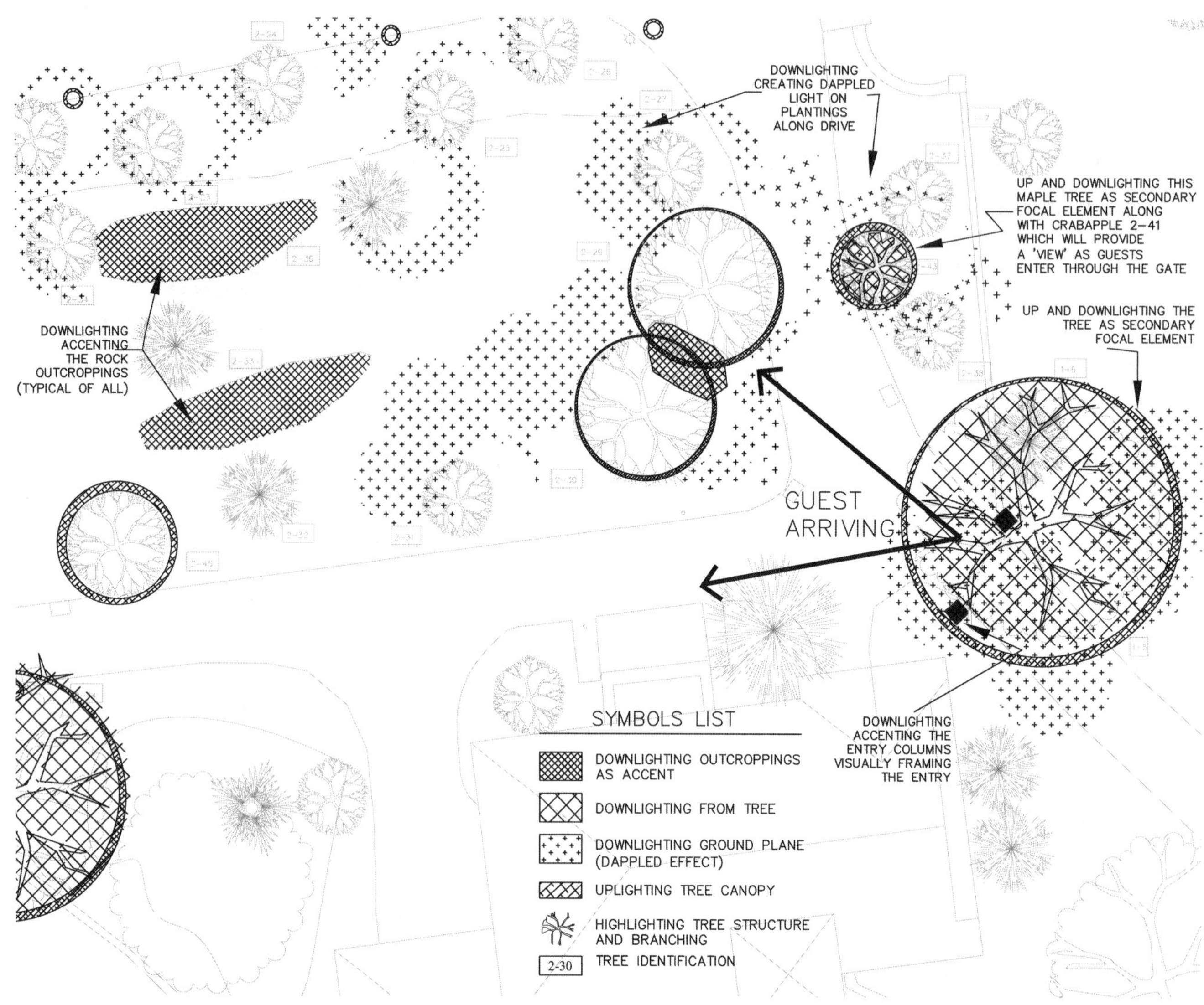

Figure 4.9. *An example of a shading technique master plan drawing (color adds clarity). Lighting Design: Janet Lennox Moyer, MSH Visual Planners; Drawing: Insiya Shakir.*

A variety of software exists for producing contract documents and for many other documentation purposes. All sorts of calculations can be done for parking lots and roadways, but, these programs have little use in landscape lighting. Calculating the way lighting will make a tree look isn't feasible. No graphics program can accurately illustrate the lighting effects intended for a tree (see Figures 4.5A–C & 4.6A–C).

CONCEPTUAL DESIGN PHASE DOCUMENTS

The conceptual design phase of a project begins with developing the lighting intent. It requires the designer(s) to evaluate all the client information gathered during interviews, including the intended uses of the space and the client's reactions to and preferences about light levels and lighting options as well as long-term development plans for the site. The designer must understand issues that pertain to the specific site identified during site visits, and must have discussed the landscape design with the landscape professional and studied the landscape design documents thoroughly enough to mentally visualize new gardens and the physical attributes of the site. The design team needs to have thoroughly synthesized this information collected from the client and the site in order to establish the lighting goals. This includes determining the owner's expected result(s) and identifying the lighting objectives—the specific visual elements that will result in the accomplishment of the project goals for the owner.

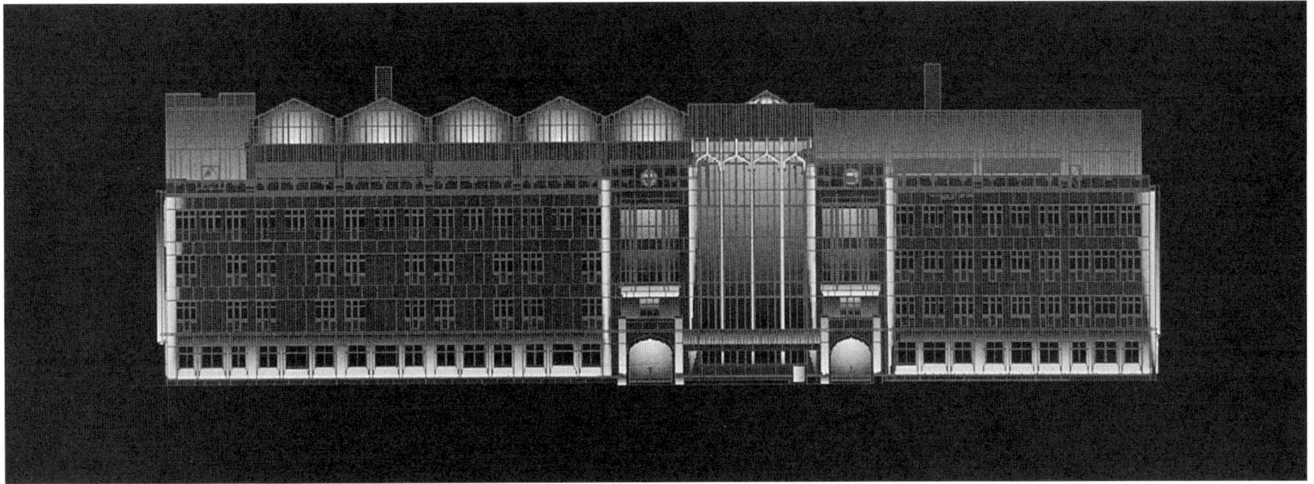

Sacred Heart Basilica
Proposed Exterior Lighting
Sponsored by:
Niagara Mohawk

MSH Visual Planners
Limited Liability Company
107 Leversee RD. 3403 Piedmont Ave. Suite 502
Brunswick, NY 12182 Oakland, CA 94611
Voice: 518.235.4756 Voice: 510.595.4360
Fax: 518.235.4756 Fax: 510.595.4361

Figure 4.10. *This computer-generated rendering of the lighting concept for the front elevation of the University of Chicago Biomedical Building clearly showed the design team and the clients how the lighting would transform the building at night. Lighting Design: Michael Stewart Hooker; Drawing: John Court & Michael Stewart Hooker.*

Figure 4.11. *A perspective rendering of the lighting concept for the Sacred Heart Basilica in Syracuse, New York, brings the building to life. The design team and clients can use this type of drawing to publicize the idea of building lighting. Lighting Design: Janet Lennox Moyer, Patricia Rizzo, Jean Paul Freyssinier Nova, & John Tokarczyk; Rendering: John Tokarczyk. Sacred Heart Basilica Proposed Exterior Lighting Sponsored by: Niagra Mohawk Power Corporation, a National Grid Company.*

TERMINOLOGY	
PROJECT AGREEMENT	A document explaining the scope of the project, the tasks to be completed, and fees to be charged
AUTOCAD	A software program produced by AutoDesk. Other programs include MicroStation and PowerCAD for Macintosh users
CAD	Computer aided design—Software for the production of architectural plans
CIVIL TWILIGHT	The time each day that electric lighting becomes necessary in order to carry on outdoor activities
CUT SHEET	Manufacturers literature defining the parts, pieces, accessories, and finish for a lighting fixture
'FURNISH'	Deliver to the job site and to the Owner or Contractor
'INSTALL'	Install material furnished by the Owner or under other parts of the Contract (or by Unknown Others)
'PROVIDE'	Furnish, store, construct, install, test, clean, adjust, and place into operation

Figure 4.12

Lighting objectives include some combination of the following:

- *Visibility*—a composite of everything that assists in sight, understanding, and recognition
- *Composition*—the organization of brightness relationships between surfaces and/or objects in space
- *Image*—a visible representation of the desired style, character, and impression
- *Mood*—an emotional response to the environment
- *Comfort*—a subjective satisfaction or freedom from pain and anxiety (including physical, aesthetic, functional, and psychological support)
- *Orientation*—an awareness of location, time, enclosure, direction, destination, and/or presence

The designer makes initial decisions based on the way he/she envisions how the lighting will sculpt landscape or how it will reveal the selected landscape elements from the dark. These ideas then translate into the number and types of lamps required to produce the effects of this imagined night scene. With effects determined, generic fixtures that will hold the lamps can be identified. General fixture and transformer or ballast locations should be identified, and control strategies as well as provisions for future system expansion need to be considered.

Organize the conceptual ideas into a master plan by areas (See Documents Appendix Figures A6 & A7) and/or lighting effects. This provides the owner with a complete, cohesive design for the mature landscape. Lighting ideas and associated costs can then be reviewed by section of the garden or by layers of light. The first priority for most projects will be to implement the required power for the master plan throughout the site. Then, lighting for selected garden areas can be implemented over the course of years.

Presentation Drawings

Presentation drawings in the form of conceptual sketches, layouts, and/or renderings help the client understand the intent of the proposed lighting. At this juncture in the project, other issues are equally important to the visual impression. Initial and maintenance costs must be prepared and reviewed with the owner. This provides them with all the information required to evaluate aesthetic and financial ramifications before proceeding to the next phase of work. A designer needs to consider how to communicate the following issues

Figure 4.13. Equipment has been laid out during the day to test more than one technique for lighting this tree. The fixtures have been lamped, connected to transformers and/or extension cords, and preaimed. Once darkness falls, the real work of testing the concept can begin. Photograph: Janet Lennox Moyer.

when selecting how to present the design intent to the client:

- Aesthetic imagery
- Functional performance
- Performance requirements of equipment and materials
- Scale and cost of the work

To express these ideas to the owner and other design team members, one or more of the following types of design documents can be utilized:

- *Visual concept statements*—a project description including an explanation of how the lighting scheme will achieve the owner's goals and objectives, overall visual impressions and those from key vista points resulting from the conceived use of qualities of light, the functional characteristics of the system resulting from the conceived qualities of light, and technical qualitative and quantitative requirements
- *Visual concept renderings*—black and white or color, hand- or computer-generated images of one or more areas of a project
- *Performance concept sketches and/or layouts*—black and white or color, hand- or computer-generated plans showing equipment location and/or installation detail
- *Basic equipment layouts*—schematic location or quantitative allocation of fixtures for general or specific locations
- *Performance specifications and calculations*—one or more of the following as necessary:
  Perceptual brightness levels
  Luminance pattern, levels, and/or ratios
  Exitance levels and/or ratios
  Illuminance pattern, levels, and/or ratios
  Visibility levels
  Contrast ratios

Figure 4.14. For either mock-up or actual aiming sessions, low-voltage stake-mounted fixtures should be laid down in the approximate location of the initial marker. Photograph: Janet Lennox Moyer.

Discomfort glare levels
Disability glare levels
Color rendering levels
Correlated color temperatures, shifts, and/or contrast ratios

- *Lighting fixture information*—generic or specific fixture imagery, scale, lamping, mounting, finish, required or potential accessories
- *Budget and estimate information*—purchase and installation costs including typical industry markups and hourly costs (typically by area), thus allowing for potential phasing of installation

The format(s) of drawings will vary based on the client's ability to understand lighting and architectural drawings and the type of project (see "Types of Presentation Drawings," below). Using presentation documentation as a tool provides a client the opportunity to review the initial ideas and either request changes or additions or approve the concept as shown. Design documents should provide the following outcomes for a project:

- The owner's understanding, acceptance, and support of the design
- The owner's and designer's ability to manage project cost
- The contractor's and supplier's understanding, acceptance, and support of the design
- The contractor's and supplier's ability to execute the concepts as intended
- The project team's ability to integrate the design with other systems and project design elements

Most of the changes the owner will request happen at this stage of the project. It is crucial that the owner understands and approves the proposed design before working drawings are produced for construction. Most frequently this approval consists of the owner's signature on a blueprint or a letter authorizing the designer to proceed with the next phase of work. In some cases, when the designer and owner have worked together previously, know each other well, and have a strong trust between them, a verbal approval is enough to authorize proceeding to the next phase of work.

Types of Presentation Drawings

Presentation drawings vary widely in technique and formality. Each emphasizes different aspects of the lighting design. Sometimes, a suite of sketches with a preliminary fixture layout and details will graphically explain a concept (see Figure 4.7A–C). In some cases, the designer may present more than one concept. When alternative schemes are presented, it may be to provide the owners with aesthetic choices, or because different schemes offer varying benefits and drawbacks that need to be discussed and evaluated (see Figure 4.8A–C).

Other types of presentation drawings include more formal approaches that give the owners a visual picture of the intended design. An earlier edition of this book included several hand-drawn techniques. This edition will concentrate on computer-generated imagery.

Perhaps the simplest technique is to shade a plan with patterns and/or colors representing a specific lighting technique. Arrows delineate the important viewing locations and text explains the concept or technique (see Figure 4.9).

Shading a photograph of the site or an elevation/perspective drawing of an element (see Figure 4.6A–C) or a section of a garden (see Figure 4.5A–C) shows graphically how a familiar daytime setting will be transformed at night. Brightness variation provides some information about the hierarchical importance of elements. Using a graphics program such as Adobe Photoshop, a daytime view can be generally translated into a composite of nighttime brightness relationships. Several fixture manufacturers make available computer programs that allow a designer to create a general night scene of a garden (see the websites for Kichler and Vista in the Lighting Manufacturers Directory).

Using a combination of commercially available graphics programs, a more realistic lighting appear-

LANDSCAPE WIRE LIST

FRONT YARD:

WIRE #:	WIRE SIZE:	AREA:
1	#10	Mesquite tree
2	#10	Mesquite tree
6	#12	Street Octaillo
7	#12	Sonoran Palo Verde-by family room
8	#12	Sonoran Palo Verde-by family room
9	#12	Drive Saguaro
10	#12	**Future– drive Saguero**
11	#12	Yucca
12	#12	**Future– Yucca**
17	#12	Saguro by front door
18	#12	Saguro by front door
19	#12	Octaillo by front door

BACK YARD:

WIRE #:	WIRE SIZE:	AREA:
3	#10	Palo Verde Tree by sewing room
4	#10	Palo Verde Tree by sewing room
5	#10	**Future– Palo Verde tree by sewing room**
13	#12	Existing tree by house
14	#12	Octaillo by wash
15	#12	Existing tree
16	#12	Existing tree
20	#12	**Future– Palo Verde tree by sewing room**

Figure 4.15. *A chart showing the actual cables installed at a site facilitates future system expansion. Drawing: Janet Lennox Moyer & N. J. Smith.*

ance can be created on architectural elements (see Figures 4.10 & 4.11). The simplicity of the building materials, compared to the complex characteristics of leaf, canopy, and trunk structure of a tree (see Figure 4.6A–C and Chapter 14) allows for relatively reasonable computer calculation of the night appearance. Producing these images is time-consuming and requires an experienced hand; this person must be knowledgeable enough about lighting to know whether the imagery being generated by the computer can actually be produced using available lamps and associated lighting equipment.

Neither hand-drawn nor computer-generated drawings capture the actual experience of lighting (see Figure 4.5). This limitation of drawings needs to be understood by the designer, and expressed to the client. When the drawings are not enough to convey the ideas, the lighting designer needs to suggest a mock-up, take the client to see other projects, or show the client photographs of other installations utilizing similar ideas.

Mock-up Sessions

During the *conceptual design* stage, the designer may need to do a mock-up, either to illustrate to the owner the potential lighting effect(s) or to determine, for the design team, if a new idea will work. A mock-up consists of bringing lighting equipment to a site and setting it up to show or test lighting ideas at night.

As a marketing tool, setting up lighting in one or more areas of a client's garden can help convince a client to hire the designer or help the client understand the lighting effect(s). A mock-up, either on-site or in a darkened office space can determine appropriate lamp selection, fixture location, and/or best technique to use in a specific situation. Mock-up sessions visually explain what clients often have a hard time understanding from drawings and written descriptions.

Issues to plan for in determining a mock-up include:

- *Time of year.* The best time of year for a mock-up is late October through early April, when darkness begins early in the day. The United States Naval Observatory, Astronomical Applications Department has a website, http://aa.usno.navy.mil, that tracks twilight (among other sun and moon phenomena) throughout the world over the course of the year. A daily or annual chart earth that lists the end of civil twilight (see "Terminology Chart," Figure 4.12) can be produced for any location on (see Documents Appendix Figures A.24 & A.25).

- *Time of day.* While the lighting setup has to wait until after dark, equipment can be packed and transported to the site during the day. Power can be extended from existing sources using extension cords, and fixtures can be prepared, including preliminary lamp selections. The actual work of a mock-up to create or test the ideas or equipment under consideration needs to be done after dark. The number of people needed and hours required to prepare, set up, test, show, and take down the mock-up needs to be planned.
- *Staffing.* The amount of equipment needed, the areas where equipment will be located, distances and complication of preparing/providing power, and the amount of work to be done after dark suggests how many people to bring. Include tasks such as retrieving items from toolboxes, cars, or even supply houses in this planning. During the course of the night setup, the number, type, and/or location of fixtures might require adjustment. Multiple fixtures might need to be set up to compare techniques or effects. The fixtures will need aiming, and this will involve moving fixtures, horizontal and vertical fixture rotation, changing lamps, adding accessories, and so on. A person needs to be assigned to take care of procuring snacks and/or meals; even in many warm climates, the temperature will cool off at night, and having a warm cup of coffee becomes an important consideration.
- *Equipment and power.* The lamps, fixtures, mounting assemblies, shielding accessories, tools, power cords, gloves, and sometimes even snowshoes need to be procured, organized, and brought to the mock-up site. Once at the site, power needs to be distributed from available sources.
- *Setup.* All the equipment that the designer(s) will need should be brought to each mock-up location and prepared for the night aiming. Fixtures should be assembled, including inserting the lamp and any shielding accessories, attaching the appropriate mount (spike, canopy, etc.), and placing the equipment how and where the designer designates (see Figures 4.13 & 4.14). Spare lamps and fixtures or alternative lamps and fixtures should be prepared so that the work effort can concentrate on creating and testing effects once it is dark.
- *Teardown.* The mock-up team and the owner need to determine how long the equipment will remain on site. All the equipment utilized in the mock-up should remain for the presentation and duration of the mock-up. Any additional equipment not utilized needs to be removed and returned.

Consider photographing the mock-up. Photography of lighting is an involved process and usually disruptive to the lighting setup. In planning, therefore, arrange to have the photographer arrive when the setup will be essentially complete. If the mock-up will remain in place for more than one night, the photography should be done on another evening. The benefits to photographing this session will be many—a reminder to both owner and designer as to what was done, an example for future reference, and a contribution to future documentation of the project.

There is one additional mock-up consideration. For all fixtures that are permanently mounted in a lighting system (for example, 120-volt ground-mounted adjustable accent fixtures, below-grade fixtures, tree-mounted fixtures, and building/structure-mounted fixtures), a locating mock-up should be done at night. This will be discussed in more detail later in this chapter.

Preliminary Budget

Clients typically don't understand the cost of lighting. Responding to this issue by offering inexpensive fixtures in an attempt to limit the project cost causes long-term discontent toward the lighting industry. Inexpensive fixtures are not manufactured to respond to environmental and site challenges. Fixtures need to withstand continual wetting and drying conditions, especially in tropical locations or in landscapes that have irrigation systems. Sockets fail, mounting arms break, and aluminum spikes completely disintegrate in the ground (often within less than one year). All too often, aiming angles are lost because fixture-locking mechanisms cannot withstand shovels or rakes. Worse, after aiming the fixtures at night, the locking mechanism can't tighten solidly enough to hold the desired angle. All these maintenance problems cause client dissatisfaction.

Instead of offering inexpensive fixtures, develop an overall master plan for the site. Organize the lighting into independent areas or phases that can be installed as the garden develops or as the client feels financially comfortable. This requires initially sizing the electrical infrastructure for the addition of future load(s) and distributing the appropriate conduit/power throughout the site (see Figure 4.15). Once a client experiences successful landscape lighting, he or she typically will be more understanding of the costs involved.

The preliminary budget includes an estimate of the purchase price of the equipment and the cost of installing the equipment. For some projects it might include the design fees. Equipment costs include fixtures and lamps, as well as accessories for the fixtures, such as louvers or shrouds, special color finishes, and mounting canopies or stakes/spikes. Each project and every fixture will have different accessory requirements. The equipment costs include wiring equipment, such as junction boxes, conduit, conduit connectors, wire, transformers, breakers/fuses, cable ties, screws, controls, and so on.

Installation costs include the contractor's labor to install all the equipment, dig ditches for conduits, and participate in the after-dark aiming session(s). Overall project costs vary greatly from one size project to another and from one site to another due to varying labor rates from one community or area of the country to another, site conditions, and the complexity of the design. There is no simple way to assign a square-foot cost based on the equipment and quality of the system, as designers often do for interior lighting systems. Cost estimating is one of the many situations where a computer aids the designer. A cost program can be set up that allows input of all the equipment and installation variables on a given project to produce a useful preliminary budget.

Some designers look at all the costs from previous similar jobs and determine a cost per fixture that includes all the costs of the project. This factor can then be multiplied by the anticipated number of fixtures to get a ballpark cost estimate. This fixture unit price helps in revising the project when the owner wants to add to or simplify the lighting at any stage of the project. This per-fixture method, while useful, can be dangerous if trying to apply it as an actual budget. Integrating the cost of transformers, complicated control systems, difficult site power distribution issues, and other wiring items into a per-fixture cost does not always translate directly to the actual project costs. It is often wise to list the control system, which is often a large-cost item, as a separate item in preliminary budgets.

The designer starts by requesting a price for all the fixtures from one or more manufacturers. This pricing comes from an independent company that acts as a manufacturer's representative. The designer must be cautious to request a specific price estimate. This will typically be one of three costs: either the price at which the representative will sell the equipment to an electrical distributor, an estimated cost that the electrical contractor will pay, or an estimated cost to the owner.

In the lighting industry, there are several intermediary layers of business entities that the equipment passes through before reaching the client. The typical path starts with the manufacturer selling to the manufacturer's representative, who sells to an electrical distributor, who sells to the electrical contractor, who sells to the owner. At each point along the way, a cost is added to the original selling price from the manufacturer. On large projects, the general contractor will add a percentage on top of everyone else! The typical markup percentage varies with the business entity and by geographical area. The designer must understand what cost type is being provided and add in all the appropriate markups when computing the estimated purchase price for each fixture.

Clients tend to remember the preliminary budget estimate number and expect that is what the project will cost. The designer needs to make clear to the owner that the budget is an estimate and that the actual cost will be determined by the electrical contractors bidding on the construction documents.

DESIGN DEVELOPMENT PHASE

The conceptual phase of work is followed by design development. The work in this phase refines the lighting ideas. Often, some research may be needed to determine how to produce an effect or how to build a custom fixture. The designer will meet with manufacturers or manufacturers' representatives to discuss how conceptual custom fixtures would be constructed. At this time, the designer should request current fixture costs to update the preliminary budget and advise the client as to any changes in project costs.

The designer reviews and determines the final type and quantity of fixtures. Associated equipment gets identified and located including remote transformers, ballasts, and/or intermediate junction boxes. Control strategies get defined and developed. The schedules required for all equipment get produced, always including provisions for future expansion of the system.

This phase of work culminates in translating the conceptual ideas into working drawings or contract documents that show the locations of fixtures and prescribe the equipment to be used for the project.

CONSTRUCTION OR CONTRACT DOCUMENTS

The purpose of this documentation is to provide the contractor with information about what material and equipment to purchase and where and how to install it. A designer should never assume that a contractor understands something or knows what the designer wants. Everything required for the project needs to be clearly indicated and explained on the drawings or in the specifications. The contract documents for lighting projects

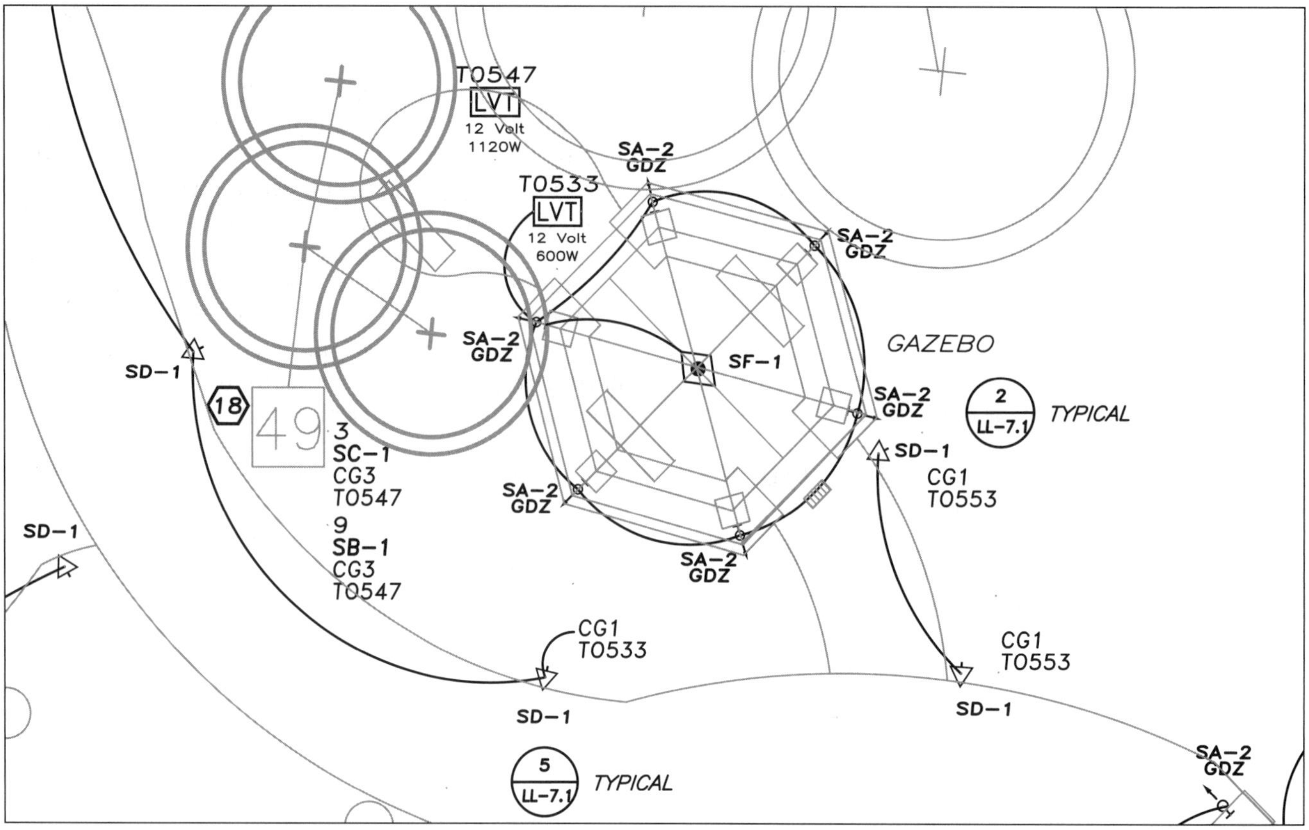

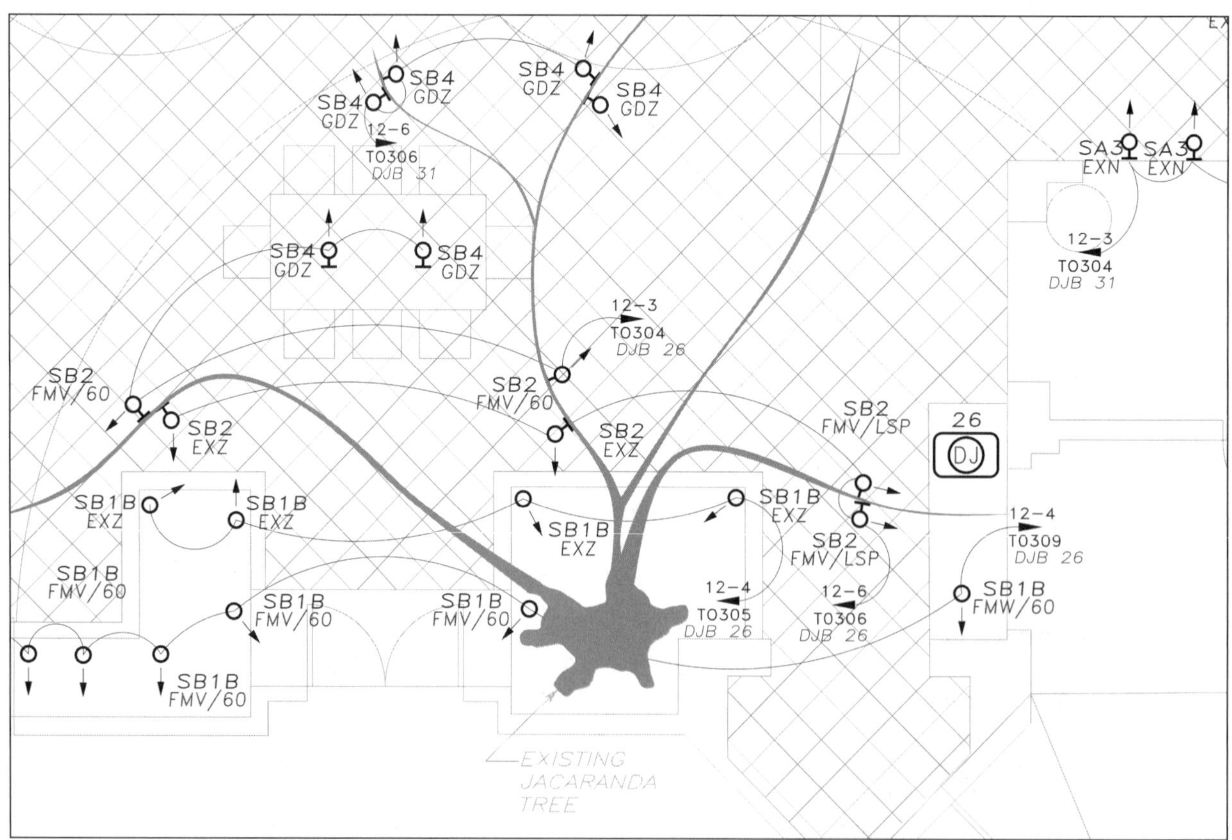

Figure 4.16A&B. *These two drawings show examples of alternate ways to provide lighting fixture, transformer, and controls information on contract document layout sheets. Lighting Design: Janet Lennox Moyer & Michael Stewart Hooker: Drawings: Elizabeth Krietemeyer & Andrew Johnson.*

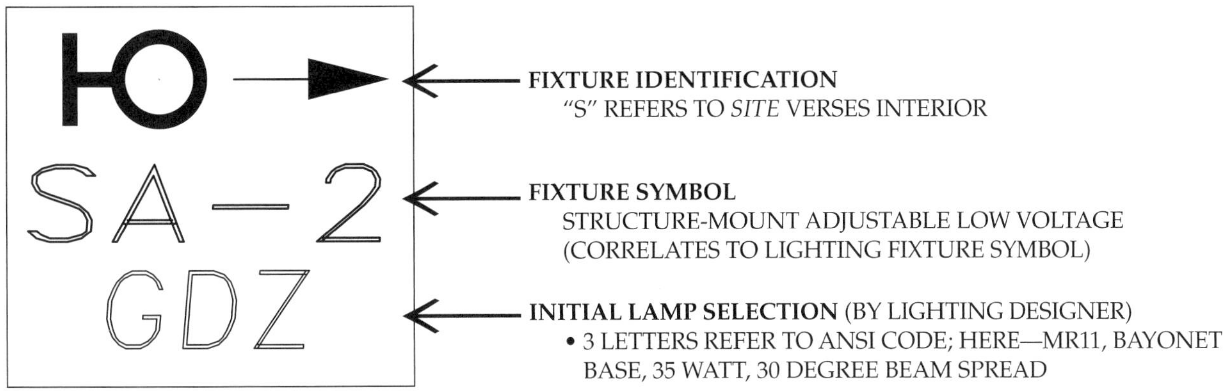

12-3
SB2
FMV/60
T0304
DJB 26

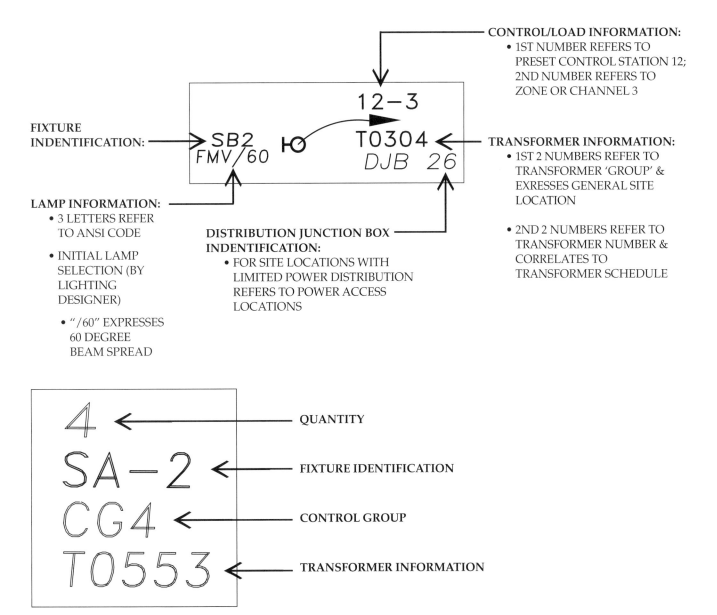

CONTROL/LOAD INFORMATION:
- 1ST NUMBER REFERS TO PRESET CONTROL STATION 12; 2ND NUMBER REFERS TO ZONE OR CHANNEL 3

FIXTURE INDENTIFICATION:

TRANSFORMER INFORMATION:
- 1ST 2 NUMBERS REFER TO TRANSFORMER 'GROUP' & EXRESSES GENERAL SITE LOCATION
- 2ND 2 NUMBERS REFER TO TRANSFORMER NUMBER & CORRELATES TO TRANSFORMER SCHEDULE

LAMP INFORMATION:
- 3 LETTERS REFER TO ANSI CODE
- INITIAL LAMP SELECTION (BY LIGHTING DESIGNER)
- "/60" EXPRESSES 60 DEGREE BEAM SPREAD

DISTRIBUTION JUNCTION BOX INDENTIFICATION:
- FOR SITE LOCATIONS WITH LIMITED POWER DISTRIBUTION REFERS TO POWER ACCESS LOCATIONS

4 — **QUANTITY**
SA-2 — **FIXTURE IDENTIFICATION**
CG4 — **CONTROL GROUP**
T0553 — **TRANSFORMER INFORMATION**

Figure 4.17. *Examples and explanation of varying symbology used in Figures 4.16A&B. Drawing: N. J. Smith.*

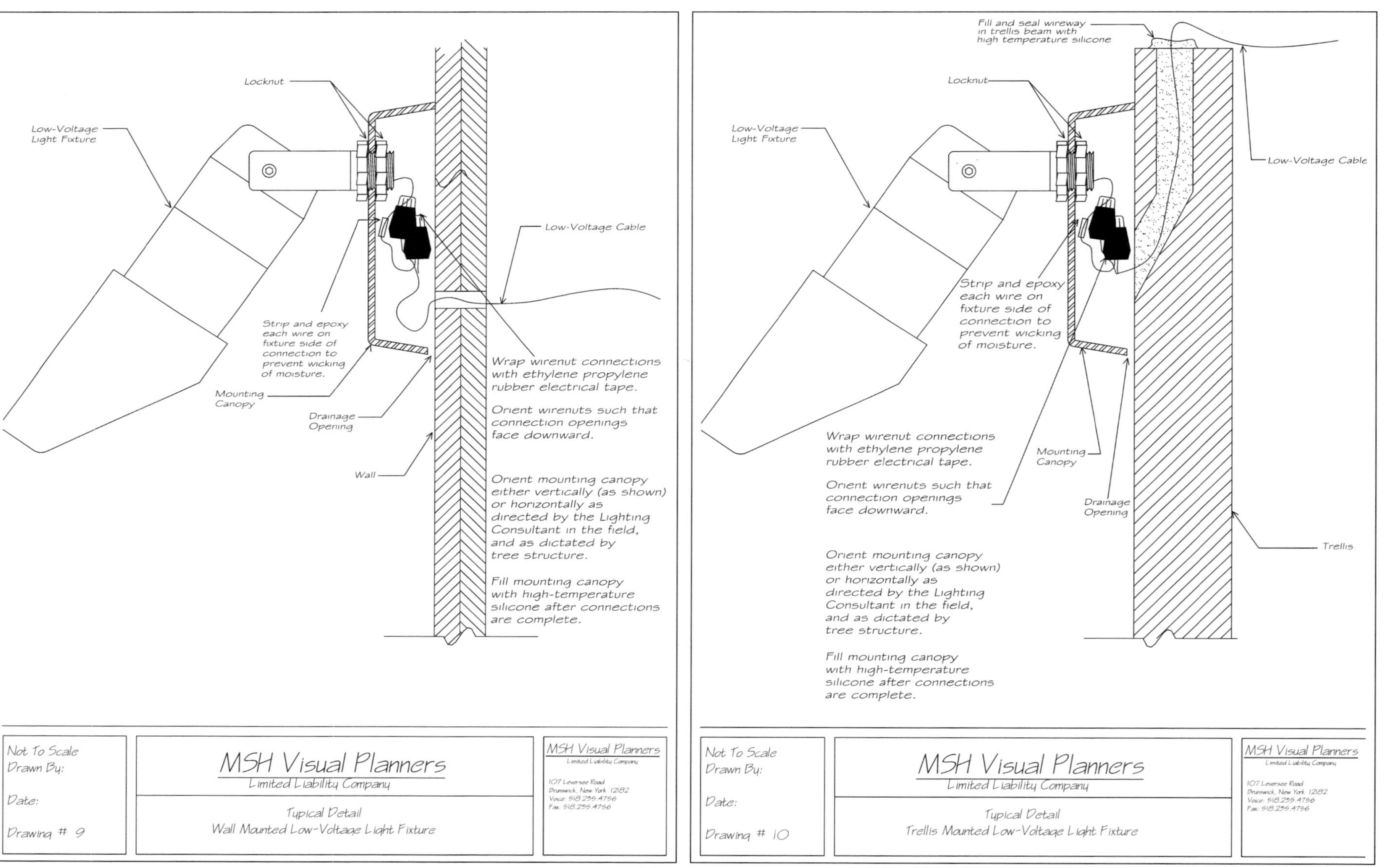
Locknut
Low-Voltage Light Fixture
Low-Voltage Cable
Strip and epoxy each wire on fixture side of connection to prevent wicking of moisture.
Mounting Canopy
Drainage Opening
Wall
Wrap wirenut connections with ethylene propylene rubber electrical tape.
Orient wirenuts such that connection openings face downward.
Orient mounting canopy either vertically (as shown) or horizontally as directed by the Lighting Consultant in the field, and as dictated by tree structure.
Fill mounting canopy with high-temperature silicone after connections are complete.
Not To Scale
Drawn By:
Date:
Drawing # 9
MSH Visual Planners
Limited Liability Company
Typical Detail
Wall Mounted Low-Voltage Light Fixture
MSH Visual Planners
107 Leversee Road
Brunswick, New York 12182
Voice: 518.255.4756
Fax: 518.255.4756

Figure 4.18. *Typical detail of a wall-mounted fixture showing aesthetic and installation requirements. Drawing: MSH Visual Planners.*

Fill and seal wireway in trellis beam with high temperature silicone
Locknut
Low-Voltage Light Fixture
Low-Voltage Cable
Strip and epoxy each wire on fixture side of connection to prevent wicking of moisture.
Wrap wirenut connections with ethylene propylene rubber electrical tape.
Orient wirenuts such that connection openings face downward.
Mounting Canopy
Drainage Opening
Trellis
Orient mounting canopy either vertically (as shown) or horizontally as directed by the Lighting Consultant in the field, and as dictated by tree structure.
Fill mounting canopy with high-temperature silicone after connections are complete.
Not To Scale
Drawn By:
Date:
Drawing # 10
MSH Visual Planners
Limited Liability Company
Typical Detail
Trellis Mounted Low-Voltage Light Fixture
MSH Visual Planners
107 Leversee Road
Brunswick, New York 12182
Voice: 518.255.4756
Fax: 518.255.4756

Figure 4.19. *Typical detail of a trellis-mounted fixture showing aesthetic and installation requirements. Drawing: MSH Visual Planners.*

Figure 4.20. *Placing a photographic image of a fixture onto a photograph of the building can show exactly where and how a fixture should be located and installed. Drawing: Insiya Shakir.*

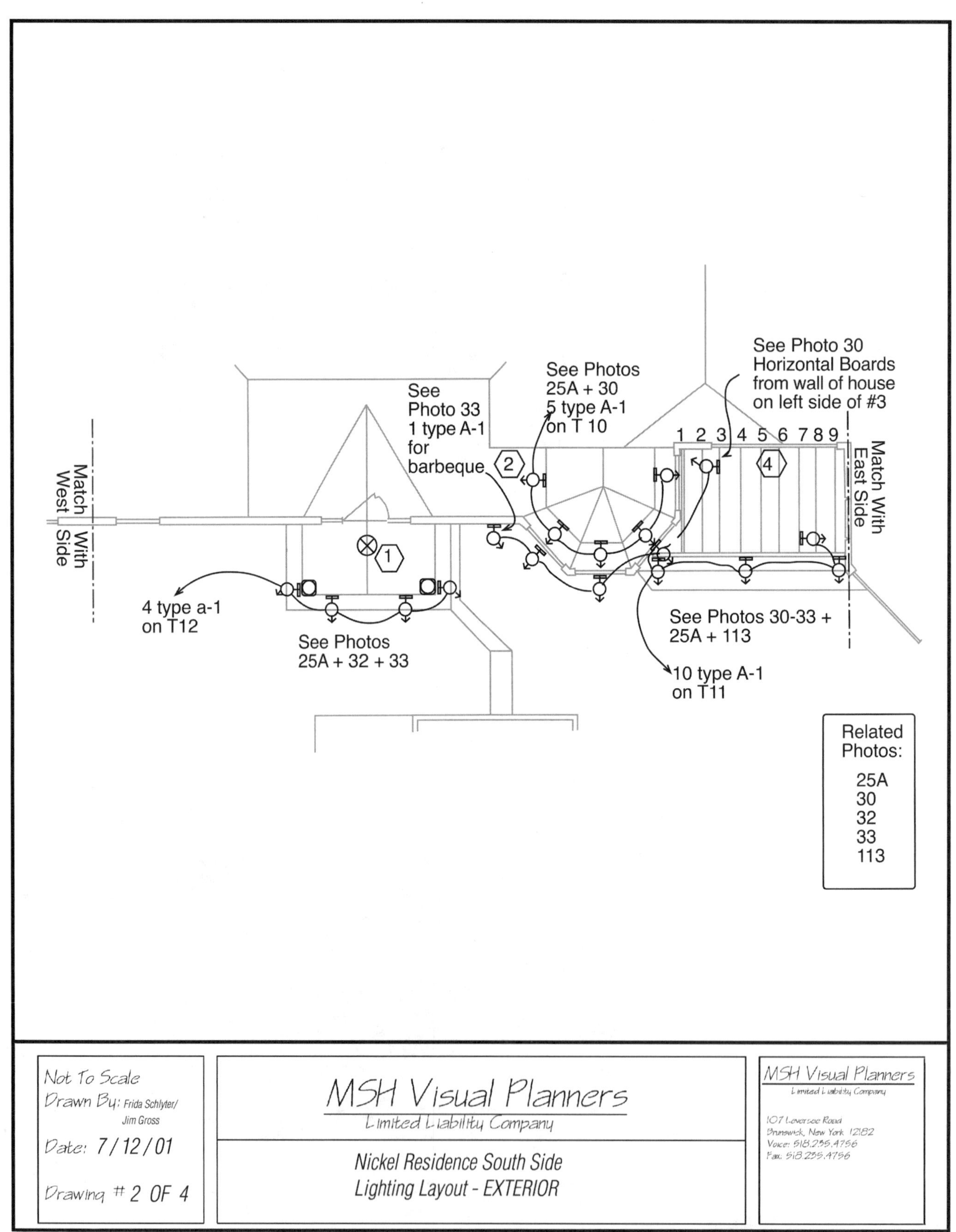

***Figure 4.21.** A sketch showing locations of fixtures on a building keyed to related photographs that illustrate actual installation locations. Lighting Design: Janet Lennox Moyer & Frida Schlyter, MSH Visual Planners; Drawing: Frida Schlyter.*

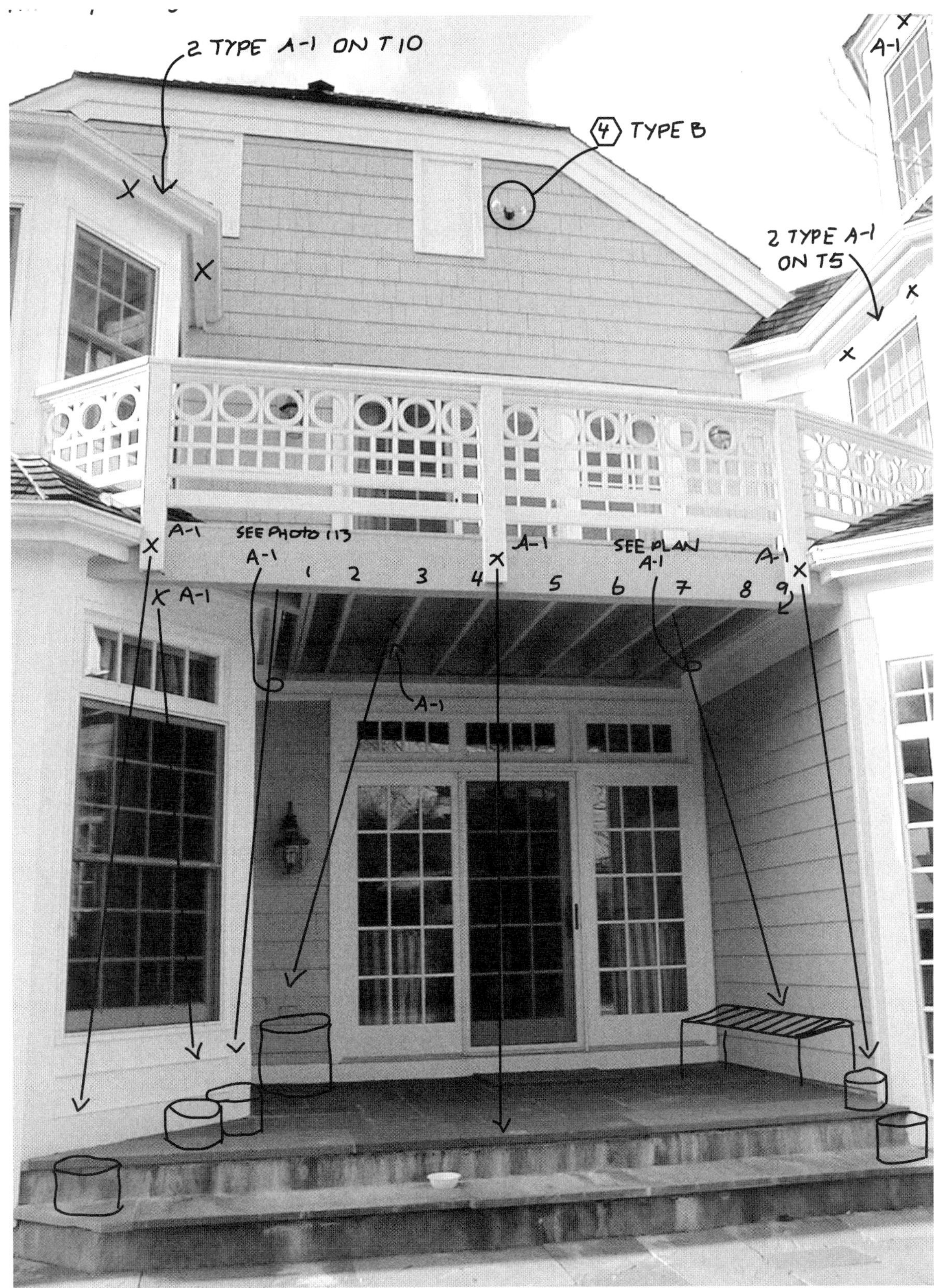

Figure 4.22. *A photograph that accompanies the sketch illustrated in Figure 4.21. This format provides the owner and contractor with location and aiming information. Lighting Design: Janet Lennox Moyer & Frida Schlyter, MSH Visual Planners; Drawing: Frida Schlyter.*

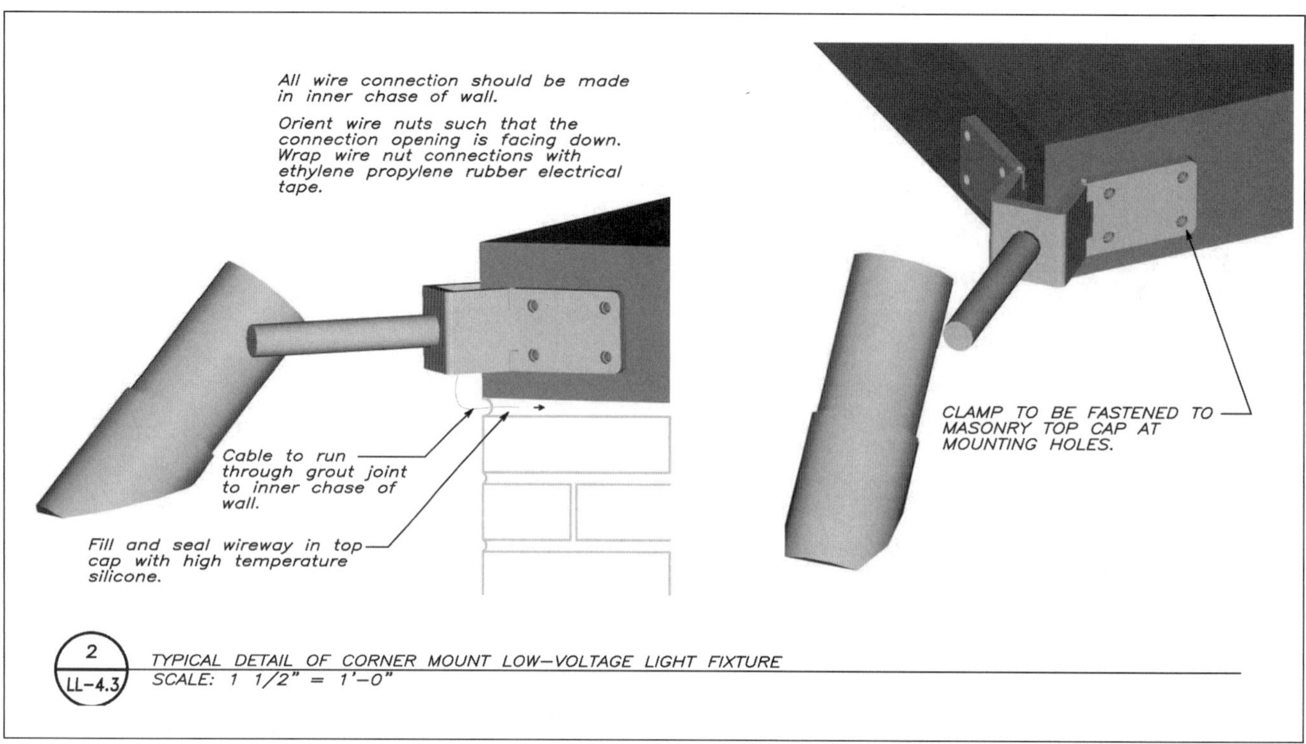
All wire connection should be made in inner chase of wall.
Orient wire nuts such that the connection opening is facing down. Wrap wire nut connections with ethylene propylene rubber electrical tape.
Cable to run through grout joint to inner chase of wall.
Fill and seal wireway in top cap with high temperature silicone.
CLAMP TO BE FASTENED TO MASONRY TOP CAP AT MOUNTING HOLES.
2
LL-4.3
TYPICAL DETAIL OF CORNER MOUNT LOW-VOLTAGE LIGHT FIXTURE
SCALE: 1 1/2" = 1'-0"

Figure 4.23. *Detail showing the concept of an adjustable corner mounting bracket. Lighting Design: Janet Lennox Moyer & Dan Dyer, MSH Visual Planners; Drawing: Dan Dyer.*

Figure 4.24. *The actual mount and MR8 fixture designed by Hiroshi Kira of H. Kira Design & Manufacturing. Photograph: Janet Lennox Moyer.*

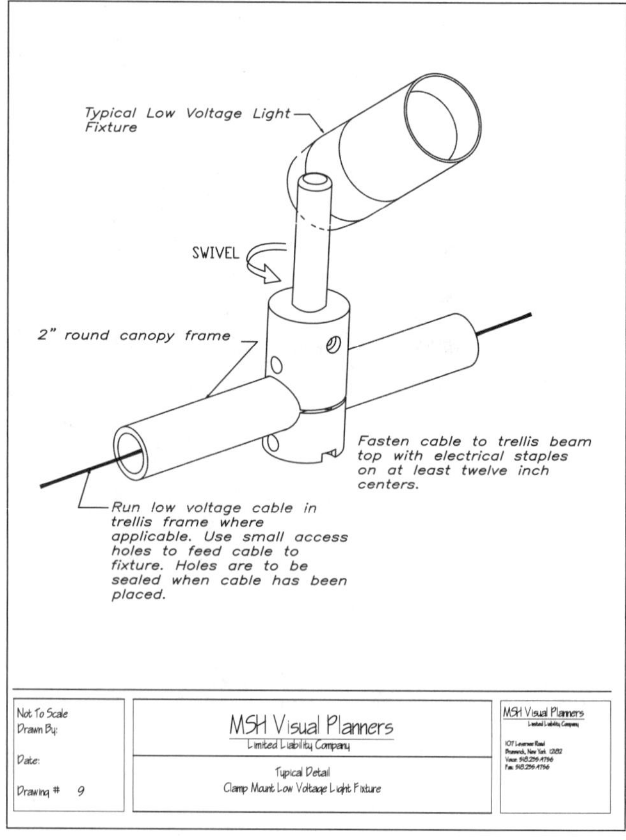
Typical Low Voltage Light Fixture
SWIVEL
2" round canopy frame
Fasten cable to trellis beam top with electrical staples on at least twelve inch centers.
Run low voltage cable in trellis frame where applicable. Use small access holes to feed cable to fixture. Holes are to be sealed when cable has been placed.
Not To Scale
Drawn By:
Date:
Drawing # 9
MSH Visual Planners
Limited Liability Company
Typical Detail
Clamp Mount Low Voltage Light Fixture
MSH Visual Planners

Figure 4.25. *A detail drawing showing the detail for an adjustable clamp-mounting bracket (available for both round and square canopy/frames). Drawing: Dan Dyer.*

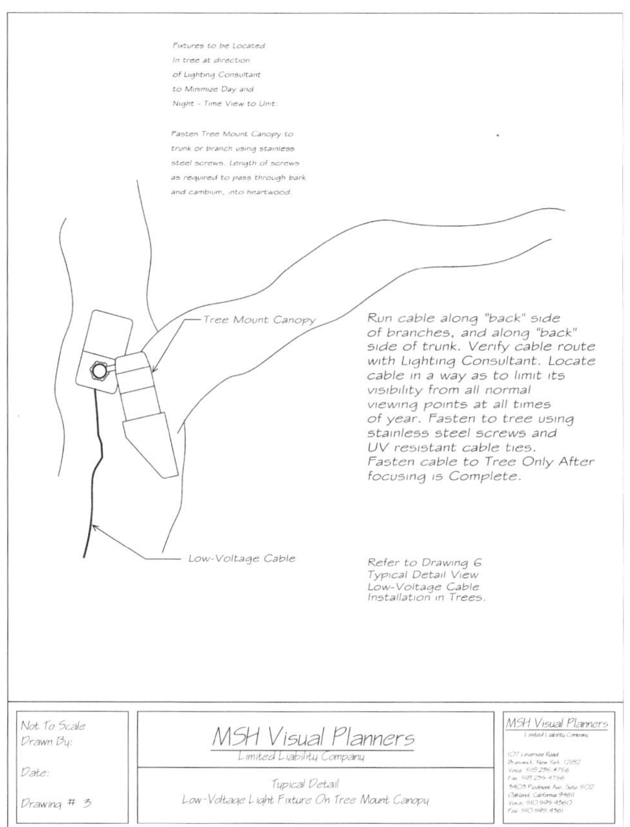

Fixtures to be Located
In tree at direction
of Lighting Consultant
to Minimize Day and
Night - Time View to Unit.
Fasten Tree Mount Canopy to
trunk or branch using stainless
steel screws. Length of screws
as required to pass through bark
and cambium, into heartwood.
Tree Mount Canopy
Run cable along "back" side
of branches, and along "back"
side of trunk. Verify cable route
with Lighting Consultant. Locate
cable in a way as to limit its
visibility from all normal
viewing points at all times
of year. Fasten to tree using
stainless steel screws and
UV resistant cable ties.
Fasten cable to Tree Only After
focusing is Complete.
Low-Voltage Cable
Refer to Drawing 6
Typical Detail View
Low-Voltage Cable
Installation in Trees.
Not To Scale
Drawn By:
Date:
Drawing # 3
MSH Visual Planners
Limited Liability Company
Typical Detail
Low-Voltage Light Fixture On Tree Mount Canopy
MSH Visual Planners

Figure 4.26. *A detail drawing showing a typical area on a tree for mounting a fixture. Using the trunk or branch as a shield both during the day and at night, the fixture becomes less obvious than the location illustrated in Figure 4.27. Drawing: Dan Dyer.*

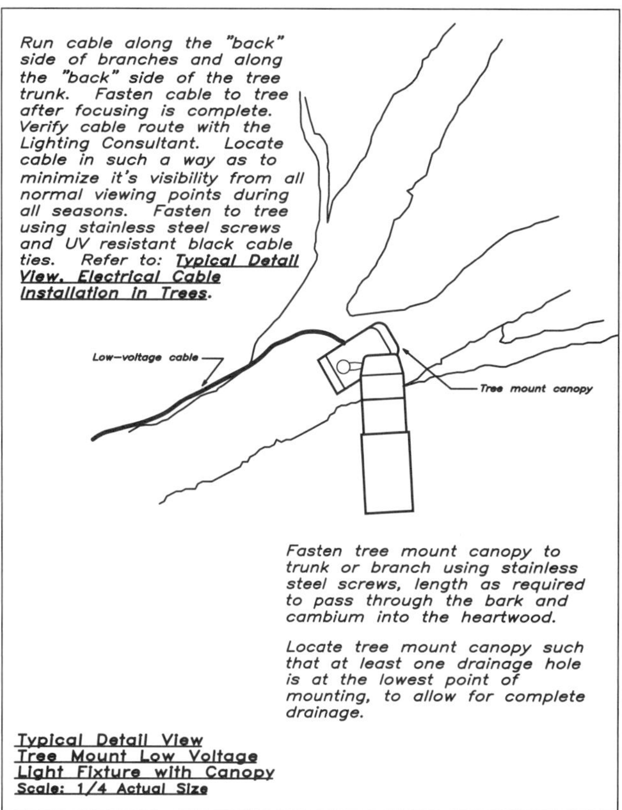

Run cable along the "back" side of branches and along the "back" side of the tree trunk. Fasten cable to tree after focusing is complete. Verify cable route with the Lighting Consultant. Locate cable in such a way as to minimize it's visibility from all normal viewing points during all seasons. Fasten to tree using stainless steel screws and UV resistant black cable ties. Refer to: Typical Detail View, Electrical Cable Installation In Trees.
Low-voltage cable
Tree mount canopy
Fasten tree mount canopy to trunk or branch using stainless steel screws, length as required to pass through the bark and cambium into the heartwood.
Locate tree mount canopy such that at least one drainage hole is at the lowest point of mounting, to allow for complete drainage.
Typical Detail View
Tree Mount Low Voltage
Light Fixture with Canopy
Scale: 1/4 Actual Size

Figure 4.27. *A sketch showing a bad location for mounting a fixture in a tree. The fixture hanging down beyond the tree trunk or branch becomes much more obvious against the skylight during the day, and the back side has nothing to prevent viewing the brightness of the inside of the fixture at night. Drawing: Dan Dyer & N. J. Smith.*

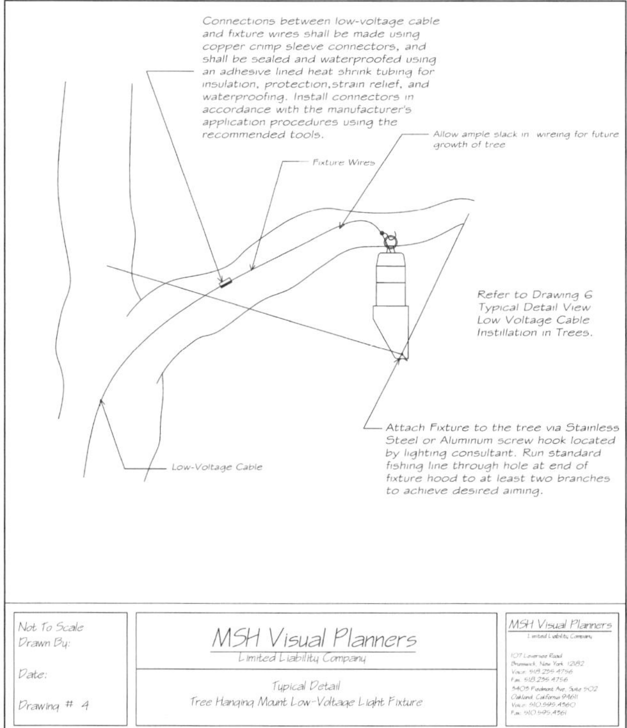

Connections between low-voltage cable and fixture wires shall be made using copper crimp sleeve connectors, and shall be sealed and waterproofed using an adhesive lined heat shrink tubing for insulation, protection,strain relief, and waterproofing. Install connectors in accordance with the manufacturer's application procedures using the recommended tools.
Allow ample slack in wireing for future growth of tree
Fixture Wires
Refer to Drawing 6
Typical Detail View
Low Voltage Cable
Instillation in Trees.
Attach Fixture to the tree via Stainless Steel or Aluminum screw hook located by lighting consultant. Run standard fishing line through hole at end of fixture hood to at least two branches to achieve desired aiming.
Low-Voltage Cable
Not To Scale
Drawn By:
Date:
Drawing # 4
MSH Visual Planners
Limited Liability Company
Typical Detail
Tree Hanging Mount Low-Voltage Light Fixture
MSH Visual Planners

Figure 4.28. *A sketch showing the detail for installing a ring-mount low-voltage fixture. Drawing: Dan Dyer.*

Figure 4.29. *Close-up view of a ring-mounted fixture installed in a tree. Drawing: Dan Dyer.*

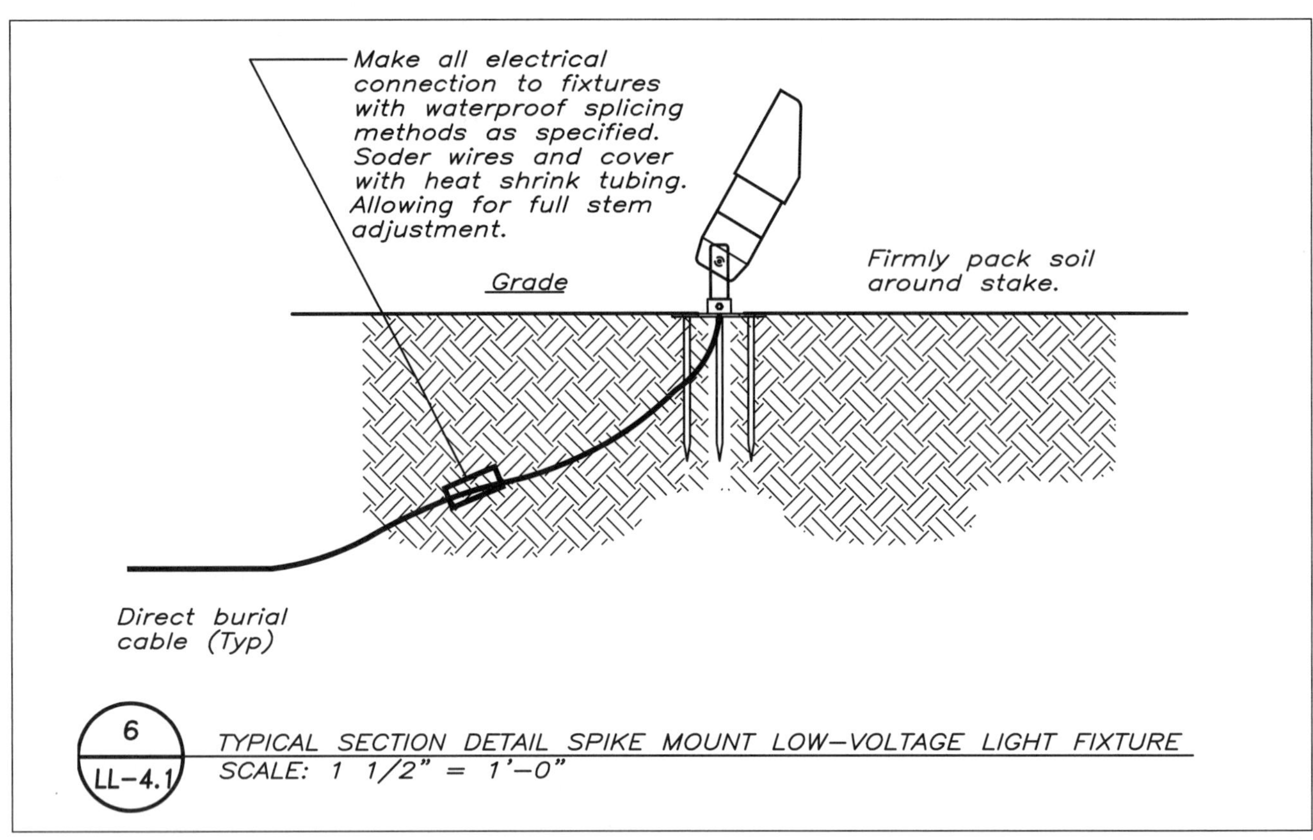

Figure 4.30. *A detail drawing showing the aesthetic and installation requirements for a standard three-prong spike-mounted low-voltage fixture. Drawing: Dan Dyer.*

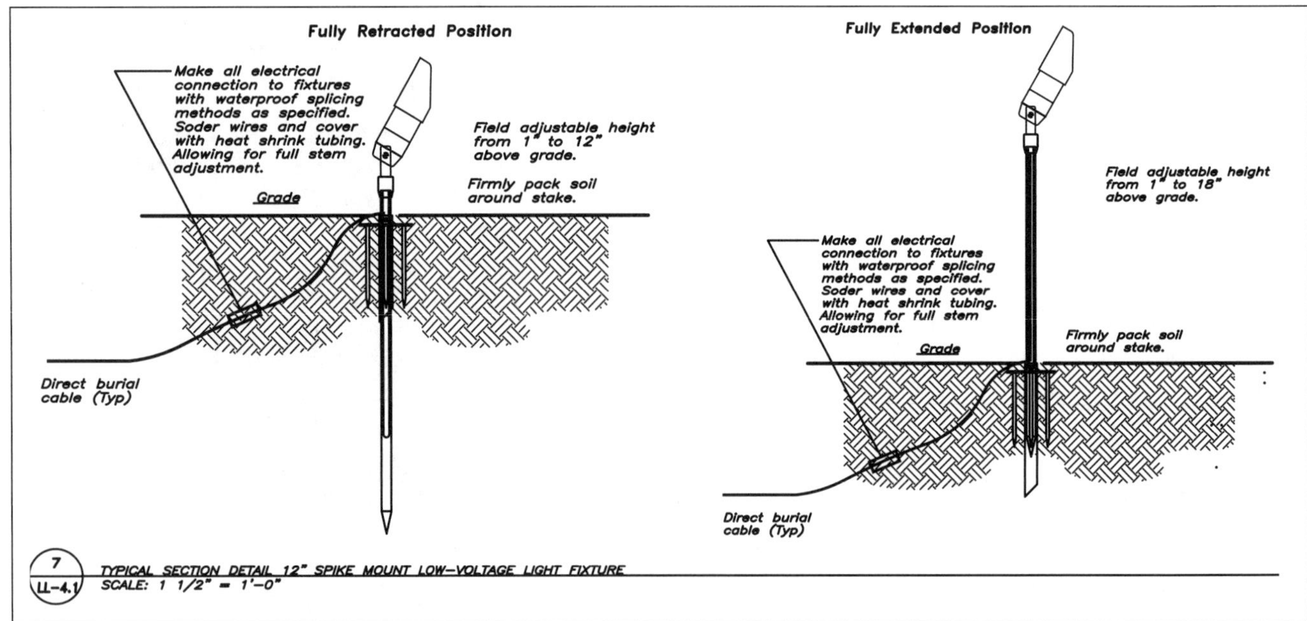

Figure 4.31. *A detail drawing showing the aesthetic and installation requirements for an adjustable three-prong spike-mounted low-voltage fixture. Drawing: Dan Dyer.*

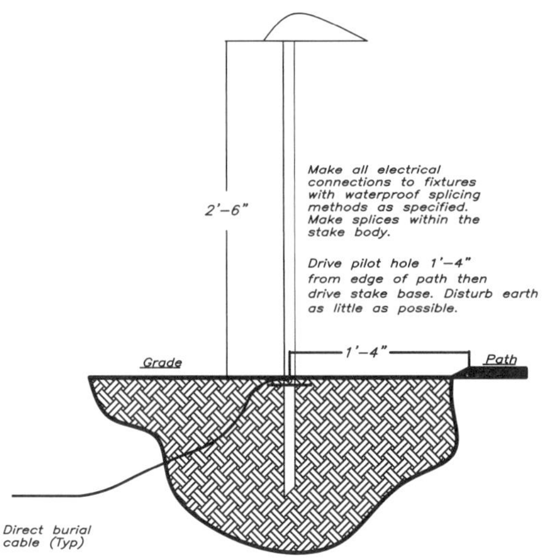
Make all electrical connections to fixtures with waterproof splicing methods as specified. Make splices within the stake body.
Drive pilot hole 1'-4" from edge of path then drive stake base. Disturb earth as little as possible.
2'-6"
1'-4"
Grade
Path
Direct burial cable (Typ)

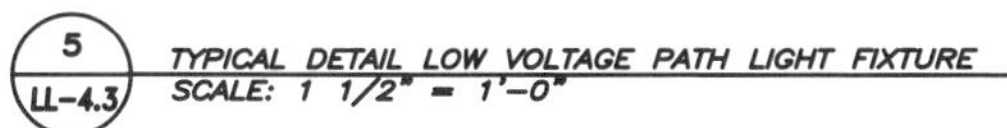
5
LL-4.3
TYPICAL DETAIL LOW VOLTAGE PATH LIGHT FIXTURE
SCALE: 1 1/2" = 1'-0"

Figure 4.32. *A sketch showing the detail for a low-voltage spike-mounted path light fixture. Drawing: Dan Dyer.*

Figure 4.33. *Example of placing a marker for fixture locations on a site.*

normally include two basic elements: drawings and specifications. The goal in documentation is to efficiently produce clear, concise, precise, and definitive information about the project work. In accomplishing this goal, the designer can use written specifications and/or notes, plans, schedules, details, and photographs.

All the documents produced into a contract document set represent the legal basis of agreement between the Owner and the contractor of the work to be done and the terms and agreement, including the mutually accepted price for the work. Contract documents should include a description of all administrative requirements and all projected construction work, and show the location, sizes, and dimensions for construction. Plans and specifications should reflect only the elements you, the lighting designer, and the owner

Figure 4.34. *Photograph of a completely shielded, custom path light fixture. The splayed sides of the top and the overall shape of the top provide soft, wide light distribution. Courtesy of Escort Lighting.*

fully understand and choose to require. The requirements must be scientifically measurable. Subjective requirements such as "aesthetically pleasing" or "adequately proportioned" cannot be included in any drawing detail or written specifications.

Contract documents include three types of information:

- *General terms and conditions*
  a. General areas of concern that relate to the project and which define the general administrative and technical requirements
  b. A detailed definition that describes the acceptable equipment materials, fixtures, and fabrications to be incorporated into the project
  c. A detailed description of the expected execution of the work, including the manner and location in which the products are to be incorporated into the project
- *Plans*—drawn performance and technical requirements
- *Specifications*—written general, performance, and technical requirements

The format and content of contract documents will vary based on the project requirements. Determining what documents are needed and the format of these documents is one of the important decisions a lighting designer makes for each project.

Plans or Working Drawings

The drawings, out of necessity, will include other organization information such as:

- Index of drawings and standard details
- Symbols and standard abbreviation lists
- Notes, which could include general notes, numbered notes, and/or sheet notes

Index of Drawings
This is a schedule listing all the drawings in the set of documents with a drawing number and descriptive title. The schedule includes an issue date so that each team member knows which drawings they should have and the most recent version (see Documents Appendix Figure A.1A). This information helps to keep the project organized and allows team members to converse more easily over extended distances.

Project Layout Key
On large-scale projects, produce a schematic site diagram that identifies all the project areas. Show diagrammatically how the areas have been apportioned. This *key drawing* helps team members easily determine to what part of the site a specific drawing refers (see Documents Appendix Figure A.7).

Standard Symbols and Abbreviations
All sets of working drawings should include a symbols list that explains every notation on the drawing, including general drawing symbols such as detail designations, all abbreviations used, fixture symbols, controls symbols, etc. (see Documents Appendix Figures A.1A & B, A.2–A.5). Because an industry-wide standard list of symbols does not exist for landscape lighting, designers can use any symbols they want as long as they are indicated on the symbols list and are used consistently through all the drawings for the project. Typically, the symbols list appears only once on a set of drawings. In addition to defining each symbol used on the drawings, this list should also define every abbreviation used on the drawings (for example, "O.C.," which means "on center").

The accepted standard practice (in the United States) for identifying lighting equipment is to use symbols to identify mounting and voltage. For example, all 120-volt below-grade fixtures would have one symbol and 12-volt below-grade units would have a different symbol (see Documents Appendix Figure A.3). Then, each specific fixture will be assigned a fixture type, such as "SB1." In this case, the "S" refers to "site," the "B" is an alphabetical ordering, and the "1" refers to the first in a series of this type of fixture. Within a series the difference may be mounting type, lamping, finish color or type, accessories, and so on. The fixture type and transformer designation symbols include important information the contractor needs (see Figures 4.16 & 4.17).

Notes
Working drawings also can include a list of *general notes, numbered notes,* and/or *sheet notes.* General notes provide information about the overall project, while numbered notes provide information about a specific situation or location on the drawings. Sheet Notes refer to information specific to items on that sheet.

Important notes to include on all sets of landscape lighting drawings include but are not limited to:

- Fixture locations shown on the lighting plan are conceptual. It is not prudent to show the location of any ground- or tree-mounted accent light on a working drawing. Each tree varies in the way that it has grown, as well as the way it gets placed into its planting hole. There is no conceivable way to predetermine the location of fixtures for new trees. The complexity of tree branching structure does not lend itself to two-dimensional drawings. Showing fixtures in tree branches or on tree trunks is not practical.
- The contractor must refer to mounting details included in the set of drawings. Human nature is to not follow instructions. Details are made by the designer for a purpose, and finding that those instructions were not followed after the fact can cause significant cost or other problems for an installation.
- All actual fixture locations for ground- or tree-mount adjustable accent fixture types will be marked on the site at the direction of the designer in conjunction with the installing electrical contractor. A flag (or other marker) represents each initial fixture placement. The fixture type, transformer number, and/or initial lamp selection is identified on the flag. The designer needs to stress with the contractor that these are initial locations that serve as a starting point for the aiming session(s). Each fixture should be temporarily placed and no cables should be buried yet (see Figure 4.14).
- The cable location for tree mount fixtures must be determined at this time, before any fixtures are installed (see Figure 10.13).
- For path fixtures, bollards, post fixtures, sconces, and other permanently mounted fixtures that provide general lighting but do not light specific objects in the landscape, the designer may want to list dimensions for the approximate location. However, the general notes should require that even for these fixtures, the exact location should be marked by the designer with the electrical contractor at the site.

Lighting Layout, Schedule, and Detail Sheets
Plans or working drawings consist of all the drawings necessary for the installing contractor to construct the

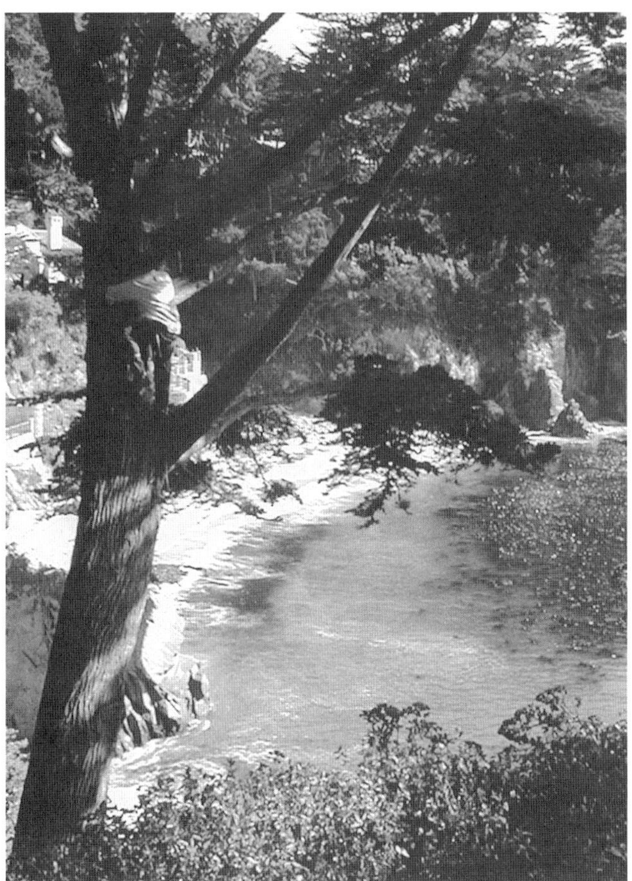

Figure 4.35. *Photograph showing a tree climber getting into position for locating fixtures in a tree overhanging a cliff on the Monterey, California, coast. Photograph: Janet Lennox Moyer.*

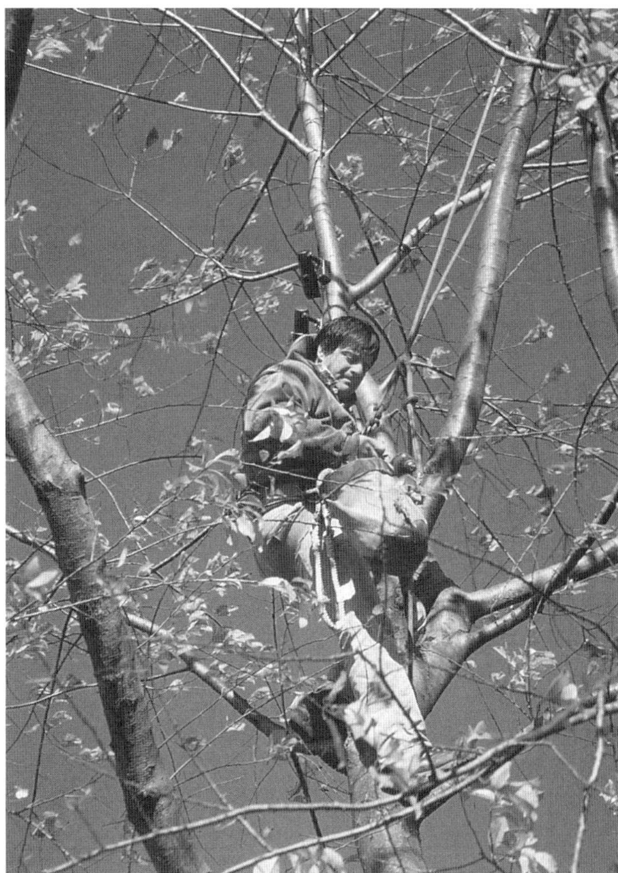

Figure 4.36. *Photograph showing a tree climber installing a fixture in a tree location. Photograph: Janet Lennox Moyer.*

design. The actual type and number of drawings will vary from project to project, but should include the following information:

- Fixture type and location, including any important location dimensions
- Remote transformer designations and schedules
- Control load designations and schedules
- Fixture control group designations and schedules
- Schematic wiring diagrams
- Custom or modified fixture details
- Special systems such as neon or fiber optics
- Installation details

On a project of any scale, having an area name designation allows the various parties involved in the project to communicate from a distance and provides the initial breakup of the site into separate drawings for the lighting plans, schedules, and details. Within the designated areas, all architectural spaces and all major trees should be identified for easy reference. Trees can be labeled either by a number that corresponds to a tree schedule or by Latin/common name (see Documents Appendix Figure A.9). All transformer, electrical load, and control groups need to be developed and shown in a consistent and logical manner that incorporates spare capacity for future plant growth and project development. The level of detail the lighting designer needs to include on the wiring for the system depends on other professionals included in the project. When electrical engineers are also working on the project, they will normally produce the wiring plans.

An important aspect of this documentation for all parties involved (designer, client, and installer) to understand is that landscape lighting fixture placement typically cannot be accurately shown on a lighting layout plan. One reason for this is that landscape elements, including pathways, stairs, plantings, and/or other elements, often change during construction. A designer needs to stay in close contact with the landscape designer and installing landscape contractor during construction to know what elements

4.37

4.38

4.39

4.40

Figure 4.37. *Photograph showing an electrician using a ladder to get to a fixture location in a tree. Photograph: Janet Lennox Moyer.*

Figure 4.38. *Photograph showing an electrician mounting a fixture in a tree. Photograph: Janet Lennox Moyer.*

Figure 4.39. *Photograph showing an electrician using a ladder to get to a fixture location in a tree. Photograph: Janet Lennox Moyer.*

Figure 4.40. *Close-up showing an electrician mounting a fixture in a tree. Photograph: Janet Lennox Moyer.*

Figure 4.41. *A lift truck being delivered to a job site. Photograph: Janet Lennox Moyer.*

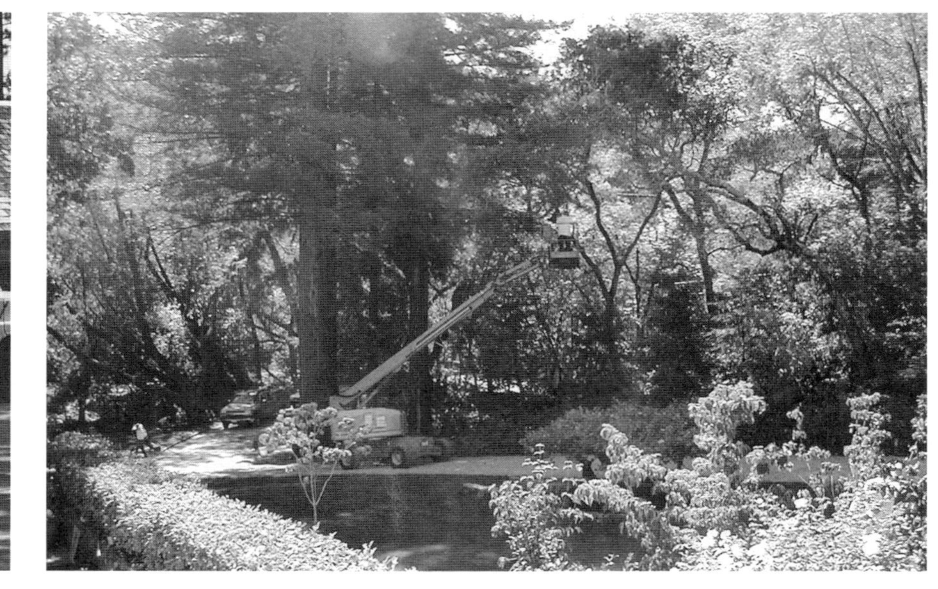

Figure 4.42. *Articulated lift trucks can maneuver easily into difficult positions, but they are often sensitive to a slight grade pitch. Photograph: Janet Lennox Moyer.*

Figure 4.43. *Articulated lift trucks often have incredible range, along with nearly unlimited maneuverability. Lift trucks can speed up installation of easily accessible trees with multiple fixtures located high up into tree canopies. Photograph: Janet Lennox Moyer.*

Figure 4.44. *The lighting designer can accompany the installer in the lift truck to show exactly how and where to mount the fixture(s)—as long as the designer isn't afraid of heights. . . . Photograph: Janet Lennox Moyer.*

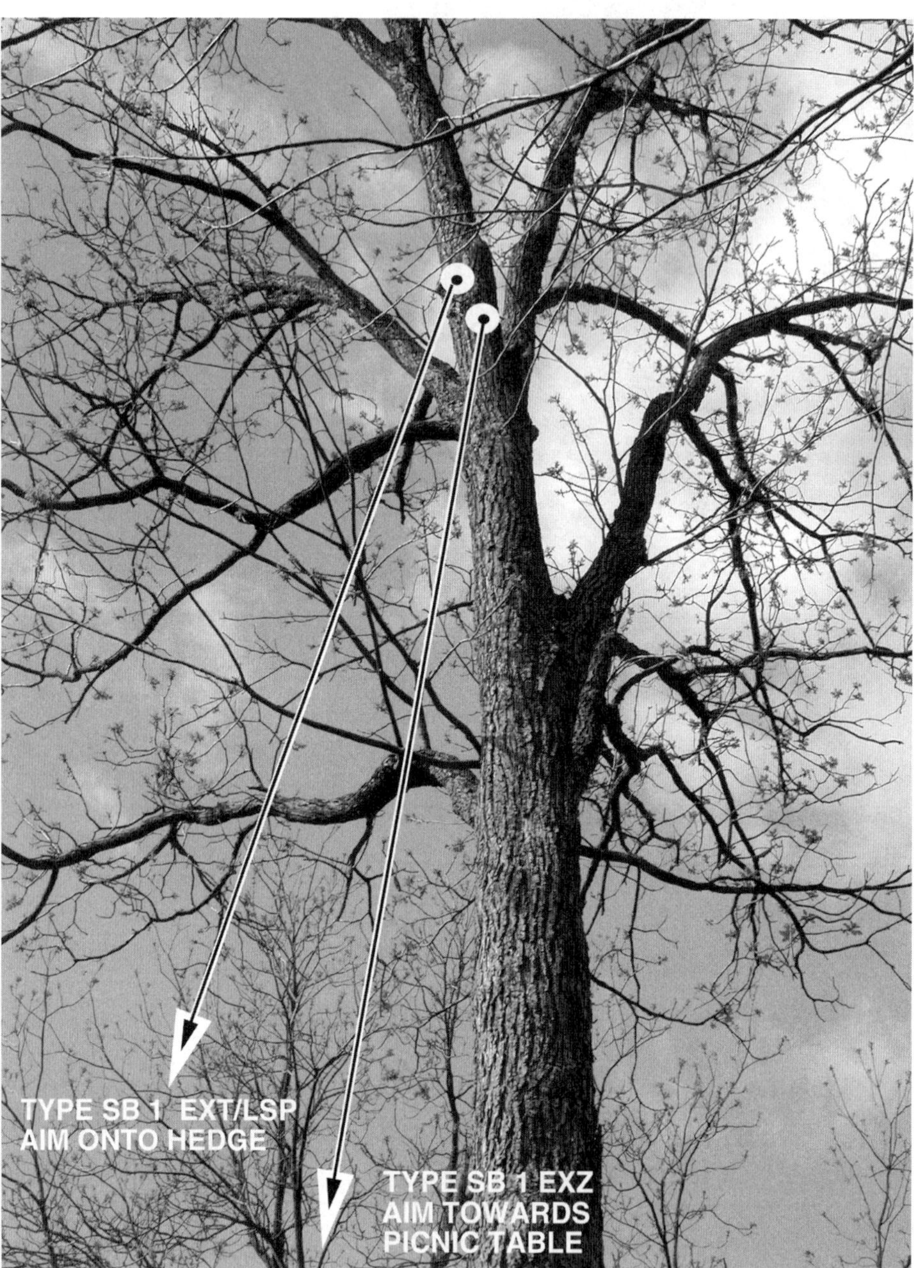

Figure 4.45. This drawing showing fixture locations in a specific tree can serve as an alternative to the lighting designer working on site with the installer. Actual on-site location is always preferable. Drawing: N. J. Smith.

change. Another difficulty in showing fixture location on a plan is the nature of individual trees, including size and physical characteristics (see Chapter 14, "Plant Materials").

On any plan some fixture information can be scaled and shown. When the designer chooses to show individual fixtures on the plan, the scale of the plan will need to be at least ⅛ inch equals 1 foot, but preferably ¼ inch equals 1 foot or larger. Most landscape drawings are shown at ⅛ inch equals 1 foot, 1:10 scale, or 1:50 metric scale. Using a scale smaller than these makes it difficult to show the fixture, its wiring, and its controls information clearly.

When the designer chooses not to show individual fixtures, a notation can be located by the element intended to be lit, such as a tree or sculpture. The notation includes the quantity and type of fixture, the transformer identification (for low-voltage fixtures), and the control load and/or zone identification. Another option is to use numbered notes that include the quantity and type of fixtures and any notes about installation or aiming that will be helpful to the installing contractor.

Pathway fixtures can be located on a large enough scale drawing (¼ inch minimum) with dimensions from paving edges and with typical paving pattern indi-

FOCUS CHECK LIST

Deadline:
Number of Sessions Anticipated?:
Scheduled Dates:
Meeting and Ending Times:
Crew
  Participants from design firm:
  Participants from electrical contractor:
  Tree Climber:
Is Client Participating?
All Fixtures Installed &Working?
All Accessories on site: Lamps, Louvers, Lenses, & Shrouds?
Are Fixtures fitted with lamps, louvers Lenses & Shrouds?
Has voltage drop been checked?
Is Control System Functioning?
Is wiring to fixture locations in trees ready?
Number and size of ladders:
Truck Lift
Tools:

☐ Leather Gloves	☐ Flashlights
☐ Spare Batteries	☐ Electrical Tape
☐ Screwdrivers	☐ Spare lamps, louvers, & Lenses
☐ Welders Glasses	☐ Spare Shrouds
☐ Wrenches	☐ Wire Nuts
☐ Wire Strippers	☐ Spare Wire
☐ Voltage Meter	☐ Welder
☐ Hammer	☐ Pruning Shears
☐ Paper Towels	☐ Saw
☐ Solvent	☐ Anti-Seize Compound
☐ Spare Gaskets	☐ Lubricating Compound
☐ Permanent Ink Pens	☐ Epoxy

Copies of Plans for Marking Lamping & Aiming Info.
Appropriate Clothing:
☐ Sweater or Jacket ☐ Hat ☐ Waterproof Shoes
Food
☐ Nearby Restaurant—Name & Phone Number:
☐ Thermoses With Coffee or Tea
Snacks:
Accommodations:
☐ Hotel: ☐ Phone Number:
☐ Reservation Confirmation:
☐ Location:

Figure 4.46

cated. Fixtures mounted on structures such as walls, eaves, and trellises can be dimensioned on the plan. However, each installation type requires at least one detail to express the actual location. For wall-mounted fixtures, an elevation is required to show the height to the center of the junction box and the coordinating horizontal distance from some architectural reference.

For tree-mounted fixtures, providing a note is all that can be done unless someone is willing to draw a plan and one or multiple sections showing the trunk and branching structure of the tree. The note should include the quantity and type of fixture, the transformer identification (for low-voltage fixtures), and the control load and/or zone identification.

Details Including Schedules

The type and quantity of details included in the working drawings vary from project to project. Details provide a closer look at a specific issue on the drawings (see Documents Appendix Figures A.12–A.15) or standard procedures required for the project (see Documents Appendix Figure A.10). Details include large-scale drawings of construction or connection techniques (see Figure 4.18), typical or specific mounting techniques (see Figures 4.18–4.32), and schematic one-line drawings that show basic wiring layouts (see Documents Appendix Figure A.11 and the one-line diagrams in Figure 10.2). Organize related details onto a detail sheet (see Documents Appendix Figure A.10).

Some detail information shows best in the form of a schedule. One or more of the following are typically required: Low-Voltage Transformers (see Documents Appendix Figures A.18 & A.19), Control Loads (see Documents Appendix Figure A.21), Control Schedules (see Documents Appendix Figures A.22 & A.23), and Approved Lamps (see Documents Appendix Figure A.20). Fiber optics, when used in landscape lighting, typically have an entirely separate specification section and require a number of schedules (see Documents Appendix Figures A.16 & A.17).

All these schedules need to account for anticipated system expansion over time. Some changes that affect general and/or specific systems sizing can be anticipated ahead of time, such as plant growth, while others may not be predictable, such as the owner's addition of a new path, sculpture, structure, site furniture, or garden area (see Chapter 15). The designer needs to discuss fixture issues and gauge expansion capacity required. This will affect individual fixture placement and load, which affects cable size and length, transformer size, control system loads, and so on.

Some projects can be handled with very little or no initial documents from the lighting designer. For a small site with no existing site or garden plan, the designer may walk the gardens with the owner, landscape designer, and installing contractor and make all the lighting decisions. A project description with sketches of layout and marked-up photographs to clarify mounting locations can then be provided to the

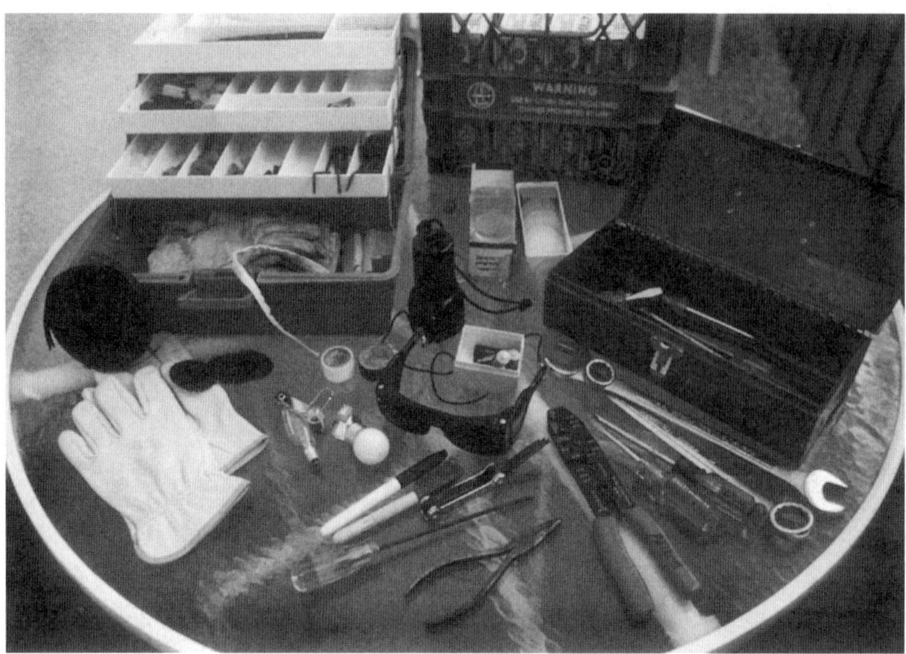

Figure 4.47. *Some of the tools used during aiming and adjusting phase of a project. Photograph: Janet Lennox Moyer.*

owner and contractor. These documents should show all the information that is necessary for contracting, purchasing, and installing the lighting system as determined in the walk-through meeting (see Figures 4.20–4.22).

Another option is for the contractor to take the responsibility to note the design as decisions are made throughout a site walk-through, to provide the correct number and type of fixture in the approximate location with the discussed controls, and to provide the record documents. With this approach, the owner and lighting designer must have extreme confidence in and experience with the contractor's understanding of landscape lighting, capability to install the project properly, and ability to provide documents after the installation that will serve as record plans.

Another issue to remember about documents is the physical size of the drawings. These plans spend an enormous amount of time outdoors at the site. It will nearly invariably be moist, which deteriorates the quality of the drawings. Typically, there is not a good work surface for laying out large drawings to reference on the site. So, consider preparing a set of drawings in 11″ by 17″ or 8½″ by 11″. This allows areas to be planned individually and handed out to a contractor assigned to that area. This size plan is easy to work with on site and can be easily laminated. Other sizes of plans can be laminated at printers or using clear contact paper but will still be awkward.

Specifications

In addition to the drawings, the contract documents will also include a set of specifications. In general, all dimensions, locations, and physical relationships should be shown on the drawings, and all materials, quality and installation standards, and methods should be listed in the specifications. To avoid contradictions between the drawings and the specifications, no information should appear in more than one place.

On projects where the lighting is only one portion of the construction work, the lighting specifications are included in Division 16 of the standard Construction Specifications Institute (CSI) specification format. This section of the specification document will have a general section that describes the responsibilities of the contractor, the work to be performed, and all processes to be followed. In this section, the designer puts all project-wide requirements for any and all equipment: products, fixtures, lamps, transformers, ballasts, lenses and louvers, mounting hardware, fiber optics, neon, light-emitting diodes, and/or electrical wire and cable (See Documents Appendix Figure A.28). The designer needs to determine which of these needs to be included and what information is pertinent for each type of equipment.

When the project consists of only lighting design, the specifications can either be a separate document in 8½″ by 11″ format or be included on the drawings. The

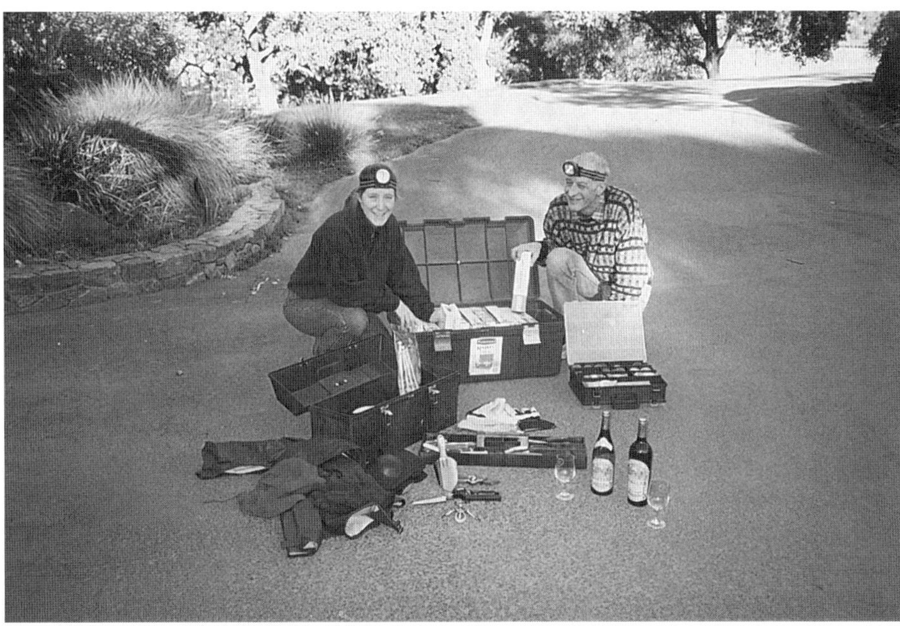

Figure 4.48. *Lighting Designers Michael Stewart Hooker and Janet Lennox Moyer getting equipment ready for a night focus session.*

information normally included in the general section may be integrated into the list of general notes.

General Section

The general section (or general notes) includes information such as acceptable fixture finishes; the processes required for those finishes; acceptable or required lamp, ballast, and transformer manufacturers; a time period in days for fixture orders to be placed and submittal drawings to be provided to the designers for approval by the contractor; and a description of the aiming and adjusting work to be done by the contractor, specifying that the work will be done after dark and listing the number of labor hours to include in the bid.

Lighting Fixture Section

Division 16 will also have a lighting fixture section that identifies and describes the equipment corresponding to the symbols and fixture identification tags on the drawings. Appendix Figure A.26 lists factors to consider in this specific description by equipment type. As with the general section, not all items on the list will be required for each piece of equipment listed on a specification. All standard features, required accessories, and modifications or custom features need to be identified in the fixture specification. The designer must determine which items are important for a specific project and include those in the specification.

This lighting fixture section may be shown on the drawing as a fixture legend rather than contained in the overall project specification for either large or small projects. There are at least three types of fixture specifications: one-name, multiple-name, and performance. Each has benefits and drawbacks, and only one type will be used for any given project.

Three Typical Fixture Specification Formats

A *one-name specification* lists only one manufacturer and fixture ordering number for each fixture. This provides the owner with the advantage of specifying the highest-quality product or the most appropriate product for the situation. It requires the specifier to be thorough in describing all important considerations that warrant the fixture being the only one under consideration. The disadvantage to the owner is that the cost may be higher than if several manufacturers were bidding against each other for the project. This method is used for private properties and is often not permitted for projects owned by public agencies.

A *multiple-name specification* lists at least two and typically three to four manufacturers for a given product. The benefit to the owner of a multiple-name specification is typically a lower cost per unit. The drawback is that the products being compared are often different in one or more features or characteristics, which can affect the quality of the installation. For example, one manufacturer's fixture might vertically adjust 360°, while another's may be limited to 110° due to the construction of the fixture. Another example might be an anodized finish versus a powder coat finish. A third example might be the wattage capacity, with one fixture accepting up to 300 watts, while the other only accepts up to 150 watts based on its UL (Underwriters Laboratories; see Chapter 7) rating.

The last type, the *performance specification,* is the most rigorous. It consists of a construction description of each product and should include the light distribution or photometrics for each fixture, but lists no manufacturers or fixture numbers. This gives both the client and the designer a firm position for rejecting inferior products or good-quality products that do not have all the required capabilities or features. This type of specification is typically required on federal government projects and can be required for state and local government projects or on large commercial projects to provide equal opportunity to all contractors and manufacturers.

No matter which specification type is used, a pitfall to avoid is the use of the phrase "or equal." This essentially opens up the bidding to anyone. A safer phrase is "or approved by the lighting designer." This requires a bidder to request permission from the designer to substitute another manufacturer's fixture for the one listed. In the general section of the specification, require that substitutions be submitted to the lighting designer within a specific time frame prior to the bid submittal date. In discussing this requirement of prequalifying substitutions, consider what type and format of information should be required, including whether a sample needs to be provided for review.

Cut Sheets

Including copies of the manufacturer's catalog literature (called "cut sheets" in the trade) on each fixture, ballast, transformer, lamp, and control device aids the contractor in understanding the required equipment.

The accepted practice in the lighting industry is for the designer to make copies of the manufacturer's catalog sheets for all parts of the equipment and then to highlight all required features, such as finish color or accessories. This process of identifying all the specified characteristics and parts/accessories will further ensure that the contractor understands the complete requirements.

With the aid of computer technology, designers can produce a composite sheet for a specific product describing all the important characteristics, parts, and accessories with drawings and/or photographs of these important elements (see Documents Appendix Figure A.27).

BIDDING PROCESS PHASE

The specifications should be introduced by a document, called an *invitation to bid,* that outlines the general requirements of a contractor to provide a bid on the project. This document typically includes some or all of the following issues:

- A statement of the type of work to be done, such as "the final electrical engineering and installation of a lighting system to be done in [one, two, three] phases for . . ."
- The owner's right to select or reject any bid
- A due date and location for the bids to be submitted
- Whether the price is to be a *lump sum* or *time and materials*
- Whether a not-to-exceed provision shall be included
- How the price shall be submitted, including separating the fixture and installation costs or providing a unit cost per fixture, in case fixtures might be added or deleted at any time during the project
- When change orders will be accepted and how change orders will be handled
- A requirement for the bidders to inspect the site to ensure that they have an understanding of the scope of the project and to determine the method of proceeding with the work
- Whether substitutions will be allowed, when they will be accepted, and how they are to be presented
- Whom to contact for questions or clarifications
- How to obtain additional sets of drawings and the cost of these drawings
- A statement to the effect that the bidder fully understands the requirements of the project and that no additional charges will be accepted from the contractor unless either a condition could not be reasonably detected from the drawings and review of the site or changes are requested by the owner
- A requirement to post a performance bond and to have a certain type and amount of insurance, including liability, property damage, and personal injury or workers' compensation policies
- A requirement for a payment bond that protects the owner against liens on the property by subcontractors or suppliers that do not get paid by the general contractor (even though the owner paid the general contractor for its services or products)
- The time that the owner has to accept the bid and initiate work
- The time or date when the work is expected to begin and end, sometimes accompanied by a financial incentive or penalty clause
- A place for the bidder to sign and date the form

In order for contractors to reasonably bid a landscape lighting installation, they must become familiar with the site and know how they will distribute power with minimal disruption to existing site conditions and plantings. For all low-voltage loads, they need to review specified transformer locations. The difference in location of 120-volt versus 12-volt power throughout a site can dramatically affect cost. They need to understand all the specified mounting details and be clear what kind of equipment (such as ladders or lift trucks) and additional help (such as tree climbers, landscape contractors, etc.) will be required (see Figures 4.35–4.44).

How the bidding is handled and who is invited to bid varies from project to project. On large projects, the general contractor may invite several electrical contractors to put together prices for the electrical portion of the project and then include those bids as a part of the total project bid. On small projects, the designer typically recommends that the owners solicit bids from several electrical contractors. If the owner does not know any qualified contractors, the designer will often provide a list of contractors. In some cases, the owner may already have a relationship with a contractor, whom the owner will use unless their bid is unreasonable.

On public projects, the designer is often not involved in the bidding process. However, on smaller projects, the bids are often presented to the designer. In this case, the designer reviews the bids and then presents them to the owner. The owner then selects the contractor but may ask the designer to provide an appraisal of the bids and even a recommendation as to which contractor should be selected.

CONSTRUCTION PHASE

In the construction phase, part of the control of the project passes from the designer to the contractor. The designer typically observes the construction, checking that everything is installed properly and in the correct location. However, the contractor is responsible for ensuring that everything is installed and functioning properly. It is imperative that the designer make it clear to the contractor the kind of communication and coordination expected. For example, the exact location of fixtures that will light plant materials cannot be determined until all the major plantings have been installed. The electrical contractor needs to coordinate with the landscape or planting contractor to determine when this will occur and to advise the designer. Then a meeting can be arranged to mark the location of the fixtures. The location of fixtures for lighting sculptures, stairs, structures, or any other kind of feature should also be coordinated in this manner.

Throughout the construction process, the decisions and procedures discussed in all meetings should be documented. Designers need to be as available as possible to avoid delaying the progress of construction. Job sites today have fax machines and/or computers with e-mail and often a Web-based project management site, so clarifications, revised drawings, or additional information the contractor or other team members need can be provided from the designer or other team members quickly and easily.

Submittal Drawings and Samples

Submittal drawings provide information on each fixture specified for a project. They are supplied by the manufacturer to the electrical contractor, who passes them on to the designer for final review and approval. These drawings are produced to ensure that the products being supplied to the job are correct. The specifications include the required procedure for submittal drawings to be supplied from the contractor to the designer. The designer reviews the submittal drawings and fills out a cover form approving the submittal, requesting more information, or rejecting it (see Documents Appendix Figure A.28). If a submittal is rejected, the designer lists each fixture that is not acceptable and notes the irregularities. At the designer's discretion, the contractor will resubmit to the designer either the entire package or just the revised sheets on the items that were rejected.

On projects requiring custom or modified fixtures, the specifications may also require samples for approval. When a large number of custom fixtures will be made for a project, the specifications often require that one prototype fixture be produced for review and approval. This prototype, if accepted, will count as one of the final fixtures for the project. This occurs primarily when a large number of the fixtures will be made. If a special finish is required on a fixture, the specification should require a finish sample for approval.

Construction

After the contract has been awarded, the designated construction foreman and the designer should walk through the site together to familiarize the foreman with the project. In this site visit, transformer or junction box locations can be set, fixture locations can be approximated, and any initial questions can be discussed. Throughout the construction, the designer should visit the site to check progress, answer questions, and ensure that proper power distribution, including future provisions, and installation techniques and details are being followed.

The actual construction process for installing lighting equipment includes several phases of work. In the case of a site being newly developed, control locations need to be determined in all areas of the buildings prior to installing Sheetrock. Junction boxes and wiring to the boxes need to be installed. Conduit needs to be installed from the inside of the building to the outside wherever power will be required around the buildings, as well as under any permanent outdoor surfaces such as driveways and patios. These sleeves provide access for power to all areas of the site in the future.

Locating Fixtures on Site

Whether the job involves new construction or the renovation of a landscape, fixtures intended to light plant materials should be installed after planting has been substantially completed, but prior to the planting of ground covers (see Figures 4.33 & 4.45). Since each 120-volt above-grade fixture and each below-grade fixture is permanently mounted, the location of these fixtures should be marked after the plants that each will light have been installed. This location needs to be done at night with a working sample of the exact lamp/reflector assembly (if necessary) to allow visual determination of appropriate locations.

Low-voltage fixtures, which are somewhat portable, should be placed in an approximate location based on the plant they are intended to light. All these fixtures should be supplied with enough cord to provide movement within the predetermined area listed in the general notes (typically). These fixtures' spikes should not be firmly packed into the ground, nor should the wiring for these fixtures be buried (see Figure 4.14). The final installation needs to be done after the night aiming session, as fixtures might need to be moved slightly or substantially in order to create the desired effect on the plant material.

Locating Tree-Mounted Fixtures

Each tree-mounted fixture should be temporarily attached to the trunk or branch in a location identified by the designer at the site (see Figures 4.36 & 4.44). This location is the most critical of all fixtures. Depending on the size of the tree and the mounting height or extension out onto a branch, one of three methods for locating tree-mounted fixtures needs to be selected. For fixtures mounted less than 20 feet above grade and typically on a main trunk or easily accessible branch location, the installing contractor can locate the fixture using a ladder (see Figures 4.35, 4.36, & 4.41–4.44). For fixtures above 20 feet and located at an extreme branch location, either a tree climber or a lift truck needs to be employed (see Figures 4.35 & 4.36). Lift trucks can quickly move from one location to another but require essentially flat ground. Few work on even the slightest slope. Another issue to consider with lift trucks is the maneuverability. It is imperative that the bucket can extend to all required locations and maneuver through the branching structure. For locations where lift trucks cannot be utilized or to keep the noise down in quiet neighborhoods, tree climbers can install the fixtures (see Figures 4.35 & 4.36).

When the designer cannot be on site for the entire tree-mounted fixture installation, an option is to take photographs using a Polaroid or digital camera (if there is a printer on site). In this case, the designer needs to provide thorough details for each fixture location. Mark the exact place on the branch that the installer should place the mounting canopy; the preliminary lamping, aiming, and shielding information; and enough information as to where the photographer stood when shooting the image to allow someone to find the location again (see Figure 4.45).

In all cases, the fixtures need to be preassembled with the preliminary lamp selection, all distribution lenses and shielding devices such as louvers and hoods, the mounting canopy, and the appropriate length of wire to reach the desired location in the tree. As the fixtures are being installed, the designer needs to be cognizant of how well it is hidden in the tree from all viewing angles, and a preliminary aiming and glare-shield adjustment should be made.

This helps to limit the amount of night aiming required for tree-mounted fixtures. However, all tree-mounted fixtures need to be easy to move during the aiming and adjusting session, if necessary, in order to create the desired effects.

AIMING AND ADJUSTING THE LIGHTING SYSTEM

Near the end of construction, the electrical contractor notifies the designer of the anticipated completion date so that a mutual schedule (including all team members and the owner) can be determined for aiming and adjusting the fixtures. Before this session takes place, the contractor must confirm that all fixtures and the control system function properly. The aiming and adjusting session must be done after dark, as the effects cannot be seen during daylight.

Decisions made during the adjustment phase determine the success of the lighting. In order to streamline the process, all aspects of the session need to be planned by the designer. Perhaps the first decision is how many people are needed and with what skills. For example, when installing a large number of fixtures in trees, using professional tree pruners with tree-climbing equipment can make the process move more quickly. While one climber is attaching a fixture and then moving on to the next fixture location, the designer can be working with a second climber at another location.

A schedule listing the order of work and assigning a person to each task needs to be developed by the designer and explained to each participant. On large projects, setting up more than one team to do the focusing can shorten the length of these sessions.

Aiming and adjusting sessions can often last for many hours. The number and length of sessions should be planned by the designer, keeping in mind that the participating members often have to be back at work the next morning. When all the participants work an 8-hour day before the focusing, restricting the length of the session to approximately 4 hours makes sense. When the site is out of town, the sessions can often be longer, as much as 8 hours or sometimes more (depending partially on the length of darkness), if the participants will not be returning to work the following day and can rest during much of the next day until the next evening session begins.

The designer must make sure that each person knows how to dress for these sessions. Some sites will get cold at night, and people need to have the appropriate clothing to avoid getting chilled. The designer needs to plan work breaks when sessions will be long, and provisions need to be made for snacks or food.

The designer must also make sure that all the equipment and supplies necessary to complete the work are brought to the site (see Figures 4.47 & 44.48). The required tools, ladders, fixture accessories, spare lamps, and other supplies will vary by project. A toolbox and maintenance kit stocked with everything that might be needed helps make sure that nothing gets left behind. Compiling a checklist of tools and supplies (such as those listed in Figure 4.46 and illustrated in Figures 4.47 & 4.48) helps ensure that the all the essential equipment necessary for a focusing session will get packed and brought to the site.

During the focusing session, the contractor adjusts each fixture to create the desired effect at the designer's direction. This adjustment can include placing low-voltage stake-mounted fixtures, then aiming them in the proper direction and at the proper angle, changing the lamp to create the desired effect, adding lenses to change the light distribution (such as spread lenses to widen and soften the effect or linear spread lenses to create a line of light rather than a circle of light), adding louvers or shrouds to shield people's eyes from the lamp brightness, and even changing the lamp (in incandescent fixtures) to properly balance brightness relationships from one area to another. For tree-mounted fixtures, the contractor moves the fixture until the correct placement is found and then completes the fixture aiming. At the conclusion of locating and aiming each fixture, the electrical contractor tightens the fixture's aiming mechanism to secure it. This session also includes setting the control system equipment, such as the operation times on time switches and presetting dimming levels on multiple-scene controllers.

As these adjustments are being made, the designer needs to check the brightness balance, overall composition, and potential glare from all viewpoints in the landscape, from all view locations inside buildings, and when necessary from the street as well as from neighboring properties. On large projects, using two-way radios can help the process move more quickly and save the participants' voices.

The last task to be completed during these sessions is to document the final settings on control devices, lamping selections for incandescent fixtures, and aiming directions (often including what the fixture is highlighting) for all adjustable fixtures. These data are transferred onto as-built plans that are supplied to the owner and maintenance staff, with a copy retained by the designer for future reference or maintenance.

5

Follow-up Work: Record Documents and Project Maintenance

After the project installation has been completed, the designer needs to provide a few more services: an as-built plan of the final lighting layout, updated equipment schedules, a meeting to familiarize the client and/or maintenance staff with the lighting system, and development of an ongoing maintenance schedule. The deliverable in this phase of a project consists of a set of Record Documents. These documents include all the information and instructions the client requires to maintain the lighting system and the lighting composition as originally designed and to respond to inevitable change (see Chapter 15). They also help the designer respond to any and all future developments in the landscape.

Record Documents represent the only hope the owner has to maintain the integrity of the property's lighting design. The information provided in the Record Documents is only useful if it is updated to reflect existing conditions every time any change occurs. The design and installation team must initially provide clear, concise, and thorough documentation of the final lighting installation and a maintenance manual. Over time, all parties involved in the maintenance and further development of the lighting system must strive to keep all these documents accurate throughout the life of the landscape lighting system.

The owner and maintenance personnel need to understand the importance of this maintenance and be prepared to do these tasks on a regular basis. The designer should discuss maintenance with the owner during the initial interview and again in conceptual design to ensure that the owner understands the nature of ongoing maintenance for landscape lighting. The designer will need to remind the client about this work throughout the design and installation process to ensure that it doesn't come as a complete surprise during the maintenance review meeting.

The content and organization of the Record Documents should provide the maintenance and repair personnel with an understanding of the system, all the work to be done, and a schedule for the maintenance tasks. The designer meets with the project maintenance staff to review the system and express the importance of the maintenance staff's efforts in the continuing functioning of the system. The information the designer should provide to keep the lighting system producing the intended effects includes:

- A description of the finished system
- A description of the system operation
- Updated drawings showing actual equipment type, size, and location
- Updated equipment and material schedules
- Maintenance and repair procedures
- Aiming adjustment tasks and schedule
- Design adjustment tasks and schedule

The designer should schedule a final meeting with the owner and maintenance staff to review these docu-

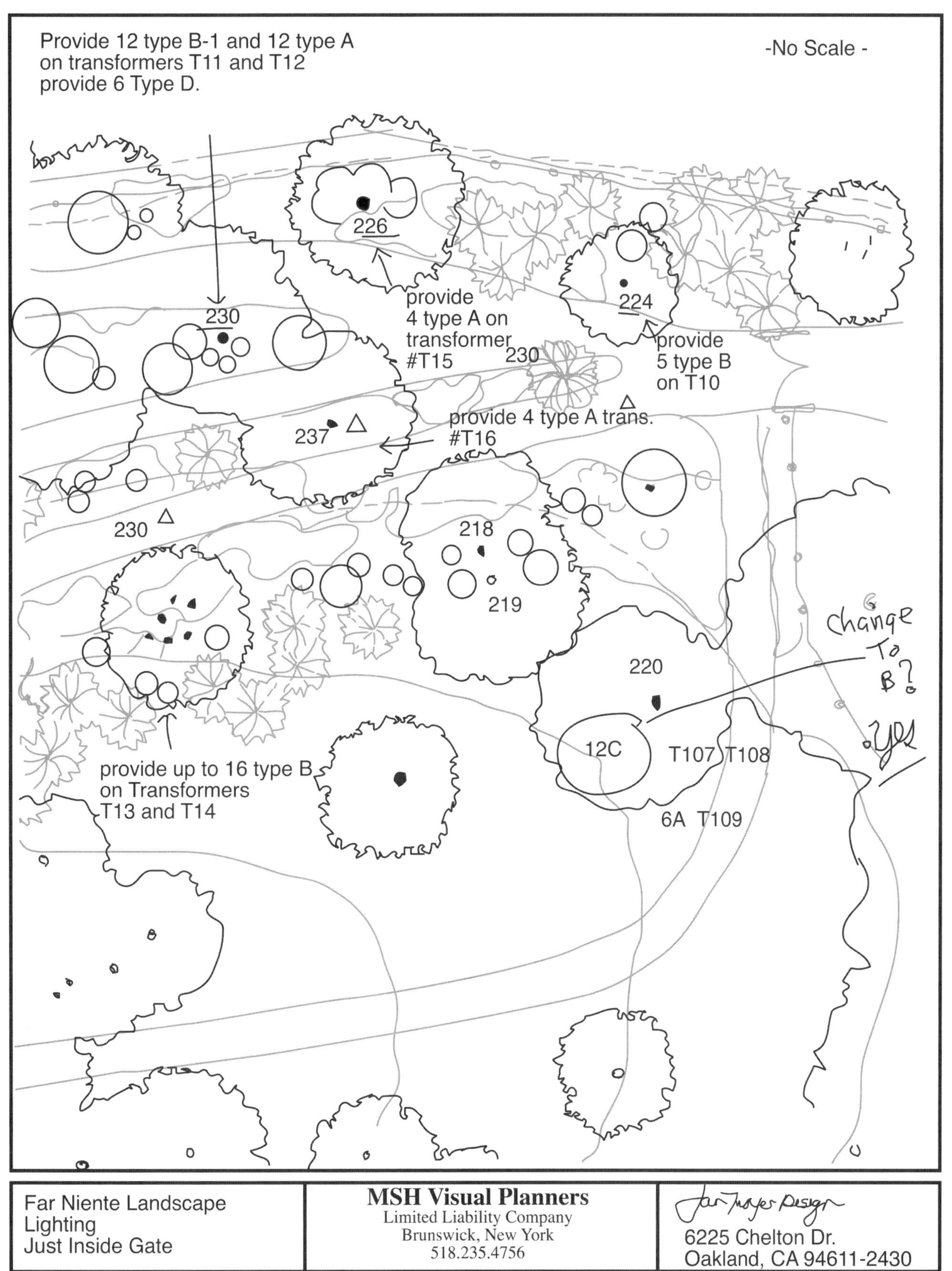

Far Niente Landscape Lighting Just Inside Gate	**MSH Visual Planners** Limited Liability Company Brunswick, New York 518.235.4756	Jan Moyer Design 6225 Chelton Dr. Oakland, CA 94611-2430

Figure 5.1. *Lighting information marked up on a hand-drawn site plan. Note the information for Tree 226. Lighting Design: MSH Visual Planners; Drawing: Jim Gross & N. J. Smith.*

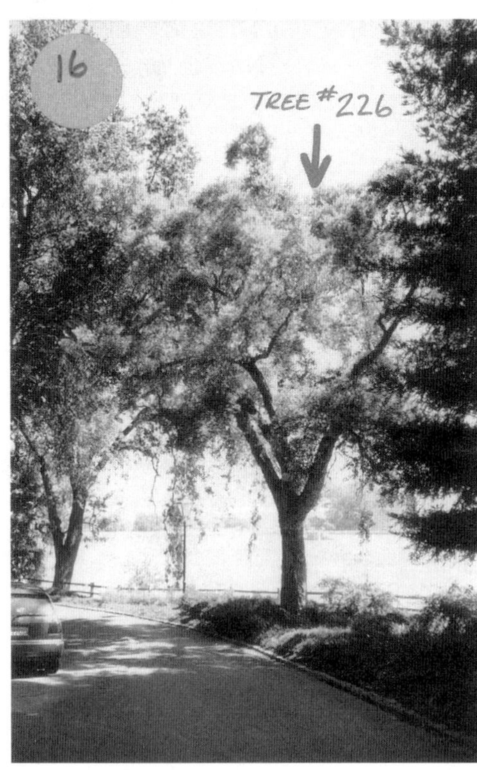

Photo 16
Tree #226

Standing just inside the main gate at the end of the upper road.

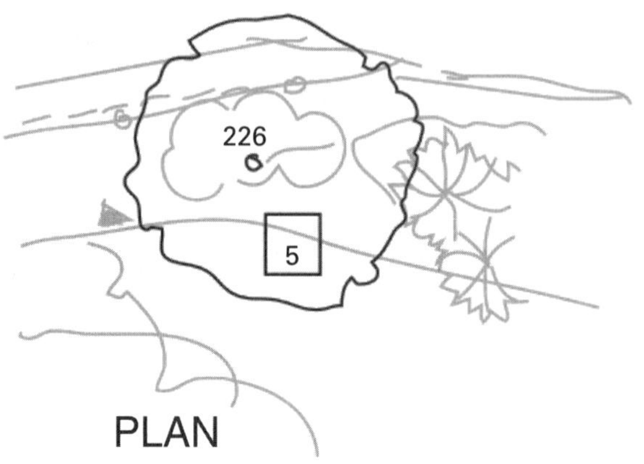

Photo 18
Tree # 226
2 Type A

Standing behind Tree #226, on lower road. For the planting below.

Far Niente Landscape Record Documents							
Page #	DWG #	Photo #	Tree #	Location & Fixture Purpose	Fixtures	Lamps	Trans #
3	5	16, 17, 18	226	Just inside main gate on right side Downlights in Tree 226	4 Type A	4 FSV	T15

Figure 5.2. *At the end of the project in Figure 5.1, the Record Documents information is shown using the revised plan of Tree 226 with the accompanying photographs and schedule. Drawing: Jim Gross & N. J. Smith.*

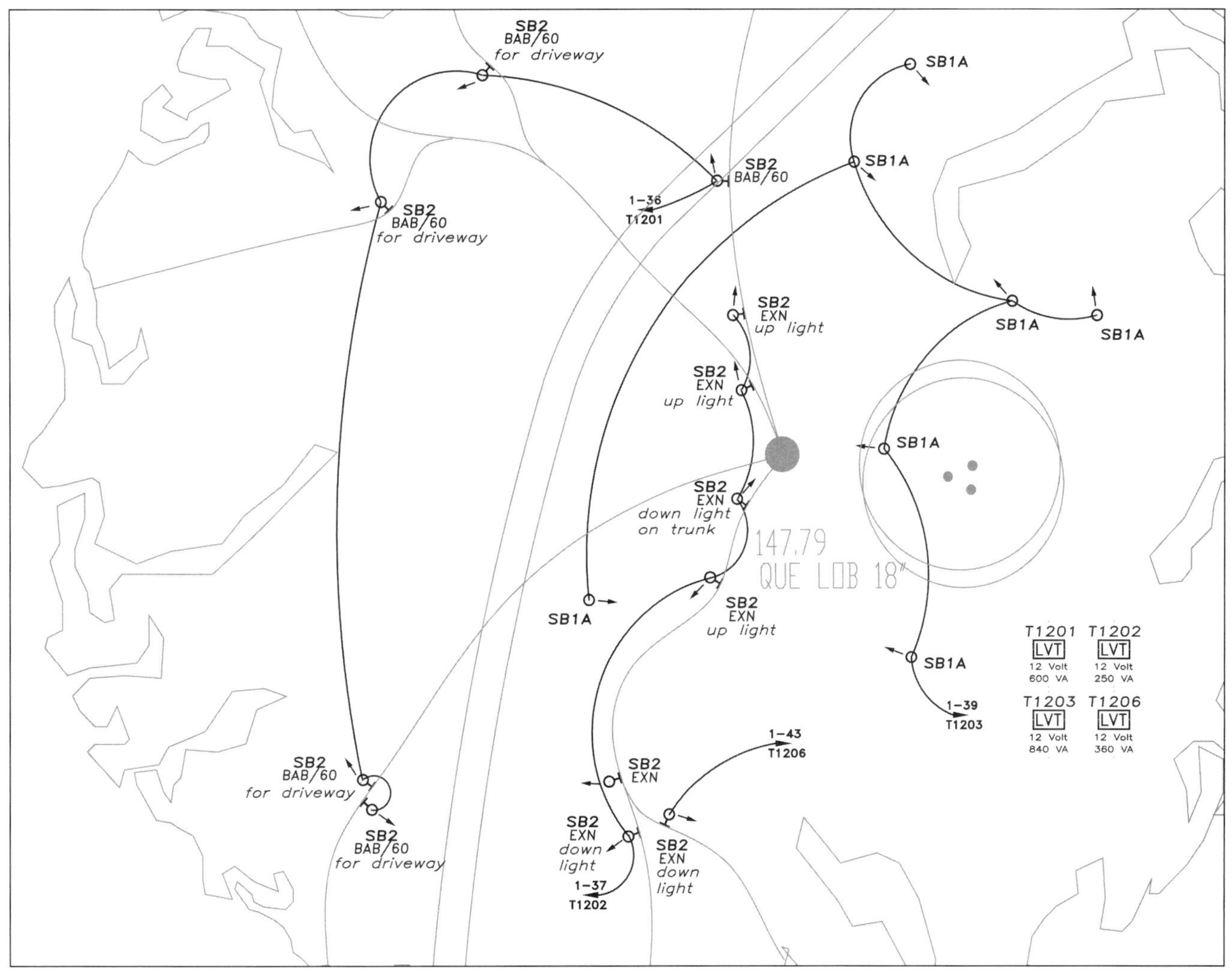

Figure 5.3. On this Record Documents plan, final lamping, aiming directions and notes, and updated controls/transformer information has been shown. Lighting Design: Michael Hooker & Paul Schreer, MSH Visual Planners; Drawing: N. J. Smith.

ments. During the meeting the designer should explain and demonstrate each maintenance task that needs to be done now and as the landscape matures. This will help everyone understand when specific tasks need to be done and the reason for each task.

RECORD DOCUMENTS PACKAGE

The purpose of Record Documents is to provide all the pertinent project information needed to keep the newly installed lighting system properly functioning and all the information needed to respond to any and all site changes affecting the lighting system in the future. Documents issued as a part of the package consist of updated design and installation documents and all maintenance guidelines.

Updated Design and Installation Documents

These documents should include:

- All the design, construction, and site changes that occurred during construction
- A record of all existing site conditions that pertains to the lighting
- Final locations, sizes, and types of equipment
- Information including installation and operation manuals for equipment use
- Controls adjustment records and settings
- Fixture aiming and shielding data

The set of information will vary by project, based on the equipment and systems utilized and the form of the contract documents provided. It should always include

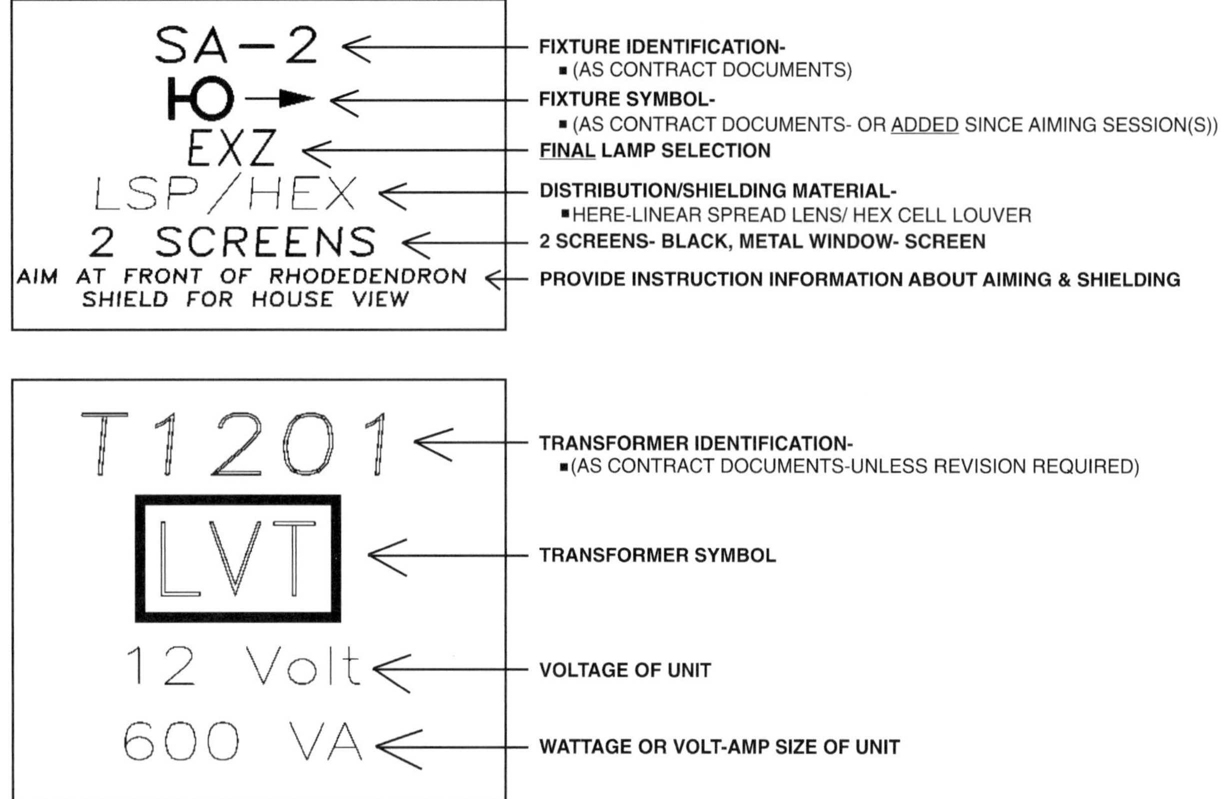

Figure 5.4. *Record document information can be shown as part of the fixture symbol information on a plan including fixture identification, final lamping, distribution/shielding materials, and aiming/shielding instructions. Any changes to the transformer should be included at the actual transformer location on the plan including the identification, voltage, and size. Drawing: Jim Gross & N. J. Smith.*

updated lighting plans, all fixture and control systems information, and the maintenance information and supplies.

Some changes may have occurred in fixture and/or transformer selection at almost any phase of design and construction. Including a copy of the revised/new cut sheet for the fixture(s) and/or transformer(s) may be helpful for the owner's future reference to identify the proper item when procuring additional units or spare parts in the future.

Typically, changes do not occur to the schematic wiring and installation details shown on detail sheets within the drawing set. Any drawings, schedules, and/or cut sheets that don't have changes do not need to get issued as part of the Record Documents. The designer and the owner should review the condition/existence of the owner's copy of the contract documents. If there is any doubt that the owner will have a complete set, all documents may need to be reissued. Especially on a large project, providing duplication of existing, unrevised documents can be extensive and become a significant project cost. Whenever possible, integrate new documents into the existing document set to save the project additional expense.

Updated Lighting Plans

The updated lighting layout plan(s) will show all the following information:

1. Actual lighting fixture locations
2. Installed lamp(s) and all distribution/shielding accessories
3. Aiming information
4. Shielding information
5. Actual low-voltage transformer and lighting fixture interconnections
6. Actual lighting control interconnections
7. Actual low-voltage transformer locations
8. Actual control equipment locations
9. Actual wiring distribution routing and cable sizes
10. Actual pull box and junction box locations
11. Actual service trench and sleeve locations
12. Actual electrical distribution panel locations

Project: Harlan West Winery
Area: Parking Patio
Location: Tree 5 - Tree

Exterior Lighting System
Focus Record

Focused By: PFS
Recorded By: PFS
Date: 6/1/99

Fixture ID	Type	Mounting Location	Lamp Type	Lens Type	Louver Type	Filter Type(s)	Shielding Remarks	Aiming
1	SA1	Tree - Down	MR11 - FSV	N/A	BLK Hexcell	N/A	Parking / Patio	Parking Area
2	SA1	Tree - Down	MR11 - FSV	N/A	BLK Hexcell	N/A	Parking / Patio	Parking Area
3	SA1	Tree - Down	MR11 - FSV	N/A	BLK Hexcell	N/A	Parking / Patio	Parking Area
5	SB2	Tree - Up	MR16 - FNV	N/A	BLK Hexcell	N/A	Parking / Patio	Up NW
6	SB2	Tree - Up	MR16 - FNV	N/A	BLK Hexcell	N/A	Parking / Patio	Up W
7	SB2	Tree - Up	MR16 - FNV	N/A	BLK Hexcell	N/A	Parking / Patio	Up SW
10	SB2	Tree - Down	MR16 - FMW	N/A	BLK Hexcell	N/A	Parking / Patio	Down Trunk
11	SB2	Tree - Down	MR16 - FNV	N/A	BLK Hexcell	N/A	Parking / Patio	Down between Trees

MSH Visual Planners, LLC
© 1999

Page 1 of 1

Figure 5.5. *A Focus Record schedule represents another way to document final installation information. Lighting Design: Michael Stewart Hooker, Janet Lennox Moyer, & Paul Schreer, MSH Visual Planners; Drawing: N. J. Smith.*

The contractor needs to provide the designer with all the final information regarding items 5 through 12 above for inclusion in the Record Documents. Typical changes to that equipment include the quantity, type, size, and location. For example, the installing contractor may determine during construction that a transformer location must be moved. This might mean changing from an interior location to an exterior location. Any changes must be shown on the plans and in all affected schedules. These important electrical data can be provided directly to the owner as a separate set of documents and inserted into the Record Documents binders or incorporated into the lighting documents before the binders are given to the owner.

Fixture Location

The way each installed fixture becomes documented varies by project. It can be shown by a note on the updated plan (see Figure 5.2), by revising/updating fixture symbols on the lighting layout plans (see Figure 5.3), via photographs (see Figures 5.2), or by utilizing a combination of these techniques.

Revising the location of fixture symbols on a plan needs to show the approximate location of stake-mount adjustable accent fixtures. These fixtures are specified to provide movement flexibility as plants grow and/or to respond to other site condition changes that require fixture relocation (see Chapter 15). Since the initial fixture location will likely change as specific plants and overall garden plantings mature over time, documenting dimensions for these fixtures becomes superfluous.

Show the approximate location for adjustable, stake-mounted fixtures with the symbol arrow identifying the aiming direction. To better identify each fixture symbol, consider providing a notation of the selected lamping, any relevant aiming directions and fixture brightness shielding information. Either show or update the transformer information (for low-voltage fixtures) and any/all load/controls information (see Figures 5.2–5.5). This data provides an at-a-glance overall view of all the important information needed for future maintenance and system expansion (see Chapter 15).

Using Photographs to Locate Lighting Equipment

For projects without accurate drawings, provide lighting information notation by individual trees and other site elements on a project sketch (see Figure 5.2) and then utilize photograph(s) to show the actual installed fixture locations with lamping, accessories, and aiming notations (see Figure 5.2). This notation approach generally works well for tree-mounted fixtures. Showing even a general tree-mount fixture location on a

Mountainwood — Revised Transformer Schedule — Revised 1/2/03

Spencer Lane Trust Landscape Lighting											
Transformer Schedule — for RECORD DOCUMENTS											
Updated 2002	Transformer Number	Size (VA)	Fixture Type	Quantity	Max Fixture wattage (Watts)	Total Watts	Actual Load	Transformer Location	Load Number	Sheet Number	Transformer Use
Feb 26 03	T170	500	Type SB3	5	50	250	160	DB Near Tree #23	L100	LL 2.1.1	Entry Court For Tree #23
Feb 26 03	T171	500	Type SB3	3	50	150	105	DB Near Tree #24	L100	LL 2.1.1	Entry Court For Tree #24
Feb 26 03	T172	300	Type SA2	2	35	70	40	DB Near Entry Way	L220	LL 2.1	For Entry Gate Post and Address Number
Feb 26 03	T173	840	Type SA1	16	35	560	440		L210	LL 2.2	For Tennis Court Deck
Feb 26 03	T174	500	Type SA1	12	35	420	240	DB Near Riding Ring	L208	LL 2.2	For Riding Ring Deck
Feb 26 03	T175	500	Type SA1	12	35	420	240	DB Near Riding Ring	L209	LL 2.2	For Riding Ring Deck
Feb 26 03	T176	500	Type SB1	2	50	100	100	Garage D Attic	L211	LL 2.2	For Barn Drive Area
Feb 26 03	T177	500	Type SB1	3	50	150	60	Garage D Attic	L203	LL 2.2	For Barn Path By Garage
Feb 26 03	T178	500	Type SB1	3	50	150	60	Garage D Attic	L103	LL 2.2	For Area By Caretaker/ Tree #68
Feb 26 03	T179	500	Type SA1	10	35	350	200	Tennis Court Closet	L216	LL 2.2	For Tennis Court Plaza
Feb 26 03	T180	500	Type SA1	10	35	350	200	Tennis Court Closet	L216	LL 2.2	For Tennis Court Plaza

5/31/04 — Page 1 of 1

Figure 5.6. *For ease of maintenance and future project expansion, all data should be updated on a transformer schedule. Lighting Design: Michael Stewart Hooker, Janet Lennox Moyer, & Paul Schreer, MSH Visual Planners; Drawing: N. J. Smith.*

LOAD SCHEDULE - for RECORD DOCUMENTS												
Updated 2002/ 2003	Load No.	Location	Description: Fixture Type	Qty	Load Type	Voltage	Transformer T#	Max Watts	Total Watts By Item	Load Total	Sheet Number
Dec 27 02	L77	Pool House Eaves	A	14	MLV	12	T74, 75	35	490	490	2B-E 2.1
Feb 26 03	L78	Mud Rm Eave/Family Entry Trellis	SA1	30	MLV	12	T38,9,8,3,5	35	1050	1050	LL 2.1.1, LF 2.4b
Feb 26 03	**L79**	**Trellis, Staff Building Walk, & Tree 60**	**SA1**	**29**	**MLV**	**12**	**T2, 4, 6, 7, 68**	**35**	**1015**	1645	LL 2.1.1 LL 2.1.3
			SA2	**5**	**MLV**	**12**	**T114**	**35**	**175**		
			SB1	**5**	**MLV**	**12**	**T112**	**50**	**250**		
			SC1	**2**	**MLV**	**12**	**T112**	**50**	**100**		
			SF3	**7**	**INC**	**120**	**NA**	**15**	**105**		
Dec 27 02	L80	Staff Building Eave	A	10	MLV	12	T1	35	350	350	LL 2.1.1
Dec 27 02	L82	Garage B Exterior	D	4	INC	120	NA	13	52	52	LL 2.1.1
Feb 26 03	L89	Master Bedroom/Laundry/Lib Eave Flood	L	6	INC	120	NA	250	1500	1500	LF 2.4b
Feb 26 03	L90	Living Room Eave Flood	L	7	INC	120	NA	250	1750	1750	LF 2.4a

•LOADS 85 THROUGH 91 SHALL BE CONNECTED WITH THE ALARM SYSTEM TURNING LIGHTS ON WHEN SYSTEM IS BREACHED. LIGHTS WILL THEN BE TURNED OFF BY THE ALARM SYSTEM KEYPAD.

• *ND MEANS NON-DIM. ALL FLUORESCENT LOADS REQUIRE AN INTERFACE DEVICE.

•LOADS 78 & 79 SHALL BE CONNECTED VIA AN ASTROMICAL TIMECLOCK.

•ALL LANDSCAPE LOADS SHALL BE ON/OFF ONLY, EXCEPT WHEN DIMMING IS DESIGNATED ON THE PRESET CONTROL SYSTEM OR BY A DIMMING SWITCH ON THE PLANS.

•INTERIOR LOADS THAT REQUIRE DIMMING HAVE DIMMING SWITCHES OR ARE SHOWN ON THE PRESET CONTROLLER SCHEDULE.

• ALL LOADS OVER 1920 WATTS SHALL BE FED WITH TWO CIRCUITS.

Spencer Lane Trust Revised Load Schedule 5/31/04 3:00 PM 1 of 1

Figure 5.7. *For ease of maintenance and future project expansion, all data should be updated on a load schedule. Lighting Design: Michael Stewart Hooker, Janet Lennox Moyer, & Paul Schreer, MSH Visual Planners; Drawing: N. J. Smith.*

LAMP COORDINATION							
CLIENT: Pawling Penthouse Suites							
FOCUS DATES: May 26, 2004 - June 4, 2004							
WATTS		LETTER ID	PROJECT TOTAL	REMAINING INVENTORY	25% SPARE STOCK	STOCK NEEDED	STOCK ORDER DATE
	MR 16 LAMPS						
20	Very Narrow Spot	EZX	20	5	5	0	–
20	Narrow Spot	ESX	100	25	25	0	–
20	Flood	BAB/60	60	7	15	8	–
	MR 11-BAYONET BASE						
20	Narrow Spot	FSS	40	12	10	6	–
	Spot	FST	24	0	6	6	–
	Narrow Flood	FSV	64	16	16	0	–
	CDM METAL HALIDE						
100	Flood	N/A	120	20	30	10	–
100	Wide Flood	N/A	20	5	5	0	–
70	Spot	N/A	32	8	8	0	–
	Quartz PAR 38 LAMPS						
45	Spot	N/A	44	4	11	7	–
90	Flood	N/A	24	4	6	2	–
250	Spot	N/A	100	0	25	25	–

Figure 5.8. *A Lamp Coordination form provides a client with a summary of all the lamps used on their project for procuring stock and staying organized for future maintenance. Forms such as this need to be updated anytime work is done on the site. Drawing: N. J. Smith.*

two-dimensional drawing becomes difficult. Trying to draw a specific location on an individual branch becomes a cumbersome process for more than a few tree-mounted fixtures on a project. Instead provide a photograph showing the general location of the tree on a site to orient someone and an accompanying close-up of the tree showing the fixture locations (see Figure 5.2).

Lamping Information

Provide information about the lamp installed in an individual fixture or by an appropriate grouping. For example, list the quantity of the specific lamp for several fixtures in a tree or for a discrete area when all fixtures utilize the same lamp. This notation placed by the fixture symbol or fixture group designation on a plan allows the maintenance staff to bring the appropriate replacement lamp to be installed as the burned-out lamp is removed (see Figure 4.16). Knowing the initial lamp utilized to create a specific lighting effect serves as a record of the original design intent and provides a guide to use when needing to revise the aiming and/or relamping to re-create that original effect as the planting matures (see Chapter 15).

Aiming Notation

Next in importance after the location and lamp selection, the aiming of an accent fixture helps determines the success of the lighting effect. When the aiming will not be obvious from looking at the documentation, providing a notation to describe it records the intent of the original effect composition (see Figure 5.5 & Documents Appendix Figure A.29).

Shielding Notation

Shielding notation usually refers to the placement of an angled hood to prohibit or minimize view to the inside of a fixture. Seeing the interior surface brightness of a fixture will distract from the overall lighting composition (see Figure 5.5 & Documents Appendix Figure A.29).

Updated and New Project Schedules

At the completion of construction, the design and installation team must update all informational data sched-

PROJECT DIRECTORY

CLIENT: FAR NIENTE		
Far Niente Winery (just off Oakville Grade)		OFFICE: (707) 944-2861
P.O. Box 327		FAX: (707) 944-2312
1 Acacia Drive	ACCOUNTING FAX:	(707) 944-2563
Oakville, Ca 94562		1-800-363-6523
Cynthia, Gina		
	VINEYARD HOUSE:	(707) 944-9406
CONTACTS:		
Owner: Gil Nickel		
Beth Nickel		
Winemaker: Dirk Hampson		
Katherine, Gina		
Elan		
Cynthia Waters		
Beth's Assistant: Sherry Viner	FAX:	(707) 771-8705
CAVES GENERAL CONTRACTOR		
Al Burtleson Construction	OFFICE:	(707) 942-5834
2245 Palmer Drive		
St. Helena, CA 94574		
CONTACTS:		
Alf Burtleson		
Cave Digger: Dale		
ELECTRICAL CONTRACTOR:		
Vintage Electric	OFFICE:	(707) 942-0751
600 Petrified Forest Road		
Calistoga, CA 94515		
CONTACT:		
Eddie Burhans (& Judy)	CAR PHONE:	CAR PHONE:(707) 486-4276
P.O. Box 454	FAX:	FAX: (707) 942-0670
Calistoga, CA 94515		
LANDSCAPE ARCHITECT:		
Jonathan Plant		
71 A LaFayette circle	OFFICE:	(925) 283-5574
LaFayette, CA 94549		
St. Helena Office:	OFFICE:	OFFICE: (707) 963-8313
1230 Pine Street	FAX:	FAX: (707) 9631230
ARCHITECT:		
Ron Nunn	OFFICE:	(707) 963-0899
	FAX:	(707) 963-3431
	TIB:	(415) 435-2115
TREE SERVICE:		
Joseph Borden		(707) 486-6004
Of Britton Tree Service	PHONE:	(707) 963-7578
	FAX:	(707) 963-7599
	CAR:	(707) 486-6004
	CELL:	(707) 695-5022
	PAGER:	(707) 944-6667
CONSTRUCTION MANAGER:		
Patrick T. Green		
1910 West Myrtle Street	OFFICE:	(707)942-0548
P.O. Box 1040	FAX:	(707) 942-0549
Calistoga, CA 94515		
INTERIOR DESIGNER:		
Caroline Ross		
Rossi Designs	PHONE/FAX:	(415) 776-7620
2186 Vallejo Street, #2		
San Francisco, CA 94123		

MacHD/Addresses/Clients/Far Niente 5/31/04 1

Figure 5.9. *A Project Directory with all contacts from the owners to all designers, installers, and suppliers helps all team members service the project over the years. Drawing: N. J. Smith.*

ules produced for the Contract Documents. All changes that occurred during design and construction need to be documented. Project maintenance and future expansion depends on the accuracy and availability of these documents. The schedules provide not only a record of the existing conditions for maintenance, but also a guideline for the future expansion of the lighting system. This includes all schedules for fixtures, transformers, loads, control systems, etc. (see Figures 5.6 & 5.7).

During the lighting system planning, the designer and owner must discuss future garden development issues that will affect the need for expansion in the lighting system. The anticipated additional capacities will then get integrated into the electrical system infrastructure, including the total power available at the electrical panel, the sizing of electrical wire/cable capacity for estimated future additional load, and the sizing of transformers and load/control channels for estimated additional loads. These allowances should be easily identifiable in any project schedule (see Documents Appendix Figure A.19). Of course, it is impossible to anticipate all future landscape changes, but discussing it during conceptual design helps prepare the electrical power distribution system with available load to eliminate or at least minimize the need to dig up the lawn or garden at a later date.

The designer should review all contract document schedules to determine necessary updating and revision, including:

- Lighting Fixture Schedule
- Transformer Schedule
- Load Schedule
- Control Schedule
- Electrical Distribution Panel Schedules
- Cable, Conduit, Pull Box, and Junction Box Schedules
- Lamp Coordination Forms (documenting lamps used and spare lamp requirements)

The lighting designer will have produced some of the schedules; the electrical engineer or electrical contractor may produce others. All the schedules originally provided for the project need to be updated and included in the issue of Record Documents.

There are two schedules the lighting designer might produce after the aiming sessions. A Focus Record Schedule records the aiming and shielding data determined during the nighttime focusing session(s). On small or simple projects, this data can be included on the plans at each fixture location or listed in the revised project description (see Figures 5.2–5.4 & Documents Appendix Figure A.16).

The second new schedule, called a Lamp Coordination Schedule (see Figure 5.8), tracks the lamps used for a project. The form tallies the quantity of each lamp type used and the quantity of each remaining after the aiming session(s). The remaining quantity represents the project's spare lamp stock. The amount of stock to keep on hand depends on the hours of operation and the relative availability of each lamp (see "Maintenance Planning and Instructions," below). Typically, having 25 percent spares should allow a client to provide spot-relamping (see below) and not have to panic, as a lamp burns out (see "Lamp Life" in Chapter 6). At the end of the initial installation, the designer needs to coordinate with the owner as to who should be responsible for stocking the first set of spare lamps and all maintenance supplies.

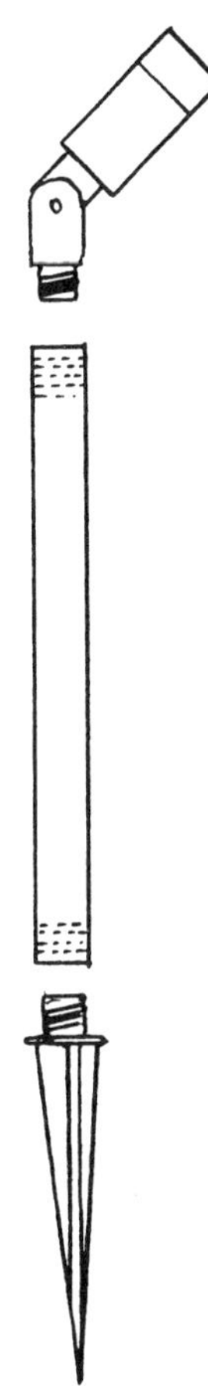

Figure 5.10. *Adding a stake segment can raise a fixture above the ground when the initial plant material will be tall or it grows higher than the fixture over time. Drawing: Lezlie Johannessen.*

Unusual lamp types or fixtures requiring group relamping (see below) in less than one year might warrant keeping a higher percentage of spares. Projects in remote areas should have either a higher percentage of spare lamps or a reliable supplier that can quickly ship the type and quantities of spare lamps that will be needed. The name and phone number of a supplier should be included in the Project Service Directory.

Project Service Directory

A list of all the people and companies that comprised the design, procurement, and installation team for the project should be provided at the front of the Record Documents. For each party, include name, company affiliation, address, phone numbers (office with extension, cell, and home, with a note which to try first), e-mail address, and so on. This allows anyone working on the system instant access to the others involved at all times (see Figure 5.9). As with all other documentation, if parties change or new parties become involved in the project, their name and contact information should be added to the directory.

Controls Adjustments and Settings

The control system selected for a landscape lighting system can vary dramatically from a simple system consisting of one on/off switch (sometimes fed with multiple contactors) to a sophisticated computer driven multiple-preset-scene system. The notation required varies based on the system selected. All Controls Schedules must be updated and any dimming or preset scene data must be recorded (see Document Appendix A.23 and Chapter 9).

Maintenance Documents

Lighting designers and property owners must understand that landscape lighting systems require ongoing maintenance. Each landscape lighting project is different, and the proper maintenance tasks and schedule need to be planned at the end of the initial lighting installation and implemented immediately. The planning includes deciding who will do the work and the time frame for all tasks.

Maintenance is critical to keeping the equipment functional and to retain the lighting effects. A regularly scheduled review of the property during the day can easily identify burned-out lamps. A night review will show fixtures that are no longer aimed properly and effects that need to be reworked.

As the designer is planning the maintenance, the owner needs to identify who will lead each type of maintenance. Often, the owner will request that the garden maintenance staff or the installing contractor provide ongoing maintenance services following the maintenance manual directions provided by the designer.

Maintenance Issues

Regularly occurring maintenance, such as pruning the growth of plants surrounding fixtures and cleaning debris buildup on fixture lenses, can be done by the garden staff during normal garden maintenance. Other tasks, such as reaiming of fixtures, needs to be done by the lighting designer or other trained party. If the owner prefers to do this, the designer needs to show the owner how to manipulate the fixtures to retain the effects. This includes educating the owner about aiming angles, lamp wattage, and beamspread, when to consider changing the lamp beamspread or wattage, and the importance of tightening each fixture's adjustment points.

Over time, as some plants grow, they begin to disrupt the lighting. Plant growth can begin to block light from reaching an intended object (see Figures 14.34–14.36). To remedy this problem, either the fixture needs to be moved or the plant needs to be pruned. Moving the fixture can entail either locating the fixture farther from the plant it lights or adjusting the stake height to avoid blocking the light distribution (see Figure 5.10, the adjustable stake in Figure 7.27, & Figure 14.36).

A decision needs to be made by someone familiar with the garden and/or the specific plant (the owner, landscape architect, gardener, and/or arborist) and the lighting designer as to which is the preferable action. In some cases, any pruning will disfigure the plant, while at other times it will not negatively affect the appearance of the plant and offers the simplest solution. If pruning is the correct solution, the gardener needs to be shown the intent of the pruning and instructed to include it as part of the regular maintenance routine.

Other related grounds maintenance issues that affect lighting include the need to regularly cut back ground cover plantings to avoid fixture lenses becoming buried in foliage. Hedges may need to be trimmed away from pathlight fixtures. The lower branches of young trees may need to be pruned as the tree grows (see Figure 15.40D&E).

All pruning of trees should not affect the health or the aesthetic beauty of the branching structure. Any pruning done for lighting should accentuate the beauty of the tree. Whenever there is a question about pruning and the health of the tree, the lighting designer should ask the project landscape designer or arborist.

Specimen plants may also outgrow the beamspread or aiming of a fixture. As this happens the lighting becomes less effective or totally useless. While variation in brightness throughout the canopy of a tree can be effective, excessive brightness variation is at best distracting. The maintenance response will involve either changing the lamp to a different wattage or beamspread, moving the fixture location farther away from the plant, or a combination of both steps.

In newly planted gardens, young plants often grow quickly, making the lighting outdated within a year or two. As plantings grow and change over time, fixtures may need to be added or removed from the site. When plants die, the fixtures lighting them can be used in another location or kept in the same place if a similar plant replaces the dead one. As plants grow, additional fixtures may be required to light the larger plants. In mature gardens, the lighting can work for many years before readjustment becomes necessary.

Maintenance also includes the replacement of burned-out lamps. This can be done on a fixture-by-fixture basis as each lamp fails or by group relamping. For small projects, replacing lamps as they fail makes good sense for fixtures at or below grade. For larger projects and for fixtures mounted in trees or any other hard-to-reach location, the designer should suggest to the owner that these fixtures be relamped as a group to maximize efficiency. In most cases, when even one lamp burns out, it affects the appearance of the lighting.

Another condition that requires care is the attachment of fixtures, wires, and any other equipment to trees. As trees develop they will start to grow around anything attached to them. To protect the tree and any equipment and wiring, the nails or screws that attach any equipment to the tree must be regularly loosened (see Figure 10.23). How often this must be done depends on the type of tree(s), their age, and how quickly they are growing. The time can range from approximately 1 to 3 years. Sometimes animals that live in or near the trees will bite the wiring and can actually chew through fixture cords. This is something to check for when an existing lamp is not functioning and a new lamp does not work.

The lighting designer needs to become familiar enough with the plantings in the landscape, and how the site will be used, to advise the client of the recommended maintenance schedule. During this discussion, the designer can help the client evaluate whether an ongoing maintenance agreement with the designer is necessary or whether the owner's gardeners and the owner can take care of the system.

Maintenance Equipment and Spare Parts

The Record Documents should include the owner's manuals and operating instructions for all lighting system equipment, such as the control system. A list of tools needed for maintaining the fixtures, cleaning supplies to keep fixtures functioning and in good condition, and all spare parts to keep the overall lighting system functioning properly should be included. Most tools needed to maintain lighting equipment are standard, such as screwdrivers or Allen wrenches for aiming and locking the fixtures. However, sometimes required types or sizes of tools are unusual. In either case, a set of tools should be kept with other system equipment.

The designer should review all supplies that will be needed to service the lighting equipment. This includes solvents for cleaning fixture lenses and housings, antioxidant compounds for coating joints and joining mechanisms, and lubricating compounds for coating metal parts such as fixture sockets and lamp bases. It also includes any spare parts that might be needed over time such as spare lamps, distribution lenses, shielding louvers, accessory retaining rings, gaskets, fasteners, fuses, mounting parts, ballasts, transformers, and so on.

MAINTENANCE WORK

The following guidelines will outline the work that needs to be done to keep the landscape lighting system functioning properly. Two basic types of maintenance work need to be provided: focus adjustment and design adjustment.

Focus Adjustment

This includes all maintenance tasks required to keep the lighting functioning as originally designed. The work consists of:

- Lamp replacement
- Fixture cleaning
- Maintaining the proper fixture aiming
- Restocking maintenance supplies

The owner needs to assign a responsible party to provide the services. This party should contact the lighting designer regarding all plant growth or maintenance conditions/situations arising that do not fit into the category of ongoing normal maintenance in order to retain the original design intent and appearance.

Lamp Replacement

This refers to the process of verifying that all fixtures function properly and replacing any burned-out lamps with new functioning lamps. There are two kinds of lamp replacement: spot relamping and group relamping.

Spot relamping refers to replacing any burned-out lamp found during the normal review process. This type of relamping should be done for all incandescent fixtures at grade, below grade, or easily accessible by

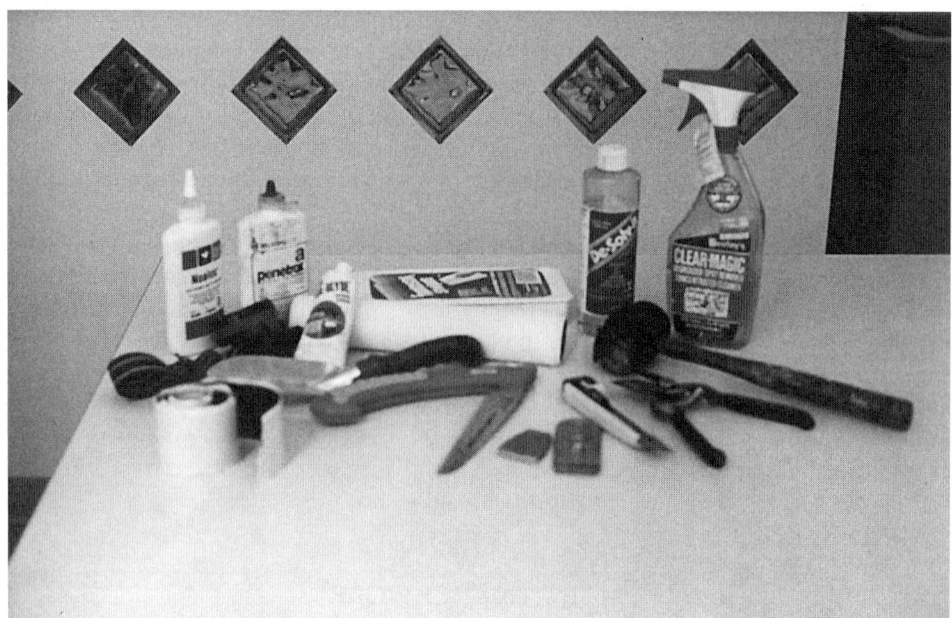

Figure 5.11. Additional equipment for maintaining an installed lighting system includes cleaning materials and pruning tools. Photograph: Janet Lennox Moyer.

ladder. The time frame for this review should be scheduled based on the site conditions. Typically, it could be as often as once a month, but should be done at least once every three to four months. The party assigned to do this relamping service would be responsible to provide all the replacement lamps and accessories as required. This means either taking the responsibility for the spare stock or providing a list of stock needed to the appropriate party after any lamp replacement work.

Group relamping refers to replacing all lamps within an area at the same time once any lamp(s) in that group start burning out or on a regularly scheduled basis. This applies to all tree-mounted incandescent fixtures requiring access by ladder, lift truck, and tree climber. Again, a specific party should be identified to be responsible to provide this service and all lamps and accessories as required.

The intended hours of operation determines the timeframe for this type of relamping. For example, a time switch activates a group of fixtures along a drive/entry walkway each night at dusk via an astronomical clock and remains activated until the selected time, say 11:00 PM. In the summer months the hours of operation will be less and in the winter they will be longer. The actual hours depend on the geographical location of the site. For the purpose of this example, in the summer the lights will be activated at 8:00 PM, so the hours of operation will be three. In the winter, if the on time is approximately 5:00 PM, the hours of operation become six. This averages out to approximately 1,640 annual hours of operation. A typical MR16 lamp life today is 6,000 hours. If no dimming is involved (which extends lamp life), the average lamp should last nearly four years. If you de-rate the life to 80 percent, then the relamping would be just under three years. All these issues need to be considered when determining the hours of operation and recommending to a client the relamping schedule.

The following text is from a winery maintenance manual prepared in 1999 (note the lamp life for the MR16 lamps have improved significantly since that time—these manuals require updating). The first section addresses tree-mounted incandescent fixtures requiring access by ladder, lift truck, and tree climber, but not the below-grade accent lights for a group of Olive trees or the high-pressure sodium lamps illuminating the main winery building. These two groups have longer operating hours, and the high-pressure sodium lamps have a much longer life of 24,000 hours. This means that for this project there were three conditions to consider, and each had a different relamping time frame. The recommendation for those two groups follows the tree-mount fixture section:

(1) ***Incandescent Group Relamping.*** This section will address the time frame for replacing all incandescent lamps on the winery site, *except* for those in the fixtures for uplighting the Olive trees (see below).

   (a) The time frame for relamping incandescent fixtures is estimated to be every 2 years based on 1,500 hours annual usage. This translates to 4 hours per day and includes usage during (winter and other inclement) evenings when dinners are held indoors at the winery and the

Maintenance Materials

Lens & Glass Cleaner: Use to clean lenses and glass that have "caked-on" film of varying natures.

Recommended Product:
'De-Solv-it', A citrus based organic cleaner.
Manufactured by Orange-Sol: 1-800-877-7771

Typically **available** at hardware/big-box stores

Anti-Seize Compound: Lubricant used to prevent corrosion and seizing of aluminum threads. Resists high temperature. Use on fixture housing threads between housing and bezel. We recommend doing this everytime you open the fixture.

Typically sold through automotive stores for use on spark plugs, manifold and head bolts, etc. Sold through most stores in small quantities. Larger quantities typically can be ordered from specialized automotive stores. We recommend using the larger containers which come with applicator brushes.

Recommended Products:
Locktite 'Anti-Seize Lubricant'
Permatex 'Anti-Seize Lubricant'
NAPA Auto Parts 'Anti-Seize' Lubricant

Also available through electrical distributors as conduit joint compound.

Recommended Products:
Burndy 'Penetrox'
Ideal 'Noalox'

High Temperature Lubricant: Lubricant used to waterproof and prevent corrosion and seizing of lamp contacts and sockets. Resists high temperature and moisture. Use on 12 and 120 volt screw base and bayonet base lamp sockets. Use on anything with metallic base and metallic socket.

Typically sold through automotive stores for use on brake parts, cables, belts, etc.

Recommended Products:
American Grease Stick Company 'Sil-Glyde'
Sta-Lube 'Synthetic Brake Caliper Grease'

Figure 5.12. *Suggested cleaning and lubricating materials to use each time a fixture is handled. Drawing: N. J. Smith.*

landscape lighting is turned on for guests to enjoy as part of viewing the gardens.

(b) There might be areas, such as the Cabernet Terrace bar that uses the lighting fewer hours or the Chardonnay Garden kitchen, which might use more hours. For any special cases, we can set up separate schedules within these guidelines with input from [*insert client contact name here*].

(c) MSH Visual Planners and [*insert maintenance party name here*] would like to conduct a relamping of all landscape lighting equipment this year, 1999, and then [*insert maintenance party name here*] should track the conditions over the next two years to verify if this is the proper timeframe.

(d) This 1999 overall site relamping will be supervised by MSH Visual Planners to determine if the tree mounted fixtures have remained tightly locked and therefore will remain properly aimed when relamped. If not, then future group relampings of tree mounted fixtures will require similar supervision by MSH Visual Planners to retain the proper aiming. This site relamping will also determine how much input MSH Visual Planners will need to provide on reaiming of all fixtures.

(e) If two years does represent the correct time frame for incandescent relamping, this schedule will be: spring 2001, 2003, 2005, 2007, 2009, etc. If conditions determine otherwise, [*insert maintenance party name here*] shall keep MSH Visual Planners informed, and a revised schedule will be brought to [*insert client contact name here*] for approval.

(f) Based on approval from [*insert client contact name here*] to proceed with relamping the entire site (including the proposal from [*insert tree service provider name here*]), [*insert maintenance party name here*] shall replace all lamps in fixtures accessed by ladder or lift truck and oversee [*insert tree service provider name here*] or other approved tree service company in the replacement of lamps for all fixtures requiring tree climbing for access.

(2) ***Group Relamping for the Olive Trees.*** The Olive trees have predominantly FMW MR16 lamps and some BAB MR16 lamps. The lamp life on these lamps is approximately 4,000 hours for the FMW and 5,000 hours for the BAB.

(a) Based on 8 hours usage in the winter and 4 hours in the summer, the annual total hourly usage would be 2,190 hours. At that rate, we should replace those lamps every year and a half.

(b) These fixtures are being changed over from stake-mounted to below-grade fixtures due to the change of ground cover around the trees. The below grade fixtures will be located, lamped, and aimed this spring (1999). Thus, the schedule for relamping will be as follows: fall 2000, spring 2002, fall 2003, spring 2005, fall 2006, spring 2008, fall 2009, etc.

(c) [*Insert maintenance party name here*] should track the conditions over the next two years to verify if this is the proper timeframe. If conditions determine otherwise, [*insert maintenance party name here*] shall keep MSH Visual Planners informed, and a revised schedule will be brought to *insert "client contact" name here* for approval.

(3) ***Group Relamping for the High-Pressure Sodium Floodlights.*** Based on the annual usage of 2,190 hours, as listed above of the incandescent lighting for the Olive trees (above) and a 24,000-hour average life,[1] these should be replaced every 10 years.

(a) Replacement includes all ground-mounted building floodlights (total of 8) and all grade-mounted fixtures for the wall (total of 30).

(b) These lamps were installed in 1997, so the next time they should need to be replaced is 2007.

(c) [*Insert maintenance party name here*] should track the conditions of these lamps to verify if this is the proper time frame.

For another project, the actual hours of operation are included in the description. Many years later, this helps everyone to not have to recall the hours of operation and rethink the math.

(1) ***Incandescent Group Relamping.*** This section will address the time frame for replacing the tree-mounted fixtures (see below).

(a) The time frame for relamping incandescent lamps is estimated to be every 2 years based on 2,200 hours annual usage. This translates to 6 hours per day based on start of 5:00 PM in the winter with off at 10:00 PM and on at 9:00 PM in the summer and off at 10:00 PM. The lamp life, based on reducing the voltage of all the tree mount fixtures transformers to 11 volts, becomes 6,198 hours. Dividing this by the hours of usage (2,190), the lamps would last approximately 3 years.

(b) However, lamp life is based on averages and lumen output degrades over time, so to keep the garden looking reasonable, we should change the lamps every 2 years. We just changed all the lamps in May 2002. I recommend changing the lamps again in October 2004.

(c) In 2004 (or earlier if [*insert maintenance party name here*] notices that lamps are burning out prematurely—if this is the case, please advise MSH Visual Planners) we should evaluate this relamping time frame.

(d) If 2 years does represent the correct time frame for incandescent relamping, this schedule will be: fall 2004, 2006, 2008, 2010, etc.

Fixture Cleaning

A knowledgeable party needs to walk through the site regularly to check the condition of the fixtures. This can be done during the site review to check for burned-out lamps. The time frame needs to be determined and listed in the maintenance manual.

Any accumulated debris on or around the fixture body should be removed. The outside of the fixture needs to be kept clean primarily to minimize any corrosion potential. Plant debris, such as leaves, fruits, flowers, and nuts, may fall onto the lens and need to be wiped off. Accumulation on the lens can severely diminish the fixture light output. Water spray from rainfall, snow, fog, irrigation, or other sources can deposit minerals onto the lens surface. Such deposits affect light output and distribution. Deposits should be removed with nature- and fixture-friendly solvents (see Figures 5.11 & 5.12), when possible. In some site conditions, the only way to remove these deposits is to scrape the lens surface with a straight, sharp blade.

Whenever a fixture is opened for relamping or any other kind of maintenance, several maintenance prevention efforts need to be done. The lens and body of the fixture should be cleaned of debris. The socket or lamp base should be lubricated with a high-heat compound to avoid seizing of the metals that could prevent removing the lamp at a later date (see Figures 5.11 & 5.12). The connection points of separate fixture parts, such as the threads of a fixture's bezel and body, should be coated with an antioxidizing compound to prevent seizing that could make access into the lamp compartment difficult at a later date (see Figures 5.11 & 5.12). Gaskets should be checked and replaced if they are worn or compressed and cannot continue to provide a good seal.

Maintaining the Proper Fixture Aiming

Wear and tear from the environment and usage knocks fixtures out of adjustment. A knowledgeable party should periodically check the aiming of all fixtures at night to retain the originally designed lighting effect. Reaiming includes changing the horizontal rotation and/or the vertical angle of the fixture to maintain the original effect. Any time a fixture is reaimed, all locking mechanisms on the fixture should be tightened securely. This process should be directed by a maintenance party assigned by the client and trained by the lighting consultant. Any questions about aiming should be directed to the lighting consultant, by phone or written communication, by scheduling a meeting, or during a normally scheduled design adjustment walkthrough.

Stocking and Restocking Supplies

The maintenance party becomes responsible to stock all lamps, lenses, louvers, gaskets, antioxidizing compounds, high-heat lubricants, all cleaning supplies, and all aiming and tightening tools necessary to conduct the relamping, cleaning, and reaiming as described above.

Whenever possible, the owner should designate a place on site with access by the maintenance party to locate all the spare lamps, accessories, parts, tools, and cleaning supplies. The Record Documents should be kept here, allowing easy access to the lighting plans for getting spare lamps for fixtures with burned-out lamps and for access to the Lamp Coordination Schedule for restocking proper quantities of lamps after relamping.

DESIGN ADJUSTMENT

This work includes all maintenance work that tracks the development and growth of the landscape. The work responds to all changes in the landscape, providing visual and functional continuity in the lighting system.

Unlike focus adjustment tasks, this work *must* be led by the lighting designer. The start of this work and the frequency of this work depend on the maturity of the garden and how quickly things grow and change in the garden. Changes in the garden that trigger this lighting maintenance include:

- Plant growth
- Adding, repositioning, deleting, or death of plant materials
- Adding, repositioning, or deleting site furniture, paths, stairs, water features, structures, sculptures, etc.

When a change triggers the need for design adjustment, the lighting designer needs to review the site at night to assess what, if any, design renovation needs to be done. The frequency of this kind of review depends on the maturity of the garden plantings and the occurrence of changes to the gardens. Once the garden becomes mature, meaning that plant growth has slowed considerably, the size and appearance of individual plants or plant grouping change less rapidly, and once the owner stops expanding, changing, or adding garden areas, this work slows down.

For a newly planted garden, this design review should typically happen once a year until plant growth slows. For mature gardens that have installed lighting, after a one-year check to make sure the system does hold up well, the review could be three to five years. For mature gardens with new plantings, renovations, or additions to existing gardens, or new gardens, the design review time frame becomes more frequent again.

Each of the following tasks will be discussed below:

- Reaiming existing fixtures
- Relamping existing fixtures
- Relocating existing fixtures
- Removing existing fixtures
- Adding new fixtures (and associated equipment)
- Updating the Record Documents

Reaiming Existing Fixtures

As plants grow and change in size and shape, the original aiming may no longer produce the desired effect. Fixture reaiming includes adjusting the horizontal rotation and/or vertical angle to regain the intended lighting effect. Plant growth may also require relamping or relocating fixtures (see below). If the aiming has changed significantly, it might require updating the aiming notation in the Record Documents.

Relamping Existing Fixtures

The increased physical size and/or a shift of a plant's importance as a feature can require relamping one or more fixtures that light a specific plant. Relamping consists of changing the wattage and beamspread of a lamp to either re-create the existing effect on the larger plant or to create a new effect if the plant's importance in the overall lighting composition has changed. This is normally done in conjunction with reaiming, as it is not likely that simply changing the wattage and beamspread of a lamp within a fixture will be effective in recapturing the original effect or creating the desired new effect. Update the Record Document plans and schedules with any and all changes.

Relocating Existing Fixtures

An increase in physical size of a plant will often require relocating one or more fixtures, in conjunction with reaiming and/or relamping, to reproduce the original lighting effect. As a plant grows, its importance as a feature in the overall lighting composition may change, requiring relocation of a fixture(s) (see Chapter 15). This situation often involves reaming, relamping, and/or adding more fixtures. Update the Record Document plans and schedules with any and all changes.

Removing Existing Fixtures

Removing a fixture becomes necessary when plants or other features die or are removed. This means the fixture can be used elsewhere on the site. Deleting a fixture frees up space on the electrical circuit, the controls, and/or the transformer (if low-voltage). This kind of change needs to be documented in the Record Documents to keep that information accurate and current.

Losing an element in the landscape requires careful evaluation of the overall lighting composition and possible lighting changes to make sure that visual cohesion is retained. After the designer has evaluated the effect of the lost element, any recommended changes need to be presented to the client, and approved by the client, prior to the installing contractor commencing this work.

Adding New Fixtures

This normally occurs due to growth or additions to the landscape and is required to maintain existing effects or to respond to landscape changes that call for lighting composition changes. All recommended changes will be presented to the client, and approved by the client, prior to the installing contractor commencing this work.

UPDATING THE RECORD DOCUMENTS

All changes to the landscape lighting need to be reflected in the current Record Documents for all future maintenance efforts. These documents are only as good as the information in them. Because human memory fails and staff changes, accurate and current information is part of maintaining a landscape lighting project. Any change, deletion or addition of a lamp, or changes in the lamp's aiming, accessories, fixture location, load on transformers, or controls must be reflected in the Record Documents.

Part of the designer's value to a client is the designer's understanding of the construction process, along with the ability to coordinate that process and to see that the project is completed in a timely fashion with high-quality work. In order to practice landscape lighting, a designer must understand the technical side of lighting (discussed in Part II), the issues pertinent to specific applications (discussed in Part III), and the issues and techniques that apply to specific features of a landscape (discussed in Part IV). Since landscape lighting is still a young design field, all designers interested in this field need to educate themselves as much as possible about the appropriate lighting technology, the lamps and fixtures used for landscape lighting, the types of projects and their characteristics, and the elements of all projects that will need to be addressed. Understanding, communicating, planning, and leading the maintenance effort is another value the lighting professional should offer the client.

REFERENCES

1. Michael S. Hooker, "The Design Process," presentation to Light Fair International, San Francisco, 1999.

II

MATERIALS AND TECHNOLOGY

6

Light Sources

This chapter is devoted to describing the types of available light sources used in landscape lighting, the operating and physical characteristics of these lamps, and how they are typically used. Selecting a specific light source is the most important decision made in landscape lighting, as it is the lamp that creates the visual effect. Lamps can be evaluated by several characteristics, including beamspread, candlepower, physical size and shape, color rendition, and efficacy.

Often in interior lighting, efficacy (the amount of lumens produced per watt) is a major criterion for lamp selection due to the need to provide high-quality task lighting at minimal watts per square foot. In exterior lighting, other issues often have greater importance. In selecting lamps for landscape lighting, candlepower, fixture size, the availability of low-wattage lamps, a lamp type available in a variety of beamspreads and wattages, and color rendition are more important than efficacy.

PHYSICAL CHARACTERISTICS

A lamp consists of three parts: the glass envelope or bulb; a filament, electrodes (for producing an arc), or an arc tube; and a base. Low-voltage incandescent lamps and neon lamps also require a transformer, and fluorescent and high-intensity discharge (HID) sources need a ballast for operation. The shapes and sizes of bulbs and lamp bases vary, as do filament shapes and HID arc tubes. Understanding the characteristics and importance of each part of a lamp helps a designer select lamps that will provide the best effect and last outdoors.

Bulb or Envelope

Most incandescent bulbs are made from a soda-lime or other soft glass. This type of glass cannot withstand physical impact or temperature shock (from cold water touching it when it is hot) and does not provide for maximum light output efficacy. Tungsten-halogen lamps use a hard glass around the filament, which permits a higher filament temperature, resulting in increased lamp efficiency. Lamps rated for outdoor use in open fixtures have borosilicate glass, which is heat resistant and hard. Bulbs can be clear, frosted, coated, or colored. Clear lamps produce the greatest amount of light. To soften the appearance of an operating lamp, manufacturers will etch the glass surface or apply a coating. As the etching or coating thickness increases, the light output becomes more diffuse and less efficient. Fluorescent lamps are also typically made from a soft glass. Most of the HID sources use hard glass for the outer bulb and either quartz or ceramic glass for the arc tube.

Shapes and Sizes

Lamps' shapes and sizes vary based on the desired light distribution and, for incandescent and HID sources, the lamps' filament design or arc-tube design.

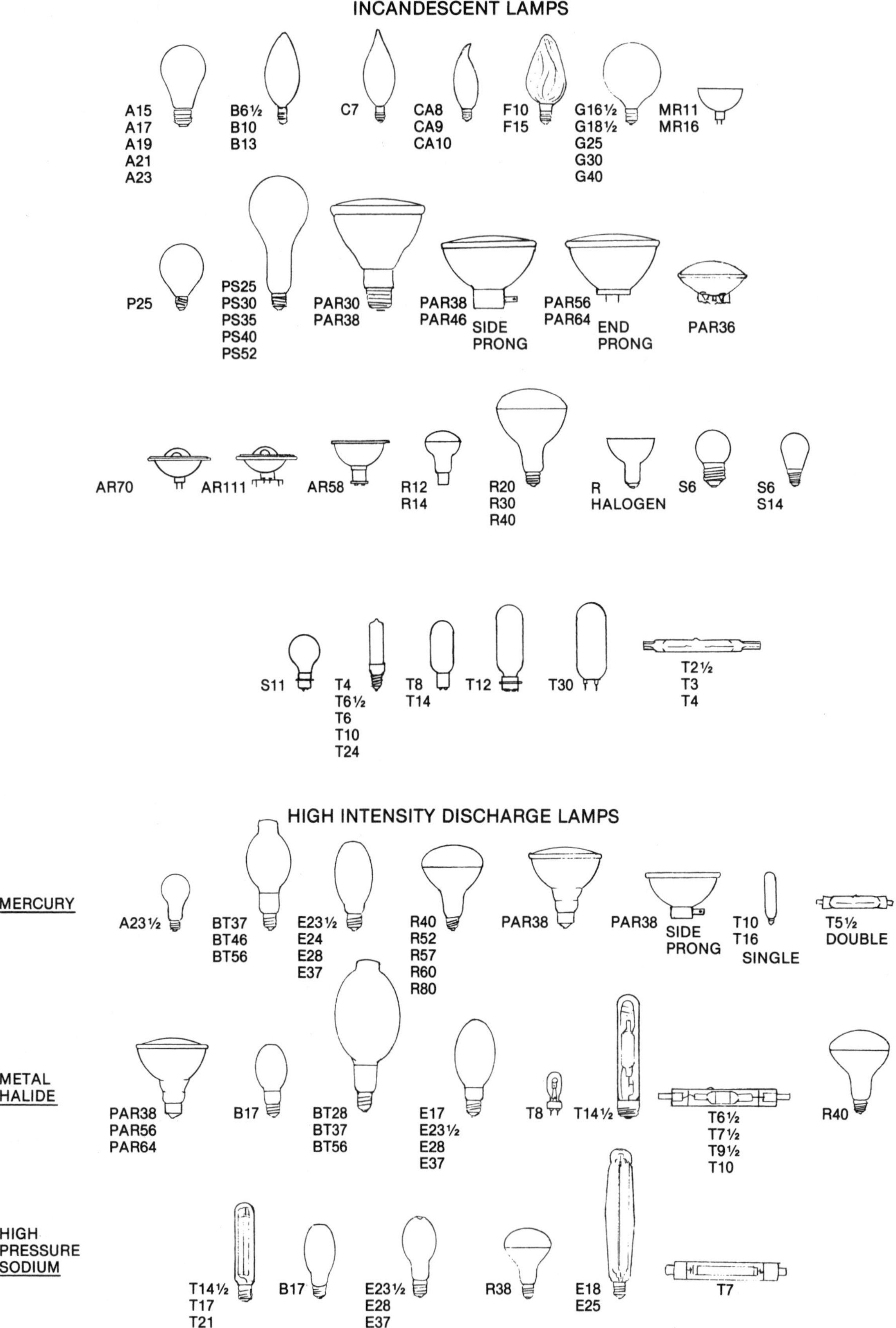

Figure 6.1. *Examples of incandescent and HID lamp shapes. Drawing: Lezlie Johannessen.*

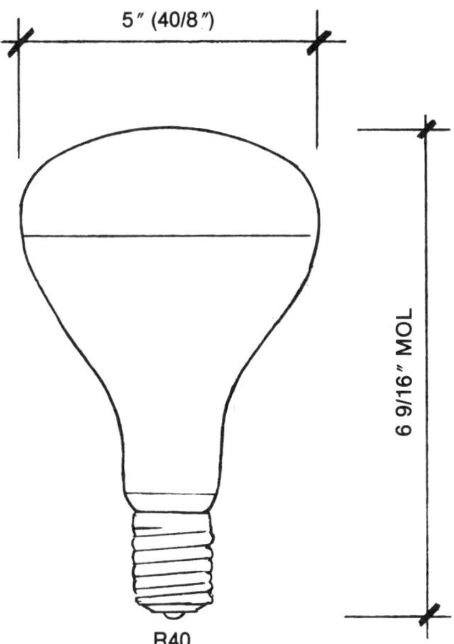

Figure 6.2. Example of lamp measurements. Part of the lamp designation, in this case an R40, is the measurement of the widest point of the lamp in eighths of an inch. A second measurement is maximum overall length (MOL). The third measurement, light center length, does not apply in a lamp with a frosted bulb. Drawing: Lezlie Johannessen.

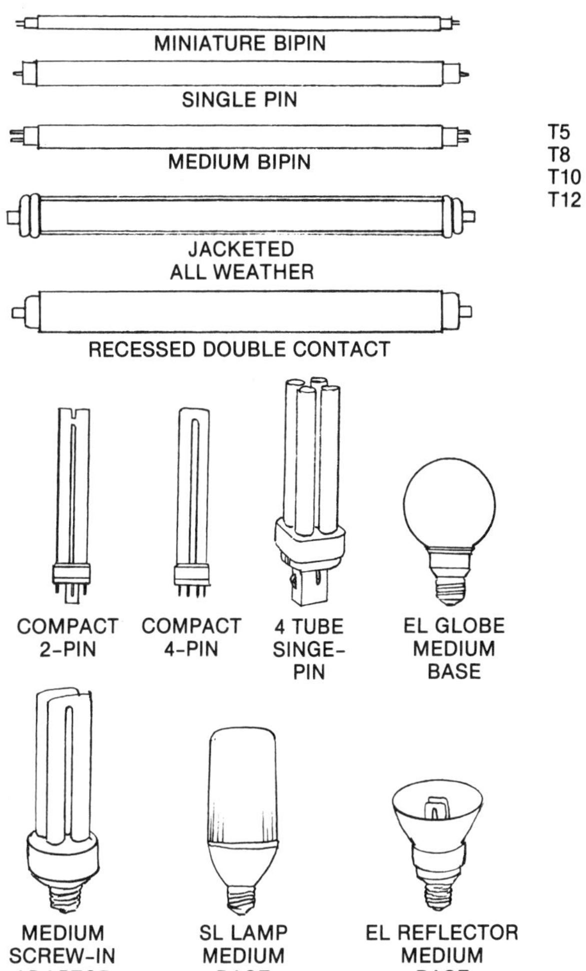

Figure 6.3. Examples of fluorescent shapes and bases. Drawing: Lezlie Johannessen.

Incandescent and HID lamps are named using one or more letters followed by a number. The letters typically indicate lamp shape. For incandescent they include S—straight side, F—flame, G—globular, T—tubular, PAR—parabolic aluminized reflector, R—reflector, MR—multimirror reflector, A—arbitrary. For HID, they include primarily BT—bulbous tubular, E—elliptical, and R—reflector types (see Figure 6.1). The number indicates the diameter of the lamp in eighths of an inch at its widest point. For example, an R40 is a reflector shape 40/8 or 5 inches at its widest point (see Figure 6.2).

Fluorescent lamps are named in the same manner, but the shapes of these lamps are quite different. Fluorescent lamp designations start with the letter *F* followed by the wattage, then the shape, diameter (except in compact types), and color designation. For example, F7BX/SPX35 is a 7-watt compact lamp with an improved color of 3500 K. Fluorescent lamps are linear sources, so their shapes are typically long and narrow. Some lamps bend the tubing into various shapes to make the overall size of the lamp smaller. The available shapes include T—tubular, U—U-shape, C—circular, and a variety of other shapes (see Figure 6.3).

There is no consistency in the way lamp manufacturers designate HID lamps. Many simply use trade names for the various HID sources. For example, in metal halide lamps, Osram and Philips use the name "metal halide" and the designation "MH"; Venture uses the name "Pro-Arc" or "Super-Pro-Arc" but the designation "MH"; General Electric uses the name "Multi-Vapor" or "Halarc" and the designation "MV" or "MX"; and Sylvania uses the name "Metalarc" and the designation "M" or "MS." This adds confusion to the identification of lamps. The confusion is compounded by fixture manufacturers, who typically use "MV" for mercury vapor, "MH" for metal halide, and "HPS" for high-pressure sodium when listing lamps available for their fixtures in their catalogs.

Because there are so many lamps available, and in some cases (such as the HID sources) the designations between manufacturers are not consistent, designers need to keep themselves up to date on all the latest innovations and lamps that are available. The only way to really understand the designations that a particular manufacturer uses, as well as the color, candlepower, life, and all lamp characteristics, is to request technical data and photometric distribution charts from the man-

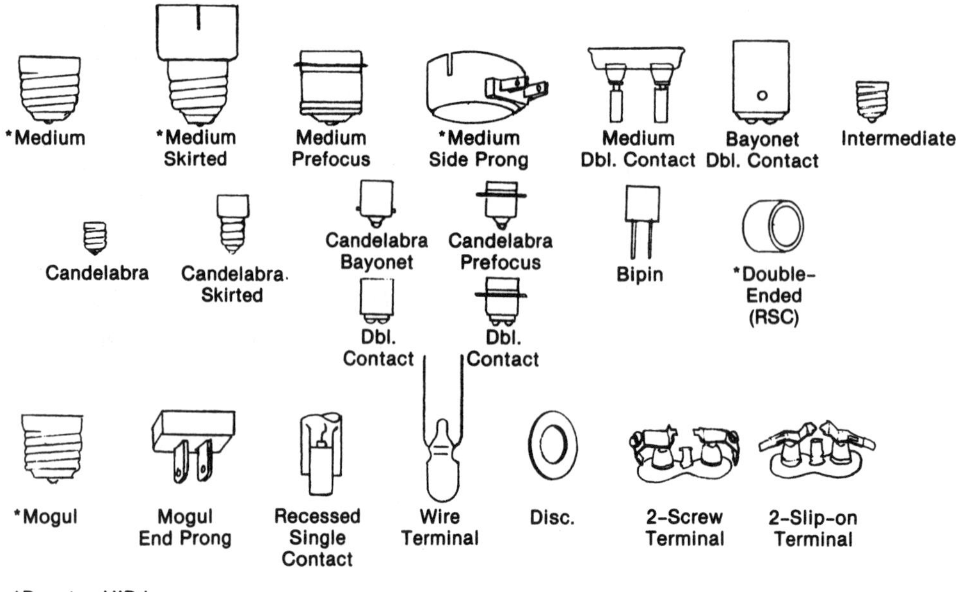

Figure 6.4. *Examples of incandescent and HID bases. Drawing: Lezlie Johannessen.*

ufacturer and then see the light source functioning out in a landscape.

Base

The base connects the lamp to the fixture socket and provides a path for electricity to reach the filament or arc tube. Base types vary from one lamp type to another and within lamp types (see Figures 6.3 & 6.4). One of the reasons that manufacturers make differing bases is to prevent a lamp from being installed in a fixture not meant to drive that lamp. The base on a lamp affects the ease of maintenance and lamp interchangeability. When selecting a lamp and fixture combination, the designer needs to check that the lamp base matches the socket supplied with the fixture.

Filament, Electrodes, and Arc Tubes

A filament is the wire in an incandescent lamp that actually produces the light. When a lamp is turned on, the filament heats up, producing a glow of light. This process of burning the filament also destroys the filament over time, causing the lamp to fail. Filament design must balance light output with lamp life. To produce light efficiently, the filament needs to be heated to a high temperature. The common material used today for filaments is tungsten, which combines a high melting point and slow filament evaporation.

One type of halogen lamp has a dichroic coating on the filament tube, which allows all the visible light to pass and redirects the infrared radiation back onto the filament. Because of this, fewer watts are used to keep the filament hot, increasing the candlepower that can be produced. For example, a 60-watt lamp using this technology produces candlepower equivalent to a 90-watt standard halogen lamp.

Filaments are designated by a letter(s) indicating filament type: S—straight, C—coiled, CC—coiled coil (see Figure 6.5). In coiled filaments, there is more wire and it is more closely spaced, which conserves heat and increases both efficacy and filament stability. Most incandescent lamp filaments become softened when heated during operation. Vibration and shock may damage or break the filament in this condition.

All discharge lamps, including fluorescent and all types of HID lamps, do not have a filament. They use electrodes to produce an electric arc through gas. In fluorescent lamps, the arc occurs inside the glass tube. In all the HID sources, there will be an inner bulb called the arc tube that contains the arc (see "High-Intensity Discharge Lamps" below).

TYPES OF LAMPS

Two basic categories of lamps can be identified: filament and discharge types. In the filament category there is only one family of lamps: incandescent. In the discharge category there are two subcategories: the high-intensity discharge group (HID), consisting of mercury vapor, metal halide, and high- and low-pressure sodium, and the low-pressure discharge group, consisting of fluorescent, cold cathode, and neon.

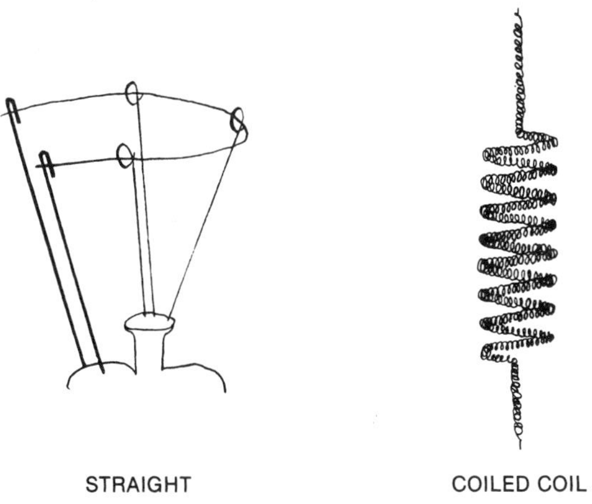

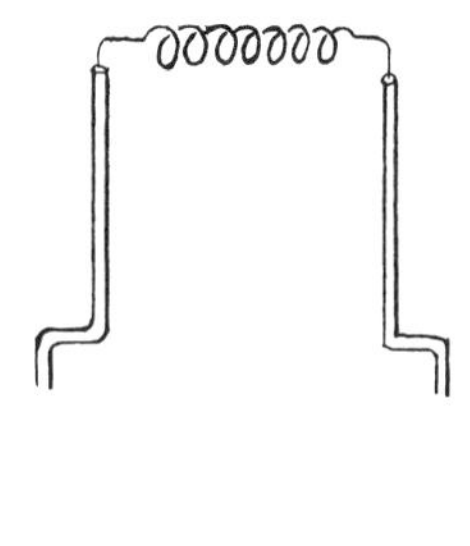

Figure 6.5. *Examples of the three kinds of incandescent filaments. Drawing: Lezlie Johannessen.*

Filament Lamps

Filament lamps produce light by heating a tungsten filament in a vacuum- or gas-filled envelope. A wide variety of shapes and sizes is available in the incandescent type (see Figure 6.1). Many types of lamps are available in this category, from less than ½ watt to 1,500 watts. However, few fixtures are available for incandescent lamps over 500 watts because at those wattages, it makes more sense to use a discharge-type lamp. The advantages of incandescent lamps include the availability of a wide range of beamspreads, tight beam control due to their small optical source (which translates into higher candlepower in a controlled beamspread at a lower wattage), easy and inexpensive dimming capability, and a color that favors human skin tones and is familiar to people since most residential interior lighting to date has been from incandescent sources. The weaknesses of these lamps include their inefficiency and the amount of heat they produce.

Tungsten-Halogen Lamps

These lamps, sometimes also called *quartz lamps,* offer a more balanced white light color (see Figure 6.6), higher efficiency, more compact size, longer life and higher lumen maintenance than conventional incandescent lamps in both standard and low-voltage varieties. Tungsten-halogen lamps have a halogen gas pumped in around the tungsten filament, which picks up and redeposits evaporated tungsten back onto the filament. Called the *tungsten-halogen cycle,* this process allows the filament to operate at a higher temperature and keeps the bulb clean, increasing lamp life. However, this occurs only when the voltage applied to the lamp is 90 to 100 percent of its rated voltage.

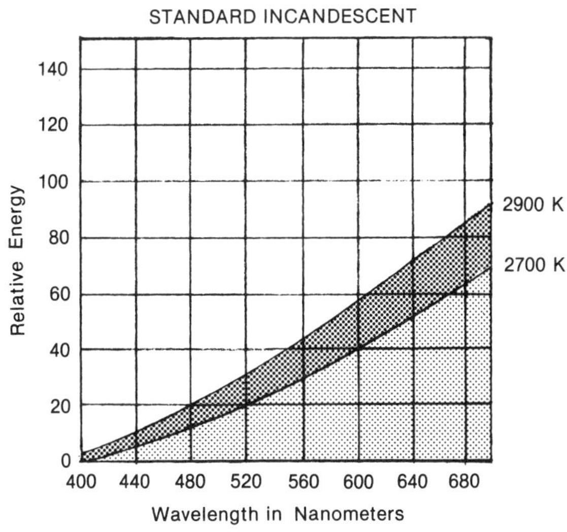

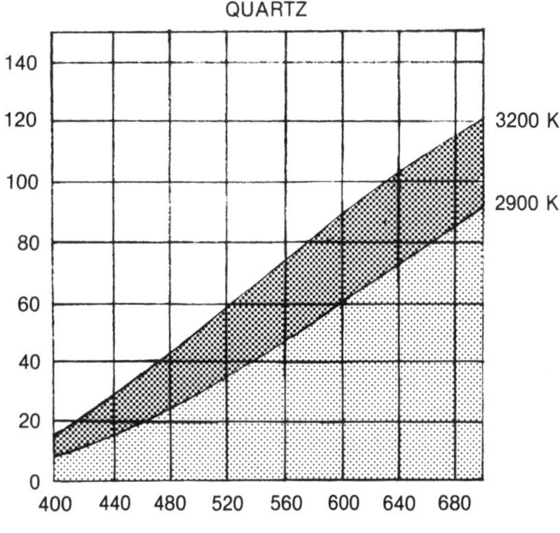

Figure 6.6. *Incandescent and quartz spectral distribution. Based on material from the* IES Lighting Handbook, Reference Volume, *Illuminating Engineering Society of North America, New York, 1984. Drawing: Lezlie Johannessen.*

Halogen lamps are particularly sensitive to shock damage when operating, which means that people need to avoid treating fixtures roughly during focusing—do not kick a fixture to change its aiming position or use a hammer to drive a stake into the ground. If rough treatment is warranted due to soil conditions or other circumstances, make sure that the fixtures are turned off and the lamps have cooled, or remove the lamp from the fixture.

Frequently Used Types

The most frequently used incandescent lamps are the MR, PAR, R, and miniature lamps. The MR, PAR, and R types all have a built-in reflector offering varying light output distributions. The ability to vary beamspread within one lamp shape and one size provides the designer with the flexibility to use any of the lamp wattages or beamspreads available in that lamp family in the same fixture throughout the site as well to change the wattage or beamspread to respond to the changes in the landscape.

MR Lamps These lamps have a multifaceted mirrored reflector surrounding a subminiature lamp. Variations in the reflector permits many beamspread and wattage options in one lamp size. This lamp's compact size allows the fixture to be small, so it can be used in areas with limited space more easily than larger fixtures. For example, these smaller fixtures can be more easily hidden in trees, and they will create less stress on the trees than heavier standard-voltage fixtures.

All MR lamps are tungsten-halogen lamps, which provide improved color (over standard incandescent lamps) flattering to plants and generally accentuating the color of any object. Most MR lamps are low-voltage, and these are the ones used primarily for landscape. Some MR lamps are open and others are closed, but for outdoor use all must be used in enclosed fixtures.

MR lamps are available in two sizes: MR16 (2-inch diameter) and MR11 (1⅜-inch diameter). MR16 lamps come in 20, 35, 42, 50, and 75 watts with at least three beamspreads (approximately 12°, 24 to 28°, and 36°) in each wattage. Some fixtures can take all the wattages, but most have a 50-watt maximum capacity (due primarily to limited heat dissipation). The wide range of options available in the MR16 makes it a very useful lamp in landscape lighting for all purposes. The MR11 comes in 20 and 35 watts, but many outdoor fixtures can use only the 20-watt lamp, due to the fixture size and limited heat dissipation. The tiny size of the MR11 lamp allows a fixture to be squeezed into tight spaces previously not usable for fixture mounting locations, such as between boards in a trellis, where it can continue to offer some adjustment capability.

These lamps are designated by a three-letter American National Standard Institute (ANSI) name. The letter designations are arbitrary but identify the lamp by beamspread and wattage. For example, a BAB is a 20-watt lamp with a 38° beamspread.

PAR Lamps The letter designation of this lamp stands for *parabolic aluminized reflector.* These lamps come in a variety of sizes, some standard-voltage and some low-voltage, and all have a heat-resistant glass that makes them acceptable in open fixtures (see Figure 6.2). The sizes include low-voltage PAR36 (4½-inch diameter) and standard-voltage PAR20 (2½-inch diameter), PAR30 (3¾-inch diameter), PAR38 (4¾-inch diameter), PAR46 (5¾-inch diameter), PAR56 (7-inch diameter), and PAR64 (8-inch diameter) sizes. While their glass can withstand the temperature shock from rain, irrigation water, and snow, some of the lamps (especially the smaller PAR20 and PAR30 sizes) are susceptible to corrosion due to water entering the lamp from air holes at the base. It is wise to always use all PAR lamps in enclosed fixtures to ensure long-term functioning.

PAR36 lamps have a wide range of tight or spot beamspreads (varying from a 3° diameter spread to a 40° by 5° spread) that can throw extremely long distances and still create bright, small accent effects on small objects. Often, they are too controlled and too bright for most landscape needs. Flood distributions are also manufactured, but these have limited intensity and need to be used in close-up situations such as washing low walls. At least one manufacturer makes a PAR36 that is not a glass-enclosed lamp. This lamp offers more light output in the flood distributions but must be used in an enclosed fixture.

PAR20 and PAR30 lamps are small compared to the other PAR lamps. They are available in 50 or 75 watts. They do not produce an even spread in flood types; they retain a hot spot in the middle of their beamspread. This limits their use for wallwashing or downlighting walkways, but makes them very useful for accentuating sculptures or plants.

PAR38 lamps work well in both spot and flood distributions to uplight large trees, sculptures, and structures, and they come in a wide range of wattages: from 45 to 250 watts in tungsten-halogen, or 75 to 150 watts in standard incandescent (some specialty lamp manufacturers offer them in higher wattages).

PAR46, 56, and 64 lamps are used in many submersible fixtures and are especially effective at lighting tall fountain sprays or waterfalls. They range in wattage from 150 watts (PAR46 size) to 500 watts (PAR64 size). For nonsubmersible fixtures, when higher wattages are required in flood distributions, using one of the high-intensity discharge sources makes more sense.

PAR lamps are used when excellent optical control and high candlepower is required. Although using the HID lamps makes sense in high wattages for flood distributions, they cannot produce the equivalent intensity and controlled beamspread.

R Lamps Reflector lamps have a parabolic shape with a silver or aluminum coating applied to the internal wall of the envelope, which serves as a reflector. These lamps provide a very smooth, very wide flood distribution. Both 120-volt and low-voltage types are made. The spot types are not as controlled as MR or PAR lamps. R lamps use soft glass for their envelope and aluminum for their bases, which means that they must be in an enclosed fixture if they will be exposed to water. They can be used in a damp location fixture if they will be protected from direct contact with precipitation (see "Labels" in Chapter 7). These lamps are not used as much as PAR lamps primarily because they are too fragile.

Miniature and Subminiature Lamps This refers to a large number of small-sized lamps typically used because of their size and their low wattages. Available both in 120-volt and low-voltage types, they normally range from less than ½ watt to 20 watts and are used primarily in small step lights, walkway fixtures, and strip-light fixtures.

Comparing 120-Volt and Low-Voltage Lamps for Landscape Use

Incandescent lamps are designed by the lamp manufacturer to operate at a specific voltage. Manufacturers produce lamps for a variety of voltages, including 5.5, 6, 12, 14, 24, 120, and 130 volts. Several factors influence the selection of a 120-volt lamp versus a low-voltage lamp—physical size of the lamp, available wattages, candlepower and beamspread, life, and installation and wiring methods and requirements.

For most of the time that landscape lighting has been practiced, 120-volt lamps have been the main incandescent sources used. The PAR38 lamp served as the prime type of lamp for landscape lighting until recently, because it is a glass-enclosed lamp suitable for outdoor use. Another reason 120-volt lamps were used was a lack of low-voltage lamps with high output in flood distributions. In addition, few fixture manufacturers made fixtures for the smaller low-voltage lamps.

Currently, the low-voltage MR lamps provide great flood distributions, and a wide variety of low-voltage fixtures are available from many fixture manufacturers. The smaller size of this lamp compared to a PAR38 lamp means that the fixture can be much smaller and more easily hidden in the landscape.

Another difference between the two classes of lamps is light output. Low-voltage lamps are available in lower wattages that provide the desired low light levels. They are also available in a large variety of wattages and beamspreads. In many small commercial and most residential projects the lowest-wattage 120-volt PAR38 lamp available, the 45-watt lamp, still produces too much light. However, when lighting large trees such as redwoods or palms with tall trunks and wide canopies, using a standard-voltage spot lamp with a strong main beam and lots of fill light around the main beams may provide the best effect.

Another advantage found in many low-voltage lamps is longer life. For example, in the MR family of lamps, the average lamp life is 4,000 hours, compared to 2,000 hours for PAR38 lamps. However, low-voltage lamps need transformers to provide the proper operating voltage. This requires not only a more thorough plan from the designer, but also that the installer know how to size the wiring to avoid voltage drop. The chapter on wiring discusses installation and wiring requirements.

Essentially, when the project involves new construction, either 120-volt or a combination of 120-volt and low-voltage makes sense. In renovations, especially when the site has a well-established garden with closely planted specimen plants, low-voltage wiring is preferable because it can be installed without significant damage to the planting.

Discharge Lamps

Discharge lamps include all the HID lamps (mercury vapor, metal halide, and high- and low-pressure sodium) and the low-pressure lamps (fluorescent, cold cathode, and neon). Discharge lamps create light by sending an electric arc through a gas between two electrodes. An electrical device called a ballast provides a high-voltage pulse required to start the lamp, then limits the amount of current to the lamp to prevent the lamp from drawing a destructive amount of current (see "Ballast" in Chapter 7).

All discharge lamps are more efficient than incandescent lamps at gross light output (lumen production). This makes them very useful for floodlighting and accent lighting on large-scale commercial projects. Drawbacks of discharge lamps include the fact that precise optical control is not possible (without the used of large reflectors and bulky equipment) because the source size is so large, wattages are often too high, wattages cannot be interchanged without changing the ballast in a fixture, color and color consistency can be poor (especially with metal halide lamps), the cost is high for the lamp and fixture, and they are not easily dimmable.

High-Intensity Discharge Lamps
High-intensity discharge lamps can be divided into four lamp families: mercury vapor, metal halide, high-pressure sodium, and low-pressure sodium (technically, low-pressure sodium is a group all by itself, but it is included here to simplify the discussion). All the lamps in this group are more efficient than incandescent, but mercury vapor typically produces slightly fewer lumens per watt than the others (see Figure 6.7). In addition to high efficacy, these lamps have a relatively compact size considering the amount of light they produce.

HID lamps produce light by creating a relatively small electric arc, so they are considered point sources. This means that their light output is more easily controlled than that of a linear source such as fluorescent. Each of these lamp types requires a reflector or refractor to control its candlepower distribution.

Some HID lamps have clear bulbs, while others have a coating. The color of light produced by lamps with clear bulbs is dependent on the characteristics of the gas used in the lamp. For example, mercury vapor lamps use mercury gas, which creates a blue-green light. Lamp manufacturers use phosphor coatings on the outer bulb to change or control the color of light produced by the lamp. For example, a coating on a mercury vapor lamp can add red, which makes the color a more balanced white. However, this also increases the source size because the entire lamp, rather than the arc tube, now serves as the source.

HID lamps all require an initial warm-up period when turned on, and if power is lost, they require a cooling period before restriking their arc (see Figure 6.7). This delay in operation must be considered when selecting lamps for outdoor use, especially when they will be used for security lighting of walkways, stairs, parking lots, or sports facilities. Some fixtures permit the installation of a supplementary incandescent quartz lamp to provide safety light in the case of power failure or other type of power interruption.

Mercury Vapor Mercury vapor lamps produce light by passing an electric arc through mercury vapor. This type of lamp produces light predominantly in the blue and green regions of the electromagnetic spectrum (see Figure 6.8) and in the ultraviolet region. Some of this ultraviolet radiation can be transformed into visible light by a phosphor coating added to the outer bulb of the lamp. Some manufacturers make these types of color-improved lamps, which produce an acceptable white light.

The mercury vapor lamp has a long life but is not particularly efficient (see Figure 6.7), and it will lose up to two-thirds of its light output as it ages. It is seldom used for interior lighting at this time.

Mercury's main strengths are its long life, typically 24,000 hours, and the blue color it produces, which is similar to natural moonlight. Its weaknesses include its limited color range, large physical size compared to other HID sources, limited efficacy compared to other HID sources, and limited availability (not all lamp manufacturers continue to make it and production runs are sporadic).

Metal Halide This type of HID source produces light by passing an electric current through mercury gas and scant quantities of specific combinations of metal halides. The halides widen the emitted color spectrum of these lamps. The metal halide lamps offer the most balanced white light color of all the HID sources. The addition of halides also greatly improves the lamp's efficiency but shortens the lamp life (see Figure 6.7). Manufacturers typically offer several color variations.

One of the problems with metal halide lamps is that there tends to be color variation from lamp to lamp and a color shift over the life of the lamp due to manufacturing inconsistencies and inconsistencies in voltage from ballast to ballast. It is difficult for the manufacturers to control the exact amount of each halide added because they use such scant quantities. Metal halide lamps are sensitive to voltage variation. A slight drop in voltage can cause the lamp to extinguish. Metal halide lamps can take up to 20 minutes to go through the cooling and restrike period before reattaining full output. To minimize these problems, electronic ballasts can be used. They aid in controlling color shift, can stabilize life, and prevent unwanted interruptions of light output.

Metal halide lamps are used for uplighting trees, lighting buildings, and providing task lighting at sports stadiums. They are less efficient and have a shorter life than high-pressure sodium, which limits their use for lighting freeways, but they are used for street lighting in downtown areas, car sales lots, shopping areas, or other outdoor areas where color rendering is important. Metal halide lamps are also the best choice for promoting plant growth due to the spectrum of light they produce (see "Lighting for Plant Growth" in Chapter 13).

High-Pressure Sodium This lamp type produces light by passing an electric arc through sodium vapor. The lamp manufacturer increases the gas pressure inside the arc tube to a level higher than for low-pressure sodium lamps (which produces a monochromatic yellow color). Increasing the gas pressure broadens the color spectrum to include the entire visible portion of the electromagnetic spectrum. However, since this lamp produces most of its light in the yellow range of the spectrum, its color appears as a golden yellow.

Color-improved lamps are available that approach a balanced white color. As with any color improvement,

LAMP COMPARISON CHART						
LAMP CATEGORY CATEGORY	WATTAGE RANGE	EFFICACY (lumens per watt)	LIFE in hours	TRANSFORMER BALLAST	START/POWER INTERRUPTION	INTERCHANG-ABILITY
INCANDESCENT	Less than 1–1,500+	7–24 17 avg.	750–2,000 Special lamps: as low as 10 hours	120–135 volts None required All voltages below 120 require transformer; quantity of lamps per transformer based on lamp wattage	Immediate start No restrike delay	Within same base type up to fixture max. wattage
FLUORESCENT	4–220	20–95 Standard F40 magnetic ballast: 60–75 Electronic ballast: 40–95 Compact type: Mfrs. don't list	7,500–20,000	Ballast required Up to 3 lamps per ballast	Immediate start Preheat: few seconds' delay No restrike delay	Within same base type: voltage and wattage only
MERCURY VAPOR	40–1,000	50–60 Good color and/or low wattage as low as 20	16,000–24,000 Self-ballasted: 12–16,000	Ballast required 1 lamp per ballast	Start and restrike: 3+ minutes	Within same base, voltage, and wattage
METAL HALIDE	70–1,500	75–125	6,000–20,000	Ballast required 1 lamp per ballast	Start: 2–5 minutes Restrike: 10–20 minutes	Within same base, voltage, and wattage
HIGH-PRESSURE SODIUM	35–1,000	80–100 Low wattage: as low as 50	24,000 Good color: 10,000	Ballast required 1 lamp per ballast	Start: 3–4 minutes Restrike: 1/2–1 minute	Within same base, voltage, and wattage
LOW-PRESSURE SODIUM	18–180	Up to 180	10,000–18,000	Ballast required 1 lamp per ballast	Start: 7–15 minutes Restrike: 1 minute	Within same base, voltage, and wattage

Figure 6.7.

efficiency and life are typically reduced. High-pressure sodium lamps offer long life and are the most efficient source other than low-pressure sodium. When this type of lamp reaches the end of its life, the ballast continues to start the lamp, but it cannot maintain the arc without excessive voltage. The lamp will then extinguish, cool down, restrike, and come almost up to full light output. At this point, a protective circuit will extinguish the lamp again. This phenomenon is called *cycling*. Prolonged on-off cycling can damage the ballast. It is important to replace the lamp at the first sign of cycling to avoid ballast damage.

High-pressure sodium lamps are typically used only for lighting parking lots and freeways, due to their color limitations. The color they produce makes plants look dull and lifeless and creates an eerie atmosphere.

Low-Pressure Sodium This sort of lamp is not technically grouped with the other discharge lamps, but put in a category by itself. It is a monochromatic light source producing only yellow light. While it is the most efficient light source available today, its inability to render any colors well should discourage designers from using it.

Fluorescent Lamps

A fluorescent lamp consists of a tubular bulb with an electrode sealed into each end and a combination of mercury (at low pressure) and argon (or a mixture of gases), which help in starting the lamp. As voltage is applied, an arc of primarily ultraviolet radiation occurs between the electrodes. The lamp walls are coated with fluorescent powders that are excited by the ultraviolet radiation to produce colors within the visible spectrum. By varying the phosphors, many colors of fluorescent lamps can be produced. The choice of colors in the compact lamps (the ones most used in landscape lighting) are limited.

Fluorescent lamps produce several times the amount of gross light per watt compared with incandescent sources, but since the light source is large it is difficult to control the light beam. They offer a long life, ranging from 10,000 hours in the compact types to 20,000 hours in the larger-sized lamps (see Figure 6.7). Some manufacturers make self-ballasted lamps that can be used in incandescent fixtures as an energy-saving retrofit. Before using them, a designer should consider the change in brightness that will occur at the fixture lens.

The advantages of fluorescent lamps include their ability to produce an even wash of light and the small size of the compact types. The high efficacy of fluorescent lamps means that these compact lamps can be used instead of incandescent lamps, producing plenty of light while saving energy. For example, many manufacturers are making fixtures, especially walkway, stair, and surface-mounted types, for these compact lamps, using 5-, 7-, 9-, 11-, and 13-watt lamps to replace incandescent lamps of 20 watts or higher. Weaknesses of fluorescent lamps include the length or large size of most types, the lack of lamp interchangeability, the fact that they produce too much light for outdoor use in the larger-sized lamps, the inability to easily control or direct their output, and the fact that dimming is expensive and limited in range.

Jacketed, Aperture, and Reflector Types Three kinds of special fluorescent lamps are used in landscape lighting. The first type is a group of lamps designed for low-temperature operation called jacketed lamps. Fluorescent lamps are temperature sensitive. A low ambient temperature as well as wind can affect both the starting capability and the lumen output, so a fluorescent lamp needs to be protected. Some all-weather lamps have a glass jacket to protect them from air movement and provide heat retention to ensure that they reach the proper operating temperature. Lamp manufacturers identify these lamps in the catalog by adding a "J" to the description of the lamp—for example, F48T10J/CWX (GE) or FJ48T12/CW (Sylvania). Some of these lamps can be difficult to start at temperatures lower than 50°F/10°C, 32°F/0°C, or 0°F/–18°C. Low-temperature ballasts must be used for most fluorescent lamps operated outdoors.

Reflector and aperture types of fluorescent lamps are used in flood lighting because of their controlled beamspread and concentrated output capabilities. The reflector type of lamp has an internal layer of white powder between the phosphor and the tube, covering most of the envelope wall. This layer reflects a high percentage of the total light produced out through a small area of the envelope that has only the normal phosphor coating (see Figure 6.9). The aperture variety of lamp is similar, except that it has a section of clear window area along the glass envelope. This increases intensity or candlepower by up to 10 times over a standard lamp.

Cold Cathode, Including Neon This luminous tubing is similar to the fluorescent lamp. It is also a long, tubular lamp, but it runs at higher voltages (between 9,000 and 15,000 volts, typically) and produces less light per watt. The advantages of this group include the ability to make very long pieces in any shape. These lamps are used primarily for decorative purposes in landscape lighting: for signs, decorative features on fixtures, outlining buildings, and other unusual uses.

This group of lamps has the ability to produce many different strong, clear colors. Color is produced by a combination of one or more of the following: the

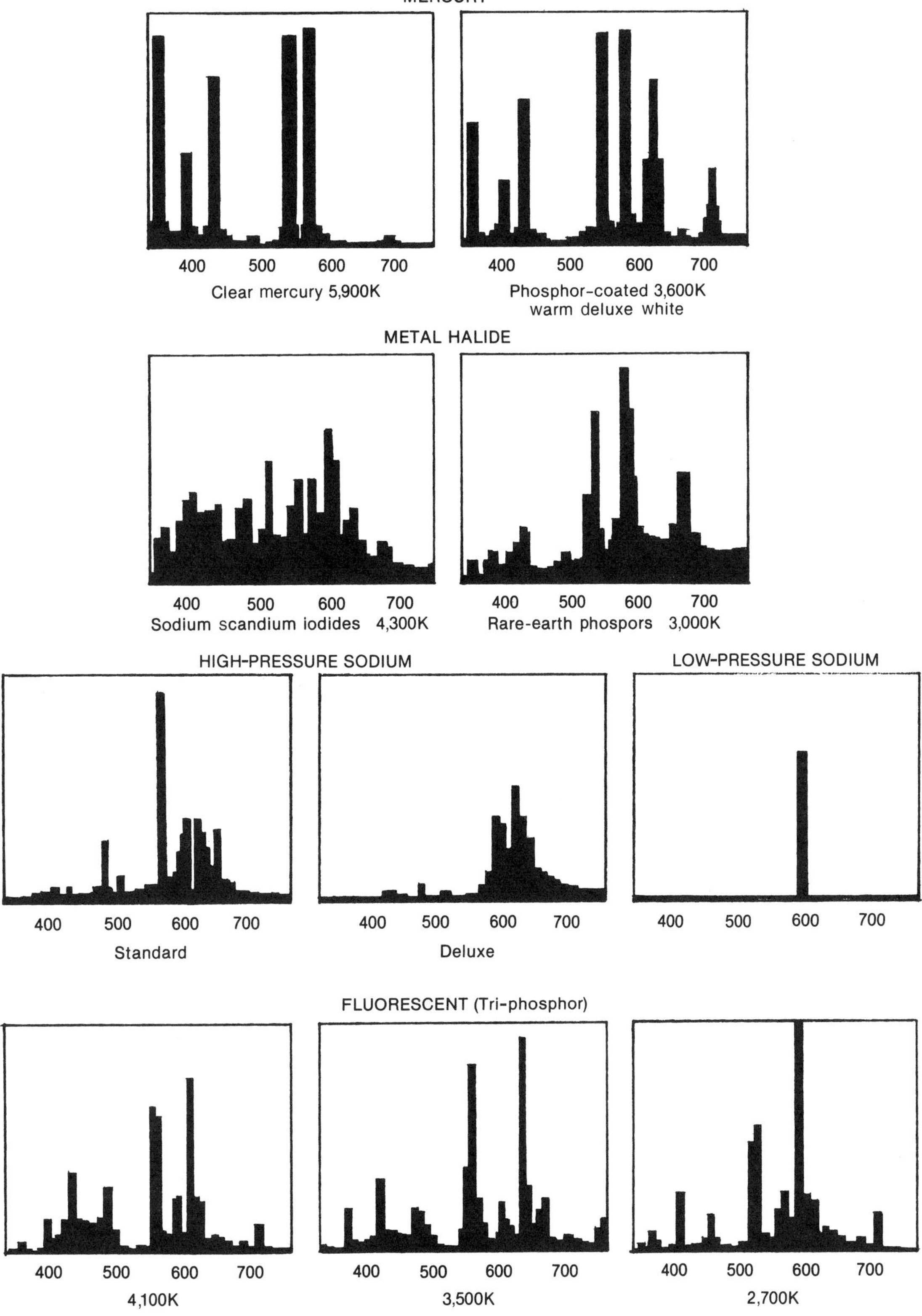

Figure 6.8. *Examples of HID and fluorescent spectral distribution. Portions are based on material from the* IES Lighting Handbook, Reference Volume, *Illuminating Engineering Society of North America, New York, 1984, and portions are courtesy of Osram Corporation. Drawing: Lezlie Johannessen.*

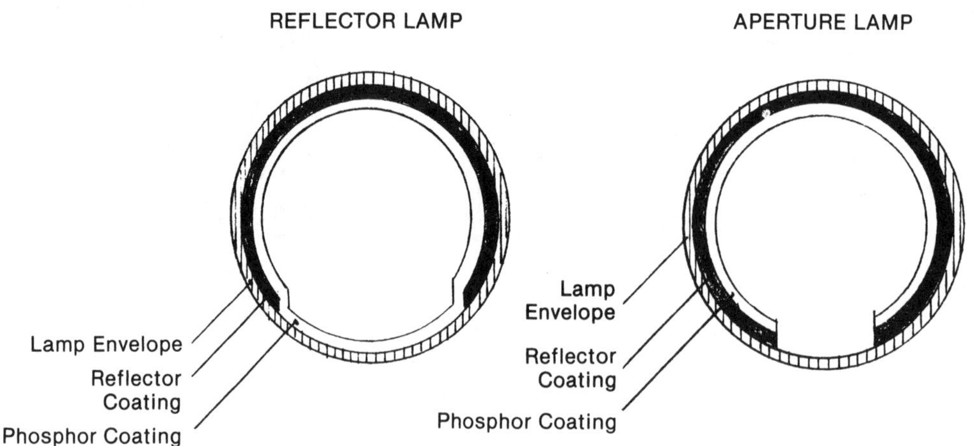

Figure 6.9. *Drawing: Lezlie Johannessen.*

type of gas used in the tube, the specific phosphors used to coat the inside of the tube, or the color of the glass.

The prime advantages of these light sources include their flexibility in size and shape, the availability of many colors, the ability to produce more than one color per tube (by changing phosphors or splicing in a different color glass), and their low energy consumption. Although they do not produce high lumens per watt, they also do not use many watts per unit length (typically, 4 watts per foot or 13 watts per meter for neon and up to 8 watts per foot or 26 watts per meter for cold cathode). This means that these lamps consume considerably less energy than do fluorescent lamps. However, they also produce less light than fluorescent lamps.

These lamps must always be enclosed to protect them from moisture and cold temperatures and to protect people from their high voltages. They are always custom-made and often cost more than other sources. Their transformers are usually large and noisy, so they must be located in a place where their noise will not be heard by people. Some electronic ballasts are quiet, making their placement less critical.

FUNCTIONAL AND OPERATING CHARACTERISTICS

There is considerable technical information on lamps available from organizations such as the Illuminating Engineering Society (see *IES Handbook* and other books in the Bibliography) and from lamp manufacturers (see "Lighting Manufacturers Directory" in the Appendix). This section will discuss some of the more important technical points to understand about lamps for landscape lighting applications.

Physical Dimensions

In order to know if a lamp will fit in a fixture and whether the lamp brightness will be visible, a designer needs to know the lamp's physical dimensions. The two standard dimensions of a lamp are *maximum overall length* (MOL) and *light center length* (LCL). Both dimensions are listed in the manufacturers' catalogs for reference (see Figure 6.10). MOL is the maximum dimension of a lamp measured from the tip of the bulb to the end of the base (see Figure 6.2). Knowing a lamp's MOL helps determine how deeply recessed the lamp will be in a particular fixture or if the lamp will fit in a specific fixture. LCL is the dimension from the center of the filament to a designated location on the base which varies with the lamp type. This information is important if a lamp will be used in a fixture with a reflector controlling the light distribution pattern. Lamps with the same LCL can be interchanged in a fixture, wattage permitting.

Operating Characteristics

Several operating characteristics need to be considered in selecting a lamp, including operating position, temperature, and voltage. Position and temperature are characteristics of the lamp that direct how it is used and what type of fixture is acceptable for it. Voltage is something that can be varied either by dimming, by the selection of a specific voltage ballast or transformer, or due to variation in voltage as provided by the utility.

Lamp Operating Position

Most lamps can be used in a wide range of positions within a fixture—base up, base down, or horizontal. However, some mercury and metal halide lamps must be burned only in certain positions in order to maximize efficiency. Additionally, metal halide lamps may

Bulb	Base	Ordering Code	Description	Volts Watts Amps	Case Qty.	Additional Information	Filament Design	MOL (in.)	LCL (in.)	Rated Avg. Life Hours	Approx. Int.	Lumens Mean
150 WATTS												
T-3	RSC	>19378	Q150T3/CL	120	5	Clear-2850K. HORIZONTAL [101]	C-8	3 3/16	1 [LCL]	1500	2400	—

Figure 6.10. *Example of a lamp catalog. Courtesy of GE Lighting.*

require a specific position to stabilize color production. High-pressure sodium lamps are not affected and can generally be operated in any position. The lamp manufacturer's catalog will stipulate any burning position restrictions in the "Additional Information" column (see Figure 6.10).

Bulb-Wall and Base Operating Temperature

Lamps need to be operated at or within specific temperature tolerances to maximize efficiency, prevent melting of the bulb glass or fixture parts, minimize base cement deterioration or base loosening, retain spring tension, and to minimize damage to the fixture socket or surrounding wiring. Fixtures are designed to dissipate lamp heat up to the maximum rated wattage listed in the manufacturer's literature. Using higher-wattage lamps can cause any of the problems listed above, potentially shortening lamp life and possibly destroying the fixture.

Fluorescent lamps perform best at specific temperatures that vary with lamp type. Light output and wattage decreases with either an increase or decrease in this optimal operating temperature. Information on operating temperature is not printed in lamp catalogs. It is provided to fixture manufacturers for their use in developing fixtures. Their fixtures are tested (see "Testing" in Chapter 7) to see that they meet the requirements. The fixture manufacturer then lists the lamps that are acceptable for each fixture.

Voltage

Utilities are allowed a slight variation in the actual voltage they provide to any premise. It is important to test the voltage at the electrical panel and to research whether the site is prone to spikes or surges. The power company should be able to provide this information. Because some lamps and other equipment such as transformers and ballasts are sensitive to variations in voltage, knowing this can determine whether surge or spike protection is necessary.

Varying the voltage to an incandescent lamp has several effects. Using a higher voltage than the manufacturer's rated operating voltage increases light output, shifts the color of light toward blue, and dramatically decreases life. A lower voltage decreases light output, shifts the color of light toward red, and increases life. A dimmer changes the voltage to a lamp. When an incandescent lamp is dimmed, the shift in color and reduced light output will be apparent. This is a useful way to extend lamp life or reduce the amount of light.

Designers can sometimes use a decrease in voltage to their advantage to extend the life of some lamps (see life versus voltage calculation in Figure 10.7). For example, if a lamp is rated at 28 volts and has a 2,000-hour life, selecting a 24-volt transformer extends the life to over 15,000 hours. Transformers are not available in every voltage, so the designer must check if an acceptable voltage is available for this purpose.

Lumen Maintenance

Lamp manufacturers list two categories of lumen output for most lamps in their catalogs: initial lumens and mean lumens. *Initial lumens* is the quantity of lumens a lamp will produce after 100 hours of operation. *Mean lumens* refers to the gross light output at between 40 to 50 percent of life, depending on the lamp type (see Figure 6.10). Most lamps produce the most light they can when first turned on and gradually lose lumens as they operate. In incandescent lamps other than tungsten-halogen, burned-off tungsten deposits on the lamp envelope, blackening the bulb and reducing light output. Fluorescent lamps and all the HID sources also emit less light over time. This lamp lumen depreciation is most serious in the mercury vapor lamp and least critical in the high-pressure sodium and fluorescent lamps.

Life

Lamp manufacturers print in their catalogs an *average rated life* measured in hours (see Figure 6.10). The number is called an average because that is the time at which 50 percent of lamps tested will fail. This means that lamps used on a project may fail before reaching that number of hours in use or may last longer.

Dimming increases the life of an incandescent lamp (see Figure 10.7) but does not appreciably affect lamp life of HID or fluorescent lamps. Fluorescent lamp life can be shortened, however, by turning the lamp on and off frequently.

Color of Light Produced

Designers need to consider the color a lamp produces, because the apparent color of everything in the landscape will be determined by the color of light striking it. If the color of the object is not in the spectrum of the light source, the appearance of the object will be changed. For example, when low-pressure sodium light strikes a red car, the car will appear to be brown. However, an object's color can also be enhanced by the color of light striking it. The improved color of tungsten-halogen over standard incandescent lamps accentuates the appearance of flowers and most trees.

Designers can use the color-producing characteristics of lamps to influence how people feel about a space. For example, the blue color of mercury vapor shining through trees mimics the color of moonlight and can simulate a moonlit night. Some plants have a lot of blue-green pigment, which can be accentuated by mercury vapor lamps at low light levels. At higher light levels, however, this color makes the plants appear too blue and unnatural. Mercury vapor needs to be kept away from areas frequented by people, because its poor color-rendering ability makes them look like ghosts. Variation in color from one light source to another can be used to expand or limit depth in a space or add a creative touch.

The color of light a lamp produces determines the color an object will appear. If a plant has red flowers, a light source with little red radiation, such as mercury vapor, will dull the color of the flower. Lamp manufacturers produce *spectral energy distribution* charts that show the amount of energy produced at each wavelength of light over the visible range of the electromagnetic spectrum (see Figure 6.8). Incandescent lamps and natural daylight produce smooth, continuous spectra, whereas HID sources produce light primarily in lines, and fluorescent lamps produce a combination of continuous and line spectra. In general, a continuous spectrum or source with many lines of radiation across the electromagnetic spectrum produces the most balanced white light. This is true because white light is a combination of all colors of light. To produce white light, a light source needs to have relatively balanced quantities of all light waves throughout the electromagnetic spectrum.

The designer must also understand that the human eye is more sensitive to light in three specific bands of light wavelengths. The three bands are specific, narrow bands in the blue-violet, pure green, and orange-red areas of the electromagnetic spectrum. Lamps called *prime color* are made with strong output in each of these three regions.

Manufacturers also rate the *color temperature* of lamps. Color temperature is a comparison of the color produced by a light source to a standard (blackbody) source heated to a particular temperature. It is measured in kelvins (K), with low numbers referring to warm color and high numbers referring to cool color. This rating system provides the designer with basic information about the color produced. If a lamp is listed at 3,200K, the designer knows that the color produced by that lamp will favor the warm end of the spectrum. If the lamp is listed at 4,000K, it will favor the cool end of the spectrum.

Color temperature does not provide any actual information about the color-rendering ability of the light source. Two lamps with the same color temperature can produce a color of light very different from each other. The difference will show in the spectral energy distribution of each lamp. This information provides a clearer picture of the color produced, but not of how the eye will interpret the color. The only way to clearly understand the color of a specific light source is to see it demonstrated on the plant material or structures to be lit in a landscape.

One thing that can be said with certainty in the lighting field is that lamp technology and development drive the market and therefore design. There is constant change and development of new light sources and improvements in existing sources. For designers to serve their clients well, they need to keep current with what lamps are available and their characteristics, as well as new technologies being developed. They should contact the lamp manufacturers to get their most current catalogs and technical information at least once a year. Some manufacturers have a mailing list and send out new information as they produce it. As new lamps become available, the designer needs to see the color of light and the distribution they produce. Attending seminars sponsored by professional organizations such as the IES (Illuminating Engineering Society) or the DLF (Designers Lighting Forum) or by the lamp manufacturers is another good way to see these developments.

7

Light Fixtures

A light fixture consists of a housing, a socket, and a mounting assembly (see Figure 7.1). The fixture housing will also hold any reflector assembly necessary to control the beam distribution of some incandescent and most fluorescent and HID lamps. Additionally, some fixtures will have other elements, including a lens cap or bezel and transformer or ballast compartment (see "Transformer" and "Ballast" below). The main purpose of a fixture is to hold the lamp. It protects the lamp and electrical components from the harsh outdoor environment and ensures that the lamp aims at the proper angle in the correct direction.

Fixtures can be used in two basic ways: as a decorative element and as a functional device. Currently, the lighting market offers a wide variety of fixture types and styles, and manufacturers continue to develop new concepts and products.

Selection of a fixture should include evaluation of appearance, capabilities, construction, and cost. This chapter will look at these issues along with the various types of fixtures available for different uses, accessories necessary for the fixture to function and those available as options to fulfill specific needs (such as louvers and shrouds for shielding), the various mounting locations and methods that can be used, and the safety issues that control the manufacturing and installation of fixtures, including codes, safety labels, and performance tests.

SELECTION CRITERIA

Four issues—aesthetics, function, mechanical features, and cost—comprise the basic criteria for selecting a fixture. Within each of these categories there are several issues to consider. Knowing all the issues ensures that the designer can make the best selection for a project.

Aesthetics

Appearance is important not only to decorative fixtures, but to functional units as well. In both cases, the fixture selected needs to visually complement the building's architectural style and the landscape style. Literally hundreds of fixture styles are available, from the bare-bones high-tech look to one of many historical styles meant to coordinate with specific architectural periods. Often, several different types of fixtures will be needed throughout a site, each serving different purposes. This may mean using varying sizes of the same fixture style. Large sconces may be required at a building's main entrance and a smaller version at secondary entrances, or a smaller coordinating style for post-mount walkway fixtures. Selecting a family of fixtures (a series of fixtures that coordinate in their basic shape but may vary in size or detailing) helps present a cohesive appearance to the lighting equipment.

The size of the fixture needs to be in scale with the location where it will be used. Too large or too small a fixture looks out of place and detracts from the appearance of the landscape during the day as well as at night.

Function

In evaluating whether a fixture will function properly in a specific situation, several issues should be considered. What lamp(s) does the fixture accommodate? Will the fixture accept different wattages? How adjustable is the fixture? Can the fixture readily accept accessories?

Lamp Type and Wattage

Fixtures are designed for specific lamp types or families of lamps. The physical size and characteristics of a lamp determine the size and characteristics of the fixture. For example, the small size of incandescent lamps allows a smaller fixture housing than what will be required for an HID lamp. Since many incandescent lamps have optical control built into the lamp itself, often the fixture has no need for a reflector assembly to direct the light. HID and fluorescent lamps typically need optics to control their spread of light. This usually increases fixture size.

Most outdoor fixtures need to be totally enclosed with a lens that is sealed and gasketed to the housing in order to protect the lamp from water. Most lamps are not weatherproof. Fixtures meant to use PAR36 and PAR38 incandescent lamps can be open, as the glass used for the lens can withstand the temperature shock from rain, irrigation water, and snow. However, some lamps (especially the smaller PAR20 and PAR30 sizes) are susceptible to corrosion due to water entering the lamp from air holes at the base. It is always wise to use these lamps in enclosed fixtures to ensure long-term functioning (see Figure 7.2).

Most fixtures can accept a range of wattages. However, limitations apply, such as heat dissipation in the incandescent and HID lamp families. For example, a fixture using up to a 50-watt MR16 lamp can be one size, but the size will need to increase to accommodate a 75-watt lamp because it produces more heat. Typically, fixtures are built to accept one lamp category—incandescent, fluorescent, mercury vapor, metal halide, or high-pressure sodium. In the incandescent family, the size of a fixture and the socket type will limit the lamps that can be used in the fixture. For example, a fixture made for an R40 lamp can also accept a PAR38 lamp since the PAR38 lamp is slightly smaller in overall width and uses the same base type. This fixture would not, however, accept an MR16 lamp, as the size and socket type are quite different.

In general, fluorescent fixtures are built to accommodate the size and wattage of a single lamp and its ballast. Since the 5-, 7-, and 9-watt compact fluorescent lamps are operated by a single ballast, most fixtures that accept the 9-watt lamp can also accommodate the 5- and 7-watt lamps. However, a 13-watt fixture will only accept a 13-watt lamp, and the same is true of the higher-wattage compact fluorescent lamps. In the HID family, one size of fixture can often accommodate several lamp types within a specific wattage range. However, each lamp wattage requires a dedicated ballast, so the fixture is built at the factory for one wattage only. This means lamps are not interchangeable at the job site unless the ballast is also changed. It is best to avoid this situation since it is time and labor intensive.

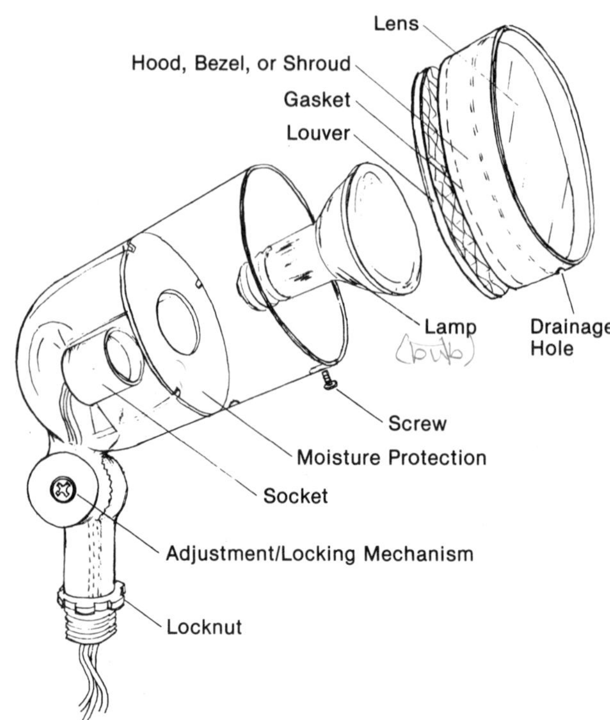

Figure 7.1. Parts of a typical incandescent fixture. Drawing: Lezlie Johannessen.

Adjustment Capabilities

To create specific visual effects on buildings, plant material, sculptures, or other features, fixtures often need the ability to adjust the aiming of the lamp or the beamspread (see Figures 7.3 & 7.4). The possible range of adjustment varies. Designers need to consider both horizontal rotation and vertical aiming capabilities (see Figure 7.3). Most, but not all fixtures have both horizontal and vertical movement capabilities. Some below-grade or submersible fixtures have limited verti-

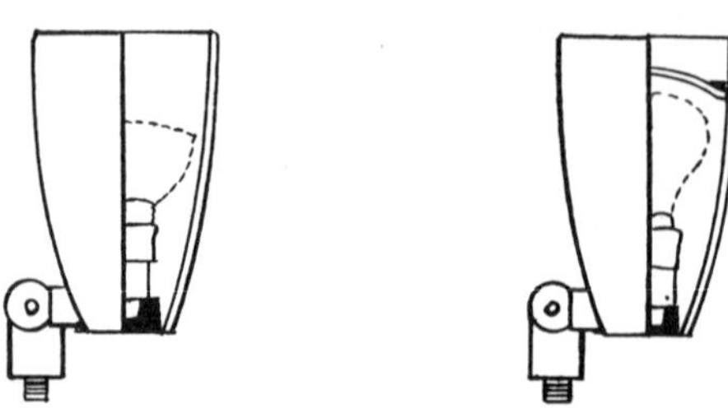

Figure 7.2. Example of an open (left) and closed (right) fixture. Drawing: Lezlie Johannessen.

cal aiming or tilt capability, typically approximately 15°, and may have no horizontal rotation. Aiming is a prime concern for below-grade fixtures, which typically have a limited range of tilt. The manufacturer's catalog information should list the aiming range. However, the best way to understand the actual movement possible is to request a sample and test it. When more than one fixture will be mounted on a single canopy, the adjustability of both fixtures may be limited.

When a fixture will be used for highlighting plants, the ability to change wattage and light distribution is important. As plants grow they expand in size and often become denser in branching and leaf overlap. Increased size often requires a wider beam distribution, while increased density requires higher wattage.

In some fixtures the lamp can actually be moved within a reflector to change the distribution (see Figure 7.4) without having to change the lamp. In some HID floodlighting fixtures, the optical chamber can be rotated in the housing to shift the lamp distribution or can be changed to another light distribution without affecting the physical appearance of a row of fixtures.

Ability to Add Accessories

Another important consideration in selecting a fixture is the ability to add accessories such as shrouds, louvers, lenses, and color media. Accessory needs for a given fixture will vary from one location to another on a site. For example, a fixture in an area of pedestrian circulation may require a louver or both a louver and shroud to eliminate lamp brightness. In other areas neither accessory may be required because the fixture aims away from people.

Some fixtures easily accommodate accessories. Many manufacturers have a group of accessories available for a specific fixture type. When the manufacturer has not provided for the adding of accessories, the designer needs to evaluate how much space is available (inside the fixture) to add accessories such as louvers and lenses, how they will attach, and whether they will need to be waterproof (if they cannot fit on the interior of the lamp compartment).

Mechanical Features

Fixtures should also be evaluated on how they are constructed. This section examines issues that affect long-term wear and access into a fixture for lamping and maintenance. Projects will have varying requirements. On some public or commercial landscapes, concern about vandalism will necessitate tamper-proof attachment and aiming mechanisms and impact-proof lens materials. A tamper-proof requirement normally means using an Allen-head screw rather than a flat-head or Phillips-head screw. On residential projects, however, the ease and simplicity of the adjustment is more important. All outdoor fixtures should minimize sharp edges where the finish could fail, and areas where water and dirt could collect and encourage corrosion. No uplight fixture, either below- or above-grade, can prevent the accumulation of dirt and debris on the lens or faceplate. However, some lens configurations slough off dirt better than others (see Figure 8.10). Keeping the fixture lens clean becomes a maintenance task that needs to be done regularly to maintain proper function.

Attachment of Lenses

The designer should determine exactly how lenses are attached to fixture housings. Sometimes lenses are attached using an adhesive that holds the lens permanently in place. Other manufacturers may use thin metal tabs to hold the lens. These tabs can break off or loosen, allowing the lens to slip out of position. On decorative fixtures, a crooked lens is unsightly, but on functional fixtures, the waterproof seal of the lamp compartment may be compromised.

Access to Lamp, Transformer, and Ballast Compartments

The designer also needs to understand what tools are required to open the fixture and what parts will be affected. Some fixtures require too many tools: one (or more) size and type of screwdriver, one (or more) wrench size, and one (or more) type of pliers. On other fixtures the lamp bezel twists off and a single tool is necessary for locking the aiming adjustment. Sometimes all or part of the fixture must be disassembled to gain access to the lamp. The more parts and pieces that someone must keep track of during lamp installation or fixture maintenance makes working on the fixture more difficult and successful reassembly less likely.

Examining sample fixtures and disassembling them is the best way to determine whether the fixture will be easily maintained in the field. This issue is important for all fixtures since parts can be easily lost in the soil or plantings surrounding a fixture. Remember, too, that when parts are set down, they can become covered with soil; they then require careful cleaning to ensure a tight seal when the fixture is reassembled. However, ease of maintenance becomes especially important for fixtures mounted on or under eaves, high above the ground on any structure, or in trees, because maintenance of these fixtures typically occurs on ladders, where there is no space to set down all the disassembled parts. The easier the fixtures are to maintain, the better the odds are of having a lighting system that continues to function for a long time.

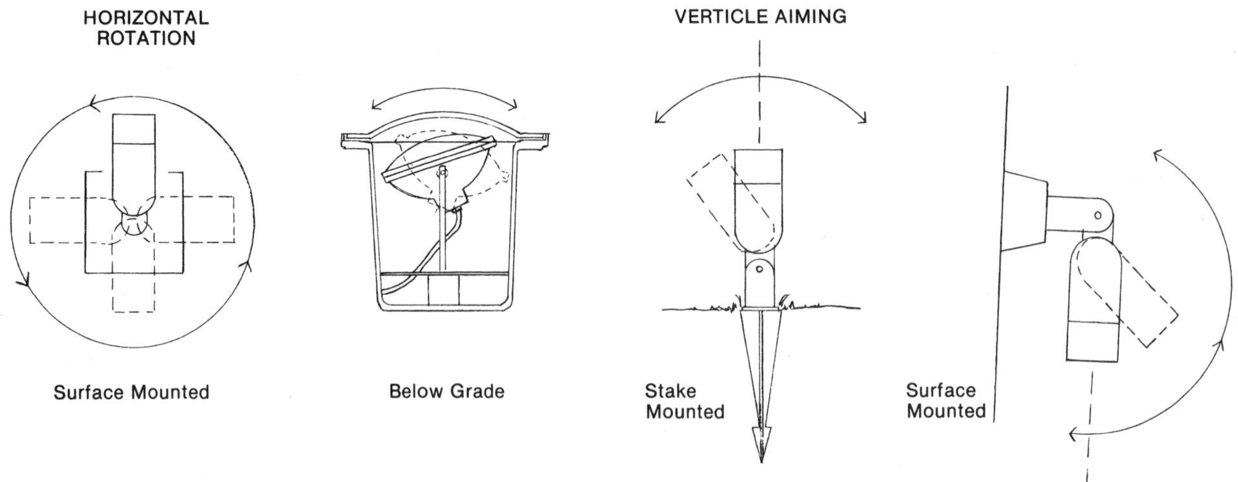

Figure 7.3. *Examples of typical fixture adjustments. Drawing: Lezlie Johannessen.*

Waterproofing

Some controversy exists in the lighting industry regarding the entry of water into fixtures. Some manufacturers approach water entry as unavoidable and provide drainage from the lamp compartment to accommodate moisture buildup. Other manufacturers enclose the fixture and seal all the connection points to eliminate water entry. Regardless of the manufacturer's approach to moisture in the lamp compartment, all openings into the fixture need to be as water resistant as possible.

For a fixture that is designed to allow water to enter or build up in the lamp compartment, review the way the manufacturer has provided for drainage. Are there enough holes, and are they large enough to let water out? Is the project located in an area where these holes become an invitation to insects to take up residence in the fixture and then die inside the housing, affecting the functioning of the fixture? If so, watertight fixtures may be more appropriate.

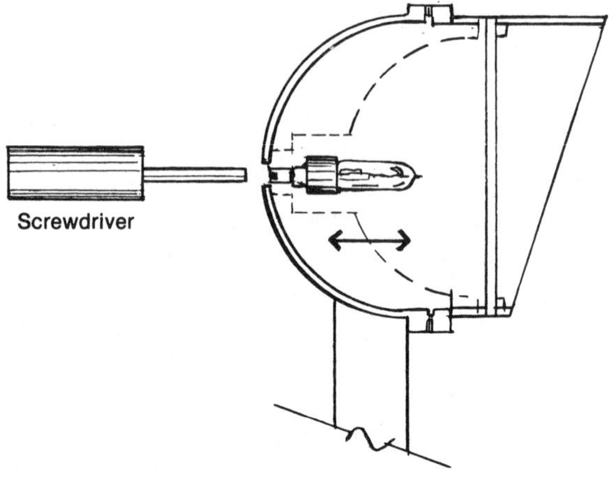

Figure 7.4. *In this fixture the lamp can move back and forth in the housing. When the lamp is positioned toward the back of the housing the beamspread is wide; as the lamp moves away from the back the beamspread narrows. Drawing: Lezlie Johannessen.*

Waterproofing is important, as it prevents internal corrosion of the fixture housing and damage to parts such as the socket or lamp. Sockets are typically metal and susceptible to corrosion. When a socket fails, the fixture will not function. Lamps can also fail due to water exposure. Cold water striking a hot lamp can crack the lamp jacket, causing lamp failure. Water accumulation can corrode the lamp base, preventing an electrical connection. Lamps with odd sockets such as the MR incandescent or the HQI metal halide are especially susceptible to corrosion and failure. The bipins of MR lamps corrode and can physically separate from the lamp, preventing an electrical connection.

All potential openings into a fixture need to be examined to determine whether it is waterproof. How does the lens attach to the housing? Since the materials used for the lens and fixture housing are different, a sealant with high heat properties is needed. The sealant must be able to change shape and still maintain the seal as temperature varies (due primarily to lamp heat), stand up to ultraviolet radiation from the sun, and withstand changeable weather conditions over a long period of time.

How is the fixture faceplate or the bezel sealed? Look at the gasket type and material to make sure that the material can stand up over time. Make sure that the gasket will not become crushed due to the pressure of the lamp closure, which would prevent a good seal the next time the fixture is opened and reclosed.

How are the wire entrances into the lamp compartment sealed? Again, a sealant should fill the opening to prevent water entrance. Have the ballast or transformer compartments been filled with a sealant to prevent water entrance and water movement to other parts of the fixture? (See Figure 10.16.) Are the wires themselves treated to prevent water from being drawn into the housing? (See Figure 7.5.)

Each fixture will have differing solutions to these issues. There is not one right way to approach waterproofing. When evaluating waterproofing, a designer needs consider how the manufacturer has approached each of these issues and what materials they have chosen to use. Chapter 8 discusses characteristics of materials and finishes to help the designer evaluate the materials used by manufacturers.

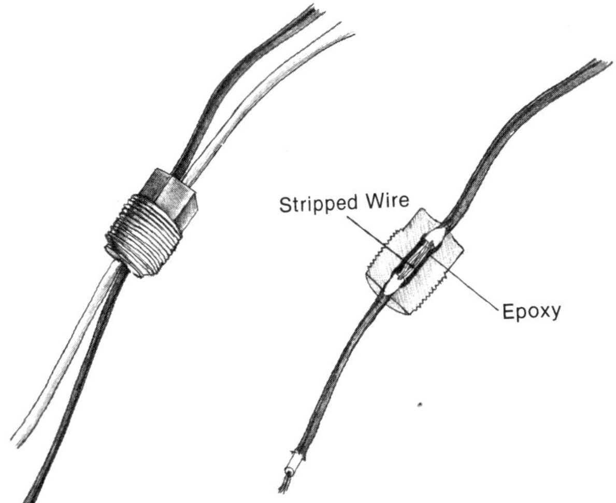

Figure 7.5. This antiwicking plug breaks the potential path of water along the inside of the wire jacket by potting the stripped wires in epoxy. Drawing: Lezlie Johannessen.

Locking Mechanisms

Accent fixtures must maintain the required aiming angle over time. A small change in the angle can destroy the effect and therefore the overall luminous composition. The fixture needs to have a secure locking mechanism, but one that can be changed if and when necessary. Locking mechanisms vary widely from one manufacturer to another. One good locking mechanism consists of joining toothed knuckles and securing the connection with a mechanical locking device such as a screw, a bolt, or a wingnut (see Figure 7.6, top). Another good locking mechanism uses an Allen-head screw to tighten and secure two flat surfaces (see Figure 7.6, bottom).

Lamp Shielding

Another consideration in fixture selection is how the lamp is positioned in the fixture housing. The lamp needs to be recessed enough to shield a person's view of it without restricting the lamp's beam distribution. When the fixture will be aiming away from people's normal view, such as aiming at a dense hedge at the back of the property, lamp shielding is not an important issue. In many situations, however, people will be walking by the fixture or the fixture lens will be in their field of view. If the lamp is not shielded, its brightness will attract a person's eye and either detract from the scene or impair the person's ability to see.

Some manufacturers provide shielding by offering bezels of different depths, recessing the lamp away from the lens deep into the housing (some manufacturers offer more than one lamp recess location for one fixture style), or offering accessory shrouds that can be attached to the fixture. In some cases, deep bezels or deeply recessed lamps restrict the lamp's light distribution. A shroud will also affect distribution. Even with one of these shielding media, a louver may be required to minimize lamp brightness.

Optics

In some fixtures the lamp is solely responsible for the distribution of light. This is the case with most fixtures using incandescent lamps. Other fixtures require reflectors or a reflector assembly to control the distribution of light. Most fluorescent and HID lamps, most quartz lamps, and many of the compact and subcompact incandescent lamp types require reflectors to sculpt the emitted light beam.

Reflectored fixtures vary in quality. Some reflectors simply push the light forward out of the housing, while others have multiple facets or carefully controlled shapes that direct the light in desired ways. For exam-

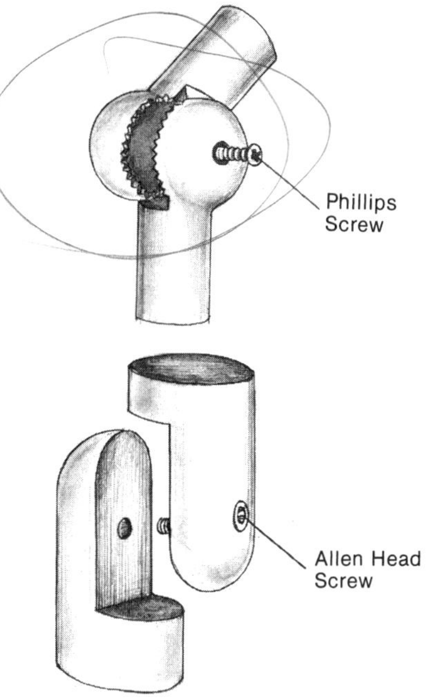

Figure 7.6. Examples of good locking mechanisms. Drawing: Lezlie Johannessen.

ple, with some HID lamps a narrow spot distribution is produced using a parabolic-shaped reflector system. One of the factors that determine the quality of fixtures is the control of direct lamp brightness or "cutoff."

One of the interesting features to look for in an HID accent fixture is the choice of several reflector assemblies for the same fixture. This allows the designer to use the same fixture type in several areas of a large site even though the fixtures are serving different purposes. Some fixtures also permit changing the position of the optics within the lamp housing to offer flexibility in distribution.

Environmental Considerations

The conditions that a fixture will be exposed to is an important consideration for all fixtures used on a project, but some more than others. Factors such as soil type (amount of clay, silt, and sand) along with additives in the soil (including salts, chemicals, and water), temperature and temperature variation, and exposure to ultraviolet radiation, wind, rain, and snow all affect fixture selection. The fixture must be designed to fit the harshness of the environment. For example, in soils that have a high percentage of clay (which retains moisture), the fixture must have good corrosion resistance (see corrosion section in Chapter 8).

Thermal Considerations

Heat buildup in a fixture is an important issue to consider. If the fixture housing is too small, it will not dissipate enough of the heat generated by the lamp. The increased temperature surrounding the lamp can shorten lamp life, affect the ballast or transformer, and damage wires or sockets. Some materials are sensitive to heat and will not last when exposed to either high heat or heat sustained for a long time. For example, if a lamp with too high a wattage is installed in a fixture made for a tubular quartz lamp or HID source, the fixture lens material may discolor, crack, or burn (see Figure 8.22).

Manufacturers are required to perform heat tests on fixtures as a part of the testing for UL or ETL labels. The tests determine the acceptable lamps and maximum acceptable wattage for the fixture. This information is listed on the fixture manufacturer's catalog sheet. Installing a lamp wattage higher than this can cause serious problems to the fixture or wiring system and violates the label. Using a different lamp than those listed by the manufacturer can also void the label. Often with incandescent fixtures, a group of lamp types and wattages will work in the fixture up to the maximum stated wattage. In listing the maximum wattage, the manufacturer is not recommending use of that wattage. The lamp selection depends on the needs of the project for each fixture. On the catalog page for an HID fixture, the manufacturer will list all the lamps that can be used. The designer then specifies the one appropriate for the project and the manufacturer supplies the fixture with the correct ballast and socket for that lamp. If the specifier installs another lamp, the fixture will not function because of a lamp–ballast incompatibility.

FIXTURE TYPES

There are two categories of fixtures: decorative and functional. Decorative fixtures need to conform to the style of the landscape during the day and can contribute to the luminous composition at night. Functional fixtures are used to create visual effects throughout the landscape and are typically hidden from view. Some fixtures fall into both categories.

Decorative Fixtures

Decorative fixtures include several types: lanterns, bollards, and path lights, and post-mounted, wall, and hanging fixtures. Characteristics such as shape, size, lamp type and wattage, construction materials, mounting accessories, and construction details will determine whether a fixture is appropriate for a specific project. For example, in a wooden post fixture, two manufacturers may make a similar-appearing fixture, but one manufacturer may use exposed screws for connecting parts of the fixture while another uses a connection method where the hardware is concealed. The fixture with the concealed connectors may be visually more attractive. Differences such as this typically affect the cost of the fixture.

Lanterns

The lantern category includes many styles of traditional fixtures that recall outdoor lights of earlier times in history and of different cultures (see Figure 7.7). For example, the Japanese culture produced both portable and permanent stone lanterns. Today, lanterns typically provide a decorative element in the garden, but they can also add soft fill light. Some are not electrified, using candles or gas to produce light. When they are electrified, the wattage of lamps must be kept low (3 to 15 watts) to avoid having the lens or opening become too bright.

Bollard and Path Fixtures

Bollards provide task light for walkways and carry a visual design style through the site. Typically, bollards have a substantial size and strong construction to withstand the rough conditions experienced in commercial projects. Path fixtures will be smaller in size and more residential in appearance (see Figure 7.8). All families of lamps, incandescent, fluorescent, and HID are represented in this category. Bollards typically use compact fluorescent or low-wattage HID sources. The fluorescent wattages may be as high as 26 watts and the HID in the range of 35 to 70 watts. However, most path light fixtures will use either incandescent or compact fluorescent lamps. Incandescent wattages range from 7.5 to 25 and compact fluorescent from 5 to 13 watts.

Post, Wall-Mounted, and Hanging Fixtures

The main purpose of post, wall-mounted, and hanging fixtures is visual decoration, but they can provide walkway light, identification, or general illumination. Post fixtures are often used at a drive or walkway entrance, while wall and hanging fixtures often adorn entrances to buildings. The shape of the fixture needs to coordinate or integrate with the architectural design of the project, and the wattage needs to be planned to provide the light needed while not creating glare on the lens of the fixtures or hot spots on walkway surfaces below the fixtures. The wattage range of incandescent sources for residential wall-mounted or hanging fixtures should be between 3 and 25 watts. The wattage for post fixtures may be slightly higher (up to 40 watts). Compact fluorescent lamps below 13 watts also work. For commercial projects, both compact fluorescent (26 watts and below) and HID (70 watts and below) sources are used (see Figure 7.9).

Functional Fixtures

Functional fixtures represent those that are designed to produce effects. These should be hidden from view both during the day and at night. When they cannot be hidden, the daytime appearance of functional fixtures needs to be planned to integrate with other stylistic details on the project. Their shape should be consistent with the architectural style and their finish color should be selected to ensure that they will blend in with the surroundings. At night, people's view of the lamp brightness needs to be minimized or eliminated.

Functional fixtures take many forms: ground-mounted adjustable, hanging, surface-mounted, ground-recessed, recessed step lights, underwater accent, and underwater niche fixtures.

Ground-Mounted Adjustable Fixtures

Ground-mounted adjustable fixtures are used to highlight structures, objects, or plant material in the garden. Fixtures are made for both 120-volt or low-voltage incandescent sources, as well as fluorescent or HID sources (see Figure 7.10). All 120-volt fixtures must be permanently mounted on either an above- or below-grade junction box unless the installation is temporary. The low-voltage incandescent group can be stake mounted. The size of the fixtures will vary tremendously according to the light source used.

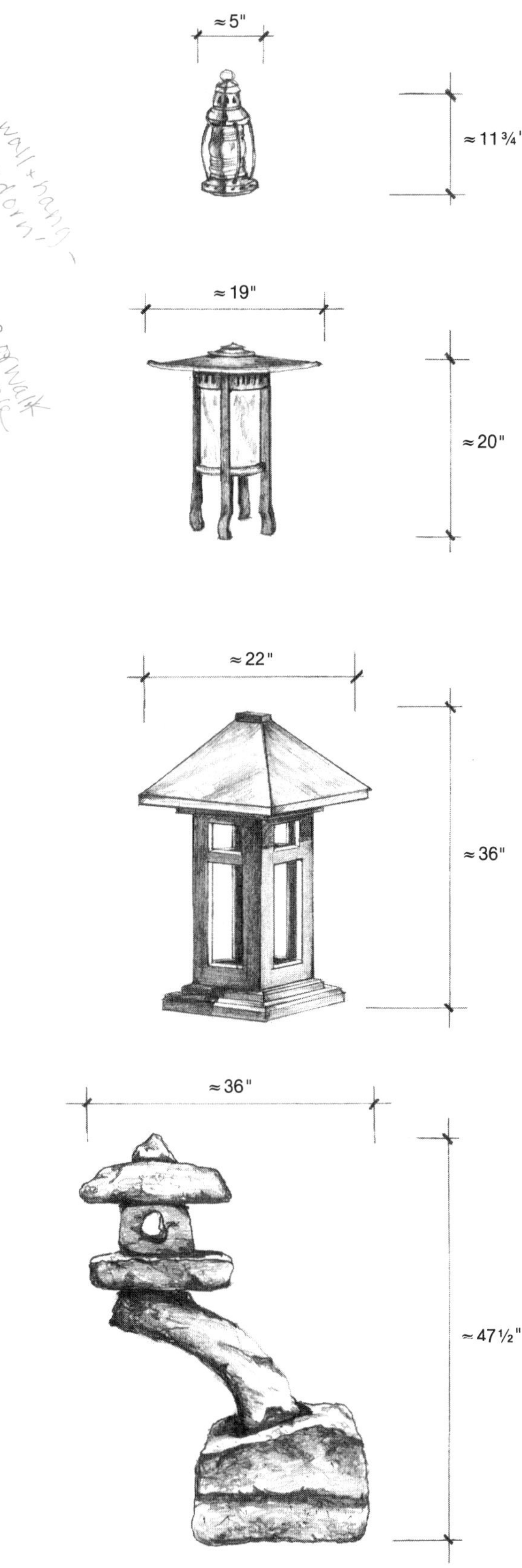

Figure 7.7. Examples of lanterns. Drawing: Lezlie Johannessen.

These fixtures are available for incandescent lamp wattages ranging from 20 to 1,000 watts and up to 400 watts for HID sources. Fluorescent fixtures are available in wattages starting with a 5-watt compact lamp and including the higher-wattage 4- and 8-foot lamps.

These fixtures need to be aimed on site to ensure that the intended effect is created. This requires easy access to the lamp compartment and a strong locking mechanism to retain the aiming of the fixture. These fixtures also require enough space between the lamp and outer lens to add accessories such as louvers and spread lenses.

Hanging Fixtures

When mounted in trees, hanging fixtures can produce a soft wash of light below them for walkway lighting or task lighting on patios, or they may create a pattern of light as they shine through tree foliage. They can create a glow or sparkle effect when the fixture has perforations in the housing. These typically use either 120-volt or low-voltage incandescent lamps (see Figure 7.9).

Surface-Mounted Fixtures

Surface-mounted fixtures are used to provide general lighting, fill lighting, or accent lighting. They can be mounted to the trunk or branches of a tree, on walls or fences, and on roofs or roof overhangs. They use either 120-volt or low-voltage incandescent lamps or low-wattage HID sources in the same wattages available for ground mounting. Higher wattages are used as the fixture is mounted farther above grade. They may be adjustable or fixed; they may be uplights or downlights, or have a combined up-and-down distribution.

Many shapes and sizes are available (see Figure 7.10), and the designer must consider how the fixture will attach to the tree or structure. The size, shape, and color of the fixture needs to coordinate with the architectural style of the project and surface where the fixture will be attached. For example, when mounting in trees, the fixture color should match or blend with the color of the bark.

Attaching light fixtures to a tree or building requires planning how power will be supplied to that location. The wiring should be recessed into the structure or hidden somehow. In new construction, the wiring can be placed in the building framework before the final architectural finish material is applied. On a garden structure such as a trellis, wiring can be located behind a removable cover or in an open raceway (see Figure 16.14).

In existing structures, the wiring location must be planned to hide it from view as much as possible. For example, when mounting a fixture to a trellis that attaches to a building, the wiring can be brought directly out of the building at the top of the trellis and run along the top member of the trellis. When mounting at eaves, the wiring can often be run inside an attic adjacent to the eaves, allowing all the wiring to be hidden.

When locating fixtures in trees, mounting accessories should be kept small (see Figure 7.12) and the wiring feed should run up the least visible side of the tree. The wire should be tucked into crevices of the tree's bark, when possible, and attached to the tree at intervals as the wire goes up the trunk. Of all the attachment accessories available, the least harmful to a tree and the easiest to maintain over the years is a cable tie. This holds the wire close to the tree but does not directly attach it to the tree (see Figure 10.23). Cable ties should be UV or sunlight resistant. In no instance should a wire or tie for holding electrical wires be wrapped around the girth of the tree. As the tree grows, this can cut through the cambium layer of the tree and kill it. The best fastener to use is a stainless steel nail, which is less harmful to the tree than a screw. Staples are an alternative to a cable tie with a nail, but they are more difficult to loosen as the tree grows.

Designers should familiarize themselves with local requirements for tree mounting. Some jurisdictions require the use of conduit to a minimum of 10 feet above grade for both 120-volt and low-voltage fixtures. In some areas there may be a fixture weight restriction or other special requirements.

Fixtures intended to illuminate steps can be recessed into either the sidewalls of stairs (see Figure 17.12 & 17.13), into the risers, or under the nose of a tread. These fixtures are often quite small in order to recess into walls of limited thickness (see Figure 7.13). Their size also needs to relate to the scale of the stairs. Several manufacturers make units the size of a standard brick so that a fixture can easily be integrated into a brick wall. These fixtures range in wattage from 20 watts (or less) in low-voltage subcompact to 60 watts (or slightly higher) in A-lamp incandescent, 5 to 26 watts in compact fluorescent, and 30 to 50 watts in HID. Designers need to examine the faceplate appearance. Any fixture with a lens will attract attention to itself rather than inconspicuously lighting the steps. Fixtures with louvers or shrouds draw less attention to themselves, but designers should test these fixtures prior to specifying them, as some cast louver shadows. Designers should consider the light distribution from the step light to ensure that the fixture will adequately illuminate the stairs.

Ground-Recessed Fixtures

Fixtures mounted below grade can be used for highlighting specimen trees, for accenting sculptures, for washing walls or fences, and for lighting low-level signs. These fixtures are usually relatively large in order to dissipate lamp heat and to provide a waterproof chamber for the lamp, transformer or ballast, and electrical connections. However, some very small units

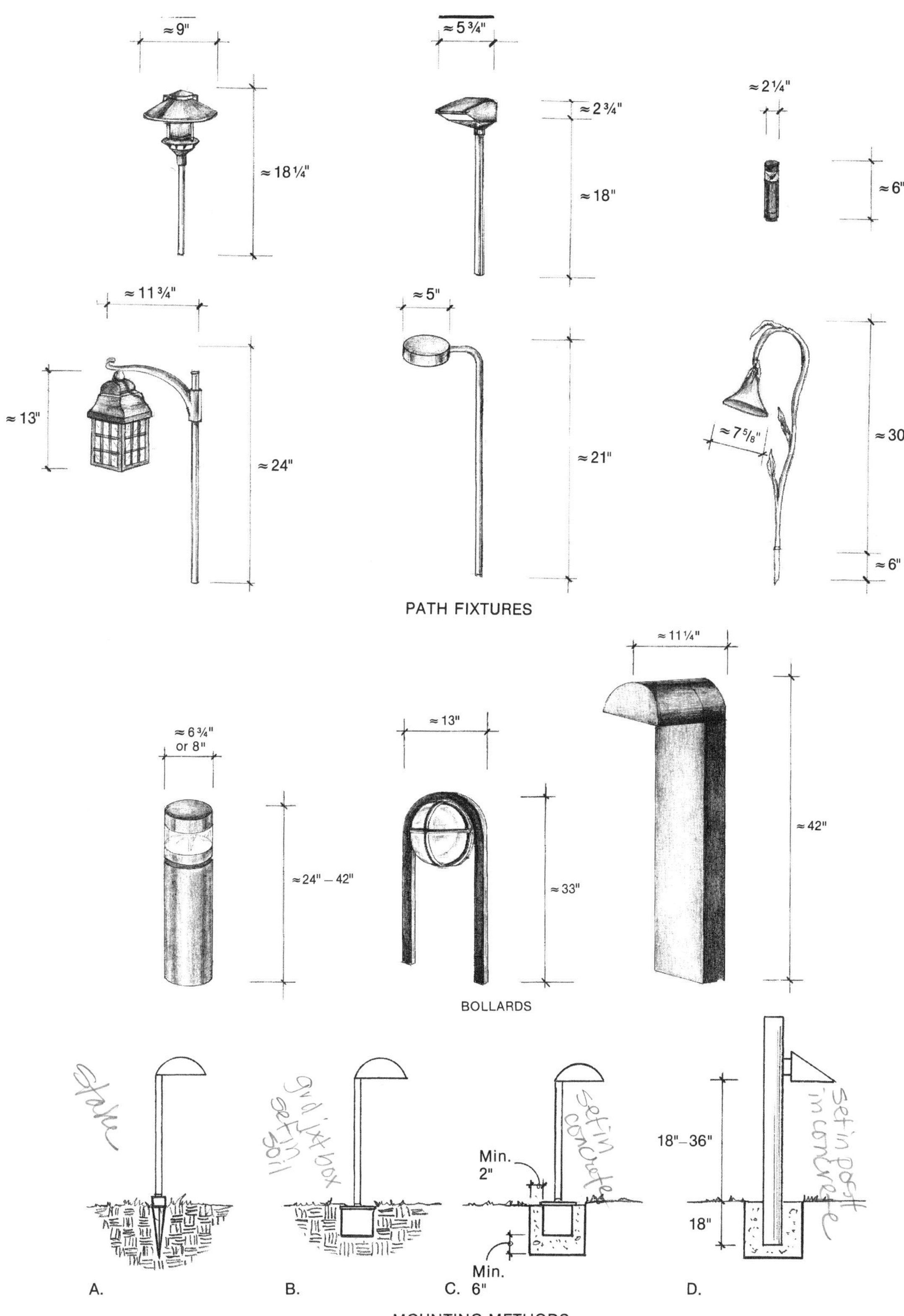

Figure 7.8. *Examples of path fixtures, bollards, and mounting methods for path fixtures. The mounting method determines flexibility or permanence. A. Any 12-volt fixture can be stake mounted, providing ease of movement. This method makes the fixture less physically stable and should not be used in any commercial installation. B. Mounting to a ground-recessed junction box provides more stability. C. Setting the below-grade junction box in concrete bolsters the permanence. D. Mounting a fixture onto another post, in this case wood, provides continuity within a site using wood detailing and strong support. Drawing: Lezlie Johannessen.*

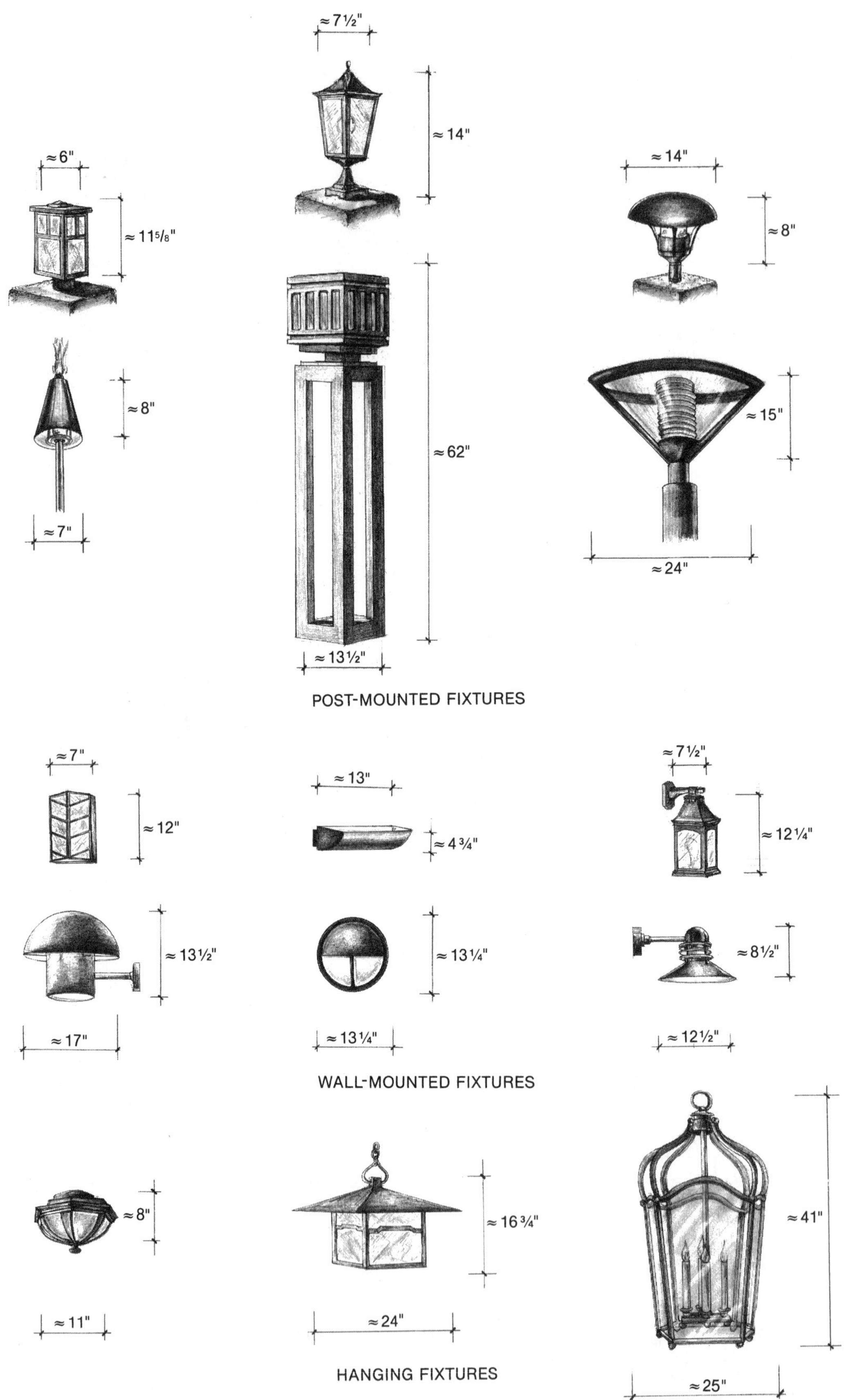

Figure 7.9. *Examples of post-mounted, wall-mounted, and hanging fixtures. Drawing: Lezlie Johannessen.*

FIGURE 7.10: GROUND- AND SURFACE-MOUNTED FIXTURES

INCANDESCENT AND HIGH-INTENSITY DISCHARGE

FIXTURE SHAPE Shape, Size, and Lamps (will vary with manufacturer)	Open or Closed	Lamp Type and Wattage	Louver and Shielding Availability and Types	Mounting Types Available
ROUND BODY				
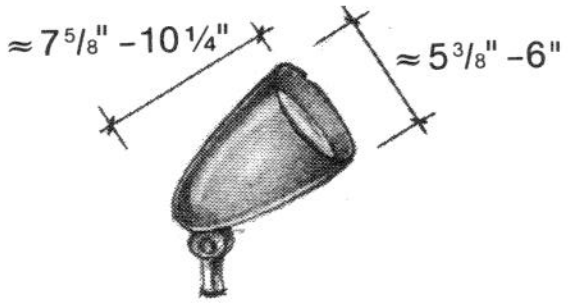 ≈ 7 5/8" – 10 1/4"; ≈ 5 3/8" – 6"	Closed or open	PAR38 45 to 300 watts	Custom louver/ short or long shroud	Stake w/splice box, above-grade junction box, surface mount
	Closed	R40 75 to 150 watts	Custom louver/ shroud required	Same as above
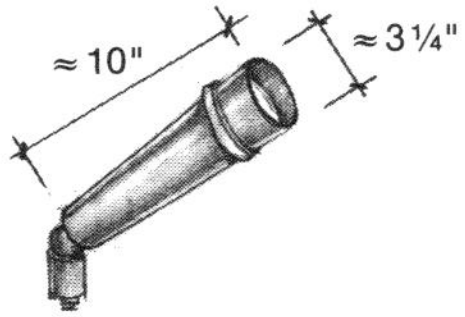 ≈ 10"; ≈ 3 1/4"	Closed	PAR20 50 watts	Custom louver/ shroud optional	Same as above
	Closed	R20 50 watts	Custom louver/ shroud required	Same as above
	Closed	MR16 20 to 75 watts	Custom louver/ short or long shroud	Stake w/splice box, surface mount, extension stem
≈ 5 1/2" – 6 3/8"; ≈ 3 3/4"	Closed	*Mercury Vapor* ER20 50 watts	Custom louver	Tree mount w/ remote transformer box,
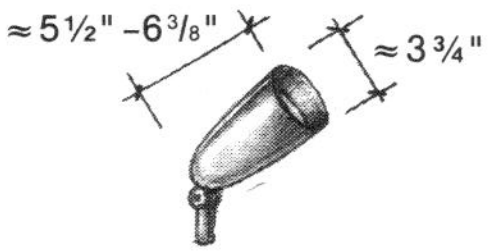	Closed	MVPAR38 100 to 175 watts	Custom louver	above- or below-grade ballast box,
≈ 10 1/4"; ≈ 6 1/4"	Closed	MVR40 100 to 175 watts	Custom louver	integral below-grade ballast box
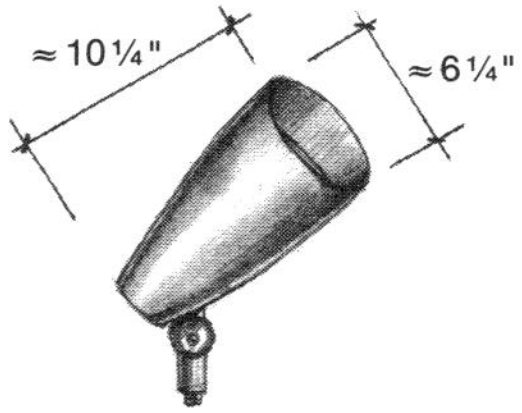	Closed	*HPS* E17 35 watts	Custom louver	Same as above
	Closed	E231/2 35 to 100 watts	Custom louver	Same as above

FIXTURE SHAPE Shape, Size, and Lamps (will vary with manufacturer)	Open or Closed	Lamp Type and Wattage	Louver and Shielding Availability and Types	Mounting Types Available
SQUARE HEAD				
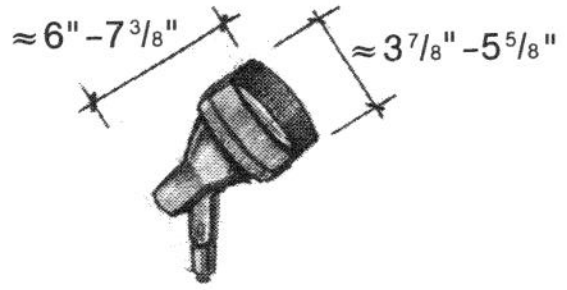 ≈ 6" – 7 3/8"; ≈ 3 7/8" – 5 5/8"	Open or closed	PAR38 45 to 300 watts	Custom louver/ shroud optional	Stake w/splice box, above-grade junction box, below-grade junction box, surface mount
	Closed	PAR20 50 watts	custom louver/ shroud optional	
	Closed	R20 50 watts	Custom louver	Same as above
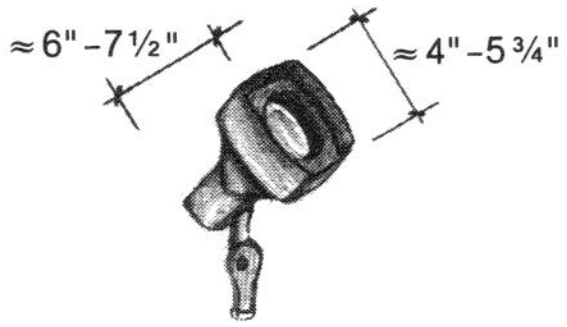 ≈ 6" – 7 1/2"; ≈ 4" – 5 3/4"	Open or closed	PAR36 20 to 75 watts	Custom louver	Stake w/splice box, above-grade junction box, below-grade junction box w/ transformer, surface mount, extension stem
	Closed	MR16 20 to 75 watts	Louver option or custom louver	
≈ 6" – 11 1/2"; ≈ 4" – 7"	Closed	MVR40 100 to 175 watts	*Mercury Vapor* Custom louver/ shroud optional	Below-grade ballast box
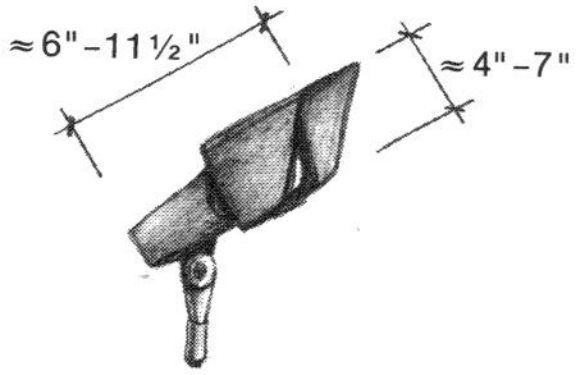	Closed	MVPAR38 100 watts	Custom louver	Same as above
	Closed	*HPS* E17 35 to 150 watts	Custom louver/ shroud optional	Same as above
	Closed	E23 35 to 100 watts	Custom louver	Same as above

* Drawings: Lezlie Johannessen

Figure 7.10.

FIGURE 7.10 CONTINUED: GROUND- AND SURFACE-MOUNTED FIXTURES

INCANDESCENT AND HIGH-INTENSITY DISCHARGE

FIXTURE SHAPE		Lamp	Louver and Shielding	Mounting
Shape, Size, and Lamps (will vary with manufacturer)	Open or Closed	Type and Wattage	Availability and Types	Types Available
CYLINDRICAL HEAD				
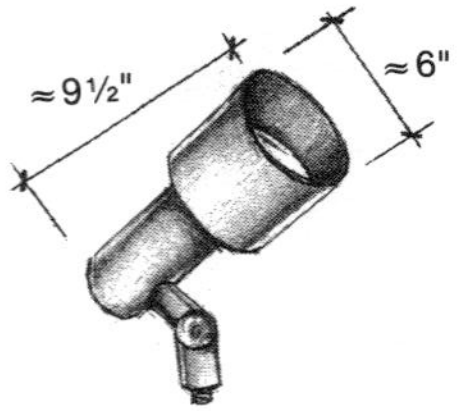 ≈9½" ≈6"	Closed or open	PAR38 45 to 300 watts	Custom louver	Stake w/splice box, above-grade junction box, below-grade junction box, surface mount
	Open or closed	PAR36 20 to 75 watts	Louver option or custom louver	Same as above may also use w/extension stem
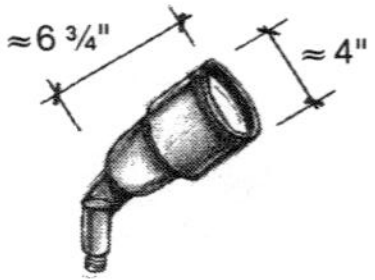 ≈6¾" ≈4"	closed	MR16 20 to 75 watts	Louver option or custom louver	Integral stake, below-grade junction box w/transformer, extension stem, wall plate
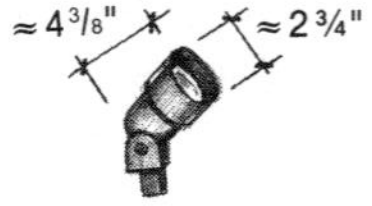 ≈4⅜" ≈2¾"	Closed	*Mercury Vapor* MVR40 100 watts	Custom louver/ shroud optional	Surface or below-grade ballast box
 ≈11⅜" ≈7"	Closed	MVPAR38 100 watts	Custom louver	Same as above
	Closed	*HPS* E17 or B17 100 watts	Custom louver/ shroud optional	Same as above

FIXTURE SHAPE		Lamp	Louver and Shielding	Mounting
Shape, Size, and Lamps (will vary with manufacturer)	Open or Closed	Type and Wattage	Availability and Types	Types Available
RIBBED BACK				
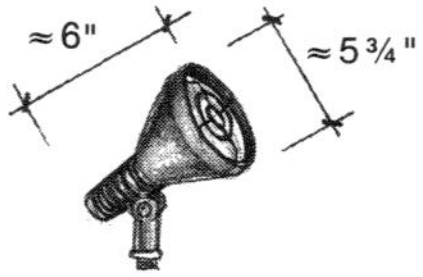 ≈6" ≈5¾"	Open	PAR38 45 to 300 watts	Custom louver/ wire guard	Stake w/splice box
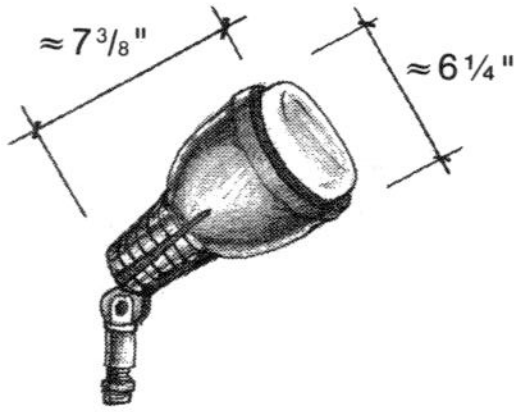 ≈7⅜" ≈6¼"	Open or closed	R40 75 to 500 watts	Custom louver/ wire guard	Stake w/slice box, extension stem
CYLINDRICAL BODY				
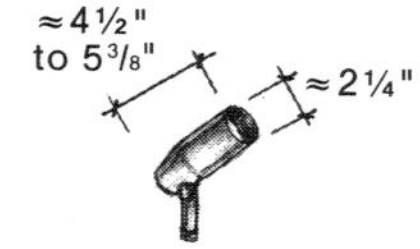 ≈4½" to 5⅜" ≈2¼"	Closed	MR16 20 to 50 watts	Louver option or custom louver	tree mount, wall plate, stake w/splice box,
	Closed	MR11 20 to 35 watts	Louver option or custom louver	stake w/junction box, extension stem, below-grade junction box
WITH CUFF				
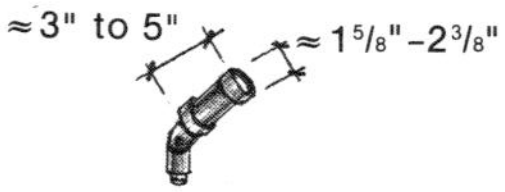 ≈3" to 5" ≈1⅝"–2⅜"	Closed	MR16 20 to 50 watts	Louver option or custom louver, extension cuff	Same as above
	Closed	MR11 20 to 35 watts	Louver option or custom louver, extension cuff	Same as above

* Drawings: Lezlie Johannessen

Figure 7.10. (continued)

FIGURE 7.10 CONTINUED: GROUND- AND SURFACE-MOUNTED FIXTURES

INCANDESCENT AND HIGH-INTENSITY DISCHARGE

FIXTURE SHAPE Shape, Size, and Lamps (will vary with manufacturer)	Open or Closed	Lamp Type and Wattage	Louver and Shielding Availability and Types	Mounting Types Available
BULLET SHAPE ≈ 5¾" – 10⅝" ≈ 4¼" – 6⅞"	Closed	PAR38 up to 150 watts	Integral shield w/lamp guard	Below-grade junction box, surface mount, spike, extension stem
	Closed	PAR30 up to 75 watts	Integral shield/ custom louver	
	Closed	PAR20 up to 50 watts	Integral shield/ custom louver	Same as above
	Closed	PAR36 12 to 75 watts	Integral shield w/lamp guard	Same as above
	Closed	MR16 20 to 50 watts	Integral shield/ custom louver	Same as above
	Closed	T4 TH up to 75 watts	Integral shield/ custom louver	Same as above
	Closed	1141 18 watts	Integral shield/ custom louver	Same as above
	Closed	1156 26 watts	Integral shield/ custom louver	
STRETCHED BULLET ≈ 5¾" ≈ 9$^{1}/_{16}$"	Closed	T4 TH 75 watts	Integral shield/ custom louver	Same as above
	Closed	A19 75 watts	Integral shield/ custom louver	Same as above
	Closed	*Mercury Vapor* 75 watts	Integral shield/ custom shield	Below-grade ballast box
* Also available in fluorescent				

FIXTURE SHAPE Shape, Size, and Lamps (will vary with manufacturer)	Open or Closed	Lamp Type and Wattage	Louver and Shielding Availability and Types	Mounting Types Available
SQUARE BODY ≈ 6½" ≈ 3⅜" – 5⅜"	Closed	PAR20 50 watts	Custom louver/ glare shield	Above-grade and below-grade junction box with transformer, stake, extension stem, tree and wall mount
		MR16 20 to 75 watts	Custom louver/ glare shield	
		AR70 50 to 75 watts	Custom louver/ glare shield	
SPHERE-SHAPED HEAD ≈ 8¾" – 10½"	Closed	PAR38 300 and 500 watts	Optional louver, shield and rock guard	Below-grade junction box
	Closed	R40 300 watts	Same as above	Same as above
	Closed	PAR56 240 watts	Same as above	Same as above
	Closed	HPS E23 ½ 150 watts	Same as above	Below-grade ballast box
	Closed	MVPAR38 100 watts	Same as above	Same as above
	Closed	MVR40 175 watts	Same as above	Same as above
	Closed	MH-E17 175 watts	Same as above	Same as above
SQUARE FACE ≈ 13" ≈ 9"	Closed	*MV* 100 to 250 watts	Integral shield/ custom louver	Yoke arm, mounting bracket
		MH 175 to 250 watts	Integral shield/ custom louver	Same as above
		HPS 150 to 400 watts	Integral shield/ custom louver	Same as above

* Drawings: Lezlie Johannessen

Figure 7.10. (continued)

FIGURE 7.10 CONTINUED: GROUND- AND SURFACE-MOUNTED FIXTURES				
FIXTURE SHAPE		Lamp	Louver and Shielding	Mounting
Shape, Size, and Lamps (will vary with manufacturer)	Open or Closed	Type and Wattage	Availability and Types	Types Available
		FLUORESCENT		
ROUNDED BODY				
≈ 9⅞" – 48⅝"; ≈ 6½"	Closed	T5 6 watts	Optional hood, Custom louver	Above- or below-grade junction box, portable spear, surface mount, tree mount
	Closed	T8 15 watts	Optional shield, Internal louver	
	Closed	T10 60 watts	Optional hood, Custom louver	Same as above
	Closed	T12 30 to 40 watts	Optional hood, Internal louver	Same as above
	Closed	Compact 9 to 13 watts	Optional hood, Custom louver	Same as above
FLAT BACK				
≈ 9" –49½"; ≈ 4"	Closed	Compact 9 watts	Custom louver	Above- or below-grade junction box, surface mount, portable spear
	Closed	(2) Compact 13 watts	Custom louver	
	Closed	T8 30 watts	Custom louver	Same as above
	Closed	T10 40 watts	Custom louver	Same as above
	Closed	T-12 40 watts	Custom louver	Same as above

* Drawings: Lezlie Johannessen

Figure 7.10. (continued)

are becoming available. Both 120-volt and low-voltage units are available for incandescent sources. For HID sources several voltages are often available.

Two types of units exist in this category: *direct-burial* and *well fixtures* (see Figure 7.14). The direct-burial type is entirely enclosed. It is usually wide but shallow in depth to minimize the size of the hole that needs to be dug to accommodate it. Direct-burial fixtures work in areas that have densely compacted soil or rock below a narrow layer of soil. They provide a clean look and do not interfere with maintenance when mounted in the midst of a lawn to uplight a tree. Direct-burial fixtures work equally well for mature dwarf trees surrounded by low-growing, controllable ground cover.

The other type of ground-recessed fixture, called a well light, consists of an open sleeve with a fixture mounted inside the sleeve. This has a smaller width at ground level than the direct-burial fixture but is deeper. This fixture relies on adequate water drainage to continue functioning. In soils with poor drainage, a thorough drainage system must be provided or well lights should not be used. Drainage for below-grade fixtures should include both vertical and horizontal drainage, especially in dense or compacted soils. This requires producing several horizontal channels from the main fixture hole (see Figure 7.14).

Fixture location is critical with below-grade fixtures as they typically have a limited aiming capacity. An aiming range from 0–10° or 15° is typical. Some newer units can aim up to 35°. Often, a larger aiming range means that the lamp is mounted closer to the top of the fixture, making shielding the lamp brightness more difficult. Well lights can sometimes be installed at a slight angle to increase the aiming range. Some fixtures actually sit with a portion of the fixture slightly above grade or have the ability to pull an inner housing up above grade when a higher aiming angle is needed (see Figure 7.15).

Below-grade fixtures work well in areas where they will not be covered by a ground cover creeping over them, or by bedding plants or shrubs expanding in size as they mature. These fixtures work well located in con-

Figure 7.11. *A clamp mount allows for flexibility in movement as the garden evolves. Lighting Design & Photograph: Janet Lennox Moyer, MSH Visual Planners*

Figure 7.12. *Example of a low-voltage fixture mounted in a tree with a small mounting canopy. Lighting Design: Janet Lennox Moyer.*

crete, brick, or stone walkways and patios, wood decks, or lawns.

The material used to make the below-grade housing varies from manufacturer to manufacturer. Some manufacturers produce all their below-grade products from acrylonitrile-butadiene-styrene (ABS). ABS does not have strong ultraviolet radiation resistance, so as long as the top of the housing is not exposed to sunlight, this material is good. The lens cap, however, needs to be made of some other material. Other manufacturers use polyvinyl chloride (PVC) or other plastics for below-grade housings. Always check with the manufacturer on the stability of the material.

Underwater Accent Fixtures

Underwater accent fixtures, often called submersible fixtures, include freestanding fixtures. Some submersible fixtures are adjustable, while others are available only in one or more fixed positions (see Figure 7.16). These fixtures have to pass stringent tests for waterproofing and must have ground-fault interruption protection when installed. All freestanding fixtures facing up in a body of water are also required to have a rock guard to protect the lens from breaking and to protect people from the heat of the lamp.

Adjustable fixtures have a range of uses, including highlighting objects above the water's surface, such as fountains, waterfalls, sculptures, or plants located within the body of water. Fixed units are typically used to create a glow under an object, such as stepping-stones, in a pool. These fixtures typically use long-life incandescent A-shape lamps, and they can be ordered with a decorative cover to prevent direct glare from viewing angles above the water when the fixture is not hidden.

Mounting of these underwater fixtures requires attention to several details. First, during the day will the appearance of the fixture in the body of water be undesirable? If so, a niche fixture recessed into the pool bottom may be more acceptable, or a recessed trough can be created to accommodate a group of fixtures in a line. When a trough is used, a grate is needed to cover it, protecting both people and the fixtures (see Figure 7.17).

Underwater Niche Fixtures

Underwater niche fixtures provide a glow of light through a body of water to highlight a pool's shape, structure, or finish. Typically, these are mounted into the wall or floor of a body of water and have special requirements for relamping required by code. They consist of a housing that is permanently embedded in the wall or floor of the pool or pond and an inner fixture assembly that is removable and is meant to be set on a dry surface outside the pool for relamping (see Figures 7.18 & 7.19). Sometimes these fixtures will be adjustable (see Figure 7.20).

Strip Light Fixtures

Strip light fixtures can be used as either a decorative element or a functional fixture. This category includes individual 120-volt and low-voltage incandescent lamps mounted inside waterproof tubing, attached to a reflector housing, or wired on a cable. It also includes fiber-optic cabling and light pipes (see Figure 7.21).

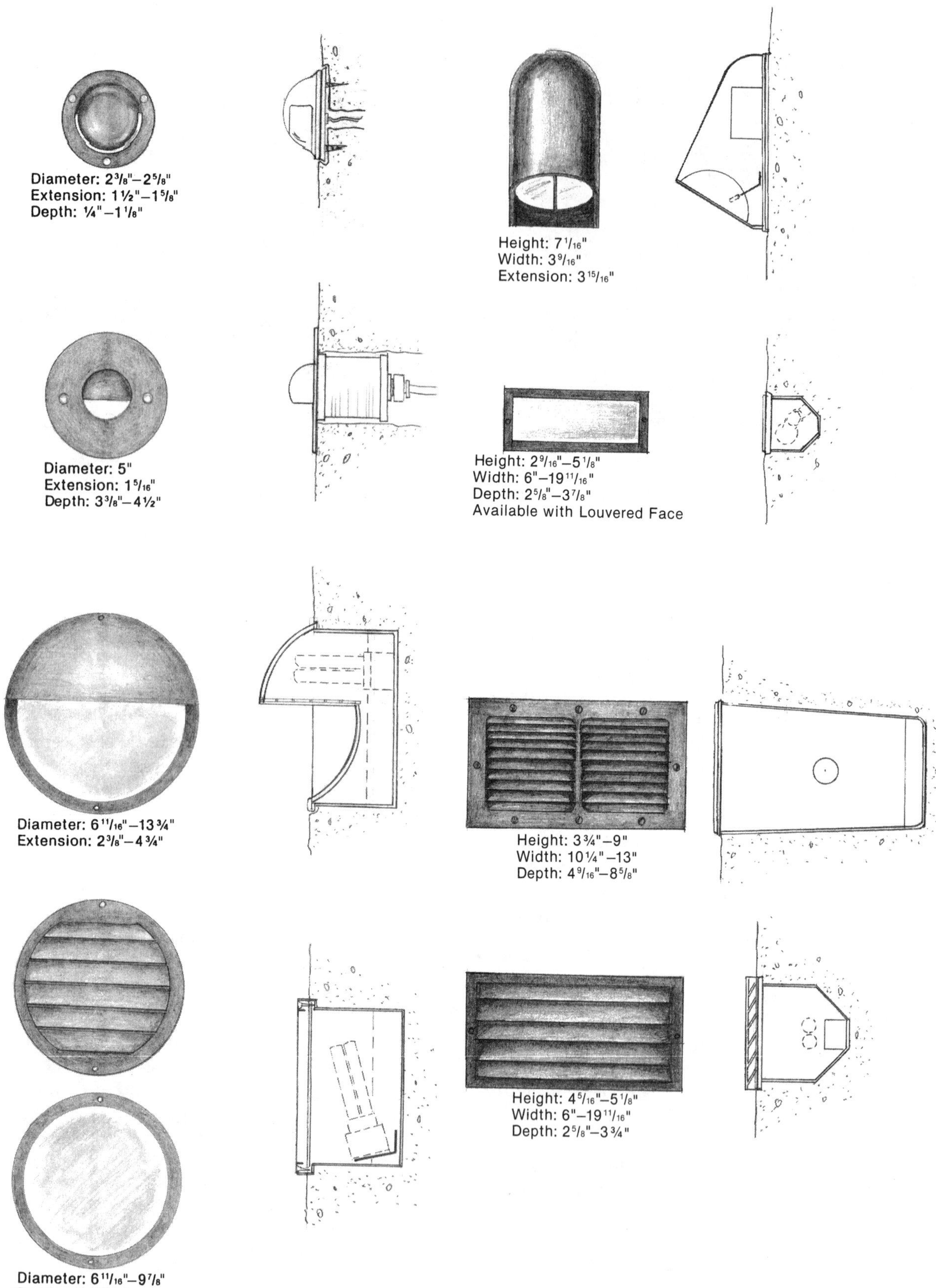

Figure 7.13. *Examples of step light fixtures. Drawing: Lezlie Johannessen.*

120-Volt or Low-Voltage Fixtures

In strip-light fixtures subminiature lamps are frequently used, allowing the fixture to be extremely small and fit into tight locations. The specifier normally has a choice of lamp spacing from 1 inch up to 12 or more inches on center. Some units will have a reflector housing to direct light output. The reflectors are typically available in different materials, from a white plastic to a polished chrome finish. The housings can also have protective lens coverings to prevent dirt buildup around the lamps and the lenses can often be sealed to make the fixture waterproof. These are typically mounted in a concealed location such as under a railing cap or under the nose of a stair tread to create a line of light. They can be mounted on the upper side of framing boards to create a soft glow on the roof structure of a pavilion or a covered walkway.

Some low-voltage strip lights use weatherproof sockets or add weatherproofing to protect the lamp base and socket connection so that the lamp does not have to be in an enclosure. This type of strip light could be used when mounting on a trellis structure woven in with a vine or around a decorative element.

Fiber Optics

Fiber optics consist of a light source in a housing and solid glass or plastic fibers of extremely high quality typically bound together in bundles to transmit light from one point to another. This allows the actual light source and fixture or *illuminator* to be remotely located in an easily accessible, weatherproof location. Light travels through the bundles by internal reflection to the location where light is desired. Common uses of fiber optics include spa and pool lights, mounting under pool coping to create an outline of a pool, embedding in the paving at the edge of a driveway, or using individual fibers to create a sparkle in a water feature (see Figures 7.22 & 19.18).

Custom Fixtures

In some instances, an off-the-shelf product might not exist that fits the need of a project from an appearance or functional standpoint. Modifications can often be made to standard products, or one of the design team members may design a custom fixture (see Figure 7.23). Typically, custom fixtures will cost more than standard products, but on projects requiring a large number of fixtures, the cost may not be significantly higher.

ACCESSORIES

All fixtures require an accessory of one type or another. Accessories include electrical components necessary to allow a lamp to function properly, mounting devices, materials that change a lamp's beam pattern or color, and materials that shield lamp brightness from view.

Ballast

All fluorescent and HID sources require a ballast for the lamp to function properly. The ballast initially provides the voltage needed to start the lamp (ranging from 1,800 to 5,000 volts for high pressure sodium). Once an arc is struck between a lamp's electrodes, the ballast also regulates the current so that the lamp does not destroy itself.

Ballasts are typically quite large and their location needs to be planned. An HID ballast can range in size from roughly 2½ by 2½ inches up to 4½ by 6 inches and sometimes larger. In some cases, the ballast will be an integrated fixture component. In many cases, the lamp housing does not have room for the ballast. In this case, the ballast can be located in the shaft of the fixture pole, in the base of the pole, mounted below grade in an accessible box, or remoted to a location inside a building. Check the manufacturer's catalog information for the maximum distances that the ballast can be remoted from the lamp compartment and the size wire that will be required for the distance away from the lamp. Ground-mounted fixtures often locate the ballast in a below-grade ballast compartment adjacent to the fixture. Whenever a ballast will be located below grade the ballast should be potted in epoxy to eliminate water problems. Always check with local inspectors to see if below-grade mounting will be allowed.

The National Electrical Code (NEC) requires ballasts to be easily accessible for maintenance. Ballasts also require ventilation to avoid overheating. Ventilation can be provided by allowing for air space around the ballast or locating it in a room where the temperature will not be abnormally high. Normal ballast operating temperature should not exceed 194°F/90°C. At this temperature a typical ballast will function for approximately 12 years. A 20°F/7°C (approximate) increase in temperature will shorten life by 50 percent, and a similar temperature decrease can double life. For outdoor use of fluorescent lamps, the designer must select a ballast that will continue to start the lamp at whatever low temperatures will be experienced at the site. For example, most compact fluorescent lamps above 9 watts require an ambient temperature of 32°F/0°C, and the lower-wattage lamps can operate at 0°F/–18°C. Ballast manufacturers list the minimum starting temperatures in their catalogs.

Transformer

This device changes the voltage from the main power source to supply a lamp with either a lower or a higher

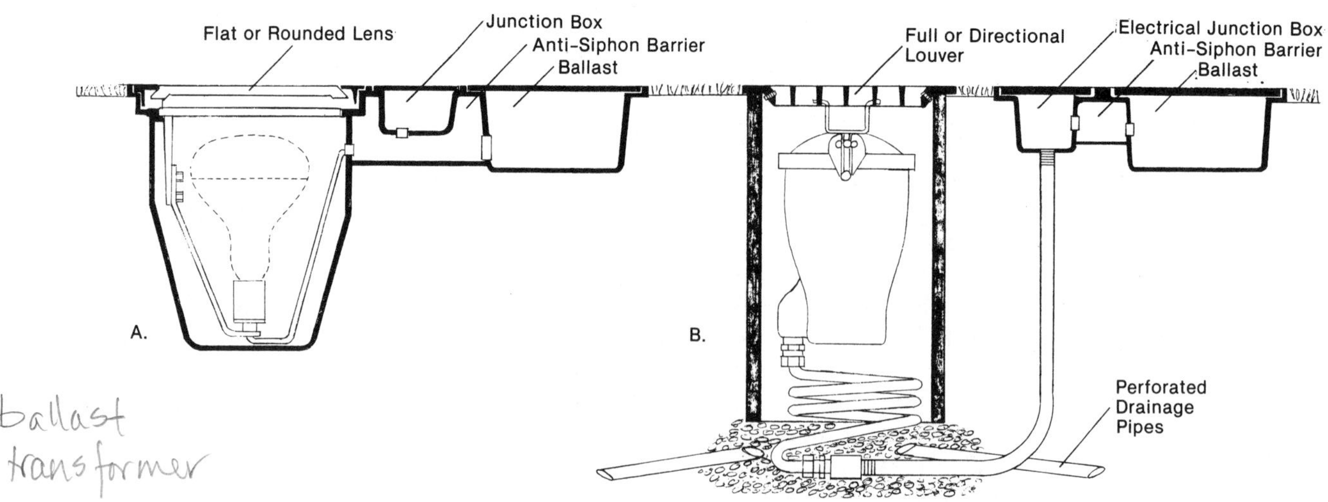

Figure 7.14. *Examples of a direct-burial fixture (A) and a well fixture (B). Drawing: Lezlie Johannessen.*

voltage. Low-voltage incandescent lamps require lowering the voltage provided by the power company. In landscape lighting, most low-voltage incandescent lamps use 12 volts. However, some of the subminiature lamps used in strip lighting require 24 volts and some PAR36 lamps need 5.5 volts. Some fluorescent lamps can operate at lower voltages as well. Having the option of driving compact fluorescent lamps at 12 volts is helpful in projects where the remainder of the equipment will be 12 volts. Neon and cold cathode sources require an increase in voltage typically to between 5,000 and 15,000 volts from that provided by the power company to function properly.

In some cases, the transformer will be located inside the fixture housing and supplying the proper voltage to one lamp only. In this case, 120 volts is supplied to the transformer at the fixture location and the transformer then reduces the voltage it supplies to the lamp. Using a fixture with an integral transformer is beneficial in retrofit situations when 120-volt power exists at a specific location, but the wiring back to the electrical panel is not accessible.

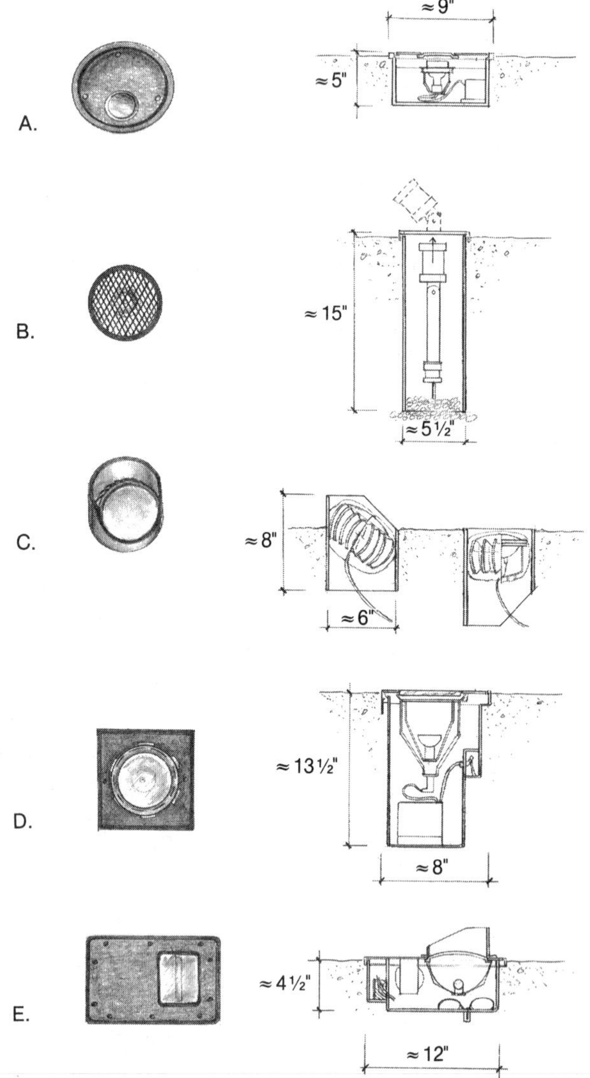

Figure 7.15. *Examples of below-grade fixtures. The size, shape, and construction of below-grade fixtures varies. A, B, & D all show units for MR16 lamps. Note the difference in size and lamp recess location between A & D. B allows the inner lamp housing to come up above grade when necessary for aiming. C shows a PAR36 lamp fixture that can have its housing mounted facing up or down to provide either a better aiming angle with built-in backside shielding or a straight uplight version. E shows an example of an HID direct-burial fixture; this one uses an HQI metal halide lamp. Drawing: Lezlie Johannessen.*

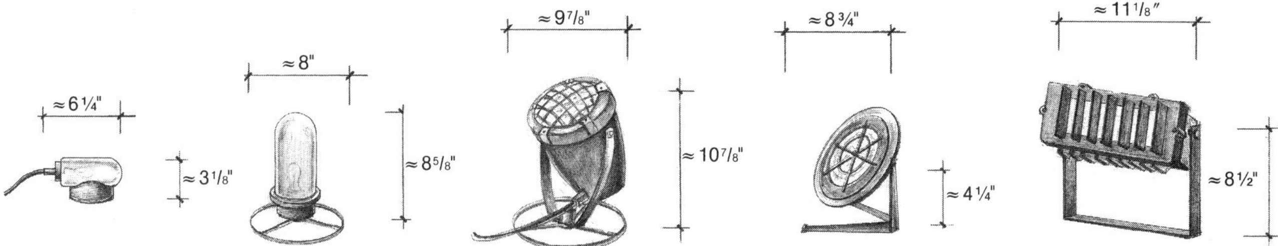

Figure 7.16. Examples of submersible accent fixtures. The first two are fixed types and are used primarily for creating a glow in the water. The last three show various adjustable units. Drawing: Lezlie Johannessen.

A more economical use of transformers is to use one transformer for multiple fixtures (see the wiring examples in Chapter 10). In this case, the transformer can be mounted in an interior weatherproof space such as a garage or pool equipment building, outside above grade in a weatherproof housing, or below grade in a weatherproof housing. Some of these transformers are available with integrated time switches, on-off switches, photocells, and dimming capabilities.

Whenever a transformer can be located inside, it invariably will save money for a project, as weatherproof transformers can be as much as four times the cost of interior-type units. Interior transformers also make the initial installation and maintenance of the transformer easier. Sometimes, however, the interior location is too far from a fixture or a group of fixtures to provide the appropriate voltage (see Figure 10.6). In this case, the transformer must be located outdoors and a weatherproof type is used. Outdoor transformers should always be placed out of view, but in an accessible location for maintenance. Mounting transformers below grade makes installation, waterproofing, and maintenance difficult. It is best to avoid below-grade installation locations if possible.

The capacity rating of a transformer is listed typically by kilovolt-amperes (kVA). One volt-ampere is roughly equal to 1 watt. Therefore, an 0.5 kVA transformer translates to a 500-watt transformer. Interior transformers are typically available in 60, 100, 150, 250, 500, 750, 1,000, and 1,500 watts. Outdoor transformers are typically available in 100, 200, 250, 300, and 500 watts.

Mounting Boxes

When a fixture is attached to a building or tree it requires a mounting box. This device serves not only as the attachment mechanism, but also as the electrical connection box (see Figure 10.12). All 120-volt equipment requires a junction box, which should, if possible, be recessed into the structure to minimize the size of the overall fixture assembly (see Figure 16.14). A surface-mounted box adds size to the fixture and makes a clean appearance more difficult to achieve (see Figure 7.24). For low-voltage fixtures, manufacturers offer smaller mounting covers that complement the fixture's appearance (see Figure 7.25).

Fixtures mounted at grade also require a mounting device. Some fixtures have an integral mounting box, but for many fixtures the manufacturer lists the fixture head separately from mounting accessories so that the designer can specify the appropriate mounting device for the location where the fixture will be used. For 120-volt equipment this must be a junction box, either an above-grade or below-grade model. The NEC requires that all above-grade boxes be located above finished grade and a maximum of 18 inches above the soil line (unless additional support for the box is provided—see Figure 7.26). Above-grade units should be used only where a fixture will be located in among shrubs taller than the box itself.

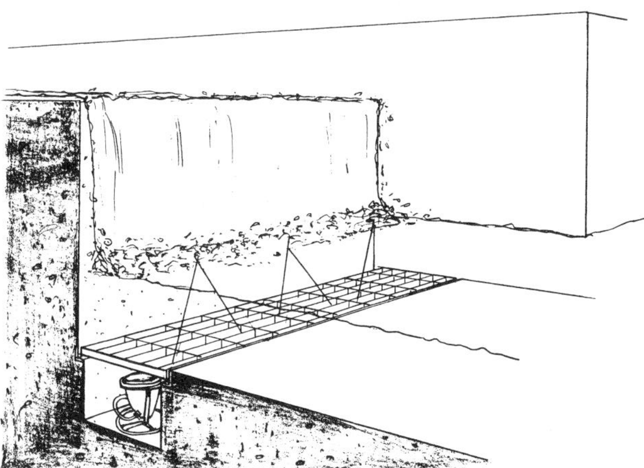

Figure 7.17. Creating a trough in the floor of a body of water minimizes the appearance of multiple submersible accent fixtures and their wiring. Drawing: Lezlie Johannessen.

Figure 7.18. Example of an underwater niche fixture. Photograph courtesy of Hydrel.

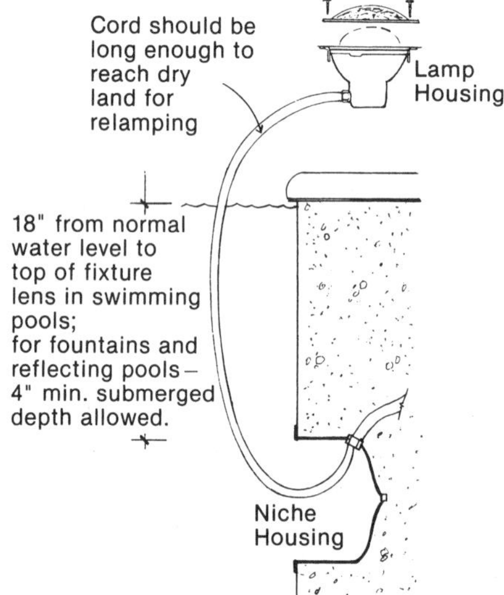

Figure 7.19. Typical detail of an underwater niche fixture. Drawing: Lezlie Johannessen.

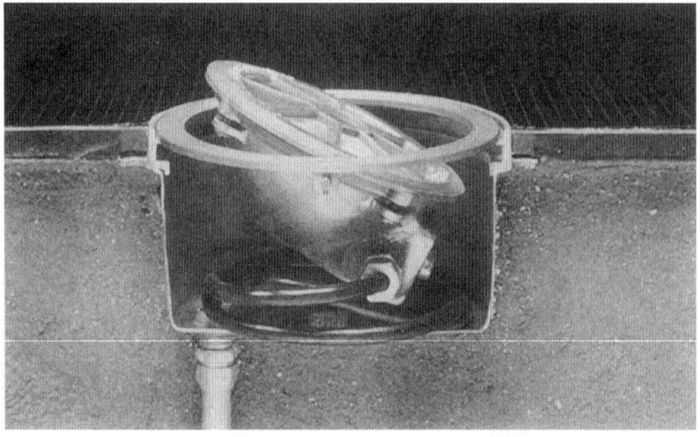

Figure 7.20. Example of an adjustable underwater niche fixture. Photograph courtesy of Hydrel.

Below-grade junction boxes present a cleaner look. However, they are significantly more expensive due to the materials and construction required to withstand the severe corrosion potential to which the device will be exposed. Boxes made from both metal and PVC are available. All 120-volt equipment should be mounted on metal boxes for stability and to provide for grounding. PVC boxes, which are less expensive than metal boxes, can be used as intermediate wiring boxes when required (see Figures 10.2 & 10.21D & E). Once again, the designer needs to be familiar with local code requirements. Some states, such as Massachusetts, do not allow below-grade connections.

Mounting Stakes

Above-grade low-voltage fixtures for can be mounted on a stake. Stakes vary in their shape and size (see Figures 7.27 & 7.28), as well as in the materials used to construct them. The standard materials include aluminum (finished with a protective coating) and PVC. Some PVC stakes are made thinner in cross section with a sharper point at the end. This makes them easier to use in compacted soils. A wider cross section adds stability in loose or sandy soils.

Fixtures often need to be raised as plantings grow. This requires the flexibility to increase the height of a stake. Some manufacturers provide stems in various lengths, prethreaded with a female connection on one end and a male connection on the other end. These can be added to the initial stake as required. Other manufacturers offer stakes that are adjustable in height (see Figures 4.31 & 7.27).

Shrouds

Some fixtures offer a shroud as an accessory. This is a shielding device that attaches to the front of the fixture housing to block lamp brightness (see Figures 14.1 & 14.2). The shape and size of these devices vary from manufacturer to manufacturer. Some shrouds require drainage. When using shrouds of this type, ensure that the drainage hole is located at the fixture's low point (see Figures 7.29 & 7.30).

Louvers

Frequently, fixtures require the addition of a louver to shield lamp brightness. Many manufacturers have settled on a product called Honeylite (Nova Industries), which uses a honeycomb configuration. The honeycomb-type louver provides either a 45° or a 60° shielding angle, depending on the depth of the material and size of the openings. Custom sizes and shapes can be made to fit almost any fixture.

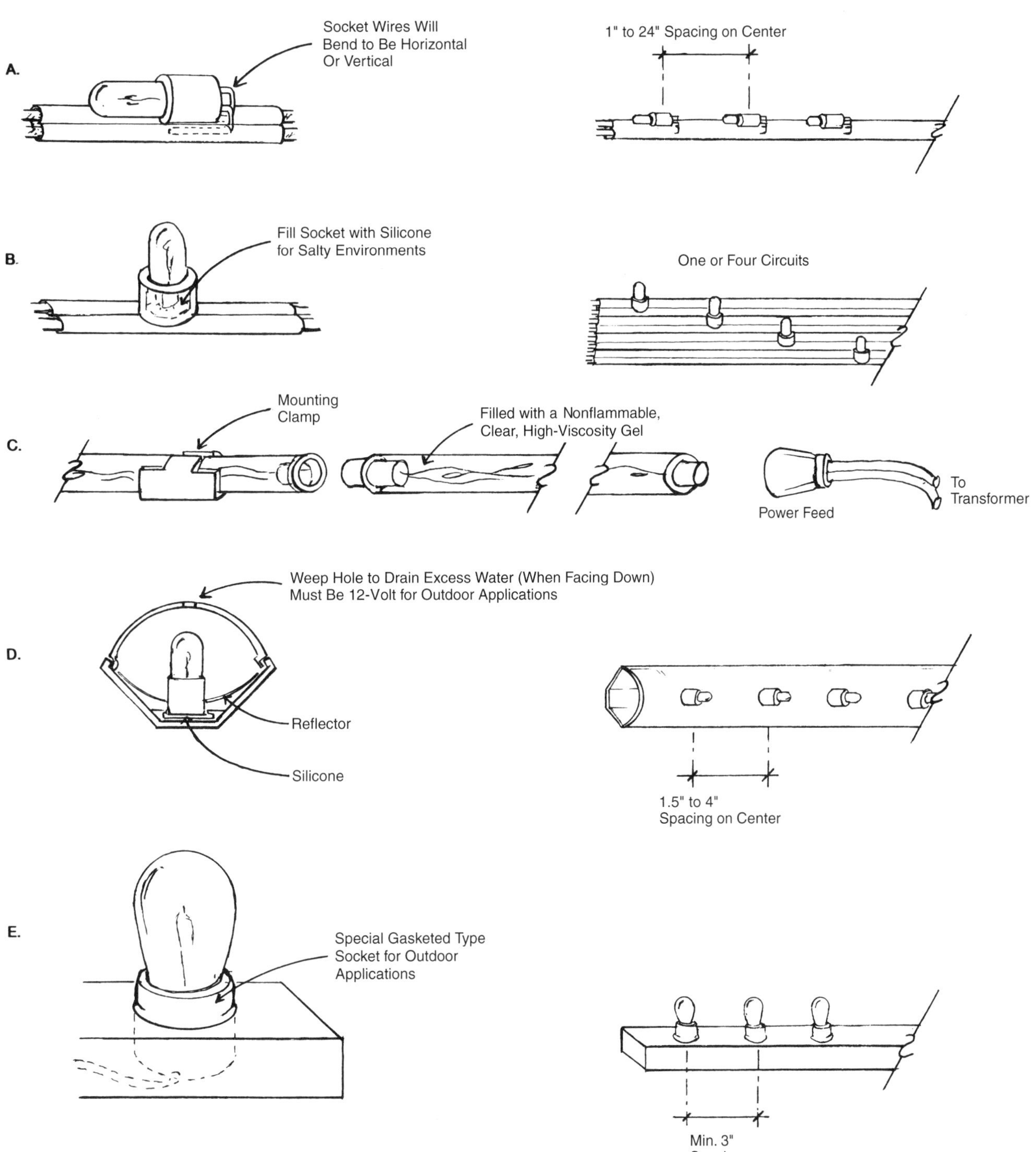

Figure 7.21. *Examples of open and closed strip lights. Examples A through D are all either 12- or 24-volt types. E is a 120-volt version. Drawing: Lezlie Johannessen.*

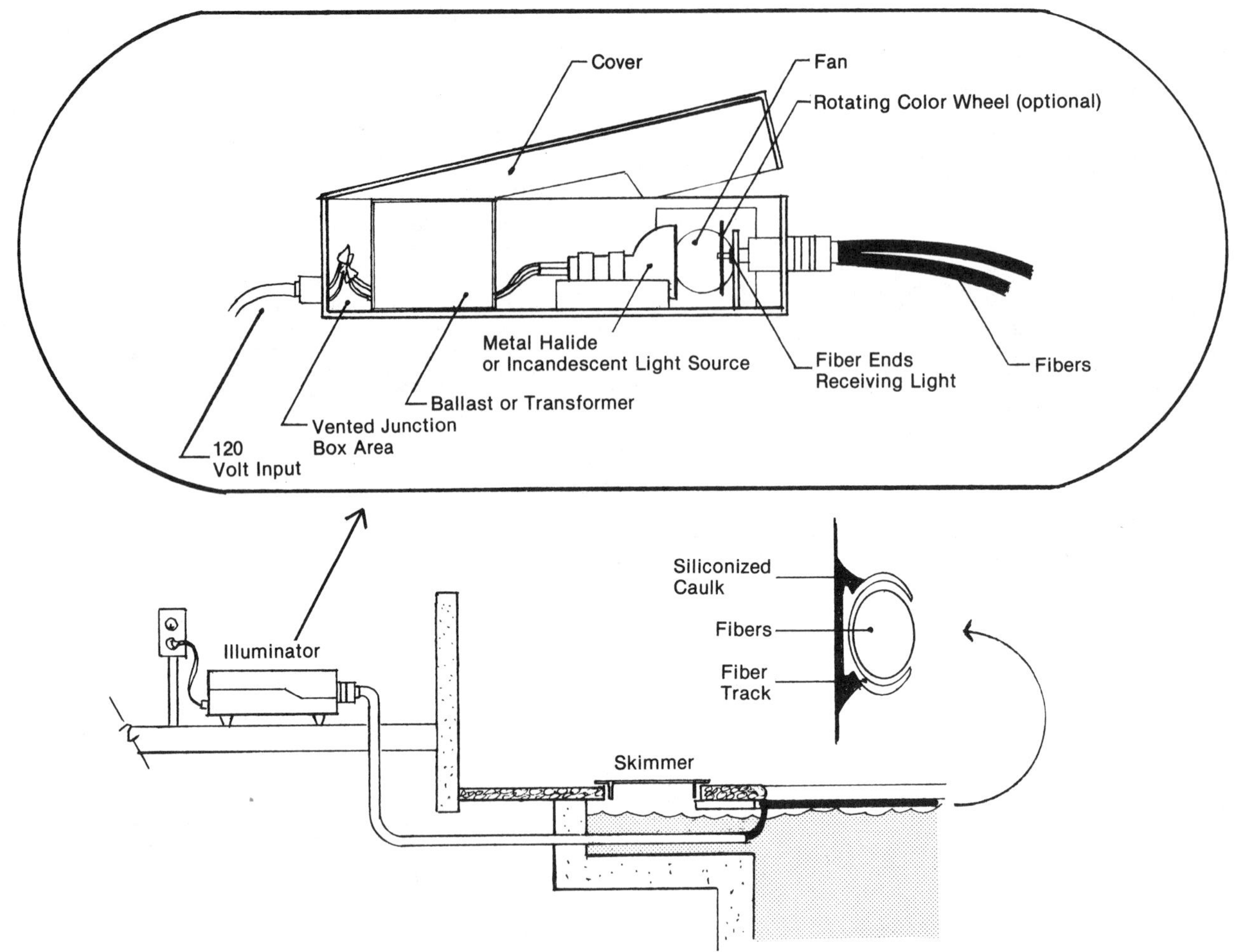

Figure 7.22. *Example of a fiber-optic fixture, called an illuminator, and the fiber-optic tubing system used for a pool. Drawing: Lezlie Johannessen.*

Lenses

Lenses serve two purposes in landscape fixtures. First, for some decorative fixtures, they enclose the housing and provide a glow of horizontal light. The selection of lens material is critical to maintain brightness balance throughout the site. When the lamp is located directly behind the lens, rather than hidden, lamp wattage and lens material must be coordinated to minimize lamp brightness. If the designer prefers to use a clear glass that makes the lamp visible, the lamp wattage must be kept low enough to avoid having the lamp become the brightest object in the composition. Whenever possible, a translucent lens should be selected. This helps soften the effect of the lamp brightness. The lens material needs to be as thick as possible, preferably 3⁄16 inch or thicker, to ensure that the lamp image will not be visible inside the fixture. Most art glass is not available in a thickness above 1⁄8 inch, but some is available in 3⁄16-inch thickness. Another type of glass, flashed opal, is made from two layers of glass. One is a clear layer and the other is white glass. In this case, the thickness of the glass does not affect the translucency, and the thinner 1⁄8 inch is preferable to minimize cost.

The second function of lenses is to change the beam distribution of the lamp. Some manufacturers offer two standard types as an accessory option: a spread lens called Crystal No. 73 or Prismatic, and a linear spread lens called Skytex. These are made from soda-lime glass, which does not have high heat resistance. For any lamp that gets extremely hot, for example, 75-watt MR16 lamps, the lens will need to be heat treated. A spread lens roughly doubles the lamp's beamspread and quarters its light output. The linear spread lens takes the lamp's round beamspread and changes it into a linear shape. Another spread-type lens available is called Solite. This is a high-transmission soda-lime glass that eliminates the green tint of the standard soda-lime glasses, which is useful when color is critical. If the manufacturer does not offer these as accessories, the designer can specify cus-

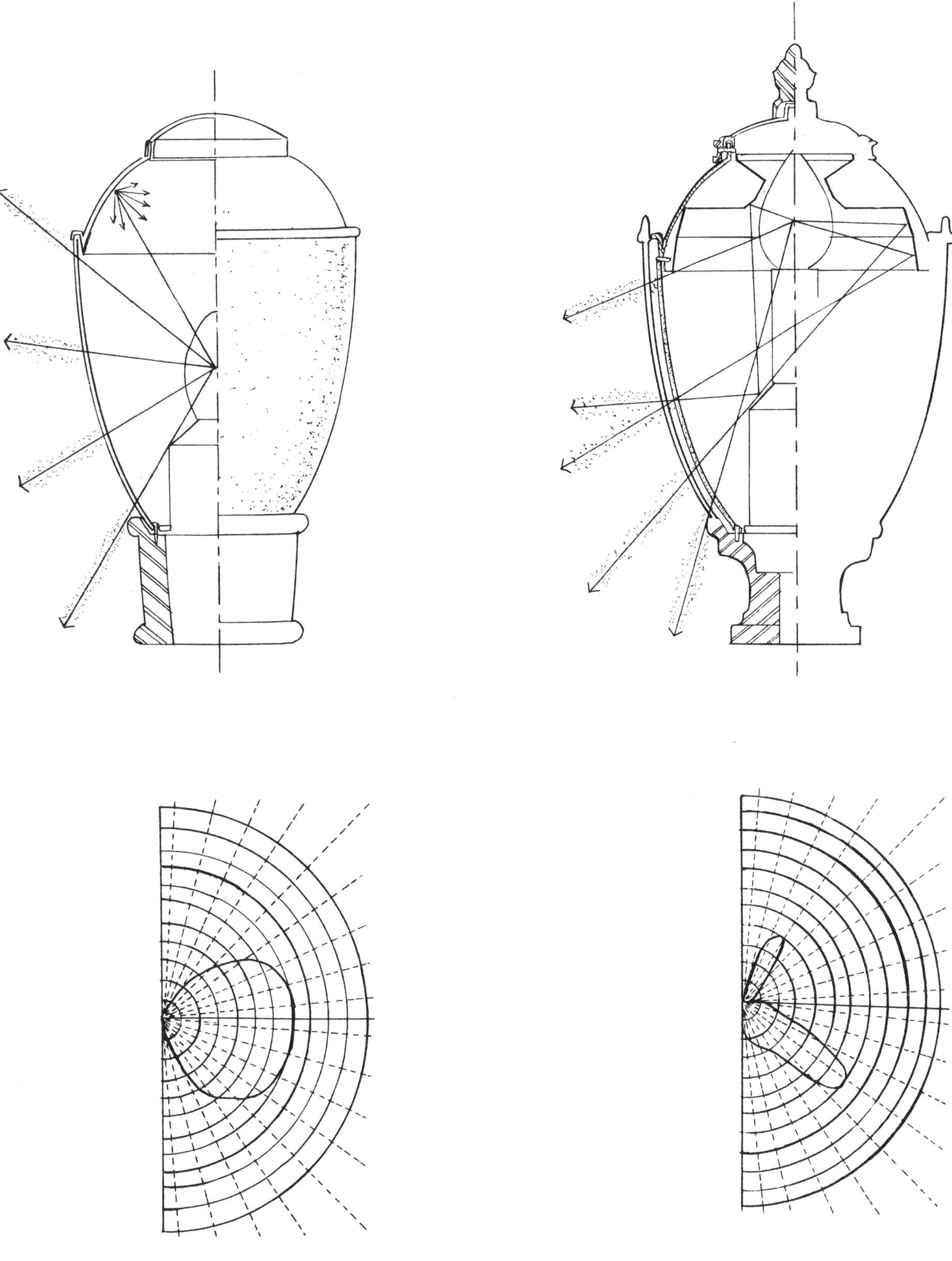

BEFORE MODIFICATION AFTER MODIFICATION

Figure 7.23. Before and after drawings of the fixture head and photometric distribution of the Battery Park fixture. The revised fixture design moved the lamp up into the top of the fixture so that it is not visible in the lens. The optics designed for the new version controlled the distribution in a more effective pattern with less glare. Lighting and Fixture Design: H.M. Brandston & Partners, Inc.

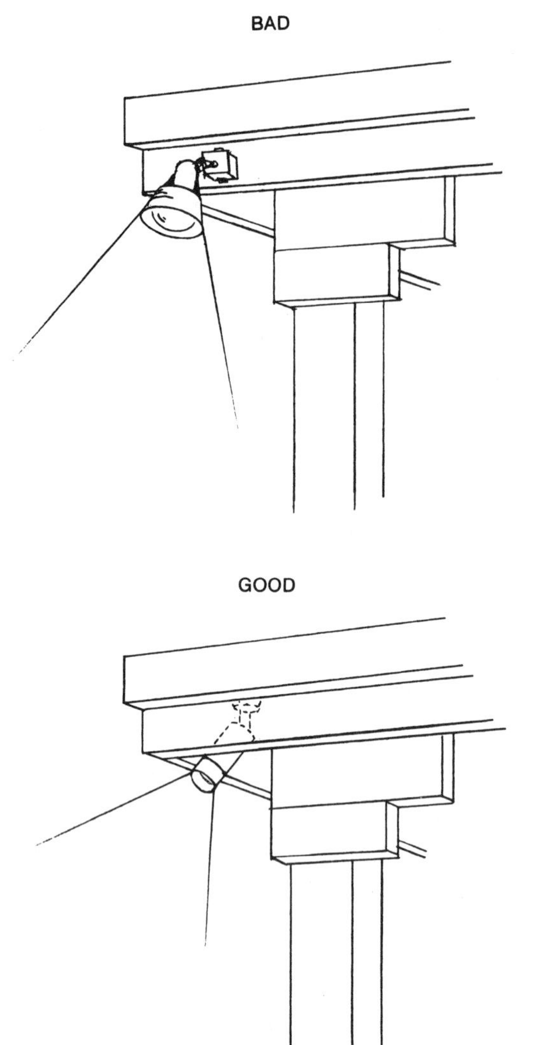

Figure 7.24. *Integrating the mounting of a fixture into an architectural structure minimizes the visual effect of the fixture. Drawing: Lezlie Johannessen.*

tom sizes and shapes from glass companies and install them on the job site during focusing.

Color Media

In some cases, the designer may want to change the color of the light from a lamp. Two basic kinds of color filters are available: glass and polyester. Whenever heat will occur, for example with most incandescent and HID sources, glass filters must be used to provide a lasting effect. The polyester filters will fade, scorch, and eventually burn through or dry out, cracking into pieces. When fluorescent sources or fiber optics are used, polyester color filters are adequate because they will be exposed to relatively little heat. Polyester filters are available from manufacturers of theatrical filter materials.

Several types of colored glass are available, including dichroic-coated and regular or art glass. Dichroic-coated glass transmits one color and reflects all other colors. This makes the transmitted color purer. Regular or art glass is available in a wider range of colors but needs to be heat treated. When used in larger than a 5-inch size it will need to be cut into strips, which are held together in a frame (to avoid breaking from expansion and contraction due to the alternate heating and cooling it will be exposed to from the adjacent lamp). Color correction lenses are also available, including booster and cosmetic types. The booster types increase color temperature, making the light appear cooler. This is sometimes used with incandescent lamps to make them produce a color closer to moonlight. Cosmetic lenses decrease color temperature and are used to match the warmer color of incandescent lamps.

SAFETY

The primary sources for safety information and requirements for outdoor lighting fixtures include electrical codes written to regulate fixture construction and installation, the labels that can be applied to fixtures verifying compliance with the safety standards required in codes, and tests done to determine compliance.

Codes

Codes vary from country to country, and within the United States from state to state and city to city. The National Electrical Code (see "Safety" in Chapter 10) sets a standard for the United States, but not all states have adopted it. Further, it sets the minimum standard. Local jurisdictions can write more stringent standards.

The NEC lists several definitions that are important to understand in specifying lighting fixtures:

- *Dry location*—primarily interior locations where fixtures will not be subject to dampness or wetness.
- *Damp location*—either an outdoor location where fixtures will be partially protected from precipitation, such as under roof overhangs, or inside in a space subject to moderate degrees of moisture, such as some basements.
- *Wet location*—outside locations where a fixture will be exposed to weather or subject to saturation with water or other liquids.
- *Rainproof*—when a fixture is constructed to prevent water from interfering with normal operation.
- *Raintight*—when a fixture is constructed to prevent water entrance.

Each of these terms will be used by fixture manufacturers, and understanding what they mean helps a

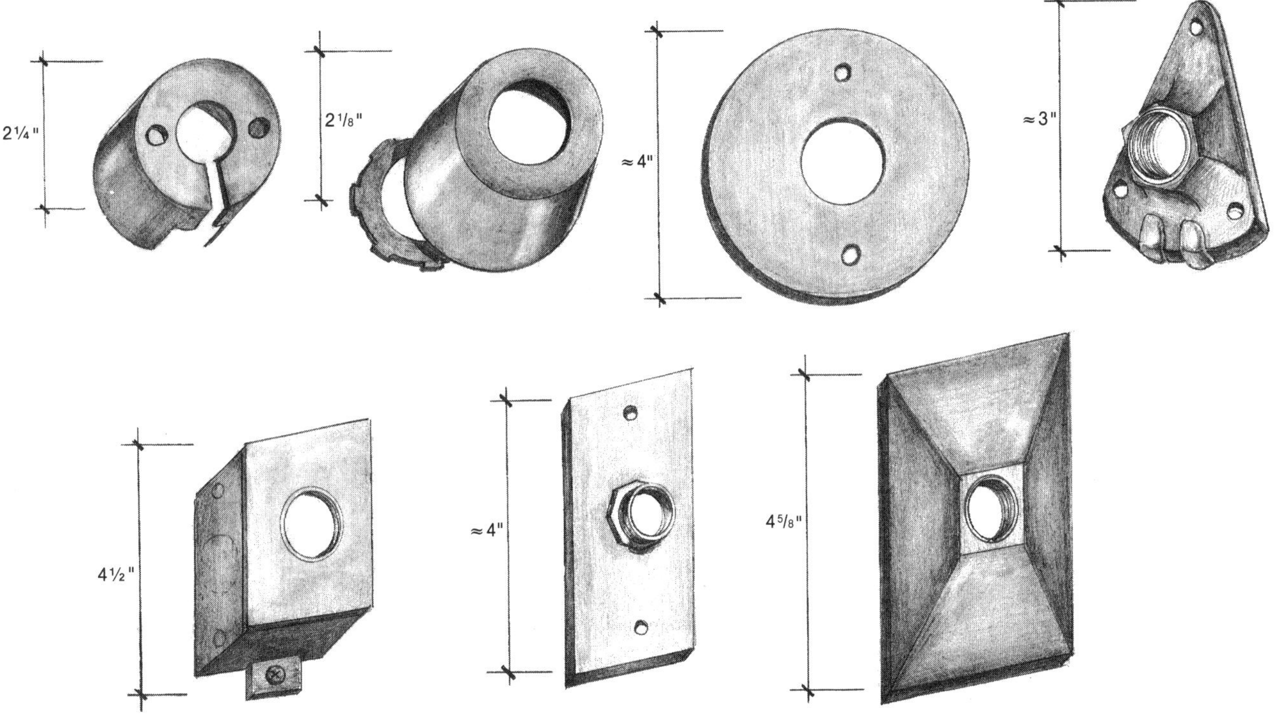

Figure 7.25. *Examples of mounting canopies. Drawing: Lezlie Johannessen.*

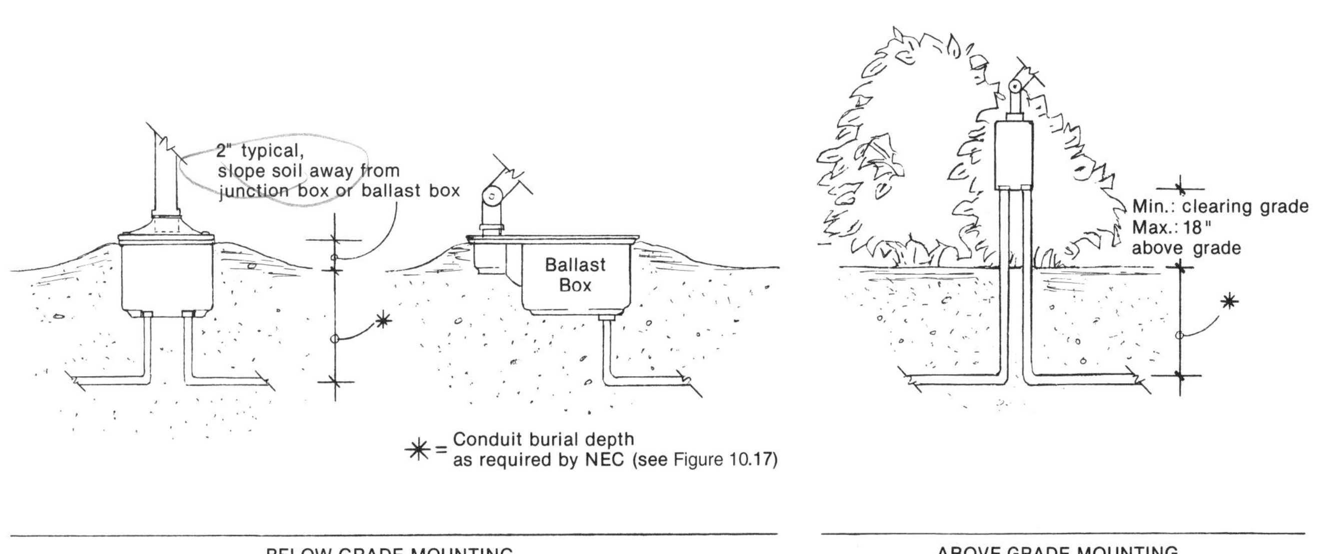

Figure 7.26. *Examples of below-grade junction and ballast boxes and above-grade mounting of junction boxes. Drawing: Lezlie Johannessen.*

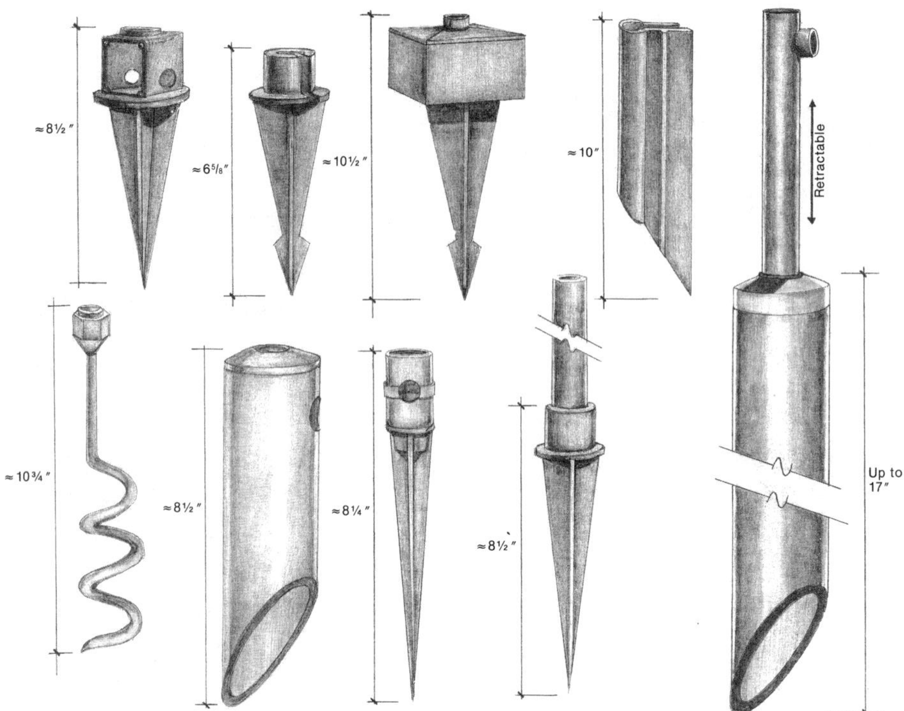

Figure 7.27. Examples of stakes. Drawing: Lezlie Johannessen.

Figure 7.28. The three prongs on this stainless steel stake provide incredible stability while allowing easy movement as fixtures need to respond to garden change. Photograph: Janet Lennox Moyer.

designer to know if the fixture will be suitable for a specific use or location. A further discussion of the NEC is included in Chapter 10.

Labels

Fixtures running at 120 volts or higher that will be used outdoors must comply with the normal standards for incandescent (UL1571), fluorescent (UL1570), or HID (UL1572) fixtures and with either the *damp* or *wet* location requirements by meeting standards set by Underwriters' Laboratories (UL). The designer needs to be familiar with state and local codes. For example, some jurisdictions do not recognize the designation "damp location." In most states, the local inspector decides what is a damp or wet location. UL has a separate standard for underwater equipment, UL676. UL has prepared a standard, UL1838, which covers all low-voltage landscape lighting systems.

Various testing laboratories, including UL and Environmental Testing Laboratory (ETL), test fixtures submitted by manufacturers and provide the manufacturers with labels that are applied to the fixture certifying compliance. A fixture that has been tested will have a testing laboratory label attached to its housing showing which UL standard it meets. Further, when a fixture is meant to be used in a damp or wet location and passes the testing for that standard, the fixture will

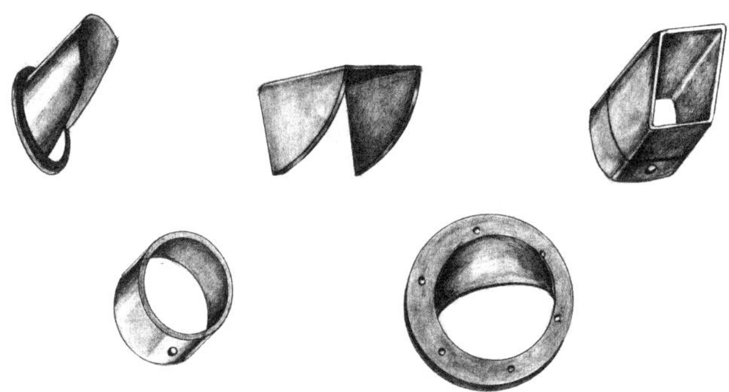

Figure 7.29. Examples of shrouds. Drawing: Lezlie Johannessen.

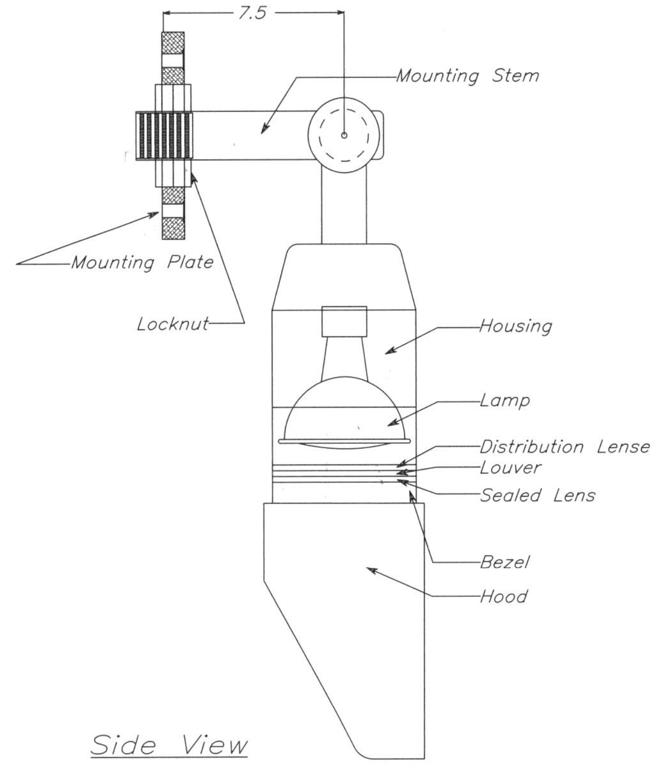

Figure 7.30. This side view of a typical low-voltage MR16 fixture shows a deeply recessed lamp, the order in which distribution accessories should be installed, and the furthest placement of an angled hood. Drawing: Michael Stewart Hooker, MSH Visual Planners.

have a label that clearly states "suitable for damp location" or "suitable for wet location."

All fixtures, including custom fixtures, must comply with these standards. The process of submitting a fixture to a testing laboratory is costly and time-consuming. Manufacturers must do it for their standard catalog units and factor the cost into their anticipated volume of fixtures. However, for a limited run of custom fixtures, field testing makes more sense than the standard laboratory testing in some cases. A field-tested fixture will not have a normal certification label but one that states "field-tested," showing that it meets the requirements for the specific location.

These labels only address the electrical safety of the fixture. They do not evaluate the quality of materials used or the construction quality of the fixture. The designer must determine the needs for each fixture to be specified and evaluate if a specific fixture meets these requirements.

Testing

The basic testing a fixture needs to pass to be approved for outdoor use falls into two categories: damp and wet locations. The testing and compliance requirements are the same for incandescent, fluorescent, and HID fixtures and can be referenced in UL1571. Fixtures that will be used underwater must meet the testing requirements in UL676.

Because low-voltage fixtures are not currently regulated, not all manufacturers have had their fixtures tested. If the fixtures do not have a label showing that they meet UL safety requirements, the designer should request documentation from the manufacturer showing that they meet the safety standards for outdoor fixtures.

Damp Location Requirements

For damp locations, all metal parts of a fixture must be protected from corrosion and the electrical insulation materials used must be of the nonabsorptive type, such as porcelain.

Wet Location Requirements

The requirements for wet locations are in addition to the damp location requirements. This section of UL1571 lists minimum acceptable coating thicknesses for various types of finishes. It requires that the fixture enclosure prevent wetting of electrical components or wiring (unless the fixture is identified for use in contact with water). The fixture lens must pass a 3-pound impact test. Gaskets and lenses must pass heat testing and thermal-shock testing. These tests ensure that the gasket retains its shape and does not compress and lose its ability to provide a waterproof seal. These tests also ensure that the lens does not lose its shape or break when subjected to cold water. The fixture must be subjected to a rain, sprinkler, or

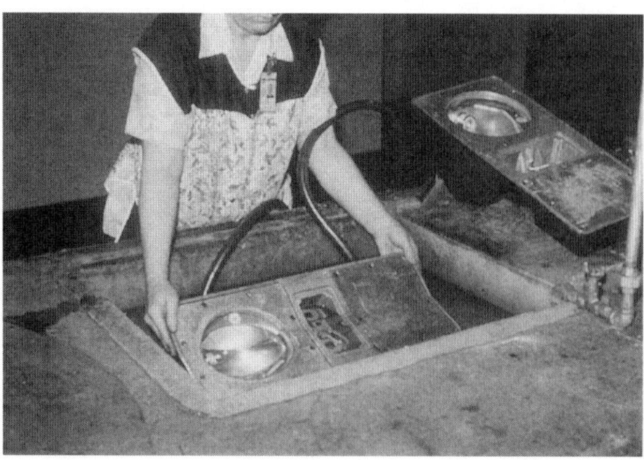

Figure 7.31. *Example of a fixture being immersed to test whether it is waterproof. Photograph courtesy of Kim Lighting.*

immersion test based on where the fixture will be located outdoors.

Below-grade fixtures must pass the immersion test. This test has a cycle of turning the fixture on for 3½ hours, then turning the fixture off and submerging the fixture in 1 foot of 41°F/5°C water for 4 hours. This procedure is then repeated twice with the fixture in a dry location for 16½ hours between cycles. The fixture passes the test if no water enters the housing (see Figure 7.31).

The rain and sprinkler tests follow a similar sequence of events with the lamp and water alternating on and off for specific time periods. The fixture passes the test if no water enters the housing. Fixtures with drain holes are allowed to have water entry as long as no inherently nonwaterproof parts are wetted. Fixtures mounted more than 4 feet above grade must pass the rain test, where water is sprayed down onto the fixture. Fixtures mounted below 4 feet above grade must pass the sprinkler test, which sprays water up at the fixture. Some fixtures are exempted from these tests when the fixture's construction shows that water cannot inherently enter the fixture.

Underwater Requirements

The operating conditions, construction requirements, and testing procedures for fixtures intended to be submerged are far more stringent than for wet locations. UL676 prescribes the type of materials and conditions that housings, lenses, and gaskets must meet to ensure a waterproof fixture that will not cause shock to a person entering the same water where the fixture is located. This standard covers issues including, but not limited to, wiring, accessibility, bonding, grounding, drainage and water leakage, lamp overheating protection, impact resistance, strain-relief requirements for all cords attached to the housing, and saltwater resistance. To ensure that a fixture is waterproof, the immersion test requires that it pass a sequence of turning the lamp on and off in half-hour cycles for 6 hours. The fixture fails if any water enters the housing.

Salt Spray Tests

UL does not have a standard for salt spray testing, as salt does not affect the safety of the fixture. Designers should require that all outdoor fixtures they use be tested for resistance to salt, especially for geographic areas with high salt content in the air or in the soil. The requirements for this testing vary based on the type of base metal and applied finish. Salt spray tests typically subject fixtures to a 5 percent salt solution that is sprayed onto the fixture at a specific temperature and rate for a specific number of hours. The time periods vary from 24 hours to over 1,000 hours. In the lighting industry, most fixtures are tested for a minimum of 1,000 hours. Failure criteria are based on the materials tested. For example, more than five pits visible to the eye or through a magnifying glass will fail aluminum. A powder coat finish fails if corrosion creeps more than $\frac{1}{32}$ inch from a line scored through the coating. Several organizations produce specifications for these tests, with some being more stringent than others.

Scratch Test

A scratch test or wet-tape test is conducted for powder coat and other applied finishes to see if the top coating adheres to the prime coat. This consists of scoring the coating in a crosshatch pattern, soaking for 24 hours, and then applying a tape to the surface. If portions of the finish adhere to the tape, the finish fails the test. Some versions of this test also check adherence prior to soaking and can fail the finish at that point.

Selecting and specifying fixtures requires attention to many issues at once. In the end, designers must evaluate each fixture planned for a project to ensure that the fixture quality meets the project needs. The fixture must be able to stand up to the environment and any abuse to justify its being selected. Materials, construction methods, and safety requirements for fixtures continue to change. Designers needs to keep abreast of the changes in order to provide their clients with the correct equipment.

8

Corrosion, Materials, and Finishes

Chapter 6 identified the types of fixtures used in outdoor lighting and discussed functional considerations to think about when selecting a fixture. This chapter will address three additional issues regarding fixture selection: *corrosion, material properties,* and *finishes.* Once the designer understands how destructive the outdoor environment is, the importance of examining site conditions and knowing what materials and finishes a manufacturer uses in making fixtures becomes clear. No one material is perfect for all situations due to varying durability, corrosion resistance, and cost. Exposure to the environment—sunlight, atmosphere, temperature, soil, water, and wind—can damage or destroy both a fixture's appearance and function. Ultraviolet radiation from the sun can fade a fixture's color affecting its aesthetic appearance. Chemicals, soil characteristics, water conditions, and pollutants can attack a fixture leading to rusting (see Figure 8.1), staining, leaking, or structural disintegration (see Figure 8.2).

When a designer sits down to specify fixtures for a project, corrosion resistance is probably the most important factor to consider. While there can be no question that physical appearance and function are critical issues, if the fixture cannot withstand environmental decaying forces, the lighting effects will not last and the client will not be well served.

Corrosion potential starts with site conditions (chemical makeup of the soil and water) and environmental conditions (temperature, temperature variation, normal humidity, rainfall, soil drainage, and amount and velocity of wind). It ends with material selection and fixture design to minimize or eliminate negative corrosion effects. Corrosion resistance varies according to the combination of materials selected, finishes implemented, fixture design, and site conditions. This chapter will look at corrosion—how it occurs, the damage it causes, and how to prevent it—and will then discuss the strengths and weaknesses of materials and finishes used for outdoor lighting equipment.

CORROSION

Corrosion occurs when lighting equipment is exposed to oxygen (see Figure 8.3), water, acids, and salts. Obviously, since fixtures are outdoors, they will get wet from rain, dew, fog, splash from water features (fountains or streams), and irrigation. Adding exposure to acids or salts from either water or soil compounds, the likelihood increases that corrosion will take place. Essentially, this alerts designers that protection from corrosion is critical in the selection of fixtures.

The effect of corrosion varies from affecting the physical appearance of metal equipment to rendering the equipment nonfunctional. To fully understand the importance of potential corrosion on lighting equipment, lighting designers need to understand how corrosion occurs. There are three corrosive environments to consider—water, soil, and atmosphere. The following discussion examines corrosion types affecting lighting equipment and protection approaches to minimize or eliminate corrosion.

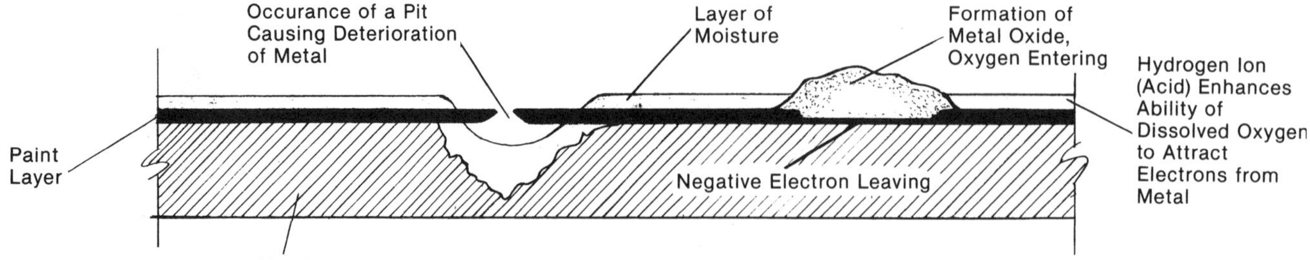

Figure 8.1. *Basic corrosion reaction. Corrosion consists of the gradual breakdown of a material by surface disintegration, including both physical and chemical interactions between the material and the surrounding environment. Fixture corrosion is primarily a chemical process in which the metal gives up electrons by reacting with another material. This leaves behind positively charged ions which easily dissolve in water and tend to combine with other negative ions near them, forming compounds such as metal salts or oxides. Common rust, shown here, is an iron oxide formed from the oxidation of iron. Drawing: Lezlie Johannessen.*

Water

The presence of water accelerates corrosion. The type of water, both fresh and salt water, and exposure time affect corrosion potential. Sites with constant wetting and drying cycles (areas with frequent rain, fog, or sprinklers) experience a higher rate of corrosion. Freshwater corrosiveness depends on oxygen concentration, pH value (see Figure 8.4 and discussion of pH below), and hardness (see Figure 8.3). Pollution in the atmosphere, such as acid rain, or direct pollution into the water can change the pH level, making it more corrosive. Clean salt water in open oceans has a relatively low corrosive potential. However, salt water in harbors and other areas near land can have much higher concentrations of pollutants, which increase corrosiveness.

Figure 8.2. *Remains of a below-grade fixture being removed from a city street. The impact of corrosion becomes obvious when seeing the complete disintegration that occurred.*

The best defense against corrosion from water is a strong finish for all fixtures except underwater fixtures. Also, select fixtures designed to encourage water runoff. For underwater applications the fixture needs to be manufactured from a stable metal such as bronze or brass.

Soil

Soil represents the largest concern for corrosion of lighting equipment for several reasons. First, the likelihood of the presence of water, salts, and other chemicals that encourage corrosion is high. Next, determining soil content is relatively difficult and soil makeup changes over time. Finally, fixtures located in soil or just above the soil line mounted on stakes or junction boxes constitute a large proportion of outdoor lighting equipment.

Soil is seldom homogeneous. It can vary in structure (see Chapter 1) both horizontally throughout the site and in depth. At the intersection of soil types corrosion of metals can occur (see Figure 8.5 & "Pitting Corrosion" below). Characteristics of soil will also change with the seasons, due to precipitation and dead plant material such as leaves, bark, and flowerheads. Corrosion in soil is influenced by four factors:

- *Presence of soil moisture.* Since water accelerates corrosion, its presence in soil aggravates other corrosion potential. Areas with high rainfall, irrigation systems, and bad drainage (clay soils are the worst) increase water content in soil. Even in geographical areas with drought seasons, water can be held above the water table by the soil particles. Avoid fixture contact with the natural water table.

MATERIALS, FINISH, AND CORROSION TERMINOLOGY	
ALLOY:	A metal combined with one or more additional elements.
CORROSION:	An electrochemical reaction of a metal exposed to water that changes the physical nature of the metal. This process requires an electrolyte—a fluid that conducts electricity. In landscape lighting, water is the normal electrolyte. Water conducts electricity readily, as it normally carries salt ions. These ions permit the transportation of electricity. Without ions in the water electricity would not be carried and corrosion would not occur. This process can also occur in the atmosphere due to humidity.
GALVANIZE:	The addition of a zinc coating by a hot dipping process providing corrosion protection. Zinc corrodes at a rate 30 times slower than steel. Additionally, when scratched, the zinc coating will corrode before the base metal. Coatings using a more noble material will cause the opposite effect of the base metal corroding first. Typically, this will cause pitting of the base metal.
HEAT TREATING:	This refers to a number of processes including tempering.
NOBLE:	The term identifying the corrodibility of a metal. The more noble a metal, the less active or likely to exchange ions it is (see Figure 7.4).
OXIDATION:	An electrochemical reaction of a metal, due to the loss of electrons, that changes the physical nature of the metal resulting in corrosion. The presence of oxygen is required, as it gains the electron(s) that the metal loses.
TEMPERING:	Heating a metal or glass and then quickly cooling. This reduces the brittleness of steel without significantly lowering hardness and strength. In glass it increases the ambient temperature the glass can withstand, as well as its resistance to shock impact.

Figure 8.3.

- *Oxygen supply.* Because the presence of oxygen accelerates corrosion, understanding how and where it occurs helps the designer know corrosion potential. The quantity of oxygen will be higher above the water table than below and will vary with soil type—high in sand, lower in clay. Movement of oxygen is greater through fine-grained soil and soil that has been disturbed by excavation (including the installation of electrical equipment). If a piece of equipment straddles two soil types with differing oxygen permeation characteristics, pitting can occur. When a fixture straddles the water table, localized corrosion can occur (see Figures 8.5 & 8.6).
- *pH value.* This expresses the acidity or alkalinity (see Figure 8.4) of a material, such as water or soil. Corrosion can occur in both alkaline (high pH) and acid (low pH) conditions, depending on the metal. A neutral pH will not cause corrosion. Reaction to pH of metals commonly used falls into one of three patterns:
  a. Iron and other acid-soluble metals have low resistance to high pH, high resistance to low pH, and a variable resistance in the middle range, based on how quickly the corrosion-producing agent can reach the metal surface (see Figure 8.3). An increase in temperature also increases iron's susceptibility to corrosion. Iron can be used for equipment such as junction boxes, where it will not be exposed to high temperatures, but it requires construction with thick walls and a galvanized or other type of protective coating.
  b. Aluminum and other metals that exhibit characteristics of both an acid and a base break down rapidly when exposed to either an acidic or alkaline solution. They exhibit resistance at pH 4 to 7 (see Figure 8.7). Aluminum is used extensively for fixture housings because it has high heat resistance, it is relatively inexpensive and easy to work with but it requires a strong protective coating to prevent corrosion.
  c. Gold and other nonreactive or noble (see Figure 8.3) metals are not appreciably affected by pH (see Figure 8.8). Although very expensive, in

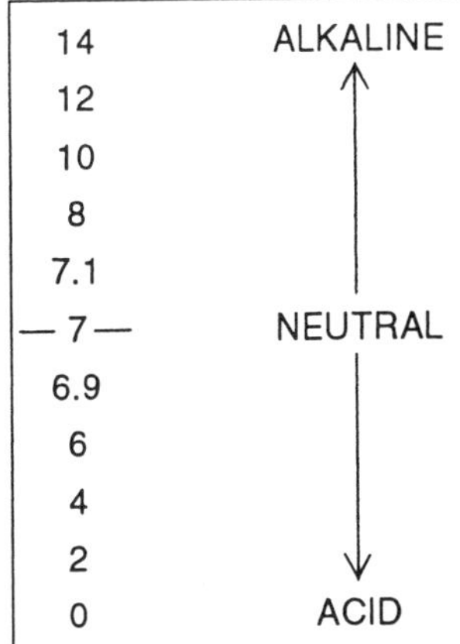

Figure 8.4. *pH chart. This is a measure of the acidity or alkalinity of water or soil expressed on this scale. With a range from 0 to 14, neutral occurs midway up the scale at 7 (based on 77°F/25°C). Moving along the scale from 7 to 0 indicates increasing acidity and from 7 to 14 indicates increasing alkalinity.*

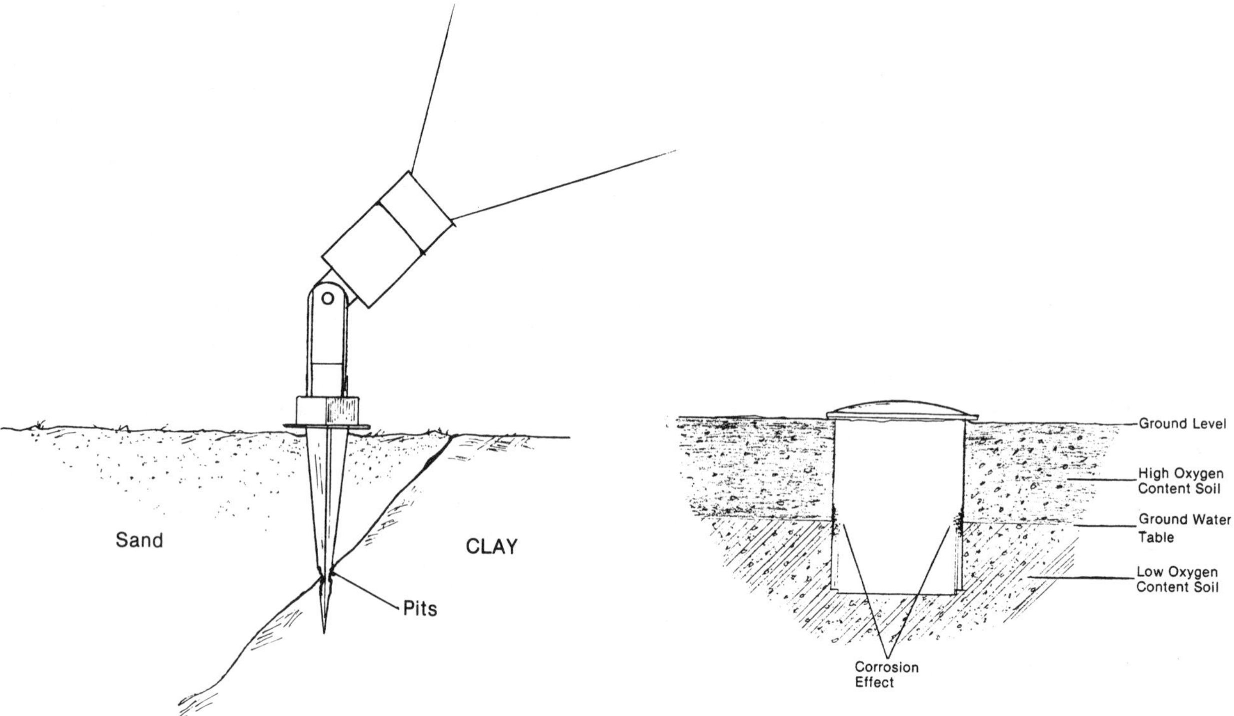

Figure 8.5. *Pitting corrosion occurs on metals at the intersection of two soil types. Drawing: Lezlie Johannessen.*

Figure 8.6. *Fixture or other metal straddling the water table encourages corrosion. Drawing: Lezlie Johannessen.*

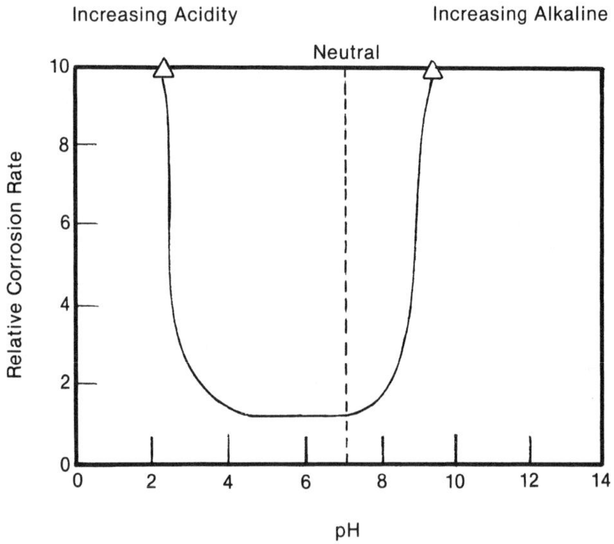

Figure 8.7. *Effect of pH on metals—that display the characteristics of both an acid and a base—including aluminum and zinc. Due to these metals' ability to form a protective coating, they will be protected from corrosion, between 4 and 8 pH. Adapted from F. Perry, Ed.,* Perry's Chemical Engineers Handbook, *6th ed., ©1984. Courtesy of McGraw-Hill, Inc.*

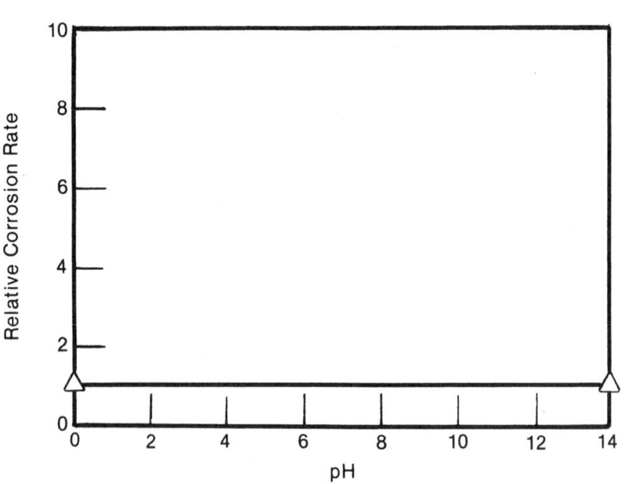

Figure 8.8. *Effect of pH on noble metals. These have strong corrosion resistance unaffected by pH. Adapted from F. Perry, Ed.,* Perry's Chemical Engineers Handbook, *6th ed., ©1984. Courtesy of McGraw-Hill, Inc.*

areas such as the Hawaiian Islands, where the atmosphere, water, and soil are extremely corrosive, brass is used consistently and gold is sometimes used for fixtures.

- *Temperature.* The rate of corrosion tends to accelerate with increased temperature. This is a cause for concern in selecting lighting fixtures, since they create significant heat while operating.

Prevention

The best protection for any metal located near soil or below-grade in soil is some kind of protective coating. The key is to seal the pores of the metal. For above-grade fixtures anodizing or powder coat painting constitute the most common finishes (see "Finishes" below).

For below-grade fixtures several options are available. An organic coating can be applied, such as bitumen, a form of plastic (including powder coat paint), or tape wrapping. An inorganic coating can be applied, including zinc, zinc–aluminum alloy, or concrete. On aluminum, a clear anodized coating as a base or prime coat with a baked enamel finish provides the strongest protection.

In addition to coating the metal, the fixture can be embedded in concrete. This provides separation from the soil. To be effective, however, the makeup of the concrete is critical, as not all concretes are corrosion resistant. Filling the area immediately surrounding the lighting equipment with sand or gravel helps minimize differences in oxygen supply from varying soil compositions but may not always be effective at reducing corrosion (see Figure 8.9).

Avoid locating fixtures in or near clay, slag, peat, or other soils rich in acid, sulfate, chloride, or organic matter. While general characteristics of the soil in a community may commonly be known, this type of information requires testing the soil (see Chapter 1). Without this precaution fixtures can disintegrate in some soils within two years.

Atmosphere

Three factors affect atmospheric corrosion: pollution, moisture, and temperature. Pollution causes problems primarily due to dirt or soot (containing acid) settling onto a fixture and ozone, a form of photochemical smog, which destroys paints and other rubber-based coatings.

Atmospheric corrosion requires moisture to cause a problem. The corrosion is caused due to dissolved substances in the water, including oxygen, sulfur oxides, sulfate, nitrogen oxides, carbon dioxide, chloride, and metal ions. At coastal locations, chloride is transported to metal surfaces as salt crystals from salt-

Figure 8.9. *This illustrates the importance of checking the concrete composition. Here, even though the metal fixture base was separated from soil, corrosion is occurring.*

water spray and from wind coming to shore over bodies of salt water. Both high humidity and precipitation (rain, snow, and irrigation splash) produce enough of a layer of water on a fixture for corrosion to occur. Cycles of wet and dry conditions further escalate corrosion rate.

An increase in air temperature generally increases corrosion effects. This can be counteracted by the addition of chromium to some metals. Chromium is one of the pretreatment coatings used in powder coat paint finishes.

Corrosion Protection

To determine what is necessary to prevent corrosion, evaluate the environment in which the equipment will be placed (see Chapter 1). Also, consider the characteristics of the fixture's materials. Metals that hold up in one environment may break down quickly in another.

Some metals, such as aluminum, form corrosion-resistant oxide films during initial corrosion. This retards further attack, except when exposed to any that will chemically react with these oxide films (most likely to occur in soils or when exposed to chemicals or solvents). In this case the film is destroyed and corrosion will continue.

The best form of corrosion protection is using a resistant metal such as copper or brass, but this adds significant cost to fixtures. The most practical form of corrosion protection is the use of an effective finish (see the discussion of finishes below) applied by careful, competent finishers.

The fixture shape can also discourage corrosion (see Figures 8.10 & 8.11). In selecting fixtures to minimize corrosion, consider three basic guidelines:

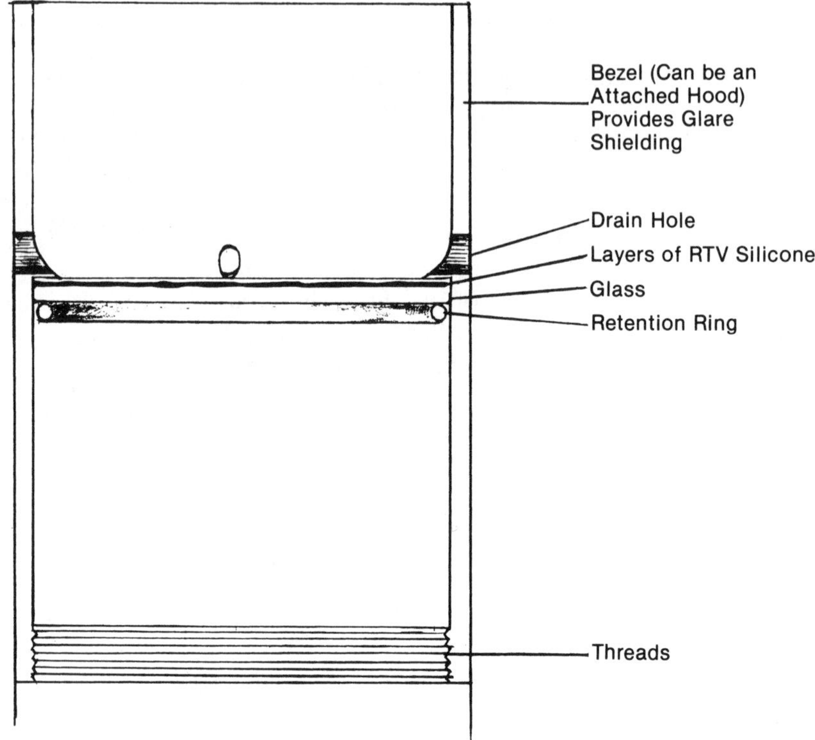

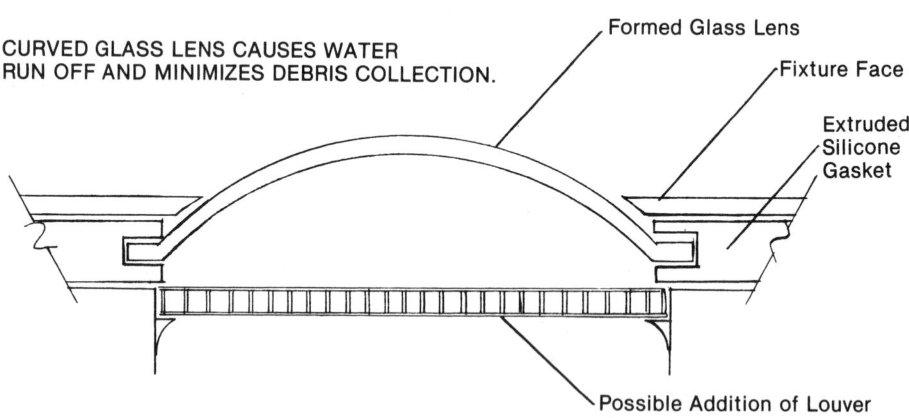

Figure 8.10. *Corrosion prevention by design—Look at fixtures to see if they avoid water and debris collection. This pair of drawings addresses one issue of corrosion prevention by design. Consider the trade-off between lamp brightness, glare shielding, and corrosion resistance. A bezel or hood provides glare shielding that curved glass will not. Some fixtures allow locating an additional shielding device (louver or baffle) within the fixture cavity. To provide equal shielding, enough depth must exist to regress the louver sufficiently. Drawing: Lezlie Johannessen.*

- *Select fixtures of the proper material.* Combine information gathered on-site with environmental conditions and material strengths and weaknesses to determine appropriateness. For example, some below-grade boxes are made of cast iron, due to low cost, using a thicker wall than necessary to allow for corrosion. Because it is buried in the ground the unsightly appearance of the corrosion is hidden. This would not be appropriate for above-grade fixtures.
- *Specify products with a minimum of pockets or crevices in the equipment where water and debris can collect.* Eliminating a place for water and other materials, such as soil, leaves, bark, and trash, to collect helps minimize several types of corrosion (see Figure 8.10).[1] When crevices must occur, make sure that a drainage hole is provided, or fill the crevice with a sealing compound.
- *Avoid products using incompatible metals.* Bimetallic corrosion occurs in moist environments and is accelerated by the continual wetting and drying that occurs outdoors.

Engineering books covering materials provide greater detail regarding conditions that either eliminate or minimize corrosion (see the Bibliography).

Types of Corrosion

Understanding the following types of corrosion that affect lighting equipment and how they occur helps in selecting appropriate lighting equipment.

Uniform Corrosion

This refers to disintegration proceeding at roughly the same rate over the entire surface of a metal exposed to a corrosive environment. It affects primarily cast iron and mild steel. This corrosion first affects appearance, then eventually the structural integrity of a fixture. Aluminum can sometimes suffer uniform corrosion, but further attack is suppressed by the resulting layer. Although this protects from further corrosion, it is unsightly.

Pitting Corrosion

This type of corrosion affects a small portion of the metal but can occur in several places on the metal surface at once (see Figures 8.5 & 8.12). It happens with most metals, including aluminum or stainless steel, and it usually results in worse damage than uniform corrosion. Due to the concentrated area affected, it can lead to perforation in a short time.

A symptom of pitting is blistering paint. Prevent pitting by choosing the proper finish. For aluminum, an anodized undercoat and baked enamel topcoat works on below-grade fixtures. A chromate conversion undercoat with a powder coat final finish works on above-grade fixtures. For stainless steel provide an electropolish finish. Since sediment depositing can encourage pitting, select fixtures that do not have places for sediment to collect.

Crevice Corrosion

Crevice corrosion occurs when a piece of equipment has a gully that will collect water or debris. It takes place due to chemical reactions encouraged by trapped moisture. This kind of corrosion can occur in a crevice where two incompatible metals are in contact (combination of crevice and bimetallic corrosion) or where a metal is in contact with a nonmetallic material such as plastic. To reduce the incidence of crevice corrosion, specify products that do not have lapping joints. Because it occurs at screw joints, make sure that a lubricant or coating is provided at the screw openings and use Teflon-coated screws. This precaution will slow corrosion. Another preventative measure is to fill any crevices with a sealing compound. When maintaining fixtures in the field, always reapply a lubricant to any surface that could corrode.

Deposit Corrosion

A frequent problem in landscape lighting, deposit corrosion occurs when moisture is held in and under a

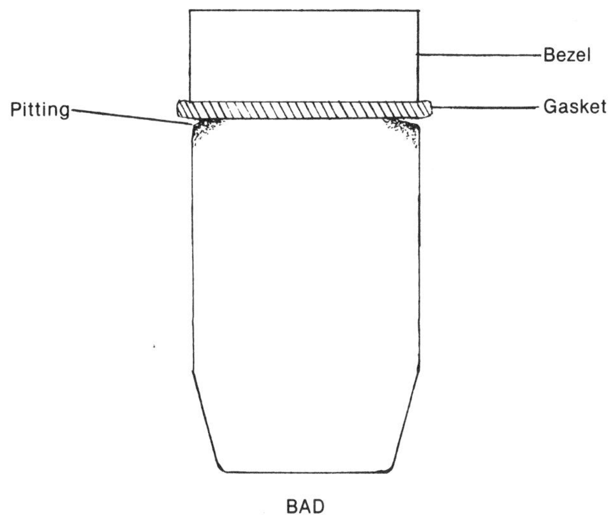

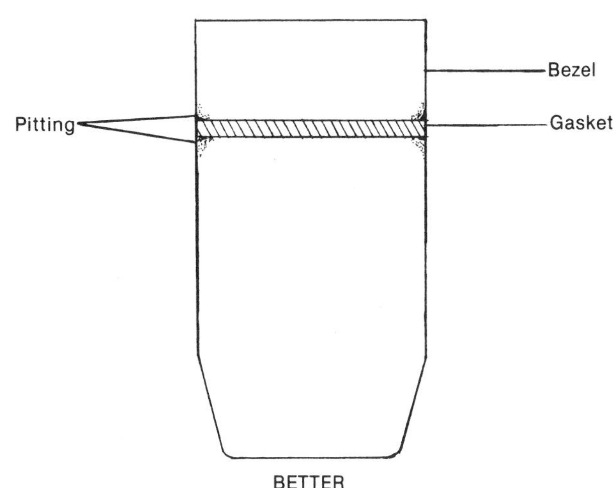

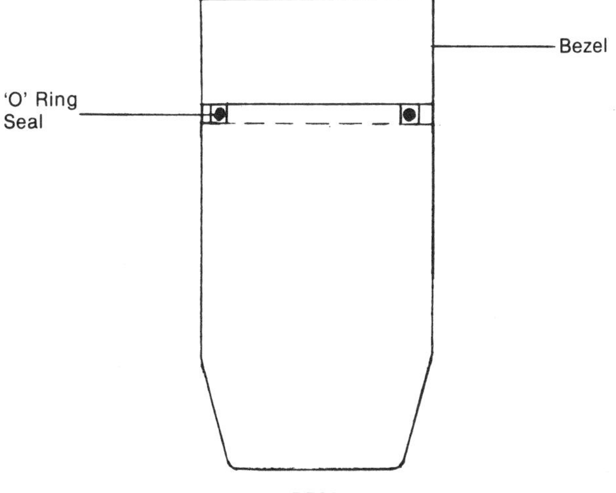

Figure 8.11. *Gasket design affects corrosion. Drawing: Lezlie Johannessen.*

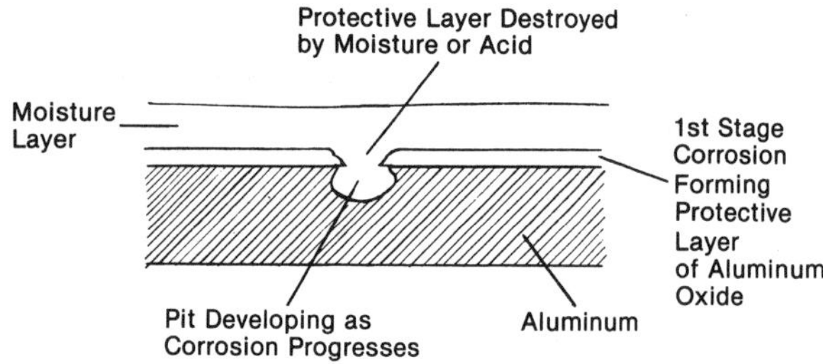

Figure 8.12. *Pitting corrosion. Drawing: Lezlie Johannessen.*

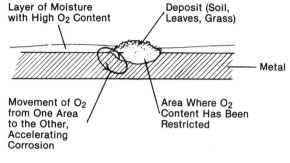

Figure 8.13. *Deposit corrosion. Drawing: Lezlie Johannessen.*

deposit on the metal. The deposit can be a small amount of soil or leaves—anything that will hold moisture (see Figures 8.13 & 8.14). To prevent this, specify equipment with a top-quality finish, and either specify no areas where debris can accumulate or ensure that the maintenance schedule includes cleaning the debris from the fixture on a regular basis. While cleaning the fixture may only be needed once or twice a year to combat corrosion, cleaning the lens may need to be done more frequently to ensure that light is not blocked.

Erosion Corrosion

Erosion corrosion is caused by the flow of liquid over a surface and is an issue to consider for underwater fixtures. Water pressure (from waterfalls or waterways) can remove protective films on the fixture and allow corrosion to proceed. The best prevention is to select fixtures made from high-quality brass or bronze with strong corrosion resistance.

Bimetallic or Galvanic Corrosion

This corrosion takes place when dissimilar metals (see Figure 8.15) are in contact and exposed to water (see Figures 8.16 & 8.17). If the surface is dry, no corrosion occurs, but a moisture film forming on a light fixture, even from dew, can be enough to cause the problem. Bimetallic corrosion is a special concern with all underground fixtures, as well as with above-grade fixtures in marine atmospheres and salty environments (including areas that put salt on roads for snow removal and where fertilizers are added to the soil to aid plant growth).

Lighting specifiers need to evaluate fixture construction to ensure that this type of corrosion will not prevent a fixture from functioning in the field. A potential problem would be when stainless steel screws secure a faceplate onto an aluminum fixture body. Without some form of separation, *freezing* or *seizing* will occur between the two metals, preventing the removal of the faceplate to change the lamp. In some cases, insulating dissimilar metals with a protective finish, gasket, or washer can prevent this type of corrosion. For instance, when mounting an aluminum fixture in a tree, stainless steel nails minimize stress to the tree. Adding a washer to separate the aluminum from the stainless steel and lubricating the nailhead and shank will help ensure separation of the dissimilar metals.

Stray-Current Corrosion

Stray electric currents are those that follow paths other than the intended circuit. For example, a weak electrical connection of wire segments in underground electrical wiring can cause current to seek an alternative path through the soil and adjacent metal objects. Corrosion occurs where the current leaves the metal to enter the soil or water. Stray currents can be quite large in the

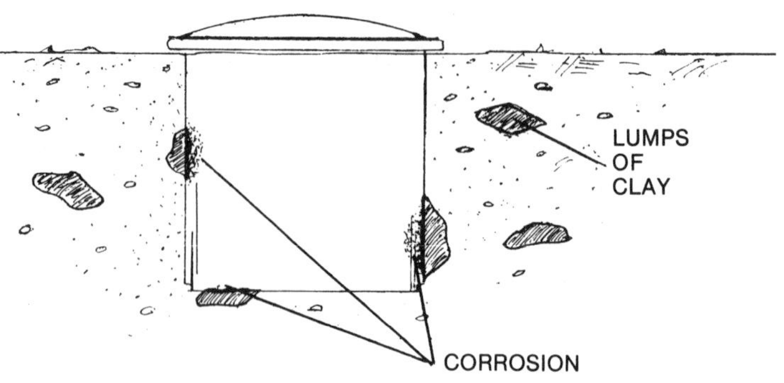

Figure 8.14. *Variation in soil content can cause deposit corrosion. Drawing: Lezlie Johannessen.*

vicinity of high-voltage transmission lines, electrically driven subway or light rail lines, or other sources of large electric currents. In a typical landscape environment, however, the major source of stray currents is from poorly connected or corroded segments of in-ground electric wiring. Stray current corrosion can best be prevented by ensuring that all metal parts of a lighting system in contact with soil or water have a strong electrical and mechanical connection. For instance, in interior locations, twisting the electrical wires together and covering the wires with a locknut forms good electrical and mechanical connections. In exterior locations, a better approach includes either soldering the wires, then putting on a locknut and covering the connection with a rubber mastic tape, or inserting the wires into a direct-burial wiring kit that surrounds the wires with a waterproof plastic.

Selective or Dealloying Corrosion

This problem occurs in metal alloys when components of the alloy corrode at different rates. Most frequent in landscape lighting is the dezincification of brass. The zinc is dissolved selectively, while the copper is left as a porous mass having poor structural strength. Salt water and air encourage this type of corrosion. To prevent this, select a stable brass material (see "Brass" below).

MATERIALS

Materials commonly used in the construction of outdoor lighting equipment include ferrous and nonferrous metals, and plastics. Specifiers need to evaluate a fixture material's chemical, physical, and mechanical properties (see Figure 8.18) for a specific site. These characteristics, based on atomic structure and relative stability, vary from one material type to another and influence a material's strength and corrosion resistance (see Figure 8.19).

Ferrous Metals

Ferrous

Ferrous metals are those containing iron, a reactive metal. With a tendency to lose electrons (forming ionic compounds), they have a higher corrosion potential than nonferrous metals.

Cast Iron

This family of metals has limited use in landscape lighting equipment. While relatively inexpensive, they have low structural strength and low corrosion resistance to the high temperatures experienced in fixtures due to lamp heat. Cast iron's primary use is for below-grade

	Magnesium
	Magnesium alloys
	Zinc
	Galvanized steel or galvanized wrought iron
	Aluminum 7072 (cladding alloy)
	Aluminum 5456, 5086, 5052
	Aluminum 3003, 1100, 6061, 356
	Cadmium
	Mild steel
	Wrought iron
	Cast iron
LEAST	Ni-resist iron
NOBLE	13% Cr stainless steel, type 410 (active)
	50-50 lead tin solder
	18-8 stainless steel, type 304 (active)
	18-8 3% Mo stainless steel, type 316 (active)
	Lead
	Tin
	Muntz metal
	Manganese bronze
	Naval brass (60% copper, 39% zinc)
	Nickel (active)
	78% Ni, 13.5% Cr, 6% Fe (Inconel) (active)
	Yellow brass (65% copper, 35% zinc)
	Admiralty brass
	Aluminum bronze
	Red brass (85% Cu, 15% Zn)
	Copper
	Silicon bronze
MOST	5% Zn, 20% Ni, 75% Cu
NOBLE	90% Cu, 10% Ni
	70% Cu, 30% Ni
	88% Cu, 2% Zn, 10% Sn (composition G-bronze)
	88% Cu, 3% Zn, 6.5% Sn, 1.5% Pb (composition M-bronze)
	Nickel (passive)
	78% Ni, 13.5% Cr, 6% Fe (Inconel) (passive)
	70% Ni, 30% Cu
	18-8 stainless steel type 304 (passive)
	18-8 3% Mo stainless steel, type 316 (passive)
	Hastelloy C
	Titanium
	Graphite
	Gold
	Platinum

Legend of Element Abbreviations

Ni	Nickel	Zn	Zinc
Cr	Chromium	C	Carbon
Fe	Iron	Sn	Tin
Cu	Copper	Mo	Molybdenum
Pb	Lead		

Figure 8.15. *Galvanic series—comparison of the corrodibility of metals. This standard is based on metals in seawater. The farther apart metals occur in this listing, the greater the potential for corrosion of the anodic or less noble type. Reprinted with permission from the National Association of Corrosion Engineers, Houston, Texas.*

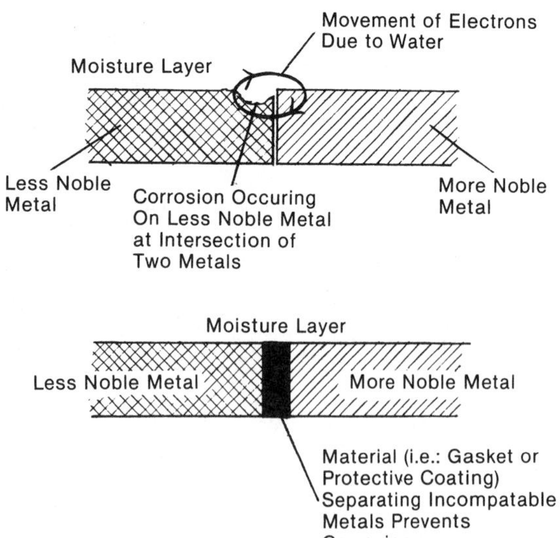

Figure 8.16. *Bimetallic corrosion. Drawing: Lezlie Johannessen.*

boxes. The boxes are typically cast with thick walls and galvanized to retard the progression of corrosion. This also adds weight to the box, which helps stabilize fixtures mounted onto the box. Until recently, they were the only below-grade boxes available. Now plastic (see "Polyvinyl Chloride" below) boxes are available in a variety of sizes at a lower cost.

Stainless Steel and Alloys

Stainless steels have limited use in landscape lighting equipment, because the metal is expensive and difficult to work with. It consists of a family of iron-based metals with varying amounts of additives, which can help combat corrosion. Many standard and alloy (see Figure 8.3) types exist with widely varying characteristics and strengths. Three types of stainless steel alloys are generally recognized (see Figure 8.20),[2] of which austenitic (see Figure 8.21) is the type generally used for lighting equipment.

Stainless steel alloys are not as thermally conductive as some other metals, which limits their use with some lamp types and wattages. However, some manufacturers use austenitic alloys as an inner lamp chamber for underground and underwater locations, where it will be protected from soil attack or stagnant water exposure. In this situation, thinner cross sections can be used, allowing precise forming for both optics and accurate sealing. Used this way, stainless steel offers good dimensional stability (to retain a tight seal). As well, this alloy is nonmagnetic and nonporous, which provides good corrosion protection.

Stainless steels are generally susceptible to pitting, deposit, crevice, and stress cracking corrosion. To counteract these corrosion problems, verify that the manufacturer uses a proper alloy and select a fixture with no crevices or places for deposits to build up on the metal. In selecting fixtures, note that welds in steel rather than flanges increase the corrosion resistance, but the welds must be cleaned of oxides that form during processing.

Nonferrous Metals and Alloys

Nonferrous metals and alloys are less corrosive than ferrous metals, making them more useful in outdoor lighting equipment. They include those listed below.

Aluminum and Alloys

Most outdoor lighting equipment is made from aluminum, due to its many beneficial characteristics, including low cost, ease of fabrication (including forming, die and sand casting, and extruding), high strength, high heat conductivity, and the ability to form a corrosion-resistant film on its surface.

Aluminum became available as a construction material later than most other metals and was originally

GALVANIC CORROSION POTENTIAL BETWEEN COMMON CONSTRUCTION METALS

	Aluminum	Brass	Bronze	Copper	Galvanized steel	Iron/ steel	Lead	Stainless steel	Zinc
Aluminum	—	1	1	1	3	2	2	3	3
Copper	1	2	2	—	2	1	2	1	1
Galvanized steel	3	2	2	2	—	2	3		3
Lead	2	2	2	2	3	3	—	2	3
Stainless steel*	3	1	1	1	2	2	2	—	1
Zinc	3	1	1	1	3	1	3	1	—

1—Galvanic action will occur with direct contact
2—Galvanic action may occur
3—Galvanic action is insignificant between these metals

* Active stainless steel

Figure 8.17. *Courtesy of* Fine Homebuilding *magazine.*

MATERIAL PROPERTIES				
	Chemical	Physical	Mechanical	Dimensional
Metals	Composition Characteristics Corrosion resistance		Strength Toughness Formability Rigidity Durability	Available shapes Available sizes Available surface texture Manufacturing tolerances
Plastics	Composition Fillers Flammability Chemical resistance	*Melting point* *Thermal* *Magnetic* *Electrical* *Finish required*	Strength Heat distortion Compression strength Creep resistance	Manufacturing tolerances Stability Available sizes
Ceramics	Composition Porosity Binder Corrosion resistance		Strength Compression strength Fracture toughness Hardness	Available shapes Available sizes Manufacturing tolerances Available surface texture

PROPERTIES OF MATERIALS TO CONSIDER		
	Composition	The percentage of various elements making up the metal. Varying amounts of differing elements impact the corrosion resistance, strength and formability of metals. Knowing the makeup allows evaluation of the appropriateness for a specific situation.
Chemical	Microstructure	This explains the condition of the metal surface and structure (grain size, condition of heat treatment, and inclusions, among others). This information provides information on the adherance of finishes to metals.
	Crystal Structure	This provides temperature resistance and chemical stability information.
	Corrosion resistance	This indicates the nature and degree of corrosion potential.
	Thermal conductivity	This describes how well a material transmits heat. It is important when a material is expected to perform a heat transfer function (such as the body of a fixture acting as a heat sink).
Physical	Thermal expansion	This refers to the rate at which a material changes shape due to temperature change. It becomes important when dissimilar metals or metals and plastics will be fastened and then heated.
	Heat distortion Temperature	This describes the temperature and rate of deformation that occurs for a material. It primarily affects plastics.
	Water absorption	Some materials, primarily plastics, can absorb water, causing a severe change of shape.
	Strength	Several types of stength can be considered. Tensile refers to a material's resistance to being pulled apart; stress resistance to crushing or collapsing; shear resistance to cleavage.
Mechanical	Formability	This characteristic determines how easily a material can be shaped and by what methods.
	Rigidity	This describes the ability to maintain a predetermined shape.
	Toughness	This describes how well a material can endure tension or strain.
	Durability	This describes the resistance to decay or change and is determined by hardness tests.

Figure 8.18.

Materials	Nonoxidizing or reducing media					Oxidizing media		Liquids: Natural waters				Gases		Comments
			Alkaline solutions, e.g.					Fresh water		Sea water		Steam		
	Acid solutions, excluding hydrochloric, e.g., phosphoric sulfuric, most conditions, many organics	Neutral solutions, e.g., many non-oxidizing salt solutions, chlorides, sulfates	Caustic and mild alkalies, excluding ammonium hydroxide	Ammonium hydroxide and amines	Acid solutions, e.g., nitric	Neutral or alkaline solutions, e.g., persulfates, peroxides, chromates	Pitting media, acid ferric chloride solutions	Static or slow-moving	Turbulent	Static or slow-moving	Turbulent	Moist, condensate	Ambient air, city or industrial	
Cast iron	1	3	4	5	0	4	0	4	3	4	2	4	3	Normally used hot-dip galvanized and with thick wall for corrosion allowance. Corrosion resistance can be improved by adding Ni or Si, but may still be weak against acids (Ni added), or caustic/mild alkalies and ferric chloride (Si added).
Basic austenitic stainless steel (302, 304,304N) 18 Cr, Ni type	3	4	5	6	6	6	0	6	6	2	5	6	5	Corrosion and heat resistant.
Austenitic stainless steel w/Ni (305), and Mo (316, 316F, 315L, 316N) added 18 Cr, 12 Ni, 2.5 Mo type	4	5	5	6	5	6	1	6	6	3	5	6	6	Corrosion and heat resistant.
Austenitc stainless steel w/ higher % Cr and Ni (308, 309, 309S, 310, 310S) 20 Cr, 29 Ni, 2.5 Mo, 3.5 Cu type	5	6	5	6	5	6	2	6	6	4	6	6	6	Corrosion and heat resistant w/ increased resistance to several corrosive media. In soil, must be isolated; in atmosphere, should be protected.
Aluminum and aluminum alloys	1	3	0	6	0–5	0–4	0	4	5	0–5	4	5	5	Corrosion resistance dependent on type. All above-grade fixtures must be protected. All below-grade fixtures require protection or allowance in thickness for corrosion (e.g., in stakes).
Copper	4	4	4	0	0	4	0	6	5	4	1	6	5	Normally used for decorative fixtures; quickly forms a patina that continues to develop slowly due to limited corrosion resistance to acids. Alkalides should not be used below grade or in proximity to soil.
Bronze and brass	3–4	4–5	2–4	0	0	3–4	0	6	6	4–5	5	6	5	Many types avail. w/varying qualities, check with fixture mfr. for composition of metal, strengths and weaknesses. Both are used under water. In marine environments, leaded red brass, leaded and high-leaded tin bronze perform best. In fresh water the types listed above plus leaded semi-red brass are recommended.

Figure 8.19. *General corrosion properties of some metals and alloys. Chemical makeup and corrosion characteristics of specific metals used for lighting fixtures should be investigated with the lighting manufacturer for complete, accurate knowledge of corrosion resistance before specifying the fixture.*

rather rare. Now it is a relatively inexpensive, common metal that is used in most fabricating processes (including those listed in the paragraph above). A large number of alloys are available and differ in their characteristics. While the alloys provide improved mechanical properties over the pure material, corrosion resistance is typically lower. Manufacturers tend to use alloys (having greater strength when exposed to high temperatures) and then overcome corrosion susceptibility by applying strong, resistant finishes.

Aluminum has a strong tendency to react with its surroundings. However, during initial exposure to a corrosive medium, aluminum forms a layer of film on the metal's surface that protects the metal from further decay. While the film produced during initial corrosion protects the metal and would allow continued functioning of lighting fixtures, the appearance of this film is not visually attractive. It has low resistance to many mineral acids or highly caustic solutions, and salts in water or soil.[3]

Continual exposure to atmosphere, soil, and water gradually breaks down the metal. Most aluminum fixtures are finished either by a paint finish or an anodized finish in order to provide a desired color and to bolster corrosion resistance.

Aluminum has high thermal conductivity, making it useful for light fixtures using lamps that produce high heat and for reducing the size of the fixtures. This factor, along with its low cost and ease of workability, makes it a widely used metal for exterior lighting fixtures. Above-grade fixtures are often die-cast, while below-grade fixtures may be sand-cast. Sand casting provides thicker walls to extend life, and often the aluminum will be clear-anodized (sealing pores to slow any potential corrosion). Encapsulating in concrete, to isolate the metal from soil, helps slow corrosion as well.

Aluminum light fixtures do not hold up well in coastal areas with salt water—Florida, most coastal areas, and Hawaii, for example. Additionally, acid soils and high temperatures such as in Arizona's and California's high desert impair corrosion resistance.

Aluminum does not normally experience uniform corrosion, but it can occur rapidly when exposed to a pH lower than 4.5 or greater than 8.5 (see Figure 8.4).[4] Pitting is a more common type of corrosion with aluminum. When exposed to atmosphere, pitting occurs rapidly for a period of up to a few years and then stops. The damage tends not to influence usability but alters appearance. Pitting due to water exposure, especially stagnant water, can cause serious damage to a fixture.

Aluminum is susceptible to bimetallic corrosion (see "Bimetallic Corrosion," above) when combined with more noble metals (especially copper but also carbon steel and stainless steel). While a problem in any outdoor atmosphere, this type of corrosion accelerates when a fixture is in a continuously wet or damp environment (areas with high or continuous rainfall such as Seattle or constant fog such as San Francisco). The influence will be pronounced in marine environments or where fixtures could become submerged (i.e., when located in a low point of a property in an area subject to flooding). If dissimilar metals are used on a fixture, make sure that a gasket or some other protective measure separates the two metals.

Crevice corrosion can occur when rainwater is allowed to collect. Aluminum oxide forms, causing a discoloration on the metal's surface that is either difficult or impossible to remove. Discoloration also occurs when fixtures become covered with road salt or are exposed to salt water or salt air.

Copper and Alloys

A relatively expensive material, copper is normally chosen for aesthetic appearance. It exhibits high thermal and electrical conductivity, as well as strong resistance to corrosion in soil. It is used both in natural form and alloyed with other metals to produce varying appearance or to improve such characteristics as strength. Addition of zinc produces brass. Other copper alloys include bronzes and cupronickel. All exhibit excellent low-temperature properties.

Copper and its alloys offer good corrosion resistance. All have high resistance to marine atmospheres, seawater, alkalis, and solvents. Exposure to oxygen-rich water or acids can cause discoloration, which affects the aesthetic appearance of copper. A protective finish can prevent or delay this problem. All copper alloys are susceptible to stress-induced cracking in the presence of ammonia. Do not locate fixtures where dogs can get to them!

New untreated copper has a patchy appearance that is not always aesthetically acceptable. The more preferred appearance, an even, darkened color or patina, is a form of corrosion that occurs over time due to carbon dioxide exposure. The patina effect develops at differing rates on vertical, horizontal, and sloping surfaces. In marine environments this takes place within 7 years. In atmospheres without salts this can take many years to develop. If this finish is desired, it can be chemically induced during fixture production.

Brass

Brass is often used for underwater fixtures and above-grade fixtures in very corrosive environments due to its structural strength and corrosion resistance. This group of alloys is formed from a combination of copper with other metals or elements, including zinc and nickel. An important consideration in specifying brass equipment is the nickel content of the alloy. When brass contains less than 15 to 20 percent nickel, corrosion resistance

THREE TYPES OF STAINLESS STEEL ALLOYS	
MARTENSITIC:	Consists of 12–20% Cr with limited amounts of C and other additives (example: Type 410). These can be hardened by heat treatment increasing tensile strength. Least corrosion resistant. Can be used in mildly corrosive situations such as fresh water.
FERRITIC:	Consists of 15–30% Cr with low C content (example: Type 430). Corrosion resistance improved due to higher Cr content. Strength can be improved by cold working, but not heat treating. Can be machined and welded, but requires skilled operators. Some lighting manufacturers have computer controlled machining processes. Corrosion resistance good, except against reducing acids like hydrochloric acid.
AUSTENITIC:	Typically contains Fe, 16–26% Cr, 6–22% Ni, and limited amount of C. This is the most corrosion-resistant alloy. Can be hardened by cold working, but not by heat treating. Fabricated by all standard methods, but not easily machined—requires rigid machines, heavy cuts, and high-speed work. Welding can be performed, but may cause depletion of some of the chromium lowering corrosion resistance in some environments. This can be overcome with heat treatment (solution annealing) or with the addition of Ti, Nb, or Ta (example: Types 321, 347, and 348). Another approach is to lower C content (example: Types 304L, 316L). The addition of Mo (example: Types 316, 316L, 317, and 317L) offers improved corrosion resistance, especially against pitting.

Figure 8.20.

will be as good or better than that of copper with higher tensile strength. When the nickel content increases to 20 to 40 percent, corrosion resistance lowers and becomes subject to dezincification and stress corrosion cracking, especially when ammonia is present. (Ammonia is often released into soil from fertilizers.)

Dezincification refers to the selective leaching of zinc from the alloy, which weakens the metal significantly. Contact with water or exposure to an outdoor environment can cause this, while chloride and high temperatures accelerate the degradation.

Another important consideration in specifying brass is the zinc content, which can vary from a small percentage up to 40 percent. Brass becomes susceptible to dezincification when the zinc content is above 15 percent. Resistance increases with the copper content. Brass with more than 85 percent copper will be resistant, even in salt water.[5] Resistance to dezincification can be helped by adding a small amount of an arsenic inhibitor or phosphorus to brass with a high copper content. This does not work with low-copper-content brasses. Lighting fixtures for very extreme environments, such as Hawaii, benefit from the use of high-quality brass to provide long fixture life. The only way to know the quality of the brass manufacturers use in their equipment is to ask them the alloy content.

TYPES OF AUSTENITIC STAINLESS STEEL

Type	*Analysis Built Up from Basic Type*
301	Cr and Ni lower for more work hardening
302	Basic type, Cr 18%, Ni 8%
302B	Si higher for more scaling resistance
303	S added for easier machining
303Se	Se added for easier machining
304	C lower to avoid carbide precipitation
304L	C lower for welding application
304N	N added to increase strength
305	Ni higher for less work hardening
308	Cr and Ni higher with C low for more corrosion and scaling resistance
309	Cr and Ni still higher for more corrosion and scaling resistance
309S	Cr and Ni increased for high temperature
310	Cr and Ni highest to increase scaling resistance
310S	Higher Cr and Ni than 310
314	Si higher to increase scaling resistance
316	Mo added for more corrosion resistance
316F	0.1% S for improved machining
316L	C lower for welding applications
316N	N added to improve strength
317	Mo higher for more corrosion resistance and strength at heat
317L	C low for welding applications
318	Nb, Ta added to avoid carbide precipitation
321	Te added to avoid carbide precipitation
329	Cr increased and Ni reduced to resist SCC
330	Ni added to resist carburization
347	Nb, Ta added to avoid carbide precipitation
348	Similiar to 347, but low Ta content (0.10%)
384	High Ni for easier cold heading

Legend of Element Abbreviations

C	Carbon	S	Sulfur
Cr	Chromium	Se	Selenium
Fe	Iron	Si	Silicon
Nb	Niobium	Ta	Tantalum
Mo	Molybdenum	Te	Tellurium
Ni	Nickel	Ti	Titanium
N	Nitrogen		

Figure 8.21. *Types of austenitic steel. Adapted from the* Stainless Steel Handbook, *©1951, Allegheny Ludlum Steel Corporation (now Allegheny Ludlum Corporation).*

Bronzes

Another material used for submersible fixtures, bronze is typically a copper alloy with tin as the major alloying element. Other elements can also be used as the major alloying element. Aluminum and silicon bronzes combine good strength and corrosion resistance. Nickel-aluminum bronze suffers dezincification. Other bronzes may also be susceptible to dealloying corrosion. Many bronzes provide excellent corrosion resistance in saltwater and salt air environments (see Fig. 8.19).

Bronze and brass have similar characteristics, except that bronze has better corrosion resistance and is not as affected by stress corrosion cracking. Bronze, not typically available as sheet material, is normally cast. This means that some underwater fixtures may be made from a combination of brass and bronze. While the initial appearance of the two metals may vary, they both darken and will be similar in appearance after a short time.

Zinc

Zinc is used primarily as an additive to or coating on other metals to increase their corrosion resistance. Zinc has an extremely high resistance to atmospheric corrosion.

Glass

In lighting fixtures, glass is used primarily in lenses. It is produced from a mixture of silica, sand, and oxides (including soda, lime, magnesia, alumina, lead oxide, and boron oxide) fused together at a high temperature. The properties of a specific glass stem from the ingredients used, processing, and heat treating (see Figure 8.3). Any glass used in outdoor fixtures must be able to withstand the combination of heat and thermal shock from cold water impact. Additionally, the glass needs to be chemically stable to avoid color shift. Most fixtures will use borosilicate glass or other high-temperature-stabilized types. All glass material used for functional fixtures should be tempered (see Figure 8.3), which strengthens the glass, preparing it for the varying conditions that it will regularly undergo outdoors.

Many lenses are shaped to prevent debris from accumulating on the lens or to modify the beamspread from a lamp. Domed shapes discourage debris collection. Ridges formed in the glass surface can direct light. Linear spread lenses, for example, modify a narrow beam of light into an elongated streak of light. Opal glass lenses or sandblasted lenses spread the brightness of a lamp.

The importance of familiarity with these materials can be illustrated by the example of a simple modification to the lens of an underwater fixture. Normally, a fixture mounted in the sidewall of a pool will show distracting or glaring lamp brightness. Aiming a lamp at a slight angle inside a fixture *with a flat lens* (rather than the normal curved lens) eliminates excessive lamp brightness due to refraction of the light passing from air through the glass to water (see Figures 19.1 & 19.2).

Plastics

The plastic class of materials consists of two basic types: *thermoplastics* and *thermosets.* Thermoplastic types become fluid at elevated temperatures, which allows reshaping. Thermosetting types will not flow at elevated temperatures. They char or burn. Additionally, thermosetting materials cannot be recycled. Between the two plastic types there are about 15 basic families of plastics. Hundreds of commercial plastics are made using slight chemical variations.

Plastics are utilized in several forms for outdoor equipment. In a solid form they are used as housings for equipment (only when not exposed to lamp heat), lenses, or gasket material. A liquid changing to a solid form is utilized for gasketing lenses to fixtures or for potting (filling a compartment with electrical connections to isolate them from water intrusion). Liquid forms provide a protective coating used to isolate dissimilar materials preventing seizure (binding or freezing of parts to each other) and to aid in waterproofing.

Although plastics do not corrode the way metals do, they still disintegrate. Some chemicals attack plastics, causing structural failure. Many plastics are not resistant to ultraviolet (UV) radiation, which can cause the plastics to become brittle, loosening connection threads and cracking housing walls. A primary concern with plastics is deterioration due to heat exposure. Heat also causes cracking and deformation, which endangers waterproofing, since the expansion rate of plastics differs from that of metals. Also, some plastics experience stress-induced cracking in salt air.

In specifying lighting equipment, two other issues regarding plastics require consideration. The first is a condition called *creep*—the tendency for some plastics under sustained loads to deform permanently. This can affect the waterproof capabilities of a lighting fixture. A similar problem occurs with *compression setting* in some plastics. Gaskets, expected to expand and contract (according to the amount of pressure applied to them) to provide a water seal, can become permanently flattened due to the effects of pressure and temperature over time. This hinders the gasket's ability to keep water from entering the fixture.

When specifying a fixture with plastic components, investigate the specific material a manufacturer uses. Great variation in quality is available in plastics. The following identifies some plastics commonly used in lighting equipment:

Polyvinyl Chloride (PVC)

In the lighting industry, PVC is used for fixture housings, junction boxes, and other containers. PVC is available in many forms, all nonflammable with good corrosion and UV resistance, but not all forms offer strength. Rigid PVC, a thermoplastic that is easily molded and fabricated, has significant strength and stiffness. For example, extruded PVC pipes are used for irrigation and electrical conduit, as well as for equipment boxes. PVC offers low cost and long life in environments that would be corrosive to metals. Its lack of toughness is considered a drawback, but in the landscape lighting industry, it means that PVC can easily provide knockouts and other penetrations necessary for wiring. PVC offers resistance to acids and bases, but not to some organic solvents and organic chemicals. PVC is heat sensitive and, in lighting use, must be isolated from the heat of most lamps and auxiliary equipment such as transformers.

Acrylonitrile-Butadiene-Styrene (ABS)

ABS is a form of polystyrene offering excellent toughness with good strength, stiffness, and high corrosion resistance. It can be formed, extruded, and molded. Many do not have resistance to UV, limiting their use above ground in landscape lighting. Some manufacturers have begun making well-light housings from ABS to lower fixture cost. It should not be used when a watertight seal to the lamp compartment is required.

Epoxy

Epoxy is a resin with a low shrinkage rate, useful for adhering and potting. It provides excellent adhesion to metals and other materials along with chemical resistance and waterproofing characteristics. In lighting, it is typically used in the potting of anti-siphon chambers (filling the chamber after electrical connections have been made) and to isolate electrical wires (see Figures 10.15 & 10.16). This prevents wicking (the movement of water along a path between the wire and wire insulation coating), which can allow water to enter the lamp cavity of a fixture housing (see Fig. 7.5).

It can also be used to stabilize the aiming mechanism on a lighting fixture. In this case, after the aiming has been completed, application of a liquid epoxy cements the knuckle. Later, if the aiming needs to be changed, the bond of the epoxy can be broken to permit reaiming.

Epoxies can be used in high-performance coatings but will chalk under elevated temperatures. This limits their acceptability as a topcoat paint finish for lighting fixtures.

Silicone

For lighting purposes, silicones are available as pastes and greases offering superior thermal stability. They can be used for lubrication to provide corrosion protection of sockets and threads, for example. As adhesive gasket material, silicone has flexibility under pressure (low compression set), allowing memory of its original shape. This characteristic is critical for gasketing, as pressure needs to be applied to make a waterproof seal.

Silicones have high heat resistance and low moisture absorption, functioning between –150°F (–47°C) and as high as 500°F (260°C).[6] This means that in all weather conditions fixtures will experience, silicones will continue to perform. Most are UV stable and remain unaffected by oxygen or ozone. RTV (room-temperature vulcanized) silicone, used for sealing lenses, offers good expansion and memory. It stands up well to the continual heating and cooling that fixtures experience due to lamp heat. RTV has been treated with a sulfur compound to harden at room temperature. This provides a good seal with high temperature resistance (up to approximately 220°F/105°C). Always, check the heat rating of specific RTV, as well as any greases or adhesives, when considering adding them as socket or thread protection in the field.

Polymethyl Methacrylate (Acrylic)

Polymethyl methacrylate offers extreme clarity, good light transmission, impact resistance, and high UV resistance for lens use. Sometimes, inexpensive types are used for fixture lenses that will be protected from vandalism. The inexpensive types break more easily than polycarbonate, scratch easily, and are temperature sensitive. Heat tolerance is below 200°F (90°C). With poor coordination of lamp wattage and housing size, yellowing and cracking of the lens can occur (see Figure 8.22).

Polycarbonate (Lexan)

Used for lenses, polycarbonate offers high impact strength, rigidity, stability up to 240°F (115°C), and good clarity. UV-stabilized forms hold up well in outdoor environments.

Ethylene Propylene Diene Monomer Rubber (EPDM)

While thought to have good weathering properties, aging resistance, and good heat properties,[7] in practice EPDM does not hold up as well as other gasket materials in lighting fixtures (where high heat is a normal condition). It is good for nonheat situations such as gasketing in underwater fixtures. Although inexpensive, EPDM has a lower temperature range and less ability to retain its original shape than PVC.

Neoprene

A gasketing material rated at 150°F (65°C—UL rates some appropriate to 200°F/90°C), neoprene is susceptible to compression setting. It works as a great one-time gasket—when a fixture will never be opened again. If it is used on a fixture that will be reopened, the gasket should be replaced each time the fixture is opened.

FINISHES

Most metals used for lighting equipment require a finish to provide corrosion resistance, weatherproofing, or finish color. The type of finish depends on the metal selected, the environment the fixture will be subjected to, and the appearance required. The type of finish used on the same metal may vary with a fixture's use. For example, most above-grade aluminum fixtures are currently being finished with a powder coat paint, but below-grade aluminum parts can be better protected from corrosion using an anodizing undercoat and baked enamel topcoat.

Most of the following discussion on finishes will apply to aluminum, since it is the workhorse metal in landscape lighting fixtures. Some other specific finishes will be included for metals discussed above.

It is difficult for a lighting designer to know the quality of a finish supplied for a specific fixture since a significant part of the quality and effectiveness of a finish relies on the surface preparation of the metal prior to applying a finish. This is handled by either an in-house or job-shop finisher during manufacturing. Surface preparation includes one or more of several types of cleaning, possibly an etching process to improve finish adhesion, and may include a prime coating to increase corrosion resistance.

Aluminum is sensitive to trace contamination. Therefore, initial cleaning of the material becomes paramount for an effective finish. From the time that the material is first treated, it needs to be kept free of contaminants. This requires a clean, controlled atmosphere in the finisher's shop and no human being touching the metal during any stage of the finishing process. Many coatings fail because the cleaning and pretreatment processes were not controlled carefully, important steps were not included, or inferior methods or materials were used in the finish process. The lighting designer is dependent on the manufacturer to know the importance of pretreatment procedures, to use a finisher that maintains high standards, and to insist on high-quality processing. The best way to ensure that the specified fixture will last is to visit the manufacturer's plant or the finisher's shop to see the conditions and discuss the process. Short of this, ask the manufacturer or representative to provide information on the pretreatment process and materials used.

Today, two major finish processes are used: anodizing and powder coat painting. The two processes have different characteristics, strengths, and weaknesses. A third process, baked enameling, has been severely curtailed due to pollution standards.

Figure 8.22. *Discoloration and cracking in this fixture probably occurred because the lens could not hold up to the heat generated by the lamp.*

Anodizing

An anodized finish deposits oxygen on the metal surface, which combines chemically with the aluminum. The process entails a series of baths for cleaning and pretreating. Any finish on aluminum needs to seal the pores of the metal to prevent corrosion. Anodizing provides a good seal by penetrating the pores and reducing their openings.

Anodizing is typically a clear finish, but color can be added with either dye or an electrochemical action caused during the processing. Both organic and inorganic dyes can be used. Organic dyes fade; inorganic dyes hold up much better. The colors that can be produced during the electrochemically induced anodizing process are limited to a range of light bronze, dark bronze, and black. Fading and limited color selection in nonfading processes are the two drawbacks to anodizing.

When a color is added in this process it penetrates through the surface of the metal. This process produces a hard finish susceptible to scratching. When a car hits and scratches a light pole, and the cut goes past the depth of the color, there is no simple, permanent way to cover the scratch.

The appearance of the coloring can vary from one alloy to another. Lighting equipment may be produced using differing alloys or forming processes (die cast, cast, extruded, and formed) for various parts of the fixture. This means that even in the same color bath, the parts could end up several different colors. A designer should request to see installations of large fixtures and samples of small fixtures to check color consistency prior to specifying the product.

Additionally, the specifier should find out the type of anodizing process used by a manufacturer. Not all anodizing processes can stand up to environmental conditions. Anodizing is sensitive to pollution and any contact with an acid. This means that a lighting designer should consider types of businesses surrounding the site—anodizing should not be used on fixtures near refineries or chemical plants. Types of anodizing processes include:

- *Clear anodize and dye.* This process uses either organic dyes (typically fugitive, fading relatively quickly) or inorganic dyes (gold or ferric ammonium oxylate, which will last longer). This process does not include corrosion protections that are used in other processes and should not be used for outdoor lighting equipment.
- *Two-step or two-step electrolytic.* This process includes several classes of anodizing: commercial, class II, and class I. Of these, only class I has a thick enough film coating and seal to withstand outdoor conditions.
- *Duranodic (Alcoa) or Kalcolor (Kaiser).* This type of anodizing produces a harder finish but costs more than two-step. It works only on a few aluminum alloys.

Either a class I/two-step or Duranodic/Kalcolor type of anodizing may provide a lasting finish. Ask the fixture manufacturer which type of anodizing process it requires from its finisher. Two factors that help determine if the anodizing is appropriate are the film thickness (it should be no less than 7 mils) and the type of seal applied at the end of the anodizing process. It should be either a nickel acetate bath, which blocks the aluminum's pores with a hot water bath finish to seal the pores (temperature needs to be minimum 210°F/100°C), or a chemical seal.

Powder Coat

This paint finish consists of a powder resin heated to a temperature of between 375°F/190°C and 400°F/205°C to form a strong, durable, but somewhat porous finish. This process requires a conversion coating, applied during the pretreatment, to ensure long-term performance and corrosion protection (see Figure 8.23). Three types of conversion coatings are available: chromate (identified by a yellow appearance on the unpainted metal), phosphate, and oxide. Chromate provides both corrosion protection and improves the adhesion of the final paint coat, eliminating the need for an intermediate coating. Neither the phosphate nor the oxide reacts as well with aluminum.

Resins serve as the base material. Resins are chemically synthesized, usually transparent or translucent, and electrically nonconductive. Paint manufacturers offer several types with differing characteristics: epoxy, hybrid, urethane, and polyester (see Figure 8.24). Hybrid and urethane are typically not used for exterior uses because they do not perform well against corrosion outdoors.

While having excellent corrosion resistance in dry environments and good scratch resistance, epoxy is more susceptible to overbake (which weakens the finish) and does not hold up when exposed to UV. It breaks down by forming a loose powder on the surface called *chalking*.

TGIC (triglycidal isocyanurate), a type of polyester, is a good choice for outdoor lighting equipment. This type of polyester combines a small amount of epoxy-curing resin with the polyester resin to provide additional corrosion and solvent resistance. TGIC does not chalk, is resistant to heat and UV, resists overbake, and performs well in outdoor environments in both durability and corrosion protection (see Figure 8.24).

A fifth resin type, acrylic, has no real weaknesses in outdoor application, but creates problems in paint shops. Its incompatibility with all other resin material prohibits equipment to be used with acrylic and then any other resin material. Most powder coat finishers do not offer acrylic resin for this reason.

As with anodizing, the quality of powder coat painting depends heavily on the preparation steps used and the control implemented at each step. The metal surface needs to be clean, making sure that all rust, mill scale, or contaminant is removed. The surface needs to be adequately rough for a primer, when required, to adhere. Throughout the process, the metal temperature needs to be controlled to eliminate any risk of condensation. The thickness of the paint coating needs to be properly determined and applied within a specified tolerance. Finally, the adhesion of the paint coating needs to be verified using a pull-off test (see "Testing" in Chapter 7).

Symptoms of poor pretreatment conditions or inferior pretreatment materials include paint blistering, chipping, peeling, pitting, crevice corrosion, and deposit corrosion.

Verdigris or Verdi Green

Both a natural aging process and a treatment applied to brass and copper, verdigris produces a green or bluish appearance called "patina." The process depends on the formulation of the chemical compound applied to

Figure 8.23. *Tanks at Kim Lighting's factory that are used to clean fixture parts and apply a chromate conversion coating. Once the process has started, the parts are not handled by humans. The atmosphere is controlled completely, eliminating any potential contamination of the metal's surface. Photo courtesy of Kim Lighting.*

	EPOXY	HYBRID	URETHANE	POLYESTER
Hardness	Excellent	Very good	Good	Very good
Flexibility	Excellent	Excellent	Excellent	Excellent
Overbake Stability	Fair	Good	Very good	Excellent
Exterior Durability	Poor	Poor	Excellent	Excellent
Corrosion Protection	Excellent	Very good	Good	Very good
Chemical and Solvent Resistance	Excellent	Good	Good	Good
Ease of Application	Very good	Excellent	Very good	Excellent

Figure 8.24. *Powder coat resin performance characteristics. TGIC polyester performs best for outdoor lighting fixtures. One resin type, acrylic, is not included, as it is typically not available from powder coat shops. Reprinted courtesy of Fuller-O'Brien from their "Powder Coatings" brochure.*

the metal surface, as well as controlled humidity and temperature, to induce the reaction. Typically, the compound will be a combination of salts and acids. Some metals require sandblasting to encourage the reaction. Some manufacturers apply a verdi green paint coating onto metals such as aluminum (over a powder coat finish) that will not develop a natural patina or when they cannot meet the appropriate state or federal environmental pollution requirements.

Temporary Finish

When using copper, brass, or bronze, providing a temporary finish helps ensure that the product reaches the job site in top condition. Three types of film forming agents can provide this temporary protection—water based, oil, and fluid. They are applied by dipping, spraying, or brushing. Water-based agents deposit a thin, typically oily film on the surface, which will wash off in rain. An oil finish normally consists of a mineral oil with an inhibitor providing a nondrying film that can be easily removed with an organic solvent. The fluids are composed of fat, oil wax, or resin together with a corrosion inhibitor. These will eventually wear off.[8]

Designers need to plan for lighting equipment to last for many years. Since the outdoor environment presents harsh conditions, integrating the information in this chapter into a designer's normal thinking process helps ensure that the client's installation will continue to function. It cannot be stressed enough that designers need to press manufacturers for more information on the materials and finishes they use in making fixtures, so that designers can make appropriate choices in specifying them.

REFERENCES

1. Einar Mattson, *Basic Corrosion Technology for Scientists and Engineers,* Ellis Horwood, Chichester, West Sussex, England, 1989, p. 122.
2. Kenneth G. Budinski, *Engineering Materials Properties and Selection,* 3rd edition, Prentice Hall, Englewood Cliffs, N.J., 1989, pp. 397–398.
3. Ibid., pp. 502–503.
4. Ibid., p. 503.
5. Einar Mattson, *Basic Corrosion Technology for Scientists and Engineers,* Ellis Horwood, Chichester, West Sussex, England, 1989, p. 116.
6. Kenneth G. Budinski, *Engineering Materials Properties and Selection,* 3rd edition, Prentice Hall, Englewood Cliffs, N.J., 1989, pp. 108–109.
7. Ibid., p. 129.
8. Einar Mattson, *Basic Corrosion Technology for Scientists and Engineers,* Ellis Horwood, Chichester, West Sussex, England, 1989, p. 117.

9

Controls

Controls, along with wiring, fixtures, and lamps, constitute the *hardware* of a lighting system. The controls represent an important part, as they determine how easily the lighting system will function. Controls consist of a device wired to one or more fixtures that activates or dims the lamps in the fixtures. Control needs vary based on the type of project and how the landscape will be used. This chapter will explore what control systems can do, the issues to consider in selecting specific controls, and the types of control devices available.

CONTROL SYSTEM ISSUES

Controls regulate which fixtures will turn on and off together and provide the opportunity to alter the level of light. Further, controls can regulate one group or multiple groups of light fixtures manually or automatically. Control devices are available with a variety of features, from the simplest on-off function to a complex multiple-zone, multiple-scene preset dimming system or a multiple-group timed system that turns various groups of lights on and off at differing times of day, week, or year.

The simplest control device is an on-off switch. This switch can be replaced with a *dimmer* switch, which allows the amount of light output to be varied. Some dimmers offer a *preset* capability. These devices have a separate dimming and on-off mechanism that allows users to decide what light level they prefer and then always turn the fixtures on and off at that level. If a need or desire exists to separately control some of the fixtures in a landscape, *zones* or *channels* can be identified. A zone or channel is a group of fixtures wired together. Using a multiple-zone dimmer, each zone can be dimmed separately. The next level of control is to use a multiple-scene preset dimmer. This device can preset the dimming level of each zone in several different configurations, providing various *scenes*. Essentially, a scene is a predetermined level of light for each of the fixture zones. This introduces the ability to dim each group of lights or zone to a desired light level at the touch of one button.

Dimming is not the only control function to consider. Three other automatic controls can be used in landscape lighting: photocells or photoelectric controls, time switches, and motion detectors. A photocell is a device that automatically turns lights on and off based on the level of surrounding light. A time switch turns fixtures on and off at specific times of day. Motion detectors turn lights on and off when movement is detected within a specific area monitored by the device.

Any of these control devices can be used together. A group of lights can be turned on with a time switch, set at a preset light level with a dimmer, and then turned off by a photocell, for example. Deciding what type of device or devices to use and the level of control sophistication depends on the project and how the clients intend to use the space.

Some spaces need simple controls because the lighting requirements for the space do not dictate a need for flexibility or because multiple users will be expected to operate the controls. For many landscape lighting situations, when the lighting is well designed initially and the brightness properly balanced during the focusing sessions, dimming will not be required, nor will any type of complicated controls. Controls strategy and dimming become important for clients to consider for properties with multiple functions, in areas where the annual seasons affect the use and/or appearance of the garden, and when the use shifts from outdoor activities in one season to view out interior windows in another. Keeping the controls simple helps ensure that the lighting will function properly and look its best.

With the advent of computer miniaturization and advanced technologies, controls have become very sophisticated, with almost unlimited capabilities. Computer-driven control systems account for an ever increasing percentage of the market, and the software capabilities are nearly limitless. This family of controls has become more affordable as overall computer technology has advanced. Such sophisticated or complex control systems often require considerable skill or understanding to operate. Because of this, a client may not take advantage of all the system's capabilities. For a highly trained or knowledgeable user who will be monitoring the system regularly, the designer can consider using such sophisticated systems. If the operators may change over time, or when multiple users will have access to the control system, the system needs to be easy to understand and operate.

The lure of a sophisticated system with multiple functions and presets can backfire for a designer on a project when the owner or operator(s) does not understand how to use it. As the need for control options or capabilities increases, it is imperative that the designer select a system that operates without the need for special training or reference to a manual. Additionally, the more sophisticated the system becomes, the more expensive it will be. The designer must weigh the cost of controls with the actual day-to-day needs of the system.

DESIGNING CONTROL SYSTEMS

The first step to take in planning the controls for a site is to identify how the space will be used each night as well as throughout the week and year. The designer should know the types of activities that will take place, at what time of night, and how often the types of activities vary. Some of this information is learned during the initial client interview, but the bulk of it develops as the project proceeds.

The client must have decided how the interior spaces and landscape areas will be used, which often cannot be determined until the architectural design drawings are substantially completed. There will also be times that the actual functioning of a space may not be clearly determined until after the space is occupied. In that case, the control system needs to offer the flexibility to respond to changing or developing needs.

The activity pattern (or lack of a pattern) directs the type of control device(s) to choose. For example, if a regular pattern happens each day and the schedule of use does not change from one week to another or involve special events on specific dates during the year, an automatic 7-day time switch may offer all the control needed. Controls need to be designed concurrently with the lighting layout. Fixture placement and control group designations must have been determined prior to starting the controls strategy. Trying to design the controls too early in the project can waste time and the client's money. However, discussing the available con-

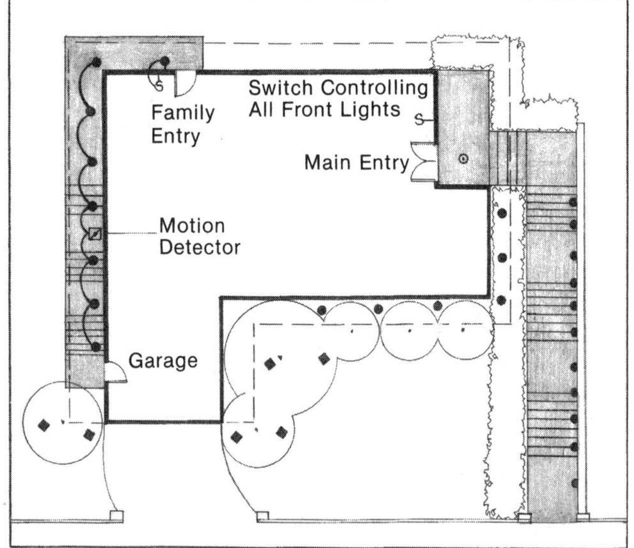

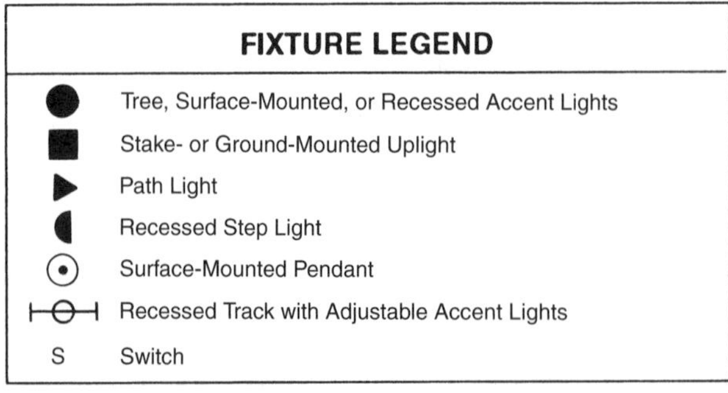

Figure 9.1. *This residence has two separate pathways—one for the family entrance and one for the public entrance. Due to the remote location of the family entrance, a motion sensor ensures that the path to the family entrance will always be lit. Drawing: Lezlie Johannessen.*

trol options early in the project helps determine a basic direction.

The next planning step is to identify each potential entry or egress location to the landscape from buildings and other exterior spaces, traffic routes through the landscape, and viewing location(s) from an interior space out to the landscape (see Figures 9.1 & 9.2). These locations, along with the way the spaces will be used, identify where controls should be located. The fixtures being controlled should be visible from the switch location. There may also be auxiliary buildings on the site, such as guest houses, barns, garages, or cabanas, that require local control for some or all of the landscape lighting. Typically, landscape controls are located inside buildings, often alongside the interior lighting controls. In this case, the two sets of control devices should coordinate in style and color.

In a residence there may be a main entrance, several side or back doors, and doors onto enclosed patios, decks, or balconies. Additionally, there may be areas

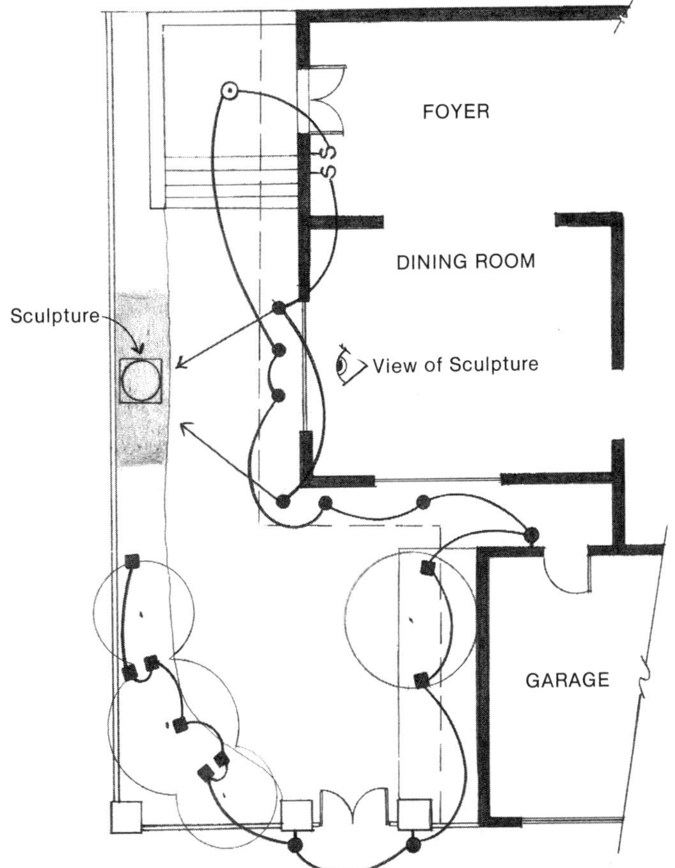

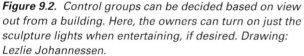

Figure 9.2. *Control groups can be decided based on view out from a building. Here, the owners can turn on just the sculpture lights when entertaining, if desired. Drawing: Lezlie Johannessen.*

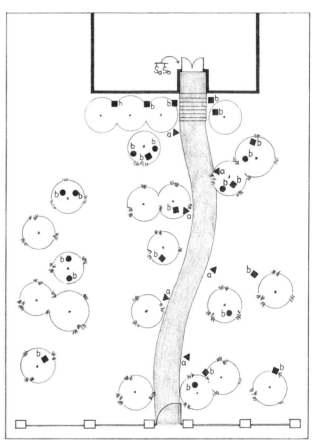

Figure 9.3. *Yard with two on-off switches where the path lighting is controlled separately from the accent lighting, for functional reasons. Drawing: Lezlie Johannessen.*

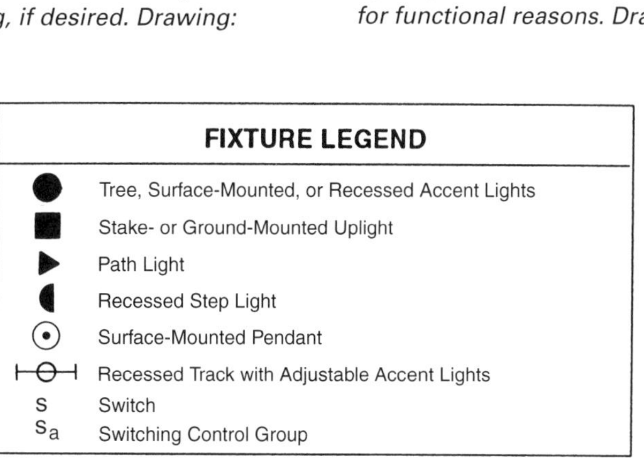

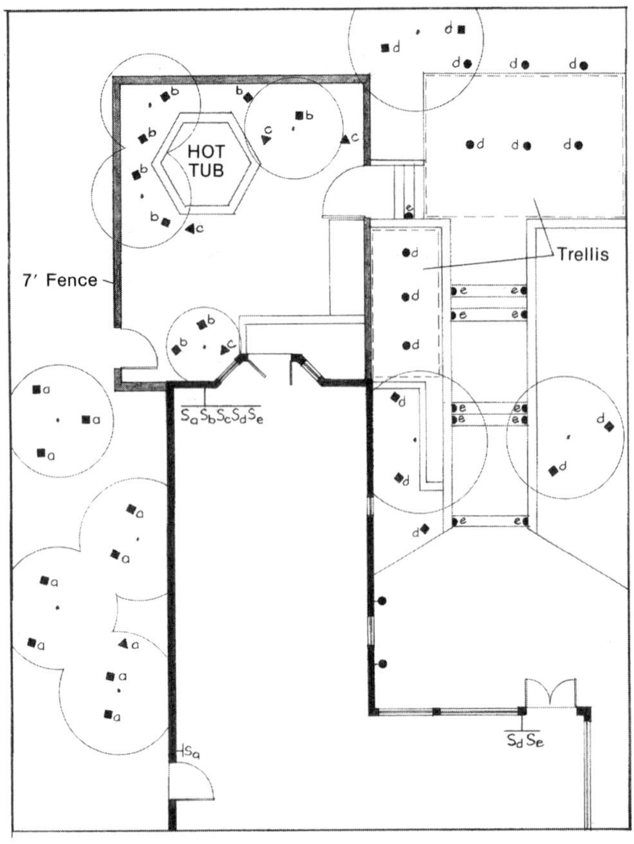

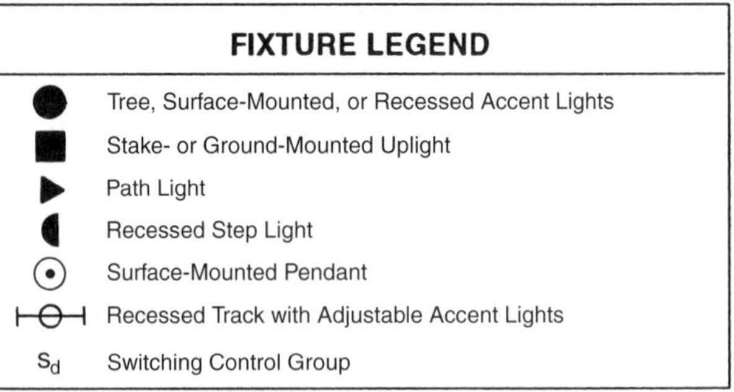

Figure 9.4. *On a large piece of property, local on-off switches are useful. By the door to the hot tub the owner can separately turn on fixture groups for any area of the yard accessible from that location. Additionally, the owner can choose to turn on only the path or accent lights for the hot tub area when using the tub. Drawing: Lezlie Johannessen.*

that have important views, such as the kitchen, master bedroom, living or dining rooms, or special rooms such as entertainment areas or ballrooms. The lighting at these areas may require separate controls. The decision of what kind of control occurs at each location depends on how the traffic flows through the space and the lifestyle or needs of the client.

For example, many clients never actually use their front door for day-to-day family activities. Therefore, locating a main control panel at the front door may be inconvenient for the owner. However, local controls for all the front-yard lighting or the walkway lights may be appropriate. Many residences run the household from the kitchen, and locating the master controls in that room may be more appropriate.

Providing local controls for portions of the landscape lighting system at view locations or traffic entrances provides flexibility of use. Luminaires lighting the landscape just outside a window can be activated, providing a view without turning on the entire system. For example, when entertaining, an owner may want to feature a sculpture outside a dining room window without turning on all the surrounding lights (see Figure 9.2).

Additionally, providing a master on-off control switch or group of switches at one or more locations provides psychological comfort and practicality. This allows homeowners to turn on all the exterior lights quickly at the flip of a switch when they fear that an intruder is on the property. It also provides them a convenient way to turn off all the lights that may have been left on at the end of the evening without making the rounds of the household.

The next step, before actually laying out the control system, is to plan how much flexibility will be required in the system. The number and type of uses direct the need for flexibility. The more functions that occur and the more varied they are, the greater the number of switches, dimming capability, or preset capabilities that will typically be required. Once the designer has a clear understanding of how the landscape will be used, entry and egress locations, views and traffic paths, and the flexibility required for a project, the control system can be laid out on a drawing (see Figures 4.16 & 4.17).

Residential Spaces

Residential properties rarely have a predictable schedule of events occurring daily or on the same day from week to week. They also have a wide range of activities that will occur in the landscape. These two conditions require a control system that provides a flexible

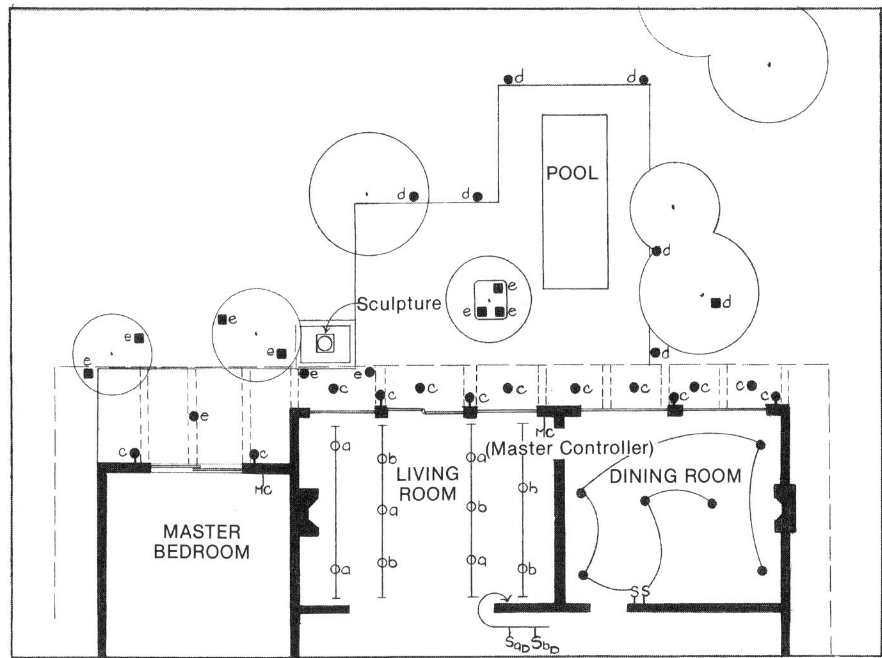

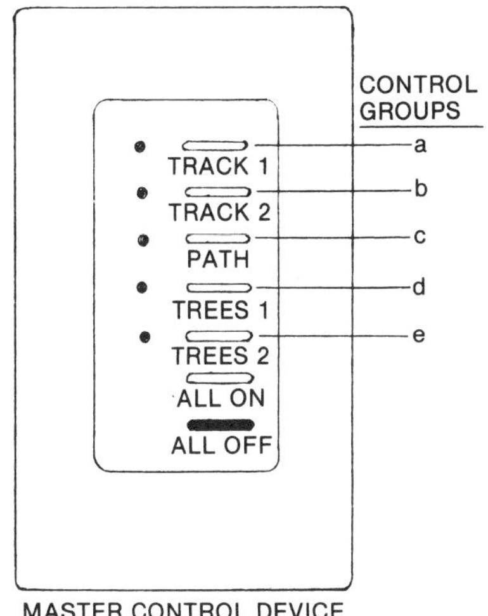

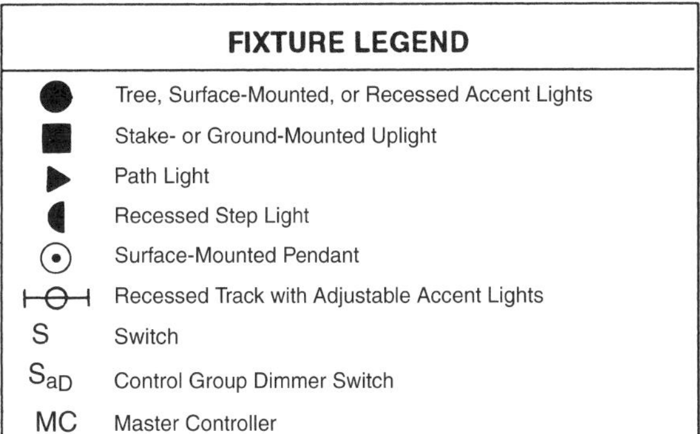

Figure 9.5. *In a renovation project (or new construction), a single-gang switch location becomes a multiple on-off master control station. Some systems can interface with dimmers, as shown, for interior control groups a & b. Drawing: Lezlie Johannessen.*

response to impromptu activity. In residential projects, there often is a need for turning on functional lighting separately from aesthetic lighting. For example, the pathway lighting might be on a separate switch so that the owner can take the dog out for a walk in the evening without lighting up the entire garden (see Figure 9.3). Another situation would be when the owner wants to control some of the front-yard lights when a guest shows up unexpectedly or as guests depart at the end of the evening. Yet another example would be turning on fixtures that highlight plants and sculptures visible to people relaxing in the hot tub or pool, but leaving off aesthetic lighting not visible from that area (see Figure 9.4).

A large portion of the expense in control systems is the capability to dim lights. In residential spaces, even though activities may vary, when the design is cohesive and lighting levels are balanced with the neighborhood through the selection of lamp beamspread and wattage, dimmers frequently sit unused. Using multiple on-off switches introduces the ability to create differing effects based on which fixtures are activated.

For example, in a renovation project, an existing on-off switch can be replaced with a master control switch that individually controls several groups of fixtures. Figure 9.5 illustrates how a master control switch could be used. In this case, lighting was added in the living room and in the landscape. Three groups of landscape fixtures and two interior groups were connected to the controller. The three exterior groups related both to use of the landscape and view out into the landscape. One group activated walkway and terrace lights for traffic movement and food display during parties. The second group activated the lighting of mature trees at the perimeter of the property to expand the view from the living and dining rooms. The last group controlled plantings and specific focal points viewed primarily from the master bedroom suite as well as from the living and dining rooms. This arrangement provides a great deal of flexibility without involving the use of dimmers.

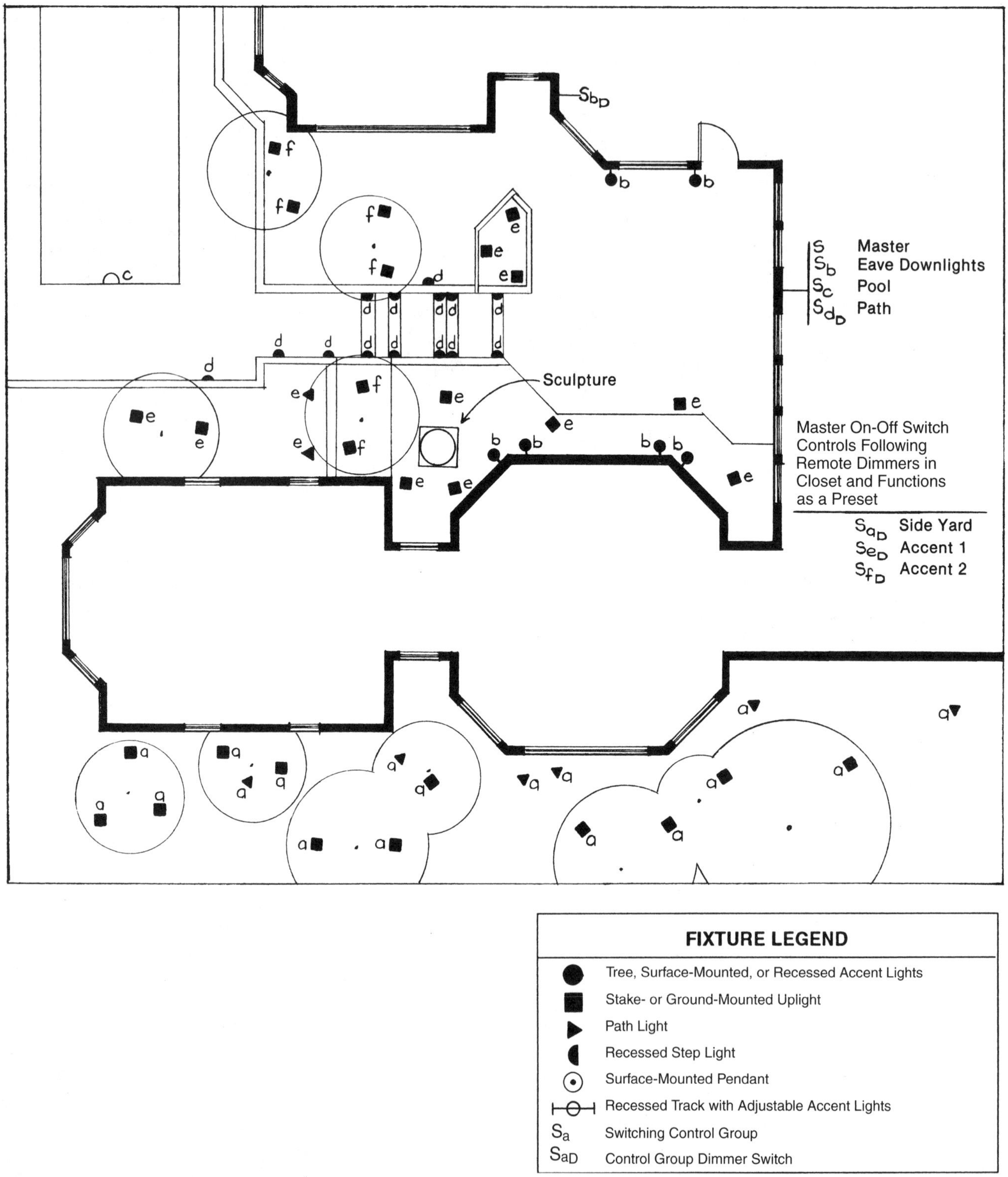

S_{b_D}

S Master
S_b Eave Downlights
S_c Pool
S_{d_D} Path

Sculpture

Master On-Off Switch Controls Following Remote Dimmers in Closet and Functions as a Preset

S_{a_D} Side Yard
S_{e_D} Accent 1
S_{f_D} Accent 2

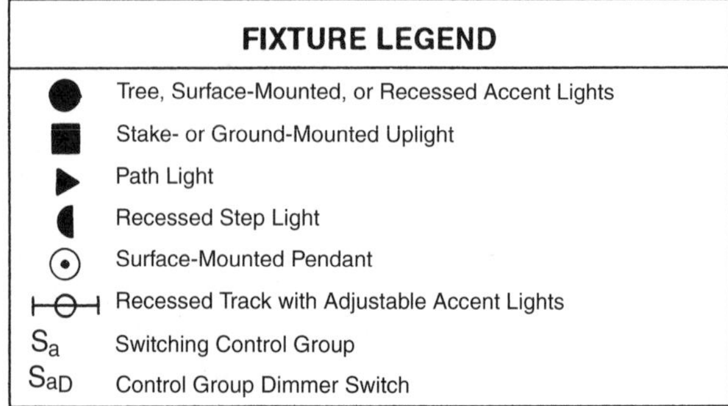

Figure 9.6. *A more sophisticated control system uses a single master on-off switch to control several groups of fixtures that provide accent lighting. Dimmers for these separate groups are located remotely in a closet. The owner can preset each accent group's light level for normal use and change the dimming level for special occasions. Drawing: Lezlie Johannessen.*

Location	Control Type	Time On	Control Type	Time Off
Parking lot	Photocell	Dusk	Time switch	Midnight
Grounds	Photocell	Dusk	Time switch	10:00 PM
Building	Photocell	Dusk	Time switch	2:00 AM
Security Zone	Photocell	Dusk	Photocell	Dusk

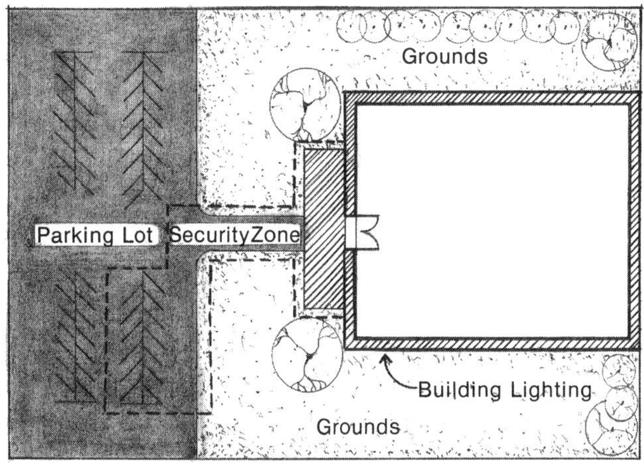

Figure 9.7. On commercial projects, a multiple-circuit, multiple-purpose time switch provides the ability to turn separate groups of fixtures off at varying times. Mechanical units require that the fixtures be turned off manually. Digital units turn each group off automatically at the specified time and can also turn each lighting group on at differing times. Drawing: Lezlie Johannessen.

A situation where dimming is helpful would be a large, secluded property where the owners entertain frequently and host several different types of events. For example, a family might host large benefit parties, invite small groups of friends to play tennis or croquet followed by a barbecue, and also have more formal dinners on the terrace. Some of these activities require high light levels in one area and a lower level or no light in another. When playing tennis, path lighting might be needed, while the grounds lighting may not need to be on. When hosting large benefit parties, the lighting level on the terrace might need to be higher than when enjoying a more quiet evening with friends (see Figure 9.6).

Commercial Spaces

Commercial spaces often have a regular schedule of events that are repeated every day or are consistent on each day of the workweek. For example, the parking lot lights, path lights, facade or building lighting, and grounds lighting may need to turn on and off at specific but varying times (see Figure 9.7). This type of project benefits from a control system that automatically controls each group of lights without needing a person to operate it. Properties that cater to the public, such as hotels and restaurants, may benefit from a control system that also automatically dims lights at predetermined times or to specific levels on a preset scene activated at the touch of a button.

Security lighting is an important issue for commercial spaces. The security lighting system can be a separate group of fixtures or it can consist of one or more groups of fixtures used in the overall lighting system. The type of business, the location of the building, and how the occupants use the building help determine the security lighting needs. For example, a business that has workers in the building 24 hours per day needs to have a security lighting system that lights pathways to and from at least one section of the parking lot. This lighting is typically controlled automatically, turning on at dusk and off at dawn.

Single-Use Spaces

When the landscape has only one function or several similar functions, the lighting controls should be simple. For example, at a hotel, there may be a patio by the pool. Here, people may lounge, enjoy a drink, and swim. The controls should turn the fixtures for this area on when the patio is open and off when it closes. An automatic control, such as a time switch, eliminates the need for the hotel operator to remember to turn the lights on and off each day. In single-use spaces such as this, control options include using a manual on-off switch or switches, a time switch, or a combination of a photocell and time switch. Often, the ability to turn the lights on and off will often be all that is required. Dimming, when needed, can be integrated into many manual or automatic systems.

Multiple-Use Spaces

For a space that has multiple functions, the control system may need to provide several options of either on-off or dimming for multiple groups of light fixtures. At a school property, the administrators may want the controls to turn certain areas on and off automatically each weekday at specific times as well as respond to a manual command to operate lights in one or more areas for special events not regularly scheduled. Additionally, they may want only some of the groups of fixtures to turn on during weekend nights.

Many commercial spaces may want the ability to have a nightly routine but skip specific days such as Saturday and Sunday and use a different time schedule or control different groups of fixtures on holidays. These type of needs require a time switch that has the ability to turn multiple groups on and off at different times, turn the same set of fixtures on and off more than once in a 24-hour period, and respond to different days of the week or dates in a year.

Often, residential spaces have several landscape entertainment areas that need to be controlled separately. With multiple entertainment areas, the owners may want to turn on only the fixtures in one area, dim the lights in one area of the landscape, or have each group of fixtures automatically dim to predetermined levels for the specific activity that will occur.

When people entertain indoors, the exterior lighting levels need to be high enough to balance with the interior levels or the landscape will not be visible. When entertaining occurs outside on a patio, the ability to dim the lights at the patio allows brighter lighting on plants and sculptures to serve as the view. At the same time, they might want to dim the lights at the pool house, so that it does not create a dark spot in the scenery but also does not distract the guests' eyes from the plants and sculptures. The designer needs to evaluate all the options and sort out what level of control sophistication is appropriate for each project.

TYPES OF CONTROL DEVICES

The devices available for controlling lighting loads include manual on-off switches, manual dimmers, preset dimming controls, photocells, time switches, and motion sensors. Manufacturers develop control devices to fit specific needs. Some types are meant for commercial use, some for residential. Devices meant for residential use tend to be more aesthetically detailed and many have a limited load capacity. Products designed for commercial use often look less refined, are physically larger, handle larger loads, and often offer more options for automatic functioning.

Additionally, some control equipment is wired at 120 volts and other equipment uses low-voltage signaling wiring. A distinction needs to be made between the voltage of the wiring and the voltage that the device is controlling. Control equipment that uses low-voltage signaling can carry a large load and use a small device for the control unit. The manufacturer's literature will specify if low-voltage wiring is appropriate for the device. Dimmers are rated by the type of load they can control, 120-volt or low-voltage.

Manual Switches

A manual switch turns on and off one or more groups of fixtures. It consists of the switching unit, a faceplate, and a junction box (see Figure 9.8). Manual switches nor-

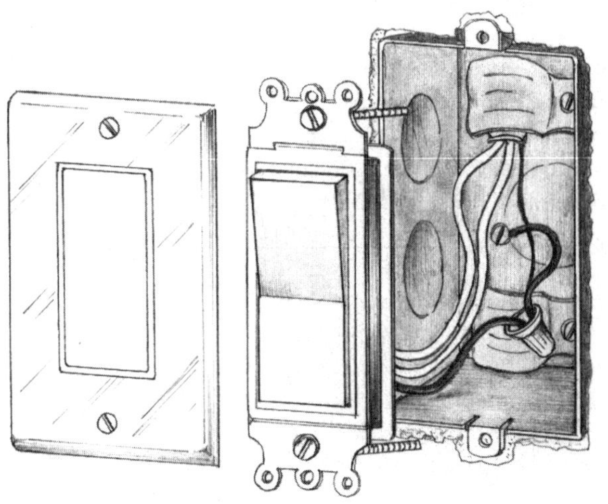

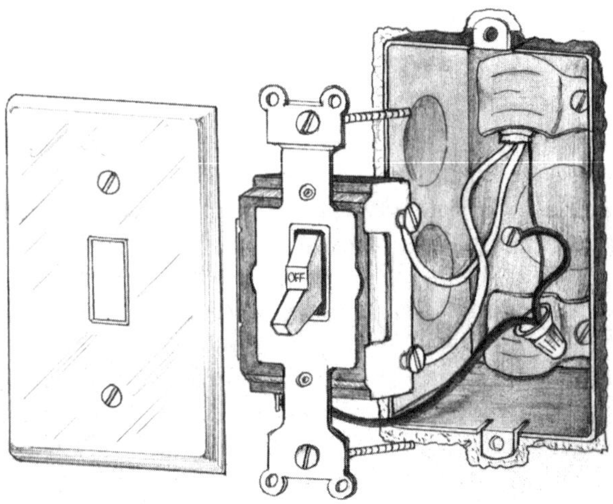

Figure 9.8. Components of a switch. A switch consists of a junction box (the wiring compartment), the switch device, and a cover plate. Two standard types are shown: on the left, a rocker switch with a decorator cover plate; at right, a toggle switch and toggle cover plate. Drawing: Lezlie Johannessen.

mally handle up to either a 15- or 20-ampere load (see "Wiring Approaches" in Chapter 10 and Figure 10.20). A prime advantage to a manual switch is low cost.

The size of manual on-off switches has been standardized by the National Electrical Manufacturers Association (NEMA). A single manual switch normally fits over a single-gang junction box. Multiple switches can be ganged together using one faceplate for the group. Some manufacturers make standard plates for commonly occurring numbers of switches and then provide most any other number required as a custom item. For example, manufacturers make standard plates for up to 10 toggle-type and 8 decorator-type switches (see Fig. 9.8). The physical dimensions of junction boxes and dimensions for faceplates are normally listed by switch manufacturers in their catalogs.

Flexibility can be added to the lighting control system by using devices suitable for multiple-location control which are called three- and four-way switches. Additionally, some manufacturers make master-control units for handling multiple groups of fixtures from one device (see Figure 9.5). Again, standard size combinations are available from manufacturers. The specific number of controls per panel and the actual size of the panel will vary with the manufacturer. One available master control unit has 5, 10, 15, or 20 switches per plate. As the number of switches per plate increases so does the junction box size. For example, the 5-switch units fit on a single-gang junction box, while the 10-switch units require a double-gang box.

Some manufacturers produce devices that fit in standard junction boxes. Other devices will require special-size boxes. When specifying, the lighting designer must check the manufacturer's data for appropriate dimensions and junction box sizes. Some of the multiple-switch devices have an all-on and an all-off button as well as the individual switch buttons. From manufacturer to manufacturer the load capacity will vary. Some units are limited to 1,000 watts; others can handle multiple 20-ampere circuits. Often multiple-switch units can interface with dimmers, photocells, and time clocks.

Another interesting possibility is using controllers manufactured for pool and spa equipment to control the landscape lighting loads. This equipment typically costs less than lighting controls. One limitation, however, is that pool control systems rarely provide the capability to interface with dimmers.

Dimming Switches

The ease, effectiveness, and cost of dimming vary from one light source type to another. In landscape lighting, the need to dim is limited and typically is necessary only for incandescent lamps. Dimming incandescent lamps is relatively easy and does not require a special device other than the dimmer. Dimming for fluorescent and HID sources requires special dimming ballasts and special dimming devices. This section will briefly discuss some issues of dimming fluorescent and HID lamps but focuses on dimming incandescent sources.

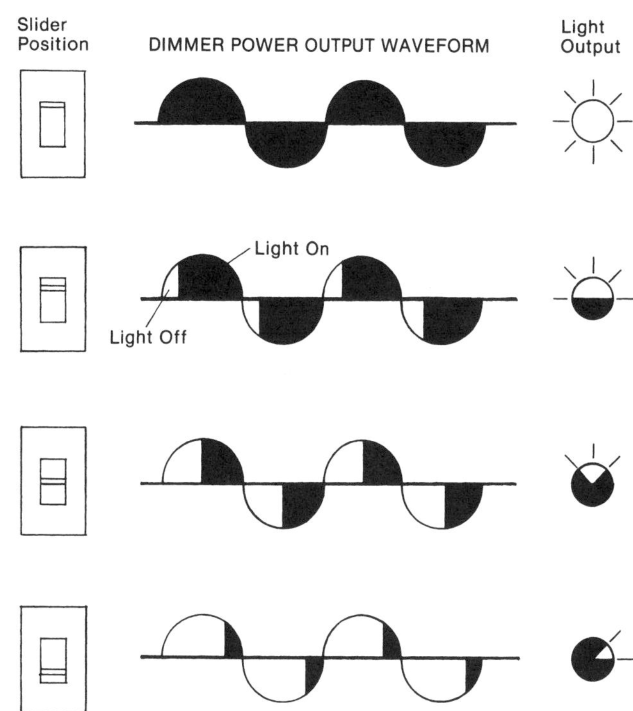

Figure 9.9. *Graphic representation of how an electronic dimmer produces a dimmed effect by "chopping" the sine wave. Courtesy of Lutron Electronics.*

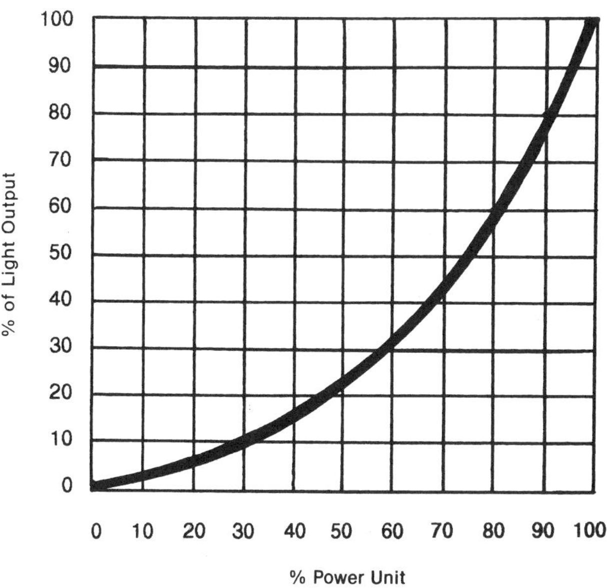

Figure 9.10. *Reducing light output uses less power. Courtesy of Lutron Electronics.*

Incandescent Dimming

As any incandescent source is dimmed, the color of the light produced becomes warmer. One of the benefits of dimming incandescent sources is that lamp life is increased (see Figure 10.7). Incandescent dimming switches are both more complicated and more expensive than on-off switches.

Several technologies have been developed for incandescent lamp dimmers. The technology most commonly used is the electronic or solid-state dimmer. A solid-state dimmer acts essentially as a switch. It dims by turning the power on and off 120 times per second. Dimming occurs due to the amount of time that the power is off. The longer the power is off, the more the lamps dim (see Figure 9.9). Additionally, while the power is off, electricity is saved. Dimming the light output to 75 percent saves approximately 50 percent of the potentially consumed electricity (see Figure 9.10).

The solid-state type of dimmer offers several advantages over older dimmer types. The physical size needed for a relatively large load is small. A 120-volt dimmer can handle up to 1,000 watts and fit into a single-gang junction box with a cover plate the size of a single-gang junction box. A 2,000-watt dimmer will fit into a single-gang box, but the faceplate will take up more wall space. Electronic dimmers are not sensitive to the actual load put on them up to their rated capacity. They can be easily integrated into preset units with variable fade rates. Last, they offer a long, reliable life. Electronic dimmers do have drawbacks. They produce electric noise on the wiring circuit that can interfere with sound systems and create static on radios, especially on the AM reception.

A distinction needs to be made between dimming a 120-volt incandescent load and any low-voltage load (for example, 24, 12, or 5.5 volts). When dimming a low-voltage load, additional components are required in the dimmer to avoid overheating the transformer. UL has separate requirements for 120-volt and low-voltage dimmers due to the heat concern with transformers. Additionally, two different types of low-voltage load dimmers exist—one for magnetic and one for electronic transformers. Therefore, dimmer manufacturers typically offer three basic types of incandescent dimmers in each series or quality of products they make—120-volt, magnetic low-voltage, and electronic low-voltage.

120-volt loads can be wired with low-voltage loads and controlled using a low-voltage dimmer. However, low-voltage loads are not recommended for use with 120-volt dimmers. Additionally, fixtures wired to magnetic transformers must use dimmers meant for magnetic transformers, just as fixtures using electronic transformers must use dimmers meant for electronic transformers. Always check with the dimmer manufacturer to see if their electronic-transformer dimmer will work properly with the specific transformer on a project.

A group of dimmers can be ganged in large-sized junction boxes and use one multiple-dimmer faceplate. However, when dimmers are ganged, their wattage capacity may have to be de-rated. Dimmer manufacturers list the wattage restrictions in their literature. To avoid the wattage derating, dimmers must be installed in separate junction boxes with air space between them. Again, the manufacturer's literature normally lists spacing restrictions.

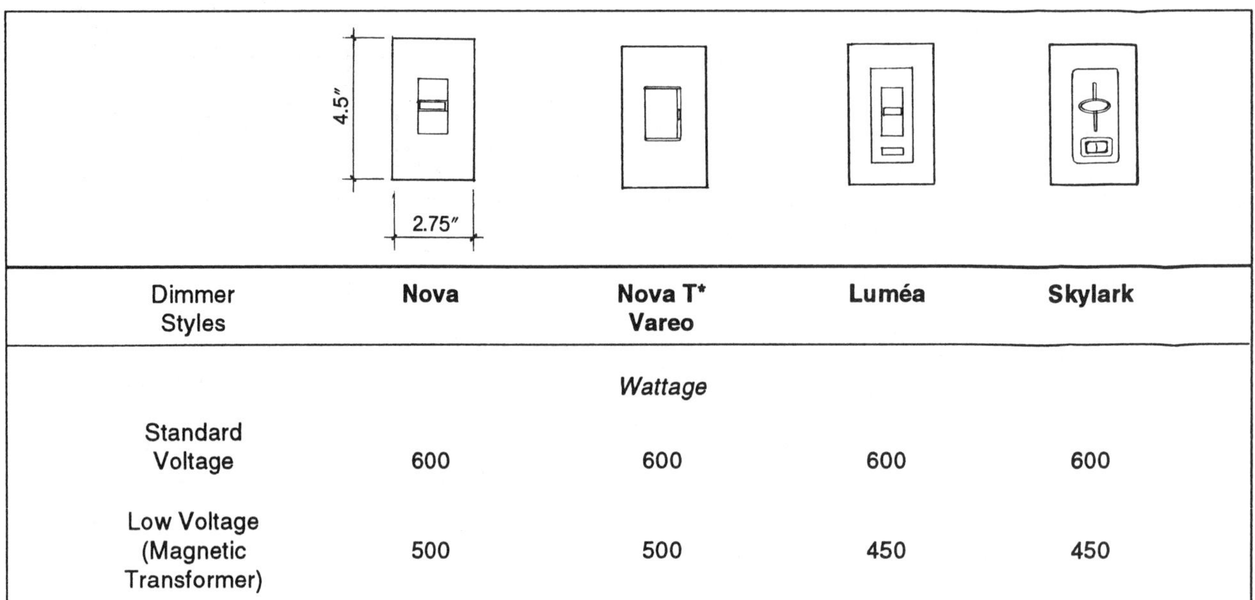

Dimmer Styles	Nova	Nova T* Vareo	Luméa	Skylark
		Wattage		
Standard Voltage	600	600	600	600
Low Voltage (Magnetic Transformer)	500	500	450	450

Figure 9.11. *Typical 600-watt dimmers. Drawing: Lezlie Johannessen.*

Manufacturers often make dimmers in several levels of quality. Available models can vary in function, size, aesthetic appearance, load capacity, and cost. For example, a high-quality low-voltage dimmer will be larger than a less expensive model and will typically have the ability to accommodate a larger wattage load. Within the series of products that a manufacturer offers, the more expensive units tend to have a more aesthetically pleasing appearance and offer a higher load capacity (see Figure 9.11).

Preset Incandescent Dimming Systems

Preset dimming systems offer the ability to automatically dim multiple groups of fixtures, called zones or channels, in a number of predetermined combinations, called scenes or presets. Three basic types of preset dimming controls are available: those that are self-contained and fit in a wall box (one unit consists of the dimming modules, preset devices, and faceplate), those that consist of a lighting control unit (light-intensity controls and faceplate) and one or more dimmer panels, and those that are managed from a computer terminal with nearly infinite capabilities.

The *self-contained* types offer the ability to dim multiple groups of fixtures manually and to preset dimming levels for each of the groups automatically at the touch of a single button. They typically handle up to four zones per panel and can be interconnected with additional panels (from the same manufacturer) to control the zones together at the touch of one or more preset buttons. They are typically restricted to a maximum of four or five scenes per panel. They are the least expensive type and work with relatively small loads. They typically have a wattage restriction for both the overall system and each zone. The overall wattage ranges from 1,600 to 2,400 watts per unit and from 600 to 1,000 watts per zone. The load restriction may make this type of system impractical for many landscape lighting situations. Often, residential and commercial projects use too much wattage for this self-contained controller.

The *control unit and dimmer panel* type offers the same functions as the self-contained type, but often has nearly unlimited load capacities per zone and for the system (see Figure 9.12). The cost is significantly more than for the self-contained system. This type of controller typically handles up to a maximum of 12 to 32 zones and 4 to 8 scenes.

The *preset control system managed from a computer terminal* typically handles from 2 to 500 zones and from 4 to over 300 scenes. This type of system often offers one or more time-activated scenes, the ability to reconfigure zones without rewiring, the ability to manually input temporary scene settings at remote locations, and photocell or motion-sensor control, among other options.

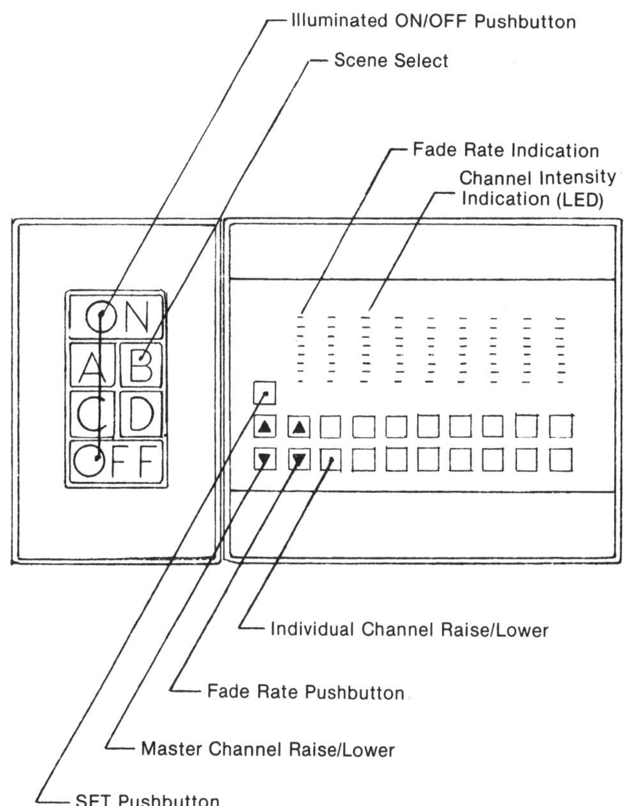

Figure 9.12. *Eight-channel, four-scene master-control station.*

Most of these controllers are more complicated and offer more control than landscape lighting projects require. These make sense for some residential interior and many commercial interior properties but are typically overkill for landscape lighting.

Fluorescent Dimming

Some limitations exist in dimmers for fluorescent lamps. For example, some dimmers can only dim down to a certain level of output (typically 50 percent) and then turn off to avoid creating severe flicker. Others can dim down to 2 percent output or less. Full-range dimming, however, is expensive. Unlike dimming an incandescent lamp, dimming a fluorescent lamp does not significantly affect lamp life. On the other hand, dimming fluorescent lamps does not shift the color of light produced, as with dimming incandescent lamps.

HID Dimming

Dimming HID sources has not been particularly successful to date. Two basic technologies exist to dim HID sources. One has a limited dimming range, typically around 50 percent light output, but maintains proper lamp and ballast life. The other, using a high-frequency or electronic ballast, can dim down to 12 to 15 percent

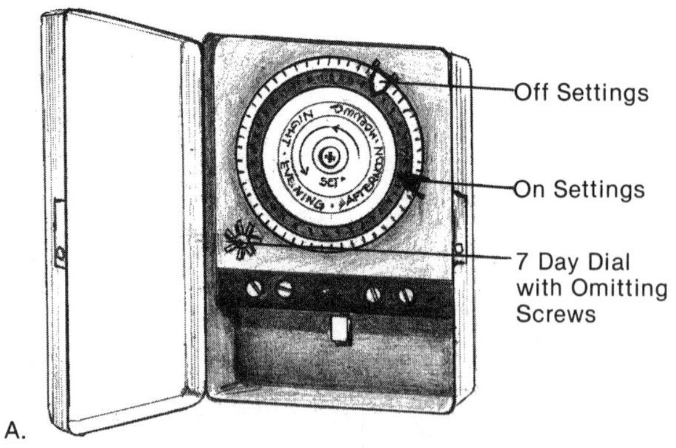

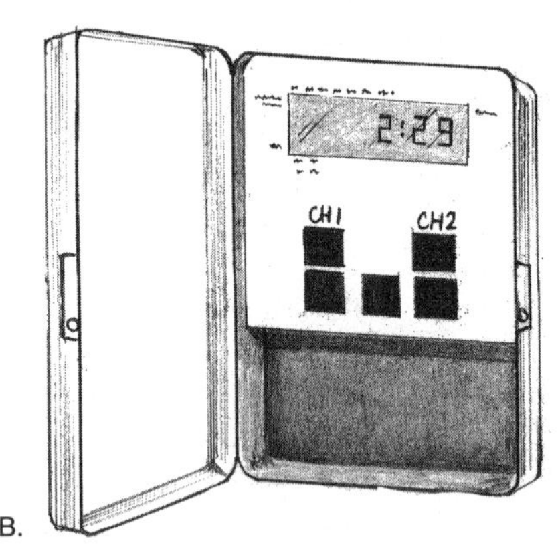

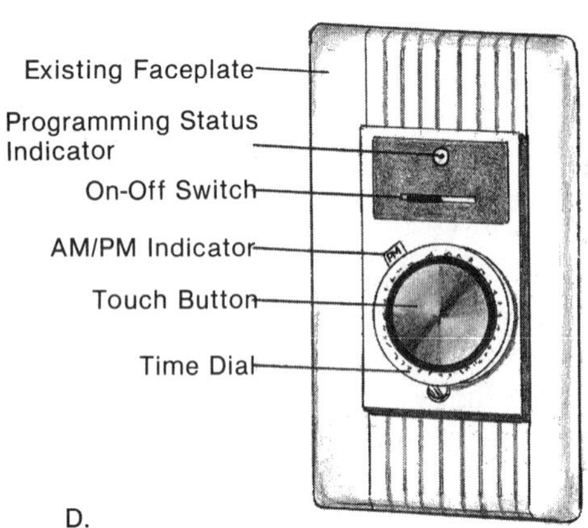

Figure 9.13. Four types of time switches. A. Mechanical 24-hour, 7-day, single-circuit device with multiple on-off capabilities and the ability to skip one or more days. B. Two-channel, multiple-purpose digital device that can turn on and off multiple times for each day of the year and can skip individual days or blocks of days. C. Electronic device that replaces a standard single-gang switch and turns a group of lights off at a timed interval such as 15 minutes or 1 hour. D. Electronic device that replaces a standard single-gang switch and can turn a group of lights on and off multiple times in a 24-hour period. This unit has a manual on-off override function as well. Drawing: Lezlie Johannessen.

output, but shortens lamp and ballast life. As HID lamps are dimmed, the color of light produced becomes increasingly monochromatic. Metal halide typically becomes more blue-green, and high-pressure sodium shifts toward orange.

Photoelectric Controls

A photoelectric control is a device that turns one fixture or a group of fixtures both on and off based on the amount of ambient light received by a photoelectric cell. Two types exist—one responds immediately and the other has a delayed reaction. The immediate-response type is normally used for individual roadway fixtures. The delayed-response type is the one used for all other types of landscape lighting loads. The delay allows the unit to avoid responding to a passing cloud or exposure to a car headlamp. The light level required to activate fixtures varies slightly according to manufacturer and model. Most units have an adjustment mechanism that allows a designer or user to select the light level on site within a range. The normal range varies from turning on at 0.75 to 2.5 footcandles up to 3 to 5 footcandles, with the unit cycling off at three times the light levels in the on mode.

Typically, this device uses a cadmium sulfide cell to detect light. The cells are sensitive to ultraviolet radiation and typically last from 3 to 5 years. Covering them with a translucent polycarbonate dome can extend the expected life. These units typically fail in the on mode. A clue that the unit is nearing the end of its life is that the foot-candle response level starts to increase and becomes inconsistent. Since the life of these devices is limited, a replacement schedule needs to be planned when designing a system using photoelectric control.

These devices can operate only a limited wattage load. For a 120-volt incandescent sources, the typical load capacity ranges from 1,500 to 3,000 watts. For sources that require a transformer or ballast (low-voltage incandescent, fluorescent, and HID sources), the load capacity ranges between 1,200 and 2,700 watts.

A photocell device needs to be placed in a location that will not invite tampering or respond to stray brightness, such as car headlamps or the landscape lighting itself. Additionally, the best way to locate it is in a place facing away from the setting sun. Both horizontal and vertical mounting types are available, plus an adjustable type that allows both horizontal and vertical positioning. Photoelectric controls can often be integrated with time switches so that the photoelectric-control turns fixtures on automatically as darkness falls and then the time switch turns the fixtures off. This combination has reduced the need for time switches that respond to each day of the year and the latitude of the building, called astronomical time switches. Both photocells and time switches need an override switch in an accessible location for times when the owner does not want the lights to come on.

Time Switches

Time switches are used to turn fixtures on and off automatically at predetermined times of day or night. Many models are available with varying capabilities (see Figure 9.13). Two technologies are available—electromechanical and digital. Both offer varying capabilities that are useful in landscape lighting.

Electromechanical units can turn fixtures on and off once a day, several times per day, or on a 7-day schedule. It can also be astronomically set to respond to sunrise and sunset at a specific latitude. Some units can skip one or more days, for example, not activating lights on Saturday and Sunday. Units that turn lights on more than once a day normally have minimum on and off time periods. This type unit has a load restriction of typically 15 to 40 amperes.

Digital units offer more sophisticated settings and more flexibility in the time settings for on-off control. These can often control multiple circuits with separate settings for each, allow an eighth standard day, providing for several holiday configurations per year, and allow one or more of the circuits to be set up for astronomic response. Each type requires battery backup to preserve the settings in the case of a power failure. The time that the battery will hold the programming varies from 24 hours to several months.

Wall-box time switches are also available. One type is a delayed-response switch that allows lights to remain on for a specific time period, such as 15 minutes, after flipping the switch to the lights-off position. An in-wall electronic time switch can be used to replace a standard single-gang on-off switch providing a timer that allows multiple on-off settings over a 24-hour time period. These typically handle limited loads (500 watts or less) and have limited program memory. This type of time switch will lose its memory with a power failure and when there is no load on the circuit (for example, if one lamp is wired to it and the lamp burns out). In this case, the timer will need to be reset.

Motion Detectors

A motion detector activates fixtures automatically when movement occurs within a specific area. This device turns lights on for a specific time period when someone crosses a passive infrared beam within the viewing range of the sensor. This can ensure that family members or guests have light to approach a home or serve as a deterrent for potential intruders. The wattage load that can be wired to the devices varies from 300 to 1,000 watts. Some have varying shapes and sizes of projection patterns that the sensor can cover (see Figure 9.14). For example, one may have a wide range but not pick up movement below a certain height, to avoid having pets and wild animals continually activating

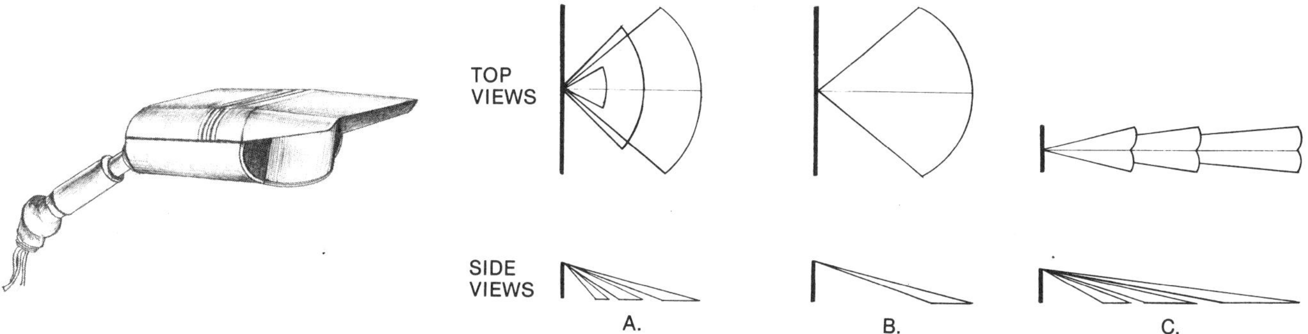

Figure 9.14. *Motion detector. Manufacturers offer multiple lens configurations for motion detectors, providing different coverage configurations. A. The standard covers a wide area and increases sensitivity closer to the unit. B. An animal alley lens permits small animals to pass undetected through most of its range. C. A longe-range lens covers a long, narrow area such as a walkway or fence. Drawing: Lezlie Johannessen.*

the lights. Others can cover a narrow but long range for narrow walkways. Some units offer several detection ranges by the selection of a specific lens. Many also offer an adjustable time of operation with the ability to turn lights on for a few seconds to 20 minutes.

Motion sensors make it easy for owners to approach their home when they use an entrance set back from the street or the garage. This controller eliminates the need to remember to turn a switch on when leaving in the morning or having the lights turn on automatically each evening with a photoelectric device. In some cases, the owners may not want the pathway to be illuminated each night or may not want guests to be encouraged to use a private entrance (see Figure 9.2).

Designing a successful control system requires the designer to evaluate the needs of the project thoroughly and then lay out a system that responds to the functions and traffic movement and is easy to operate. With so many options available to designers, a wise plan includes preparing a schematic layout that the architect, interior designer, landscape architect, or owner reviews with the lighting designer prior to finalizing the system drawings. In landscape lighting, the best control systems provide the least control. Before designing a sophisticated system, make sure that the project warrants it and that the owners want that capability. Many projects benefit from one or more of the automatic controls, eliminating the need for people to pay attention continually to the lighting.

10

Wiring

Wiring represents the critical link from a conceptual lighting design to a working reality. Any designer planning a lighting system needs to know enough about wiring to ensure that the proposed ideas will work. This chapter will look at basic power distribution, safety considerations, the critical problem of voltage drop, the differences between 12- and 120-volt systems, wire and conduit types, and planning a wiring layout. All this information helps to clarify landscape lighting wiring requirements.

POWER AND POWER DISTRIBUTION

Typically, lighting is powered by the electricity provided to buildings from the local power company (see Figure 10.1). From the main panel, electricity is directed through branch circuits to all the electrical devices planned for the building, including all the landscape lighting fixtures. In planning the wiring for landscape lighting, the designer determines the layout of wires from the building's electrical panel to the light fixtures. For 120-volt fixtures, the wire from the electrical panel typically goes through conduit directly to the fixture. Sometimes a fluorescent or HID fixture has a remote ballast that requires the wire in a conduit to run first to the ballast housing and then on to the fixture housing. Wiring to a 12-volt fixture requires running the wire from the panel to a transformer (see Chapter 7) and then on to the fixture (see Figure 10.2).

Safety

Electricity has the ability to harm or kill people. To control the use of electricity and reduce the risk of harm to human beings, the National Fire Protection Association produces and continually updates (currently every three years) the National Electrical Code. In most areas of the United States, this document serves as the basis for safety regulations. (Texas has not adopted the NEC or any other code.) Local governments sometimes lag in adopting the most current edition of the NEC. Always check which edition is currently used by a municipality.

Local areas, either cities or counties, often write more stringent regulations that either supersede or add to the NEC. For example, the city of San Diego has light-trespass regulations. Other regulations include local or state energy usage restrictions (some are based on ASHRAE 90.1-1989), or restrictions on light level or mounting height. When starting any project, always request the electrical regulations from the local authority. The local electrical inspectors have the final interpretation not only of the NEC but of all regulations. If an inspector feels that an installation is in violation of local codes, construction can be halted. Always check with the appropriate authority when a question arises about the appropriate wiring approach for a project.

Complying with the National Electrical Code

Check the requirements of the NEC carefully. The NEC is packed with technical details, and often several sections of the code cover parts of a specific issue. Finding

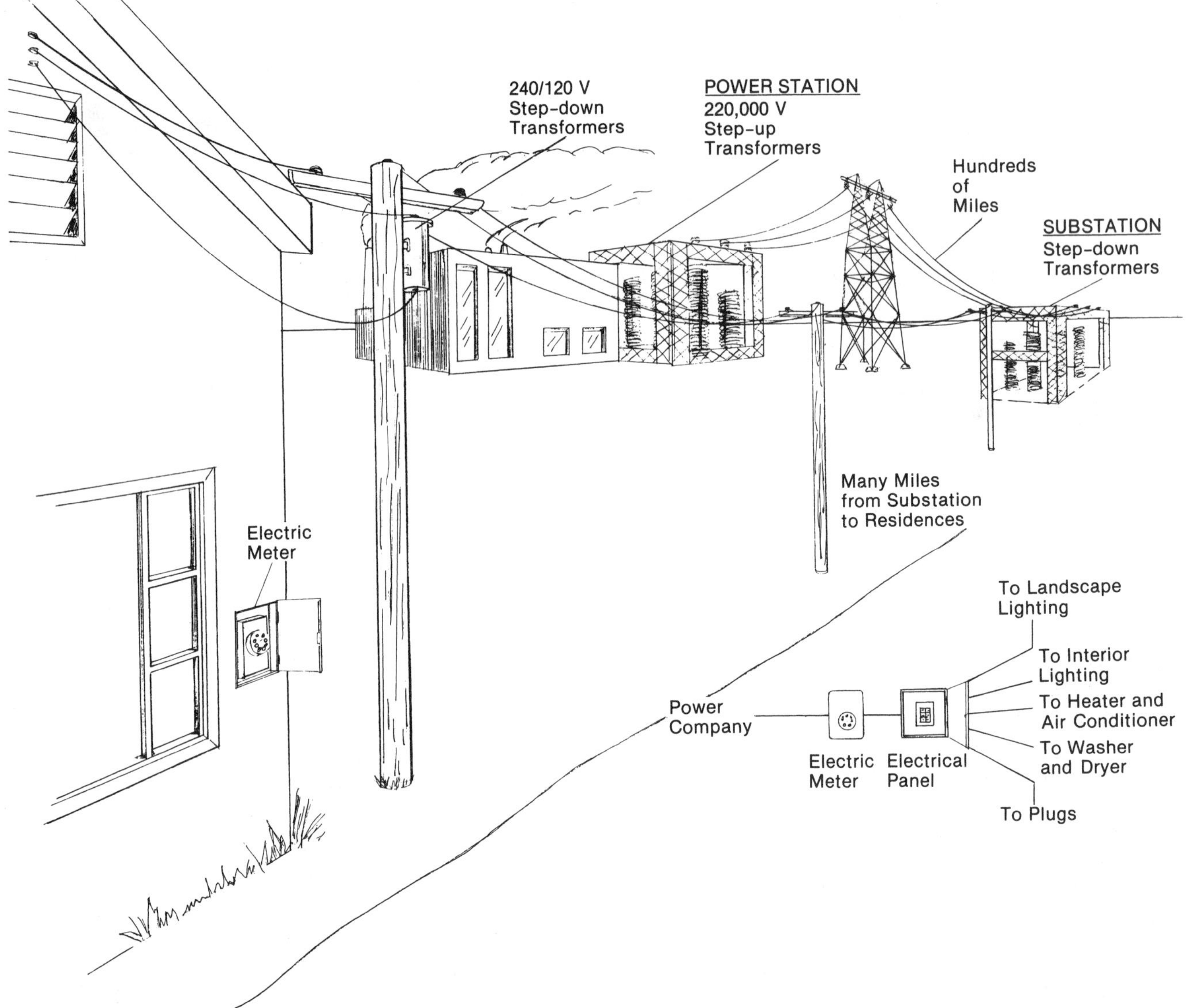

Figure 10.1. *Drawing: Lezlie Johannessen.*

specific information in the NEC requires perseverance and can be quite frustrating. Check with the local inspectors when a situation seems unclear or ambiguous in the NEC.

General wording in the NEC sometimes causes misunderstanding in the lighting industry and among inspectors. For example, in the 1987 printing, Article 225, "Outside Branch Circuits and Feeders," Section 225–26, "Live Vegetation," the code stated: "Live vegetation, such as trees, shall not be used for support of overhead spans and other electric equipment." The wording left itself open to many interpretations. A rumor circulated throughout the lighting industry that light fixtures could not be mounted in trees. The original intent of Section 225–26 was to prohibit using trees as a support for electrical service from one location to another, not to prohibit mounting fixtures in trees.

The committees that write the code, realizing this confusion, issued a tentative interim amendment before the 1987 code was released. The amendment specifically permitted mounting fixtures in trees. Then, in the 1990 NEC, the issue was addressed in two articles. First, Article 225–26 has eliminated the words "or other electrical equipment." Second, Article 410, Lighting Fixtures, Lampholders, Lamps and Receptacles," has added a sentence in section 16(h) that reads: "Trees. Outdoor lighting fixtures and associated equipment shall be permitted to be supported by trees."

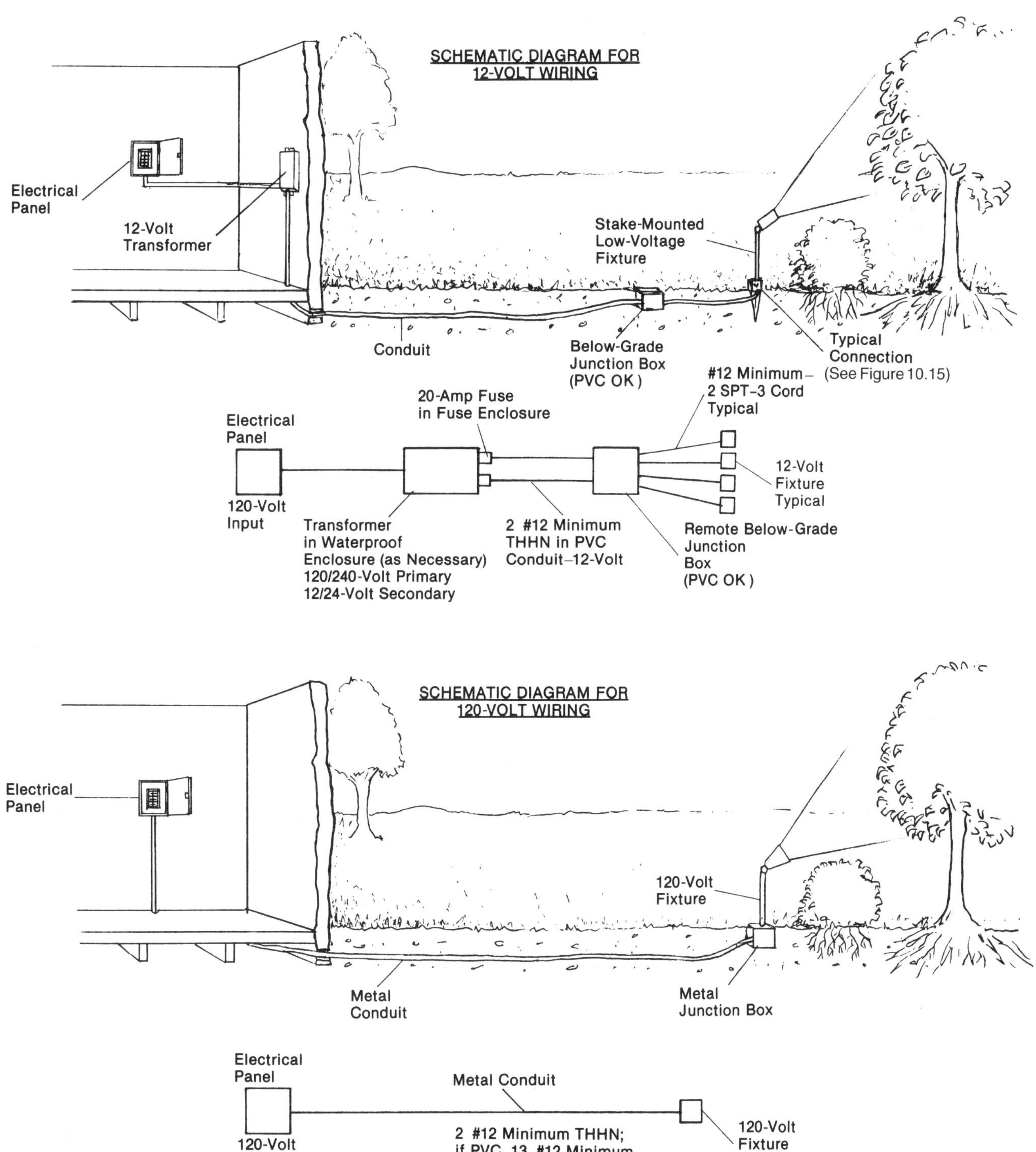

Figure 10.2. *Basic wiring diagrams for 12- and 120-volt fixtures. Drawing: Lezlie Johannessen.*

Grounding

Electricity always seeks to get to the earth's surface and takes the shortest path to get there. When a defect exists in an electrical device or in a part of the wiring system (such as an abrasion of a wire or an improper connection), and if the wire comes in contact with a person or another piece of metal that a person touches, the electricity passes through them to get to ground. In this process, the person can be seriously hurt or killed.

The point of grounding all electrical circuits and equipment is to protect people from harm. This involves bonding all metal components (not wires) that may come in contact with an electrical source and creating a path to ground. The NEC requires bonding the neutral conductor (wire) at the main electrical panel on the property to the main water service and connecting to another grounding electrode. One electrode type is a ground-driven rod typically ⅜ inch in diameter and approximately 8 feet long. The actual size of the electrode is determined by the size of the electrical service (NEC Articles 250-81 & 83 list the accepted methods).

If a ground wire is carried from the electrical panel to all the light fixtures, the fixtures will be grounded. The fixture can be bonded to a grounded metal junction box. When fixtures are mounted on PVC junction boxes, however, a ground wire must be carried to the fixture from the panel, as plastic does not carry current and the path to ground would be interrupted. All 120-volt equipment, including transformers, must be grounded. Low-voltage equipment does not require a ground wire to be carried from the transformer to the fixture (refer to NEC 250-5(a) 1 & 2).

To satisfy the NEC requirements for grounding, three separate conditions must be met. First, the path to ground must be continuous and installed permanently, providing an effective path. This portion is met by properly mounting, coupling, and terminating all equipment. Second, the wire used must be sized to safely carry any fault current that might occur (refer to NEC, Table 250-95). Last, the path must have good conductivity or low resistance. This requires the use of high-quality materials, avoiding use of two incompatible metals (providing potential for bimetallic corrosion), and adding an antioxidant to all connections to inhibit corrosion.

All 120-volt lighting, as well as being grounded, should have ground-fault protection. Wiring the circuit to a ground-fault circuit-interrupting (GFCI) device helps ensure that people will not be shocked if a problem should arise in the electrical wiring. Specify a device with a 5-milliampere tripping threshold (which is below the level that will cause physical harm to people or animals). Include a requirement in the specifications that the installer test all devices, according to the manufacturer's recommendations, to ensure that they function properly.

Fuses and Circuit Breakers

Fuses and circuit breakers interrupt power, providing safety for people and for the electrical equipment when either a short circuit or an overload condition occurs. For 120-volt systems and on the primary side of transformers, fuses and circuit breakers primarily protect the wiring from short circuits and fire hazard. At the same time, they protect people since they interrupt power, eliminating any potential for shock. On low-voltage systems, the secondary side of the transformer needs protection from overload (which could destroy the transformer) as well as from short circuits. In both cases, the breaker or the fuse should be sized for the wire load rating, not the connected load, since the connected load can change.

Protecting both sides of the transformer provides the safest condition. Either a circuit breaker or a fuse can be installed for this protection. A circuit breaker is a device that is designed to open and close a circuit. It will open the circuit automatically at a predetermined overcurrent level without damaging itself (it does not need to be replaced when it trips). Some circuit breakers react quickly, while others are built to standards that allow carrying loads over the rated capacity for a period of time before tripping.

A fuse is a device, consisting of a small strip of metal mounted in an enclosure, that completes a circuit when installed. When a short circuit or overload occurs, the metal melts and breaks the circuit (this is often accompanied by discoloration). This destroys the fuse and it must be replaced. Two types are used for lighting equipment: plug and cartridge. Plug types screw into standard medium-base sockets and are available in a variety of amperages. This type offers the advantage of easy maintenance. These can be attached to the transformer housing with a flip-up cover for easy access. Take the precaution of installing a type S fuse (a tamperproof type—it requires an adapter to fit into the standard fuse holder) to limit the high-end fuse size that can be installed.

Cartridge fuses are thin and slip into a holder that is connected in-line along the wire. The effectiveness of this type depends on the design of the holder. Some do not engage until the cover is locked in place.

Some types of fuses or fuse holders and breakers have on-off switches. This feature allows the designer to leave groups of fixtures unlit during focusing so that unaimed fixtures do not disrupt the developing luminous composition.

Pools have special protection requirements due to the extreme shock hazard. All lighting equipment in pools must be GFCI protected. Any fixtures not mounted below water must be 10 feet away from the water surface in both the vertical and horizontal directions. All submersible and wet niche fixtures must have

TERMINOLOGY	
WATT:	A measurable unit of electrical power.
VOLT:	The unit of electromotive force.
CURRENT:	A movement or flow of electricity passing through a conductor.
AMPERE:	The unit of current strength.
AMPACITY:	The current in amperes a conductor can carry continuously under the conditions of use without exceeding its temperature rating.
TRANSFORMER:	A device to raise or lower voltage. Primary side: the incoming side or the source of voltage Secondary side: the outgoing side or load voltage
SHORT CIRCUIT:	Technically a short path to ground. It refers to any defect in an electrical circuit or piece of equipment that can result in a dangerous leakage of current.
ELECTRICAL PANEL:	The distribution center of power for a site.
CONDUCTOR:	A metal wire that carries electricity from one point to another; some are bare, others have an insulation material covering them; some are solid, others stranded.
CABLE:	More than one wire (bare or insulated) covered by an outside jacket. Each conductor will be identified either by color or jacket pattern.

Figure 10.3.

a long enough cord to remove the fixture completely from the water onto a dry surface for relamping. For both these fixtures, the designer must specify the length of cord to provide an uninterrupted run back to the power source. These fixtures come with a standard length of cord listed in the manufacturer's catalog, but that length may not relate to the distances on a specific project, and splices are not acceptable by the NEC.

12 Volts Versus 120 Volts

A discussion comparing 12 and 120 volts refers primarily to issues about incandescent lighting. No HID sources are available in low voltage. Some manufacturers offer compact fluorescent lamps compatible with low-voltage wiring as a convenience to users. Both 12 and 120 volts offer benefits and have disadvantages (see Figure 10.4). Factors to consider vary from project to project, but include:

- Type, size, and condition of a site
- Lamp and fixture selection
- Amperage
- Voltage drop
- Fixture mounting
- Electrical connections

Type, Size, and Condition of a Site

Power is provided to residential buildings at roughly 115 to 120 volts and to commercial buildings from 120 to 480 volts. From the main panel, the 120-volt (or higher) power can be stepped down to 12 volts by the use of a transformer. This device, as its name implies, changes the voltage from the primary or incoming side of the device to the secondary or outgoing side. Residential properties use either 12 or 120 volts (sometimes 240 for HID light sources), while commercial properties use 12, 120, 277, or 480 volts. Voltages above 120 are restricted to fluorescent and HID light sources used in enclosed fixtures. The primary voltage used in low voltage is 12 volts, but in some situations other voltages may be used. For example, specific low-voltage specialty lighting fixtures can use 6 or 24 volts. Twelve-volt power can cause an electrical shock but not serious injury.

The 120-volt power must be used carefully, as it is dangerous and can inflict severe harm or death to people and animals. Voltages above 120 are extremely dangerous. In all fixture mountings above grade, where people have potential access (regardless of tamperproof enclosures) to the equipment, voltages above 120 volts should not be used. Higher voltages can be considered for below-grade fixtures that offer good grounding potential and for light standards (pole fixtures) that have more restricted access.

The size of a site influences voltage choice, due to the required length of wire runs and the scale of fixtures. When power must be located great distances away from the main panel, 120 volts should be selected. It has the capacity to take power over long distances with smaller cable sizes and limited voltage drop. When the overall scale of the landscape is massive, large 120-volt equipment blends into the site relatively easily. Expansive sites often have large, mature trees with broad canopies or wide areas of shrubbery that benefit from the brute strength and wide beamspreads of 120-volt lamps. When the site or trees are smaller or when mounting fixtures in trees, the smaller size of 12-volt fixtures allows hiding the fixtures more easily.

COMPARISON OF 12 VOLTS AND 120 VOLTS		
VOLTAGE	ADVANTAGES	DISADVANTAGES
120	• Minimum voltage drop • Permanent mounting locations for adjustable accent fixtures • High-wattage lamps for large trees • Wider-beamspread lamps for larger sites • Greater ampacity on wires	• Inflexibility in fixture location to accomodate changes in the landscape • Disruptive trenching required to bury conduits • The large size of fixtures limits use in small scale projects • Lamps are not available in low wattages • 120 volts is more dangerous than 12 volts
12	• A wide variety of low-wattage lamps • Small-scale fixtures that can be easily hidden in planting beds and trees as well as integrated into structures • Conduit is not required for the cables, saving materials costs • Burial depths not as deep as 120 volts, minimizing disruption and saving installation costs • Fixtures can be stake-mounted, providing movement of fixtures as the landscape changes. • 12 volts is less dangerous than 120 volts	• Increased voltage drop • Wiring must be more carefully planned, including the sizing and location of transformers

Figure 10.4.

Whether the site is newly planted or has mature plantings also guides voltage selection. Regardless of the scale of a project, if the landscape is mature, 12 volts offers the advantage of less disruption to the overall site, due to the difference in conduit burial-depth requirements (see "Conduits" below). When 120-volt power has not been distributed throughout the project, trenching, which causes significant disruption, must be done. If 120-volt power is located throughout the site, expanding the power location(s) to accommodate lighting equipment can be done without disturbing large portions of the landscape. By adding transformers at remote locations, 12 volts can still be utilized on these large, mature projects.

With new construction, the choice is less clear. Digging trenches to bury 120-volt conduit can sometimes be done at the same time as the irrigation trenching to economize on cost and minimize disruption. Once 120-volt power is provided to all areas of a site, the strengths of both voltages can be tapped.

AMPS = WATTS ÷ VOLTS

10 AMPS = 120 WATTS @ 12 VOLTS
1 AMP = 120 WATTS @ 120 VOLTS

Figure 10.5. *Amperage varies significantly from 120- to 12-volt systems, as this calculation shows. Drawing: Lezlie Johannessen.*

Lamps and Fixtures

The 120-volt lamps offer a large selection in high wattages, but become limited in low wattages. Smaller sites and many rural locations with no street lighting benefit from the wide selection of low-wattage lamps available in low voltage.

The beamspread of low-voltage lamps has greater control than that of 120-volt lamps. Using a 12-volt spot, for example, allows mounting a small fixture under a roof overhang to downlight planting or a path. If the areas to be lit have low reflectance or need high light levels, the higher wattage capability of 120-volt lamps may be the better choice.

The physical size of 120-volt fixtures is much larger than that of 12-volt units. This makes hiding 120-volt fixtures mounted in trees more difficult than hiding 12-volt fixtures. The larger fixtures are also more difficult to integrate into small sites or sites with low planting.

Amperage

Wires and cables are rated for capacity by amperage (see "Conductors" below and NEC tables 310-16 through 310-19 and 400-5(A)). This dictates the amount of wattage that can be connected to a run. The amperage carried along the wire or cable changes drastically from 120 to 12 volts (see Figure 10.5). The 120-volt systems can carry more wattage on a smaller size-wire or cable.

When wires or cables are pushed beyond their capability (by installing lamp(s) with too much wattage into fixtures) severe consequences can occur along an entire run of fixtures. For example, the addition of one fixture to a group of fixtures operating properly can exceed the wire's rated capacity. This causes the entire group of fixtures to produce a fraction of the light they produced prior to adding the fixture.

Voltage drop is a prime concern in planning the wiring of landscape lighting. Voltage drop occurs much faster with low-voltage systems and is directly related to the distance the wire has to travel, along with the total load of the run and wire size (see "Voltage Drop" below).

Fixture Mounting

Another issue to consider in voltage selection is the required flexibility of the lighting system. The 12-volt above-grade accent fixtures can be mounted on stakes, and the NEC does not require the wiring to be run in conduit throughout the site. These two factors allow low-voltage fixtures the ability to move as the plants grow or change location. Movement requires preplanning. The designer needs to predetermine the range of movement required for fixtures and specify the length of cord that should be supplied from the transformer or remote junction box.

The 120-volt equipment should be permanently mounted on junction boxes, which prohibits moving the fixture after initial installation. Remember that in landscape design, the actual plant location is determined during planting. The location of all 120-volt above-grade accent fixtures must be staked on site after the plants they will light are in the ground (see "Construction Phase" in Chapter 4).

Connections

All 120-volt electrical connections must be permanent and inside junction boxes. A cord-and-plug connection for 120-volt equipment is only allowed for temporary lighting in landscapes. When outlets have cords plugged in for an extended period of time, the risk of water entry and corrosion rises dramatically, increasing the risk of shock.

All 120-volt above-grade wiring must be in conduit outdoors up to 10 feet. Above that height, and at any height for 12-volt wiring, ultraviolet-resistant cables can be used unshielded. This limitation should discourage designers from using 120-volt fixtures on any structure where the wiring cannot be run inside the structure or mounted in trees. Conduit is difficult to hide on structures or tree trunks and detracts from the beauty of the landscape, even when painted to match.

Because outdoor low-voltage lighting is not clearly identified and addressed in the NEC, inspectors in some areas require low-voltage installations to meet all the requirements of 120-volt installations. The additional conduit required below grade and on buildings and trees, as well as junction box connections and other accessories relating to conduit runs, adds material and labor costs, stripping away some of the financial incentive of low-voltage installations.

Each of these factors should be considered in planning the lighting, but the voltage selection should not limit the ability to produce the desired lighting effects. As with all design issues, sometimes a trade-off has to be made between cost, effect, and convenience.

Voltage Drop

Voltage drop represents perhaps the most important issue in wiring. Although it occurs on both 120- and 12-volt cables, the drop is considerably faster with low-voltage systems (see Figure 10.6). Voltage drop should be calculated for all low-voltage wire runs to ensure proper functioning of the system. A 10 percent drop in voltage can be visually detected as less light. An inconsistency of voltage throughout a site (using incandescent lamps) will be noticeable since the color of light shifts toward yellow as voltage drops.

Voltage drop, as the name implies, means that under certain circumstances the voltage at the beginning of a length of wire (with fixtures attached) may be higher than at the end. Avoiding voltage drop requires the proper selection of a wire size based on the total load on the wire and the length of the run.

In some cases voltage drop can be used to advantage. For example, in a project for a private resort at Lake Tahoe 120-volt incandescent fixtures were mounted in trees 40 to 50 feet above grade. To extend lamp life, all the fixtures are slightly undervoltaged. A 10 percent drop in voltage extends lamp life by approximately four times. At the same time, it reduces light output by roughly 30 percent (see Figure 10.7).

Several different calculation methods exist to determine voltage drop. Two field guides for electricians—the *Electrician's Vest Pocket Reference Book* (see Figure 10.8) and *Ugly's Electrical References* (see Figure 10.9)—produce answers within a close tolerance. A third method, used by many manufacturers in the lighting industry, produces results allowing runs as much as 50 percent longer than do the other two methods (see Figure 10.10). For example, when 200 watts on a 12-volt system is calculated, the first two methods determine that the maximum length of run should not exceed 22 feet, but the third method allows up to 46½ feet. Whenever there is a possibility that the lighting system might

MAXIMUM WIRE LENGTH FOR ACCEPTABLE VOLTAGE DROP

AMPS X FEET X CONSTANT = VOLTS DROPPED

WATTS	WIRE SIZE	12 VOLT	120 VOLT	WATTS	WIRE SIZE	120 VOLT
50W	#12	4.17 x 88' x 3380 = 1.2	.42 x 8480' x 3380 = 12.0	750W	#12	6.25 x 570' x 3380 = 12.0
		4.17 x 89' x 3380 = 1.3	.42 x 8490' x 3380 = 12.1			6.25 x 580' x 3380 = 12.3
	#10	4.17 x 138' x 2150 = 1.2	.42 x 13,335' x 2150 = 12.0		#10	6.25 x 890' x 2150 = 12.0
		4.17 x 139' x 2150 = 1.3	.42 x 13,345' x 2150 = 12.1			6.25 x 900' x 2150 = 12.1
	#8	4.17 x 217' x 1373 = 1.2	.42 x 20,880' x 1373 = 12.0		#8	6.25 x 1400' x 1373 = 21.0
		4.17 x 218' x 1373 = 1.3	.42 x 20,890' x 1373 = 12.1			6.25 x 1410' x 1373 = 12.3
100W	#12	8.33 x 44' x 3380 = 1.2	.83 x 4,290' x 3380 = 12.0	1000W	#12	8.33 x 425' x 3380 = 12.0
		8.33 x 45' x 3380 = 1.3	.83 x 4,300' x 3380 = 12.1			8.33 x 435' x 3380 = 12.3
	#10	8.33 x 69' x 2150 = 1.2	.83 x 6740' x 2150 = 12.0		#10	8.33 x 675' x 2150 = 12.0
		8.33 x 70' x 2150 = 1.3	.83 x 6750' x 2150 = 12.1			8.33 x 685' x 2150 = 12.3
	#8	8.33 x 108' x 1373 = 1.2	.83 x 10,565' x 1373 = 12.0		#8	8.33 x 1050' x 1373 = 12.0
		8.33 x 109' x 1373 = 1.3	.83 x 10,575' x 1373 = 12.1			8.33 x 1060' x 1373 = 12.1
150W	#12	12.5 x 29' x 3380 = 1.2	1.25 x 2,850' x 3380 = 12.0	1500W	#12	12.5 x 280' x 3380 = 12.0
		12.5 x 30' x 3380 = 1.3	1.25 x 2,860' x 3380 = 12.1			12.5 x 290' x 3380 = 12.3
	#10	12.5 x 46' x 2150 = 1.2	1.25 x 4,480' x 2150 = 12.0		#10	12.5 x 440' x 2150 = 12.0
		12.5 x 47' x 2150 = 1.3	1.25 x 4,490' x 2150 = 12.1			12.5 x 450' x 2150 = 12.1
	#8	12.5 x 72' x 1373 = 1.2	1.25 x 7,010' x 1373 = 12.0		#8	12.5 x 700' x 1373 = 12.0
		12.5 x 73' x 1373 = 1.3	1.25 x 7,020' x 1373 = 12.1			12.5 x 710' x 1373 = 12.2
200W	#12	16.67 x 22' x 3380 = 1.2	1.67 x 2,130' x 3380 = 12.0	2000W	#12	16.67 x 210' x 3380 = 12.0
		16.67 x 23' x 3380 = 1.3	1.67 x 2,140' x 3380 = 12.1			16.67 x 220' x 3380 = 12.4
	#10	16.67 x 34' x 2150 = 1.2	1.67 x 3,350' x 2150 = 12.0		#10	16.67 x 335' x 2150 = 12.0
		16.67 x 35' x 2150 = 1.3	1.67 x 3,360' x 2150 = 12.1			16.67 x 345' x 2150 = 12.4
	#8	16.67 x 54' x 1373 = 1.2	1.67 x 5,250' x 1373 = 12.0		#8	16.67 x 525' x 1373 = 12.0
		16.67 x 55' x 1373 = 1.3	1.67 x 5,275' x 1373 = 12.1			16.67 x 535' x 1373 = 12.3
250W	#12	20.83 x 17' x 3380 = 1.2	2.08 x 1,710' x 3380 = 12.0	2500W	#10	20.83 x 265' x 2150 = 12.0
		20.83 x 18' x 3380 = 1.3	2.08 x 1,720' x 3380 = 12.1			20.83 x 275' x 2150 = 12.3
	#10	20.83 x 27' x 2150 = 1.2	2.08 x 2,690' x 2150 = 12.0		#8	20.83 x 420' x 1373 = 12.0
		20.83 x 28' x 2150 = 1.3	2.08 x 2,700' x 2150 = 12.1			20.83 x 430' x 1373 = 12.3
	#8	20.83 x 43' x 1373 = 1.2	2.08 x 4,210' x 1373 = 12.0			
		20.83 x 44' x 1373 = 1.3	2.08 x 4,220' x 1373 = 12.1			
500W	#12	41.67 x 8' x 3380 = 1.2	4.17 x 850' x 3380 = 12.0	3000W	#10	25 x 220' x 2150 = 12.0
		41.67 x 9' x 3380 = 1.3	4.17 x 860' x 3380 = 12.1			25 x 230' x 2150 = 12.4
	#10	41.67 x 13' x 2150 = 1.2	4.17 x 1,340' x 2150 = 12.0		#8	25 x 350' x 1373 = 12.0
		41.67 x 14' x 2150 = 1.3	4.17 x 1,350' x 2150 = 12.1			25 x 360' x 1373 = 12.4
	#8	41.67 x 21' x 1373 = 1.2	4.17 x 2,100' x 1373 = 12.0			
		41.67 x 22' x 1373 = 1.3	4.17 x 2,110' x 1373 = 12.1			

Figure 10.6. *This chart shows the maximum distance that cables can run staying within a 10 percent voltage drop—1.2 volts for a 12-volt system and 12 volts for a 120-volt system. These calculations are based on method 2 (see Figure 10.9) from Henry B. Hansteen,* Electrician's Vest Pocket Reference Book. *©1973, 1958. Courtesy of Prentice Hall, A Division of Simon & Schuster, Englewood Cliffs. NJ.*

be expanded in the future, the more conservative calculation method will provide more flexibility.

ELEMENTS OF A WIRING SYSTEM

The wiring system starts with the power provided at the main electrical panel. Then power runs through the wires and connections (sometimes placed in conduit). At the end of the wiring system is the fixture, which consists of the lamp compartment and ballast or transformer compartment or box when required. This section will look at the wires, connections, and conduits only. Fixtures, ballasts, and transformers are discussed in Chapter 7.

Conductors

Wires consist of two parts: the metal conductor and the jacket or insulator. All the additional accessories used to connect wires to each other or to other electrical parts, such as transformers, are also considered insulators. When more than one wire is carried together in one jacket, this is called a cable. A cable can carry two, three, or more wires.

The conductor carries the current (power) from one location to another. Conductors are rated by their ability to carry electricity—called current capacity or ampacity, which is listed by amperes. The capability of metals to conduct electricity varies: gold is best, then silver, then copper. In landscape lighting copper wire is used exclusively. Copper provides higher corrosion

EFFECT OF VOLTAGE DROP ON LIFE AND LIGHT OUTPUT

Uppercase letters = normal rating
Lowercase letters = adjusted rating

LIFE

$$\frac{\text{life}}{\text{LIFE}} = \left(\frac{\text{VOLTS}}{\text{volts}}\right)^{13}$$

LUMEN OUTPUT

$$\frac{\text{lumens}}{\text{LUMENS}} = \left(\frac{\text{volts}}{\text{VOLTS}}\right)^{3.4}$$

EXAMPLES

Reducing voltage by 10% for 120-volt and 12-volt lamps

120 volt, 150 watt, PAR 38 FLOOD
2,000-hour life
2,000-lumen output

$$\frac{x}{2{,}000}\text{ hrs} = \left(\frac{120}{108}\right)^{13}$$

$x = 2{,}000 \times 1.11^{13}$
$x = 2{,}000 \times 3.88$
$x = 7{,}760$ hours

$$\frac{x}{2000\text{ lumens}} = \left(\frac{108}{120}\right)^{3.4}$$

$x = 2{,}000 \times .90^{3.4}$
$x = 2{,}000 \times .6989$
$x = 1{,}390.80$ lumens

12-volt, 20-watt, MR16 (BAB)
4,000-hour life
260-lumen output

$$\frac{x}{4000}\text{ hrs} = \left(\frac{12}{10.8}\right)^{13}$$

$x = 4{,}000 \times 1.11^{13}$
$x = 4{,}000 \times 3.88$
$x = 15{,}520$ hours

$$\frac{x}{260}\text{ lumens} = \left(\frac{10.8}{12}\right)^{3.4}$$

$x = 260 \times .90^{3.4}$
$x = 260 \times .6989$
$x = 181.7$ lumens

Figure 10.7. *Based on material from the* IES Lighting Handbook, Reference Volume, *Illuminating Engineering Society of North America, New York, 1984.*

VOLTAGE DROP DATA

Wire Size	Power Factor %	A-c Single Phase	A-c Three Phase	D-c
14 Awg	100	5880	5090	5880
	90	5360	4640	
	80	4790	4150	
	70	4230	3660	
	60	3650	3160	
12 Awg	100	3690	3190	3690
	90	3380	2930	
	80	3030	2620	
	70	2680	2320	
	60	2320	2010	
10 Awg	100	2320	2010	2320
	90	2150	1861	
	80	1935	1675	
	70	1718	1487	
	60	1497	1296	
8 Awg	100	1462	1265	1462
	90	1373	1189	
	80	1248	1081	
	70	1117	969	
	60	981	849	

Multiply the current (amperes) by the distance (feet in one conductor) by the figure in the chart for the size wire used and the type of system. Point off 6 places in the product to give the number of volts drop.

For a No. 8 wire carrying 40 amperes in a 3-phase system at 90 percent power factor, the number from the table is 1189. For a one-way run of 100 feet, the product is 40 × 100 × 1189 = 4,756,000 or 4.756 volts drop.

Figure 10.8. *Voltage drop calculation method 2. From Henry B. Hansteen,* Electrician's Vest Pocket Reference Book, *©1973, 1958. Courtesy of Prentice Hall, A Division of Simon & Schuster, Englewood Cliffs, NJ.*

V = DROP IN CIRCUIT VOLTAGE
R = RESISTANCE PER FT. OF CONDUCTOR (OHMS/FT.)
I = CURRENT IN CONDUCTOR (AMPERES)
L = ONE-WAY LENGTH OF CIRCUIT (FT.)
D = CROSS SECTION AREA OF CONDUCTOR) (CIRCULAR MILS

K = RESISTIVITY OF CONDUCTOR
A. K = 12 FOR CIRCUITS LOADED TO MORE THAN 50% OF ALLOWABLE CARRYING CAPACITY (COPPER CONDUCTOR)
B. K = 11 FOR CIRCUITS LOADED LESS THAN 50% OF ALLOWABLE CARRYING CAPACITY (COPPER CONDUCTOR)
C. K = 18 FOR ALUMINUM CONDUCTORS (30 DEGREES "C")

TWO-WIRE SINGLE PHASE CIRCUITS:

$$V = \frac{2K \times L \times I}{D}$$

THREE-WIRE SINGLE PHASE CIRCUITS:

$$V = \frac{2K \times L \times I}{D}$$

THREE-WIRE THREE PHASE CIRCUITS:

$$V = \frac{2K \times L \times I \times 0.866}{D}$$

FOUR-WIRE THREE PHASE BALANCED CIRCUITS:

$$V = \frac{2K \times L \times I}{D} \times \frac{I}{2}$$

NOTE:
1—For lighting loads: Voltage drop between on outside conductor and neutral equals one–half of drop calculated by formula for two–wire circuits.
2—For motor loads: Voltage drop between any two outside conductors equals 0.866 times drop determined by formula for two–wire circuits.
*INDUCTANCE NEGLIGIBLE

CONDUCTOR PROPERTIES	
SIZE AWG/ kcmil	AREA Cir–Mils
18	1620
18	1620
16	2580
16	2580
14	4110
14	4110
12	6530
12	6530
10	10380
10	10380
8	16510
8	16510
6	26240
4	41740
3	52620
2	66360
1	83690
1 / 0	105600
2 / 0	133100
3 / 0	167800
4 / 0	211600

Figure 10.9. *A. Voltage drop calculation method 1. This calculation consists of multiplying the conductor resistivity, the distance of the circuit, and the current in the conductor (amperes) and then dividing by the cross-section area of the conductor (circular mils). Refer to circular mil numbers from NEC Table 8, "Conductor Properties." Formula reprinted with permission from* Ugly's Electrical References, *©1990, United Printing Arts, Inc., Houston, TX 77018. B. Conductor properties reprinted with permission from NFPA 70-1990, the* National Electrical Code, *©1990, National Fire Protection Association, Quincy, MA 02269. This reprinted material is not the complete and official position of the National Fire Protection Association on the referenced subject, which is represented only by the standard in its entirety.*

resistance and better conduction capacity and is more malleable than aluminum.

Wires and cables are distinguished by type and size. Classification includes the type of metal used for the wire, the maximum operating temperature, the type of insulation material used for the jacket, and the specific uses met by the conductor (refer to NEC Tables 310-13 & 400-4). In landscape lighting, uses include above grade, below grade, in conduit, and underwater. There are a limited number of cables that are acceptable for use under each of these conditions (see Figure 10.11).

Wire size increases as the coding number decreases. The size determines how much current it can carry or its ampacity. Ampacity ratings are classified by whether the wire will be enclosed (in conduit or below grade) or in free air, by the wire metal type, and by the temperature rating of the conductor. Ampacity varies for copper and aluminum wires of the same size and type. For example, a no. 12 UF copper wire is rated at 20

$$\frac{\text{TOTAL WATTS} \times \text{CABLE LENGTH}}{\text{CABLE CONSTANT}} = \text{VOLTAGE DROP}$$

CABLE CONSTANT*	WIRE SIZE
1380	#18
2200	#16
3500	#14
7500	#12
11920	#10
18960	#8

* Double constant for twin circuit

Figure 10.10. *Voltage drop calculation method 3. Courtesy of* Hadco Landscape Manual.

amperes, and a no. 12 UF aluminum wire is rated at 15 amperes (refer to NEC Tables 310-16 through 19 and 400-5(A)).

The conductor has a jacket or insulator covering the metal wire to conduct power from the source to the load, to protect people from shock, and to prevent a short circuit from occurring. The jacket thickness can change within one cable type for different service conditions. For example, SPT cable has three different thicknesses, labeled as SPT-1, SPT-2, or SPT-3, with the higher number representing thicker insulation. All exposed (including when laid under soil and not protected by conduit or some other means) SPT used outdoors should be SPT-3 for best protection.

Some jackets provide the wire with a rating for above-ground use, some for direct burial, and some for underwater lighting equipment. When a cable will be used exposed above grade, it needs protection from ultraviolet radiation and water. Ingredients can be added to the jacket to make it UV resistant. Typically, these are stamped *sunlight resistant.* Cables located below grade need biological, water, and corrosion protection. Again, ingredients can be added to the jacket to prevent bacterial or fungal attack and corrosion. Some jackets can withstand strong chemicals as well.

The letters designating a wire or cable's name provide information in shorthand about the wires use. Typically, each letter means something and guides where the cable can be used. For example, in the name "THHN" the letters indicate a thermoplastic, heat-resistant, high-temperature, overall nylon jacket. This wire is rated for 200°F (90°C), 600 volts, dry and damp locations.

This particular wire is unusual, as most manufacturers make one type to serve two different usages and call it either THHN or THHN-THWN. The 'W' in place of the second 'H' has two meanings: It indicates a wet-location rating, and that when used in a wet location, the temperature rating drops to 160°F (75°C). This means to designers doing landscape lighting that THHN (or THHN-THWN) wire can be used inside conduit outdoors, which is considered a wet location.

Some conductors are stranded, others solid. Stranded wires have more flexibility, making them easier to install, and they withstand the movement required of landscape fixtures. Many people also feel that the additional surface area provided by stranded wires makes better connections. All SPT cables are stranded, but UF cables are not stranded until no. 8 or larger. This means that UF cables are stiff and more difficult to install.

Some types of metal-clad cables are stiff, but others have excellent flexibility, making them ideal for tree mounting. When covered with an ultraviolet-resistant overjacket, metal-clad cables can be used for mounting in trees without a conduit cover. Using a flexible type allows the cable to be snaked through deeply furrowed barks. Metal-clad cables have special fittings that are not always stocked, but if the mounting detail is designed carefully, special fittings will not be required (see Figure 10.12).

Stiffness is an issue to consider in specifying wires, as it affects how easily the wire can be handled in the field. Wire size also affects handling ease. The smaller the wire size, the easier it is to handle. Sizes over no. 12 become difficult to deal with in the field. Additionally, larger wires are more expensive and often less available.

Electrical Connections

Connections represent the weak link in electrical circuits. Loose connections can increase resistance, which will cause a reduction in voltage on the wire past the connection. Loose connections also introduce the potential for disrupting the integrity of the flow of electricity due to water exposure and corrosion.

Water can travel along the wire due to a condition called *wicking*. This refers to water migrating between the wire and its jacket. A nick in the insulation is enough to provide entrance for water. Once inside the wire insulation, the water can have a clear entry to the fixture housing. Turning the lamp on and off changes the pressure inside the lamp compartment, which will draw water into the housing. If it reaches the housing, water can cause an electrical short, lamp failure due to water buildup, and corrosion.

The only way to prevent wicking is to stop the path of movement along a wire. For example, strip the insulation off the wire (see Figure 10.14) and surround it with a waterproof compound (see Figure 10.15). Manufacturers of underground lighting fixtures often provide an anti-wicking or anti-siphon chamber where wires are isolated, or simply a wicking barrier on the wire itself (see Figure 7.5).

TYPICAL WIRE TYPES FOR LANDSCAPE USE		
LOCATION	WIRE DESIGNATION	DESCRIPTION
ABOVE GRADE	UF (Sunlight Resistant)	Thermoplastic underground feeder. Must be marked as sunlight resistant. Moisture-resistant jacket must have ingredients to prevent biological (bacterial or fungal) attack and corrosion. Must be waterproof and corrosion resistant. Maximum operating temperature 60°C/140°F. Typically available in #14 or #12 aluminum through #4. NEC requires it be labeled along the entire cable exterior. Not suitable for embedding in concrete. See NEC article 339.
ABOVE GRADE AND BELOW GRADE	MC (Metal-Clad)	Shielded cable for above-grade use. Available with PVC jacket for sunlight, water, biological, and corrosion protection, as well as aesthetic appearance. Suitable as underground feed with PVC jacket. One type, CorraClad, easily rolls out and conforms to shape (for snaking in bark). Consists of flexible ribbed-aluminum sheath over insulated copper (TFN, TFFN, or THHN) conductor. Can be used as 120- or 12-volt cable up a tree without additional conduit. Meets NEC maximum operation temperature rating of 90°C/194°F. Available in #18 through #2. Number of conductors varies with size.
	SPT	Stranded service cable, parallel jacketed, all thermoplastic with 300 V rating. Available as SPT-1, SPT-2, SPT-3 (jacket thickness increases with number). SPT-3 has heaviest insulation for rough service. Available with two or three conductors (third for grounding). Maximum operating temperature rating 60°C/140°F to –30°C/–18°F. Sizes vary from #18 to #10 with varying jacket thickness. See NEC table 400-4. Not recommended for hard usage. Squirrels and other animals may chew.
BELOW GRADE	UF	See above.
	SPT	See above. For below-grade use, a special type has bacterial inhibitor in jacket material. It is both waterproof and corrosion resistant.
IN CONDUIT	THWN / THHN	Thermoplastic, heat-resistant, high-temperature, all-nylon-jacketed cable. Maximum operating temperature when wet 75°C/167°F. Most THHN meets THWN NEC 310-13 requirements. Available #14 through #1000.
	THW	Thermoplastic, heat and moisture resistant. Larger overall size than THWN. Used before THWN developed. Maximum operating temperature when wet 75°C/167°F. Still used in some fixtures with a 90°C/194°F fixture rating. Available #14 through #2000.
UNDER WATER	SO	Thermoset-insulated and jacketed hard service cord for extra-hard usage. Outer covering is oil resistant. NEC table 400-A lists it for damp location. NEC article 680-56b lists it for underwater. Available in sizes #18 through #2 (two or more conductors).
	ST	Thermoplastic- or thermoset-insulated and thermoplastic-jacketed hard-service cord for extra-hard usage. NEC table 400-A lists it for damp locations. NEC article 680-56b lists it for underwater use. Available in sizes #18 to #2 (two or more conductors).

Figure 10.11.

Consider the environmental conditions of all outdoor connections. In some case, the connection will be exposed only to damp conditions. This requires less protection than when the connection will be exposed to soil and water. Some above-grade connections require waterproofing, others do not. For above-grade connections, use a waterproof connector at all locations where the wires will be exposed to standing water. If the connection will be exposed only to moisture or passing water, a waterproof connector is not necessary.

For example, connections protected from water or where water will drain through a space do not require waterproofing. Wire nuts are sufficient for most above-grade locations not exposed to water collection. The spring inside the wire nut is corrosion resistant and is not reactive with the wires. A good practice when making wire nut connections is to ensure that the connection is solid, have the wire nut located with its opening toward ground, and then wrap in a dielectric compound or rubber mastic tape to prevent moisture from entering the wire nut space (see Figure 10.16). When connecting a solid wire with a stranded wire, insert the stranded wire deeper in the wire nut.

All below-grade connections must be waterproofed. Provide a water-resistant covering on wires to prevent corrosion and wicking. Make sure that all joints and fixture openings (such as stems) are sealed to prevent simple water entry into the transformer housing, junction box, or lamp housing. Always specify fixtures with an anti-siphon chamber.

A number of waterproof connectors are available. Direct-burial splice kits can be used for wire connections in below-grade junction boxes or for low-voltage connections buried in soil (see Figure 10.17). Two types are available at this time, one for lighting equipment below 30 volts, and one for lighting equipment up to 600 volts. Within each type, two sizes are available. These have different-sized tubes that allow various types and quantities of wires within the connection tube. The tubing material typically is not UV resistant.

When a wire in the field gets broken, it can be reconnected and then waterproofed using a heat-shrink product. This is a product with an adhesive lining that attaches to both the connector and the wire insulation. It provides resistance to water and chemicals, as well as additional strength to minimize the connection being pulled apart. Most manufacturers make two strengths of heat-shrink wrap. Only the thick-walled material should be used for outdoor and below-grade purposes.

Conduits

As discussed previously, the landscape environment is harsh and destructive. In addition to the corrosive elements that electrical equipment must withstand, wires

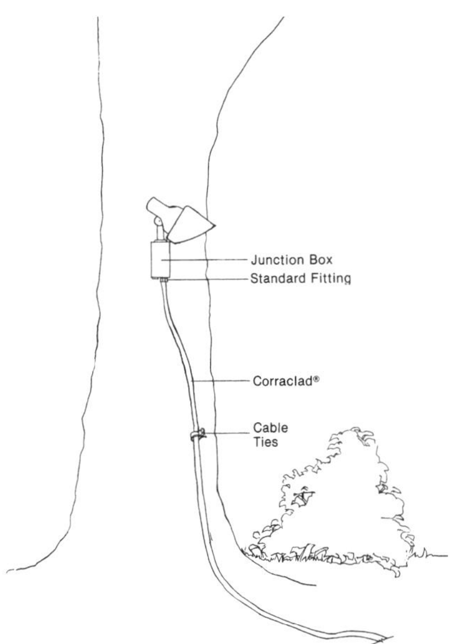

Figure 10.12. *Using a flexible metal-clad cable to provide power to a tree-mounted 120-volt fixture eliminates the need for a separate conduit. Connecting the cable to the junction box at the bottom prevents direct water entry and allows for the use of a standard fitting. Drawing: Lezlie Johannessen.*

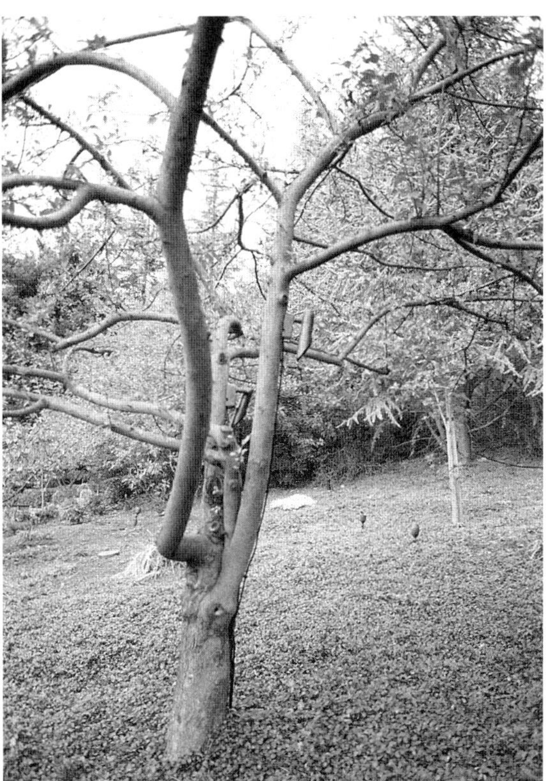

Figure 10.13. *Cable positioned on the back side of this tree and attached with cable ties allows for tree girth expansion and hides the cable from view. The fixture is located so that during the day it is not noticeable and yet lights the ground plane in front of the tree. Lighting Design and Photograph: Janet Lennox Moyer, MSH Visual Planners.*

Figure 10.14. *This close-up of an anti-siphon chamber before potting shows the electrical separation necessary to prevent wicking. Photo courtesy of Kim Lighting.*

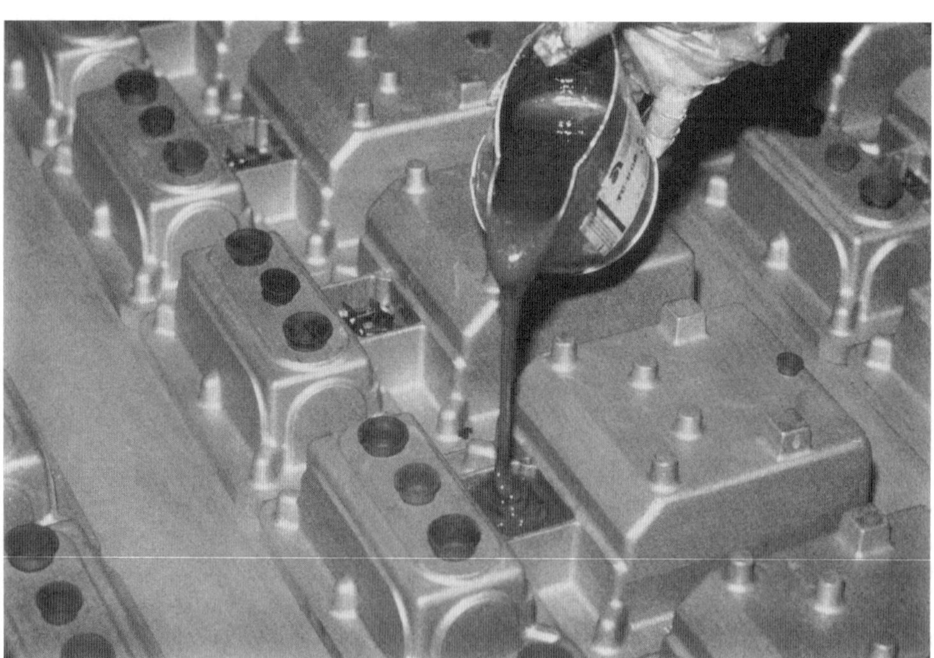

Figure 10.15. *Epoxy is poured into the anti-siphon chamber after the electrical connections have been made and the bare wire exposed. The epoxy prevents water from continuing to travel between the jacket and the wire into the lamp or ballast chamber. Photo courtesy of Kim Lighting.*

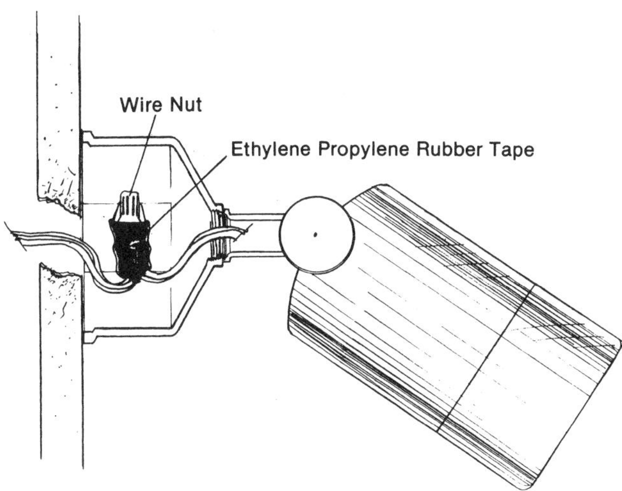

Figure 10.16. *Typical wire nut connection. Drawing: Lezlie Johannessen.*

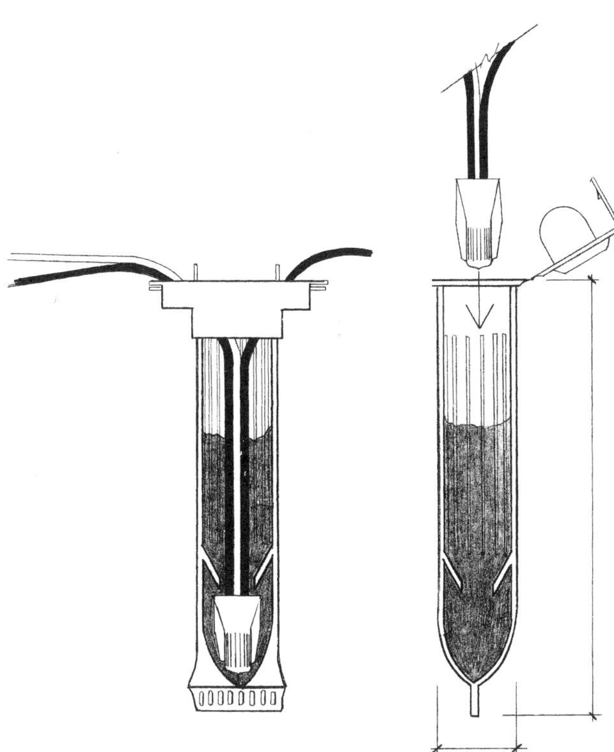

Figure 10.17. *Direct-burial splice kit. This waterproof connection kit includes wire nuts, two tubes filled with a waterproof sealant, and a chart showing the number and size wires compatible with the kit. The tube has a lid to limit water entry, and inside it are tabs that hold the wire nut in place after insertion. Drawing: Lezlie Johannessen.*

must survive shovels, picks, and other construction tools during normal maintenance or renovations in the landscape. The best protection for electrical wiring is to run the wires in conduit.

The NEC governs the use of conduit. All 120-volt systems must be in conduit when mounted on structures or trees to a height of 10 feet above grade. All 120-volt cables, except direct-burial cables, must be in conduit when located below grade. Burial depths vary based on location and type of cable or conduit (see Figure 9.17). Technically, low-voltage direct-burial cable does not have to be in conduit.

It is prudent to use conduit for both 120- and 12-volt systems in all below-grade installations in any areas where ongoing renovation or planting changes are anticipated. Landscapers cannot be expected to anticipate the locations of wires. Even diligent workers can pierce wires without realizing it. If they do not report the problem, finding the break in the system can be difficult and can either compromise safety or cause the system to fail.

Conduit is available in metal and plastic versions. The metal types offer greater strength, but they are more expensive and more difficult to work with. Bends are difficult to make and will have a wider radius. Corrosion, as usual, is an issue to consider. Additives and wraps are available to limit or delay corrosion of metal conduits.

Manufacturers make two types of PVC conduit: one for irrigation (automatic watering) systems and one for electrical systems. Irrigation conduit is white, while electrical is gray in color. Electrical and irrigation wires should not be run in the same conduit. Additionally, electrical wires should not be run in irrigation conduit. At no time combine 12-volt and 120-volt wires in the same conduit.

Only two types of PVC pipes are rated for use as electrical conduit: schedule 40 and schedule 80. Schedule 80, with 30 percent thicker walls and well over two times the crush strength, provides better protection. Neither provides the protection strength of metal conduit. PVC has several advantages over metal conduit, however. The material is less expensive; it is easier to work with because it is much lighter in weight, can be cut with saws to any length, and bends more easily with tighter radii; and it resists corrosion from organisms, water, and chemicals. In connections made in the field a solvent is used to create a cemented weld.

The decision about whether to use PVC or metal conduit involves several issues. A more complex installation with many turns or tight turns favors PVC. In new construction when the landscape has not yet been installed, digging deeper to bury PVC conduit (18 inches depth versus 6 inches required for metal) may be desirable. If major changes over time or continual

TYPE OF WIRING METHOD OR CIRCUIT					
Location of Wiring Method or Circuit	Direct-Burial Cables or Conductors	Rigid Metal Conduit or Intermediate Metal Conduit	Rigid Nonmetallic Conduit Approved for Direct Burial Without Concrete Encasement or Other Approved Raceways	Residential Branch Circuits Rated 120 Volts or less with GFCI Protection and Maximum Overcurrent Protection of 20 Amperes	Circuits for Control of Irrigation and Landscape Lighting Limited to Not More than 30 Volts and Installed with Type UF or in Other Identified Cable or Raceway
All locations not specified below	24	6	18	12	6
In trench below 2-inch-thick concrete or equivalent	18	6	12	6	6
Under a building	0 (in raceway only)	0	0	0 (in raceway only)	0 (in raceway only)
Under min. of 4-inch-thick concrete exterior slab with no vehicular traffic and the slab extending not less than 6 inches beyond the underground installation	18	4	4	6 (direct burial) 4 (in raceway)	6 (direct burial) 4 (in raceway)
Under streets, highways, roads, alleys, driveways, and parking lots	24	24	24	24	24
One- and two-family dwelling driveways and parking areas, and used for no other purpose	18	18	18	12	18
In or under airport runways including adjacent areas where trespassing prohibited	18	18	18	18	18
In solid rock where covered by min. of 2 inches concrete extending down to rock	2 (in raceway only)	2	2	2 (in raceway only)	2 (in raceway only)

Note 1. For SI units: 1 inch ÷ 25.4 millimeters
Note 2. Raceways approved for burial only where concrete encased shall require concrete envelope not less than 2 inches thick.
Note 3. Lesser depths shall be permitted where cables and conductors rise for terminations or splices or where access is otherwise required.
Note 4. Where one of the conduit types listed in columns 1–3 is combined with one of the circuit types in columns 4 and 5, the shallower depth of burial shall be permitted.

Figure 10.18. *Conduit and cable burial depths (noted in inches) required by the* National Electrical Code. *Reprinted with permission from NFPA 70-1990, the* National Electrical Code, *1990, National Fire Protection Association, Quincy, MA 02269. This reprinted material is not the complete and official position of the National Fire Protection Association on the referenced subject, which is represented only by the standard in its entirety.*

replanting is anticipated, the extra safety of metal conduit may outweigh the extra material cost and added installation difficulty.

WIRING APPROACHES

The basic guideline for wiring starts with circuit load. The total load that can be attached to a wire depends on the wire capacity (see "Conductors" above), the system voltage, and the circuit breaker size (in amperes) back at the main panel. Additionally, the NEC requires that no circuit be loaded more than 80 percent. On a 120-volt circuit, the breaker size will typically be either 15 or 20 amperes. Taking into account the 80 percent loading restriction, this translates into a total load of either 1440 or 1980 watts (see Figure 10.19). Prior to laying out the wiring approach, determine which fixtures will be controlled together and total the wattage of these fixtures. This will identify the total anticipated load for each group.

Fixtures Mounted at Grade

The ground-mounted uplights in the lighting layout shown in Figure 10.20 provide general guidelines for most outdoor wiring. In the example there are 14 ground-mounted uplights. If these are 12-volt fixtures, the maximum wattage per fixture depends on the lamp type and fixture wattage rating. For this example, the maximum per fixture is 50 watts, making the total anticipated load 700 watts.

Using a typical 120-volt fixture, the maximum wattage per fixture ranges from 150 to 300 watts (depending on the manufacturer). For this example, the maximum wattage will be 150 watts. This means that the total possible load of the 14 uplights would be 2,100 watts (see Figure 10.20A). While the lighting designer may not install a 150-watt lamp in the fixture, the load must be calculated to handle the maximum rated fixture wattage.

Daisy Chain Wiring Method

In this case, the anticipated load exceeds the capacity of a 20-ampere circuit and needs to be split into two circuits. One way to split the fixtures would be to connect the seven lights near the building on one circuit and the remaining seven at the back of the property on a second circuit (see Figure 10.20B). The total distance for the first group of fixtures is 55 feet. With a potential load of 1,050 watts, this distance is well within an acceptable voltage drop for a no. 12 wire (see Figure 10.6). The 1,050 watts translates to a 9-ampere load (see Figure 10.5 for the formula), which is within the 20-ampere allowable capacity for the various types of no. 12 copper wire (see "Conductors" above & NEC Table 310-16). For the fixtures at the back, the longest leg of the run is 64 feet. Again, this falls well within the capacity for a no. 12 copper wire and the distance for an acceptable voltage drop (refer to NEC Table 310-16 & Figure 10.20B).

Since 120-volt fixtures should be mounted on a junction box (see Figure 7.26) and not on movable stakes, the fixtures cannot move. This, and the fact that 120 volts can travel long distances, makes the daisy chain wiring method—a single wire connecting one fixture to the next—appropriate for 120-volt ground-mounted uplights.

If those same fixtures were 12 volts, they could be mounted on stakes (see Figures 7.27 & 7.28), making it possible to move them (to respond to plant growth or planting changes), and the wiring approach would change (see Figure 10.20C). The total load would be 350 watts (50 watts maximum per fixture) or 30 amperes. Using the daisy chain method would require a no. 10 wire (minimum) for wire capacity, but with a distance of 61 feet from the panel to the last fixture, the voltage drop would be almost 4 volts, which is unacceptable.

Loop Wiring Method

To avoid a voltage drop, the wiring could be done as a loop. Providing a loop feeds the group of fixtures from both ends, doubling the wire run distance (see Figure 10.21). When using this method it is critical that the polarity of the wire be maintained. Cable manufacturers make all cables so that each conductor can be identified anywhere along the cable. Common methods include having one conductor jacket marked by one or more ribs while the other conductor jacket is smooth, or by using a color variation from one conductor to the other. To maintain polarity, bring both the ribbed and smooth conductors back to their respective terminals of origin (see Figure 10.21).

VOLTS × AMPS = WATTS
NEC REQUIREMENT: LOAD CIRCUIT ONLY 80% TOTAL CAPACITY
120 VOLTS × 15 AMPS × .80 LOADING RESTRICTION = 1,440 WATTS
120 VOLTS × 20 AMPS × .80 LOADING RESTRICTION = 1,920 WATTS

Figure 10.19. *Circuit load calculation.*

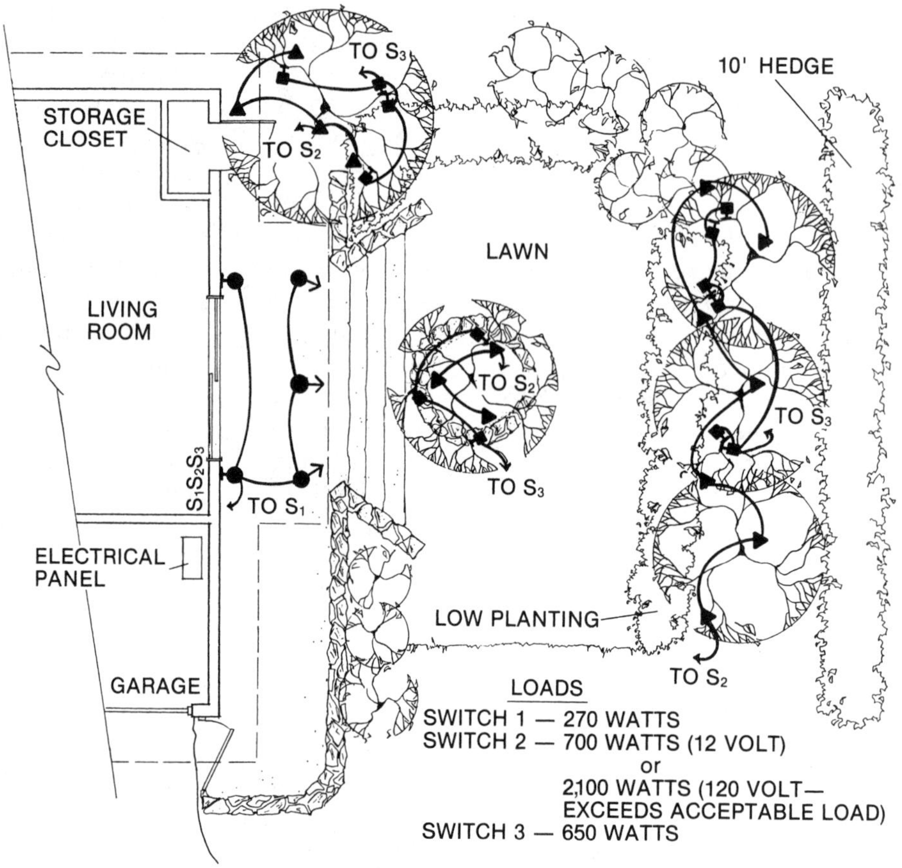

Figure 10.20A. *This layout provides an example of a potential lighting scheme. The uplights could be either 12- or 120-volt fixtures. Note that if the uplight load on switch 2 is 120 volts, it must be divided onto two separate switches.*

LOADS

SWITCH 1 — 270 WATTS
SWITCH 2 — 700 WATTS (12 VOLT)
or
2,100 WATTS (120 VOLT—EXCEEDS ACCEPTABLE LOAD)
SWITCH 3 — 650 WATTS

LUMINAIRE LEGEND FOR FIGURE 10.20 A–E

Sconce symbol	Sconce–120 Volts /60 Watts Max.
Circle symbol	Recessed Downlight–12 Volts/50 Watts Max.
Triangle symbol	Stake Mounted Uplight–If 12 Volts, 50 Watts Max. If 120 Volts, 150 Watts Max.
Square symbol	Tree-Mounted Downlight, 12 Volts/50 Watts Max.

CONTROL STRATEGY

Switch 1	Sconces and Recessed Downlights
Switch 2	All Uplights
Switch 3	All Downlights

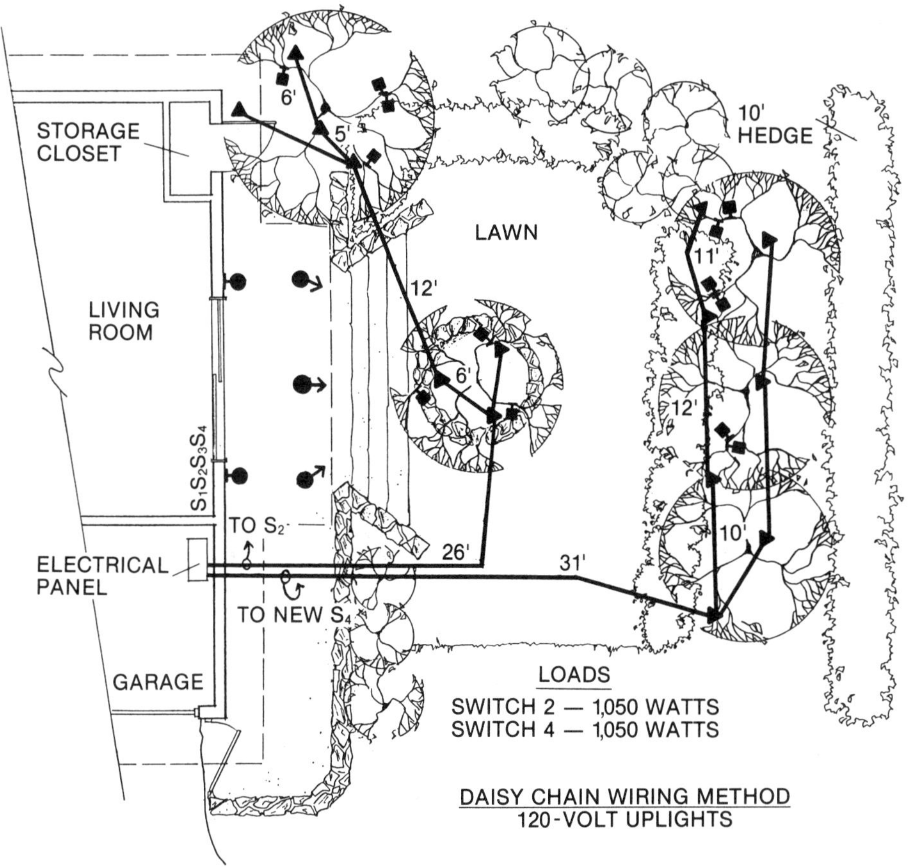

Figure 10.20B. *For this scheme, the uplights are 120 volts. This method consists of bringing wire to the first fixture, then on to the second from the first, and so on, until the last fixture is reached. Voltage drop occurs less quickly with 120 volts than with 12 volts, making the daisy chain method appropriate in this case.*

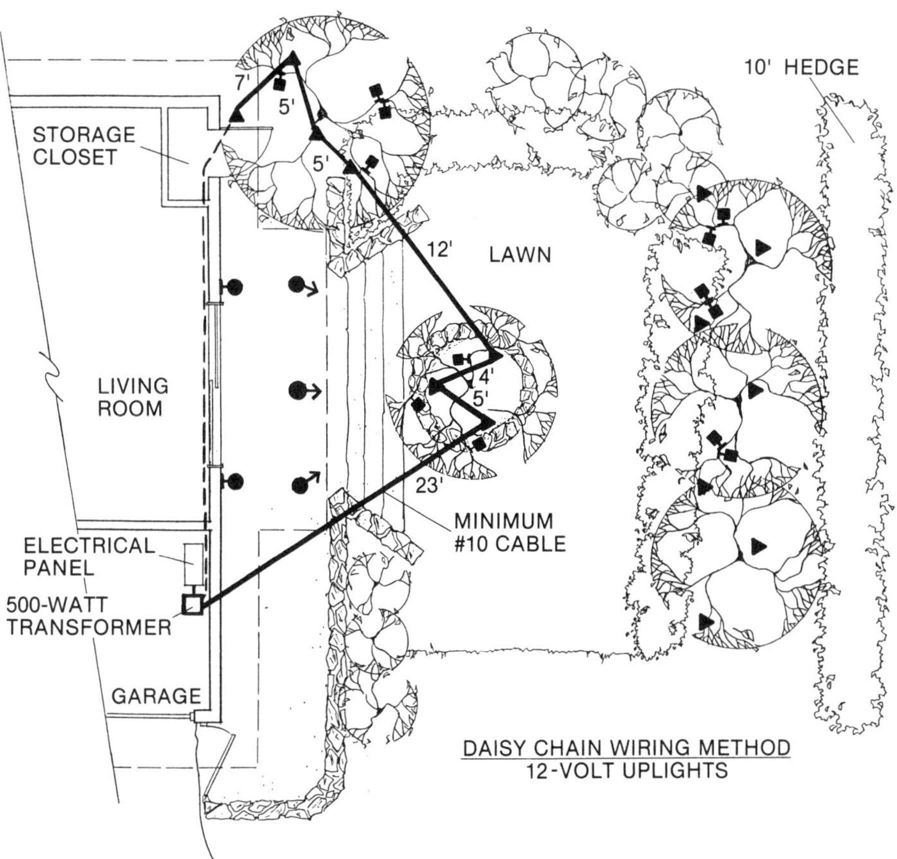

Figure 10.20C. *Using the daisy chain approach for these 12-volt fixtures limits fixture movement and the overall wire distance length possible. Here, total voltage drop is nearly 4 volts, so this scheme exceeds the acceptable 10 percent (or 1.2-volt) drop. In some cases, creating a loop, as shown with the dotted line, minimizes voltage drop to an acceptable level.*

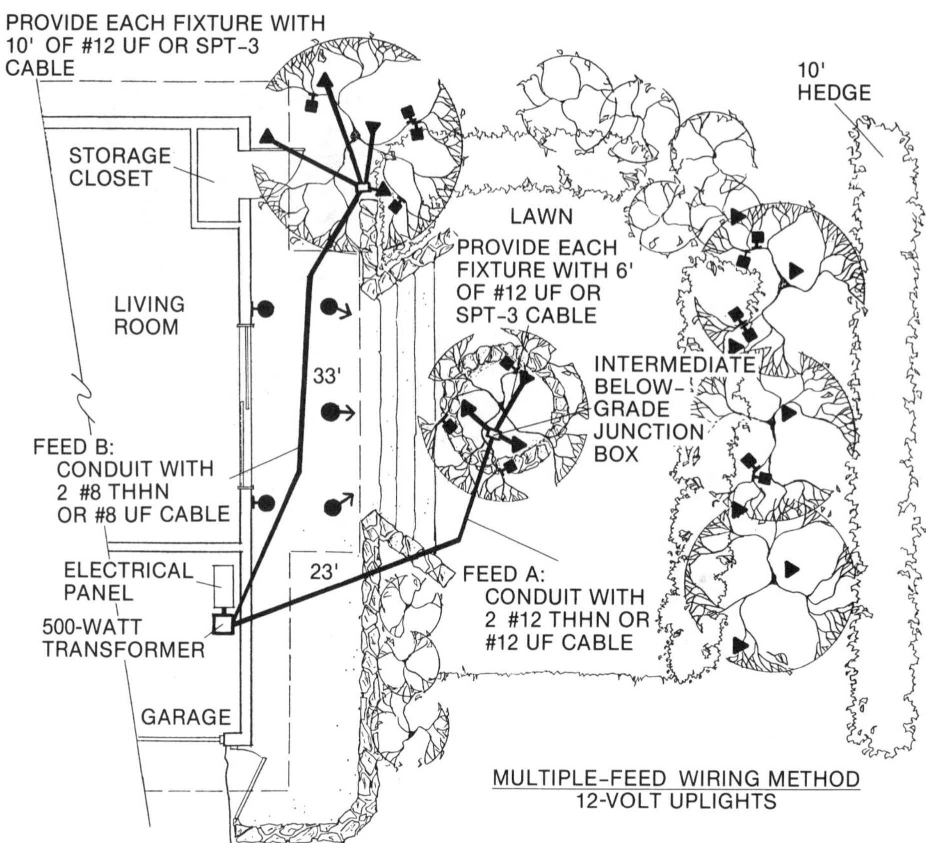

Figure 10.20D. *This scheme shows the use of two separate feeds to minimize voltage drop. A wire feeds from the electrical panel to a remote, below-grade junction box. Each fixture is then fed with a separate wire for free range of movement.*

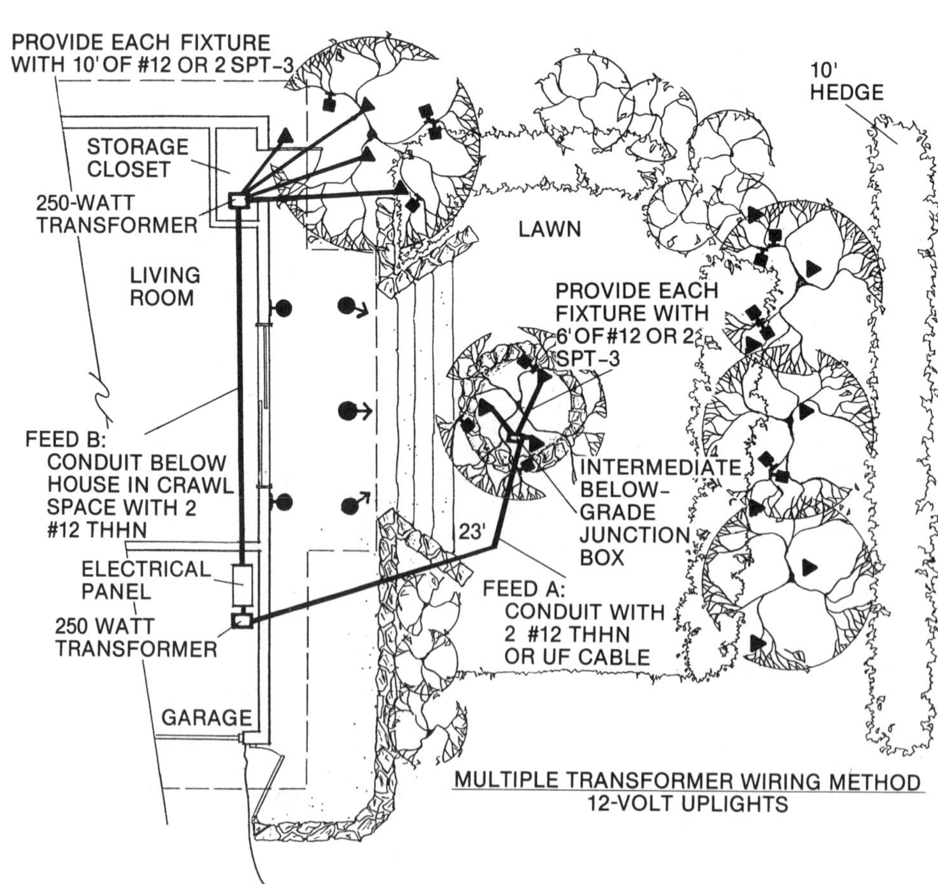

Figure 10.20E. *The best approach, in this example for 12-volt fixtures, uses not only two feeds, but takes 120 volts to a second transformer located closer to the fixtures for feed B. This allows using smaller wire sizes and greatly increases the distances possible for the individual fixture feed wires. Drawings: Lezlie Johannessen.*

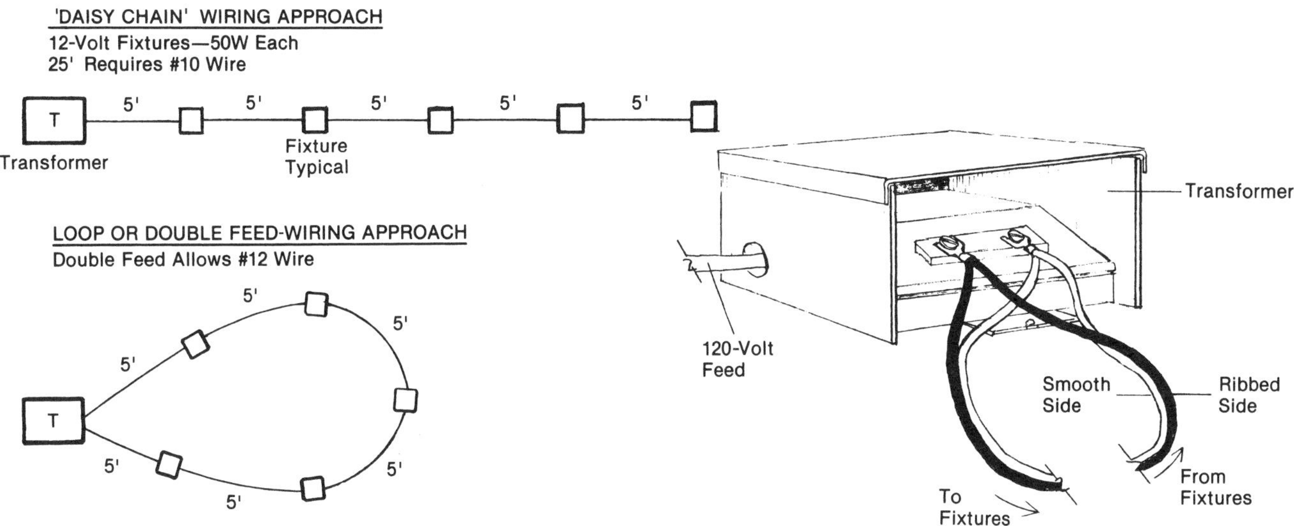

Figure 10.21. Modifying the daisy chain wiring approach to the loop or double feed decreases the wire run length. When looping a wire and returning to the origination point, wire polarity must be maintained at the transformer connection points. Drawing: Lezlie Johannessen.

Multiple-Feed Wiring Method

The best way to handle voltage drop would be to provide two separate feeds and not link the group in a loop (see Figure 10.20D). This method uses two feeds from the transformer, each running to a remote below-grade junction box located in the vicinity of each group of fixtures. The load on feed A is 150 watts and the distance to the junction box is 23 feet. Using a large wire size, voltage is preserved. The calculated drop to that junction box is 0.97 or 1 volt. From that junction box each fixture is then fed with a separate cable, allowing free movement and thus providing an advantage over the daisy chain approach.

To determine how long the cable can be from the remote junction box, the same voltage drop calculation is used starting with the 11-volt level at the junction box. The load now drops from 150 watts to 50 watts (for each fixture). Calculating from this point allows each cord to be approximately 12 feet long. In this case, only 6 feet is needed.

Feed B would require a no. 8 wire to the remote junction box, as the distance is 33 feet with a load of 200 watts. Again, from that point, the length of cord and voltage drop would be recalculated at the voltage occurring at the junction box and with the load dropping to 50 watts per fixture. The length of cord to each fixture could be as long as 30 feet and still stay within an acceptable voltage drop (see Figure 10.20D). Feeding each fixture with a separate cable increases both acceptable cable distance and the range of area each fixture can cover.

Multiple-Transformer Wiring Method

A better solution for feed B uses two transformers. The original one, located by the electrical panel, drops in size from a 500-watt unit to a 250-watt unit, since it will feed only the three fixtures (total 150 watts) located by the tree in the lawn. From the electrical panel a 120-volt feed is taken to a second transformer mounted in closer proximity to the fixtures (in the closet off the living room). This unit is also a 250-watt size to feed the four fixtures (200 watts) located by the tree beyond the porch. From that location separate feeds go to each fixture and can be as long as 88 feet using No. 12 wire (see Figure 10.20E).

Fixtures Mounted in Trees

Wiring for fixtures mounted in trees has special requirements. Make sure that the tree is physically large enough to hold the weight of the fixture and in good health to withstand the stress of attaching a fixture to it. Young trees or recently planted trees should not have fixtures attached to them. Young trees have not built a strong enough structure to handle the shock and the weight. Recently planted trees are already under stress since their root systems have been disturbed.

The strength of trees varies from one type to another. As a general rule, do not attach fixtures to trunks less than 12 inches across, but always research the specific tree under consideration. Whenever possible, try to mount fixtures on the main trunk rather than on

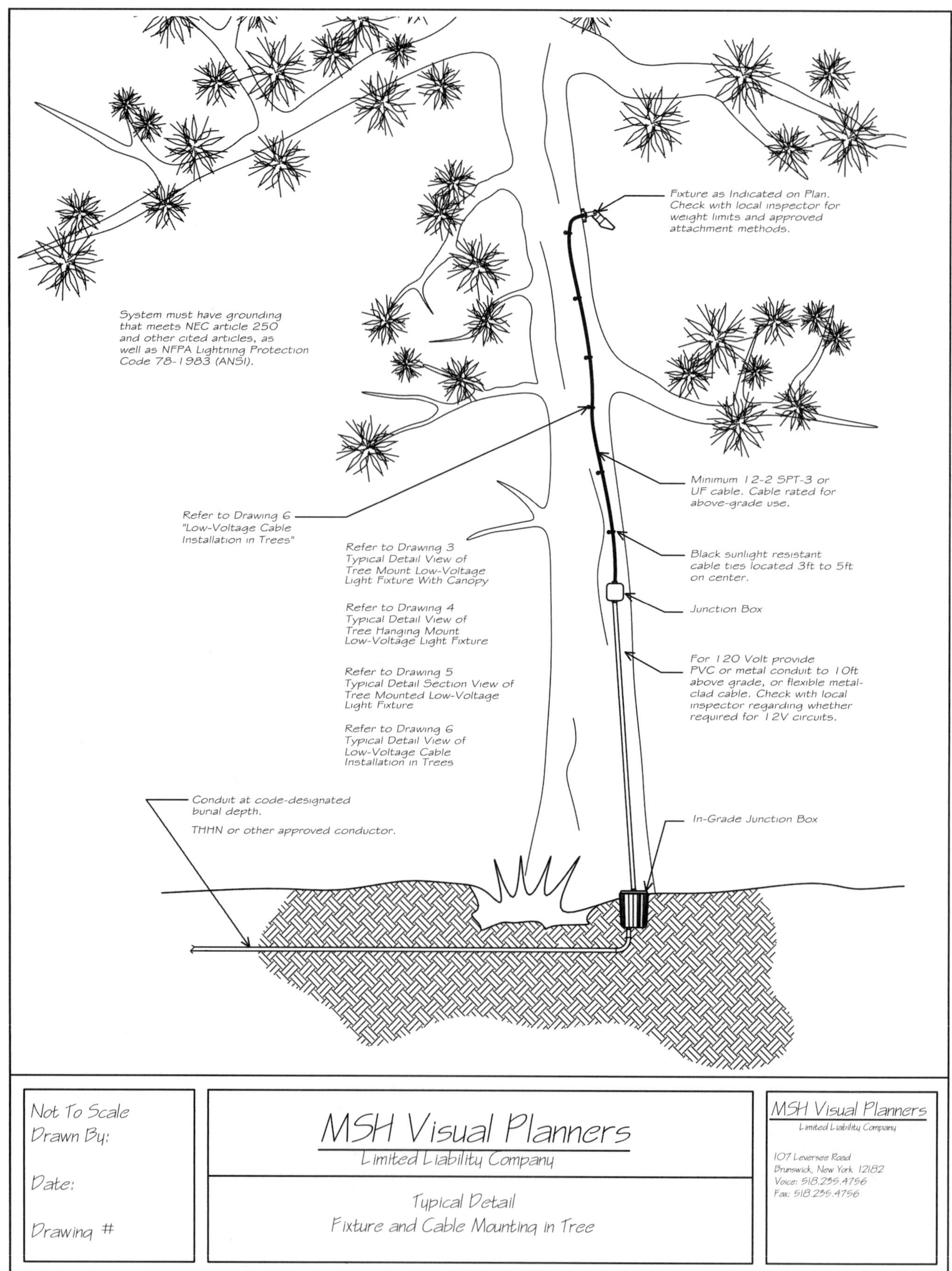
Fixture as Indicated on Plan. Check with local inspector for weight limits and approved attachment methods.
System must have grounding that meets NEC article 250 and other cited articles, as well as NFPA Lightning Protection Code 78-1983 (ANSI).
Minimum 12-2 SPT-3 or UF cable. Cable rated for above-grade use.
Refer to Drawing 6 "Low-Voltage Cable Installation in Trees"
Refer to Drawing 3 Typical Detail View of Tree Mount Low-Voltage Light Fixture With Canopy
Black sunlight resistant cable ties located 3ft to 5ft on center.
Junction Box
Refer to Drawing 4 Typical Detail View of Tree Hanging Mount Low-Voltage Light Fixture
For 120 Volt provide PVC or metal conduit to 10ft above grade, or flexible metal-clad cable. Check with local inspector regarding whether required for 12V circuits.
Refer to Drawing 5 Typical Detail Section View of Tree Mounted Low-Voltage Light Fixture
Refer to Drawing 6 Typical Detail View of Low-Voltage Cable Installation in Trees
Conduit at code-designated burial depth.
THHN or other approved conductor.
In-Grade Junction Box
Not To Scale
Drawn By:
Date:
Drawing #
MSH Visual Planners
Limited Liability Company
Typical Detail
Fixture and Cable Mounting in Tree
MSH Visual Planners
Limited Liability Company
107 Leversee Road
Brunswick, New York 12182
Voice: 518.235.4756
Fax: 518.235.4756

Figure 10.22. *Wiring guidelines for mounting light fixtures in trees. Check local codes and local requirements with electrical inspectors. Drawing: MSH Visual Planners.*

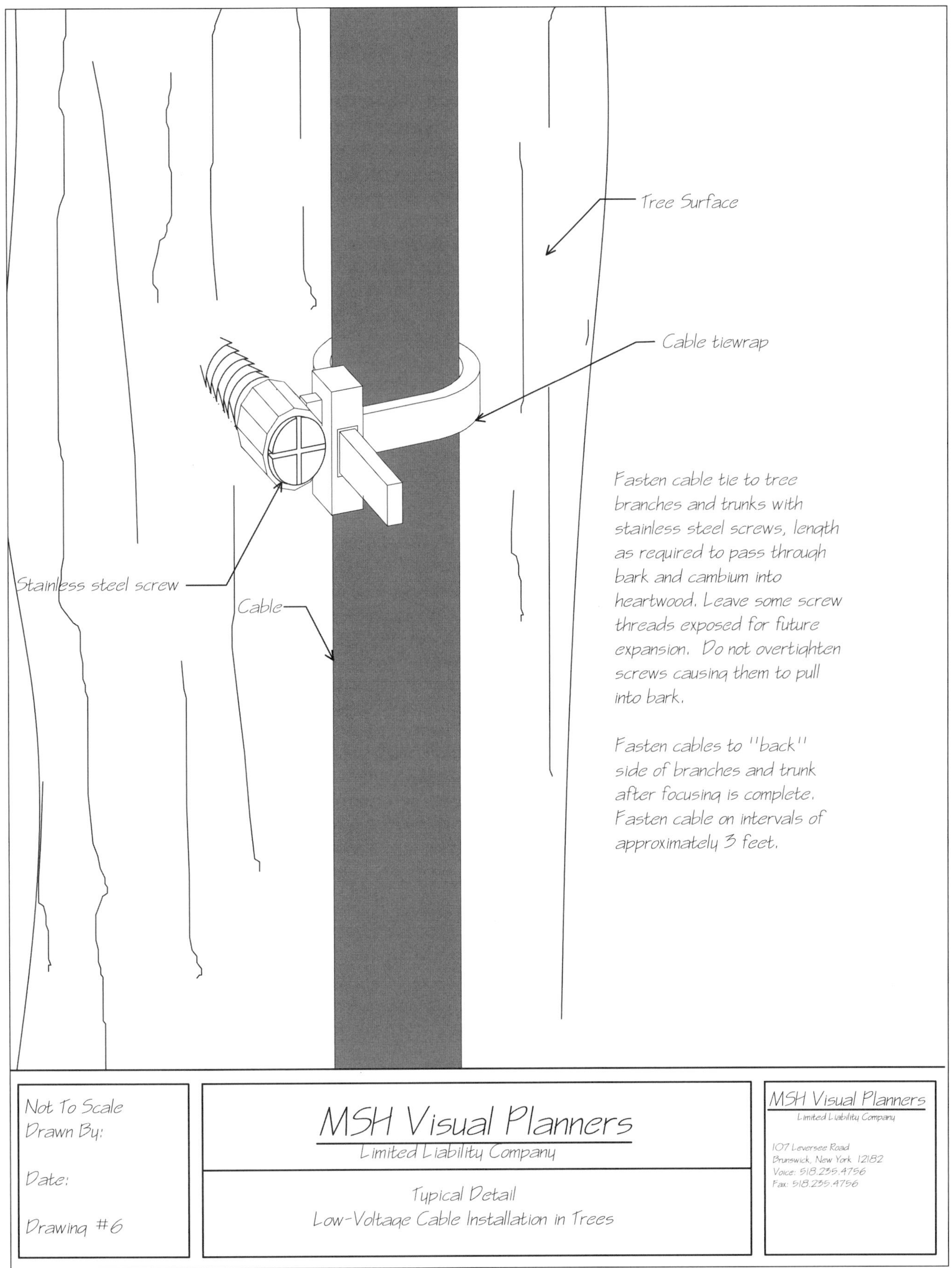

Tree Surface
Cable tiewrap
Stainless steel screw
Cable
Fasten cable tie to tree branches and trunks with stainless steel screws, length as required to pass through bark and cambium into heartwood. Leave some screw threads exposed for future expansion. Do not overtighten screws causing them to pull into bark.
Fasten cables to "back" side of branches and trunk after focusing is complete. Fasten cable on intervals of approximately 3 feet.
Not To Scale
Drawn By:
Date:
Drawing #6
MSH Visual Planners
Limited Liability Company
Typical Detail
Low-Voltage Cable Installation in Trees
MSH Visual Planners
Limited Liability Company
107 Leversee Road
Brunswick, New York 12182
Voice: 518.235.4756
Fax: 518.235.4756

Figure 10.23. *Example of cable tie installation. Drawing: N. J. Smith.*

branches. This minimizes stress and reduces the wire length.

Consider the size and condition of a tree when deciding whether to use 120-volt fixtures or 12-volt fixtures. Obviously, the smaller low-voltage fixtures blend into the tree more easily than do the larger 120-volt fixtures. Consider the weight of fixtures as well. Try to keep the overall weight below 5 pounds (again, to minimize stress).

Evaluate how the tree fits into the overall landscape and select a location around the trunk where the cable will not be noticeable to people in the landscape. Once a location has been determined, the wiring can be planned (see Figures 10.13, 10.22, & 10.23). Provide power through a below-grade conduit (using NEC-prescribed burial depths) terminating at the base of the tree in a below-grade junction box. THHN wire is suitable for use in below-grade conduit and will minimize wire cost.

From this junction box, all 120-volt power must be in conduit at least 10 feet up the side of the tree, terminating in a second junction box. Flexible metal-clad cable is an exception to the conduit requirement. It can be used from the below-grade junction box up the trunk for 120-volt fixtures. Above 10 feet, flexible, ultraviolet-resistant cable can then be used from the junction box to the fixture. Some local jurisdictions require that 12-volt systems follow this procedure; others do not. Check local codes to determine whether a 12-volt system needs to be in conduit in a specific geographic location.

The attachment method chosen for the fixture(s), wire(s), and conduit must allow for tree growth and not harm the tree. Never wrap a wire, tape, or any other material around a tree trunk or branch. The living tissue of the tree, which moves nutrients from the roots to the leaves (and vice versa) is a thin tissue layer, called the cambium, located just underneath the bark. As trees grow they expand in width. If material is wrapped around the tree, it might either cut through the cambium, killing the tree, or break if it cannot withstand the pressure of the tree expansion.

Cable ties work well for connecting wires to trees. These wrap around the wire and have a ring where a nail or screw attaches to the tree (see Figure 10.23). Select a cable tie that is sunlight (UV) resistant, as non-resistant ties will break over time. Anything driven into the tree will create a wound. Nails produce less of a wound than screws do since the cut will be clean. Also, consider the metal used. Stainless steel nails or screws are not poisonous to trees, whereas copper and brass can be poisonous to some trees. The rate of tree growth needs to be considered in lighting maintenance. If the screws or nails are not loosened, the tree will eventually grow over them.

PLANNING FOR THE FUTURE

Always plan wiring systems not only to provide the highest safety level possible, but also to respond to future needs. Over time, fixture wattages may need to be increased or additional fixtures may need to be added. Installing all wires in conduits to transformers or to remote junction boxes helps ease the difficulty of future wiring changes. A good wiring system can handle changes without significant disruption to the landscape. Plan the location of all electrical equipment to provide easy access with plenty of working room around the equipment. This aids the electrical contractor during initial installation and meets the NEC maintenance accessibility requirement.

III

APPLICATIONS

11

Residential Spaces

Landscape lighting for residential spaces has practically unlimited possibilities. Residential properties are typically smaller than public properties and the owners often want a more highly detailed end product that they are willing to maintain. Residential landscapes often have multiple uses, ranging from quiet entertaining with immediate family using limited areas of the yard, to parties for large groups that spill out into all parts of the yard, to playing a variety of sports in one or more areas of the property. The available budget for landscape lighting can vary dramatically based on the needs of the project, the importance of the lighting to the owner, and the owner's financial means. Overall, residential design requires a higher level of attention to detail from the designer and greater involvement with the owner. This chapter will look at the issues that affect residential design, starting with the knowledge and participation of the owner and then addressing the design issues that affect the development of a lighting system.

WORKING WITH THE OWNER

One of the major differences between residential design and commercial design is that the owners often want to be involved to the point of essentially becoming a member of the design team. They frequently know the site more intimately than do owners of commercial properties, use the site in more varied ways, and consider the landscape as an extension of themselves. To ensure a successful residential project, the designer must enjoy having a close working relationship with the owners of the property. The client must understand and make a commitment to maintaining the lighting effects and system (see "Maintenance" in Chapter 5). Before accepting any residential project, the designer must determine how involved the owner will want to be and then decide if the situation will work for both parties.

Sometimes, the owner will not want to be involved and will give the designer free rein. This situation is perhaps more dangerous than working closely with the owner because after the money has been spent and the design installed, the owner may not like what the designer has produced. In this type of situation, the designer needs to insist that the owner understand and approve the design before installation occurs. It may require some finesse on the designer's part to involve clients when they prefer to remain uninvolved. One way to do this is to suggest a tour of other properties, or to set up a mock-up showing the owner some ideas to gain a better understanding of what the owner expects from the lighting system.

The homeowners need to be comfortable with the lighting effects, but few are familiar with all the lighting possibilities. The designer needs to educate the owner as to the possibilities that exist in landscape lighting and then listen to the owner's response. This helps the designer develop the basic design concepts for a project. Some owners will have an idea of what they want the lighting to do, but no idea of what that actually means or how to implement it. An all-too-familiar scenario is for a lighting designer to receive a call from a

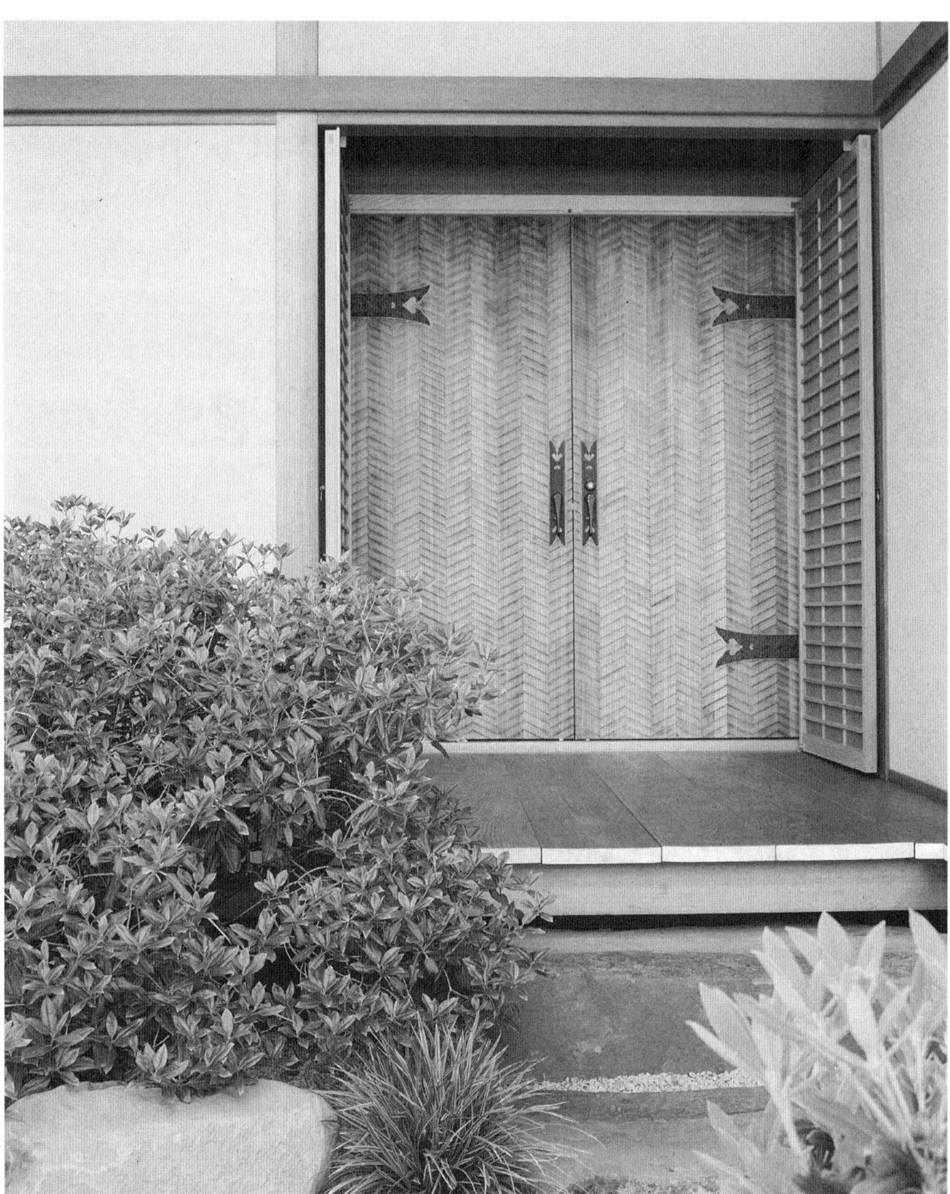

Figure 11.1. *Daytime view of the front to a home. Photograph: Kenneth Rice Photography, www.kenricephoto.com.*

frustrated homeowner who purchased a kit of lights from the local discount store and found them to be totally inadequate at producing pleasing effects.

Some owners will be familiar with construction, having remodeled their interior or built a custom home. When they have been involved in construction previously, they will have some understanding of construction costs. Many homeowners, however, have not had this experience and will need a guiding hand from the lighting designer to understand the process that will take place and the costs involved.

Often owners will not understand that there will have to be some disruption of the garden or yard to install the wiring. The maturity and type of plantings as well as the skill of the installing contractor all affect how much digging and temporary plant removal might be necessary. For example, in a mature garden, it will be difficult to install wiring without removing some roots of mature plants and often whole groups of plants.

In some cases, wiring installation can be done without permanent damage to the plants. This depends partially on whether 120- or 12-volt equipment will be used, as 120-volt equipment requires locating the wiring deeper in the ground. It also depends on how closely spaced plants are and how sensitive and careful the electrical contractor will be. The selection of the contractor is more important than might immediately be expected. Someone who has experience with plants and understands how they grow can work around the plants without harming or killing them. A contractor willing to approach the installation carefully can often install either 120- or 12-volt systems without leaving

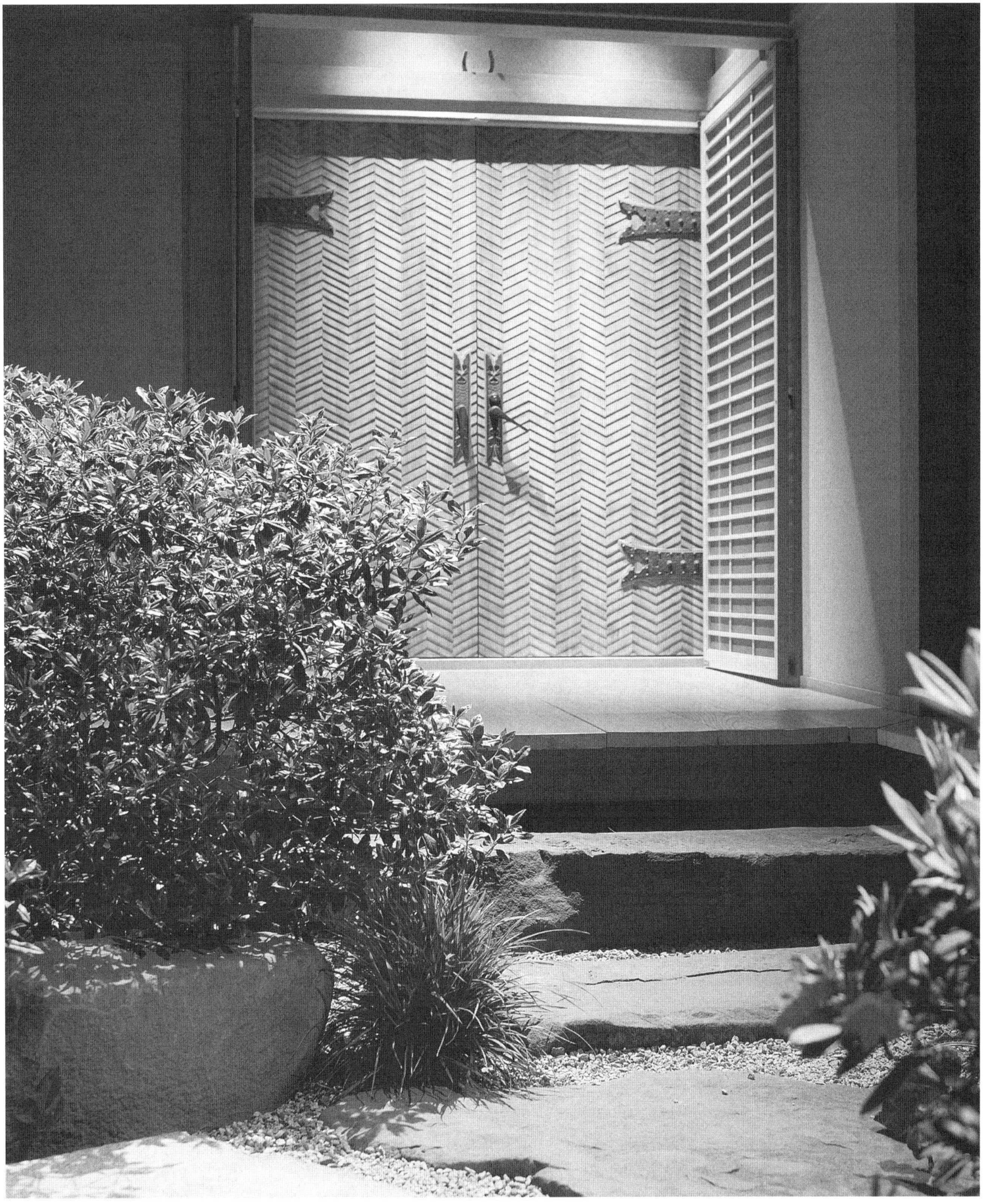

Figure 11.2. *Decisions that lighting designers make enhance architectural detailing and direct people's view through a space. Using downlights to accentuate plantings clearly illuminates the uneven pathway for safe passage. Lighting Design: Janet Lennox Moyer, Michael Stewart Hooker, & Paul Schreer; Photograph: Kenneth Rice Photography, www.kenricephoto.com.*

Figure 11.3. *In this front yard of mature redwood trees, lighting rennovations were made without disturbing the trees. On both sides of the main path, 120-volt power was available and was extended during replanting of the yard. The 12-volt transformers required for the downlighting fixtures mounted in the trees were located out of view behind trees and other plants. Lighting Design: Janet Lennox Moyer, Bash Visual Planners; Photograph: Kenneth Rice Photography, www.kenricephoto.com.*

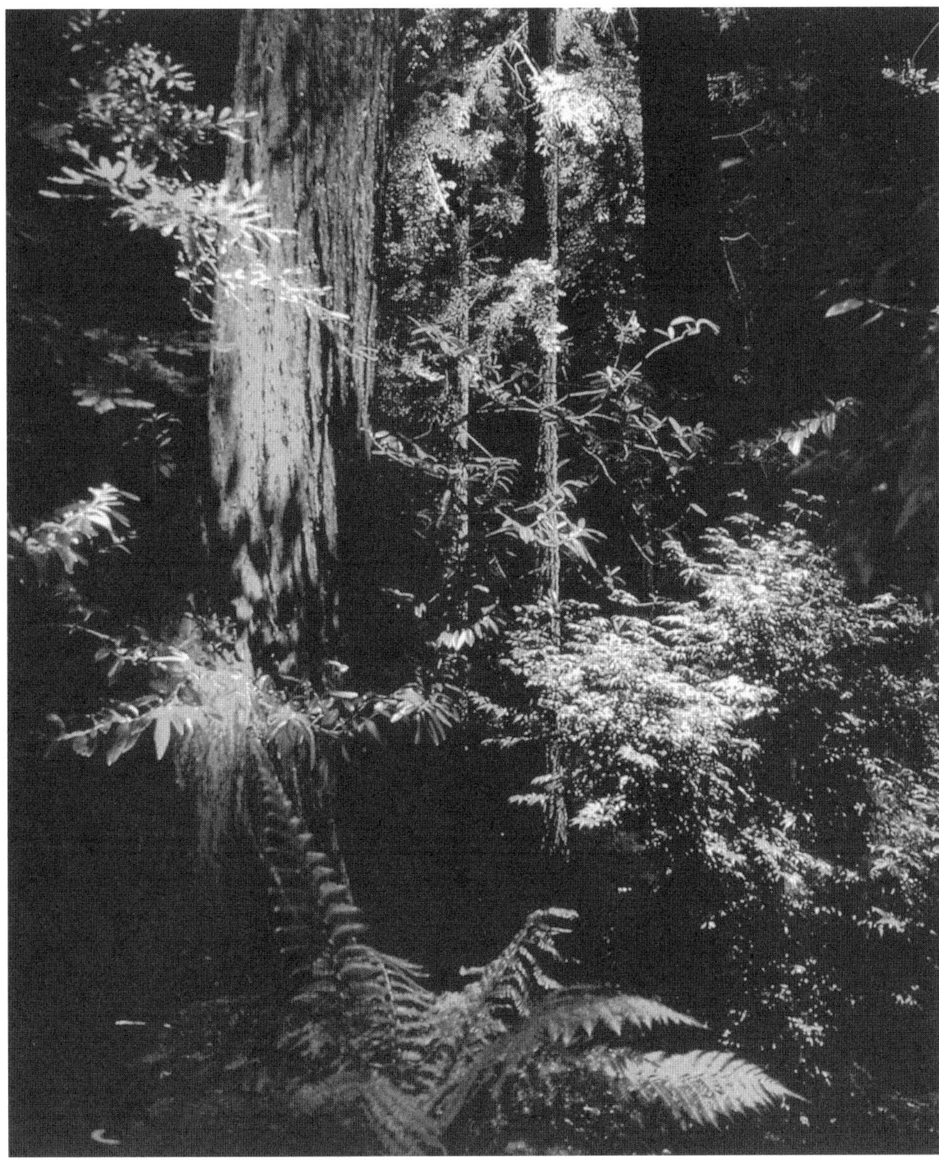

Figure 11.4. *Often landscape lighting is used to provide a view from a room inside a building out to the landscape. This view from a Piedmont, California, dining room provides a look into a quiet forest scene. 120-volt 90-watt PAR38 lamps uplight the trunks and canopies of the redwood trees, while MR16 fixtures located 25 to 30 feet up in the trees provide a soft wash onto the forest floor and smaller trees such as this Red-leaf Japanese Maple. Lighting Design: Janet Lennox Moyer; Photograph: Kenneth Rice Photography, www.kenricephoto.com; Landscape Design: Valarie Matzger.*

much, if any, trace that the work has occurred (see Figure 11.3).

The designer needs to determine the extent of the owner's understanding of the landscape, including how the property will be used; the location of furniture, sculpture, and special plants; and the owner's knowledge of all the plants used. Each of these considerations influences the basic lighting design concept. After all, lighting provides the ability to see something. When lighting a residential landscape, lighting can provide for activities from simply relaxing in an easy chair, listening to crickets, and watching the stars to playing volleyball or taking a stroll through the property.

Relaxing on a porch or patio typically requires a low, soft lighting level on the patio, along with higher light levels accentuating some of the owner's favorite plants or a sculpture as a view. Sports activities require a higher light level and proper light distribution to allow the game to proceed normally. Strolling through the property requires adequate identification of pathways and stairs so that people can walk without continual attention to where they are stepping. The path lighting should be augmented by aesthetic lighting of landscape features, providing a view along the path (see Figures 11.1 & 11.2). Each activity raises different lighting considerations, all of which can be integrated into a lighting system when clearly identified at the outset and addressed during conceptual design.

DESIGN CONSIDERATIONS

In developing a lighting system, design considerations come first. Prior to the selection of equipment, which

Figure 11.5. *Low-voltage MR11 uplight fixtures in planting beds by the stone walls graze selected elevations sculpting this home. Note that the owner has the option to leave the covered entry area dark implying that they do not expect guests. Lighting Design: Janet Lennox Moyer; Photograph: Kenneth Rice Photography, www.kenricephoto.com.*

Figure 11.6. *In an urban setting, keeping the front yard lighting to a minimum helps integrate into the neighborhood. Soft light along the entry walk leads to brighter light at the stairs and front porch, with the focus on the front door for welcoming guests. Lighting Design: Janet Lennox Moyer, Michael Stewart Hooker, & Paul Schreer; Photograph: Kenneth Rice Photography, www.kenricephoto.com.*

ultimately produces the desired effects, the design approach needs to be planned and agreed upon by everyone involved in the lighting (including the owners and the landscape, architectural, interior, and lighting designers). The lighting designer needs to keep in mind that a cohesive visual composition creates the most attractive landscape at night.

The light level needed and the techniques to implement it are directly affected by who will use the space, when they will use it, and by the activities that will occur (see Figure 11.7). For example, with large groups, the need for a higher, more even light level will increase generally throughout the site. The lighting of stairs and paths may need to be brighter and more even than when a property is used exclusively by the family. When the type of activities will vary significantly and on a frequent or regular basis, the lighting system may need to provide separate control for a number of areas with dimming capabilities within one or more of those areas (see Figure 11.5).

Creating an effective residential lighting composition nearly always relies on using more fixtures with less wattage. When the client or designer tries to light a site with a limited number of fixtures, one or more elements of composition, such as detail, cohesion, or shading—any of the special qualities that add the magic or won-

Figure 11.7. Downlighting integrated into the arbor/trellis structure creates a comfortable atmosphere for relaxing. Lighting Design: Nigel Finnimore, Hort-Couture Lighting Concepts, Sydney, Australia.

der to a design—get sacrificed or eliminated. For example, when trying to light a special tree, if not enough fixtures are utilized, the tree can look as if part of its canopy is missing, disfiguring it rather than complementing its beauty.

Property Characteristics

Both the architectural scale and style of the property influence the lighting approach. In both large- and small-scale properties, the designer must make decisions about how much of the property should be lit. It may be that only portions of the property are chosen to be illuminated rather than the entire landscape. The formality or informality of the architecture and the landscape design (including both hardscape and planting) directs the formality of the lighting. Additionally, the selection of any decorative fixtures needs to complement the architectural style of the building(s) on the site. The daytime appearance of decorative fixtures can either reinforce the landscape design theme or clash with it.

Arrival

How a property presents itself to arriving guests must be determined between the designer and the owners. Many owners want to invite guests but keep the overall appearance of the property understated (see Figures 11.6 and Color Plates 6 & 7). Downlighting from existing trees or architectural structures can highlight shrubbery along the path and allow light to spill over onto the path (see Figures 15.15 & 17.1–17.3). The front door will always serve as the focal point and should have the highest light level (see Figure 11.2). When owners want a grander appearance for the architecture, consider having a separate control group at the front door area to make a statement of privacy (see Figure 11.5).

Circulation

The designer needs to assess circulation throughout the property. Residential sites have less formal movement patterns than do public spaces. Sometimes there may not even be set paths for movement through the yard. The lighting designer needs to consider how people will approach the property and the most likely path they will take to an entry. Also, consider where and how frequently the residents or guests might circulate through the property. For example, there may be a footpath that wanders through a remote portion of the property or wooded area. Typically, paths of this nature are informal and not used frequently or regularly. The path will typically be small and be made of less formal materials than would be used in a public path. It may simply be a mulched area, consist of gravel or crushed granite, or have stepping pads of river stone or cut rounds from a tree trunk. In this case, an informal layout with a low brightness level may be appropriate. The more irregular the placement or shape of stepping pads, the more the lighting needs to ensure that each is clearly visible.

Views

The lighting designer needs to understand what parts of the landscape will be seen from inside the residence, as well as what will be seen of the interior from the landscape (see Figure 2.9 & Color Plate 60). For example, the owner may spend a great deal of time each evening in the dining room and want to be able to see the entire view out the window(s) or may prefer seeing only specific elements of that view. In either case, the portion of the landscape to be seen requires a higher light level than does the dining room and perhaps a separate control from other parts of the lighting system (see Figure 9.2). Lighting a portion of an area can provide a view and depth, increasing the apparent size of the space (see Color Plates 13, 14, & 59).

Views from one area of a property to another area need consideration as well. Minicompositions within the overall composition occur on every property. The designer needs to think through all views and ensure that the appearance is cohesive from all possible vantage points (see Figure 11.8).

Owner's Preference

The overall appearance of the landscape represents an important factor in developing a conceptual design. Lighting can replicate the way the landscape looks during daylight or create a new appearance. Owners may have an impression or mood they want to achieve with the lighting but may not understand how light can retain the daytime appearance or sculpt a new look for the property. The designer needs to discuss the importance of all the elements of the landscape, how lighting each in relation to the other will affect the overall composition, and then guide the owner as to what will work best to fit the owner's goals for the lighting (see Figures 11.1, 11.2, & Color Plates 2 & 3).

An important issue for the lighting designer to consider is the client's preference for privacy. This indicates whether the lighting should be directed only toward the client or made more available to the public. For example, some clients will not want to light the front yard or even use light to identify the front gates, preferring to concentrate the lighting in the backyard. Other clients want to highlight the front of the property as well as the back, allowing other people to enjoy the property also.

There may be a definite need for security lighting because the client travels extensively, because of the client's prominence in the community, or for a number of other personal reasons. Often, security lighting fulfills a psychological need for comfort as much as preventing any real threat. As discussed in Chapter 1, security lighting can often be integrated as one part or one layer of the overall composition. In this case, a panic switch or motion sensor can be used to activate the security lighting separately from the rest of the lighting. In other cases, it may need to be a completely separate system that does not come on with the rest of the landscape lighting, but is activated only in times of emergency (again with a panic switch, motion detector, or both).

Some owners may want to downplay the landscape and simply provide limited identification and pathway lighting. In this case, at least two options can be explored. Typically, the pathways are not the most attractive feature of the garden, but they are important from a safety standpoint. If only the paths are lit, emphasis will be directed only to that element of the landscape, at the expense of the rest of the yard. Incorporating some light on the building(s), plantings, or other features along with the paths creates a more complete visual picture. This does not need to be extensive to accomplish the goal of tying the path visually to the surroundings. For example, some downlights mounted under the eaves of the residence light the planting along the front, essentially framing the lit pathway (see Figures 11.9 & 17.2).

When the project starts, the owner may have a preconceived notion about what type of equipment should be used. For example, when mounting lights in trees to downlight lawns, paths, or plantings, often owners think that 120-volt fixtures should be used because 120 volts provide more power than 12 volts. However, because 12-volt lamps control the light being produced better than 120-volt lamps, 12-volt lamps actually perform better in this situation. Also, because 12-volt fixtures are smaller, they can be less conspicuous in the tree.

Sometimes, the owner may want to light only a certain portion of the landscape initially, due to the anticipated expense of lighting the entire property, because of a time limitation due to an upcoming event, or because the landscape is not completed in some areas. In this case the owner may want to phase the installation. Additionally, many residential landscapes continue to develop or are adjusted each year due to the nature of living plants and to changes in the owners'

Figure 11.8. Uplighting selected mature trees frames the pool pavilion garden, creating an outdoor room. Highlighting foundation trees and the architecture to a brighter level creates a sense of human scale and adds comfort to the aesthetic experience. Lighting Design: Thea Chassin, Chassin Lighting Design; Photograph: Dan Dyer.

needs and desires for the property. Landscape growth and development require that the lighting designer plan ahead for changes that might occur in the future. This can include making sure that power is planned to all areas that might be done in the future, making sure that wire and transformer sizes can accommodate additional loads in the future, and ensuring that provisions are made to install additional switches or additional loads onto existing switches and dimmers.

Equipment Selection

Once the design concept has been finalized, the lighting equipment needed to create the visual effects can be selected. This includes selecting lamps, fixtures to hold the lamps, and a control system. This process starts with the selection of the lamps because it is the lamps that actually produce the lighting effects. After the lamps have been determined, fixtures to hold the lamps can be selected, based on the needs of the location or the intended effect. Some will need to be below grade, mounted on stakes, or attached to buildings, and some may need to provide a soft light and decorative appearance during the day. The control system should be planned after the lamp and fixture selections have been made and the fixtures located on the lighting plan. Waiting until all the fixtures have been located provides an overview of the system that helps identify which fixtures should be connected together on one switch and where the switch(es) for each group of fixtures should be located.

Light Sources

Residential lighting typically utilizes incandescent light sources. Incandescent lamps offer the advantages of a wide range of beam distributions, lower wattages appropriate to the scale of small properties, and inexpensive dimming. Many types, styles, and sizes of fixtures are available for incandescent sources, making it possible to produce any desired effect. Standard incandescent

Figure 11.9. This front-yard lighting illustrates the lack of cohesion and aesthetic effect when the location of fixtures and light pattern has not been carefully planned. The house and landscape become lost behind the brightness of the decorative fixtures and behind the wash of light on the corner of the building.

lamps produce a color that is familiar to people. Quartz or tungsten-halogen incandescent lamps make a cooler, crisper color that complements the colors of foliage and flowers as well as building materials. Both types of incandescent lamps are available with a considerable range of types and wattages in both 120 and 12 volts.

Fluorescent lamps are not as frequently used, primarily because of their large size and higher light output. However, compact fluorescent lamps can augment incandescent sources in residential spaces. These lamps are available in color temperatures that are compatible with incandescent. Their small size allows the fixtures to be relatively compact. Additionally, they offer high lumen output in low wattages, making them an excellent choice for pathway lighting and floodlighting for small structures such as low walls or hedges.

HID (high-intensity discharge) lamps overpower most residential spaces, due to their large size and high lumen output. With the advent of lower-wattage lamps there may be a time in the future when the combination of a low-wattage lamp and carefully designed HID fixture may make sense for residential landscape lighting.

Fixtures

One of the most important decisions that will be made in residential lighting is the choice of fixtures. Fixtures currently available for the residential market vary significantly in construction quality. Remember that the outdoor environment is harsh and an owner's investment needs to be gauged not only by how effective the lighting will be initially but by how long the fixtures will last. Installing inexpensive fixtures that will last only a year (or less) can end up costing more in maintenance, replacement, repair, and lost lighting effects than will a more expensive fixture that meets the environmental needs of the site.

Lamp shielding is an important fixture design and construction detail to evaluate. In the night environment, a visible lamp will always be the brightest object in the field of view. Therefore, for a lighting system to be effective, the lamp needs to be hidden from view or kept at a low enough brightness (either by selecting a low wattage or by dimming separately from other lighting equipment) to integrate it appropriately with the brightness of other parts of the design. For decorative fixtures, this requires recessing the lamp up into a roofed area or down into the base of the fixture; using a thick, diffuse glass that spreads the lamp brightness evenly and hides the lamp image; or incorporating some type of optics, such as a louver assembly, to direct the light and hide the lamp. While this is important for all fixtures used, it becomes more important when a change in grade occurs on the site that will make the viewing angle to the fixture vary from place to place.

Another concern regarding the permanence of a potential lighting system is whether animals, children, or maintenance personnel may knock fixtures out of adjustment or potentially damage or harm the fixtures or the wiring system. In selecting a fixture, along with analyzing the materials used and finishes applied, consider construction details, including lamp shielding, waterproofing protections, and locking mechanisms to make sure that the lamp brightness will not overpower the scene, that the fixtures will last, and that the aiming will be retained over time (see Chapter 7).

Attention to residential landscape lighting has become increasingly common only during the last decade, so costs are not as commonly understood as are the costs of varying qualities of furniture, different types of art, and even homes of various sizes in different parts of town or the country. Fixture costs represent approximately 40 to 60 percent of the cost of residential projects. If a designer can relate the cost of the equipment to the potential effects that can be created, owners can begin to understand the value of lighting. They realize that they are buying a tangible item that adds to the aesthetic and monetary value of their property.

Additionally, as with any type of design, there is a direct correlation between cost and aesthetics. Money wisely spent produces a better end product, although an owner does not have to spend exorbitant amounts of money to have pleasing landscape lighting. The designer needs to work with the owner to plan the best system for the amount of money that the owner can or wants to spend. Sometimes a client may set a budget that the designer knows is not realistic. The budget is often determined before the designer is involved or the design concept developed and has no correlation to what could be done with the lighting or what it takes to produce the results they desire. In this case, the designer needs to explain to the client what might be gained with a specific amount of additional money. If the client insists on a budget insufficient to install the entire design, the designer should ensure that the wiring system provided (including the size of transformers when using 12-volt equipment) allows for completing the design in the future. Often, once the owners see the incomplete lighting (as restricted by their budget), they will choose to install all the equipment from the original design.

Sometimes the owner wants to light the entire property but cannot initially spend the amount of money required for the entire project. In this case, the designer can suggest phasing the lighting installation. The complete project should be designed in this case with phases identified on the drawings and a request for separate costs for each phase in the request for bids documents (see Chapter 4).

Controls

For residential properties, keeping the control system simple ensures that the owner will know how to operate the system. It also saves money that can be used to purchase more fixtures. Unless the homeowners use the landscape for multiple functions on a regular basis, it is more cost-effective to install on-off switches than to use dimmers. When light levels are balanced throughout the site during the focusing of the lighting system, dimming may not add significantly to the use of the system.

Devices that have multiple on-off switches in a master panel give owners the flexibility to use only portions of a lighting system, present a clean, organized appearance on a wall, and often fit on a single-gang junction box (see Figure 9.5). Often, this type of control panel can be connected to remotely located dimmers for one or more of the groups that might benefit from the ability to change light levels.

Motion sensors are helpful in areas such as entries, sidewalks, back service areas, or other special function areas surrounding the home. Often, having one portion of the lighting come on each evening with a photocell or in combination with a time switch provides a level of automatic control that aids the homeowner without adding significant cost to the project. Chapter 9 provides more detailed information on the types of controls available.

Residential projects often offer the opportunity to design highly individualized lighting systems with effects that enhance the homeowner's enjoyment of their property, add value to the property, and showcase the designer's talents. This type of project requires that the designer plan to stay intimately involved in the project through construction; focus the system once construction is completed; train the owner, the gardener(s), and anyone else that will be involved in the landscape on how to keep the effects working properly on a day-to-day basis; and ensure that a maintenance system is in place for the long-term functioning of the system. Additionally, the designer must enjoy working closely with individual homeowners and be prepared to deal with their individual personalities. One of the joys of residential lighting is the friendships that can develop and the referrals to other projects that occur when the project is well done.

12

Public Spaces

Landscape lighting for public spaces differs in many respects from residential lighting. In public spaces, landscape lighting needs versatility, but here versatility refers to a simple fixture layout that provides lasting effects with a minimum of attention. The types of spaces in this application category include primarily parks and plazas, but resorts and special areas such as caves, caverns, and historical sites also fit. In these projects the lighting will be viewed and, in many cases, used on a nightly basis by the general public. Because these landscapes have more human traffic and frequent or consistent activities, they demand that the lighting equipment stand up to abuse as well as to corrosion. This chapter will deal with the specific issues to consider in lighting public projects.

DESIGN ISSUES

The users of public spaces are often not the owners but people drawn to the space by the activities the owners present on the property. The owner may be more concerned about the total cost of the project than about the potential lighting effects, making the budget quite restrictive. Additionally, these spaces are usually much larger than residential spaces, requiring less thorough lighting treatment of the property. This type of project often requires using fewer fixtures with more candlepower per lamp and a wider distribution to create a cohesive appearance. As with residential projects, design considerations must precede equipment selection.

Nature of Public Projects

As with residential spaces, the style and scale of the property influences the development of the lighting concepts. Typically much larger in scale, public projects require the designer to understand clearly the needs of the project from a safety and security standpoint, as well as to plan for the aesthetic effects desired.

Public projects typically cannot use as many fixtures per area or per tree as can private spaces. For example, one fixture located between two trees may be required to light the canopy of both trees. Additionally, due to the large size of public spaces, the designer must often evaluate which areas have most importance and, perhaps, light only portions of the areas throughout the project. When limited by the number of fixtures available, the designer must carefully locate light throughout the site to provide a visual flow through the space, create an aesthetic effect, and retain a feeling of safety.

It is always important to have a brightness transition from one area to another (see Figure 12.4). Planning how light falls throughout a landscape can avoid creating dark areas that compromise the psychological feeling of safety. For example, when the plantings or other elements of the landscape have to remain unlit in some areas, select a path light that has a wide distribution so that it washes some of the plantings beyond the path's edge.

Safety and Security

Due to the larger numbers of people using public spaces, a greater need exists for users to perceive the space as

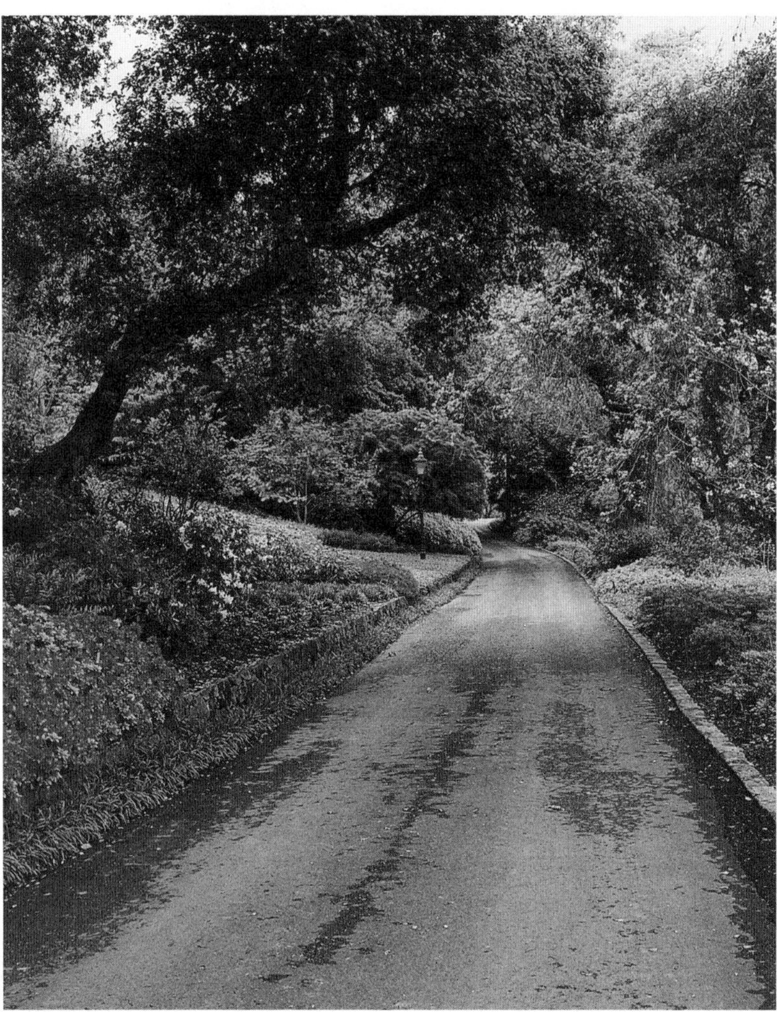

Figure 12.1. Daytime view of a roadway on the Far Niente Winery property. Photograph: Kenneth Rice Photography, www.kenricephoto.com.

safe. High light levels, in the range of 1 to 2 footcandles maintained, placed in a relatively even distribution throughout an area (or along the pathway system) provide the kind of lighting needed (see Figure 12.3). The specific level appropriate is determined by the activities occurring, the light level of the surrounding area, and requirements set by the local government or by the property owner. Sometimes the requirement may be as high as 5 footcandles (maintained, not initial). Remember that the footcandle metric is useful for regulations and comparisons, but that the visual effects of lighting result from footlamberts or reflected light. In an area with an asphalt walk, providing enough light to meet a requirement of 1 footcandle will produce roughly 0.2 footlambert. This probably will not be a high enough level to make visitors feel comfortable. Lighting designers need to consider reflectance characteristics and guide the owner as to how much light will be appropriate.

Additionally, areas of use need to be clearly identified and the lighting approach needs to respond to issues of security. The lighting must ensure that visitors feel free from a sudden approach of strangers. While the appropriate light level partially addresses safety, providing a comprehensive treatment of an area offers the best solution. This means lighting not only the paths. If the entire landscape cannot be lit, select certain areas of planting or other elements along a path and introduce light to provide the user with some information about the surroundings. Dark corners or unlit areas provide the opportunity for the unknown and create a sense of insecurity. Remember that people judge space based on a view of vertical surfaces and boundaries. If trees and shrubs around them are dark, the plants cannot be clearly seen and the boundaries become blurred. Eliminating areas of darkness will increase the perceived and probably the actual safety of an area. Safety and security lighting includes providing adequate lighting of potential obstacles in the landscape, including stairs and the boundary between land and bodies of water.

Circulation

Public projects tend to have formal traffic patterns with wider pathways than residential spaces, to handle the

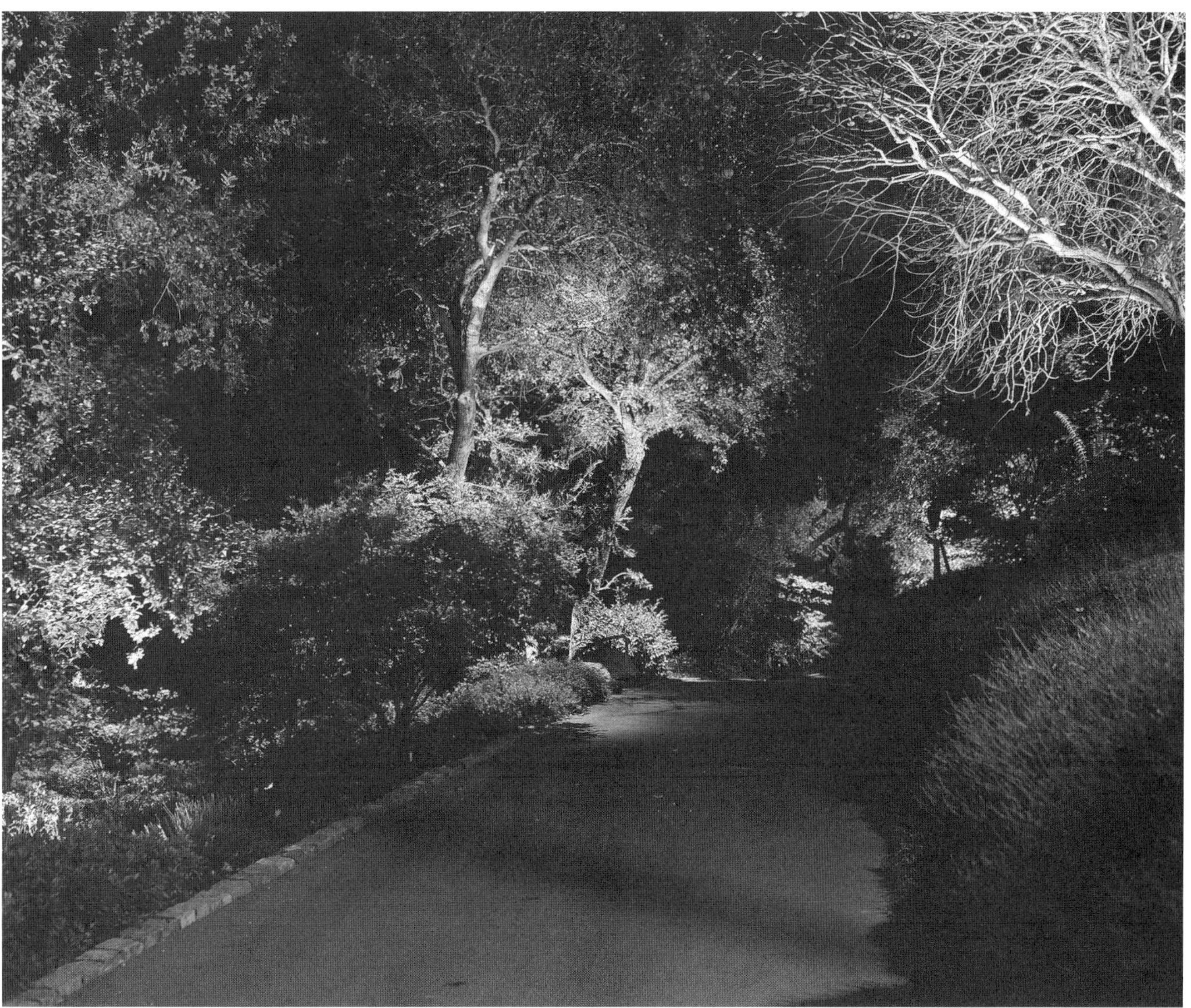

Figure 12.2. Lighting along this road allows guests to drive or walk while enjoying the gardens. The use of primarily downlighting creates a dappled effect throughout the ground plantings, but selected mature trees have uplighting, providing a vertical dimension to the composition. Lighting Design: Janet Lennox Moyer, Michael Stewart Hooker, & Paul Schreer; Photograph: Kenneth Rice Photography, www.kenricephoto.com.

heavier, more consistent traffic flow. The designer must understand all the entrance and exit locations in a project and plan the lighting to identify these areas. When the landscape has a change in pathway material to something with a higher reflectance, the lighting may not need to be altered to identify the change. One way to announce entrances is to use decorative fixtures that have some sparkle or decorative brightness to attract attention and which serve as visual markers (see Figures 12.1 & 12.2). Other approaches include using a higher-wattage lamp, more fixtures, larger-scale fixtures, or lit signage. The appropriate solution comes from the nature of the project, the landscape design concept for the property, and the lighting design concept for the project.

Anticipated Activities

All landscape lighting needs to respond to the activities that will take place in the space. In public spaces, this may include formal activities, such as performances, sports, dancing, dining, speeches, festivals, or any number of gatherings. The size of the crowd and required lighting level will vary by activity. The designer needs to identify the use clearly and respond to the visual needs that accompany the tasks in each area. This may mean that the light level and distribution will vary from one area to another in the property.

Large properties may have outdoor theaters or band shells. Often, these are used only during the day and

Figure 12.3. The lighting of Seattle, Washington's Freeway Park utilizes pole-mounted floodlights (just out of photo to right) to introduce a high general light level evenly washing the plaza and step lighting to make sure that grade changes are recognizable. The trees and water feature have higher light levels to maintain an accent role in the composition. Lighting Design: Dan Dibble, Beamer Wilkinson; Fountain Design: Richard Chaix, Beamer Wilkinson; Landscape Architect: Lawrence Halprin & Associates; Photograph: E. B. McCulley.

serious performance lighting is not required. In other cases, when performances will take place at night, depending on the type and frequency of entertainment, either provisions for power to handle both the fixtures and control system are installed, or a basic palette of theatrical equipment is provided. Even when some lighting equipment is provided, visiting performers often bring additional equipment, including towers, fixture stands, fixtures, and control systems. The basic system designed for the site needs to be able to accommodate any temporary lighting equipment that performers will bring and the loads that theatrical lighting requires. Whenever theatrical equipment is desired, a theatrical lighting consultant should be hired.

Large properties may also include sports facilities such as baseball diamonds, tennis courts, croquet lawns, horseshoe pits, or areas for any number of other activities. Typically, this lighting is installed permanently when night lighting is part of the design program. Each sports activity will have particular lighting requirements. Refer to the books listed in the Bibliography for sports lighting guidelines.

Image

Identification of a public project or the creation of an image begins with what a person sees from outside the property. What will someone see from the street or other public spaces, such as adjacent buildings or mass transit stations? Providing identification and attraction to enter the space through the use of light heightens the potential use of the space.

Image extends to what a person will see when looking at the space through the window of a nearby building, looking into windows of those same buildings from the landscape, or looking from one area in a property to another. Lighting can be used to extend or limit a view and direct the way people see a space. Light has

Figure 12.4. At a resort in the Lake Tahoe area, downlighting mounted high up in trees creates a dappled effect on the lawn, spilling onto the paving in some areas. The lighting effect provides continuity along the road and at the visual destination dubbed "Rocks 1" at the intersection of roads. Lighting Design: Janet Lennox Moyer; Photograph: Michael McKinley.

a strong effect on people's memory of a space and can be used to create a lasting impression.

Controls

Public spaces typically require automatic control systems (see Chapter 9). Usually, no one is assigned the task of waiting for darkness to fall and then turning the lights on and setting dimming levels to create moods. Parks and other areas that have multiple activities and constantly changing events benefit from having the lighting equipment connected to photocells and time switches with 365-day, multiple on-off capabilities. This eliminates the need to change settings from one season to another as activities change and the hours of sunset and sunrise change. The time switch can be preset to respond

***Figure 12.5.** A view of the main gate to the Far Niente Vineyards as guests approach it during the day. Photograph: Janet Lennox Moyer.*

to changes in use from one time of year to another. For example, parks may stay open later during certain times of the year, requiring the lights-off setting to be later than during other times of the year, or special events or holidays may require that the lights be left on longer.

Parts of projects, such as outdoor theaters within a park, may require more complicated controls or power availability with appropriate connections for lighting equipment and control systems. In some cases, a theater space will have the power provisions for shows but no control equipment. The actual performance group or company must bring and temporarily install whatever equipment is needed.

EQUIPMENT SELECTION

As with all landscape lighting, equipment selection occurs after the design concepts have been planned by the designer and approved by the authorities on the project.

Light Sources

With large-scale public projects, much of the lighting utilizes HID light sources. Their long life and high lumen output make them natural candidates for properties that cannot expect as much maintenance atten-

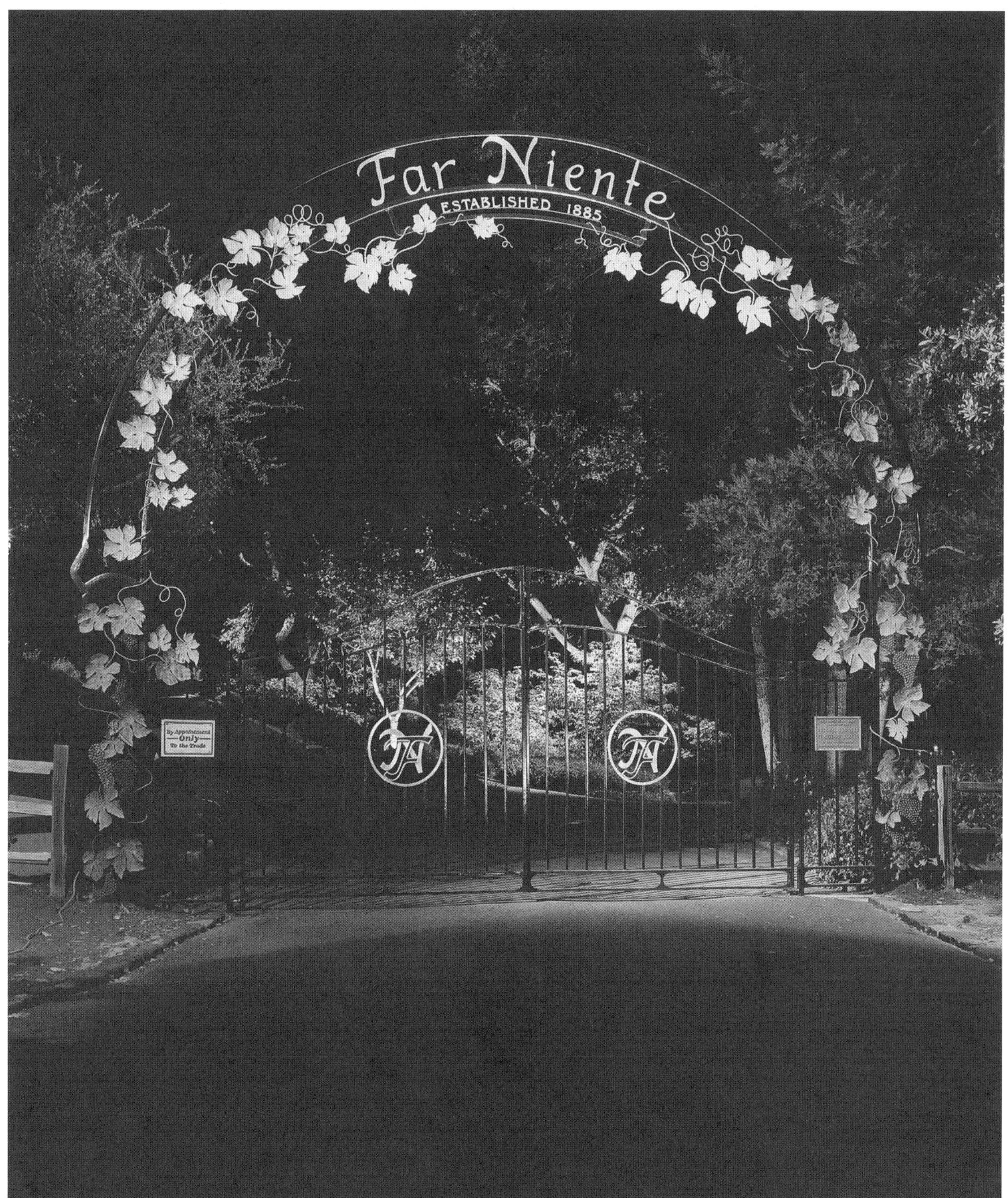

Figure 12.6. *At night, the Far Niente name and logos become featured on the gate with a glimpse into the gardens arriving guests are about to enjoy. Lighting Design: Janet Lennox Moyer, Michael Stewart Hooker, & Paul Schreer; Photograph: Kenneth Rice Photography, www.kenricephoto.com.*

tion as that of residential properties. Selection of the appropriate HID light source depends on the color of light produced by the source, as well as wattage availability and efficiency. Often, the light source needs to match the color of the source used in the surrounding street lighting or for adjacent properties. In some cases a shift in color to attract attention is desirable (for example, when highlighting flags or signage). Select HID sources carefully. Since several of them do not produce a full spectrum of color, the resulting appearance of people, plant material, buildings, and sculptures can be enhanced or harmed.

Figure 12.7 & 12.8. *At the Far Niente Winery, lighting redefines the Chardonnay Garden entertainment area. Warm incandescent undercounter lighting attracts arriving visitors to the wine and food areas. The counters and the dance floor are lit from fixtures mounted in the mature Oaks. Beyond this entertainment area, other areas are lit as mini-composition vistas. Lighting Design: Janet Lennox Moyer, Michael Stewart Hooker, & Paul Schreer; Photograph: Kenneth Rice Photography, www.kenricephoto.com.*

Using a shift in color to add to the effect or appearance of depth is a clever idea for several effects in public spaces (see Color Plate 66). Using a bluish source such as mercury vapor to accent a hedge of pines at the back of a property adds depth to a scene. High-pressure sodium on a row of palms at the back will shorten the appearance of a long narrow space. Adding color onto a building or portion of a building can emphasize some architectural detail or contrast with some other element in the landscape.

Incandescent sources are used less frequently in commercial spaces since they typically have a shorter life, lower lumen output, and more confined distribution. However, in locations close to buildings, when accenting plantings, sculptures, or even small-scale patios, incandescent may be the correct selection. The distribution of light is more easily controlled and the color is flattering to people's appearance (see Figure 12.8).

Fixtures

Fixtures in public spaces need to be able to withstand substantial abuse as well as to stand up to the corrosive outdoor environment. Due to large numbers of people visiting these spaces on a regular basis, wear and tear will be a major concern. Additionally, the regular maintenance of public-space landscapes often requires large machines that can damage lighting equipment. A greater concern than unintentional damage is the potential for vandalism. In all public spaces, this possibility exists and the lighting equipment needs to meet the challenge. Designers must specify fixtures with strong housings (choice of material or wall thickness), secure locking mechanisms (for aiming adjustments), impact-resistant lens materials, and tamper-proof screws or other accessories that prevent disassembling the fixtures. Walkway fixtures, including path lights, bollards, and post- or pole-mounted units, may need to be able to withstand impact from vehicles.

Most equipment used for uplighting in public spaces is 120-volt (or higher), which means that the fixture head on adjustable accent fixtures cannot be attached to stakes for movement. All 120-volt equipment must be permanently mounted on junction boxes. This requires locating fixtures for the mature size and shape of plant materials and careful coordination of fixture location and height to avoid an intermediary plant blocking light from reaching its target in the future.

PROJECT MANAGEMENT

Most public-space projects require that multiple contractors bid on the job. This requires supplying thorough drawings, including details of anything that may not be clear from the lighting plan alone, including mounting details, wiring diagrams, and details of custom or modified equipment. The importance of specifications becomes paramount in public projects because bidders often package the lighting equipment and try to substitute fixtures that may or may not produce the desired result.

The budget is an important item to consider in managing a public project. The owner may be more concerned with the overall project cost than with creating specific lighting effects and may not be willing to entertain additional costs for specific lighting effects. Often, financial constraints will be severe. Also, a lighting allowance may not be determined initially and the designer may be asked to design fixtures or lighting layouts that will not fit into the final budget. The designer needs to get as much budget information as possible at the beginning of the project to plan lighting that will fit both the needs and finances of the project.

The designer must also educate the client about the required qualities of fixtures to prevent substitutions that promise false savings. One of the most important jobs of a designer in public spaces is to ensure that the fixtures can hold up for many years.

On the other hand, one of the delights of public projects is that the large size of the projects often allows designing custom fixtures that, due to the quantities required, will not cost much more (if any more) than standard products. Custom fixtures often help to define the image of a project.

Key issues to keep in mind for lighting public spaces include planning the system to maximize the potential effects of each fixture and stay within the budget; selecting appropriate equipment to ensure that the lighting effects continue to function with minimal maintenance for many years; selecting light sources that have wide distribution, appropriate color rendition, and proper lumen output; and selecting light fixtures that can withstand abuse and corrosion.

The size and scale of public projects often present challenges and opportunities that smaller projects do not, such as working with artists commissioned to design sculptures specifically for the project, designing an entire series of custom fixtures for the project, or lighting massive water features. The design of such projects can take several years, as can the construction. Over this mounting number of years, it is easy to forget the ideas that went into planning the lighting. Therefore, continuous documentation of desired end results and the ways that the lighting system will need to be focused to produce the effects is a major requirement in such projects.

13

Atria

Originally, an atrium was an open central court in a home in ancient Rome. Today, new homes and commercial spaces both integrate them, but typically as an enclosed space. Since atria started as spaces open to the air, many modern atria try to simulate outdoor spaces by including plant material. Atria present a unique landscape lighting problem primarily because of their use of plants in an unnatural setting. This chapter will present information on the role that light plays in the life of plants and how to address these needs in an interior space in order to keep the plants healthy.

As with any space, interior or exterior, plants represent only one element in the space. Lighting for an atrium should address all areas and all the lighting needs of the space as part of the overall visual composition. Designers should consider all functional activities, including circulation, seating, and potential special functions, such as dancing, performances, or benefit dinners. Planning also needs to encompass lighting for focal elements, including sculptures, murals, and fountains. Composition and the lighting of specific design elements do not vary from other types of lighting situations.

Lighting interior spaces differs from landscape lighting because walls and a ceiling define the space and contribute to the lighting effects (due to reflectance of those surfaces). Atrium lighting varies from other commercial interior spaces, due to the typically large scale and unusual height. It varies from typical residential spaces because all the walls are typically glass. This chapter will not cover interior lighting issues but will address some concerns to consider for both residential and commercial atria.

RESIDENTIAL SPACES

Atria in residential spaces often visually link areas of the home by allowing view to pass through an atrium's glass walls into another area beyond. This creates a feeling of expanse. An atrium also provides a link to the outside by introducing a grouping of plants and often trees within the interior space. Often, residential atria will have a skylight covering all or most of the ceiling. This will introduce natural light into the interior. The amount of natural light usually does not fulfill the plants' lighting needs, however, and additional lighting is normally required. The light sources that work best for residential spaces are a combination of incandescent and fluorescent.

Another issue to consider when planning lighting within the atrium and in the surrounding rooms concerns the rules for viewing through glass (see Chapter 3). The balance of brightness must be carefully planned to allow a view through the atrium and into another space. Additionally, the aiming angles for all fixtures surrounding the glass must be controlled to avoid the reflection of the light source in the glass.

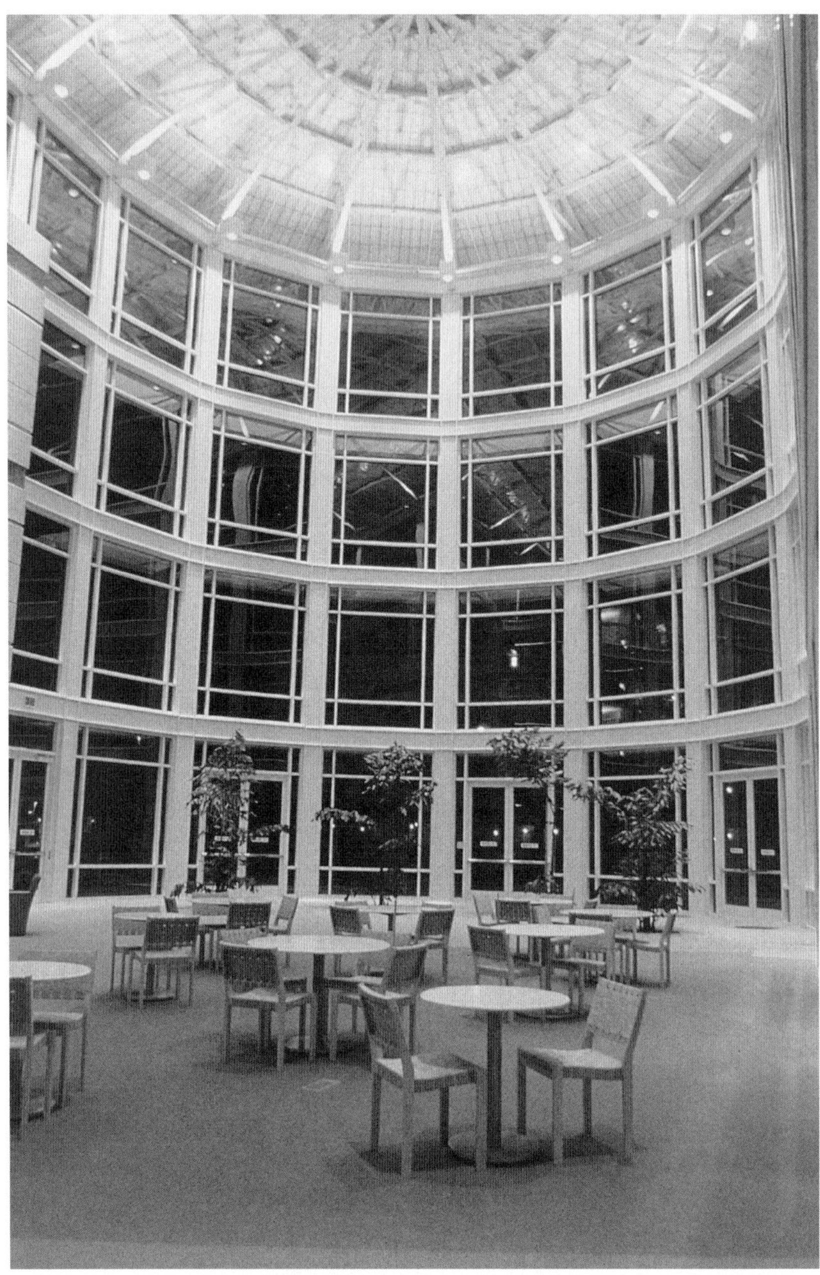

Figure 13.1. *The expansive translucent roof in this atrium space provides all the light necessary for the health and sustenance of the plants. Lighting Design: Naomi Miller, Luminae Souter Lighting Design; Photograph: David D. Miller.*

COMMERCIAL SPACES

In commercial spaces, the atrium may be a central court area surrounded by a multistory building or be an open area between two or more buildings. Often, the roof of the enclosure is or includes a skylight (see Figure 13.1). Most commercial atria are vast spaces with very high ceilings.

Commercial atria are usually public spaces, and often visitors will not be familiar with the space and will need visual direction. Light can help direct people through the space by the treatment of signage or by the hierarchy of brightnesses introduced. When signage has been well designed and thoughtfully located in an atrium, lighting aids the identification of destination points. When the interior layout includes such focal points as sculptures, water features, or other elements, the lighting for signage may not be at the highest level. As with any lighting design, the appropriate place in the brightness hierarchy for all elements needs to be thought out.

With large volumes, and especially when the height of an atrium soars above the floor, light levels need to be higher than in other spaces of similar square footage, for people to feel comfortable. The IES recommends 10 to 20 footcandles,[1] but this may not be enough for people to feel comfortable in the space. Too often, atrium lighting fails because the footcandle level is too low either at the main floor or throughout the overall volume of the space. To avoid a dark or cavernous appearance, light levels may need to be 30 to 50 footcandles.

Additionally, many atria have perimeter balconies that introduce viewing angles at multiple vertical locations throughout the space. This requires the lighting designer to anticipate all viewing angles and to make sure that glare will be minimized. A crucial mistake made in atrium lighting is to address the light level or view from only one floor level, typically, the ground floor. The aiming angle of fixtures should be carefully planned to ensure that glare will not be a distraction from any points in the space. Too often, suspended sculptures are lit from one level with a wide angle that shines right into the eyes of someone on another level.

For the long throw distances required in tall atria, HID or high-wattage incandescent sources are appropriate. Of course, the lighting designer needs to weigh the importance of energy conservation versus dimming requirements and capabilities. Aiming flexibility needs to be considered in fixture selection, as sculptures or other decorative elements in atrium spaces are often changed over the life of the building. Often, using theatrical incandescent lighting equipment offers several advantages: aiming flexibility, high-wattage sources with dimming and long throw capability, and good glare shielding due to the lamp being deeply recessed inside the fixture housing or to the addition of barn doors.

LIGHTING FOR PLANT GROWTH

Light influences many functions that affect a plant's ability to live. Three factors—the quality (spectrum and distribution), quantity (amount of light and time of exposure), and direction of light—affect a plant's health. To use plants successfully in an atrium, designers need to understand how plants respond to light. The designer needs to know the type and amount of lighting a plant receives in its natural environment. This information guides the choice of light source, light levels, time of exposure to artificial light, and direction of light. Additionally, understanding the natural conditions of the plant will also guide whether the plant will need to be specially grown under lower light levels in order to survive in the atrium.

In an atrium with a skylight, although some natural light will reach the plant, both the quality and quantity of light (including the amount of time the plant receives daylight) will be substantially reduced. The color of a skylight material will affect the spectrum of light the plants receive, as well as how much light penetrates the material. Designers need to know what material will be used and procure both spectral and transmittance data

FACTORS OTHER THAN LIGHT THAT DETERMINE PLANT HEALTH

TEMPERATURE

Plants require a specific range of temperatures over the course of approximately 24 hours. Too high or too low a temperature and too great or too narrow a range of temperatures can negatively affect the health of a plant.

AIR MOVEMENT

Plants need some air movement to avoid stagnation which could encourage disease and pest attack. Too much air movement, however, can dry out the leaves, causing discoloration or leaf death.

WATER

Plants require a certain amount of water to maintain life functions. Too much water or improper drainage can drown a plant (cutting off oxygen supply, which allows the attack of disease or pests). Not enough water causes roots to die thereby cutting off the supply of nutrients to the plant tissue (resulting in the plant's death).

NUTRITIONAL SUPPLEMENT

Plants require a continuous source of nutrients (nitrogen, phosphorous, and potassium are the main three) to maintain life. Soil mixtures are planned to provide the specific needs of a given plant, but the soil eventually runs out of these elements. To continually supply the needs of the plant a schedule of feeding and soil replacement must be implemented.

SOIL CONTENT AND TEXTURE

For each indoor plant, a proper type of soil should be provided. It needs to have the right balance of nutritional element content and appropriate texture for the correct balance of water retention, drainage, and physical support.

AIR CONTENT

Pollution in the air can harm plants the same way it can affect the health of humans.

HUMIDITY

Plants are genetically built to expect a particular range of moisture in the air. For some plants too much humidity and for others too little can cause a negative response.

PESTS AND DISEASE

When a plant becomes stressed due to an imbalance in one or more of the other factors it becomes subject to attack from pests and diseases. The best way to prevent attack is to provide the proper environment and care for the plants. If an attack occurs, measures should be taken immediately to prevent spreading.

Figure 13.2.

on the material from the manufacturer. In some cases, the amount of natural light received will be negligible. The artificial lighting system needs to provide enough light to satisfy all the plant's needs, unless a daylighting study documents that the skylight will provide the quantity of daylight and hours of exposure needed.

Although light is critical to a plant's survival, it is only one factor that determines plant health. Figure 13.2 lists other factors to consider in evaluating whether the indoor environment will be conducive to living plants. Lighting designers obviously do not have the responsibility for these other factors. However, they need to be aware of all the other factors that affect plant health.

It is a dangerous undertaking for a lighting designer to agree to design a lighting system when all other health issues are not optimal for the plants. Providing a healthy environment for plants, which includes proper lighting, is complicated and not inexpensive. Lighting is often the first issue to be questioned when plants do not fare well in an indoor environment. However, it is often not the cause, or the sole cause, of illness in a sick plant.

A designer may have to invest large amounts of time and money to test sick or dying plants. When considering whether to accept a plant lighting project, a lighting designer needs to ensure that all the factors affecting the health of the plants will be adequately addressed. Discussing all these issues with the architect and owner may be enough for them to understand that even with a well-designed lighting system, the plants may not thrive. If either the architect or owner does not understand the importance of all the factors, the lighting designer should send them some information regarding all the requirements for an environment healthy to plant life. If all these factors will not be properly handled in the atrium design, the lighting designer should decline to work on the project.

Quality of Light

One aspect of plant-growth lighting is the quality of light or the spectrum of color provided by the artificial light source. Plants respond differently than people do to the electromagnetic spectrum (see Figure 13.3). Radiation that people perceive as visible light comprises less than half the energies within a range of wavelength from 320 to 1000 nm known as the *biological window*.[2] Plants utilize energy throughout and on both sides of the range visible to people for their various life functions.

The response of plants to radiation stops at those boundaries because the energy of radiation is inversely proportional to its wavelength. Radiation of a wavelength beyond 1,000 nm does not have enough energy to allow biological processes to occur in plants. However, in some cases, heat from infrared radiation can *sunburn* plants (for example, in greenhouses with clear windows). Below 320 nm a wavelength has so much energy that it is destructive to biological photoreceptors.

Scientists do not clearly understand all the biological responses of plants to light, nor are they sure that all have been identified. What is clear at this time is that plants have photoreceptors that trigger various plant functions in response to specific wavelength ranges. Three distinct wavelength bands have been identified: blue from 380 to 500 nm, red from 600 to 700 nm, and far red from 700 to 800 nm. The amount of radiation from each of these three bands will vary from one plant function to another.

Further, most blue light receptors are sensitive to near-ultraviolet radiation (370 nm). The presence or absence of blue light appears to control several plant responses, including orientation to the light source and the growth form of a plant. The absence of blue light can cause the plant to lean or to produce thin and elongated stems or abnormally shaped or sized leaves. This can sometimes be minimized by an increased quantity of light, but selecting an artificial lamp with the required blue radiation is a better approach.

The movement of a plant or part of a plant either toward or away from light, called phototropism, is one such response. This occurs primarily due to the existence or absence of blue light in the 400 to 480 nm range. Plants that require high light levels will lean toward the source of light in low light levels. Alternatively, plants that prefer shade will bend away from too high a light level. This action can cause a plant to look lopsided and needs to be prevented in atrium lighting.

The color of daylight changes from a clear to a cloudy sky (see Figure 13.4), from morning to dusk, from one geographic area to another, from one elevation to another, from day to day throughout the year, and from exposed to protected or shaded areas. This suggests that the color of light that plants require is a reference point, not an absolute.

Shading has a strong effect on the light that a plant receives. The change from a clear to a cloudy sky shifts the color of light from a slight peak in red to a peak in blue (see Figures 2.6 & 13.4). However, although the change appears dramatic, the overall result is much like adding a neutral density filter. The intensity drops dramatically, but the shift toward blue radiation has little influence on normal plant activity.[3] Shading from an inanimate object (a building, other landscape structure, or sculpture, for example) acts similarly—it does not affect the spectrum significantly, but reduces the light level. Conversely, shading from vegetation strongly affects both intensity and color reaching a plant beneath. Plants under broadleaf evergreens receive radiation that peaks in green, while those under conifers receive radiation high in blue. This requires that the designer understand how light will reach the

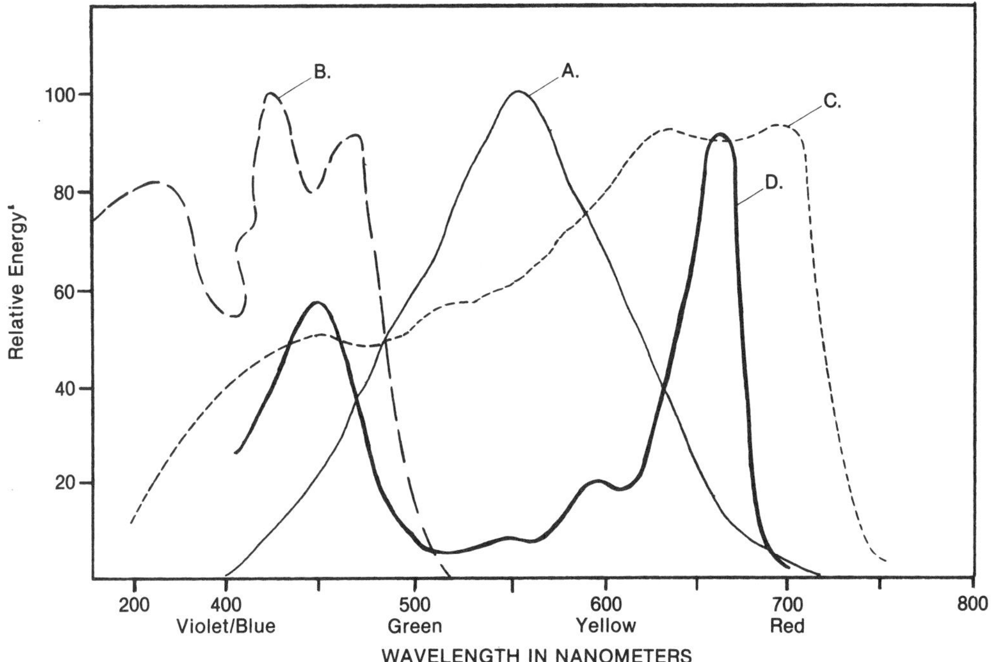

Figure 13.3. Eye response and action spectra of three plant processes.[4] A. Human vision sensitivity peaks in yellow-green. Light from artificial sources is measured according to this spectral curve. B. Phototropic responses of plants (toward or away from light). C. Spectral curve for photosynthesis, allowing green plants to absorb light energy and transform it into chemical energy. D. To have chlorophyll synthesis occur (creating the green color of foliage), plants require this combination of red and blue wavelengths. Courtesy of GTE's Sylvania Lighting Division.

smaller plants and then ensure that these plants will receive the required light quality spectrum needed to maintain healthy life.

The color of light affects atrium lighting in two ways. First, designers need to know what spectral composition the plants naturally receive in the outdoor environment. Second, the designer must ensure that the spectrum the plants receive in the new environment will be comparable to their naturally received spectrum.

Color considerations determine the selection of the proper lamp for plant growth. The best overall source for plant growth is a coated metal halide lamp. It produces energy in the three areas where plants respond to light and has the near-ultraviolet energy important to them. Metal halide lamps also offer the benefit of high candlepower in a point source format. The coating produces a diffuse light that simulates sky luminance (which produces the bulk of natural daylight). The next-best selection is a combination of incandescent and one of the fluorescent lamps. The exact fluorescent to choose depends on the spectrum required for the plants to be lit. The use of plant growth fluorescent lamps is a good choice, because they emit the proper action spectrum, which regulates all of the photo responses and provide for optimal plant maintenance.

Quantity of Light

Many plant responses depend on the spectrum makeup along with the quantity of light and exposure time. Chlorophyll synthesis, which creates the green color of plants, occurs when light has red wavelengths at 650 nm and blue at 445 nm (see Figure 13.3). In the absence of light for more than a few days, plants lose their green color and become yellow.

Light and Dark Time Periods

Red light (peak 660 nm) has a vital role in the phenomenon called photoperiodism—the influence of light and dark time periods on plant growth and development—but the prime control occurs due to the length of the light and dark periods and a change in the time of darkness. Plants have both a built-in clock and calendar. They respond to times of day and to times of the year based on the quantity and quality of light (among other factors). Although light is not strictly involved in the functions themselves, it acts as a control device to trigger the beginning or end of a function. Plants can discriminate between daylength differences of approximately 40 minutes, allowing the initiation of the same activities to occur during the same week from year to year.

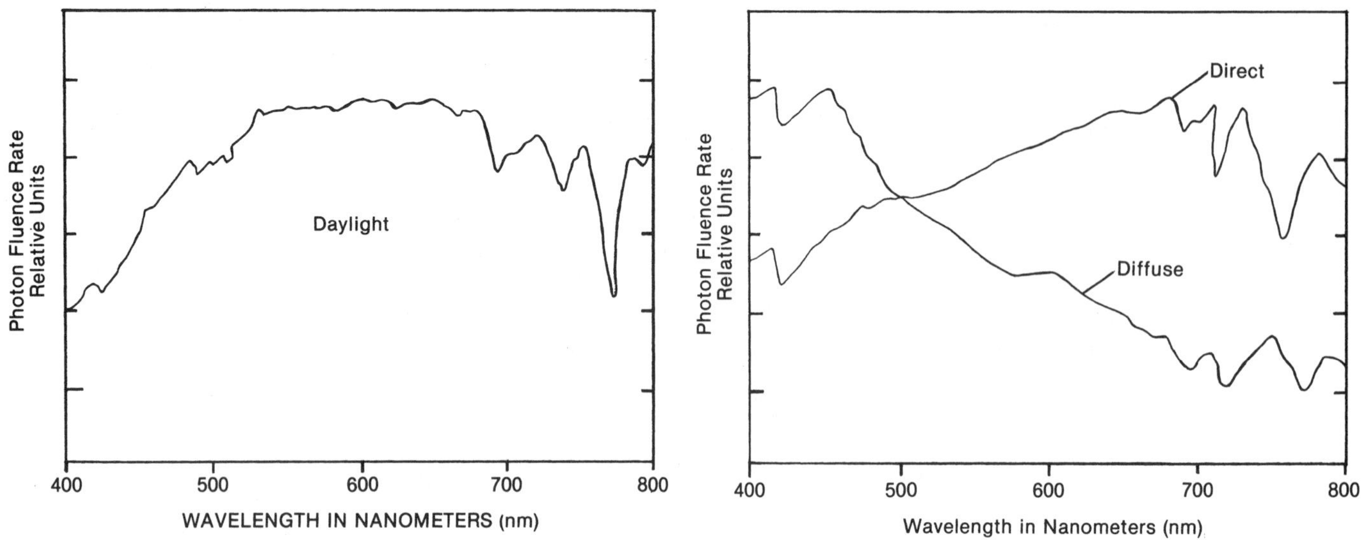

Figure 13.4. *The composition of light waves in daylight is a combination of direct (from the sun) and diffuse (from the sky) light. Adapted from J. W. Hart,* Light and Plant Growth, *© 1988 Unwin Hyman, Ltd., Courtesy of Chapman & Hall.*

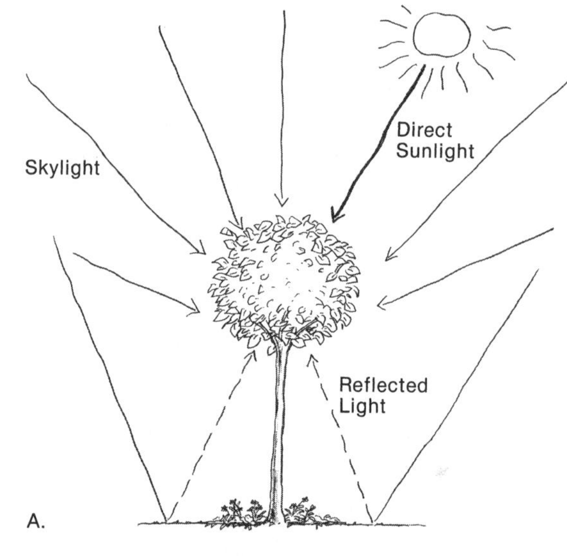

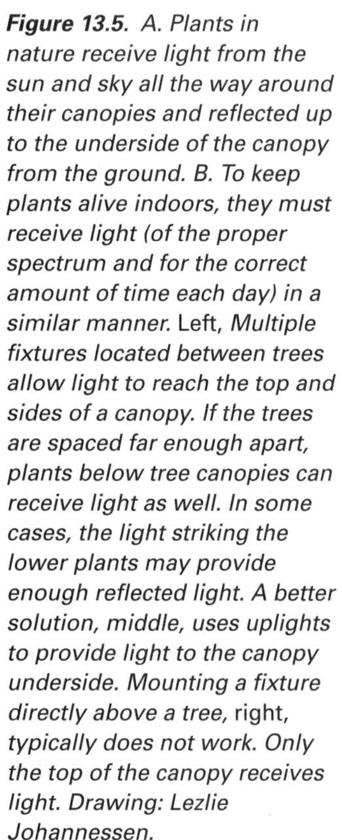

Figure 13.5. *A. Plants in nature receive light from the sun and sky all the way around their canopies and reflected up to the underside of the canopy from the ground. B. To keep plants alive indoors, they must receive light (of the proper spectrum and for the correct amount of time each day) in a similar manner.* Left, *Multiple fixtures located between trees allow light to reach the top and sides of a canopy. If the trees are spaced far enough apart, plants below tree canopies can receive light as well. In some cases, the light striking the lower plants may provide enough reflected light. A better solution,* middle, *uses uplights to provide light to the canopy underside. Mounting a fixture directly above a tree,* right, *typically does not work. Only the top of the canopy receives light. Drawing: Lezlie Johannessen.*

Figure 13.6. *In this Hewlett-Packard training facility, remodeled from a JC Penney store, the skylights admit light, but not enough to keep the mature Ficus trees alive and healthy. Supplemental lighting came from recessed, adjustable 400-watt metal halide downlights recessed into the beams and aimed at the tree canopies. Lighting Design: Naomi Miller, Luminae Souter Lighting Design; Photograph: Ross de Alessi.*

Plants function on a day measured at approximately 24 hours. To maintain normal health of plants in an interior space, plan to provide 12 to 16 hours of light and 8 to 12 hours of darkness.[5] The amount of darkness that plants experience in a 24-hour period triggers several responses. While this phenomenon affects primarily the commercial growth and flowering of plants (which is not a factor in atrium lighting), it is necessary for plants to have this rest period as a part of normal functioning. When plants do not receive the required rest period of darkness, they develop physiological stresses and are susceptible to many diseases. They can become so weakened that they die.

Intensity Levels

Normally, light level is evaluated by measuring incident light with a light meter and calculating light levels in footcandles. Since the spectral distribution useful to plants is not the same as for people, using a light meter (which measures according to the visual response of the human eye) and the metric of a footcandle will not accurately predict the usefulness to a plant.

However, a light meter and the metric of footcandles can provide a rough guide to appropriate light levels for plants indoors. As with all types of lighting, the footcandle level represents an average and should be calculated as a maintained level.[6] The following chart provides a range of footcandles based on the categories of light level that plant books state when describing various plants. These books typically list several categories, such as full sun, part shade, or shade. Use the following guideline for intensity levels:

Shade	Low level	75–150 fc
Part shade to part sun	Medium level	150–250 fc
Full sun	High level	150–350 fc

Acclimatizing Plants for Atrium Life

Plants to be used in atria need to be prepared for lower footcandle levels than they would experience outdoors. This can be done by using shade-grown plants or by adapting sun-grown plants. In several growing states, including California, Florida, and Texas, most plants for indoor use are shade-grown. Adapting sun-grown plants involves moving them to an area with approximately 40 to 80 percent shade (depending on the size and type of plant) for a set period of weeks. Research at the Agricultural Research Center in Beltsville, Maryland showed a 50 percent reduction in leaf drop with *Ficus benjamina* when acclimatized at 80 percent shade for 5 weeks. An additional 10 to 15 weeks helps, but the first 5 weeks have the strongest effect.[7] Professional growers can recommend the appropriate time period for the type and size of plants to be used.

The acclimatization process allows time for the plant to drop its sun-grown leaves and produce new, shade-grown leaves. Plants in nature have both kinds, depending on where the leaf occurs (top of canopy or under other leaves) on the plant. Shade leaves grow longer or larger with a thinner cross section and often a darker green color. Shade-grown or acclimatized plants tend to be able to tolerate the low end of the intensity-level ranges listed above and sometimes slightly lower footcandle levels.

Direction of Light

Another critical factor to consider in planning atrium lighting is the direction of light. Plants normally receive direct sunlight at varying angles throughout the day and year. They also receive a significant contribution from the sky all the way around their canopy. A final component comes from reflected light off the ground and any surrounding surfaces. Similarly, indoor plants need to receive light all the way around their canopies and from below. It is difficult to reproduce this natural reception using one fixture located directly over the top of a plant. Multiple fixtures that reach the entire top and sides of the canopy are required. Sometimes downlights can provide the reflected light needed for the underside of a tree canopy, but typically, uplights are also required (see Figures 13.5 & 13.6).

Lighting plants in an atrium differs greatly from lighting plants in a landscape for aesthetic night viewing. Designers need to use caution in accepting this type of project, and then should plan lighting that meets the plant's needs. Even more than night lighting, this type of project requires the designer to study the plants to be used in the space.

REFERENCES

1. John E. Kaufman, Ed., *IES Lighting Handbook, Application Volume,* Illuminating Engineering Society of North America, New York, 1987, pp. 2–4 to 2–23.
2. J. W. Hart, *Light and Plant Growth,* Unwin Hyman, London, 1988, pp. 2–4.
3. Ibid., p. 41.
4. Christos Mpelkas, "Indoor Landscaping for Healthy, Beautiful Workplaces," *Architectural Lighting,* Feb. 1987, p. 43.
5. John E. Kaufman, Ed., *IES Lighting Handbook, Reference Volume,* Illuminating Engineering Society of North America, New York, 1987, Chapter 9.
6. *Florida Foliage Grower,* Vol. 12, No. 9, Sept. 1975, p. 2.
7. *Sylvania Supplemental Lighting Technology Guide for the Horticultural Industry,* © 1989, pp. 1–2. The data used from this booklet was compiled by Christos Mpelkas.

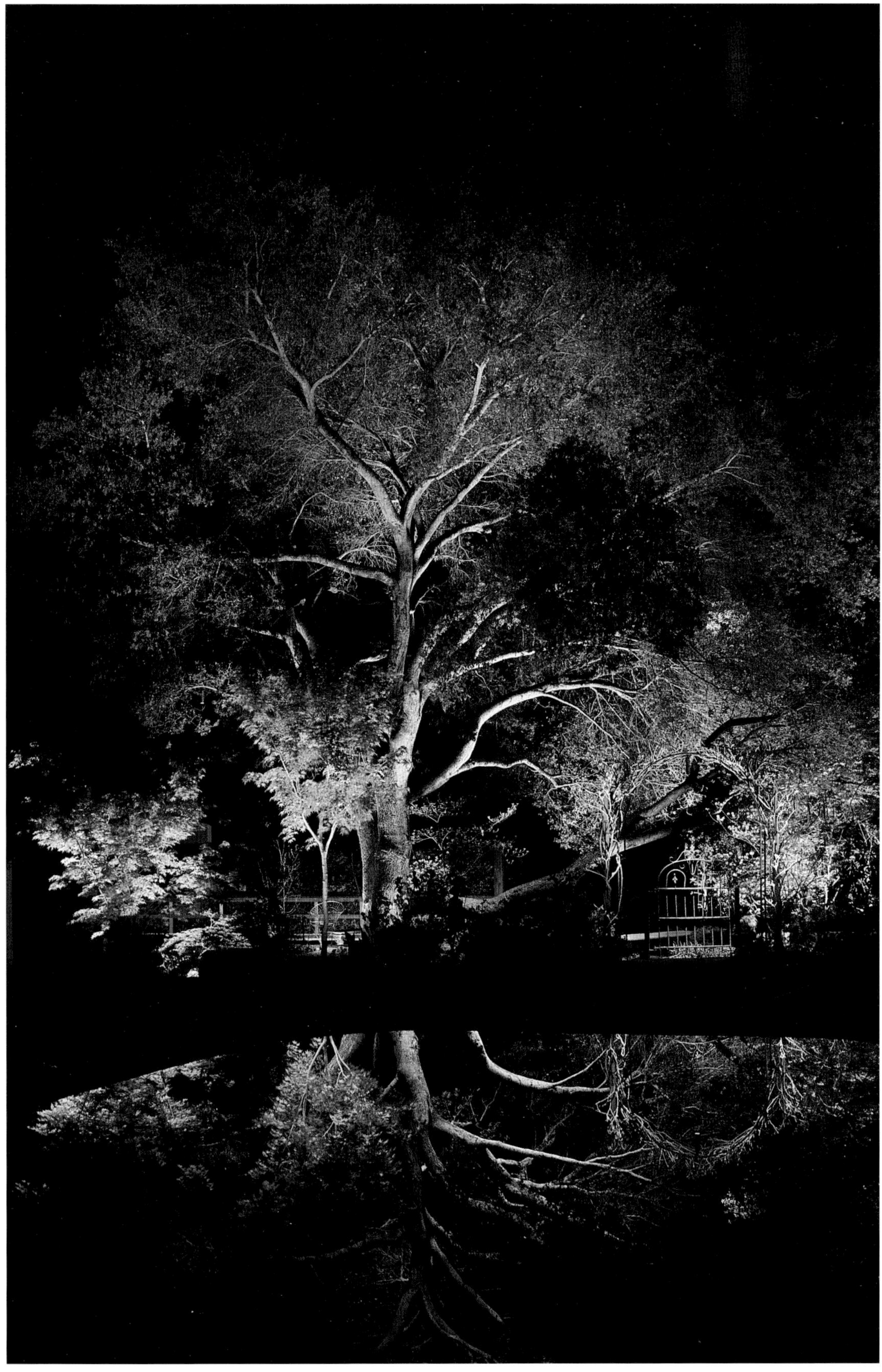

Color Plate 1. *Radical garden development can dramatically alter a tree's role in a lighting composition. Ten years of garden development have shifted the importance of the California Live Oak (*Quercus agrifolia*) from dominant feature to supporting character in this northern California garden. Lighting Design: Michael Stewart Hooker, Janet Lennox Moyer, and Paul Schreer, MSH Visual Planners; Photograph: Kenneth Rice Photography, www.kenricephoto.com.*

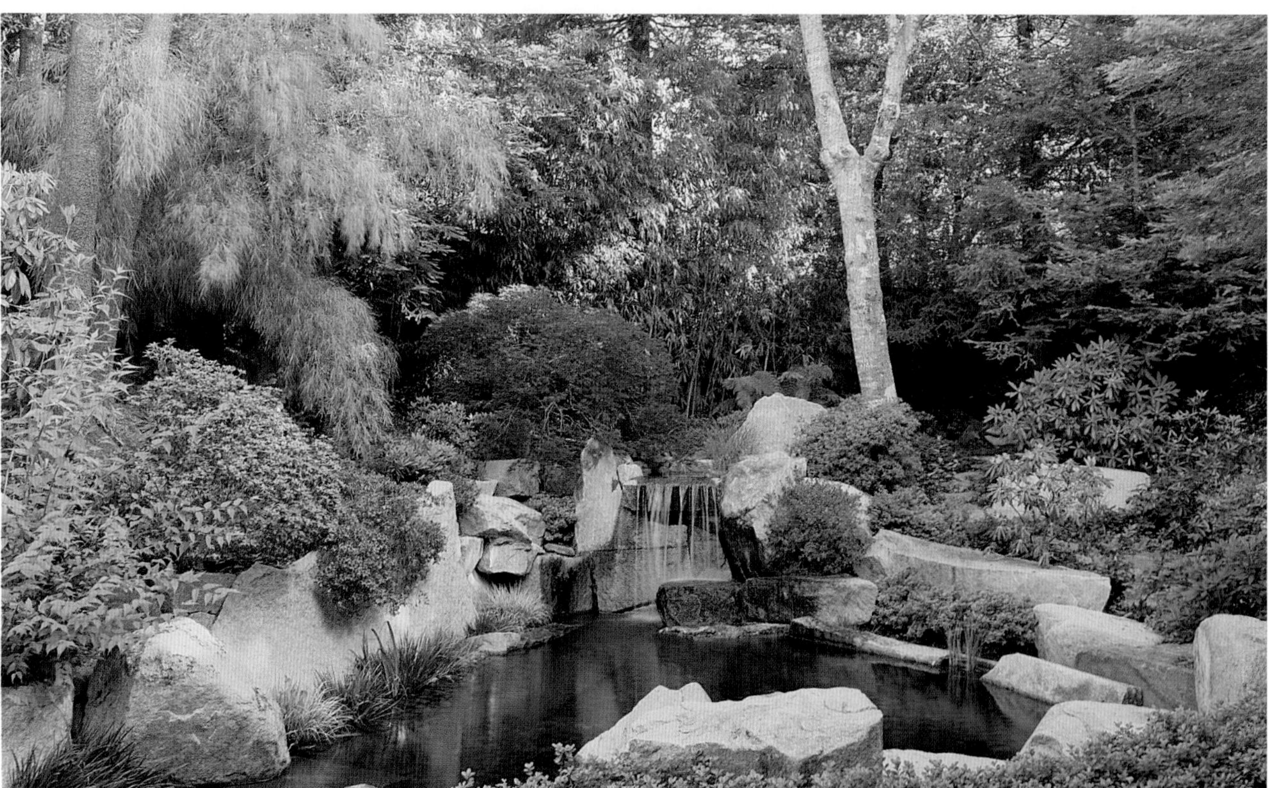

Color Plates 2 & 3. *Careful selection, placement, and aiming of lighting equipment can redefine a scene. Erasing some of the background creates a more dramatic and private scene. Lighting Design: Janet Lennox Moyer, MSH Visual Planners; Photograph: Kenneth Rice Photography, www.kenricephoto.com.*

Color Plate 4. *Providing brightness at the end of a passageway creates a visual destination. MR11 uplight fixtures tucked into a clipped hedge on the viewer's side of the arbor and aimed at the curve of the arches accentuates the structural shape and floral display. Utilizing a tight aiming angle with a deeply recessed lamp and 45° shielding louver eliminates glare as someone walks along the arbor. Lighting Design: Janet Lennox Moyer, MSH Visual Planners; Photograph: Kenneth Rice Photography, www.kenricephoto.com.*

Color Plate 5. *Visual cohesion of brightness becomes critical in gardens with a large expanse of lawn. Each separate garden has been treated as a mini-composition within the overall composition of similar brightness. This provides visual transportation for a viewer's eye. Lighting Design: Janet Lennox Moyer, MSH Visual Planners; Photograph: Kenneth Rice Photography, www.kenricephoto.com.*

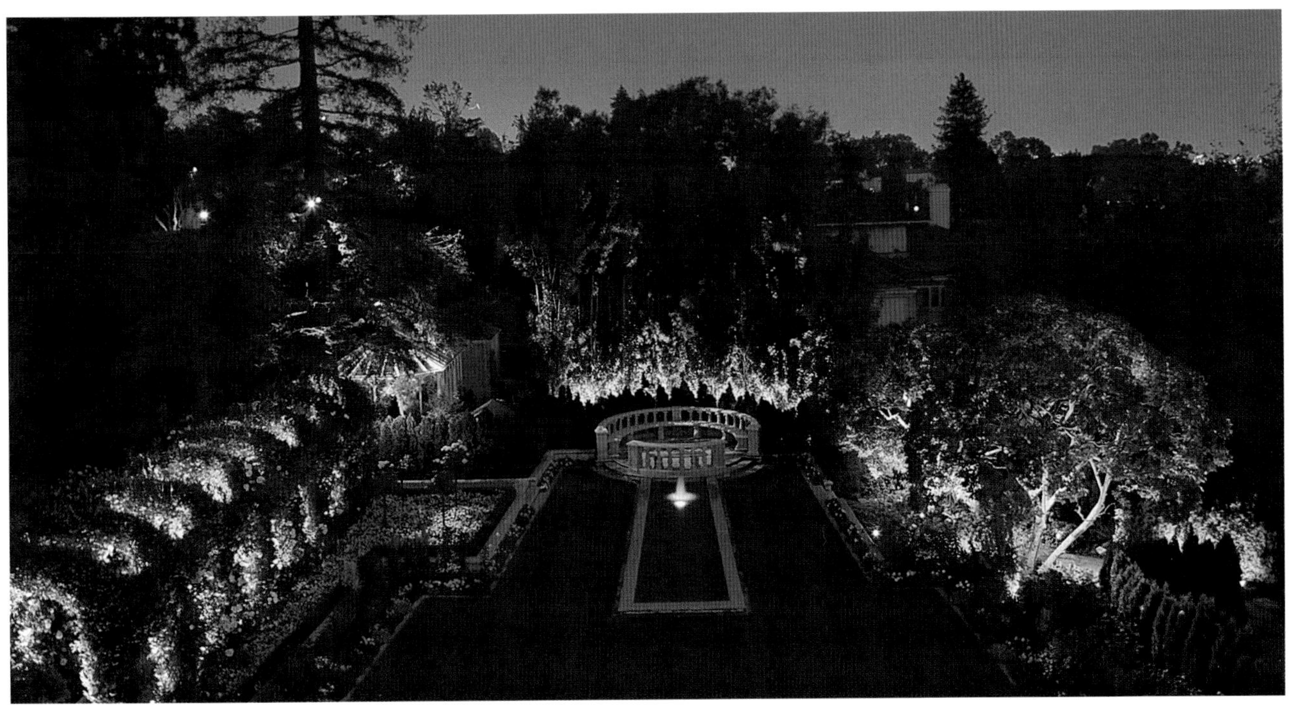

Color Plate 6. *Arrival lighting welcomes guests by including the landscape as a framework around the front door. The pathway step down at the hedge is clearly identified by utilizing downlighting mounted in the trees, as is the hedge itself. Lighting Design: Carole Lindstrom, Alan Tweed, & John Tokarczyk; Photograph: Kenneth Rice Photography, www.kenricephoto.com.*

Color Plate 7. *With a side approach to a front door, providing a path of light from the drive helps navigate an unfamiliar setting. Lighting Design: Carole Lindstrom, Alan Tweed, & John Tokarczyk; Photograph: Kenneth Rice Photography, www.kenricephoto.com.*

Color Plate 8. *In spring, the blazing red Azalea, flanked by other shrubs and the waterfall, dominates this composition. The background provides context but takes a back-seat. Lighting Design & Photograph: Tom Williams, Williams Landscape Lighting Design.*

Color Plate 9. *In summer, green foliage creates a lush, soft feeling masking the waterfall and the hillside of boulders. The lamp palette used is almost entirely 20-watt MR16 flood BABs to keep the brightness level soft. Lighting Design & Photograph: Tom Williams, Williams Landscape Lighting Design.*

Color Plate 10. *In winter, the softness and mystery of summer gets replaced with heightened texture and expansiveness as the snow defines the shapes of tumbled rock, ledge, and tree trunks. Lighting Design & Photograph: Tom Williams, Williams Landscape Lighting Design.*

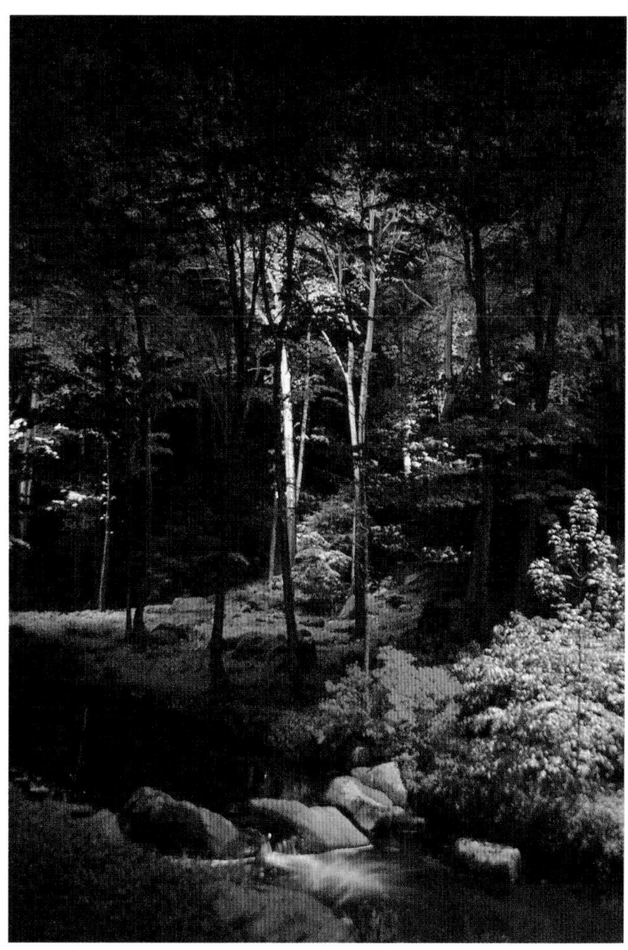

Color Plate 11. *At this front door, two 20-watt MR16 spot lamps and linear spread lenses accentuate the detailing of the bronze relief panels. Lighting Design: Janet Lennox Moyer; Photograph: Kenneth Rice Photography, www.kenricephoto.com.*

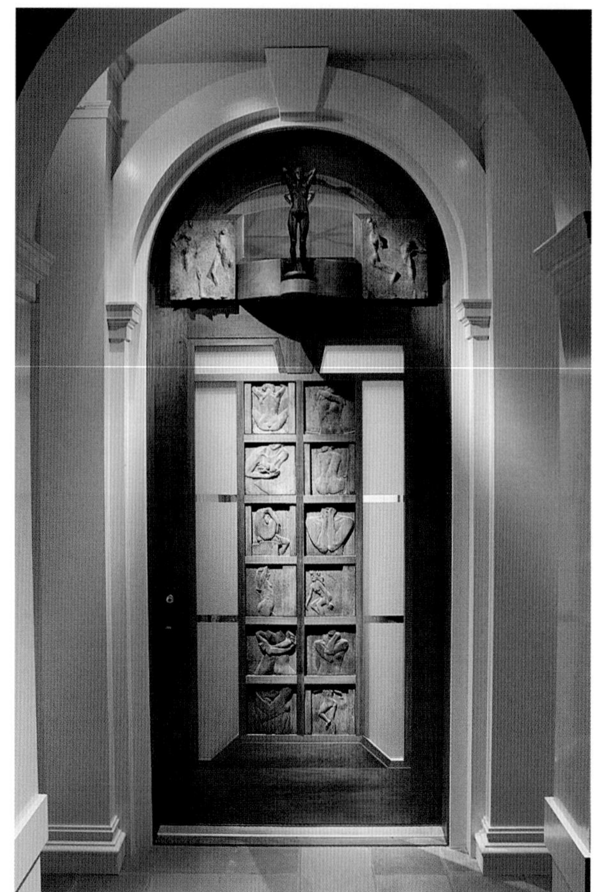

Color Plate 12. *Inside this northern California home, lighting to highlight the art and the table is carefully controlled to allow the eye to move out through the windows into the gardens beyond. Lighting Design: Janet Lennox Moyer; Photograph: Kenneth Rice Photography, www.kenricephoto.com.*

Color Plate 13. *The owners' passion for art continues out onto the upper deck. The continual motion of the two George Ricki sculptures creates a compositional tension. Soft lighting all around these sculptures frames them, providing a sense of context in the garden. Lighting Design: Janet Lennox Moyer; Photograph: Kenneth Rice Photography, www.kenricephoto.com.*

Color Plate 14. *At the lower deck, the integration of artwork continues. Here the composition is more formal, with three focal elements: the Japanese stone sculpture (left), the Deborah Butterfield horse (top middle), and the Japanese Maple (right), each lit to similar brightness. Notice that the stairs are easily visible, but the softest light level in the scene. Lighting Design: Janet Lennox Moyer; Photograph: Kenneth Rice Photography, www.kenricephoto.com.*

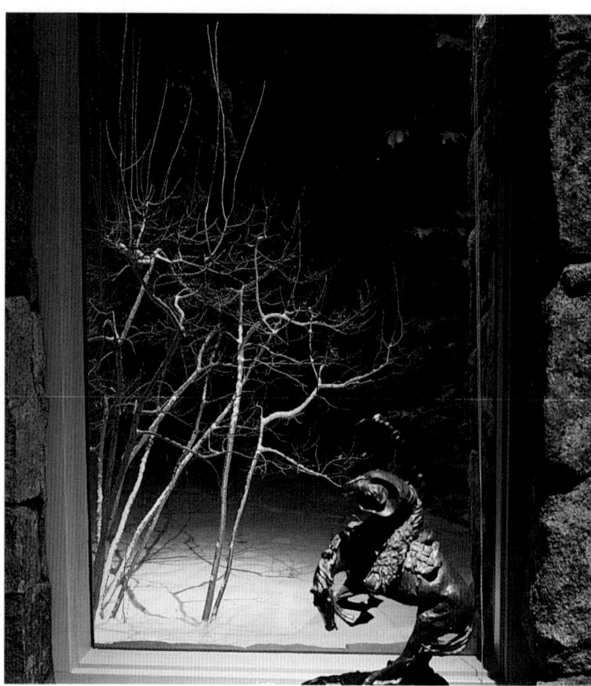

Color Plates 15 & 16. *The contrast between summer and winter effects becomes evident here in this Lake Tahoe cabin window setting. The lush foliage dominates in summer, in a way providing a sense of privacy at the window. In winter, the depth of the garden and the bones of the native Willow shrub provide a completely new view. Lighting Design: Janet Lennox Moyer; Photograph: Kenneth Rice Photography, www.kenricephoto.com.*

Color Plates 17 & 18. *In fall, the vibrant foliage color dominates this scene. In winter, when snow covers the Rhododendron, a strong horizontal line helps to focus on and isolate the specimen Japanese Maple. A blanket of snow provides a greater sense of depth due to moonlight reflecting up onto the background plantings. Lighting Design & Photograph: Tom Williams, Williams Landscape Lighting Design.*

Color Plate 19. *The balance of interior and exterior lighting levels visually integrates these two spaces. One Oak has been selected to provide a sense of depth while keeping the feeling of this pool patio private and intimate. Lighting Design: Janet Lennox Moyer; Photograph: Kenneth Rice Photography, www .kenricephoto.com*

Color Plate 20. *In a San Francisco Garden Show vignette called the "Garden of Dreams," the use of light adds to the surreal environment. Light accentuates the form of the two moss sculptures to reinforce the garden bed idea. A combination of grazing texture in some areas of the vellum clouds and strong wash in others punctuates the scene. Lighting Design: Michael Stewart Hooker; Photograph: Kenneth Rice Photography, www.kenricephoto.com.*

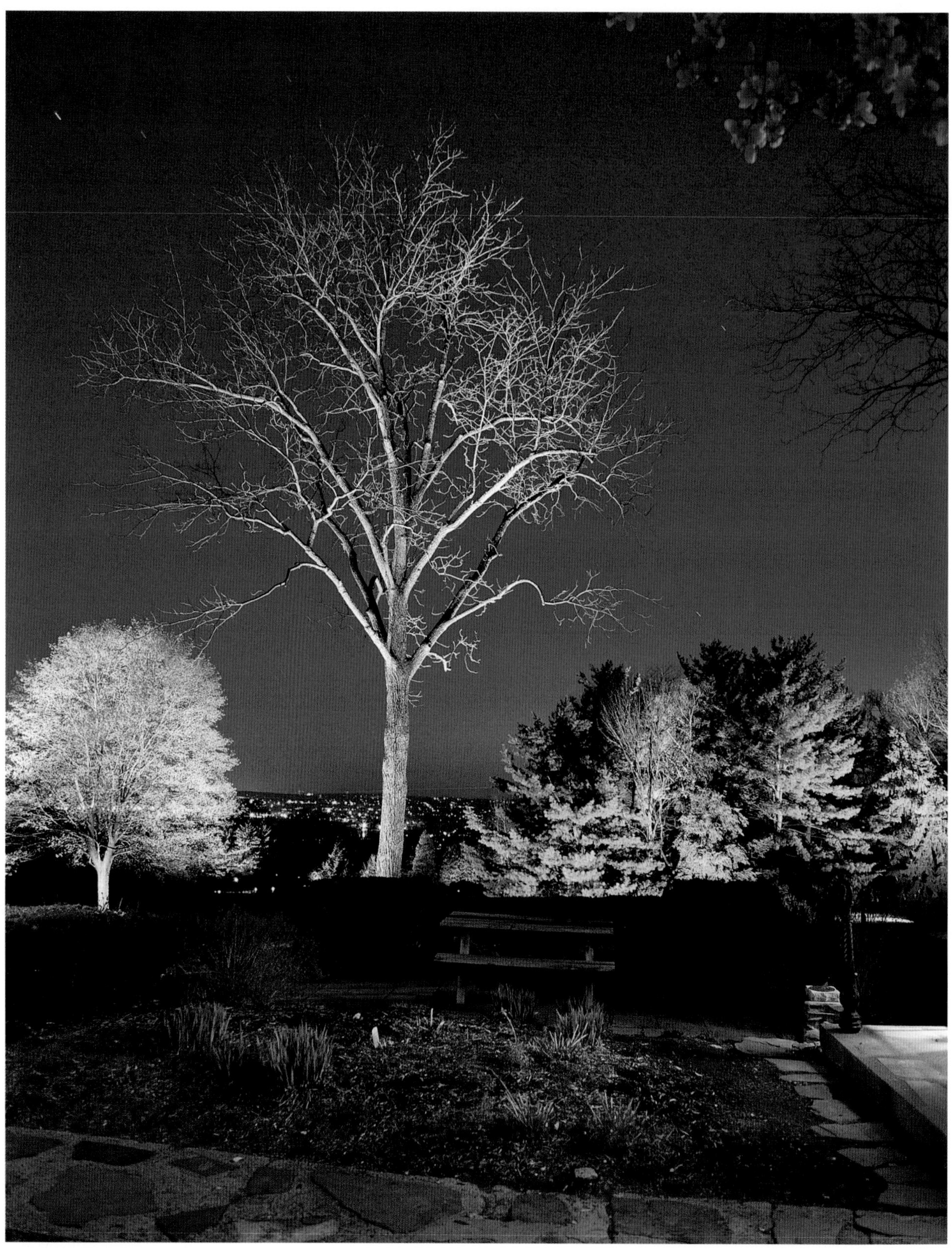

Color Plate 21. *Two groups of graduate students at the Lighting Research Center set up this mock-up. Part of their task was to coordinate their ideas between areas and create a cohesive overall scene. Their overall concept was to create a view from the main activity area of the property. Lighting Design: C. Brooke Carter, Dan Dyer, Kelly Miller, Jamie Perry, Eve Quellman, Javier Ten, & Kami Wilwol; Photograph: Kenneth Rice Photography, www.kenricephoto.com.*

Color Plate 22. *Several years later, another class of LRC students created a more defined composition at the pond area. The garden areas and the garden activities had evolved during the years between the two mock-ups. Lighting Design: Peping Dee, Brian Fuller, Francisco Garza, Sumi Han, Rohini Pendyala, & Insiya Shakir; Photograph: Dan Dyer*

Color Plates 23 & 24. *The two classes approached lighting the Colorado Blue Spruce tree differently (see Figure 15.6). The first group wanted to exaggerate its color and use it as a surprise as people wandered through a relatively undeveloped garden. The second group needed the tree to integrate with other visual elements of an overall composition. Lighting Design: groups listed in Color Plates 21 and 22; Photograph: Kenneth Rice Photography, www.kenricephoto.com and Dan Dyer.*

The Leaves: *This series of photographs illustrates how leaves with different characteristics react to direction of light.*

Summer Leaves: Color Plate 25. *Front lighting emphasizes detail and creates a sparkle when the leaf has a shiny surface.*

Color Plate 26. *Back lighting emphasizes shape and makes translucent leaves glow. Note how the opaque leaf remains dark except for the halo of light around its edges.*

Fall Leaves: Color Plate 27. *Light's effect on fall leaves varies from summer leaves and across a spectrum of leaves. Most fall leaves that change color become more translucent and react more vibrantly to light.*

Color Plate 28. *As leaves dry, backlighting emphasizes skeletal shape and the richness of fall color*

Colored Leaves: Color Plate 29. *Unusual or tropical leaves react similarly to more typical leaves. See how color, overall shape, leaf veining, and shiny finish are all emphasized*

Color Plate 30. *Backlighting on these more unusual leaves not only emphasizes shape and creates glow but exaggerates the interesting characteristics of these leaves*

The Tree: *This series of photographs illustrates how the same lighting on this Norway Maple (*Acer platanoides*) highlights the tree's seasonal characteristics.*

Summer day: Color Plate 31. *Mature, specimen Norway Maples become large trees with dense canopies.*

Summer night: Color Plate 32. *To create a cohesive canopy effect, the LRC student designers mounted fixtures up in the tree to uplight into the top canopy.*

Fall night: Color Plate 33. *Norway Maples don't have spectacular fall color. The lighting shows how the leaves become more translucent at this time.*

Color Plate 34. *A combination of front and backlighting benefits most leaves.*

Color Plate 35. *Combining front and back lighting makes leaves more three-dimensional.*

Color Plate 36. *Combining front and back accentuates all the leaf features of unusual leaves.*

Lighting Design: Janet Lennox Moyer; Photograph: Kenneth Rice Photography, www.kenricephoto.com

Lighting Design: C. Brooke Carter, Dan Dyer, Eve Quellman, & Kami Wilwol; Photographs: Dan Dyer, Janet Lennox Moyer, Kenneth Rice Photography, www.kenricephoto.com, & Kevin Simonson, www.kaperture.com.

Winter night: Color Plate 37. *In its dormant form, the tree reveals its branching structure.*

SnowStorm: Color Plate 38. *The horizontal branches hold snow and create a 'powdered sugar' effect on the canopy.*

Spring night: Color Plate 39. *Norway Maples are not known for providing a spectacular flower show in the spring, but with lighting, the effect becomes noticeable.*

Color Plates 40 & 41. *As conifers wake up in the spring, their foliage tends to be light and vibrant. This seasonal characteristic becomes more evident with lighting. Downlighting these stairs, rather than using path or steplights provides safety and allows the garden to show. Lighting Design: Janet Lennox Moyer, Dan Dyer, & Frida Schlyter; Photographs: Dan Dyer.*

Color Plates 42 & 43. *Looking down from a deck onto the conifers illustrates the different effect from spring to summer. Lighting Design: Janet Lennox Moyer, Dan Dyer, & Frida Schlyter; Photographs: Dan Dyer.*

Color Plates 44 to 46. *This Weeping Willow (*Salix babylonica*) has such a widely three-dimensional canopy that fixtures had to be located at a great distance to catch the canopy top (see Figure 15.41). Note the difference in visibility of the branching structure between late March in Color Plate 46 and mid-April in Color Plate 45. Lighting Design: Peping Dee, Brian Fuller, Francisco Garza, Sumi Han, Rohini Pendyala, & Insiya Shakir; Photograph: Dan Dyer.*

Color Plates 47 to 50. *This Mulberry (*Morus alba*) has a wispy vase shape with graceful arching branches. Lighting accentuates its form in each season. The lighting designers were careful to integrate the expanse of the branching structure for each season. Lighting Designers: Michael Myer (47), Kelly Miller, Jamie Perry, & Javier Ten (48 & 49); Photographs: Dan Dyer (47), Kenneth Rice Photography, www.kenricephoto.com (48), and Kevin Simonson, www.kaperture.com (49).*

Color Plate 51. *In 1990, this hillside represented a relatively mature hillside, planted many years previously. To light the conifers, some of the 120-volt PAR38 lamps were placed as much as 50 feet away. Lighting Design: Janet Lennox Moyer; Photograph: Kenneth Rice Photography, www.kenricephoto.com.*

Color Plate 52. *Ten years later, this garden has expanded up and down the hillside and has become an immature garden. The lighting had to be completely reconceived. The existing conifer lighting did not change, but the Crabapple lighting equipment had to be moved and/or retrofitted, and substantial equipment had to be added for the numerous trees and the extension of a small, dry streambed. Note the Oak in the upper right, which provides a transition from this hillside to the area shown in Color Plates 53 & 54 (tree at far left). Lighting Design: Michael Stewart Hooker, Janet Lennox Moyer, & Paul Schreer of MSH Visual Planners; Photograph: Kenneth Rice Photography, www.kenricephoto.com*

Color Plates 53 & 54. *Looking across the pool at the vastly renovated garden, note how the progression of 30 days in the spring affects the appearance of the gardens. In March, Color Plate 54, the branching structure dominates the scene. In April, Color Plate 53, the color and texture of the foliage starts to become prominent. Lighting Design: Michael Stewart Hooker, Janet Lennox Moyer, & Paul Schreer of MSH Visual Planners; Photograph: Kenneth Rice Photography, www.kenricephoto.com.*

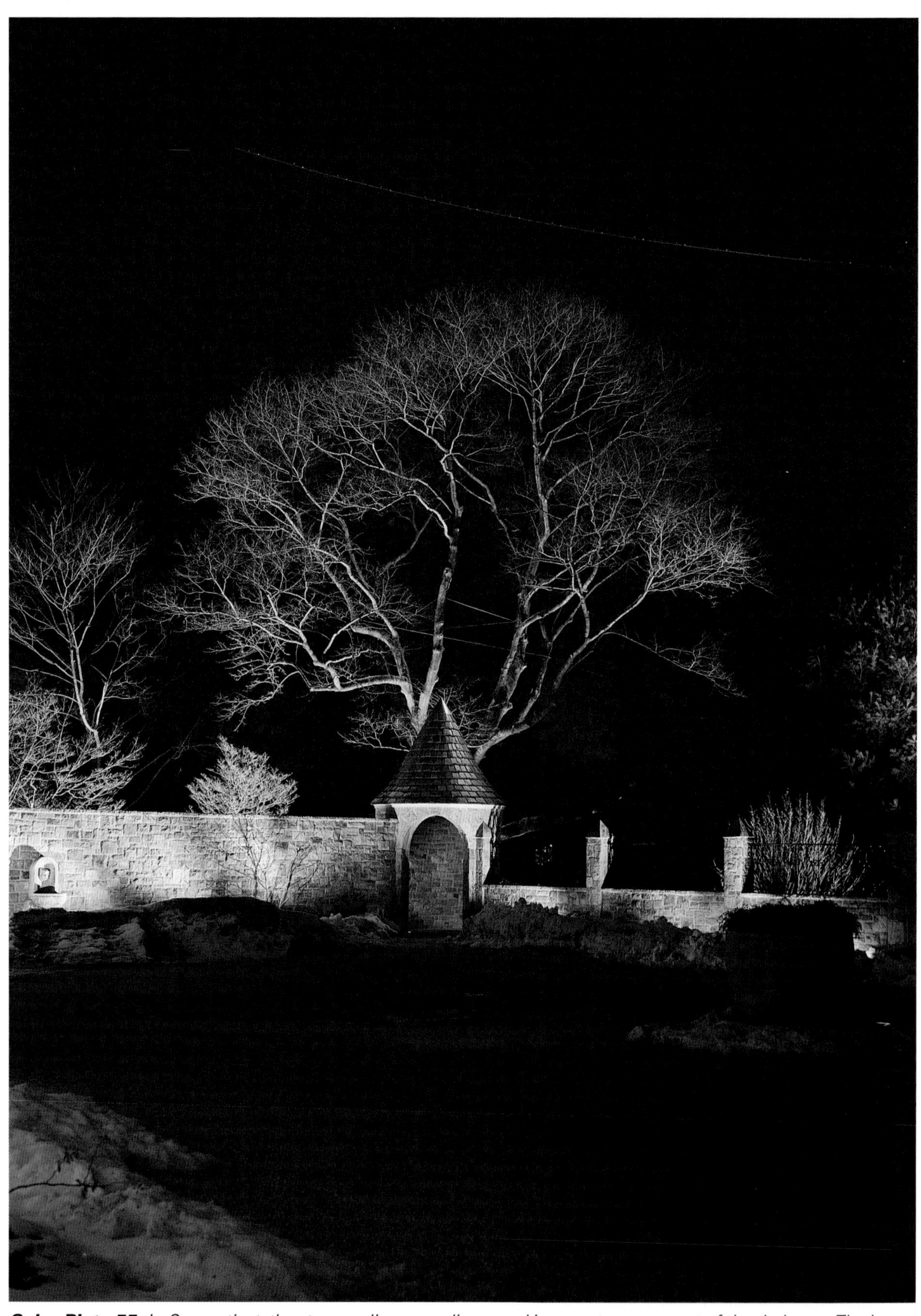

Color Plate 55. *In Connecticut, the stone wall surrounding a parking court appears out of the darkness. The large deciduous tree behind provides a sense of context but remains secondary in importance. Lighting Design: Janet Lennox Moyer; Photograph: Kenneth Rice Photography, www.kenricephoto.com.*

Color Plates 56 & 57. *At the back of this Connecticut property, the boundary consists of a row of Apple trees and conifers. Below-grade fixtures with 70-watt, 3,000°K, PAR30 ceramic metal halide wash this "hedge." Downlighting mounted to the back of the conifers' trunks punctuates the groundplane, the fence, and the pavilion. The contrast of color helps to accentuate the contrast in scale massive plant material and more diminutive architectural features. Lighting Design: Janet Lennox Moyer; Photograph: Kenneth Rice Photography, www.kenricephoto.com.*

Color Plate 58. *As the main view of this sculpture is from rooms situated above, two downlights carefully placed in an adjacent overhanging tree reveal and reinforce the lines of this sculpture. One fixture aims onto the face from the front, while the other aims onto the tail from the rear. Spill light from the two 50-watt narrow-spot lamps spills over onto the patio, providing context around the sculpture. Lighting Design: Janet Lennox Moyer; Photograph: Kenneth Rice Photography, www.kenricephoto.com.*

Color Plate 59. *At the Far Niente Vineyard gardens, minicompositions throughout the property serve as views from other areas, as well as functional spaces. The bridge visually connects the pavilion and the Oak. Each of these three elements has similar overall brightness to stabilize the composition. Lighting Design: Michael Stewart Hooker, Janet Lennox Moyer, & Paul Schreer, MSH Visual Planners; Photograph: Kenneth Rice Photography, www.kenricephoto.com.*

Color Plate 60. *This covered walkway has substantial foot traffic, requiring a high and even lighting treatment. MR11 fixtures integrated into the arbor structure provide the functional lighting and show the architectural and planting features surrounding the walkway. Lighting Design: Michael Stewart Hooker, Janet Lennox Moyer, & Paul Schreer, MSH Visual Planners; Photograph: Kenneth Rice Photography, www.kenricephoto.com.*

Color Plate 61. *In this California backyard, the stage serves as a focal point when not being used as a performance space. Uplighting two Maples flanking the stage begins the visual integration of the focal structure into the landscape. Two planting borders along the sides of the lawn provide a framework and visual transportation back to the viewing patio. Downlighting mounted in the large Oak creates the light patterns on the back wall through the arbor and on the ground around the stage, further anchoring the stage into its setting. Lighting Design: Michael Stewart Hooker, Janet Lennox Moyer, & Paul Schreer, MSH Visual Planners; Photograph: Kenneth Rice Photography, www.kenricephoto.com.*

Color Plate 62. *Guests arrive at the main gate to the Far Niente Vineyards at the end of a long road. Two fixtures with narrow-beam lamps punctuate the winery name and the two logos in the gate. Beyond, soft uplighting and down-lighting introduce the interior road that will bring guests to the activity areas. Lighting Design: Michael Stewart Hooker, Janet Lennox Moyer, & Paul Schreer, MSH Visual Planners; Photograph: Kenneth Rice Photography, www.kenricephoto.com.*

Color Plate 63. *From the main lawn or from the highway, the main winery building is sculpted using clear high-pressure sodium, as Gil Nickel, the owner, insisted. To anchor the building to the ground, the stone wall is treated similarly with HPS. The row of Olive trees is uplit with multiple MR16 fixtures as a color contrast. Lighting Design: Michael Stewart Hooker, Janet Lennox Moyer, & Paul Schreer, MSH Visual Planners; Photograph: Kenneth Rice Photography, www.kenricephoto.com.*

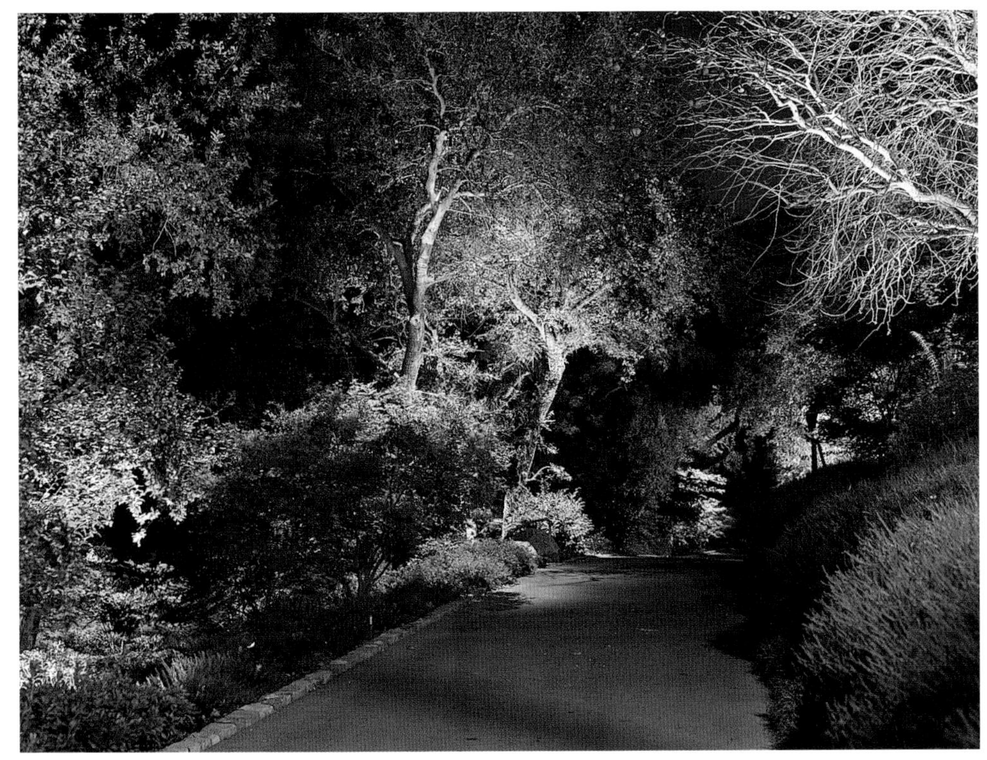

Color Plate 64. *The interior roadways at Far Niente are bordered by dappled light at the forested planting areas. Predominantly involving downlighting, the concept centers on showcasing the beautiful gardens while people visit the winery. Carefully selected specimen trees are uplit to include height to the scene. Lighting Design: Michael Stewart Hooker, Janet Lennox Moyer, & Paul Schreer, MSH Visual Planners; Photograph: Kenneth Rice Photography www.kenricephoto.com.*

Color Plate 65. *During the first week of class, a group of LRC master's candidates were assigned to design and install a mock-up of this chapel in less than three weeks. They utilized a combination of low- and high-voltage halogen and various ceramic metal halide sources to include all the elements of this structure. Note how they integrated the rooflines and carefully balanced brightness relationships to accentuate, form, detail, and texture. Lighting Design: Peping Dee, Brian Fuller, Francisco Garza, Sumi Han, Rohini Pendyala, & Insiya Shakir; Photograph: Dan Dyer.*

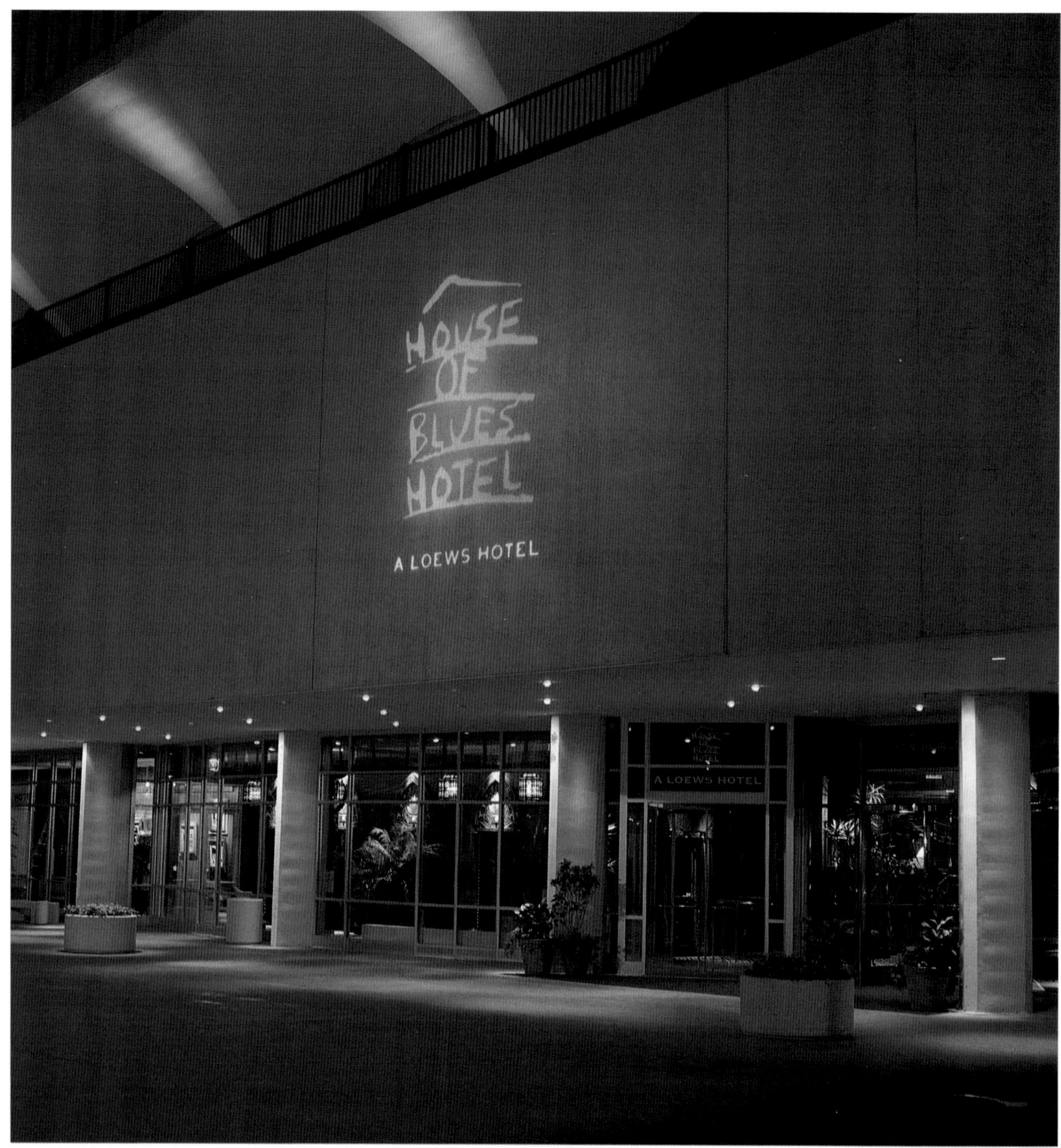

Color Plate 66. *The House of Blues hotel in Chicago comes to life at night (see daytime shot, Figure 18.11). All the general lighting is a deep, moody blue. The hotel logo is created using multiple projections (see fixture location in Figure 18.12). The hotel lobby lighting reverts to white light to flatter people and deep colors on art and architectural features to continue the HOB funk. Lighting Design: Michael Stewart Hooker & Paul Schreer; Photograph: Kenneth Rice Photography, www.kenricephoto.com.*

IV

ELEMENTS OF DESIGN

14

Plant Materials

Plant material represents one element to consider in a landscape lighting composition (others include hardscape, architectural structures, water features, and sculptures). Maximizing the beauty of the landscape and ensuring that the design works during all seasons of the year, as well as throughout the life of the landscape, requires an understanding of the plant material. The importance of knowing the characteristics of all the plants listed on a planting plan cannot be overemphasized, as a lack of this knowledge can cause a lighting scheme to fail. This chapter will cover a variety of lighting techniques that can be used to light plant materials and discuss the issues necessary to understand plant material in order to select appropriate lighting technique(s).

TECHNIQUES FOR LIGHTING PLANTS

The appropriate lighting technique to use on a specific plant is determined by the role the plant plays in the lighting composition and by the visual effect desired for the plant. Variables to consider include direction of light, fixture location, and quantity of light. Direction of light consists of either uplight, downlight, or sidelight. The selection of a direction affects the appearance of the plant but does not dictate a mounting location. The selection of up- versus downlighting is usually irrelevant. Sometimes, though, the desired mounting location may not exist. For example, to downlight a tree requires either a tree or an architectural structure taller than the tree. No downlight mounting location will exist for a large tree in the middle of a lawn. Sometimes an uplight will not work for a tree because a walkway or patio comes too close to the base of the tree.

The designer must decide whether the plant should retain its daytime appearance or make a new statement when lit at night. Downlight produces shadows on the underside of leaves, echoing how the sun lights the plant (see Figures 14.1 & 14.2). Both downlighting and uplighting can mimic daylight on an overcast day by putting a wash of light on the plant. Typically, though, uplighting changes the plant's appearance from its daytime look. It makes tree foliage glow when light shines up through the leaves. It produces shadows on the top of leaves, emphasizing texture or form, making a more dramatic visual effect (see Color Plates 47–50).

Fixture location requires consideration of the luminaire's position as it relates to the plant—in front, to the side, behind, or a combination of locations. Deciding how many fixtures should be used and their placement affects the appearance of the shape, color, detail, three-dimensionality, and texture of the plant being lit. Start by finding the "line" of the tree. This refers to the location(s) around the trunk with no branching as far up the tree as possible. Introducing soft up- or downlighting here visually connects the tree to the ground (see Figure 14.4). From this starting point, the quantity and location of canopy fixtures can then be determined.

The last variable, amount of light, refers to the importance of the plant in the overall design. As the importance of a plant increases in the composition, so should

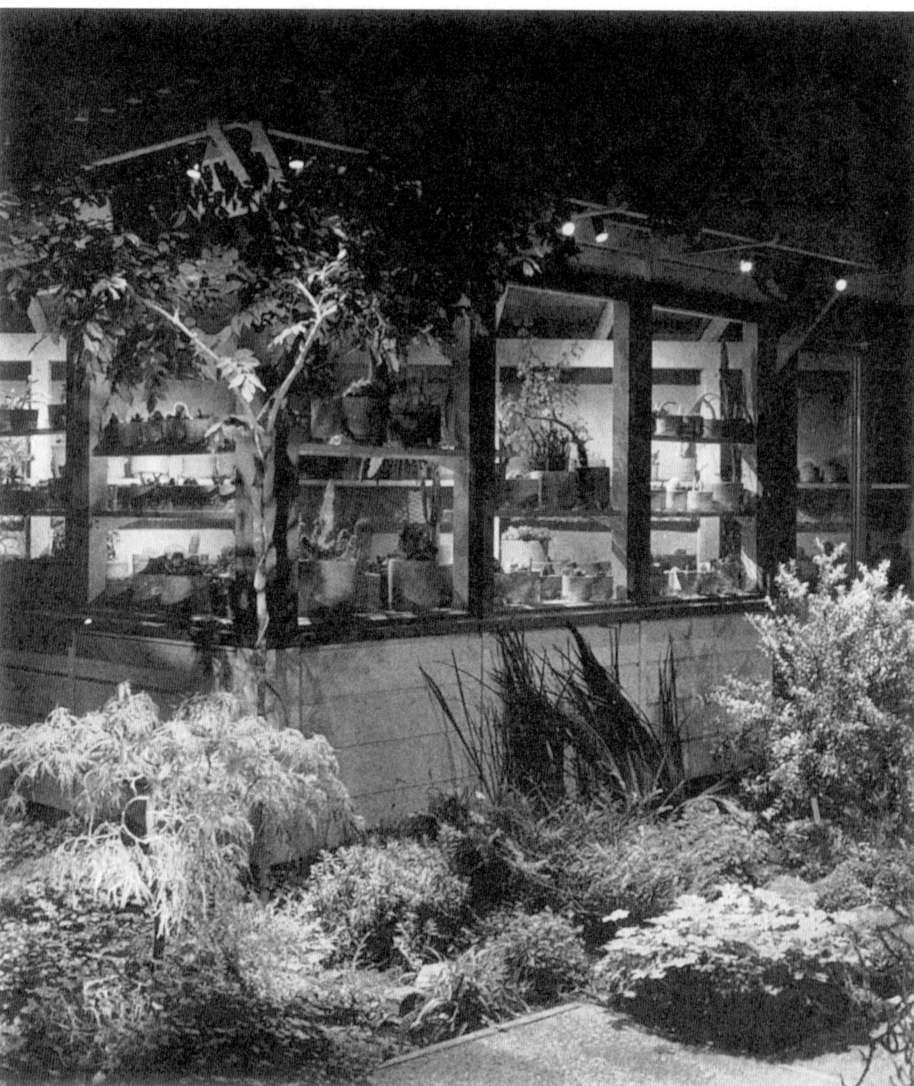

Figure 14.1. Downlighting naturally highlights the planting and accentuates foliage and flower color, simultaneously providing walkway lighting. In tight locations such as trellises, using MR8 or MR11 lamps minimizes fixture size, allowing the fixtures to practically disappear. Lighting Design: Janet Lennox Moyer, MSH Visual Planners; Photograph: Kenneth Rice Photography, www.kenricephoto.com.

the luminance of the plant. Recall that what the human eye sees is reflected light. Plan how much light to shine onto the plant, therefore, based on its role and its reflective characteristics (see Chapter 3).

Designers should also be aware that plants are sensitive to light for many functions of life. They require a regular cycle of light and darkness to maintain growth and strength and even to bloom (see Chapter 13).

EVALUATING PLANT MATERIALS

Each plant used in the landscape represents a part of the overall composition. One or more plants will represent feature elements and some will serve as secondary or support elements, while other plants might remain unlit. All plants listed on the planting plan should be considered, whether intended to be lit or not. A careful look at all plants allows the designer to complete the image of the landscape, just as furniture and accessories complete the view of an interior space.

The process of studying all the plants will help identify which should be lit, provide an understanding of the relationship of one plant to another in the landscape, and identify useful relationships or potential conflicts between the planting and the lighting equipment. A plant may be located so that it will hide lighting equipment. Other times the location of a plant may conflict with the optimal fixture location. In an immature garden, a plant located between a luminaire and a plant to be lit may not initially disrupt the light distribution. However, after growing for several months, a year, or several years, it can start blocking the light from reaching the intended plant (see Figures 14.35 & 14.36). Since this plant is close to the fixture, the level of light hitting it will be high, thus creating a "hot spot" of light that will distract from the more important elements of the composition.

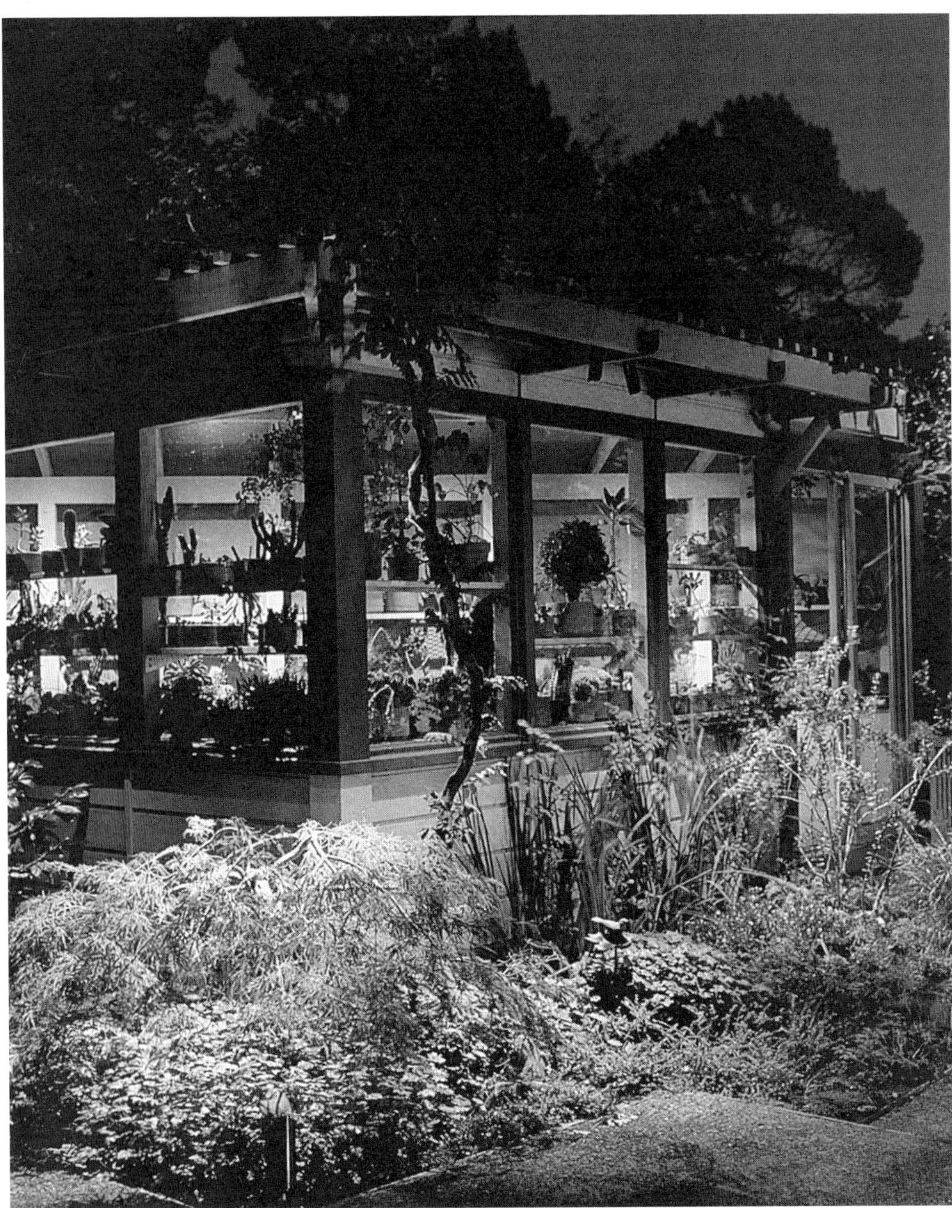

Figure 14.2. Adding an angled hood eliminates the visible brightness on the inside of the fixture body. Lighting Design: Janet Lennox Moyer, MSH Visual Planners; Photograph: Kenneth Rice Photography, www.kenricephoto.com.

Plants are categorized within the plant kingdom using Latin names, called *botanical names,* that are relatively standard throughout the world. For the purposes of landscape lighting, three of these names need to be understood: genus, species, and variety. *Genus* is a grouping of plants that are related by characteristics and the first name listed for a plant. Genus names always begin with a capital letter. *Species* refers to a subgroup within a genus and will be the second name listed. Species names always begin with a lowercase letter. *Variety* refers to a specific characteristic(s) that separates this plant from the others in the species and is the third name in a plant listing. Not all plants will have a variety name. For example, the White Pine or Eastern White Pine is called *Pinus* (genus) *strobus* (species). Varieties of Pinus strobus include 'Nana' (a dwarf variety), 'Pendula' (a weeping variety), and 'Prostrata' (a low, spreading variety). Variety names are shown in single quotes with the first letter capitalized. Each of the common or English names for the plant begins with a capital letter.

Plants within the same genus (and often within the same species) can be radically different from each other in appearance and in growing habits (see Figures 14.23 to 14.25). Two individuals of the same genus, species, and variety may grow differently due to geographic location, climatic and growing conditions (such as soil type, irrigation or natural precipitation, temperature variation, and environmental imbalance, including smog and acid rain), as well as to genetic influences. A

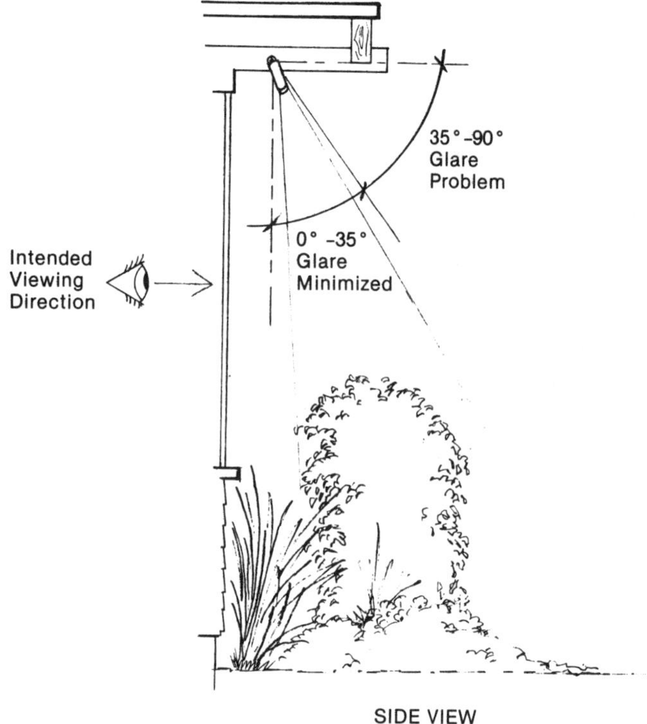

Figure 14.3. Detail and color technique. *Downlighting plant material creates a natural appearance featuring the shape of plants or groupings of plants, colors, and details against the night darkness. The sketch shows aiming angle guidelines for controlling glare. Only when people in the landscape will not see the brightness of the fixture or in adjacent properties should the higher aiming angles be used. The aiming angle guidelines apply to fixtures mounted in trees as well as on structures. Drawing: Lezlie Johannessen.*

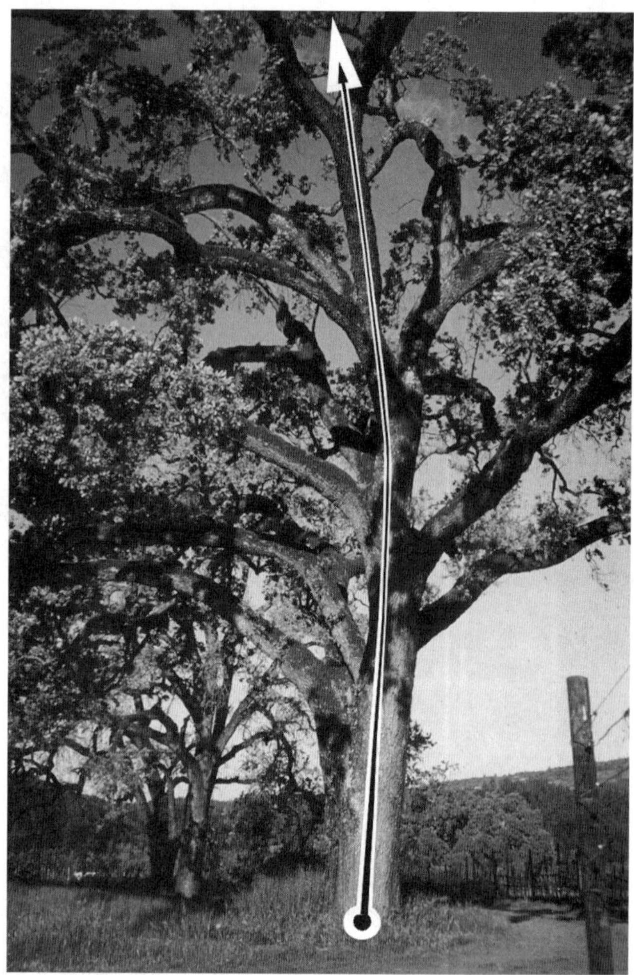

Figure 14.4. *This Oak provides a good example of a clear line up a tree from the ground. Starting with soft light grazing the trunk along this line sets up the foundation of the tree structure. Drawing: N. J. Smith.*

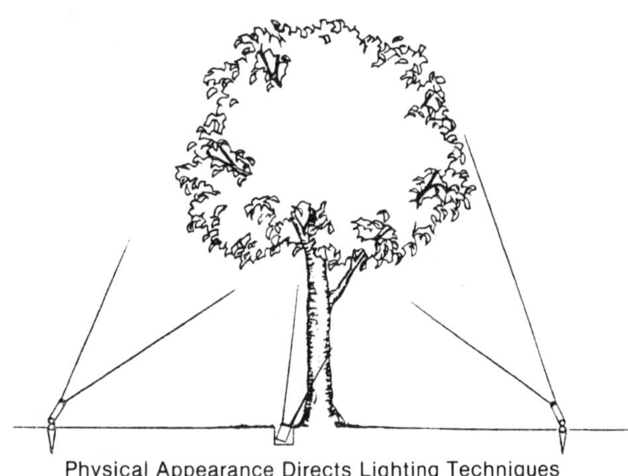

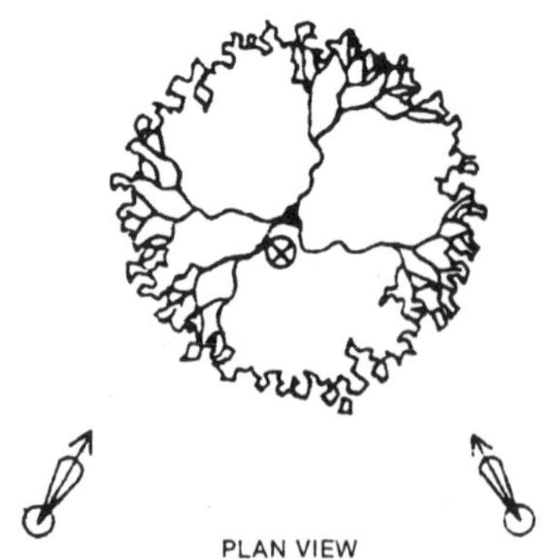

Figure 14.5. *A tree's physical appearance influences the technique a lighting designer uses on the tree. Here, a high, dense canopy and interesting trunk texture direct the designer to highlight the trunk and wash the canopy. Drawing: Lezlie Johannessen.*

Figures 14.6 & 14.7. *This fixture has been carefully placed, aimed, and shielded to light the branch that extends over the road without anyone seeing any brightness from the fixture body or lamp. Photograph: Janet Lennox Moyer.*

pine may grow quickly to 100 feet in the Pacific northwest but perhaps reach only a height of 20 feet in an area with different conditions.

A planting plan will list plants by *caliper* or *container* size. This gives the lighting designer a reference to the initial size of the plants due to arrive at a site. The local practice of designating plant specifications varies. Check how the landscape architect plans to specify for a particular project. The American Association of Nurserymen sponsored the development of standards for nursery stock that, among other things, lists a range of heights for shade trees by caliper. The standard is published by the American National Standards Institute (ANSI).

Neither caliper nor container size provides definitive size information. Discuss the initial height and width with the landscape architect, who has often selected an individual specimen and may have a photograph of the exact plant. When available, a photograph provides the best information about a plant's size and appearance.

The caliper size of the trunk confirms the feasibility of mounting lights in the tree. Use caution with trunks less than 12 inches in diameter. Confirm that they can handle the stress and weight of adding lighting equipment.

When studying the plants listed on a planting plan, discuss the overall shape, growth rate, and mature size of the plant with the landscape architect. Also discuss whether the size and shape of the plant will be controlled by pruning, and any intent to change plant material, either regularly throughout the year or as the garden matures (see Figures 14.20 & 14.21).

A good way to compile all the information on plant material for a project is to research the plants in books. Because plants are living, their statistics and characteristics vary from region to region. This complicates the search for information, because not all books will agree on statistics and characteristics about specific plants. So look to several sources for information on each plant. Hundreds of plant identification books are available from booksellers and book clubs. Local libraries, book-

Figure 14.8. *Many deciduous trees, including Flowering Dogwood (*Cornus florida*), look best in leaf. This Dogwood lacks interest and looks awkward during dormancy and should remain unlit. Other deciduous trees, such as Harry Lauder's Walking Stick (*Corylus avellana *'Contorta'), look intriguing or beautiful when dormant. When in leaf, its huge, misshapen leaves obscure this tree's best feature—the gnarled, twisting branches. Drawing: Craig Latker, Magrane Latker Landscape Design.*

sellers, and the landscape architect provide good sources for plant books to research if your library of books is not yet complete (see the Bibliography).

The same tree lit several different ways makes varying statements. With thousands of plants available to the landscape architect, the characteristics of the plants on a project can vary significantly. Evaluating the characteristics of a plant makes the lighting designer aware of the visual effect(s) that can be achieved, thus guiding how to light the plant. With some plants the structure or leaf characteristics limit how light should be applied, while the characteristics of other plants offer several options.

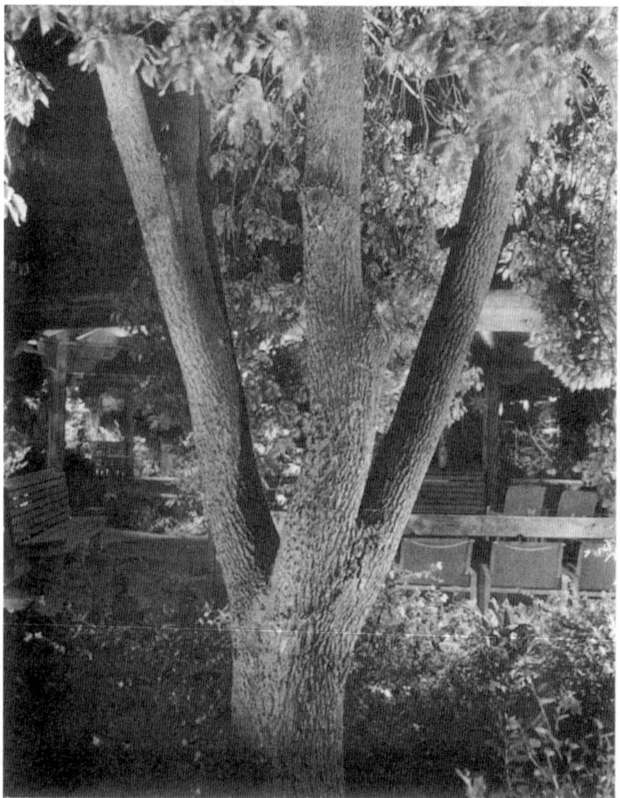

Figure 14.9. *Uplighting the trunk on this Carob (*Ceratonia siliqua*) demonstrates emphasizing a patterned trunk. Lighting Design: Janet Lennox Moyer, MSH Visual Planners; Photograph: Kenneth Rice Photography, www.kenricephoto.com.*

For example, consider a tree with deeply furrowed bark, a dense canopy impenetrable by light, and branches starting at roughly 10 feet above ground. Locating fixture(s) close to the trunk brings out the texture of the bark and creates a visual link from the canopy to the ground. Locating additional fixtures out away from the edge of the branches washes the canopy (see Figures 14.5 & 14.9).

Physical Characteristics

Characteristics of plant material to consider include:

- *Texture.* Texture consists of a somewhat subjective view of leaf size and form, branching pattern, overall scale, and openness of leaf overlap.
- *Leaf type.* This includes shape, color, size, overlapping pattern, density, translucency, or opacity. Leaves may be thick and leathery or thin and diaphanous. They may have a dull or shiny finish on one or both sides. These considerations will direct the choice of light source and appropriate lighting technique (see Color Plates 23–39).
- *Branching pattern.* The plant may have dense branching or open branching; the branching configuration may be inherently beautiful (worth highlighting) or a mangled mess that should not have attention brought to it. This consideration applies for both evergreen plants and deciduous

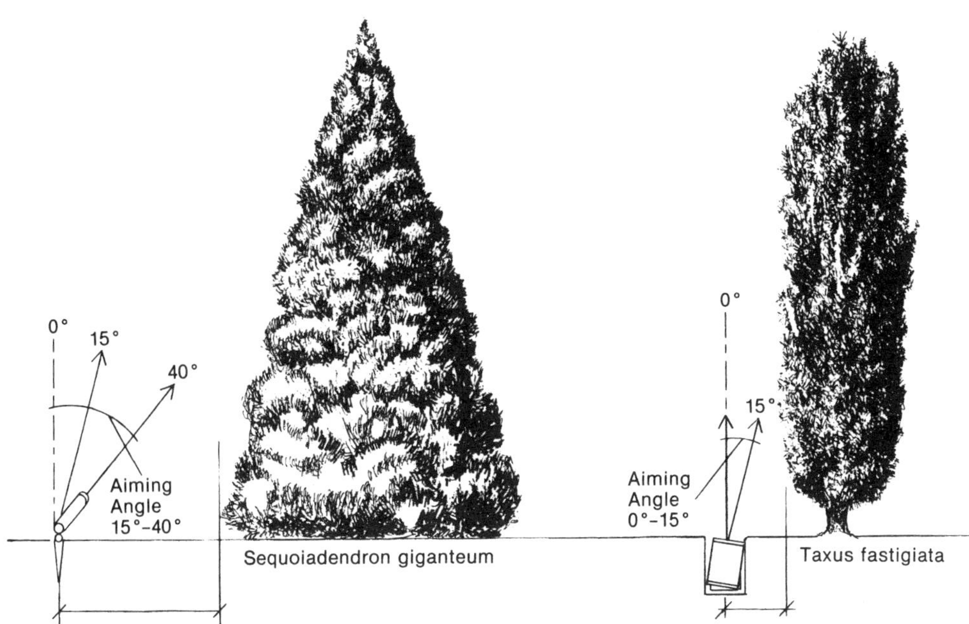

Figure 14.10. *To emphasize the shape of a Giant Sequoia (*Sequoiadendron giganteum*), left, wash the canopy, aiming fixtures between 15° and 40° off vertical. Graze an upright Irish Yew (*Taxus fastigiata*) using narrow-beam lamps in fixtures aimed approximately 15° from vertical to emphasize foliage texture. Plan the fixture distance from the tree (either stake-mounted or direct-burial) based on the plant's growth habit, including initial and mature size and planned maintenance. Drawing: Craig Latker, Magrane Latker Landscape Design.*

plants, in both the dormant and leafed-out stages (see Figures 14.6–14.8).

- *Foliage color.* This translates, in lighting terms, into reflectance characteristics. Foliage color also directs the choice of light source to enhance the color. Find out if the color changes during the year. Some foliage changes color from fresh growth to mature growth, when going dormant in the fall, and/or during the flowering period. Some plants vary from one side of the leaf to the other. For example, some varieties of Southern Magnolia (*Magnolia grandiflora*) have a tan-colored, wooly-textured growth (called indumentum) on the underside of the leaf. Uplighting makes this Magnolia look dead. Other trees, including Silver Maple (*Acer saccharum*) and some Birches and Poplars, have a silvery underside that makes the plant almost sparkle when lit from below. Varieties of a plant may have differing leaf colors. Sometimes, one plant will have multicolored foliage.
- *Branch/trunk characteristics.* Some trees have color or pattern formations that provide interest and add to the beauty of the plant when lit. The trunk may be striped or patterned. The bark may be peeling, flaking, mottled, deeply furrowed, or cracked. This feature could be emphasized during the dormant period of deciduous plants (see Figures 14.9 & 14.26).
- *Flowering characteristics.* When does a tree or plant flower during the year, for how long, and what is the flower color? What are the size and shape of the flowers? Are the flowers striking or inconspicuous? This information helps determine the light source to use and the nature of emphasis, if any, that flowers should have in the lighting composition.
- *Light requirements.* For outdoor landscapes, this is an issue not for growth but for flowering. Some plants are sensitive to light periods in relationship to flowering. Night lighting may help or hinder the tendency to come into flower. For indoor landscapes, in atria, lighting is mandatory to support life (see Chapter 13).
- *Growth rate.* Determine how quickly and by how much the plant will vary in size and shape over its life. Some plants grow only inches a year; others grow by feet. Some plants may start out 3 feet tall in a new landscape and at maturity (10 or more years later) attain a height of 4 to 5 feet. Others may grow to 100 or more feet (see Figures 15.20–15.22).
- *Dormancy characteristics.* This refers to a resting period that some plants experience in winter. Some plants go dormant in the fall by losing their leaves, others by disappearing entirely for the winter. Some plants in their dormant form look spectacular, others do not (see Figure 14.8). In garden areas with annuals, biennials, and/or perennials, bare dirt may be the norm for many months. This may influence the control strategy for the lighting.
- *Shape.* The basic shape of the plant also provides hints on lighting technique. Tree shapes can vary significantly from young form to mature form. Some young trees have no distinct form and gradually grow into a beautiful shape. Others shift from one distinct shape to another quite different shape at maturity. Figures 14.27 to 14.30 show examples of some basic tree shapes (at maturity) with a rep-

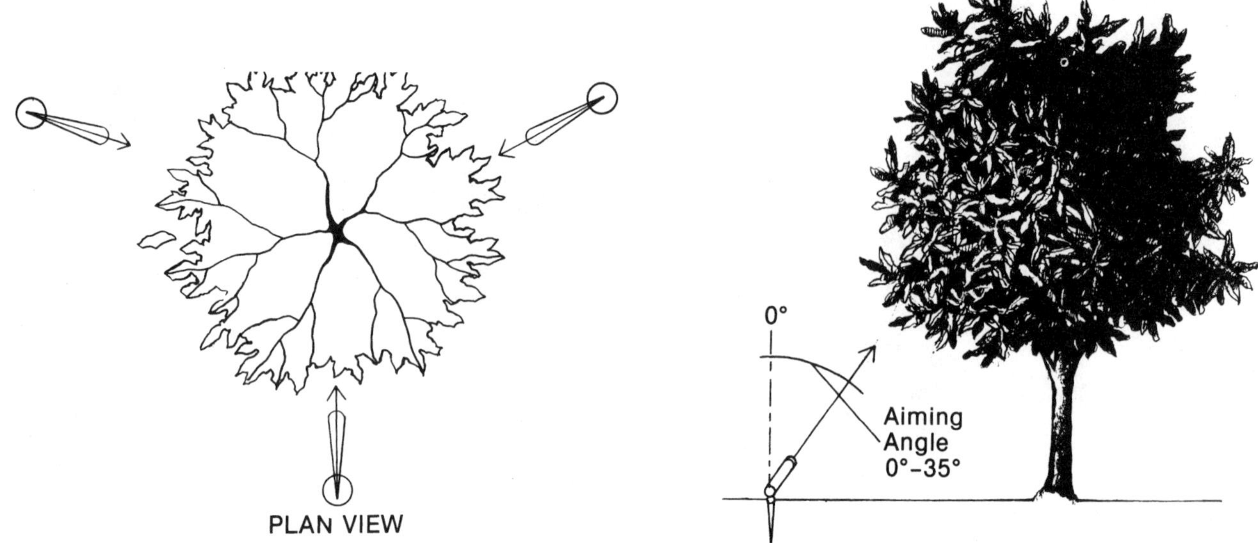

Figure 14.11. *Trees with dense, rounded forms, such as the Southern Magnolia (*Magnolia grandiflora*), require multiple fixtures outside the canopy. Use 35° off vertical as the maximum aiming angle in the following situations: viewing at close range, viewing from several sides, and when the fixture lens is visible to the viewer. Drawing: Craig Latker, Magrane Latker Landscape Design.*

resentative listing of trees that fit each type and a brief description of typical lighting approaches for that shape tree.

Physical Appearance

All these plant characteristics guide how the plant should be lit. As an example, if a plant has dense overlapping leaves, this suggests that fixtures must be located outside the tree canopy to wash the foliage. When a tree has translucent leaves, lights mounted below the canopy make the foliage glow.

Mature size and shape significantly influence lighting technique. Plants with a narrow, upright shape and dense branching best express their texture and shape when lit by a grazing light. Some Yews, for example, have a stiff upright shape. When they are pruned to maintain that shape, lighting fixtures placed close to the edge of the tree bring out their rough texture. The upright shape allows light to reach the treetop (see Figure 14.10). Use a lamp with a narrow beamspread on upright trees, especially on tall Palms (see Figures 14.37 & 14.38).

Trees with a pyramidal shape, such as many Redwoods, are best lit with fixtures moved back away from the edge of the tree. Optimal distance varies—from a few feet to 10 or 20 feet—depending on the angle of the tree's overall shape and on the tree's height (see Figure 14.10).

Plants exhibiting a rounded form with a dense leaf overlap and thick leaf structure benefit from a wallwash technique. Moving fixtures out away from the canopy accentuates the shape of the tree (see Figure 14.11) but diminishes texture. Lights placed under the canopy on dense trees will create a wash of light on the bottom of the canopy only, as light cannot penetrate the branches (see Figure 14.13).

Dense shrubs often serve as minor focal points, background elements, or transition plants between two larger specimen trees. Locating fixture(s) a minimum of 2 to 3 feet away from these plants provides soft fill light. Always calculate the distance required based on the shape and height of the plant. In some cases, the distance will be 15 feet or more. If the fixture aims away from the viewer or the plant has enough height to block the fixture, use a relatively horizontal aiming angle (see Figure 14.12).

Trees with translucent leaves and an open branching pattern glow when lit from directly under their canopies. Fixtures located under the canopy filter light up through the branches, accentuating the tree's shape and enhancing the three-dimensional qualities of the tree (see Figures 14.16 & 14.17). This creates a sensational effect in a garden, especially when the tree is a major focal point. However, if several trees are lit this way, there is a risk of creating a dramatic, but spotty scene. Use fill light to tie the scene together.

An exception to locating lights directly under the canopy applies when rounded, open trees have interesting characteristics at the outer edge of the canopy. For example, the Crape Myrtle (*Lagerstroemia indica*) produces long conical-shaped flowers at the end of its

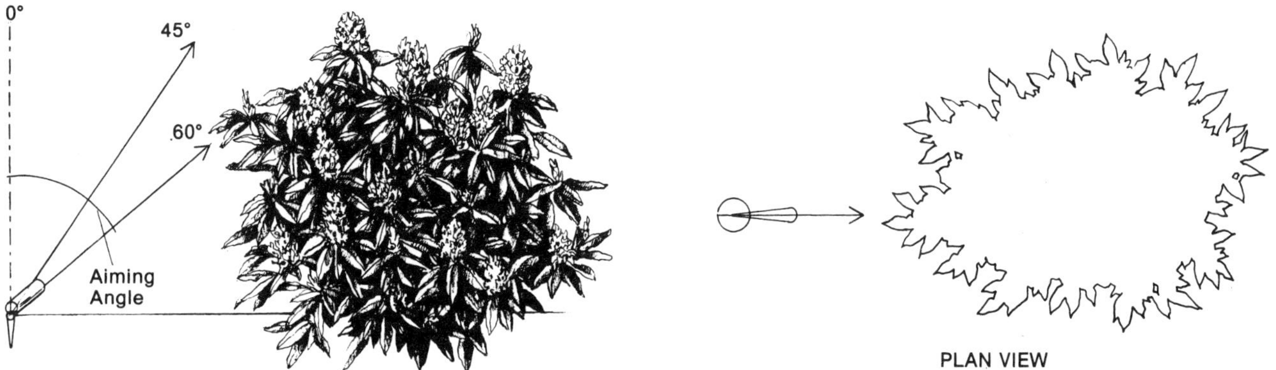

Figure 14.12. Dense shrubs such as Rhododendrons, tall enough to block any view of the fixtures, look best washed. Move fixtures away from foliage and aim between 45° and 60° off vertical. When viewing the tree is restricted to one side, one fixture will suffice. If the view encompasses more of the plant, utilize more fixtures to complete the shape. Drawing: Craig Latker, Magrane Latker Landscape Design.

branches. The open form and somewhat translucent leaves suggests locating fixtures outside the canopy both to provide light for the flowers and to filter light through the canopy. This approach accents the flowers when the tree is in bloom and provides full, balanced light for the tree when not in bloom (see Figures 14.44 to 14.46).

When a tree produces branches close to the ground, fixtures should be placed away from the canopy to light the tree from the ground to the top. The aiming angle can be relatively flat, aiming as much as 45° to 60° from vertical, since the tree will block potential glare. However, for plants that start branching a foot or more above the ground, the aiming angle needs to be a steep angle, no more than 35° from vertical, to avoid creating glare and to minimize fixture brightness (see Figure 14.11). When other plants or objects block the view of these fixtures, the angle may be more horizontal (see Figure 14.34).

For trees serving as focal points, plan to have fixtures encircling the tree to provide depth. Small trees with a mature canopy width of 5 to 15 feet require a minimum of three fixtures (see Figure 14.16). Trees with canopy widths from 15 to 50 feet require 5 to 10 fixtures or more, depending on the mature size and shape of the specimen (see Figure 14.47 to 14.49, 15.25 & 15.26).

When a large tree functions as a transition or background element, a smaller number of fixtures can potentially be utilized effectively. This approach creates a dramatic but understated effect on the tree. Pay attention to the tree's characteristics and locate fixtures carefully. This technique works when the lighting accentuates the tree's appearance (see Figure 14.22). Use caution, though, as trees can easily become visually disfigured when using a small number of fixtures (see Figure 14.14).

Trees located close to a wall often have restricted canopies, potentially reducing the required number of fixtures. Often, the wall behind the tree reflects enough light to provide depth. Place fixtures to light both the canopy and the trunk (see Figure 14.18, 14.22, & 17.3).

When accent lighting a tree, always include the trunk (see Figure 14.9), as leaving the trunk unlit causes the tree to look disjointed from the ground. Many trees have interesting trunk characteristics. The bark may be mottled, striped, thorny, peeling, deeply furrowed or cracked, multicolored, and/or flaking (see Figure 14.26). The growth pattern of the main trunk and the main branches may be striking or unusual.

Trunk lighting can be either subtle or strong, depending on the appearance of the trunk and how the trunk lighting ties in with the rest of the tree lighting. Placement of fixtures as well as the lamp type and wattage depends on the desired effect. Trunk lighting techniques include creating crisp edges through sidelighting or frontlighting for detail and color (see Figure 14.64).

Growth

In selecting a lighting technique the decision is based partially on the size of a plant. The designer needs to remember that plants grow and change shape over time. Understanding how quickly a plant grows, its eventual mature size and shape, and how the plant will be maintained or pruned helps guide the selection and location of the luminaires.

A Japanese Maple (*Acer palmatum* 'Dissectum') in a 5-gallon container may arrive 3 feet tall by 5 feet wide. This plant may be a mature tree growing an additional 6 inches to 2 feet over the next 10 years (see Figure 14.31). Alternatively, it may be a young tree that in the

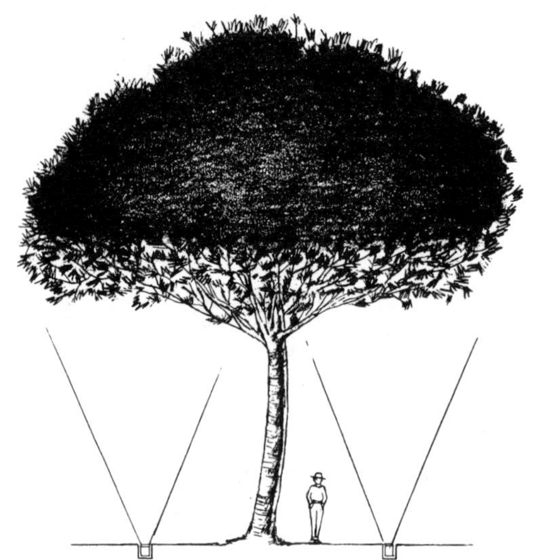

***Figure 14.13.** Italian Stone Pines (*Pinus pinea*) reach 40 to 80 feet in height and produce a dense, rounded canopy when mature. Uplighting under the canopy creates a wash on the trunk and underside of the canopy. Drawing: Lezlie Johannessen.*

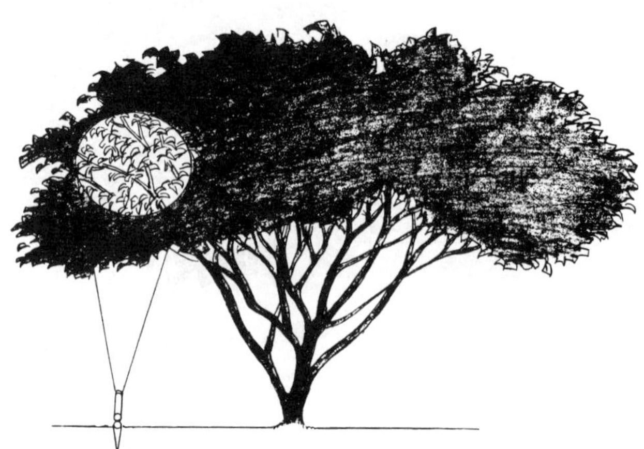

***Figure 14.14.** A graceful, spreading tree lit with one fixture creates a hot spot on a small area of the canopy while the rest remains in darkness. This creates a disfigured, ugly appearance. Drawing: Lezlie Johannessen.*

same time period multiplies several times in size (see Figure 14.32).

Japanese Maples comprise a large group of trees with a myriad of sizes and shapes. Examining this group of trees provides information to consider for most trees. Some people prefer to prune young specimens to maintain a particular size or develop a specific shape. They often prune the foliage to open up the structural shape of the trunk and branches. Others prefer allowing the tree to form a larger, thicker canopy naturally. Most Japanese Maples, including the red forms, have translucent leaves that look beautiful when lit through the canopy. However, when Japanese Maples have thick canopies, locating fixtures below the foliage does not work.

For a mature Japanese Maple, direct-burial fixtures offer advantages. These trees often branch close to the ground or have weeping branches that fall to the ground. In either case, below-grade fixtures will offer wider light distribution and less chance of burning leaves (see Figure 14.31). For a young tree, use stake-mounted fixtures with an extra length of cord so that the fixture may be moved away from the tree as it increases in size (see Figure 14.32).

Often, specimen trees planted in lawns are young or slow-growing and much smaller than they will be at maturity. This leads to a dilemma in deciding fixture location. Fixtures located for the initial tree size will become nonfunctional as the tree grows beyond the fixture and the foliage smothers the light (see Figure 14.33). Fixtures located in a reasonable position for the mature size of the tree often cannot aim far enough off vertical to hit the tree for the first few years. One solution is to locate fixtures for the mature tree size and delay activating the fixtures until the tree has matured. A second solution requires the selection of a fixture with full-range aiming capability and the ability to raise and lower the fixture within the burial can (see figure 7.15b). This approach allows lifting the fixture up to, or slightly above, the soil line and aiming it at the required angle to hit the tree immediately. It can be pushed back down into its housing and readjusted as the tree grows. Two possible concerns with this approach include increased lawn maintenance and potential glare created by a low aiming angle.

General garden growth presents a challenge to the lighting designer. Most people understand the need for garden maintenance, but they do not realize the impact that plant growth has on their garden lighting. As plants increase in width and height they can quickly start blocking light, bury a fixture, or upset the lighting effect. Discuss this problem with both the client and landscape architect in the initial planning stages of the project. Everyone must be aware of the need for a maintenance schedule which includes pruning or removing plant material that interferes with lighting equipment. Sometimes, entire plants may need to be removed due to interference.

Use of vertically adjustable stakes offers a solution to plant interference that least affects the planting. These stakes raise the fixtures as the plant material grows to keep the fixtures from becoming buried. Do not raise

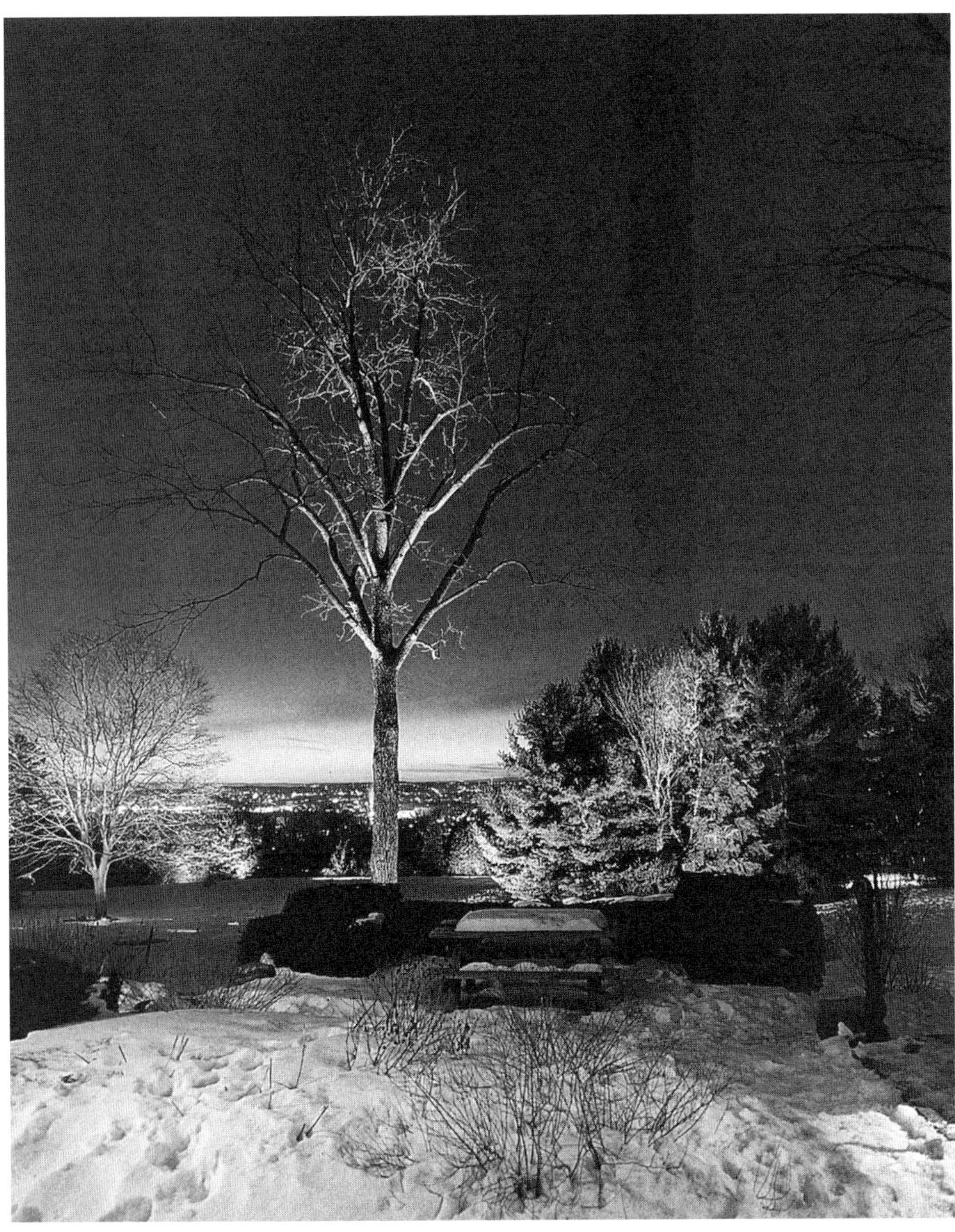

Figure 14.15. *Using too few fixtures or lamps with too narrow a beamspread compromises the tree's form and structure.*

the fixtures completely above the planting so they become obvious. Keep them tucked into the top of the plant material, still relatively hidden, but not covered by the plant (see Figure 14.36).

THE PLANT'S ROLE IN COMPOSITION

How a plant fits into the composition determines the quantity of light the plant should receive and how the plant should be treated with light. Will the tree be a major focal point, minor focal point, transition element, or background element? A beautiful tree that forms the heart of a daytime view may need to blend into the background, leading the eye to another location in the landscape at night. The characteristics of the tree, location in a landscape, and requirements of the composition dictate this shift. For example, directing visitors to the front entry can take precedence over accenting a specimen tree (see Figures 14.22 & 17.1).

Trees that act as a major focal point should be lit so that they appear brighter than less important elements in the composition. Once a role has been established, determine the amount of light required to state the plant's importance. To create a major focal point, trees with dark leaves will require more light than trees with light-colored leaves. Conversely, to avoid distracting a viewer's eye from a dark focal tree, use restraint in selecting the wattage to light secondary trees when they have lighter-colored leaves.

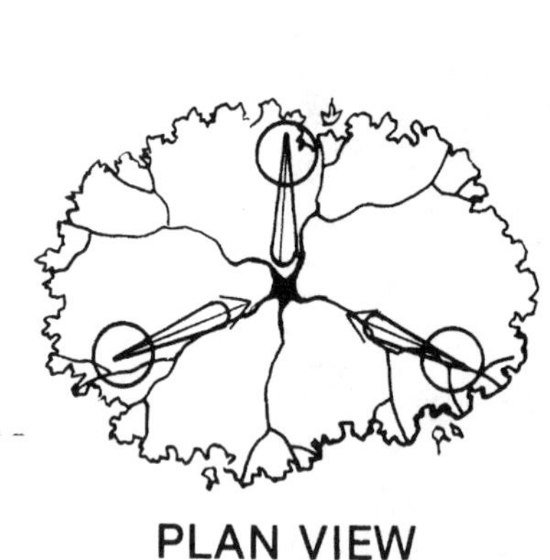

Figure 14.16. Acer palmatum *'Omuryana' grows into a rounded, willowy form, 10 to 15 feet tall by 15 to 20 feet wide. With an open, cascading foliage pattern and translucent, brilliant green leaves, it glows when lit from inside the canopy. Use a minimum of three fixtures to show the full shape of the tree. Drawing: Craig Latker, Magrane Latker Landscape Design.*

The location of a plant and how it will be viewed further directs the lighting approach. If a tree will be seen from only one viewing direction, locate fixtures in front of that portion of the canopy visible to viewers. If people will view all sides of the tree, locate fixtures around the entire canopy.

In determining the desired appearance for a tree, decide whether to show the plant naturally or to create a new artistic appearance. Follow this basic rule: Show plants serving as a primary or major focal point realistically (see Color Plates 21, 31–39, & 44–50). Secondary focal trees, background trees, or groups of trees can be shown either naturally or artistically as their role and appearance guide (see Figure 14.19, 14.22, & 14.51).

Location of light fixtures will affect a plant's appearance. The location of fixtures can be in front, to the side, or behind the plant.

Frontlighting starts to show or create shape, ties areas of a composition together, and provides detail and color to the view of a plant. Additionally, it can either reduce or emphasize texture based on fixture distance from the plant (see Figures 14.50 to 14.55).

Backlighting brings interest to the scene. It can add depth by separating a plant from the background, complete the shape started by frontlighting, or emphasize shape when using the halo technique (see Figure 14.64 & 14.65). With the silhouette technique, backlighting creates drama by eliminating color and detail and showing only form (see Figures 14.42 & 14.43).

Sidelighting emphasizes texture on plants and creates shadows on either vertical or horizontal adjacent surfaces (see Figures 14.61 & 14.62). These shadows either add interest or distract from the composition. Consider how shadows will affect the scene. For example, use shadows as fill to tie focal areas together and create an interesting pattern on a plain surface (wall, lawn, or paving).

Additionally, whether the plant is uplit or downlit can affect appearance. Some effects can be created by either uplighting or downlighting, including a wash, grazing, showing texture, creating a halo, and silhouetting. Creating a glow in foliage can be done only with uplighting. Producing shadows on a vertical surface, can also be done only with uplighting. The dappled lighting effect can only be created with downlighting (see Figure 14.66). Accentuating detail and color is best accomplished with downlighting.

In deciding whether to uplight or downlight, consider the desired appearance, maintenance required to keep the fixture functioning, and the length of life required from the system. An uplight located in ground cover or behind a fast-growing plant may quickly become buried in foliage. Regular maintenance will keep this fixture functioning, but is this desirable? Typically, downlights located out of the way of most activity in the landscape require less maintenance than do uplights.

Uplighting creates dramatic effects on plants—sometimes effective, but not always. Creating a glowing canopy on a tree with translucent leaves emphasizes the foliage shape and color, as well as the overall canopy shape (see Figure 14.63). Uplighting dense plants, however, has limitations. A fixture located close to the foliage creates shadows on the tops of the leaves (unlike

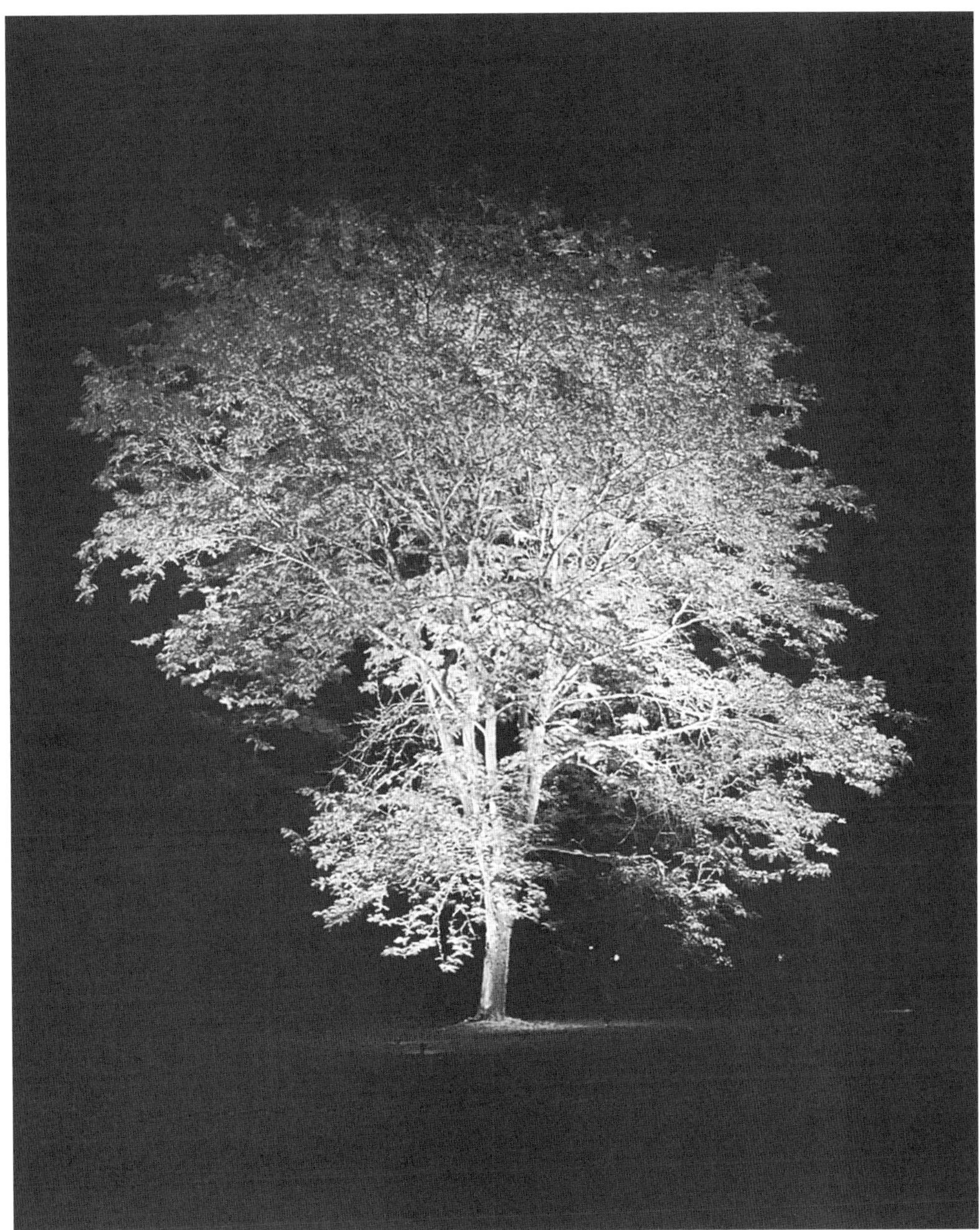

Figure 14.17. *For his first attempt at lighting at tree, Jason Neches mounted several low-voltage MR16 fixtures in the mature Honey Locust to downlight the trunk and ground plane. He used a series of stake-mounted fixtures to fill in the canopy. The mock-up fixtures can be seen and would be below-grade fixtures in a permanent installation. Lighting Design: Jason Neches; Photograph: Dan Dyer.*

sunlight, which creates shadows on the bottom side of the leaves). While dramatic, it produces an unnatural, often undesirable appearance. Consider washing this type of plant by moving the fixture(s) away from the plant. This reduces unnatural shadows. Uplighting can create many artistic effects, including grazing (see Figures 14.56 to 14.58), texture (see Figure 14.59 & 14.60), halo (see Figures 14.64 & 14.65), silhouette (see Figure 14.42 & 14.43), and shadows (see Figures 14.61 to 14.63).

Downlighting, following the direction of the sun, provides a natural appearance. It can provide strong accent lighting or soft fill light (see Figures 3.2 & 14.1). Downlighting also provides the opportunity to create lighting effects—wash (see Figure 14.53), graze, texture

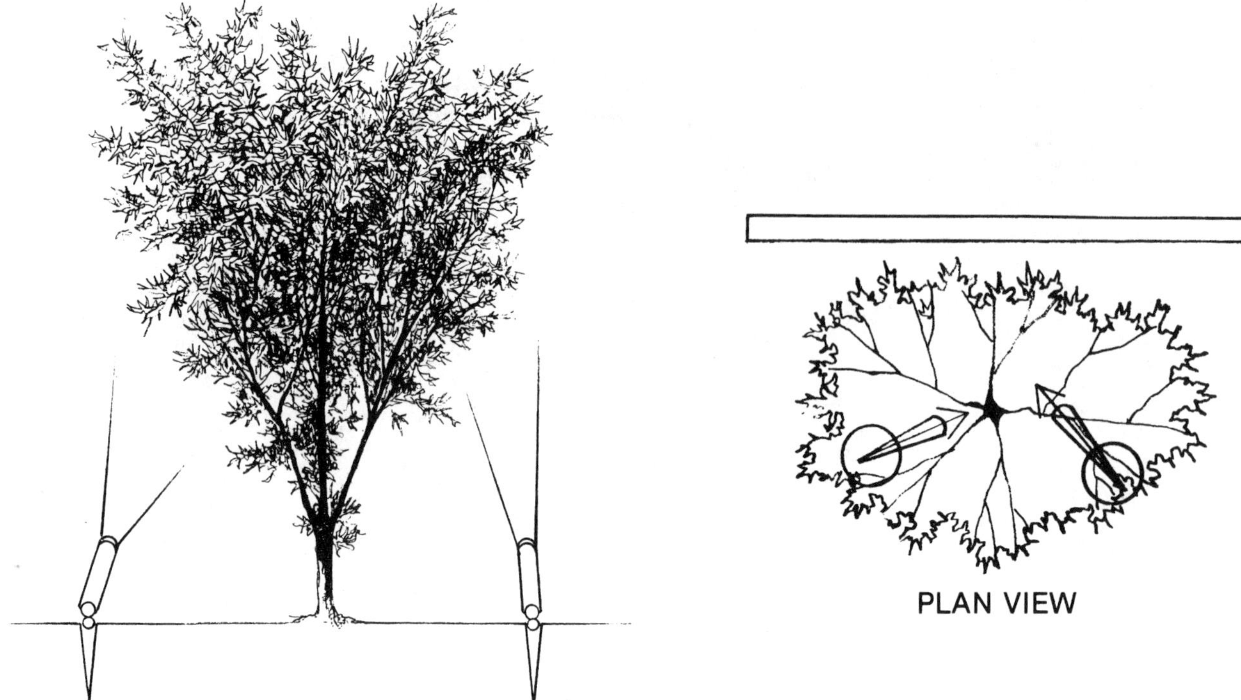

Figure 14.18. *Acer palmatum 'Butterfly' grows upright to 10 feet tall by 3 to 4 feet wide with an open foliage pattern and cream to pale green foliage—another perfect candidate for uplighting from inside the canopy. When situated close to a wall, two uplights may be sufficient. Drawing: Craig Latker, Magrane Latker Landscape Design.*

(see Figure 14.42), halo, silhouette, dappled light (see Figures 14.66 & 14.67), detail, and color—while hiding fixtures. In cold climates, snow will not affect downlighting, but as snow piles up, it can obscure uplighting until the snow melts.

In many cases the decision to uplight or downlight will be determined by the availability of a mounting location for downlighting. Trees (see Figures 10.22 & 10.23), buildings, or other structures provide downlight locations. In selecting, consider the daytime appearance of both the fixture and the wiring. The scale and appearance of a fixture should complement the architecture. Plan the installation details to hide electrical wiring (see Figure 16.14). To minimize fixture glare in the field of view, restrict aiming angles off vertical to between 0° and 35° (see Figures 14.3 & 14.1).

The Role of the Transition Plant

On large properties, creating a cohesive composition often requires using a specimen as a "transition plant" to provide a visual connection from one part of a garden to another. With multiple viewing angles within a garden or areas that are separated by some distance, this plant provides a "brightness connection" (see Figure 15.19 & Color Plates 21 & 52).

This plant may or may not be considered a specimen or focal tree. That importance can change over time as the garden naturally matures or as people further develop the gardens.

Boundary or Divider Role

Garden designers often use large masses of plants and/or hedges to create the boundary of a garden or to divide a space into multiple areas or rooms. Several approaches can be used in lighting these masses/hedges. Often a soft wash will be used to simply denote the boundary and to create a sense of depth (see Figure 3.7). At other times, the plant material or combination of architectural and plant material may merit more importance (see Figure 14.58). A combination of washing and grazing can be used to create more definition and depth for a combination of deciduous and evergreen trees (see Figure 15.10).

The type of fixture and location varies with the site conditions. When the boundary trees are part of a large planting bed, above-grade or stake-mounted fixtures

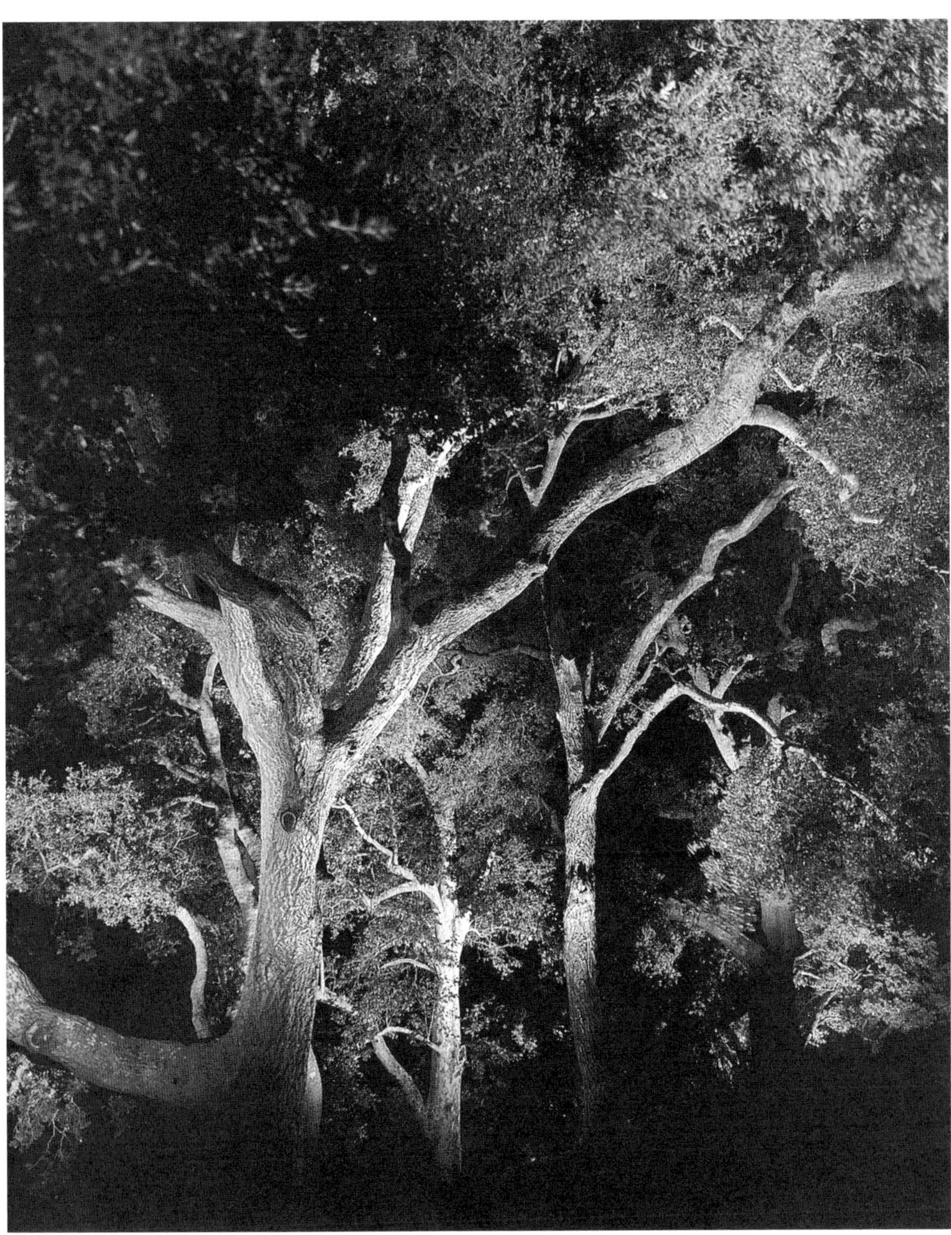

Figure 14.19. *For someone moving along a private driveway, this group of trees provides an overall dappled forest view. Varying the brightness from one to another but keeping it within a reasonable contrast ratio allows this unfocused approach to work. Lighting Design: Janet Lennox Moyer, Michael Stewart Hooker, & Paul Schreer, MSH Visual Planners; Photograph: Kenneth Rice Photography, www.kenricephoto.com.*

can be used (see Figures 15.4 & Color Plates 51 & 52). For a project in California with mature conifers, some of the fixture locations were 20–30 foot from the front edge of the conifer. Often, there isn't that much room available in a planting bed, and either multiple fixtures are needed to create the effect or the fixtures must be located in lawn. In this case, below-grade fixtures become necessary (see Color Plates 56 & 57).

As with most design, visual compositions often incorporate several effects and techniques. For example, the utilization of both uplighting and downlighting in one composition provides more visual definition and interest in the view (see Figure 3.2).

The lighting of plant material as one element in the landscape must be integrated with the rest of the composition. Consider how people will view the plants. When the plant will be seen from several areas or from several different heights, make sure that the plant looks good from all the various angles of view. Always make sure that the appearance of a tree is accentuated and becomes pleasing to the eye of a viewer. With an imbalance of light on a tree or surrounding the tree, the lighting can become eerie or frightening, wasting the owner's money. Carefully planned lighting design adds to the beauty of plant material and increases the enjoyment and value of the garden.

ISSUES TO CONSIDER ABOUT PLANTS
a. Name including Genus, Species, and Variety
b. Deciduous or Evergreen
c. Form
d. Leaf Density and Overlap
e. Size at Planting
f. Mature Height and Spread
g. Growth Rate
h. Special Features

Figure 14.20. *Each of these issues is important to consider for all plants on a project. Studying the plant's characteristics, initial size, growth rate, and special features helps the designer determine whether and how a plant should be lit. An understanding of a plant's form, how it changes appearance from one season to another, and how it will develop over time directs the selection of lighting techniques. These issues, along with an understanding of the mature size of the plant and how its role may evolve over time, direct the designer in planning the amount of spare power needed for adding more fixtures or higher-wattage lamps in the future. The more issues designers can familiarize themselves with in a garden plan, the more successfully they can plan a lighting system for the long term.*

ISSUES TO CONSIDER ABOUT A SPECIFIC PLANT ON SITE
a. Location on Site
b. Health
c. Size
d. Specific Growth Pattern/Form/Habit
e. Importance to Visual Composition
f. Interference Regarding Light Distribution
g. Future Growth
h. Pruning Plan

Figure 14.21. *Once specimen plants have been selected and tagged at a nursery, the designer can start making final evaluation decisions about how to light an individual. The location on the site and how the plant is placed affects the type and number of fixtures initially required. The health of a tree influences whether it should be uplit and if downlights can be installed. If there is any concern about health, the designer should consult with an arborist to determine if the stress of installing fixtures will adversely affect the stability of the tree. The plant's size, future growth expectations, and pruning plans all direct the selection of lighting technique and amount of initial and future equipment needs. The way the trunk and branching structure develops on an individual tree directs how to accentuate its appearance and determines potential mounting locations. Sometimes another plant will conflict with a fixture placement, interrupting the light. This needs to be studied, understood, and rectified in the initial planning of lighting equipment locations. Any future interference needs to be anticipated as much as possible.*

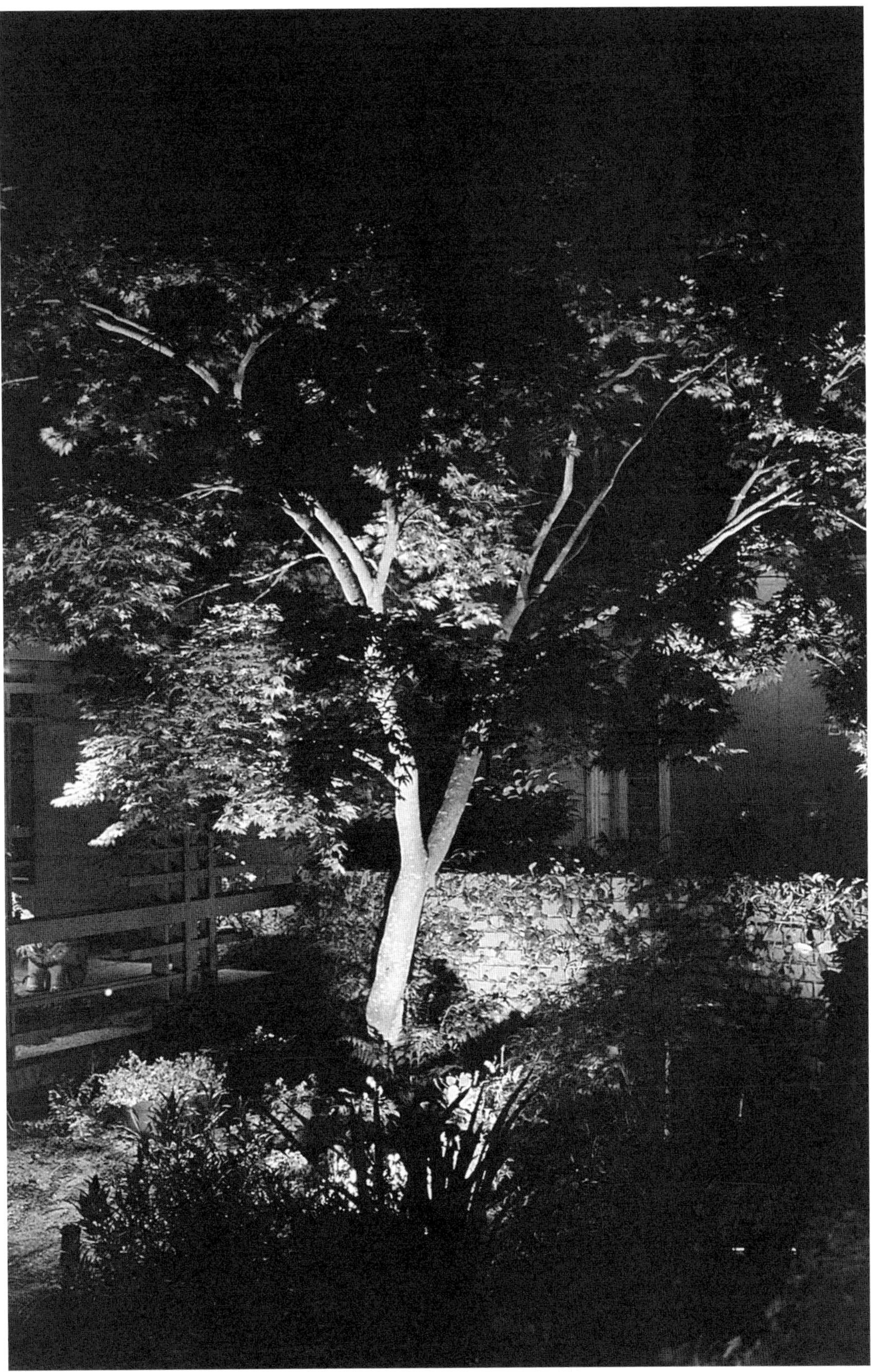

Figure 14.22. *This Japanese Maple, although a large, beautiful specimen, serves as a transition tree in this lighting design (see Figure 17.3). The prime lighting goal, directing visitors to the front door, required the tree lighting to remain subtle. The use of five low-voltage uplights (using MR16 lamps) retains the tree's overall shape by showing the trunk's branching pattern (see Figure 14.64) and softly washing portions of the canopy. Lighting Design: Janet Lennox Moyer.*

Figure 14.23. *Plant variation within the same genus and species. Two mature birch trees, European White Birch on the left, 'Trost's Dwarf' on the right, display no family resemblance although both are of the same genus and species (*Betula pendula*). Drawing: Craig Latker, Magrane Latker Landscape Design.*

Figure 14.24. *Plant habit variation within the same genus. Italian Cypress (*Cupressus sempervirens*) (A) typically has a pyramidal growth habit, but it can naturally produce pronounced lateral branching (B). The Smooth Arizona Cypress (*Cupressus glabra*) (C) has a more rounded growth habit than the Italian Cypress. Drawing: Craig Latker, Magrane Latker Landscape Design.*

Figure 14.25. *Plant habit and growth variation within the same genus. Sampling of the growing habits of Pine trees, from left to right: Mugho Pine (*Pinus mugo mugo*), Austrian Black Pine (*Pinus nigra*), and Canary Island Pine (*Pinus canariensis*). The genus Pinus refers to the Pine family, which has at least 45 species. Some grow slowly, eventually attaining a height of 40 feet (*Pinus nigra*) or only 4 feet (*Pinus mugo mugo*). Drawing: Craig Latker, Magrane Latker Landscape Design.*

TREES WITH INTERESTING TRUNK CHARACTERISTICS		
	COMMON NAME	BOTANICAL NAME
Thorned	•	*Chorisia speciosa*
	•	*Chorisia insignis*
Striped or Patterned	David's Maple	*Acer davidii*
	Snakebark Maple	*Acer capillipes*
	Amur Chokecherry	*Prunus maackii*
	Birch Bark Cherry	*Prunus serrula*
	Copperbark Cherry	*Prunus tibetica*
	Japanese Tree Lilac	*Syringia reticulata*
	•	*Betula emanii*
	Snakebark Maple	*Acer grosseri 'Hersii'*
	European White Birch	*Betula pendula*
	American Hornbeam	*Carpinus caroliniana*
	•	*Acer rufinerve*
	•	*Aloe bainesii*
	•	*Aloe dichotoma*
Peeling or Flaking	Paperbark Maple	*Acer griseum*
	•	*Betula albosinensis*
	Yellow Birch	*Betula lutea*
	River Birch	*Betula nigra*
	Paperbark Birch	*Betula papyrifera*
	Shellbark Hickory	*Carya laciniosa*
	Shagbark Hickory	*Carya ovata*
	Japanese Cornel Dogwood	*Cornus officinalis*
	Green Hawthorn	*Crataegus viridus*
	Amur Maackia	*Maackia amurensis*
	America Hop Hornbeam	*Ostrya virginiana*
	Prickly Paperbark	*Melaleuca stypheloides*
	Chinese Quince	*Chaenomeles sinensis*
	European Mountain Ash	*Fraxinus excelsior*
	•	*Betula jacqumountil*
	Madrone	*Arbutus menziesli*
	Lemon-Scented Gum	*Eucalyptus citriodora*
	Scotch Pine	*Pinus sylvestris*
	California Sycamore	*Platanus racemosa*
Mottled	Chinese Quince	*Chaenomeles sinensis*
	Korean Stewartia	*Stewartia koreana*
	Tall Stewartia	*Stewartia monadelpha*
	Japanese Stewartia	*Stewartia psuedocamellia*
	Persian Parrotia	*Parrotia persica*
	London Plane	*Platanus acerifolia*
	Lacebark Pine	*Pinus bungeana*
Crape Myrtle	*Lagerstroemia indica*	
	Tulip Tree	*Liriodendron tulipifera*
	•	*Eucalpytus maculata*
	Cabbage Gum	*Eucalyptus pauciflora*
	Chinese Tallow Tree	*Sapium sebiferum*
Furrowed or Cracked	American Smoke Tree	*Cotinus obovatus*
	Three-Flower Maple	*Acer triflorum*
	White Orchid	*Bauhinia forficata*
	Turkish Hazel	*Corylus colurna*
	Mountain Silver Bell	*Halesia monticola*
	Persimmon	*Diospyros virginiana*
	Hardy Rubber Tree	*Eucommia ulmoides*
	Blue Ash	*Fraxinus quadrangulata*
	Chinese Cork Tree	*Phellodendron amurense*
	Swamp White Oak	*Quercus biocolor*
	Shingle Oak	*Quercus imbicaria*
	Bur Oak	*Quercus macrocarpa*
	Cork Oak	*Quercus suber*
	Scotch Elm	*Ulmus glabra*
	Japanese Elm	*Ulmus japonica*
	Chinese Elm	*Ulmus parvifolia*
	Black Locust	*Robinia pseudoacacia*
	Tupelo	*Nyssa sylvatica*
	Hackberry	*Celtis sinensis*
	White Oak	*Quercus alba*
	Tulip Tree	*Liriodendron tulipifera*
	Pecan	*Carya illinoensis*
	Douglas Fir	*Pseudotsuga menziesii*
	Tea Crab	*Malus hupehensis*
	California Pepper Tree	*Schinus molle*
	Brazilian Pepper Tree	*Schinus terebinthifolius*
	Bunya Bunya	*Araucaria bidwillii*
	Australian Tea Tree	*Leptospermum laevigatum*

*These plants have no common name

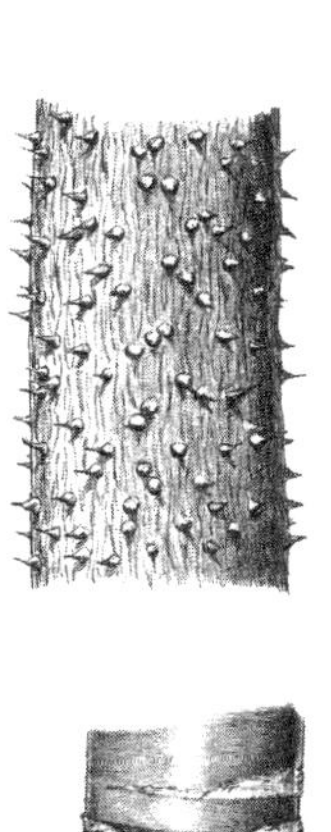

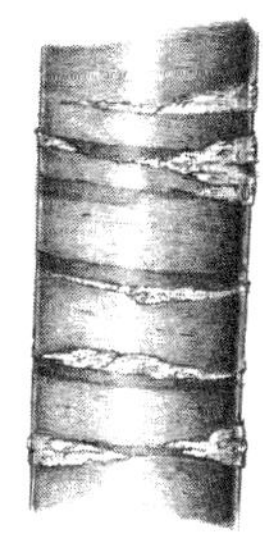

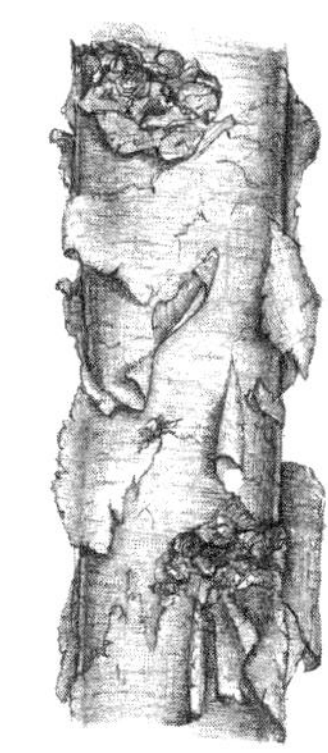

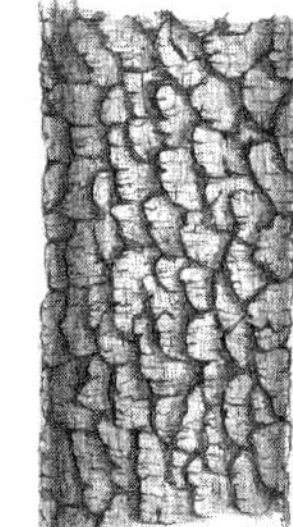

Figure 14.26. *Striking or intriguing trunk patterns accentuates a tree's lit appearance. This list presents a representative sampling of trees that would benefit from special attention on their trunks. Drawing: Lezlie Johannessen.*

GROUP ONE: BALL AND ROUNDED SHAPE

DENSE FORM

D Chinese Pistache / *Pistachia chinensis*
D Sycamore Maple / *Acer pseydoplatanus*
E Victorian Box / *Pittosporum undulatum*
E Evergreen Pear / *Pyrus kawakami*
E Holly Oak / *Quercus ilex*
E Camphor Tree / *Cinnamomum camphora*
D Norway Maple / *Acer platanoides*
D Common Horsechestnut / *Aesculus hippocastanum*
E Cork Oak / *Quercus suber*
D America Beech / *Fagus grandiflora*
D Tupelo / *Nyssua sylvatica*
D Silver Linden / *Tilia tomentos*
D Saucer Magnolia / *Magnolia x soulangeana*
D Sugar Maple / *Acer saccnaarum*
E Strawberry Tree / *Arbutus unedo*
E Loquat / *Eriobotrya japonica*
E Carob / *Ceratonia siliqua*
E Globe Willow / *Salxi matsudana* 'Umbraculifera'
E Olive / *Olea Europea*
E Brazilian Pepper / *Schinus terebinthifolus*
D Japanese Pagoda Tree / *Sophora japonica*
D Red Maple / *Acer rubrum*
D White Oak / *Quercus alba*

OPEN FORM

E Cape Pittosoporum / *Pittosporum viridiflorum*
D California Sycamore / *Platanus racemosa*
E Lacebark Pine / *Pinus bungeana*
D California Black Oak / *Quercus kelloggii*
E California Pepper Tree / *Schinus molle*
D London Plane / *Platanus acerifolia*
E Princess Flower / *Tibouchina urvilleana*
D Oregon Maple / *Acer macrophyllum*
D Moraine Locust / *Gleditsia triacanthos* 'Moraine'
D Tree of Heaven / *Ailanthus altissima*
D Amur Cork Tree / *Phellodendron amurense*
D European Larch / *Larix decidua*
D * / *Gleditsia triacanthos* 'Shademaster'
E Texas Mountain Laurel / *Sophora secundiflora*
D Japanese Maple / *Acer palmatum* (some)
D White Poplar / *Populus alba*
D Black Poplar / *Populus nigra*
D Common Golden Chain / *Laburnum anagyroides*
D European Hackberry / *Celtus australis*
D Chinese Quince / *Chaenomeles sinensis*
E California Live Oak / *Quercus agrifolia*
D Valley Oak / *Quercus lobata*
E Canyon Oak / *Quercus chrysolepsis*
D Eastern Redbud / *Cercis canadensis*
D Western Redbud / *Cercis occidentalis*
D Chinese Redbud / *Cercis chinensis*

Legend: * No common name typically used
E Evergreen
D Deciduous

This list refers to shape of mature trees. The list is not exhaustive, but representative.

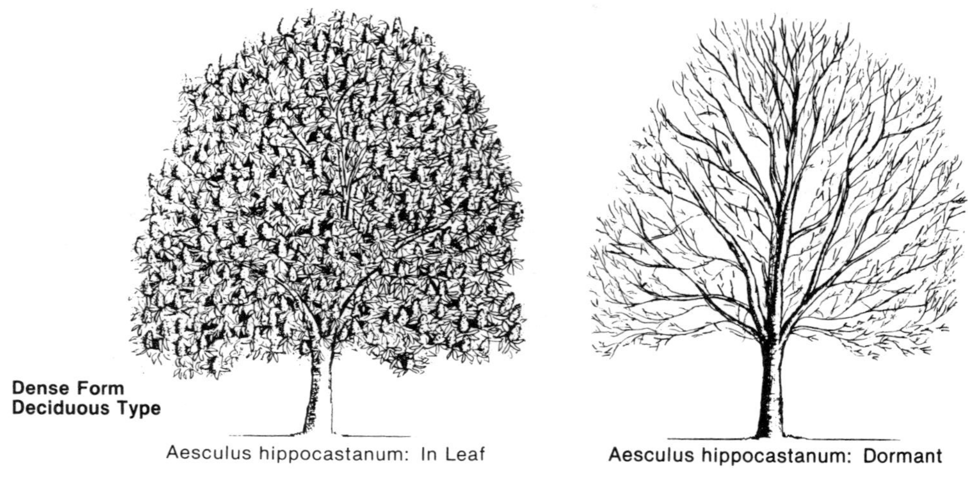

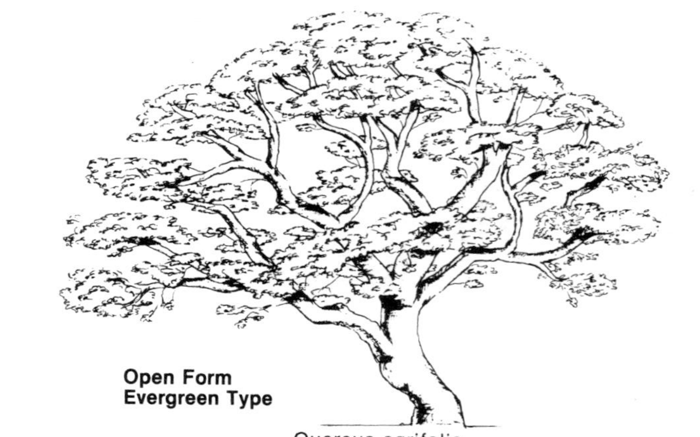

Figure 14.27. *Group one—ball or rounded tree. Uplight dense trees in this category from outside the branching structure of the tree (see Color Plates 1, 55, & 57). Fixture location depends on canopy dimensions, starting height above the ground, and appearance. Consider highlighting interesting trunks (see Figure 14.9). Locate fixtures inside the canopy for trees with open branching and translucent leaves (see Color Plates 21 & 31–39). Make sure that the outer edges of the canopy appear lit. When necessary, provide additional lights outside the canopy. Large mature trees can provide a mounting location to downlight foundation planting, walkways, or lawn. Drawing: Lezlie Johannessen.*

GROUP TWO: PYRAMIDAL, COLUMNAR, AND UPRIGHT SHAPE

DENSE FORM

E	Alberta Spruce / *Picea glauca* 'Conica'
E	Norway Spruce / *Picea abies***
E	Incense Cedar / *Calocedrus decurrens*
E	Douglas Fir / *Pseudotsuga menziesii*
E	Giant Sequoia / *Sequoiadendron giganteum*
E	Aristocrat Pear / *Pyrus calleryana* 'Aristocrat'
E	Capitol Pear / *Pyrus calleryana* 'Capitol'
D	Pin Oak / *Quercus palustris****
E	Deodor Cedar / *Cedrus deodora*
D	Little Leaf Linden / *Tilia cordata*
D	Tulip Tree / *Liriodendron tulipifera*
E	Austiran Pine / *Pinus nigra*
D	Lombardy Poplar / *Populus nigra* 'Italica'
E	Brisbane Box / *Tristania conferta****
E	Coast Redwood / *Sequoia sempervirens*
E	English laurel / *Prunus laurocerasus*
D	* / *Acer lobelli*
D	Italian Alder / *Alnus cordata*
E	Chinese juniper / *Juniperus chinensis*
E	White Cedar / *Thuja occidentalis*
E	Irish Yew / *Taxus baccata* 'Stricta'
D	Upright English Oak / *Quercus robur* 'Fastigiata'
E	Common Juniper / *Juniperus communis*
E	Italian Cypress / *Cupressus sempervirens*
E	Western Red Cedar / *Thuja plicata*
E	Lawson Cypress / *Chamaecyparis lawsoniana*

OPEN FORM

E	Canary Island Pine / *Pinus canariensis***
E	Tarata Pittosporum / *Pittosporum euginoides*
E	Black Stem Pittosporum / *Pittosporum tenuifolium*
E	Jelecote Pine / *Pinus patula*
E	Yew Pine / *Podocarpus macrophyllus*
D	Quaking Aspen / *Populus tremuloides*
D	Gray Birch / *Betula populifolia*
D	Maidenhair Tree / *Gingko biloba*
D	American Sweet Gum / *Liquidambar styraciflua*
D	Katsura Tree / *Cercidiphyllum japonica*
D	Tupelo / *Nyssa sylvatica***
D	Chinese Parasol Tree / *Firmiana simplex*

Legend:
* No common name typically used
** Pyramidal when young
*** Upright becoming rounded with age
E Evergreen
D Deciduous

This list refers to shape of mature trees. The list is not exhaustive, but representative.

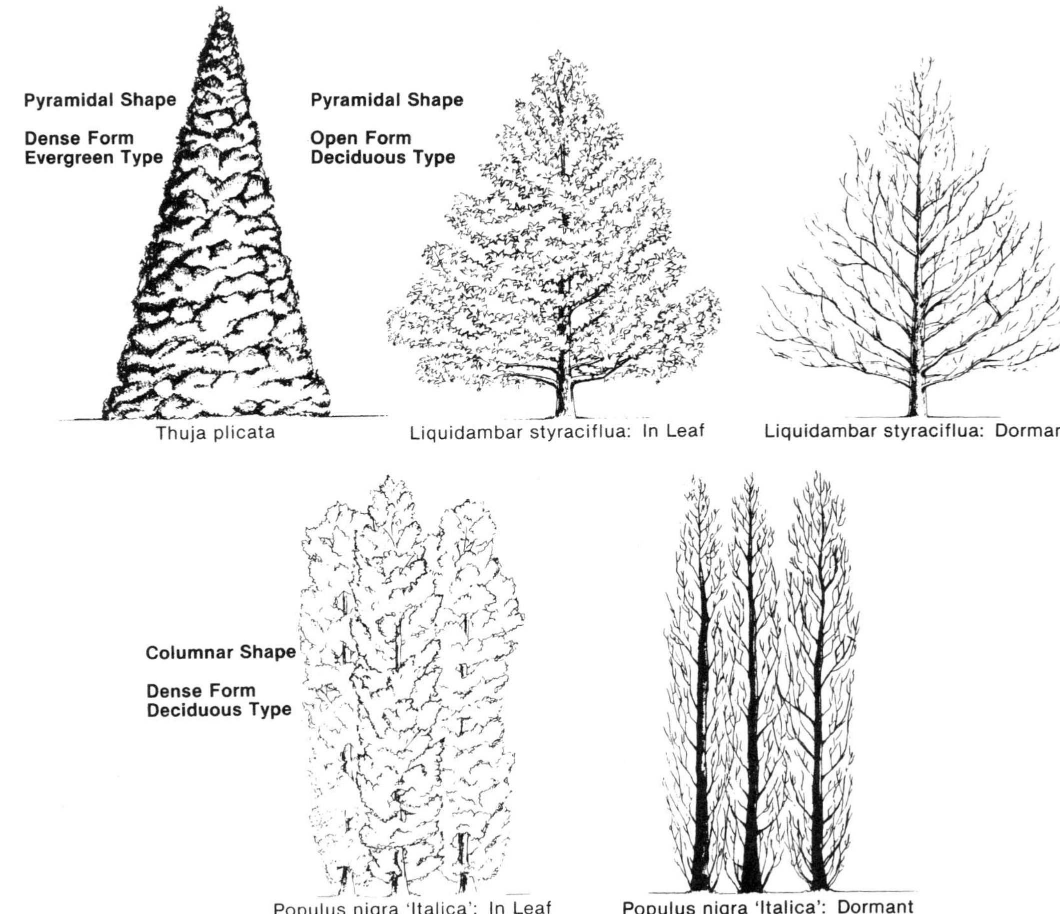

***Figure 14.28**. Group two—pyramidal or columnar/upright tree.* Pyramidal. *Approach dense trees from outside the branching structure to show general shape. To ensure that light reaches the entire canopy, plan the fixture location away from the trunk based on the expected mature height of the specimen. With open forms, locate fixtures inside or outside the canopy based on leaf type and desired lighting effect (see Figure 14.52). Translucent leaves and interesting branching formation encourage lighting from inside the canopy. Large, mature trees can provide downlighting-mounting locations.* Columnar/upright. *Approach both dense and open forms from outside the branching structure. To emphasize texture, place fixtures close to the branching (see Figure 14.58). To emphasize shape, mount the fixtures farther away. Consider internally lighting hedges with open structure and translucent leaves so as to produce a glowing effect. Drawing: Lezlie Johannessen.*

GROUP THREE:
VASE, FOUNTAIN, AND UMBRELLA SHAPE

DENSE FORM

E	Fortune Windmill Palm / *Trachycarpus fortunei*
E	Italian Stone Pine / *Pinus pinea*
E	Queen Palm / *Arecastrum romanzoffianum*
D	Royal Poiniciana / *Delonix regia*
E	King Palm / *Archontophoenix cunninghamiana*
E	California Fan Palm / *Washingtonia filifera*
D	Sawleaf Zelkova / *Selkova serrata*
D	Van Eseltine Crabapple / *Malus* 'Van Eseltine'

OPEN FORM

E	Australian Tree Fern / *Spaeropteris cooperi*
D	Snow Cloud Crabapple / *Malus* 'Snowcloud'
D	Kwansan Oriental Cherry / *Prunus serrulata* 'Kwansan'
D	American Elm / *Ulmus americana*
D	'Mt. Fuji' Cherry / *Prunus serrulata* 'Shirotae'
D	Tea Crabapple / *Malus hupehensis*
D	'Skyline' Honeylocust / *Gleditisia triacanthos* 'Skyline'
D	Apple Service Berry / *Amelanchier x Grandiflora*
D	Crape Myrtle / *Lagerstroemia indica*
D	Jacaranda / *Jacaranda mimosifolia*
D	Yoshino Cherry / *Prunus yeodoensis*
D	Silktree or Mimosa / *Albizia julibrissin*
E	Lemon-Scented Gum / *Eucalyptus citriodora*

Legend: * No common name typically used.
E Evergreen
D Deciduous

This list refers to shape of mature trees. The list is not exhaustive, but representative.

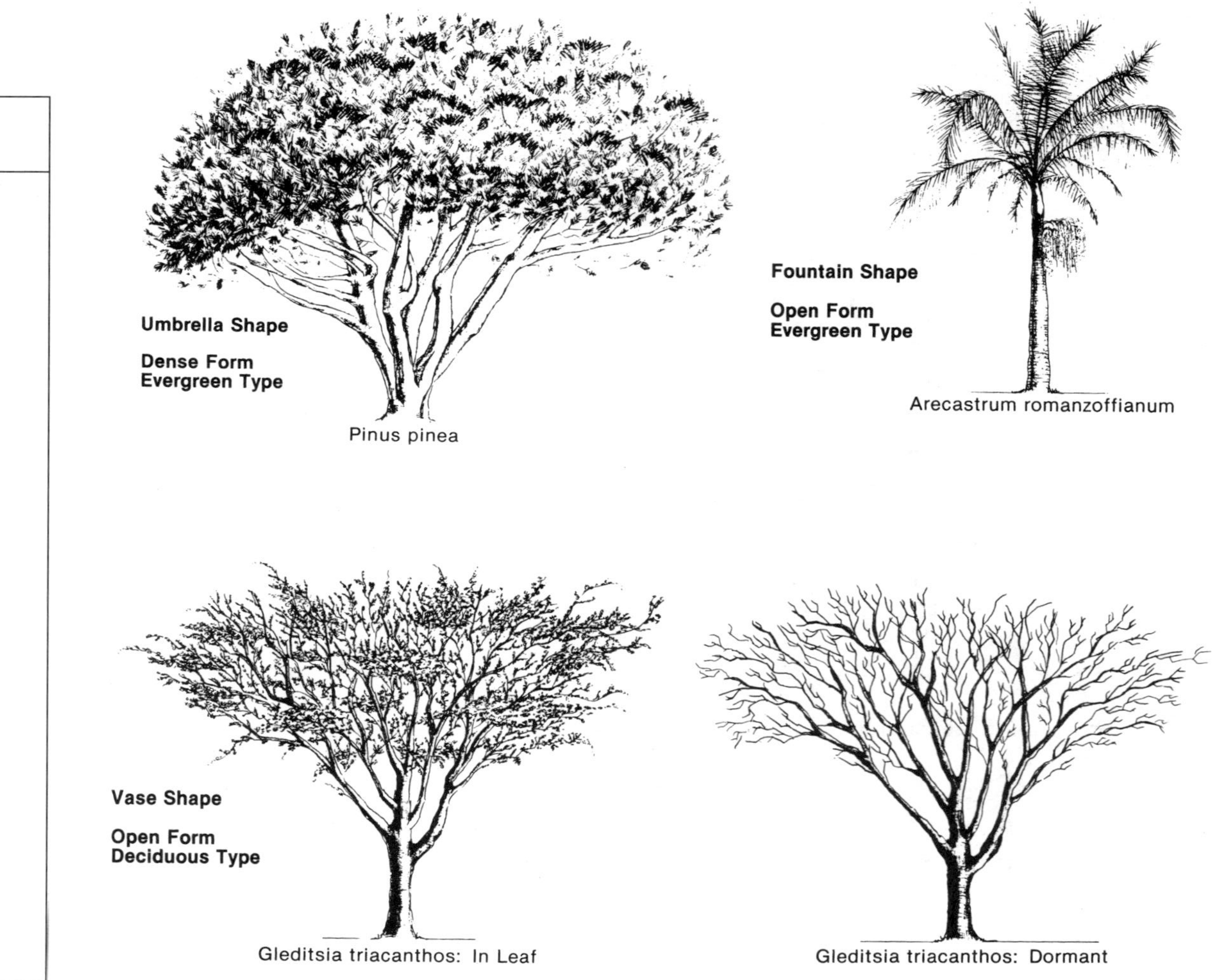

Figure 14.29. *Group three—vase/fountain or umbrella tree.* Vase/fountain shape. *Light trees with open forms, especially those with translucent leaves, from within the canopy (see Figures 14.17 & Color Plates 47–50). Dense forms require moving fixtures farther away from the trunk or outside the branching structure entirely.* Umbrella shape. *Both dense and open forms can be lit from inside the canopy. However, with dense forms, light will not penetrate the leaves (see Figures 14.13 & 15.38). For Palms, consider highlighting the trunk with a grazing technique. Some forms require additional lights for the fronds, due to the large expanse of the canopy (see Figures 14.37 to 14.41). Drawing: Lezlie Johannessen.*

GROUP FOUR: WEEPING AND BRANCHING TO GROUND SHAPE

DENSE FORM

D European Purple Beech / *Fagus sylvatica atropunicea*
D Cutleaf Beech / *Fagus sylvatica* 'Laciniata'
D Weeping Copper Beech / *Fagus sylvatica* 'Purpurea Pendula'
E Deodor Cedar / *Cedrus deodora*
D Weeping European Ash / *Fraxinus excelsior pendula*
D Tea's Weeping Mulberry / *Morus alba* 'Pendula'
D * / *Acer japonicum* 'Vitifolium'
D Weeping Gray Alder / *Alnus incana* 'Pendulum'
D Crimean Linden / *Tilia euchlora*
D Weeping Silver Pear / *Pyrus salicifolia* 'Pendula'
E Weeping Cedar of Lebanon / *Cedrus libani* 'Sargentii'
E Sargent Weeping Hemlock / *Tsuga canadensis* 'Pendula'
D Camperdown Elm / *Ulmus glabra* 'Camperdownii'
E Kashmir Cypress / *Cupressus cashimeriana*
E Canadian Hemlock / *Tsuga canadensis*

OPEN FORM

E Blue Atlas Cedar / *Cedrus atlantica* 'Glauca Pendula'
D European Weeping Birch / *Betula pendula*
D Weeping Willow / *Salix babylonica*
D Weeping Scotch Laburnum / *Laburnum alpinum* 'Pendulum'
D Young's Weeping Birch / *Betula pendula* 'Youngii'
D * / *Acer palmatum* 'Dissectum Atropurpureum Ever Red'
D Laceleaf Japanese Maple / *Acer palmatum* 'Dissectum Viridis'
D Weeping Blue Willow / *Salix purpurea* 'Pendula'
D Weeping Katsura / *Cercidiphyllum japonicum* 'Pendulum'
D Single Weeping Cherry / *Prunus subhirtella* 'Pendula'

Legend: * No common name typically used
E Evergreen
D Deciduous

This list refers to shape of mature trees. The list is not exhaustive, but representative.

Weeping Shape

Open Form
Deciduous Type

Prunus subhirtella 'Pendula': In Leaf

Branching to Ground and Weeping Shape

Open Form
Evergreen Type

Cedrus atlantica 'Glauca Pendula'

Branching to Ground and Weeping Shape

Dense Form
Evergreen Type

Tsuga canadensis 'Pendula'

Figure 14.30. *Group four—weeping or branching to the ground tree.* Weeping form. *For dense trees, locate fixtures at the edge of the branching structure to highlight foliage, texture, and to provide depth around the tree. Consider additional fixture(s) for the trunk. For open trees, especially those with translucent leaves, locate fixtures inside the canopy (see Figures 14.44 to 14.46).* Branching to the ground form. *For trees with dense branching locate fixtures outside the canopy. Either wash for shape or graze to bring out foliage detail (see Color Plates 51, 56, & 57). Consider combining the two techniques when both effects are desired. For short, dense evergreen and deciduous forms use downlighting (see Figure 14.54). Drawing: Lezlie Johannessen.*

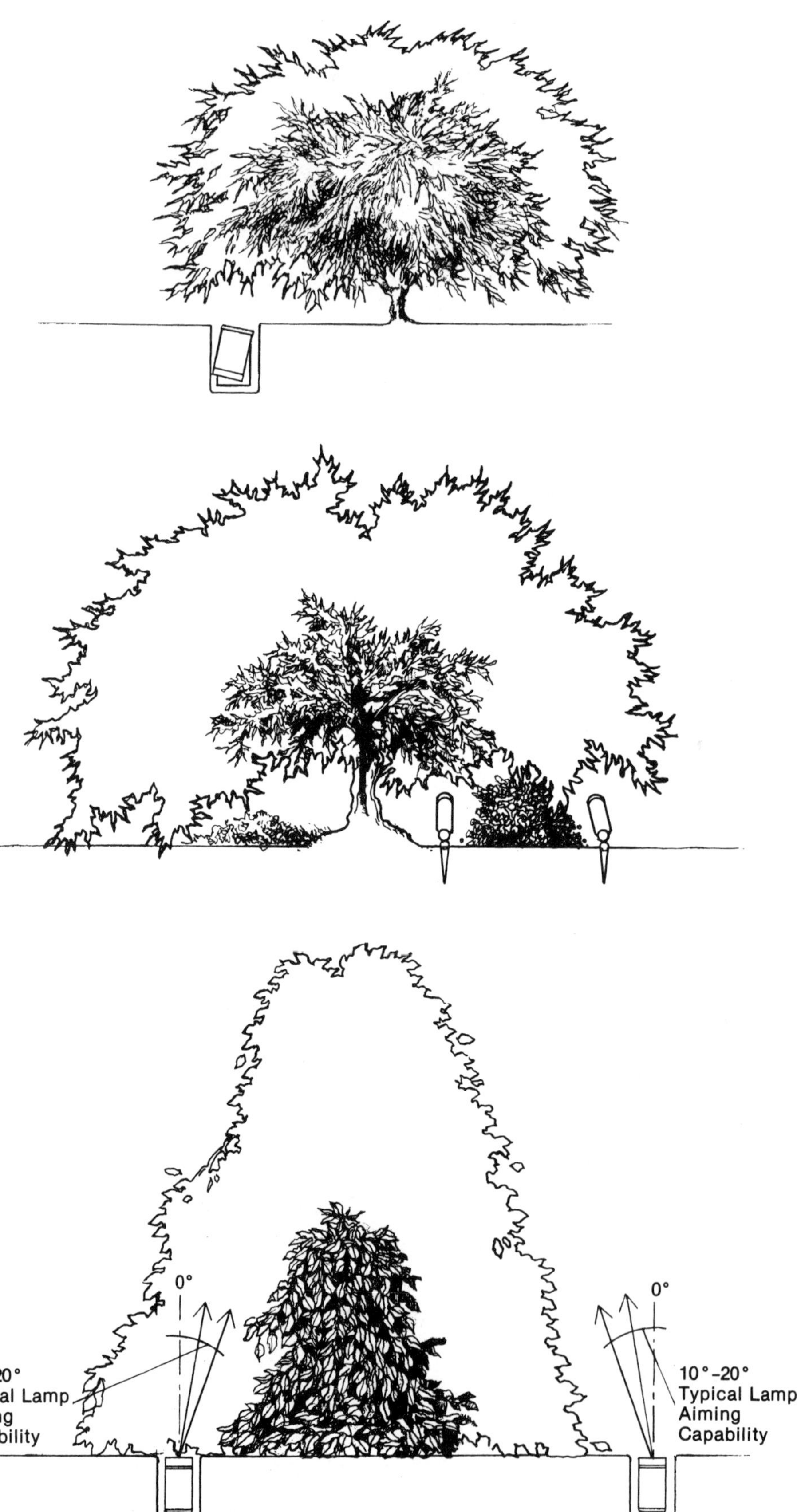

Figure 14.31. *This dwarf Japanese Maple (*Acer palmatum*) in the 'Yatsubusa' group may require many years to increase its size by a foot. Locate fixtures below grade to hide them, to increase the amount of lit canopy, and to reduce the chance of lamp heat burning leaves. Drawing: Craig Latker, Magrane Latker Landscape Design.*

Figure 14.32. *Flexibility becomes paramount for trees such as this Laceleaf Japanese Maple (*Acer palmatum*) 'Dissectum Viridis'), which may quadruple in size or more from planting to maturity. Use stake-mounted fixtures with enough spare wire to move the fixtures away from the tree as it increases in size. Drawing: Craig Latker, Magrane Latker Landscape Design.*

Figure 14.33. *Immature specimen trees, such as this dense Weeping Copper Beech (*Fagus sylvatica *'Purpurea Pendula'), often increase significantly in size. A fixture placed close to the immature tree will soon be buried and its light lost in the dense leaf coverage; a fixture properly placed for the mature tree may not be able to light the young tree for some time. Evaluate the options and determine which works best for the project. Drawing: Craig Latker, Magrane Latker Landscape Design.*

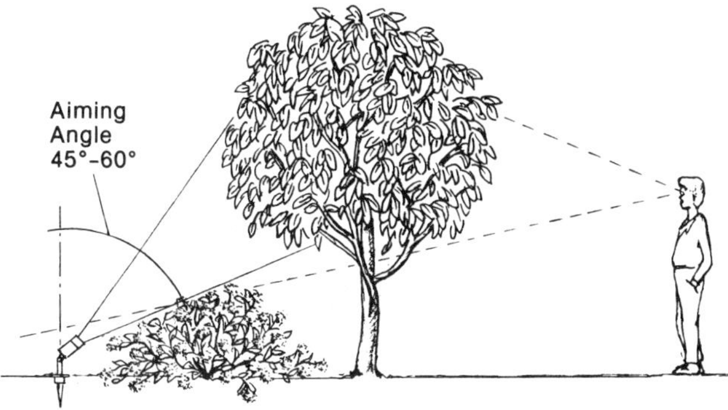

Figure 14.34. *Trees that start foliage and branching a foot or more above ground level do not block the view of the luminaires lighting them. Aim uplights between vertical and 35° off vertical to avoid glare. Locating smaller plants between the fixtures and the tree blocks the view of the fixture, allowing a wider aiming angle between 45° and 60°. Drawing: Lezlie Johannessen.*

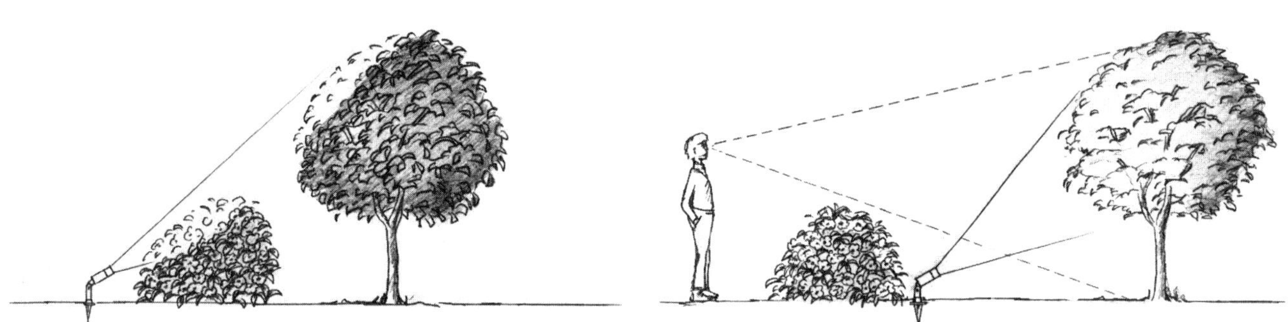

Figure 14.35. *When a plant will interfere with a fixture highlighting another plant and cannot be moved without upsetting the landscape composition, relocate the fixture. This may require using less wattage or a lamp with a wider beamspread when the fixture must move closer. Moving the fixture farther away might require a higher wattage or narrower beamspread. Drawing: Lezlie Johannessen.*

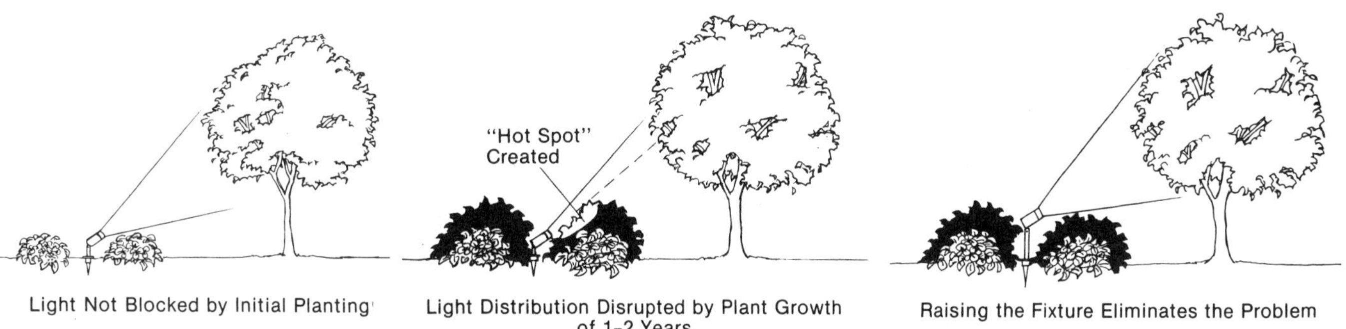

Figure 14.36. *When using a stake-mounted fixture, consider the plants surrounding the fixture. As these plants grow, they can block light from reaching the target plant. The fixture needs the ability to be moved away from such plants, raised to avoid becoming buried, or both. Drawing: Lezlie Johannessen.*

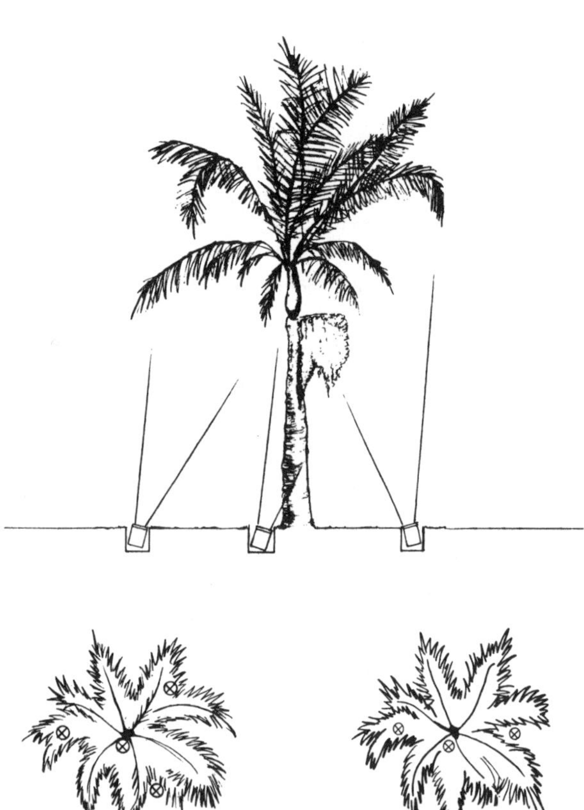

Figure 14.37. *Palms vary in size and shape, requiring differing lighting techniques as the following three examples show. The Queen Palm (*Arecastrum romanzoffianum*), with a straight, patterned trunk and rounded head of gracefully arching fronds, grows quickly to about 30 feet high. For trees situated in a lawn and viewed from all directions, locate a minimum of two lights under or outside the canopy for shape and a third to highlight the trunk.*

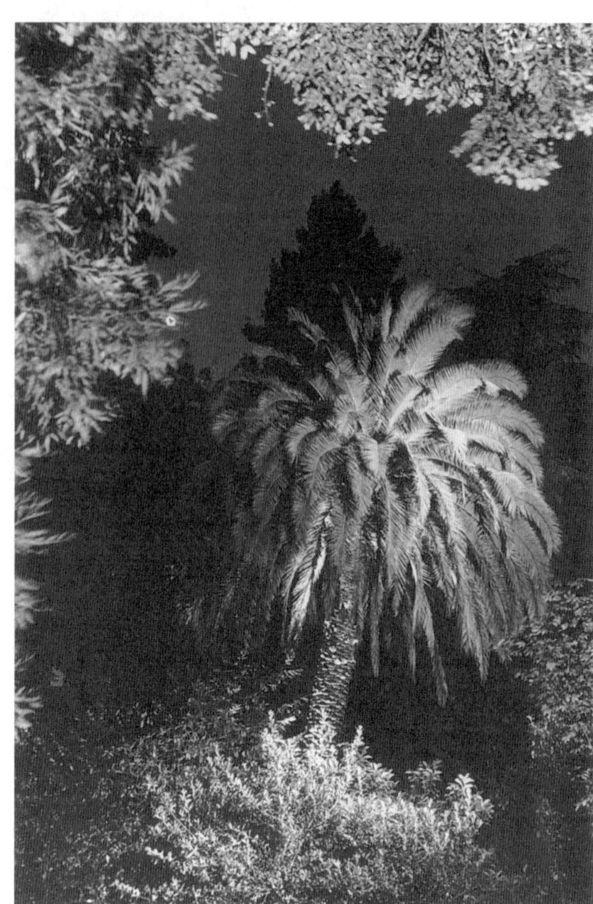

Figure 14.38. *While walking along the entry path shown in Figure 11.3, guests get a surprise glimpse into the side yard and this Palm tree. This adds considerable depth visually to the yard and shows that the versatility of the mild climate in northern California makes it possible to have these vastly different trees in the same yard. Lighting Design: Janet Lennox Moyer, MSH Visual Planners; Photograph: Kenneth Rice Photography, www.kenricephoto.com.*

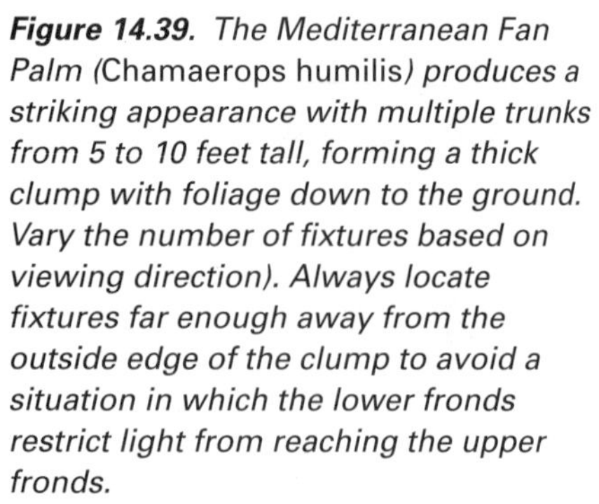

Figure 14.39. *The Mediterranean Fan Palm (*Chamaerops humilis*) produces a striking appearance with multiple trunks from 5 to 10 feet tall, forming a thick clump with foliage down to the ground. Vary the number of fixtures based on viewing direction). Always locate fixtures far enough away from the outside edge of the clump to avoid a situation in which the lower fronds restrict light from reaching the upper fronds.*

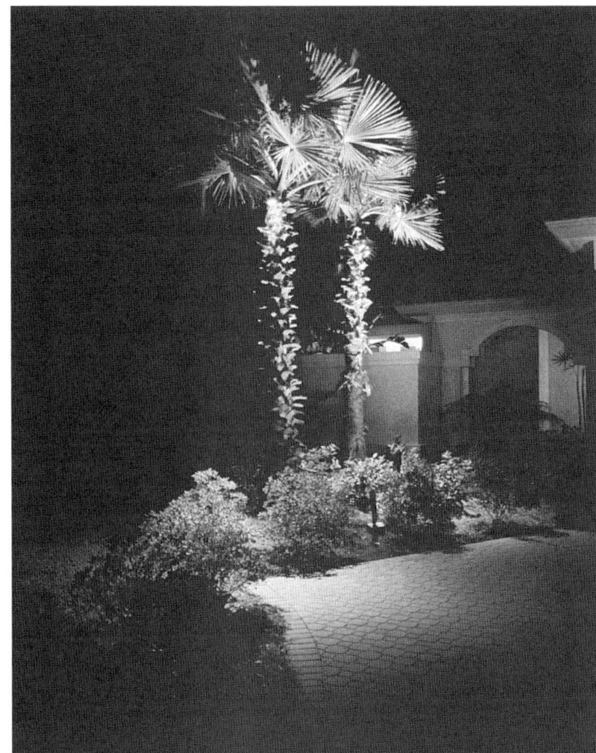

Figure 14.40. *For a mockup in Florida, two 3,000K CDM metal halide lamps—a 35-watt PAR30 set approximately 2′0″ from the trunk for the closer tree and a 35-watt PAR38 set approximately 3′6″ from the trunk for the back tree—show the varying ability to graze the trunk and cover the canopy. A prototype metal halide MR16 lamp (with multiple color filters to correct the color temperature) in a retrofitted fixture provides the downlighting from this palm onto the shrubbery along the driveway. Lighting Design: Janet Lennox Moyer & Kevin Simonson, The Lighting Research Center. Photograph: Kevin Simonson, www.kaperture.com. Photograph courtesy of The Lighting Research Center.*

Figure 14.42. *Interior lights shining through the shoji screen create a luminous backdrop for a tropical plant in this San Francisco backyard. The silhouetted fronds produce an interesting pattern in the midst of the composition. Note how the light coming from the side accentuates texture on the foreground wall. Lighting Design: Randall Whitehead, Lightsource; Photograph: Ben Janken; Landscape Design: Kimo Conant.*

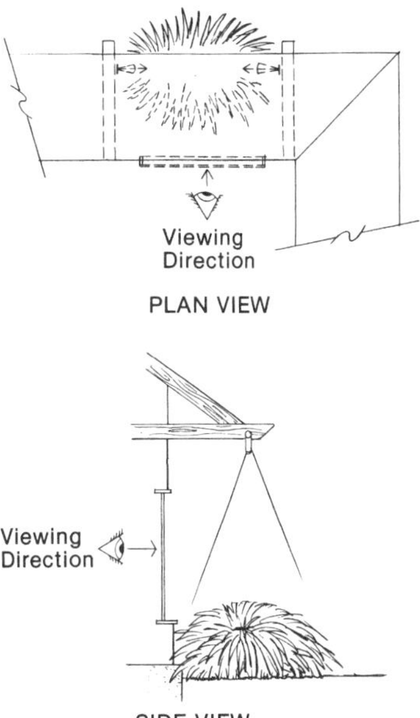

Figure 14.41. *The Sago Palm (*Cycas revoluta*), while not technically a Palm, closely resembles a Palm. It grows slowly to between 6 and 10 feet tall and creates a rounded form with arching fronds. Downlighting emphasizes form and detail. Drawings: Lezlie Johannessen.*

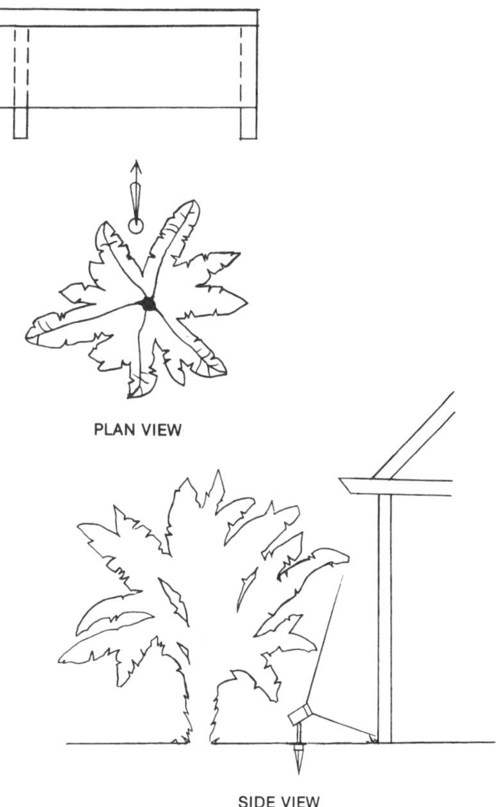

Figure 14.43. Silhouette technique. *This adds emphasis different from all other techniques. Consisting of backlighting, it shows only shape, eliminating texture, color, and detail. Locate fixtures behind the plant, washing or grazing a surface beyond the plant. This technique works best on plants with a strong shape used as a primary or secondary focal point or as an element in the overall composition. Drawing: Lezlie Johannessen.*

Figure 14.44. *Crape Myrtle (*Lagerstroemia indica*) has an open form and produces leaves at branch ends. Locate fixtures at the outer edge or beyond the canopy to highlight flowers in bloom. Light penetrates the canopy due to the relatively translucent leaves. Drawing: Craig Latker, Magrane Latker Landscape Design.*

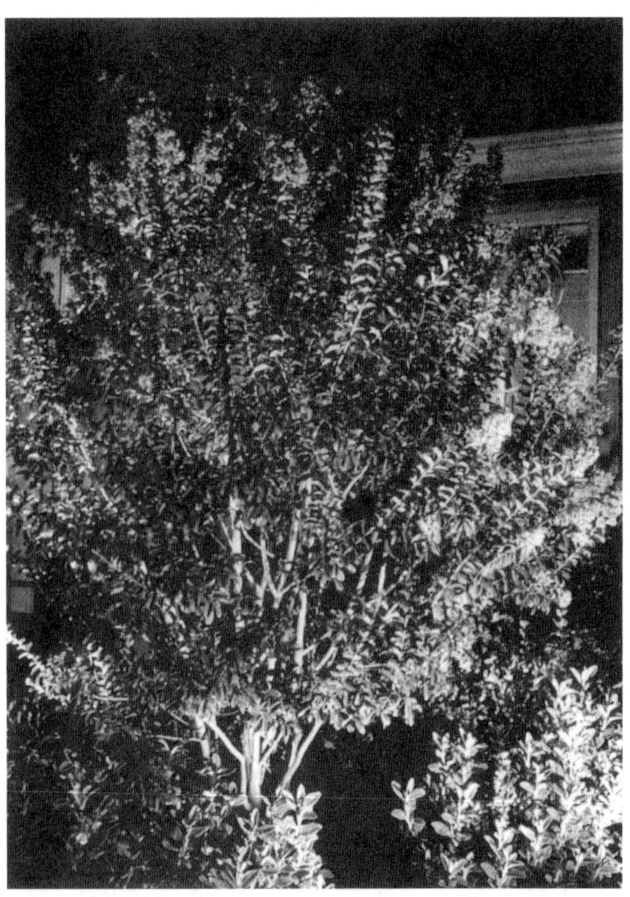

Figure 14.45. *This immature specimen of Crape Myrtle (*Lagerstroemia indica*) shows the benefit of lighting from outside the canopy. Fixtures mounted on stakes will be moved back as the tree canopy expands. Lighting Design: Janet Lennox Moyer, MSH Visual Planners; Photograph: Kenneth Rice Photography, www.kenricephoto.com.*

Figure 14.46. *Crape Myrtles can be single-trunk specimens. As they mature, their bark characteristics and branching structure become pronounced, especially when pruned for effect. This tree changed from a background tree to a focal point due to garden changes. Photograph: Janet Lennox Moyer.*

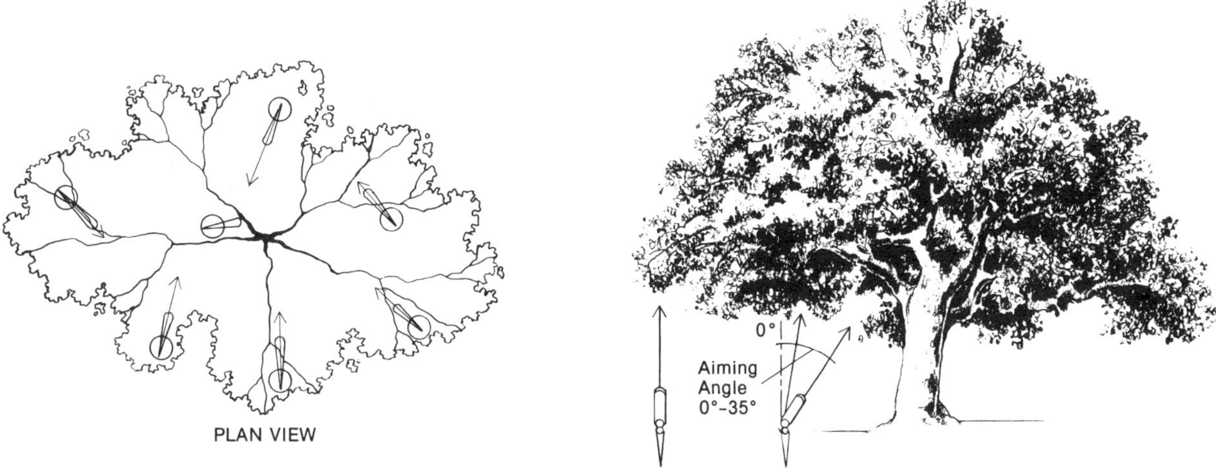

***Figure 14.47.** Large, open-form trees require 5, 10, or more fixtures to cover the entire canopy area, as shown with this California Live Oak (*Quercus agrifolia*). Restrict aiming angles to between 0° and 35° off vertical, as smaller plants typically do not grow under this tree. Drawing: Craig Latker, Magrane Latker Landscape Design.*

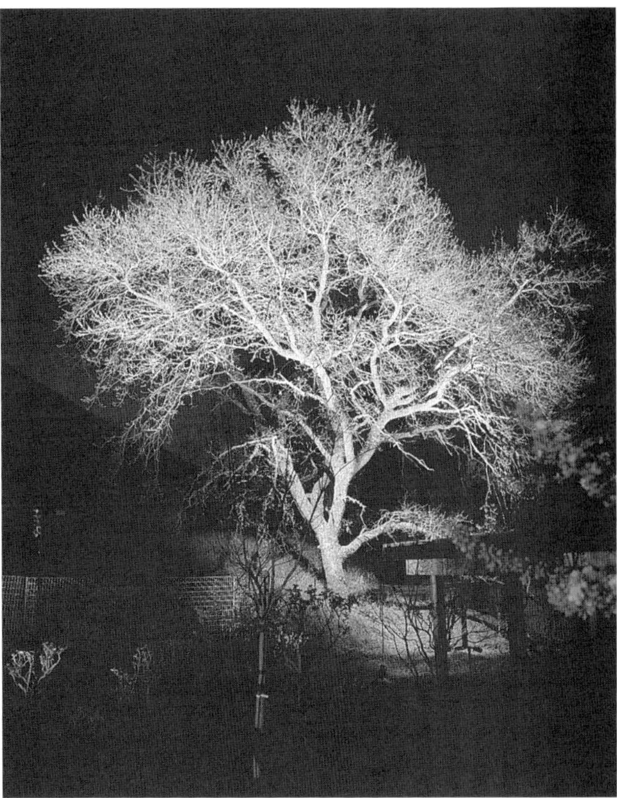

***Figures 14.48 & 14.49.** In the daytime, the overall branching structure form and canopy fullness of the Oak shows, but the tree essentially fades into the background. At night, with four 120-volt 50-watt PAR38 adjustable uplight fixtures, all located well outside the canopy and in front, the Oak's form and detailing becomes apparent. It takes on a dominant role compared to the daytime scene. Lighting Design: Janet Lennox Moyer, Michael Stewart Hooker, & Paul Schreer, MSH Visual Planners; Photograph: Kenneth Rice Photography, www.kenricephoto.com.*

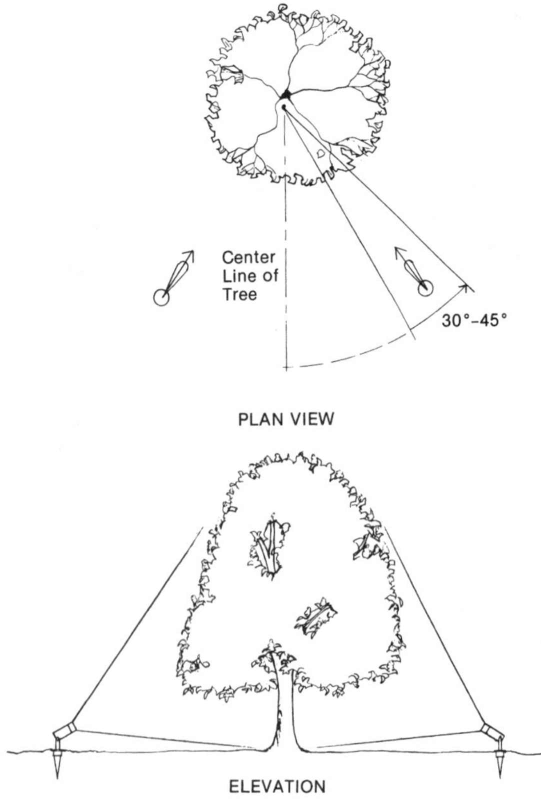

Figure 14.50. Wash technique. *Locate fixtures away from the surface to be lit to provide even lighting over a surface. It can be a bright or soft effect to fit its purpose in the overall composition. Lighting* Group One *trees requires washing the tree canopy from outside. When the tree will be viewed primarily from one direction, utilize at least two lights located 30° to 45° off center. Drawing: Lezlie Johannessen.*

Figure 14.51. *A soft wash up onto this mature Oak provides a backdrop for the parking courtyard. Lighting Design: Janet Lennox Moyer, MSH Visual Planners; Photograph: Kenneth Rice Photography, www.kenricephoto.com.*

Figure 14.52. *Fixtures 15 feet in front of the outer edge of these conifers essentially washes up the front but creates a grazing effect due to the branching characteristics of the trees. Lighting Design: Janet Lennox Moyer, MSH Visual Planners; Photograph: Kenneth Rice Photography, www.kenricephoto.com.*

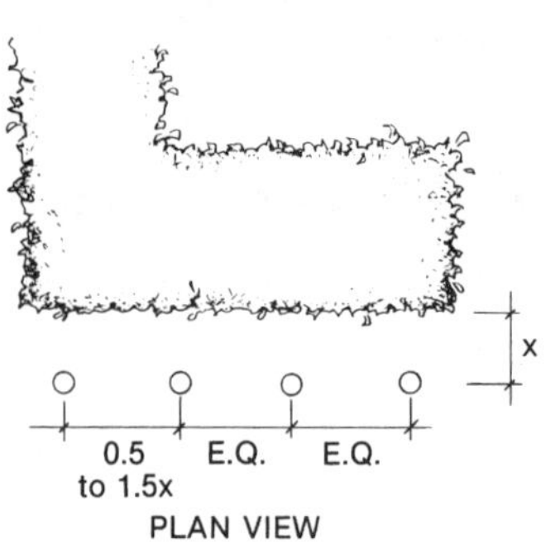

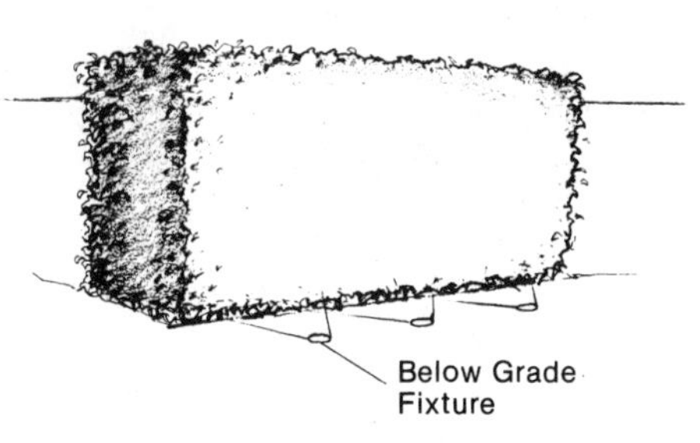

Figure 14.53. *Hedges often form boundaries of gardens. Softly washing a hedge provides a visual link with other elements in the composition as well as depth to the scene. Wash hedges that have little texture using the spacing ratio shown to ensure an even wash. Drawing: Lezlie Johannessen.*

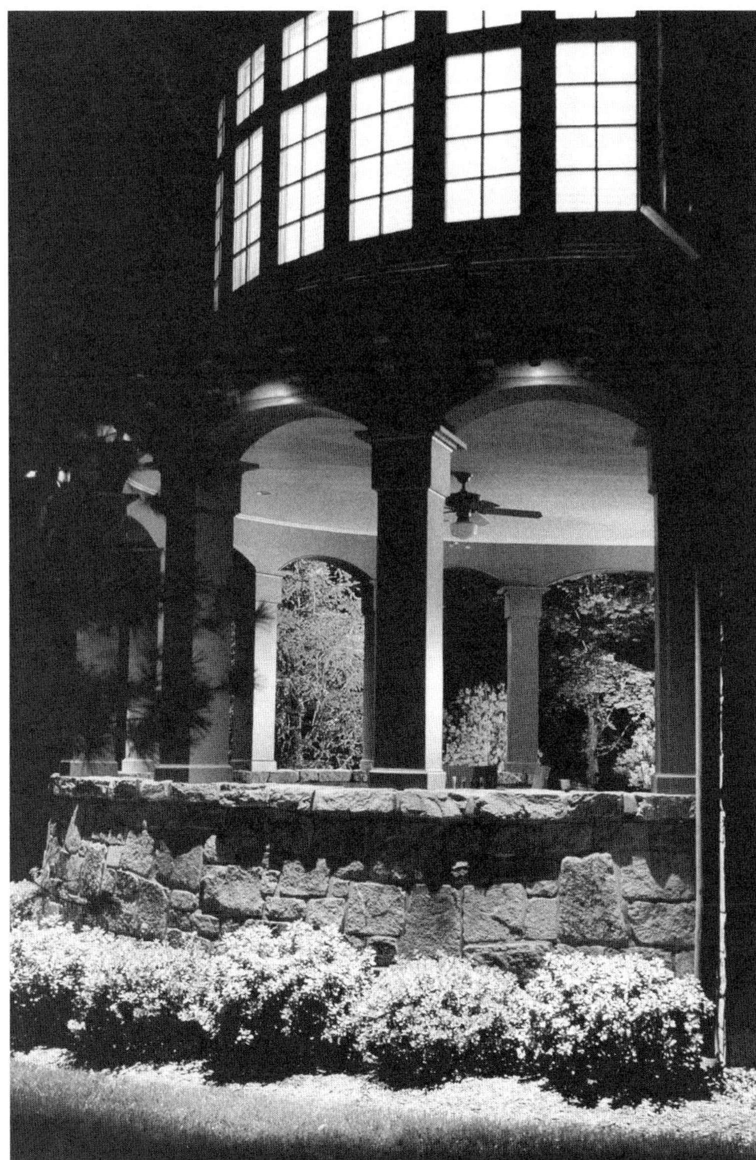

Figure 14.54. *Downlighting mounted along the arches highlights the porch railing and the hedge of Azaleas wrapping around the porch. Lighting Design: Thea Chassin, Chassin Lighting Design; Photograph: Dan Dyer.*

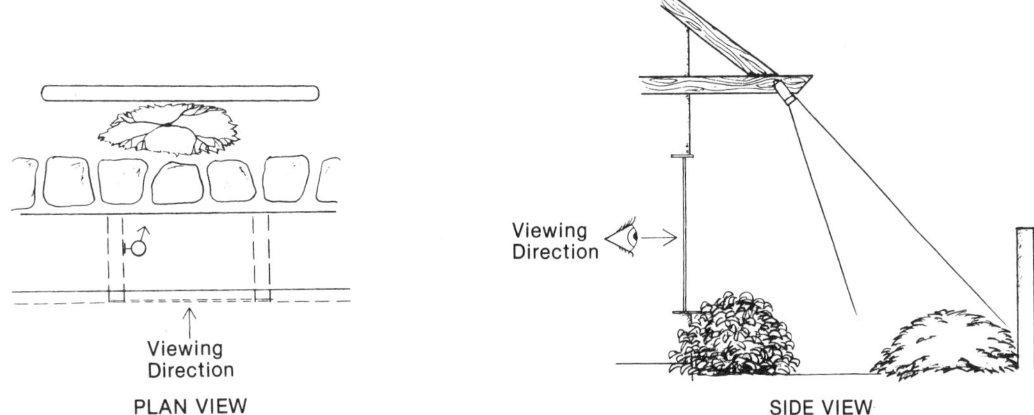

Figure 14.55. *Small dense trees, including Canadian Hemlock (*Tsuga canadensis*) from Group Four, look best downlit. Locate the fixture(s) in front of the tree, aimed away from the viewer. This creates a natural appearance. Drawing: Lezlie Johannessen.*

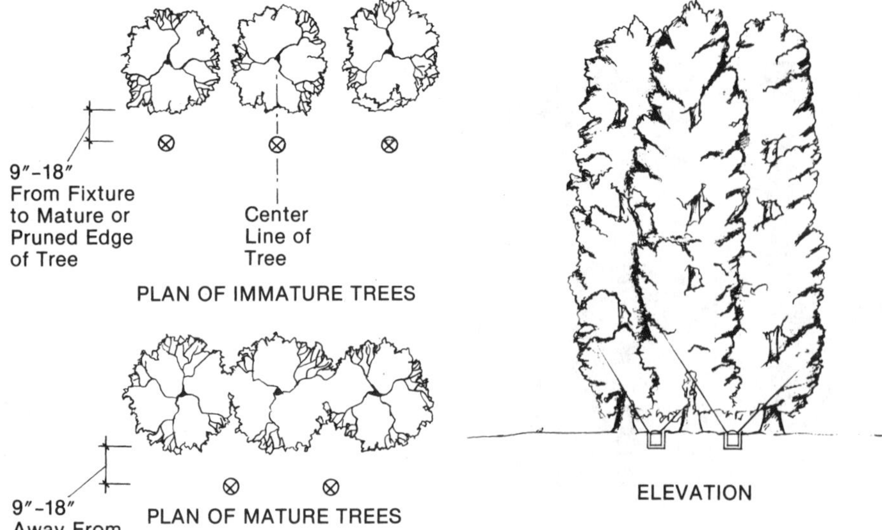

Figure 14.56. *Lombardy Poplar (*Populus nigra *'Italica'), a dense, columnar tree from Group Two, looks best uplit using the grazing technique. This accentuates its texture while defining its shape. When lighting a row of immature trees, place a fixture in front of each tree. For mature trees, place fixtures farther away from foliage and between two trees, thus minimizing the quantity of fixtures. Drawing: Lezlie Johannessen.*

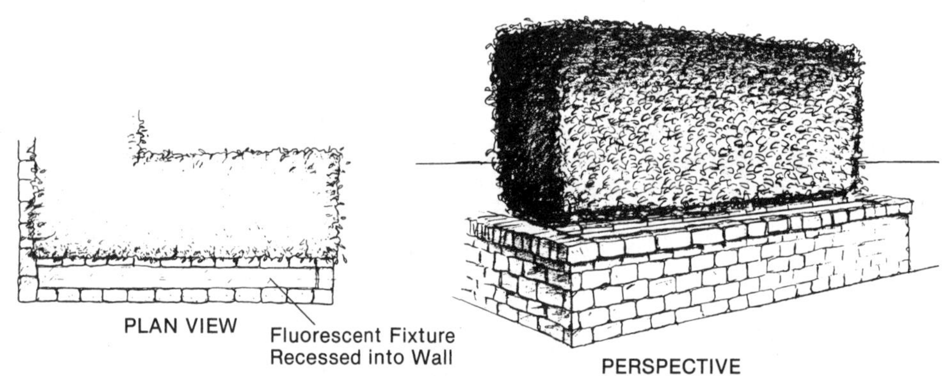

Figures 14.57 & 14.58. *When a low wall sits in front of a hedge, recess a linear light source, such as fluorescent, into the wall, creating a grazing effect along the length of the hedge. Drawing: Lezlie Johannessen.*

Figure 14.58. *Evenly spaced grazing uplight brings out the wall texture and creates positive/negative patterns leaf patterns when the hedge has leaves. Lighting Design: Janet Lennox Moyer, MSH Visual Planners; Photograph: Kenneth Rice Photography, www.kenricephoto.com.*

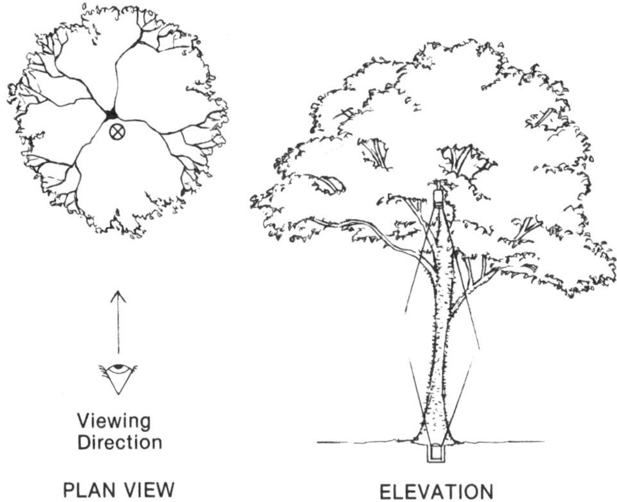

Figure 14.59A. *For trees with interesting trunk texture, locate fixtures in front of the trunk, using either up- or downlighting to accentuate pattern (see Figure 14.9). Drawing: Lezlie Johannessen.*

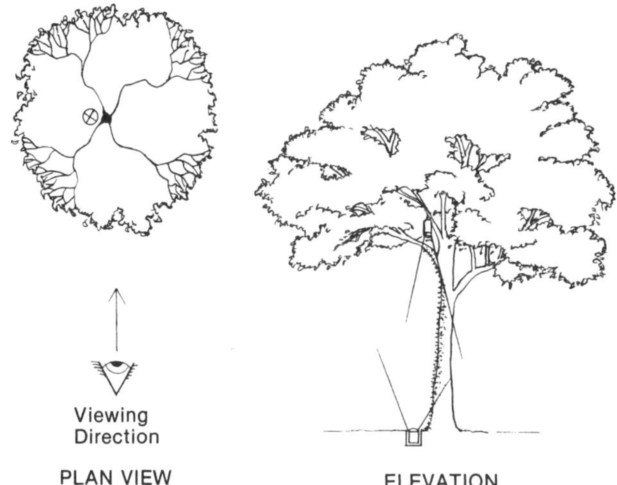

Figure 14.59B. *Mounting fixtures to the side creates a strong effect on a limited portion of the trunk. This works well with other trunk lighting techniques or alone. When used alone, it ties the tree to the ground and shows texture, but another aspect of the tree becomes visually more important (see Figure 14.64). Drawing: Lezlie Johannessen.*

Figure 14.60. *Uplighting the mature redwoods with 90-watt PAR38-spot quartz lamps accentuates the trunk texture, warm tones of the trunk, cool tones of the foliage, and softly washes the canopies up at about 50 feet above ground. Lighting Design: Janet Lennox Moyer; Photograph: Kenneth Rice Photography, www.kenricephoto.com.*

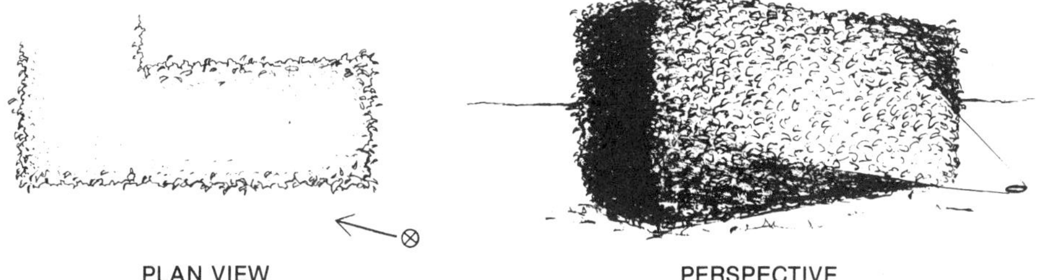

Figure 14.59C. *Texture technique. An even appearance represents the main difference between grazing and texturing. Grazing strives for an even appearance, while texturing affects a portion of a surface. Placing a fixture in front and to the side of a hedge with a narrow aiming angle emphasizes texture (see Figure 3.7). Drawing: Lezlie Johannessen.*

Figure 14.59. *Graze technique. Grazing highlights texture. Place fixtures closer to the tree or shrub than when washing. Lamps with flood distribution work on short trees, while taller trees require medium floods or spots, depending on the tree size and height.*

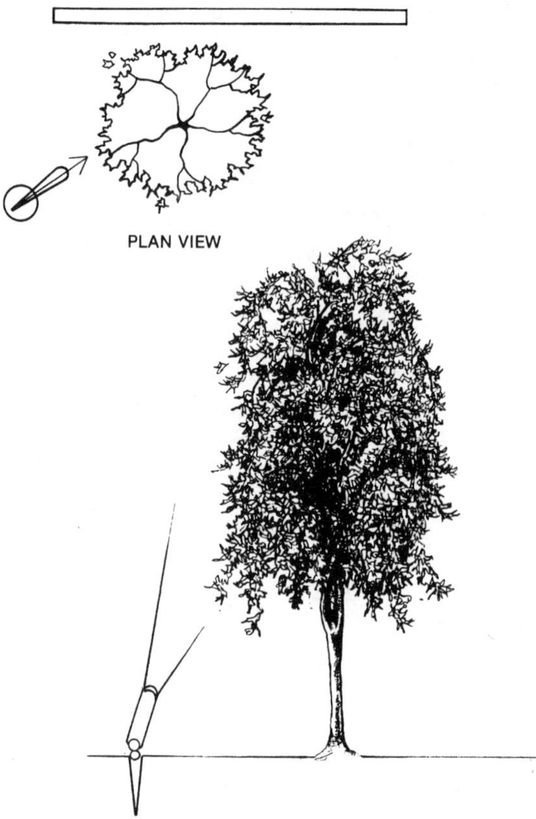

Figure 14.61. *Shadows technique. Uplighting a tree from the side produces shadows on the adjacent vertical surface. Use this as a simple way to add interest on large, plain walls. The shadow effect produced with this* Acer palmatum *'Dissectum Atropurpureum Crimson Queen' shows in Figure 14.62. Drawing: Craig Latker, Magrane Latker Landscape Design.*

Figure 14.62. *Sidelighting a tree produces shadows that break up the expanse of wall between two planting groups. Braiding the multistem trunk of this tree, along with its natural weeping form, keeps the branches compact, allowing the shadows to work both when the tree has leaves and when dormant. Lighting Design: Janet Lennox Moyer, MSH Visual Planners; Photograph: Kenneth Rice Photography, www.kenricephoto.com.*

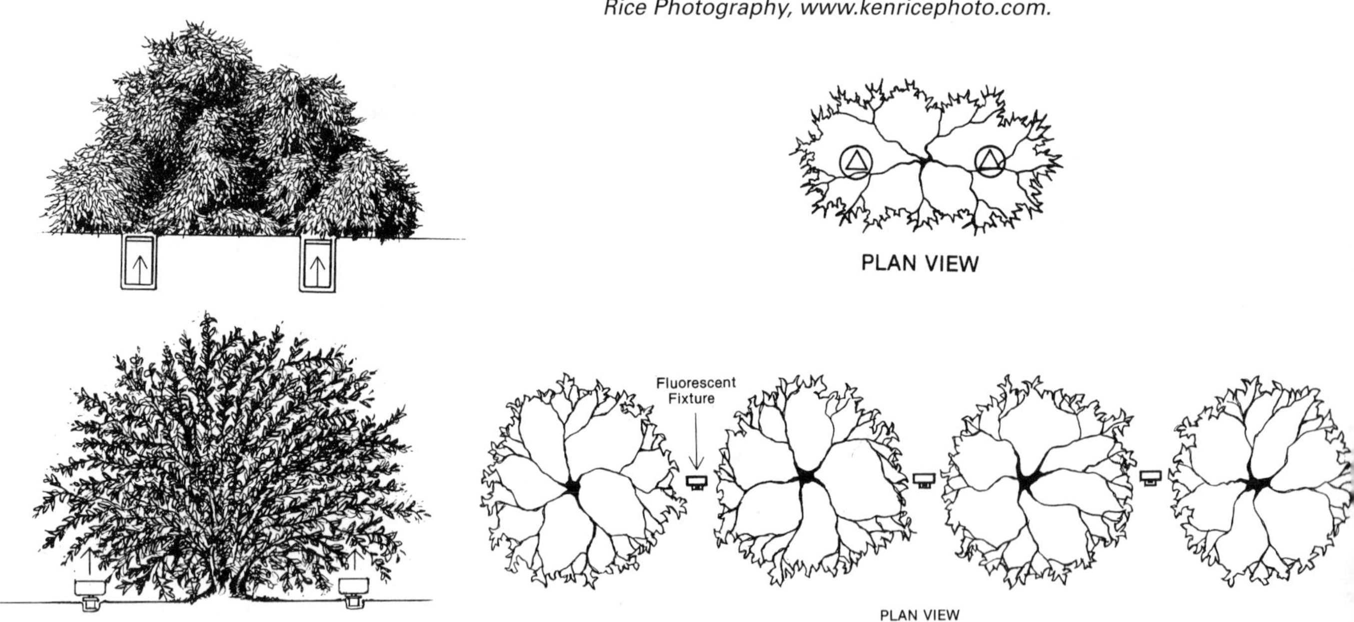

Figure 14.63. *Glow technique. A. Fixtures located under canopies of trees with an open branching form and translucent leaves create a glowing canopy effect. Recess the fixtures below grade for trees branching close to or on the ground. Use stake-mounted fixtures (see Figure 13.21) when branches start higher off the ground. B. Hedges with an open form and translucent leaves can utilize this technique. This diagram shows* Xylosma congestum *with fixtures using compact fluorescent lamps located between plants. Drawing A: Craig Latker, Magrane Latker Landscape Design; Drawing B: Lezlie Johannessen.*

Figure 14.64. This close-up view of the tree shown in Figure 17.3 illustrates combining two trunk lighting techniques: halo (on the left) and wash (on the right). Combining two techniques often creates an interesting effect. Lighting Design: Janet Lennox Moyer; Photograph: Kenneth Rice Photography, www.kenricephoto.com.

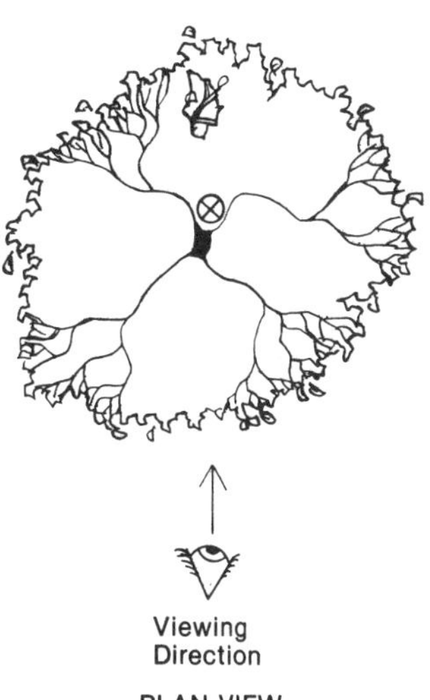

Figure 14.65. Halo technique. Lighting a trunk from slightly behind and to one side creates a sharp halo effect. Drawing: Lezlie Johannessen.

Figure 14.66. Dappled light technique. Mount fixtures high in a large tree, aiming them down through foliage and branches to create patterns on the ground below. Use this technique as fill light on lawns or for path lighting on driveways and walkways. However, directing light through foliage can easily create hot spots of light on foliage. Consider uplighting into the canopy to balance this brightness. Drawing: Lezlie Johannessen.

Figure 14.67. Downlights, using clear mercury vapor lamps (mounted in a tree not shown in this photograph), produce dappled light patterns on this patio. Mercury vapor most accurately represents the cool color of natural moonlight, but the shadowing effect can be created with any light source. Courtesy of Greenlee Landscape Lighting. Lighting Design: Doug Greenlee; Photograph: Lloyd R. Reeder.

15

Garden Evolution: Changes That Affect Lighting

Gardens evolve, and a lighting system needs to be able to respond. The issues include seasonal appearance changes for individual plants and for the overall garden, growth of individual plants and of the overall garden from one year to the next, and the human tendency to change garden layout and add new garden features or areas. Lighting must respond to these changes from the beginning.

LIGHTING SYSTEM INFRASTRUCTURE

At the inception of landscape lighting discussions, the effects of change must be considered and integrated into the planning and project documentation. Initially, this primarily affects power distribution. As a lighting design project develops, the potential future addition of fixtures (which translates to load) must be incorporated for low-voltage transformers (see Figure A.19) and controls systems.

Electrical cable can accommodate a fixed amount of load. When overloaded, the cable heats up, which can potentially cause serious damage to the electrical system. The cable will lose the ability to deliver the required power to the elements, such as 120-volt or 12-volt fixtures and their associated transformers. The symptoms of overloading in an existing system include extreme voltage drop to fixtures or total load dropout. The visual affect includes severe color shift toward yellow and dramatic light output loss. When overloaded beyond capacity, the cable will simply not be able to deliver power to the individual elements connected to it, and, they may not produce more than a dull glow, if anything.

All portions of the electrical system need to be sized for potential future loads—cable size, transformer size, and control system size. If a tree will initially have five fixtures with a maximum capacity of 50 watts each (total load 250 watts), and, in the future another five could be added, that additional 250 watts must be included in the sizing of all the system elements. The power can be accommodated by a cable large enough to handle the initial and future loads or a conduit large enough to allow for the addition of a separate cable (provided either initially or later—see Figure 4.15). Either the transformer could either be sized for the total potential load or field accommodations could be made for the easy addition of a second transformer with the installation of the additional fixtures (see Figure A.19). From the beginning, the control system needs to accommodate the potential future load.

GARDEN EVOLUTION

All plants grow at different rates and mature at different ages. The constant change in gardens requires that lighting designers consider some interesting issues. The designer needs to consider how an individual plant or group of plants changes physical appearance from one annual season to another (see Figures 15.4 & 15.6). A designer needs to identify the importance or the role of a specific plant within the context of the

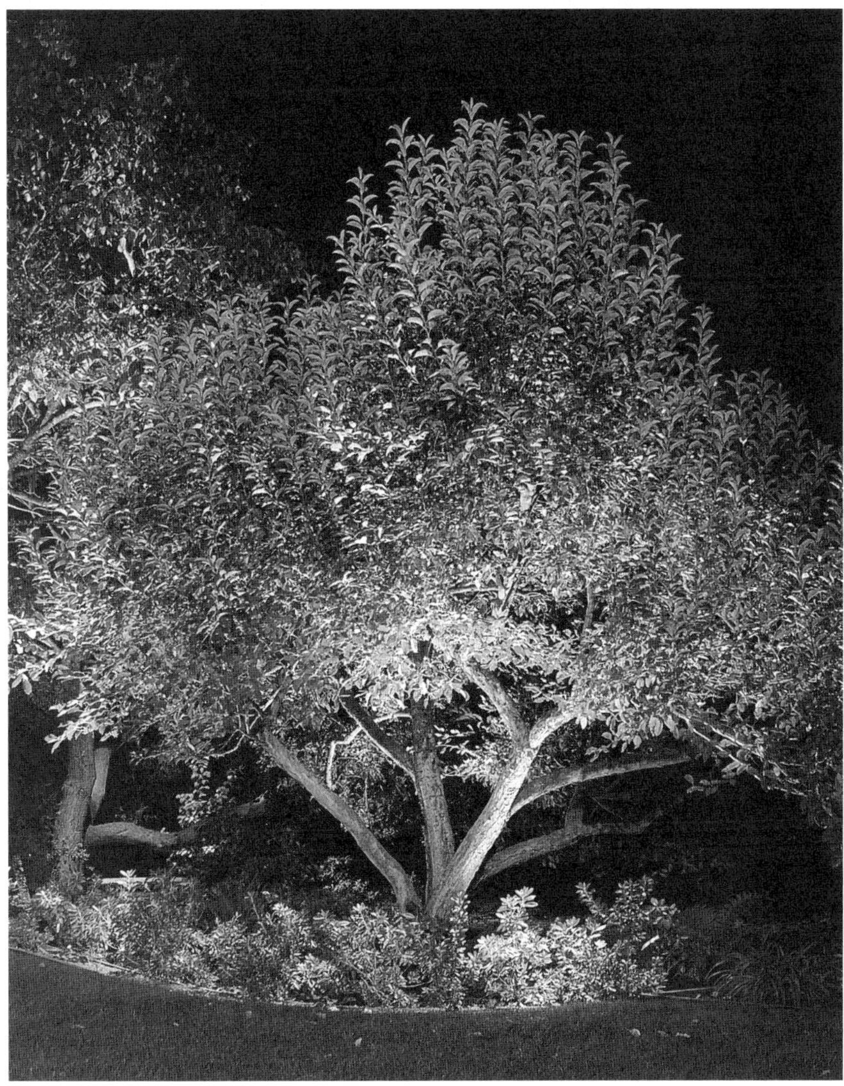

Figure 15.1. In summer, the play of light and dark on this Apple tree's leaves grabs your attention. Lighting Design: Janet Lennox Moyer, MSH Visual Planners; Photograph: Kenneth Rice Photography, www.kenricephoto.com.

overall garden composition or within a specific area. Just as importantly, the designer needs to consider how that individual plant or group changes from one year to another as the garden grows.

The effects of garden growth have substantial impact on lighting. Fixtures need to be relamped, reaimed, and/or moved. Additional fixtures and associated wiring equipment need to added (refer to Chapter 5, "Follow-Up Work: Record Documents and Project Maintenance").

CHANGES THROUGH THE SEASONS OF ONE YEAR

Most plants change their appearance throughout the seasons of a year (see Figures 15.1 & 15.2). These changing characteristics center primarily on foliage, foliage color, and flowers. Lighting designers need to understand the seasonal characteristics of all the plants in a garden. The dormant winter appearance is the best feature for some plants. Other plants release their catkins (long flowers covered in bracts) in late winter. Some plants have delicate spring foliage color that darkens for the summer and turns into a blaze in fall. Some trees have spring flowers that individually are indistinguishable and often dismissed as unimportant become spectacular when they cover the canopy (see Color Plate 9). Some plants have seasonal appeal, while others are desirable because of a single characteristic. In order to capture the essence of the plant and therefore the essence of the garden with light, these characteristics should be studied. Armed with this knowledge, the lighting designer can better select the specific lighting technique(s) for a plant within the fluid, ever-shifting overall garden composition (see Figures 15.4 & 15.6 and Color Plates 31–33 & 37–39).

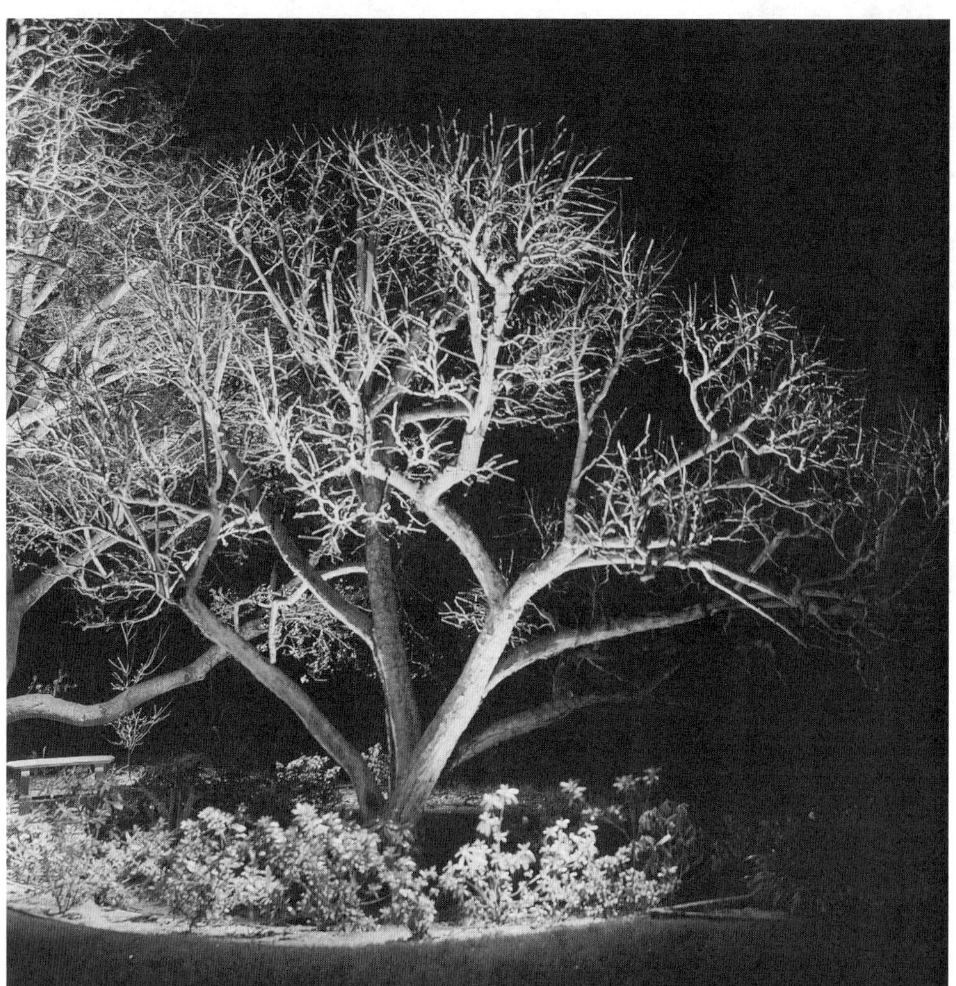

Figure 15.2. *In the winter, the overall branching structure becomes a sculpture with the way light/dark reveal the tree's form. Note that the water sprouts from a years' growing season have been pruned. Lighting Design: Janet Lennox Moyer, MSH Visual Planners; Photograph: Kenneth Rice Photography, www.kenricephoto.com.*

Figure 15.3. *Light on one tree outside a much-used room provides a visual connection to the garden in the winter months. This tree is approximately 80 feet from the window and lit with three 20-watt MR11 flood lamps. Lighting Design: Kelly Miller, Jamie Perry, & Javier Ten; Photograph: Kenneth Rice Photography, www.kenricephoto.com.*

Figure 15.4. *Soft lighting at the west side of the pond reflects in the water's still surface. At the north end, this student group left some plantings dark to accentuate the importance of the Colorado Blue Spruce lit with two 35-watt metal halide lamps. They designed and built the floating candle lanterns to provide a sense of the rest of the pond outline. Lighting Design: C. Brooke Carter, Dan Dyer, Eve Quelleman, & Kami Wilwol; Photograph: Kenneth Rice Photography, www.kenricephoto.com.*

Figure 15.5. *MR16 downlights mounted approximately 40 feet above ground softly flows over all the plants and architectural surfaces. The fullness of the leaves separates areas of the gardens. Lighting Design: Janet Lennox Moyer, MSH Visual Planners; Photograph: Kenneth Rice Photography, kenricephoto.com.*

Figure 15.6. *In March one year, warm temperatures had melted the pond and a heavy snow started late one Sunday afternoon. The layer of snow on the plants transforms the scene, exaggerating texture and heightening a sense of mass. The reflection—a lucky fluke. Lighting Design: C. Brooke Carter, Dan Dyer, Eve Quelleman, & Kami Wilwol Photograph: Kenneth Rice Photography, www.kenricephoto.com.*

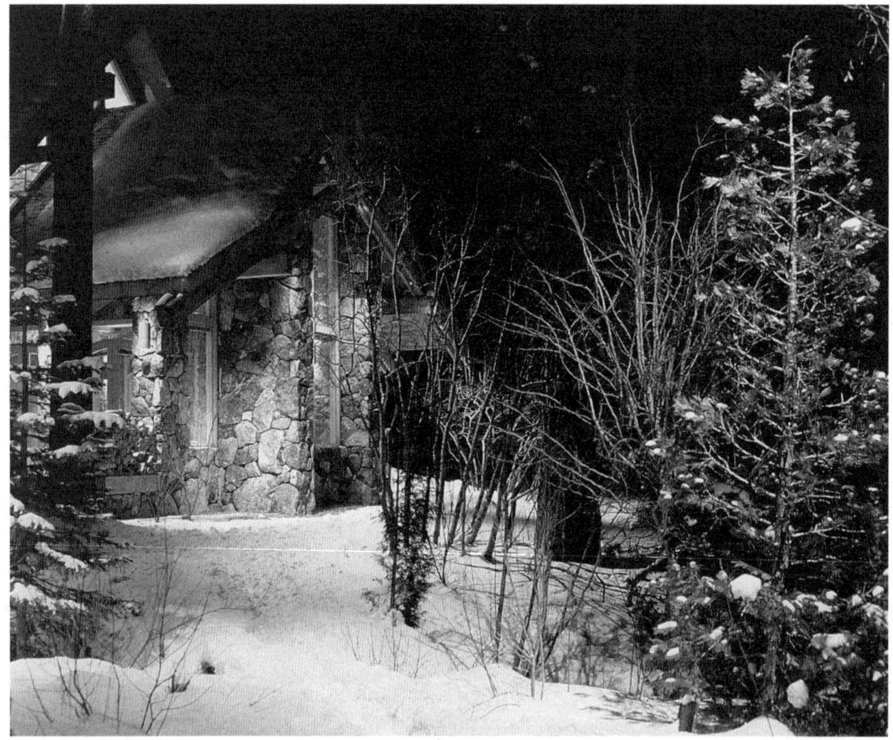

Figure 15.7. *The bare plant structure in winter and a snow pack across the groundplane opens the scene. Everything seems brighter, and depth is increased. Lighting Design: Janet Lennox Moyer, MSH Visual Planners; Photograph: Kenneth Rice Photography, www.kenricephoto.com.*

Figure 15.8. *A forest area in the summer. Photograph: Janet Lennox Moyer.*

Figure 15.9. *At dawn the next day, the snowstorm was ending, and the Northeast was left with a fleeting winter wonderland that was gone by noon. Photograph: Janet Lennox Moyer.*

Figure 15.10. *A combination of 35-watt CDM metal halide lamps wash the front of the forest with MR11 up- and downlight fixtures in the forest, highlighting specific trees and creating a footpath through the forest. Lighting Design: C. Brooke Carter, Dan Dyer, Eve Quelleman, & Kami Wilwol Photograph: Kenneth Rice Photography, www.kenricephoto.com.*

Figure 15.11. *Placement of the 35-watt metal halide fixtures becomes more noticeable in the snow-covered scene. For this photograph the students made a slight reaiming adjustment of one fixture that filled in the area in front of their footpath. Note the cohesive effect of that slight shift. Lighting Design: C. Brooke Carter, Dan Dyer, Eve Quelleman, & Kami Wilwol Photograph: Kenneth Rice Photography, www.kenricephoto.com.*

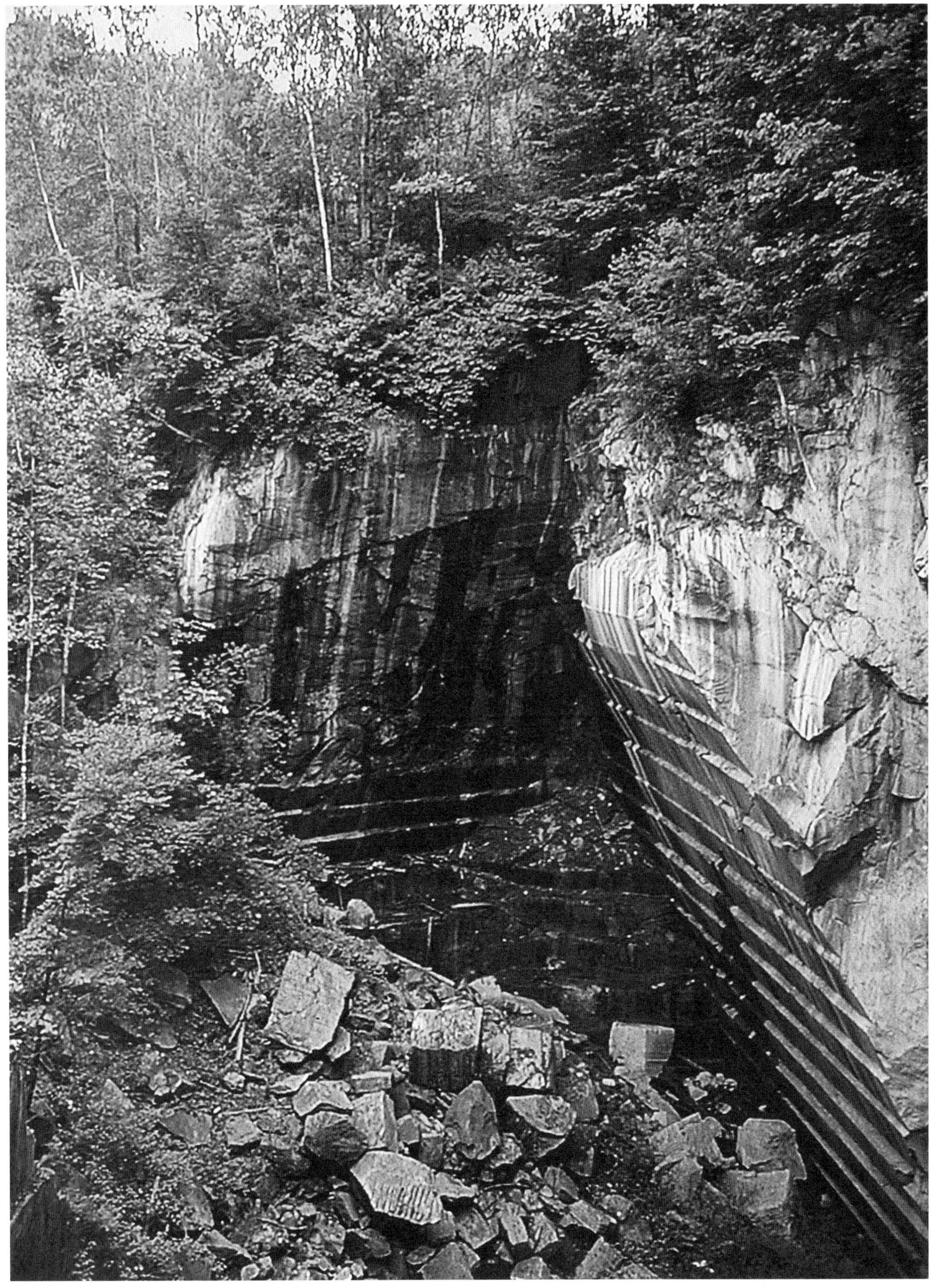

Figure 15.12. *This marble quarry in Vermont stopped being mined when the flow of water through the walls became uncontrollable. Lighting Design: Janet Lennox Moyer & Tom Williams; Photograph: Janet Lennox Moyer.*

Figure 15.13. *In the winter, the water flow through the walls freezes, creating these enormous ice formations. Light teases sparkle from the frozen water and the 70-watt CDM metal halide spot focused on the corner enhances its natural blue-green color. Lighting Design: Janet Lennox Moyer & Tom Williams; Photograph: Tom Williams.*

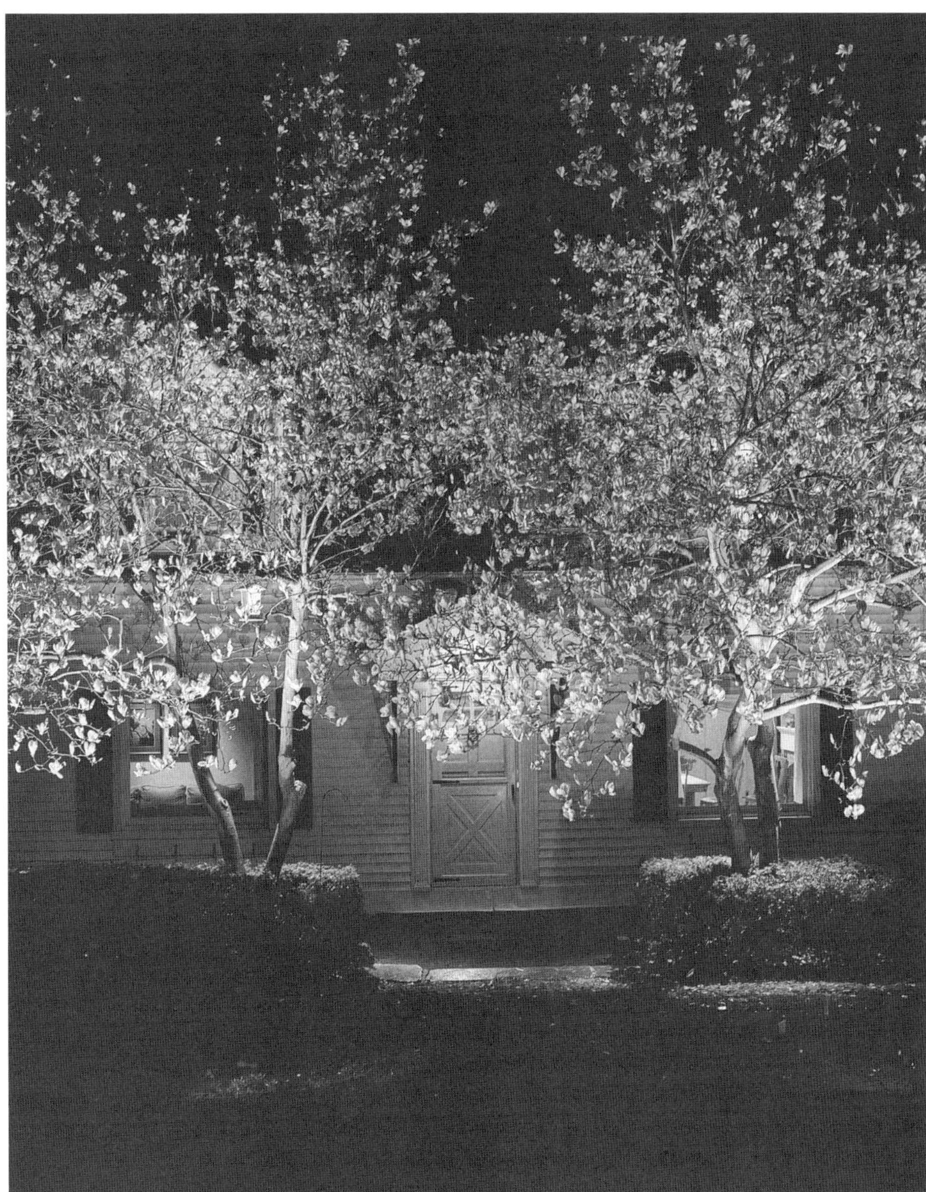

Figure 15.14. *Flanking the entry of this New York home, the floral display of these two* Magnolia soulangiana *trees dominate the scene. For this mock-up, the students astutely incorporated downlighting in the trees to define the grade change as guests approach the front door. Lighting Design: Carole Lindstrom, John, Tokarczyk, & Allan Tweed; Photograph: Kenneth Rice Photography, www.kenricephoto.com.*

People tend to start thinking about their gardens as spring approaches, and they include lighting on their summer preparation lists. Summer is a great time to utilize and enjoy landscape lighting; however, it is perhaps the *least* important of the annual seasons. Lighting can extend the hours that people enjoy a garden and provides a view out into and throughout the garden after dark in the summer months. In the nonequatorial areas of the earth, however, darkness doesn't fall until quite late in the summer months, thus limiting the useful hours of landscape lighting.

Landscape lighting becomes more important as the days become shorter. Winter, late fall, and early spring represent the important seasons for landscape lighting. In the fall, daylight hours drop at an increasing rate until the winter solstice (December in the Northern Hemisphere), with the least amount of daylight hours.

Winter

Our physical and visual connection to the garden tends to get lost in the winter. People leave their homes early in

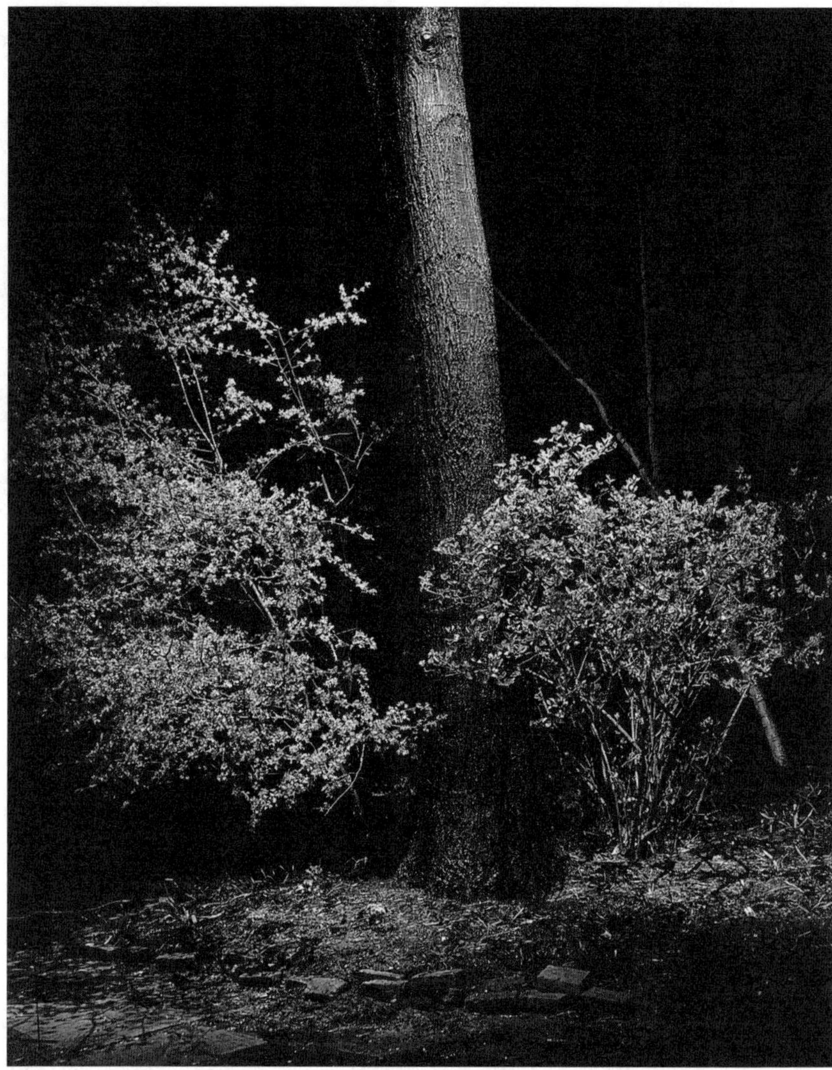

Figure 15.15. *At the driveway edge, the students chose to downlight the foundation shrubs allowing light to spill over onto the intersection of path and driveway. Note the glint of sparkle from the raindrops on the tree trunk during this rainstorm. Lighting Design: Carole Lindstrom, John Tokarczyk, & Allan Tweed, Photograph: Kenneth Rice Photography, www.kenricephoto.com.*

the morning in the dark and arrive back home late in the afternoon in the dark. Landscape lighting can aid people in getting safely to and from the house in the dark and provide them a visual connection to their gardens.

In winter, the "bones" of a garden, including hardscape elements and plant structure (form and branching patterns), become the dominant visual forms. Flowers and leaves have fallen, and many plants (annual and perennials) have disappeared completely. In some landscapes, the gardener will leave dead flower stalks of ornamental grasses and hardy perennials as a part of the garden's winter form.

The change of a garden's appearance from the lush fullness of summer to the stark structure in the winter is dramatic (see Figures 15.8 to 15.11). Light now reveals the trunk and branching structure of a deciduous tree (see Color Plates 47–49). It accentuates the lines of pathways and the visual destinations of specimen plants, architectural structures, water features, or sculptures (see Color Plates 15 & 16).

Light creates a view from inside a building to reconnect people with their gardens (see Figure 15.3). Lighting allows them to watch falling snow or driving rain. Providing this connection to the garden during the winter months can help them through the "blues" of their temporary disconnection with the garden.

When lighting in a region with snow, as with all landscape lighting, downlighting will create a more natural appearance. For safety, security, and navigating walkways from the garage to the house, downlighting provides a soft, clear path. Uplighting can be effective throughout the winter as long as the snowpack (the amount of snow that stays on the ground all winter) is not more than 24 inches deep. When a big snowstorm hits, activate the uplighting. The heat from the fixtures will melt the snow around fixtures as it collects.

Freed of foliage, the garden composition has more depth. Adding a blanket of snow on the ground further accentuates the effect of depth and increases the sense of brightness in the garden (see Figures 15.5 & 15.7 and

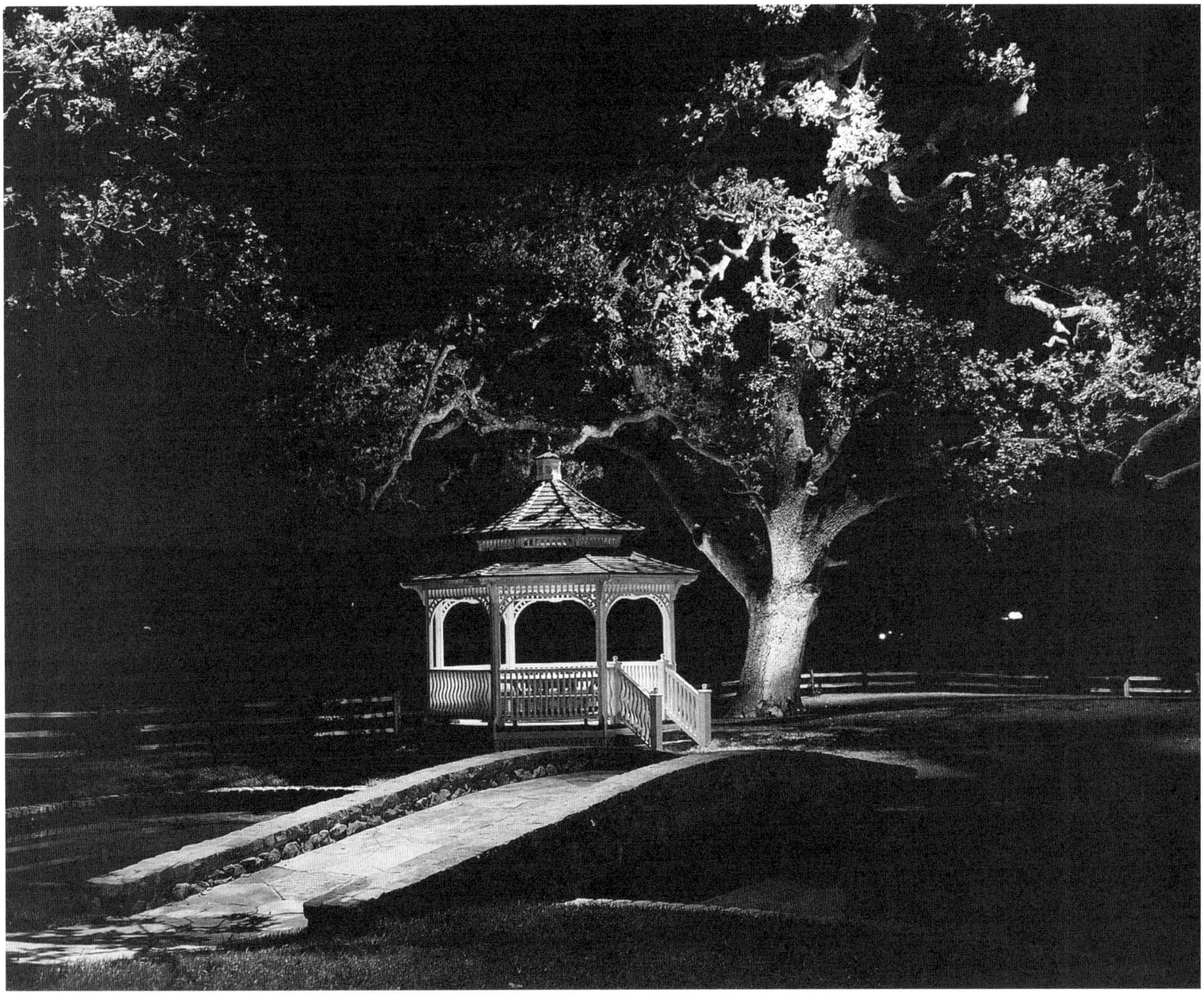

Figures 15.16 to 15.18. *As daylight shifts throughout from morning to night, the effect of light on this scene changes. At night, a carefully crafted mini-composition serves as a vista from the food and wine patio. Each of the three elements—the Oak, the gazebo, and the bridge—is lit with similar brightness, setting up a stable composition. All the lighting is from MR16 downlight fixtures mounted in the mature Oaks, except for uplights located at the base of the tree trunk. Lighting Design: Janet Lennox Moyer, Michael Stewart Hooker, & Paul Schreer, MSH Visual Planners; Photograph: Kenneth Rice Photography, www.kenricephoto.com.*

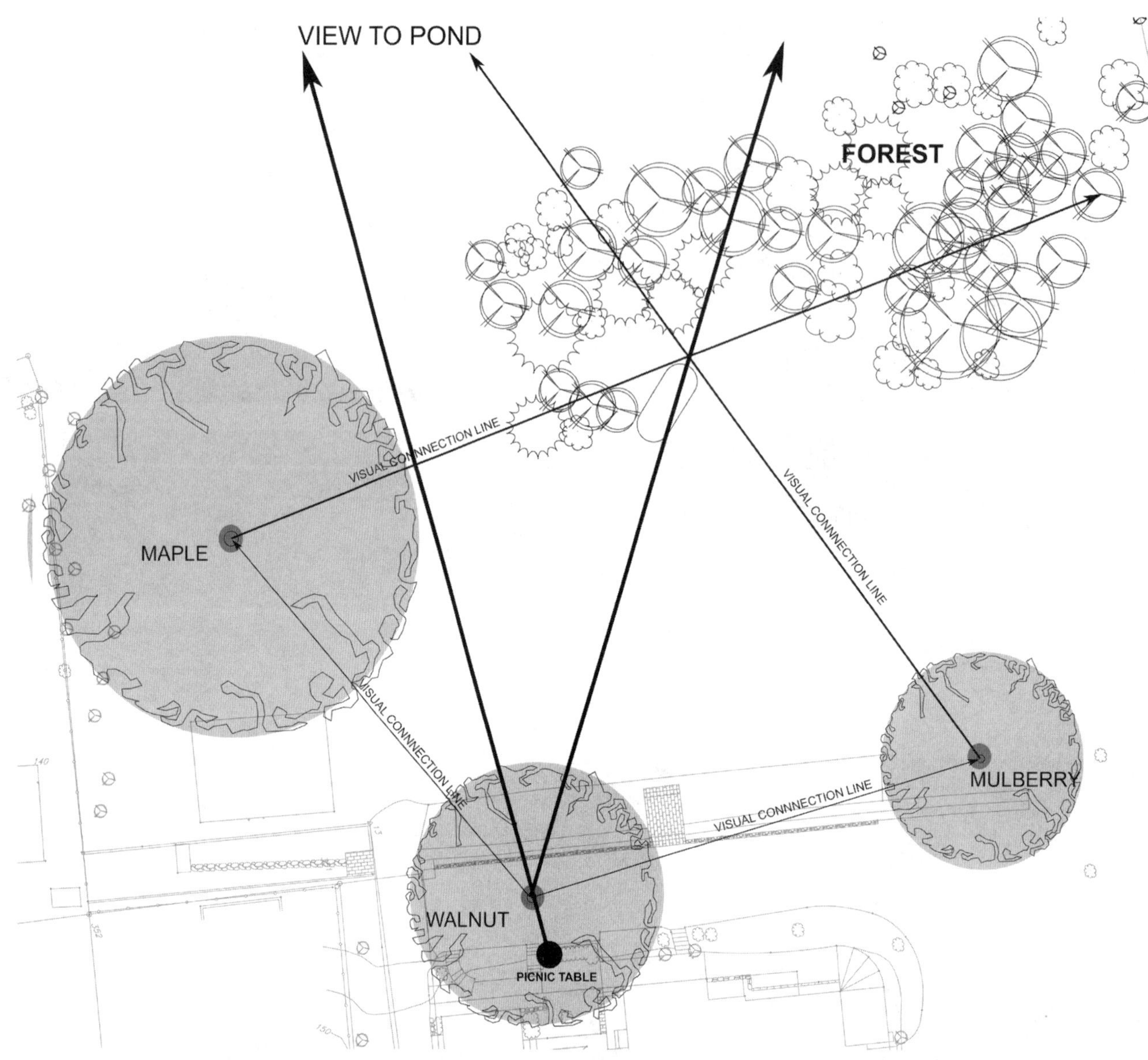

Figure 15.19. *Specimen trees can play a supporting role in a lighting composition. Selecting trees to visually connect one area of interest or activity to another creates a more comfortable, stable lighting composition. Drawing: N. J. Smith.*

Color Plates 6, 7, 15, & 16). Seeing deciduous and conifer trees blanketed in snow is wondrous (see Figures 15.8 to 15.11 and Color Plates 6, 7, 10, 18, 38 & 39). Note that the effect of snow on trees shows best on trees with strong horizontal branches. Rock formations and other grade changes become more dominant in the garden composition (see Color Plates 8–10). Sparkle glints off the crystalline structure of snowflakes and the face of ice forms (see Figures 15.12 & 15.13).

Spring

Light dances off the trunk of a tree wet from a rainstorm (see Figure 15.15) or off the raindrops themselves. In the spring, as plants start to waken and the bulbs begin to flower along the ground, downlighting can help ensure that people don't miss those exciting signs.

People tend not to notice the soft pastel foliage colors emerging on deciduous trees and shrubs and the vibrant, light new growth of conifers (see Color Plates 40–43). Often this foliage on both deciduous and evergreen plants darkens for the hot summer months, while flowers take over in importance. Spring flowers on trees, shrubs, and perennials vie for attention. Uplighting typically captures the tree flowers (see Figure 15.14), while downlighting best shows the ground plane flowers (see Color Plate 2). The garden changes so rapidly in the spring that from one day to the next attention can shift dramatically.

Betula nigra

Betula nigra				
	Age	Trunk ø	Crown	Height
Mature	60 yrs	2'-8"	78'-0"	92'-0"
Immature	18 yrs	1'-4"	24'-0"	30'-0"

NOTE: All dimensions are approximate

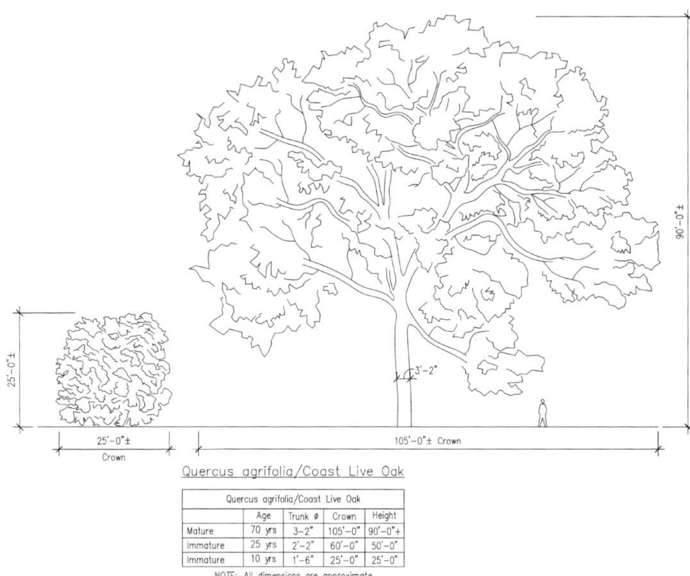

Quercus agrifolia/Coast Live Oak

Quercus agrifolia/Coast Live Oak				
	Age	Trunk ø	Crown	Height
Mature	70 yrs	3-2"	105'-0"	90'-0"+
Immature	25 yrs	2'-2"	60'-0"	50'-0"
Immature	10 yrs	1'-6"	25'-0"	25'-0"

NOTE: All dimensions are approximate

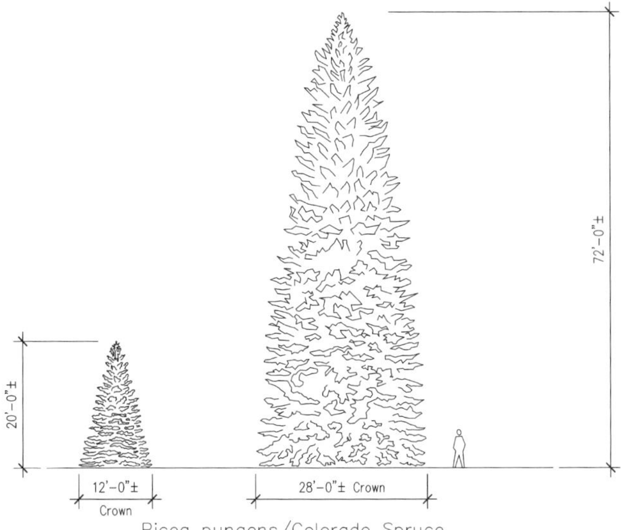

Picea pungens/Colorado Spruce

Picea pungens/Colorado Spruce				
	Age	Trunk ø	Crown	Height
Mature	80 yrs	x	28'-0"	72'-0"
Immature	25 yrs	x	12'-0"	20'-0"

NOTE: All dimensions are approximate

Figure 15.20 to 15.22. *These three tree examples show the nature of tree growth from immaturity, here between 10–25 years to maturity at 60–80 years. Some trees change shape dramatically, while others retain their shape while they grow to dramatic heights. Over the years, as a tree's form changes and its size expands, a lighting designer needs to have planned power for additional fixtures, and needs to have thought through how the lighting technique(s) will evolve. Drawings: Dan Dyer and N. J. Smith.*

Figure 15.23. *Immature California Live Oak trees have no distinguishable shape. Photograph: Janet Lennox Moyer.*

Figure 15.24. *As California Live Oak trees age, their form starts to open up and shows the trunk and branching structure. Photograph: Janet Lennox Moyer.*

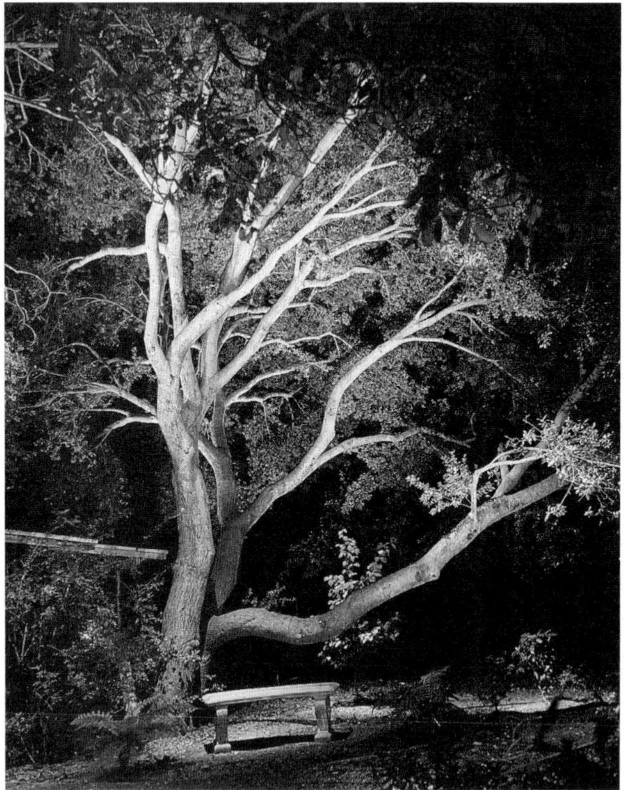

Figure 15.25. *Light fixtures mounted on the ground to uplight the canopy create a softer effect on the branching structure. Note how the density of the canopy retains all the light within, eliminating any light traveling into the neighbor's yard. Lighting Design: Janet Lennox Moyer, MSH Visual Planners; Photograph: Kenneth Rice Photography, www.kenricephoto.com.*

Figure 15.26. *At maturity, California Live Oaks have grand scale and branching structure. Their leaves are small and dense. Utilizing only fixtures mounted within the tree, due to the location of the tree in the midst of a vineyard, the lighting effect becomes dramatic. Lighting Design: Janet Lennox Moyer, Michael Stewart Hooker, & Paul Schreer, MSH Visual Planners; Photograph: Kenneth Rice Photography, www.kenricephoto.com.*

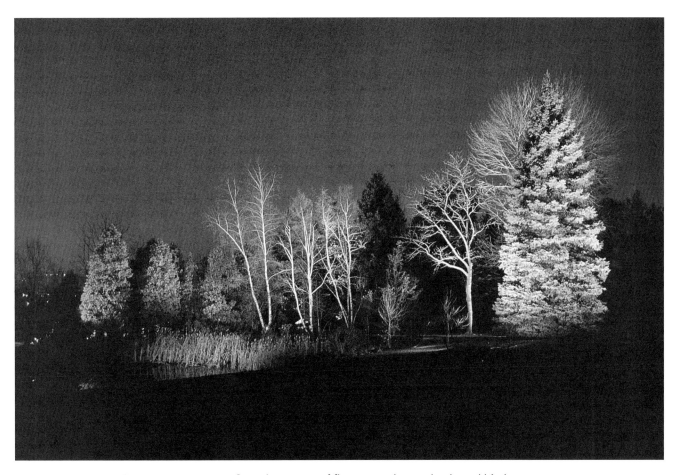

Figure 15.27 to 15.29. *Over the course of five years, the newly planted birches at the north end of this pond have grown substantially. Eventually they will replace the two Ash trees behind them as a visual element in this pond scene. At roughly 10 years old, they are still too small to serve as this connecting element in the composition. Lighting Design: Peping Dee, Brian Fuller, Francisco Garza, Sumi Han, Rohini Pendyala, & Insiya Shakir; Photographs: Kevin Simonson (15.27) & Dan Dyer.*

Figures 15.30 to 15.31. *These immature Japanese Maple and Crape Myrtle trees have been pruned to show enough form that careful, overall lighting shows their natural qualities. Lighting Design: Janet Lennox Moyer, MSH Visual Planners; Photograph: Kenneth Rice Photography, www.kenricephoto.com.*

Summer

In early summer, a riot of flowers and plant growth dominates most gardens. The fullness of the foliage remains, while the flowering effect continually flows in color and location throughout the garden. By late summer, garden plants have quieted down into the process of storing energy for the next year. Within this season, focal importance is changing nearly daily at the beginning and then settles down to a lazy pace. Lighting composition needs to include enough trees to provide a framework for the changing accents. Uplighting of trees at this time shows the combination of the trunk and the lush character of the canopy (see Figure 15.1 & Color Plate 1) as the constant, and downlighting reveals the changing floral display (see Color Plates 8 & 40–43).

Lighting takes a back seat to the daytime views of the garden flowers or long days at the beach. It still creates a magical experience late at night in a garden full of night-blooming scents. A series of photographs of the Far Niente Vineyards garden patio at midday, at dusk, and at night captures the changing nature of late summer (see Figures 15.16 to 15.18).

Fall

As plants prepare for their winter rest, they dazzle us with a display of color; as they drop their leaves or die for the season, the bones start to emerge (see Figures 15.4, 15.36, & 15.33 and Color Plates 33 & 37). Each season has inherent change. Lighting needs to respect an individual plant's response to the seasons and the overall garden's changing picture through the seasons.

CHANGING ROLES

Some plants play a supporting role in the lighting composition that serves to solidify the composition or to provide cohesion from one area to another (see Figure 15.19). Some plants serve as a focal point or visual destination at the end of a view or at a boundary. Some

Figure 15.32. In 1999, the students' lighting concept at this pond emphasized primarily a vista. They lit the back edge of the pond and limited the view and the amount of equipment they used. See the lighting layout in Figure 15.34. Lighting Design: C. Brooke Carter, Dan Dyer, Eve Quelleman, & Kami Wilwol; Photograph: Kenneth Rice Photography, www.kenricephoto.com.

plants function as the boundary, providing a sense of context, depth, or ending to the garden. Over time these roles may change. The change is primarily due to growth of the garden and people's desire to keep developing their gardens.

Growth of an Individual Plant

Plants increase in size, both in width and in height, somewhat predictably as they move toward maturity. The transformation of appearance can be dramatic from youth to maturity (see Figures 15.20 to 15.22). Then, even after they reach the age at which the horticultural world deems them mature, they continue to expand their trunk and branches, develop more branches, and/or lengthen individual branches. Over the course of one year, the Norway Maple (*Acer platanoides*) shown in Color Plates 31–33 & 37–39 expanded its canopy by more than 5 feet.

The lighting designer needs to be aware of how much a plant will grow and how it will shift in appearance. The developments can affect more than the number of fixtures required to maintain the original lighting effect. As the plant's appearance evolves, the lighting technique utilized may need to be revised. For example, as a Camellia shrub matures, it develops a beautiful branching structure. It has very dense leaves (see Color Plates 25, 26, & 34) and when young will typically be lit from outside the canopy using a washing technique. This will show the overall form of the shrub and the flowers when in bloom. Often, Camellias are pruned to open their form and show their branching structure as they mature. When this happens, fixtures can be added underneath the canopy to softly graze the trunk and branches. This

Figure 15.33. *By 2002, the garden and activities around the pond had developed significantly. This student group chose to light the area softly and encompass more of the area (see Color Plate 22). They also lit the now-present reeds along the north and south pond edges. See Lighting Plan in Figure 15.35. Lighting Design: Peping Dee, Brian Fuller, Francisco Garza, Sumi Han, Rohini Pendyala, & Insiya Shakir; Photograph: Dan Dyer.*

will give the plant more three-dimensional form as well as a new night appearance.

Within a genus some individual plants may grow slowly, while others grow quickly. The California Live Oak (*Quercus agrifolia*) grows slowly, and from a lighting standpoint it takes years to mature enough to light (see Figure 15.23). The leaves are small and dense with a dense leaf overlap, and it takes decades for the branching structure to begin to show (see Figure 15.24). At maturity, well into hundreds of years, the branching structure becomes dramatic (see Figure 4.43). This tree tends to form a rounded canopy, and it is dense due to the leaf overlap. From a lighting standpoint, this means that the interior structure can be lit from within and the canopy will remain dark on the outside. This is a useful tool or technique for respecting dark skies and neighbors' privacy, as typically no light penetrates the canopy (see Figure 15.25). When the preference is to show the exterior of an Oak canopy, fixtures must be placed well outside the canopy (see Figures 14.47 & 15.26).

Garden Evolution Influences Plant Role

During the course of garden evolution, a plant playing a supporting role in a composition can become a focal point, while a plant serving as a visual destination at one point in time can become one of several equal elements in a new destination composition. In a California garden, a California Live Oak (*Quercus agrifolia*) shifted from the role of major accent tree as viewed from several patios and porches in the 1990s (see Figure 15.25) to an anchor element in a more complicated composition in 2002 (see Color Plates 1, 51, & 52). Lighting designers need to be aware that since gardens are not static, the

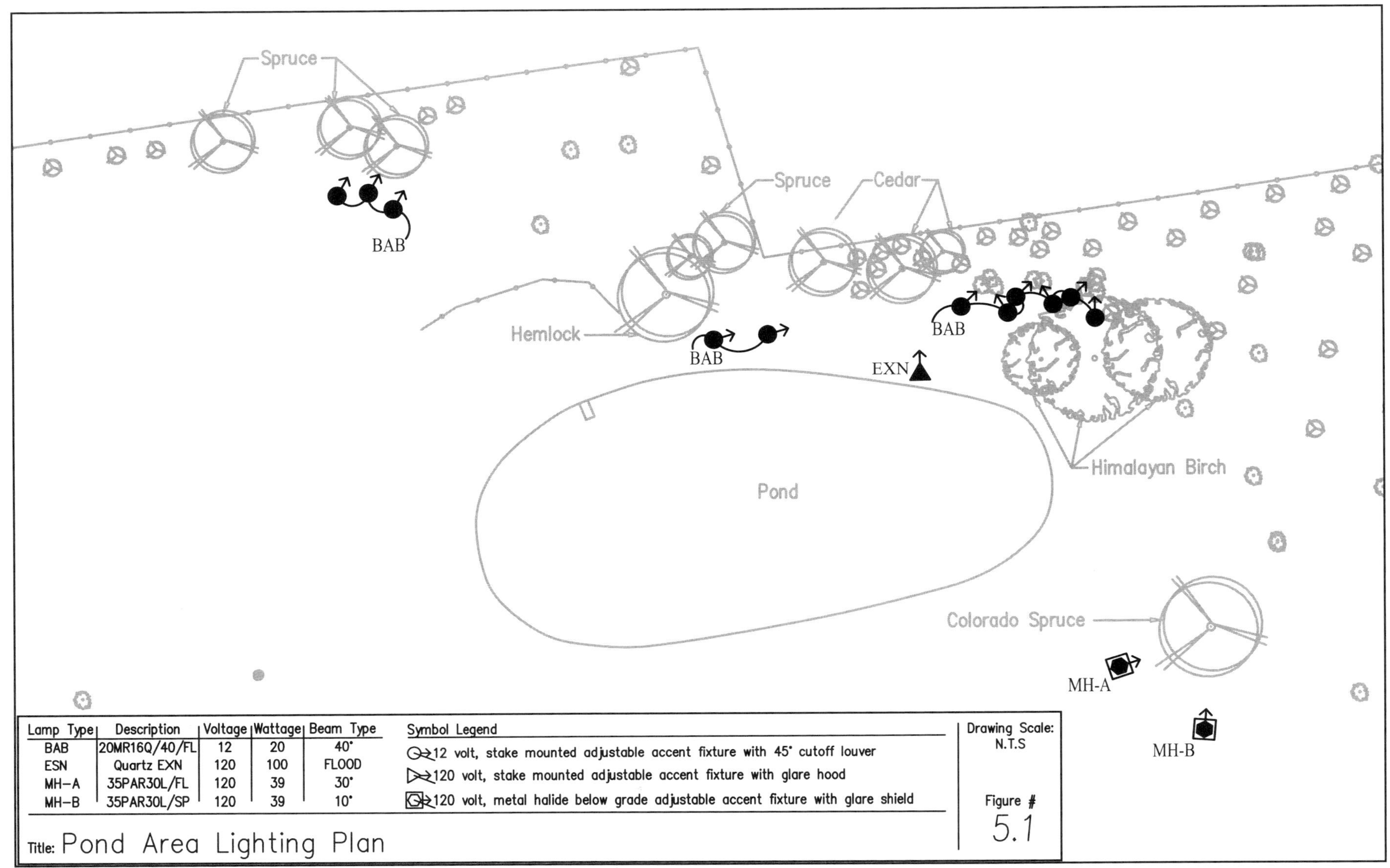

***Figure 15.34**. 1999 Lighting plan for the pond. Lighting Design: C. Brooke Carter, Dan Dyer, Eve Quelleman, & Kami Wilwol; Drawing: Dan Dyer and N. J. Smith.*

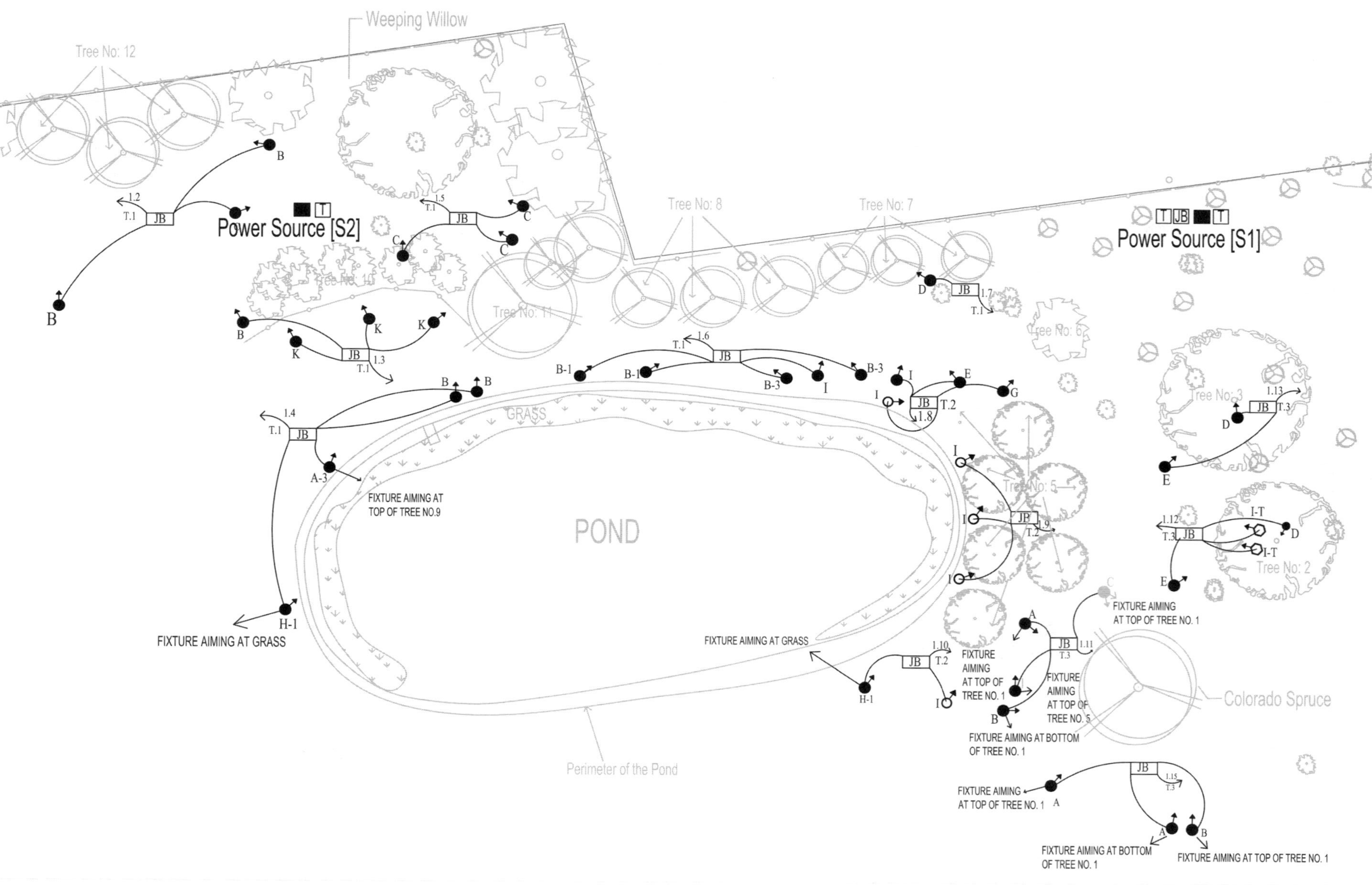

Figure 15.35. *2002 Lighting plan for the pond. Lighting Design: Peping Dee, Brian Fuller, Francisco Garza, Sumi Han, Rohini Pendyala, & Insiya Shakir; Drawing: N. J. Smith.*

Figure 15.36 to 15.37. *At the end of 10 years' time, the simplicity of this hillside garden developed in one radical change to a much more complicated garden space. The lighting system needed to respond to these changes. See Color Plates 51 & 52. Photographs: Janet Lennox Moyer.*

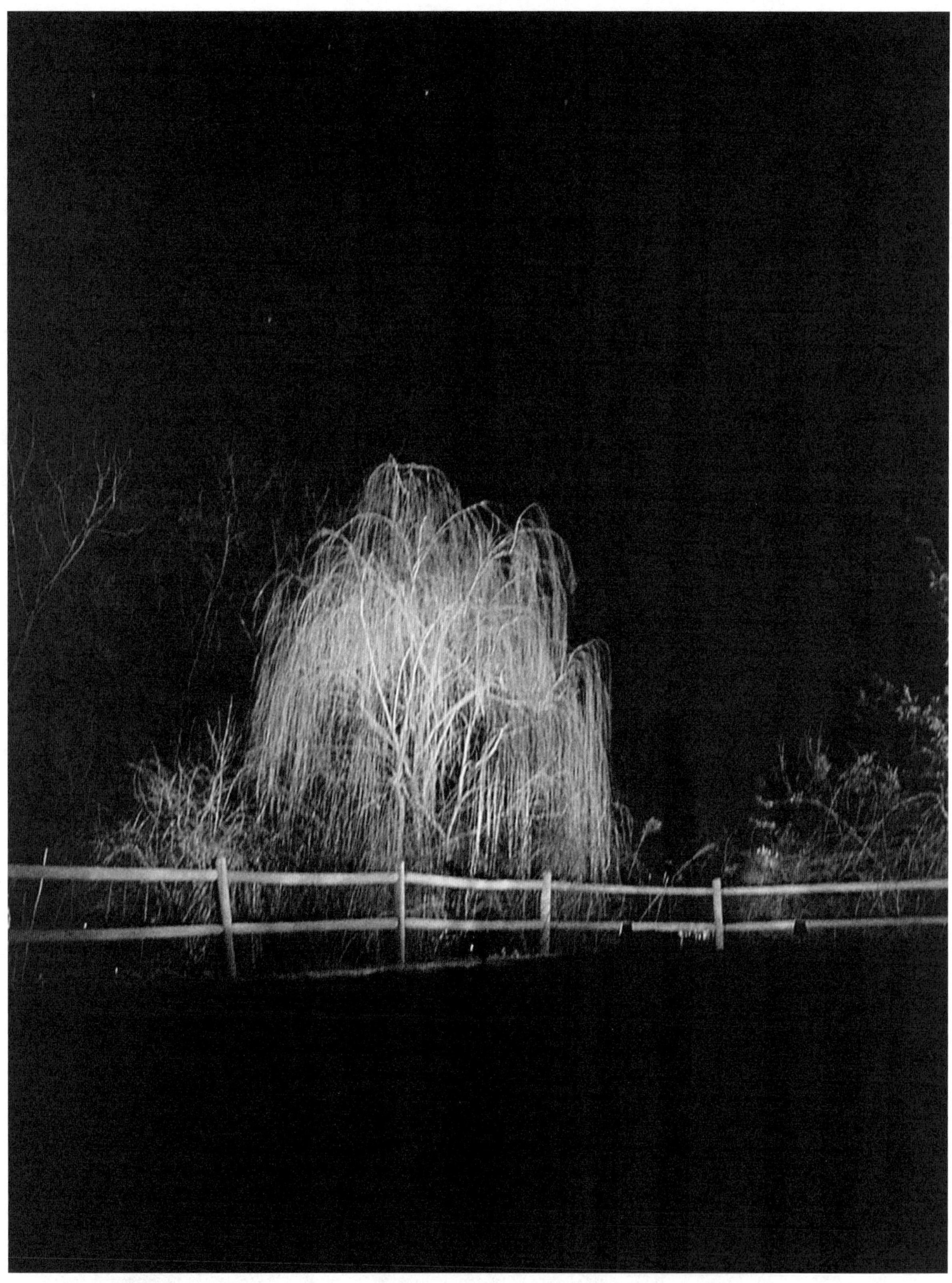

Figure 15.38 to 15.39. *The lighting mock-up for this fast-growing Willow consisted of fixtures mounted outside the canopy. The students determined when this photograph was taken in late winter that having some fixtures under the canopy to highlight the branching structure would add to the beauty of its structure. The A-3 fixture placement distance of more than 50 feet away from the tree became necessary due to the three-dimensional quality of the tree's growth habit. Any closer and the entire top of the tree fell into shadow. Lighting Design: Peping Dee, Brian Fuller, Francisco Garza, Sumi Han, Rohini Pendyala, & Insiya Shakir; Photograph: Dan Dyer.*

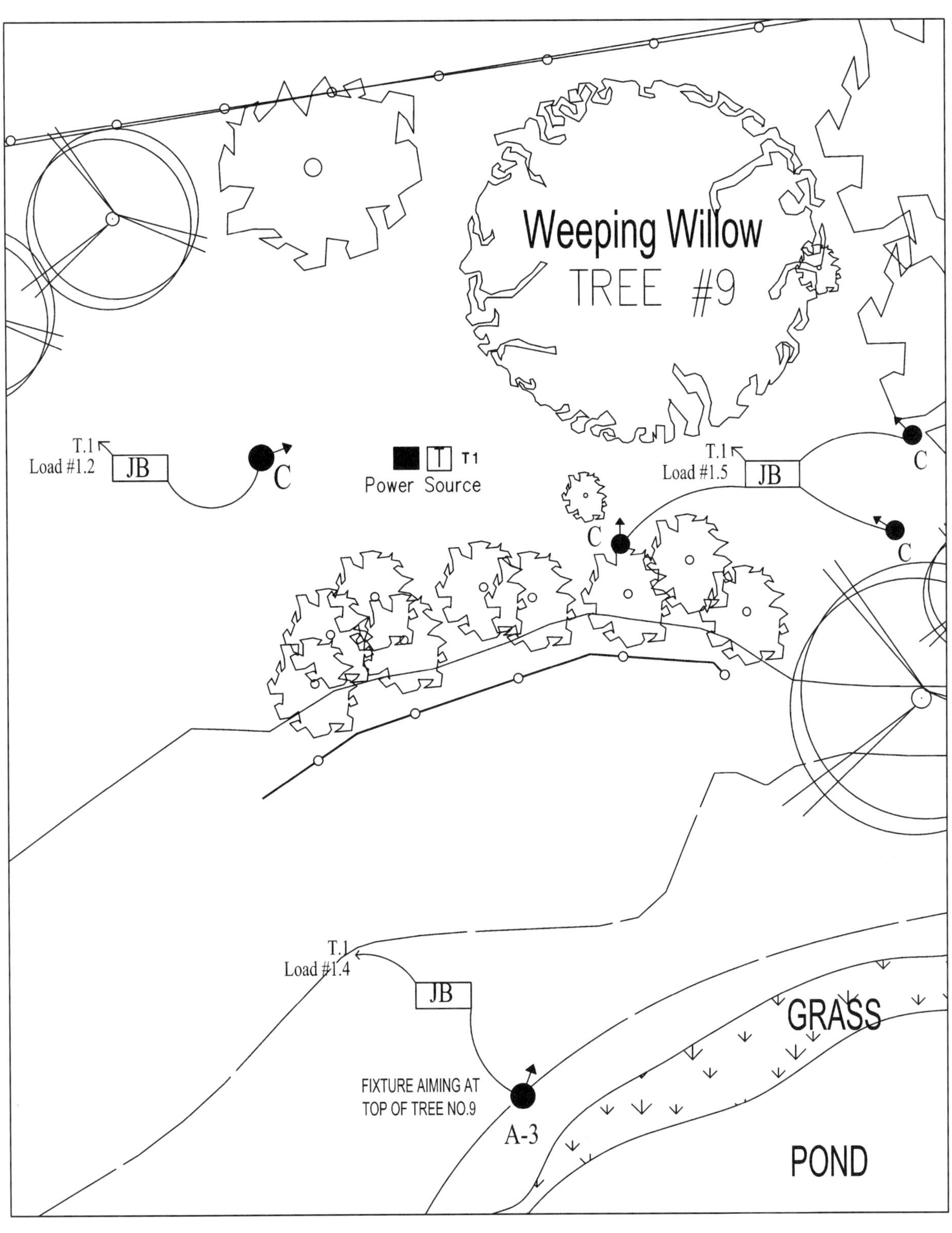

Lamp Type	Description	Voltage	Wattage	Beam Type
A3 ●	FRB	12V	35W	12 DEGREE
C ●	EXN	12V	50W	40 DEGREE

Symbol Legend

●→ 12 Volt MR16 adjustable stake–mounted fixture with glare shield

■ POWER SOURCE

JB X.XX Y.Y — JUNCTION BOX — TRANSFORMER NO. LOAD NO.

T TRANSFORMER

Title: Property Lighting Plan

Approximate current tree characteristics:
Age: 6 Trunk diameter: 16" Height: 25'–0"

Figure 15.40. *These sketches and photographs illustrate two pruning issues: thinning (A, B, C, & D) and crown raising (A, B, E, & F). Drawing: Jim Gross and N. J. Smith; Photographs: David Brearey.*

hierarchy of focal points and the organization of a visual composition will alter over time. The lighting system needs to be designed in the beginning to respond to predictable and unpredictable developments.

In a New York garden, two mature Ash trees (*Fraxinus americana*) at the north end of a pond were in decline. A grove of Heritage Birch trees (*Betula nigra* 'Heritage') planted at the edge of the pond will replace the Ashes in the day and night composition within ten years (see Figures 15.27 to 15.29).

In a different area of the California garden mentioned above, two Crape Myrtle (*Lagerstroemia indica*) trees acted as transition plants from one garden area to another in the late 1990s. In 2002, the garden began to change radically. A new staircase meant the removal of one of the two trees, and the other, now standing quite alone, became an important *transition plant* (see Figures 14.46, 15.30, & 15.31).

Gradual Change

Many gardens develop over the course of a number of years. With garden expansion come new uses, activities, views, traffic paths, structures, sculptures, water features, and garden areas. The lighting system needs to respond with power availability and the flexibility to reconfigure scenes and composition.

At a New York garden, two groups of graduate students from Rensselaer Polytechnic University's Lighting Research Center were given the assignment to plan lighting for a remote portion of the nearly 6-acre site. The garden consisted of developing plantings surrounding an existing pond. The first group of students worked on the project in 1999. At that time, they evaluated the site and determined that the pond area served primarily as a view from the main house and its accompanying entertainment areas during all seasons. They designed and set up mock-up lighting for the pond area essentially as a stage set with limited viewing directions from the residence (see Figures 15.32 & 15.34).

In 2002, when the next student group worked on the same section of the garden, several areas all around the pond had developed and were used throughout the year. A new entertaining area south and west of the pond increased the importance of the view to the pond. Two main paths had emerged for people to walk from the house to the new garden. The design team needed to consider the views from the two paths and from the new garden north to the pond. Their treatment of the planting surrounding the pond expanded from the first group's approach. They integrated the specimen Colorado Blue Spruce (*Picea abies*) instead of having it function as a surprise focal point. They also developed a mini-composition at the south end of the pond with a Weeping Willow (*Salix babylonica*) as its focal point area (see Figures 15.33–35, 15.38, 15.39, and Color Plates 22 & 44–46).

With gradual change, power expansion requirements can be relatively accurately estimated. To some extent composition issues can be anticipated. Often, however, new ideas are conceived and ferment over the years before a garden actually gets worked on. This always brings surprises with it.

Radical Change

Sometimes gardens will be developing gradually over the years and all of a sudden the landscape designer and/or the owner conceives of a grand new plan. For lighting, this can mean starting over with the composition as well as fixture locations and power requirements.

At a California garden, in January 2001, major renovations were transforming the essence of a mature garden. Mature trees had been removed, a dry streambed had been expanded to traverse the entire length of the property, a guest house had been added, a boccie court had been built and a rose garden removed, new paths now wandered throughout the entire property, and hundreds of trees and shrubs were being planted (see Figures 15.36 & 15.37 and Color Plates 51 & 52). Each of these changes affected the lighting system. Together, the impact on the lighting system was extensive.

The lighting composition had to be entirely revisited. While many mini-compositions within the entire property composition required rethinking, the existing need for cohesion from one area to another remained constant. Entire groups of fixtures had to be relocated and numerous new fixtures added. The planning for future power had not encompassed this large design shift, and additional power had to be provided to several areas of the garden. The most dramatic effect of these changes, however, was that at the end of the renovations in 2002, the garden looked less mature.

The Relationship of Pruning with Lighting

Trees benefit from pruning. Removing dead, diseased, deformed, and dysfunctional wood positively affects a tree's health. Pruning improves a tree's daytime and lit appearance. Lighting accentuates tree form. As trees grow they produce many branches that cross others, run parallel to each other, and rub on other branches. Some branches cross the main line of the tree. All of these reduce the aesthetic appearance of the tree during the day and at night.

The removal of branches close to the ground, called crown lifting, has major importance for tree lighting. When branches are too close to a lighting fixture, especially if a fixture is placed directly beneath a branch, the resulting hot spot destroys the luminance balance throughout the tree. Crown thinning helps to open the tree for light penetration. Figure 15.40 shows an example of raising and thinning the crown for lighting. Removing the lower limbs—whether established limbs, such as those shown in the drawing, or young limbs, shown in Figures 15.40E&F—avoids hot spots on lower limbs from uplighting.

Branches that cross the main line of a tree trunk impede the flow of light up to the canopy top and detract from the visual impression of the tree. Water sprouts, adventitious branches that grow straight up from a branch, detract from the day and night appearance of a tree. Removing these branches helps the lighting of a tree as well as its health. Branches that rub against each other can cut through the cambium layer, exposing the tree to attack from pests and/or diseases. All the pruning situations that designers consider for lighting positively affect the health of the tree.

The maintenance schedule for a lighting system needs to include pruning. This allows for removal of branches before they get large and branches that have grown into the path of light from a fixture since the last aiming session. The lighting designer needs to work in close concert with the garden designer and/or tree expert (typically an arborist) to plan the pruning. Pruning often needs to occur during a night aiming or maintenance focus session. When an arborist cannot attend an aiming session, the lighting designer needs enough knowledge and training to know which branches can be removed and the proper removal methodology (see *The Pruning Book* by Lee Reich in the Plant Materials section of the Bibliography). In all cases, the owner must be consulted and approve any pruning.

16

Sculptures, Architectural Structures, and Signage

Landscape architects use sculptures, architectural structures, and signage in their designs. Sculptures decorate space. In public spaces, sculptures provide recognition of a hero or make a statement about the city or landscape. They will be situated in a prominent place near the entry, in front of a building, central to a formal garden, or at the end of a vista. When placed prominently in courtyards, atria, or lobbies, sculptures can be viewed as a person approaches, as well as when inside the space. In private spaces and residential gardens, sculptures typically serve as a focal point. Location varies from a prominent vista or destination to a hidden spot tucked away as a surprise for the visitor strolling in the garden.

Structures offer more variety in their use. They can be functional: a greenhouse, pavilion, gazebo, trellis cover for a patio, or fence delineating the boundary of the space. The function varies with the structure from housing plant material in a perpetual summer environment, to a retreat from inclement weather, to a spot for entertaining. They can be representational—a grotto, triumphal arch, or a folly (see Figure 3.10)—meant to entertain the eye, but serving no use.

Signage informs people about a building's use (identifying and setting the tone for a store or restaurant, for example), directs pedestrians or vehicular traffic, or controls traffic movement or access to a space. Signs vary in type and appearance—from tasteful identification signs to domineering billboards.

In planning the lighting approach for any of these features, consider the meaning of the individual sculpture, structure, or sign in the overall setting, and its relation to other elements of the visual composition. These features can represent the main focal point(s) or minor focal points. Some structures, however, are incidental and should draw no attention to themselves. Also, consider the appearance of the feature. Will lighting add to the composition, or should it remain unlit? One of the keys to successful lighting is choosing what to light, in what order of brightness, and what to leave dark. In all cases, the lighting for these features should be an integrated part of the composition for the overall area. Remember to balance the exterior lighting with interior lighting in areas such as lobbies or atria.

Always include all pertinent people in the initial design discussions—the owner, landscape designer, or the artist. Any of them can have strong ideas about how the sculpture or structure should appear when lit.

SCULPTURES

Sculptures are individual. Each expresses the unique ideas of the sculptor. To ensure that an appropriate lighting concept will be developed, the lighting designer needs to see the sculpture or at least a photograph (accompanied by dimensions). Sculptures can take two basic forms: freestanding three-dimensional

Figure 16.1. Successful sculpture lighting requires that the sculpture be chosen and located on site prior to planning lighting. Here, accent lights built into traffic control bollards capture the sculpture's strong and subtle details. At the same time, this completes the image by reflecting the other side of the face on the polished divider. Lighting Design: Smith, Hinchman & Grylls Associates, Inc.; Landscape Design: Johnson, Johnson & Roy, Inc.; Photograph: Gary Quesada, Korab Ltd.

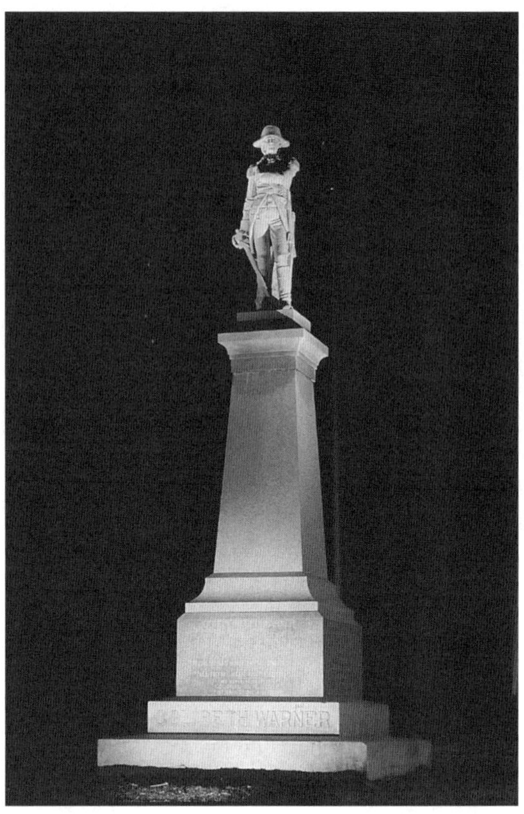

Figure 16.2. At this mock-up for a sculpture of Colonel Seth Warner in Bennington, Vermont, LRC students used multiple fixtures. One 35-watt low-voltage MR 16 spot with a linear spread lens located 6′5″ back from the base provides sufficient lighting to read the inscription and serves to ground the figure. Two 50-watt MR16 spots located at slightly varying distances (24/26′ back and at 65°/70° from center) aim at the figure to show the form. At these angles, light tucks up under his hat and onto his face. Lighting Design: David Cyr, Peping Dee, Richard DePalma, Lara Jacobson, Michael Meyer, & Jason Neches; Photograph: Peping Dee.

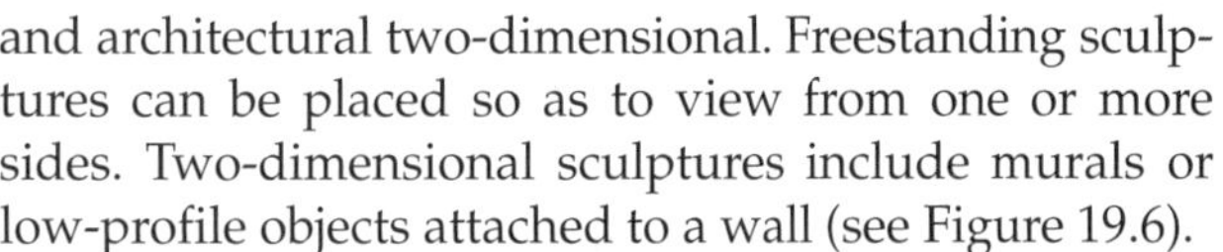

and architectural two-dimensional. Freestanding sculptures can be placed so as to view from one or more sides. Two-dimensional sculptures include murals or low-profile objects attached to a wall (see Figure 19.6).

When evaluating how to light a sculpture, a lighting designer should consider the size, physical characteristics, and any special features of the sculpture. Highlighting features of a sculpture can convey important information to the viewer or lead the viewer's interpretation. Line can communicate emotion or movement (see Figure 16.8); positive and negative space creates form or detail (see Figure 16.1); texture shows detail; facial expressions provide emotion.

For murals, the basic techniques used for hedges apply. If the mural has interesting texture, use a grazing technique (see Figures 14.56 to 14.59). Employ a wall-washing technique when either pattern or color serves as the main feature and texture either does not exist or should be deemphasized (see Figure 14.55).

Think about how the sculpture fits into the overall composition. When representing the main focal point, a sculpture's relation to other elements influences how it should be lit. Typically, the sculpture should have the brightest light level (see Figure 17.5). The lighting level on other elements should then step down in brightness to match their role in the composition. When the sculpture plays a minor role, the level of brightness applied should be softer than for the more important elements in the composition. The sculpture's importance, along with its physical and reflectance characteristics, guide the quantity of light it needs. Remember, though, that breaking rules often creates interest (see Figure 16.3).

Uplighting Versus Downlighting

Lighting can enhance the natural appearance or create a new impression of a sculpture at night. Think about how light and shadow could affect the sculpture's appearance. The direction of light influences the creation of shadows.

Downlighting maintains the natural appearance of the sculpture more easily than does uplighting (once again due to the familiarity of sunlight on objects). Mimicking daylight, downlighting creates shadows on the underside of textural details. Be careful, though, as shadows introduced onto human faces or animal figures from directly above can alter the sculpture's appearance, transforming friendly faces into frightening, unfriendly, or ugly forms (see Figure 16.4). Lighting human faces requires understanding the way the face is modeled in three dimensions. The eye sockets sit recessed into the skull, while the nose, cheeks, and lips protrude.

Lighting a face from above can create shadows that distort the face and remove the viewer's ability to read the informative expressions that people wear on their faces. Locate fixtures to shine light onto the face from the side or far enough away to minimize shadows from facial features (see Figure 16.2 & 16.3). The key to success is *fixture location,* which determines aiming angle—wide angles perform better.

For example, the deep eyebrow of a monkey sculpture required moving the accent light (located in front of the sculpture) 5 feet away from the sculpture, even though the sculpture was only about 30 inches tall (without base). A mock-up showed that any closer, the monkey's eyes fell into shadow. Two fixtures were employed: a 4405 PAR36 for the face and a 50-watt PAR36 flood to fill in the body. Both fixtures were located directly in front of and above the sculpture.

Utilizing downlight locations when available will probably provide a permanent lighting effect. Out of harm's way, fixtures are less likely to be knocked out of adjustment or vandalized. Often, though, no downlighting location exists. With no tree or architectural structure nearby for mounting lights, uplighting becomes the only answer.

Uplighting, utilized carefully, can work. Once again, fixture location and aiming angle represent the key to successful uplighting. Locating fixtures close to a sculpture means that the aiming angle will be narrow. This creates strong, extended shadows that negatively affect the sculpture's appearance. Locating fixtures away from the sculpture minimizes awkward shadows.

Locate uplight fixtures away from areas where maintenance staff or visitors could knock them out of adjustment. Below-grade fixtures best ensure permanence of fixture aim. All types of uplight fixtures require mainte-

Figure 16.3. *Artistic highlighting of this monkey accents its face and does not create disturbing shadows. Adding uplight behind the sculpture breaks the rule that the sculpture should be brightest. It makes the background become part of the sculpture itself. Lighting Design & Photograph: Janet Lennox Moyer.*

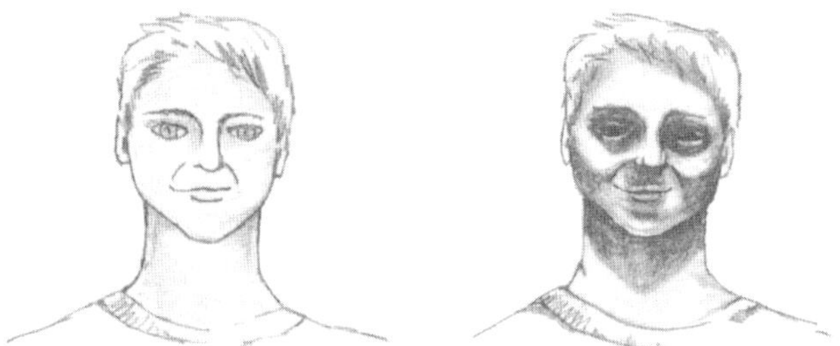

Figure 16.4. *Effect of light from the front or sides on a human face (left) versus light from above (right). Drawing: Lezlie Johannessen.*

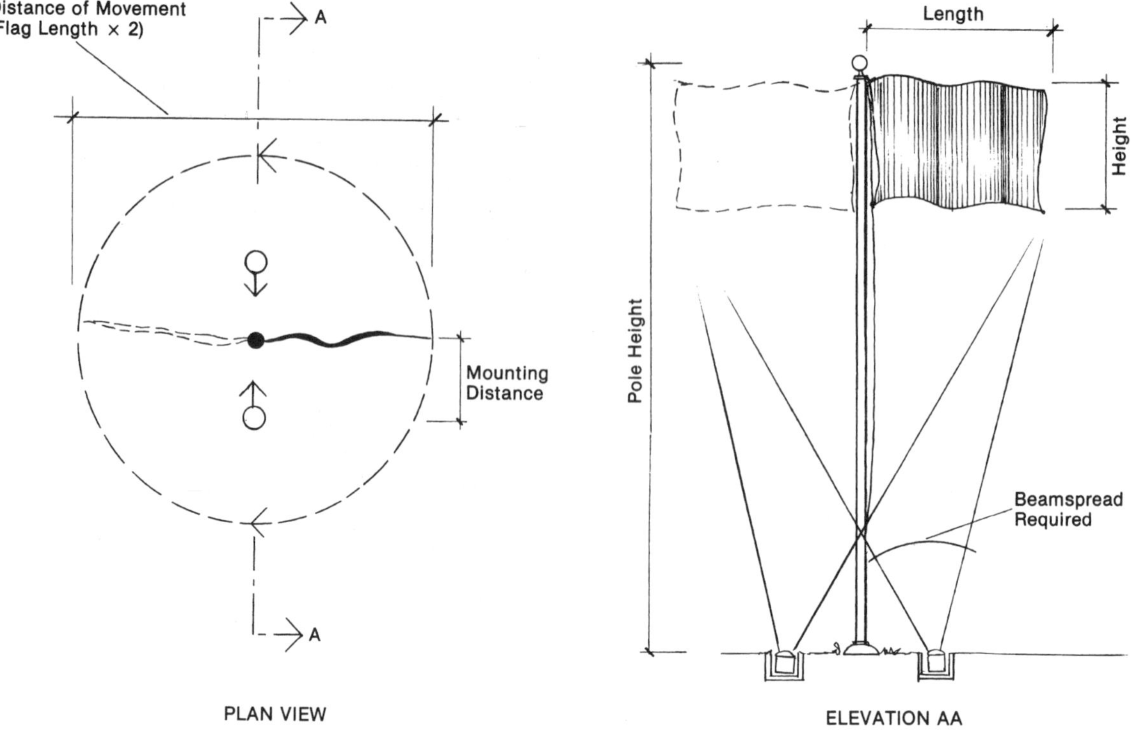

Figure 16.5. *Lighting flags (or moving sculptures) requires selecting a lamp beamspread and fixture location that will light the entire area the flag or sculpture covers. Drawing: Lezlie Johannessen.*

Figure 16.6. *Sculptures situated throughout this backyard garden are treated with similar but varying brightness levels. To visually connect all the sculptures in this asymmetrically balanced setting, foliage throughout the garden is lit within reasonable contrast range. Lighting Design: Janet Lennox Moyer, Michael Stewart Hooker, & Paul Schreer; Photograph: Kenneth Rice Photography, www.kenricephoto.com.*

nance to keep them clear of debris collecting on the lens that interrupts or eliminates the light from reaching the sculpture.

Some sculptures or other feature elements move through mechanical means, timed controls, or with wind conditions. The lighting must work for the *overall* shape and size. For example, consider a flag (see Figure 16.5). It moves both vertically and horizontally with the wind. Determine the overall width, height, and the area the flag can cover. Then plan the lamp wattage and beamspread, fixture quantity, and fixture locations.

The two brushed aluminum sculptures in Figure 16.6 move. The four pieces on the left sculpture rotate in a circle and the two pieces on the right rotate to the left and right. MR16 adjustable fixtures were located on the deck structure for the left sculpture and recessed into the deck floor for the right sculpture.

A mock-up of the lighting concept for a sculpture ensures that the lighting will enhance the sculpture's appearance rather than harming or distorting it. Testing fixture location(s) around the sculpture ensures achieving the best effect. If the sculpture is not available or has not yet been selected, provide a conduit stub at the intended location and wait to determine the actual lighting until the sculpture is on site.

Locations and quantity of fixtures required may be a surprise. When it seems logical that more than one fixture would be needed, one fixture may do the job. In some cases, fixture location may be severely restricted or the optimum location may not be available. When this occurs, fixture location availability may direct the lighting approach.

For example, a series of dog fountain sculptures stand at the edge of a swimming pool (see Figure 3.7). Locating fixtures to light them created a problem. The pool bottom was too far away to use as a mounting location and the dogs sat too far to the front of the alcove to recess an uplight in front of them. This left the alcove walls as a mounting location. The fixture had to be submersible in case the area flooded, and small enough to fit into the narrow wall area. Pool niche fixtures mounted on each side of the alcove show both the texture and shape of the dogs' bodies (see Figure 16.7). Each uses a 20-watt MR16 flood lamp, well below the manufacturer's recommended maximum 75-watt lamp. By using a low-wattage lamp, air cooling provides enough heat dissipation to allow the fixture to operate out of water. Even at 20 watts, with the fixtures so close to the sculpture, 50 percent dimming was needed to balance the lighting effect with the rest of the landscape lighting. Therefore, these fixtures dim separately. Use of niche lights in this manner required special approval from the local inspectors.

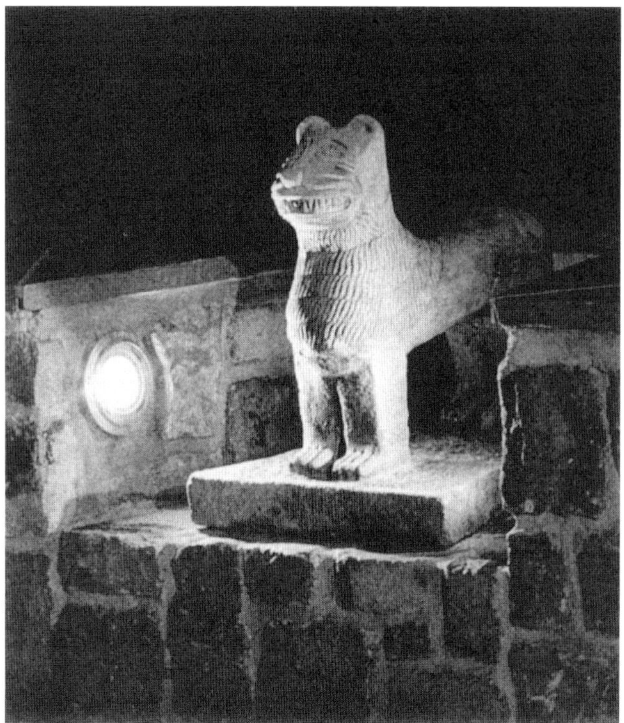

Figure 16.7. *Close-up of pool niche fixtures used to light dog fountain sculpture at the edge of a swimming pool. Lighting Design: Janet Lennox Moyer; Photograph: Kenneth Rice Photography, www.kenricephoto.com.*

Techniques

Techniques for lighting sculptures vary with every piece. Typically, this lighting will be an artistic interpretation of the sculpture. In deciding how to use light on a sculpture, remember these issues discussed previously:

- The features and characteristics of the sculpture, including shape, detailing, texture, material qualities, and color
- The sculpture's setting and how it relates to the rest of the composition

Then consider *viewing direction.* The sculpture has been placed for viewing from one or more specific angles or directions. With one viewing direction, the lighting need only address the side or sides seen from that view, but with several viewing directions, more of the sculpture needs attention to show it from all angles.

One Viewing Direction

One viewing direction typically eliminates potential fixture glare, as the fixtures are aimed away from the viewer. When visitors will walk between the fixtures and sculpture, glare remains an issue. Glare can occur

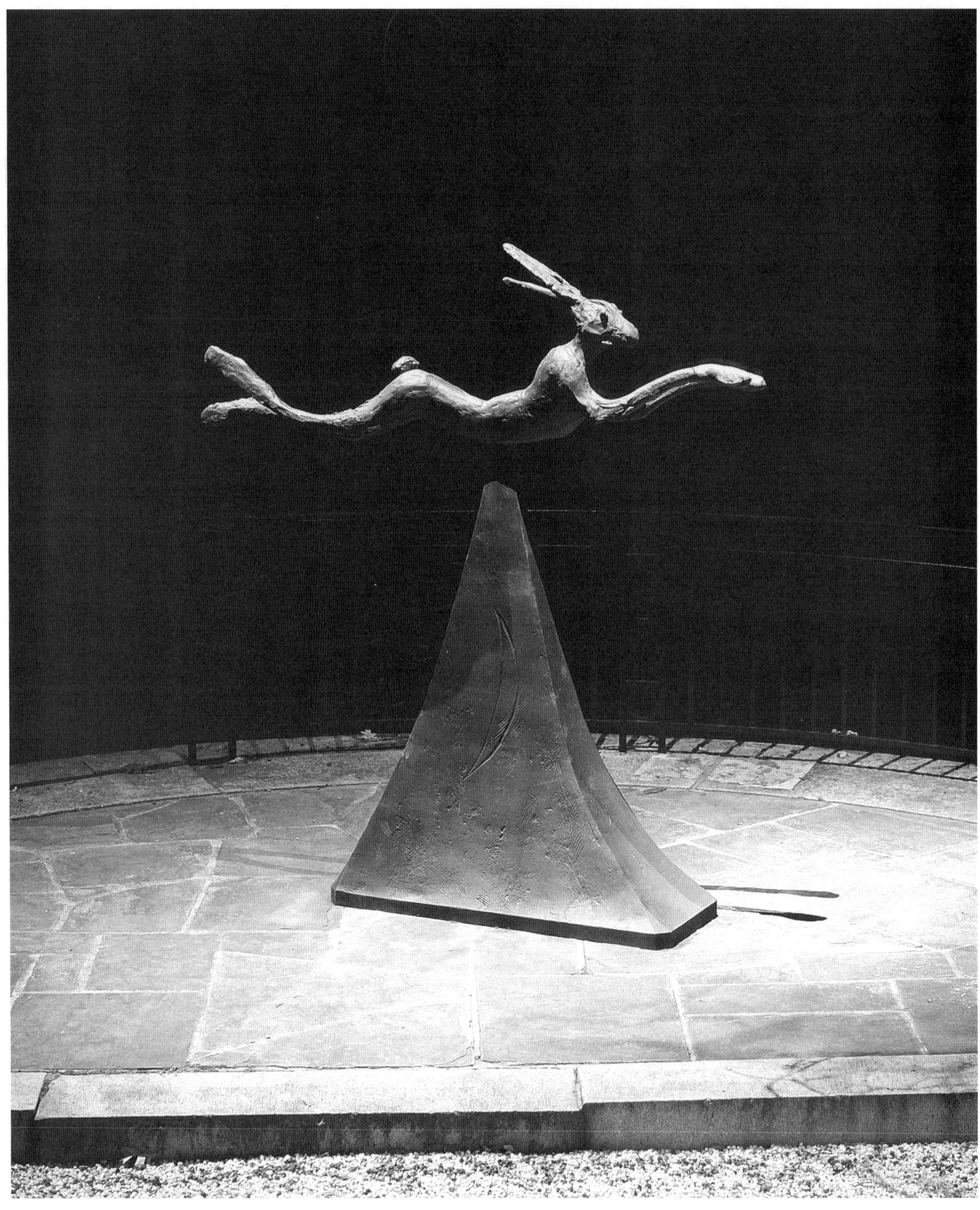

Figure 16.8. *As the main view of this sculpture is from rooms situated above, two downlights carefully placed in an adjacent, overhanging tree reveal and reinforce the lines of this sculpture. One fixture aims onto the face from the front while the other aims onto the tail from the rear. Spill light from the two 50-watt narrow spot lamps spills over onto the patio, providing context around the sculpture. Lighting Design: Janet Lennox Moyer; Photograph: Kenneth Rice Photography—www.kenricephoto.com.*

with ground-recessed uplights that either lack lamp shielding devices, such as louvers, or do not recess the lamp deeply enough into the housing. With downlights or stake-mounted uplights, aiming angle and lamp shielding determine whether glare will be a problem.

Typically, with one viewing direction, the back of the sculpture does not require lighting, since it will not be seen. When the sculpture has a wall or shrubbery immediately behind it or in the distance, consider lighting this surface to provide depth to the scene and a backdrop for the sculpture (see Figure 16.3).

The appropriate technique to select depends on the artistic impression desired and characteristics of the sculpture. With enough space to move away from the sculpture, one fixture centered on the sculpture with a flood distribution lamp washes the entire sculpture. This minimizes the quantity of fixtures, and therefore the cost, but does not emphasize specific parts or features. It shows detail but not texture or three dimensions. The distance depends on the size of the sculpture and the beamspread of the lamp (see Figure 16.9A).

One fixture located to the side shining across the sculpture emphasizes texture and highlights the closest side (see Figure 16.9B). Two fixtures spaced equally to the side from the center and aiming directly at the sculpture render a human or animal figure most naturally. This technique works with most sculptures. A variation of this technique would be to use a higher-wattage lamp or narrower beamspread on one side for additional emphasis or increased three-dimensionality (see Figure 16.9C).

Combining a side graze with a front wash emphasizes one side of the sculpture. The side light brings out texture on that side, while the wash fills in the rest of the form (see Figure 16.9D). Adding light on the background with any of these techniques shows depth and provides a visual backdrop for the sculpture (see Figure 16.9E).

Multiple Viewing Directions

Lighting becomes more difficult with multiple viewing directions because people either move around the sculpture or look at it from varying locations. This makes fixture location, aiming angle, and lamp shielding critical to ensure that the viewer will not be distracted from enjoying the sculpture because of fixture glare.

At the same time, multiple viewing angles open up a wider range of artistic options for rendering a sculpture. For example, rather than balancing light evenly around the sculpture, the designer may want to create different appearances as the viewer looks from various locations. From some viewing directions, the lighting designer may want to show just a glimpse of the sculpture—a halo outlining the shape—while highlighting the form from another viewing angle.

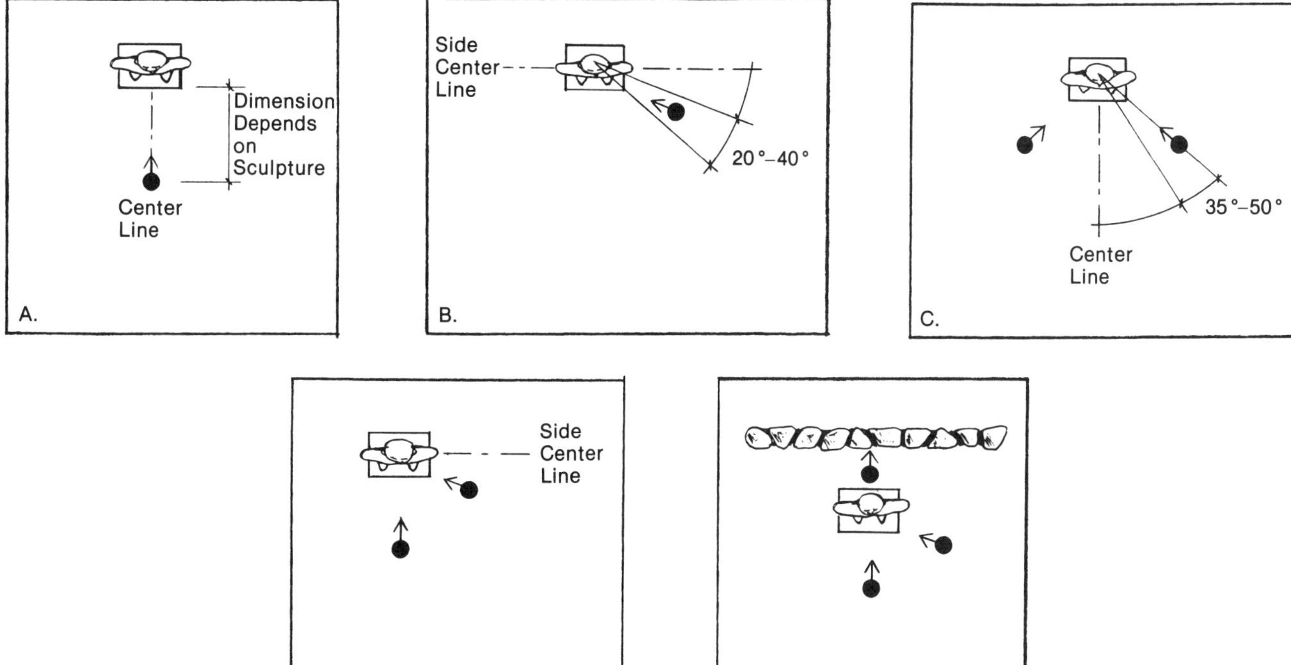

Figure 16.9. *Sculpture lighting techniques for a single viewing direction. Drawing: Lezlie Johannessen.*

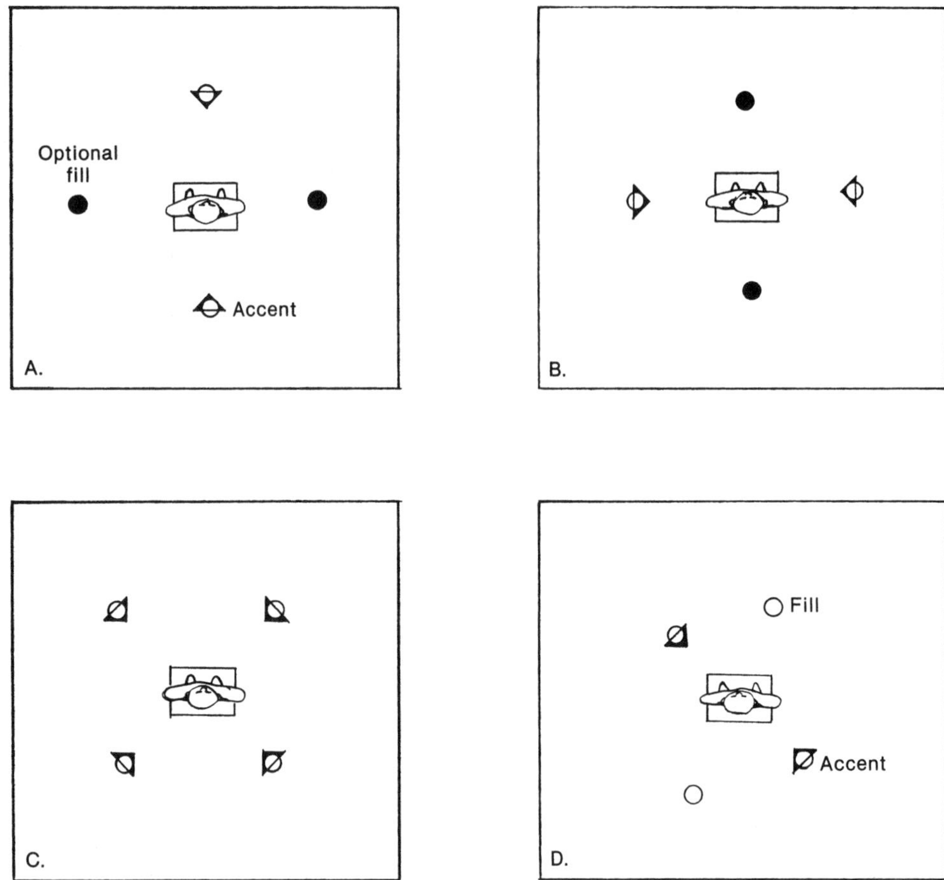

Figure 16.10. Sculpture lighting techniques for multiple viewing directions. Drawing: Lezlie Johannessen.

Depending on the desired effect, fixtures may need to encircle the sculpture, or a minimum number of fixtures may need to be located at various points to present the sculpture from specific view locations. Leaving part of the sculpture unlit can either surprise the viewer when the sculpture appears from another viewing direction or provide a silhouette from one or more viewing directions. (Like all silhouette lighting, this requires lighting a surface beyond the sculpture.) When not lighting the full shape of a sculpture, use caution, as the appearance can easily become distorted.

Figure 16.10 shows some basic techniques for full modeling of a sculpture. Accent uplights located at the front and back of a sculpture emphasize form and detail. Optional fill lights can be added at the remaining sides to soften brightness contrast and show overall shape (see Figure 16.10A). Shifting the location of the accent lights and the fill lights changes what will be emphasized. The shape, detailing, texture, and color of the sculpture guide the placement of accent versus fill light fixtures (see Figure 16.10B). Four accent lights, evenly spaced around the sculpture, provide balanced highlighting. Emphasis can still be provided to one or more sides of a sculpture using this technique by changing the lamp wattage from one fixture to another (see Figure 16.10C). Two accent fixtures placed close to the sculpture on opposite sides will emphasize shape or outline. These fixtures use either high wattage or a narrow beamspread for emphasis. The remaining two fixtures, located farther away, use lower-wattage flood distribution lamps to wash the overall shape softly (see Figure 16.10D).

ARCHITECTURAL STRUCTURES

The lighting approach for structures depends on the intended use of the structure and its visual importance in the composition. Structures without function can be approached as sculptures, providing realistic or interpretive artistic effects. Structures with functions need to address any required task lighting as well as safety and security, along with artistic effects. Always keep the users in mind. Lighting for a retirement community needs a higher, more even light level and less brightness contrast from one area to another. Resorts, parks, plazas, and other more public spaces can use higher brightness contrast to make a memorable statement or to create excitement.

When the idea of highlighting the structure as a sculpture is appropriate, use sculpture lighting techniques. Selecting one element of a structure to highlight can be effective. The construction detailing may be interesting (see Color Plate 60); a vine growing on a trellis, the rhythm of several posts in an arbor (see Color Plate 4), or an arch may be features to highlight (see Figure 16.16).

Lighting structures may require several light layers, essentially treating it as a mini-composition within the site. The main winery building for the Far Niente Winery in the Napa Valley (Color Plate 60) and the Chapel at the Oakwood Cemetery in Troy, New York (Color Plate 65) illustrate integrating the building into the overall site composition versus having the structure stand alone as a focal point. For the Far Niente main winery building, the main elevations are washed with high-pressure sodium lighting and incandescent fixtures are tucked into the eaves to highlight the dormers. The lighting level is balanced with the wall below and contrasts with the surrounding foliage to separate it as a focal point. For the chapel, a combination of low-voltage and standard-voltage incandescent sources graze the stone elevations at key areas and with varying levels to bring out the three-dimensional form of

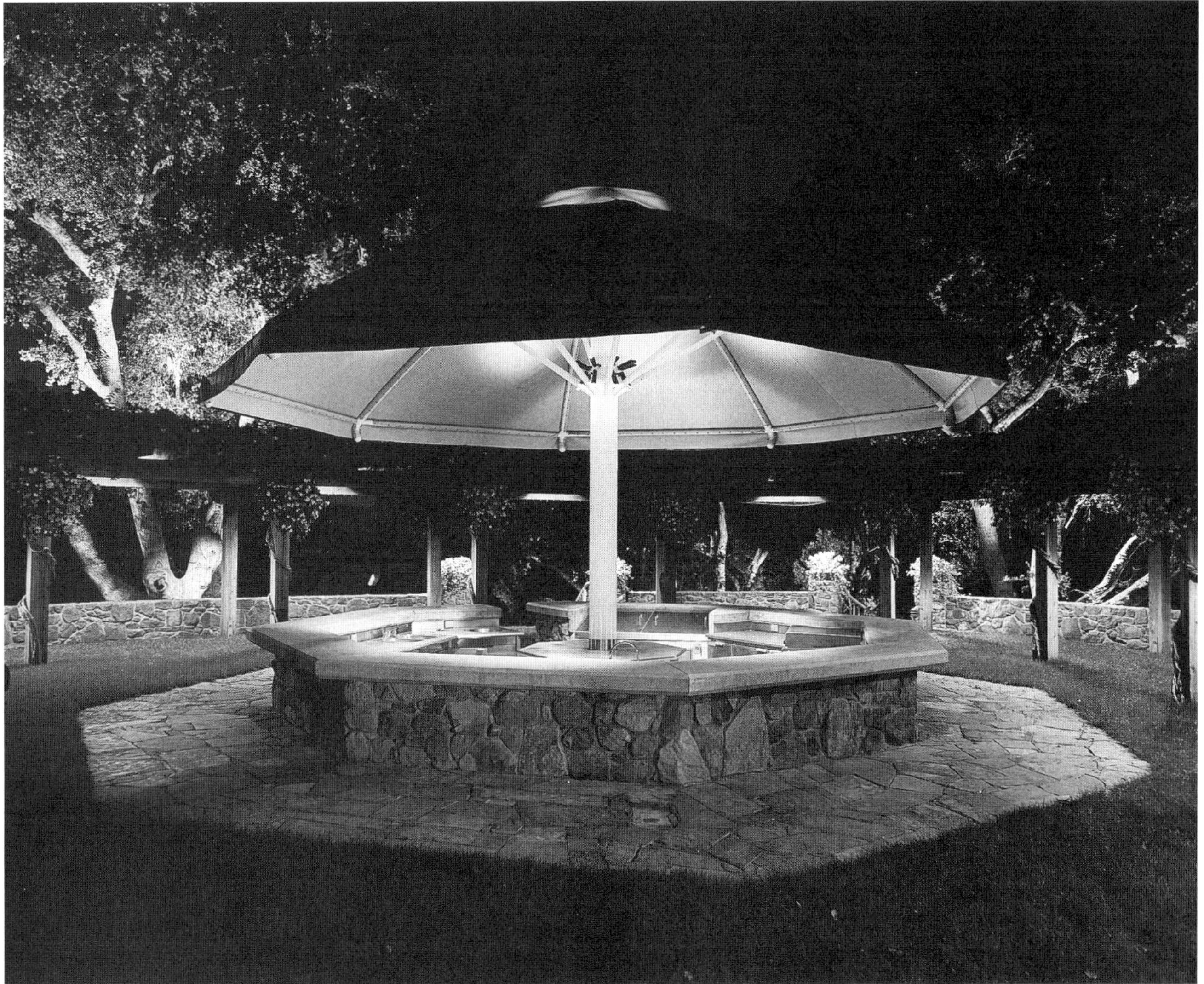

Figure 16.11. *A combination of up- and downlight low-voltage fixtures replaced large existing 120-volt fixtures. Using smaller fixtures made it possible to provide uplighting into the underside of the umbrella, while the concentrated light distribution of the downlights provided better task lighting at the work and serving portions of the counter. Lighting Design: Janet Lennox Moyer, Michael Stewart Hooker, & Paul Schreer; Photograph: Kenneth Rice Photography, www.kenricephoto.com.*

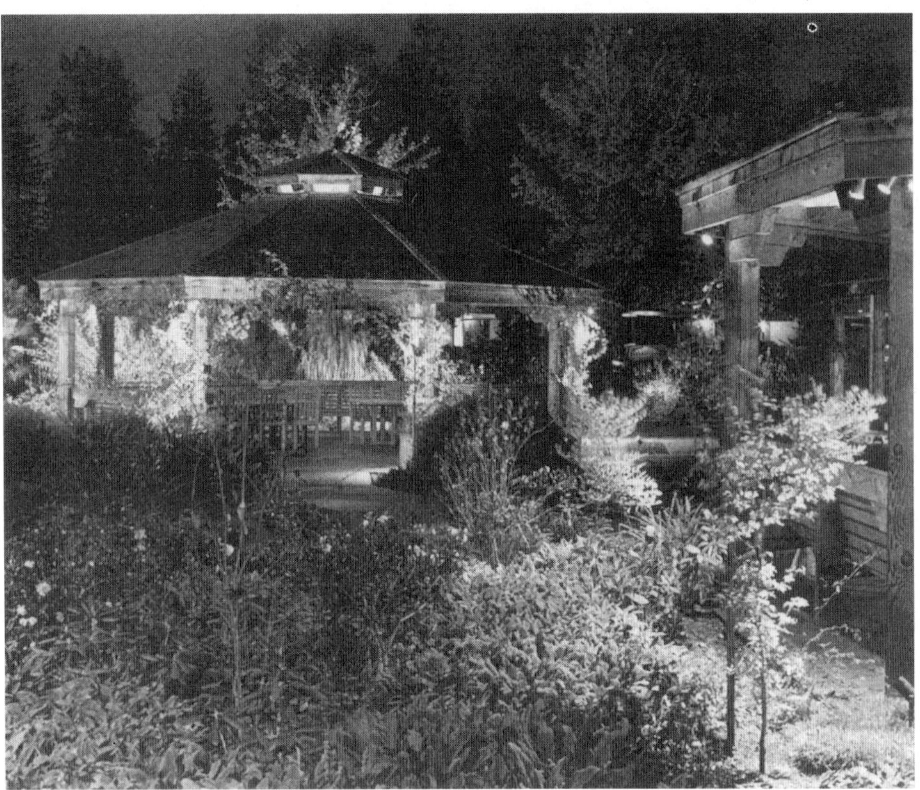

Figure 16.12. *Low-voltage incandescent adjustable fixtures with a variety of MR16 lamps, tucked under the eaves of the gazebos, highlight the plantings and accentuate the gazebos' position around the main lawn. Fluorescent uplight brackets mounted in coves inside the structure uplight the ceiling and provide a soft, nonglaring ambient light level inside the gazebos. Surface-mounted low-voltage fixtures with R14 flood lamps located in the topknot softly graze the rooflines. Stake-mounted low-voltage adjustable uplights, with MR16 lamps, highlight the vines growing up the pavilion posts. Lighting Design: Janet Lennox Moyer; Landscape Design: Michael Barclay; Photograph: Kenneth Rice Photography, www.kenricephoto.com.*

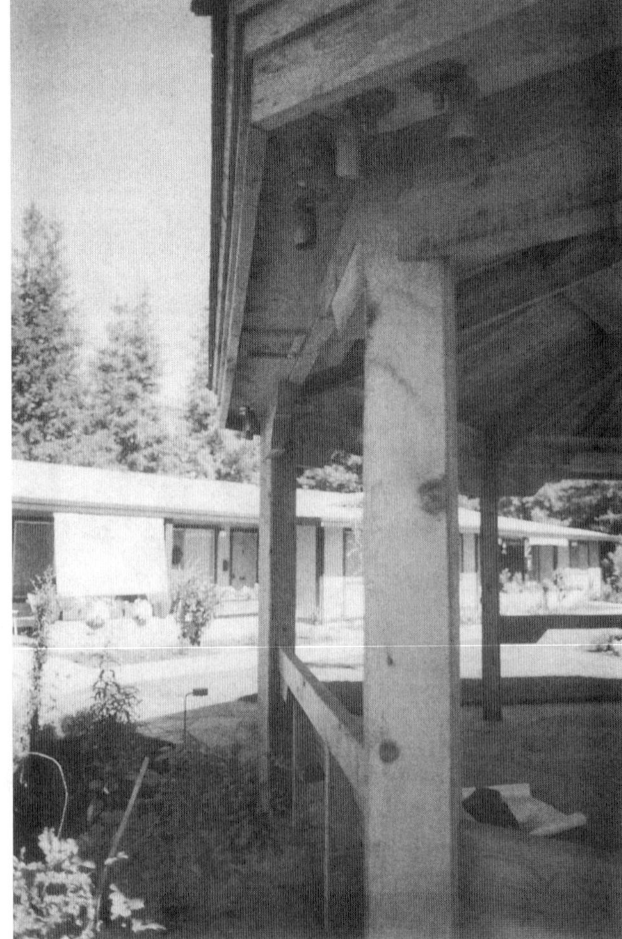

Figure 16.13. *Close-up view of one of the pavilions at a California senior-citizen complex developed by John P. Boswell shows the four adjustable MR16 fixtures painted to match the structure. Accessible by a hatch cut into the soffit, all the wiring and mounting hardware was recessed into a raceway above the ceiling (see Figure 16.14D). Lighting Design & Photograph: Janet Lennox Moyer.*

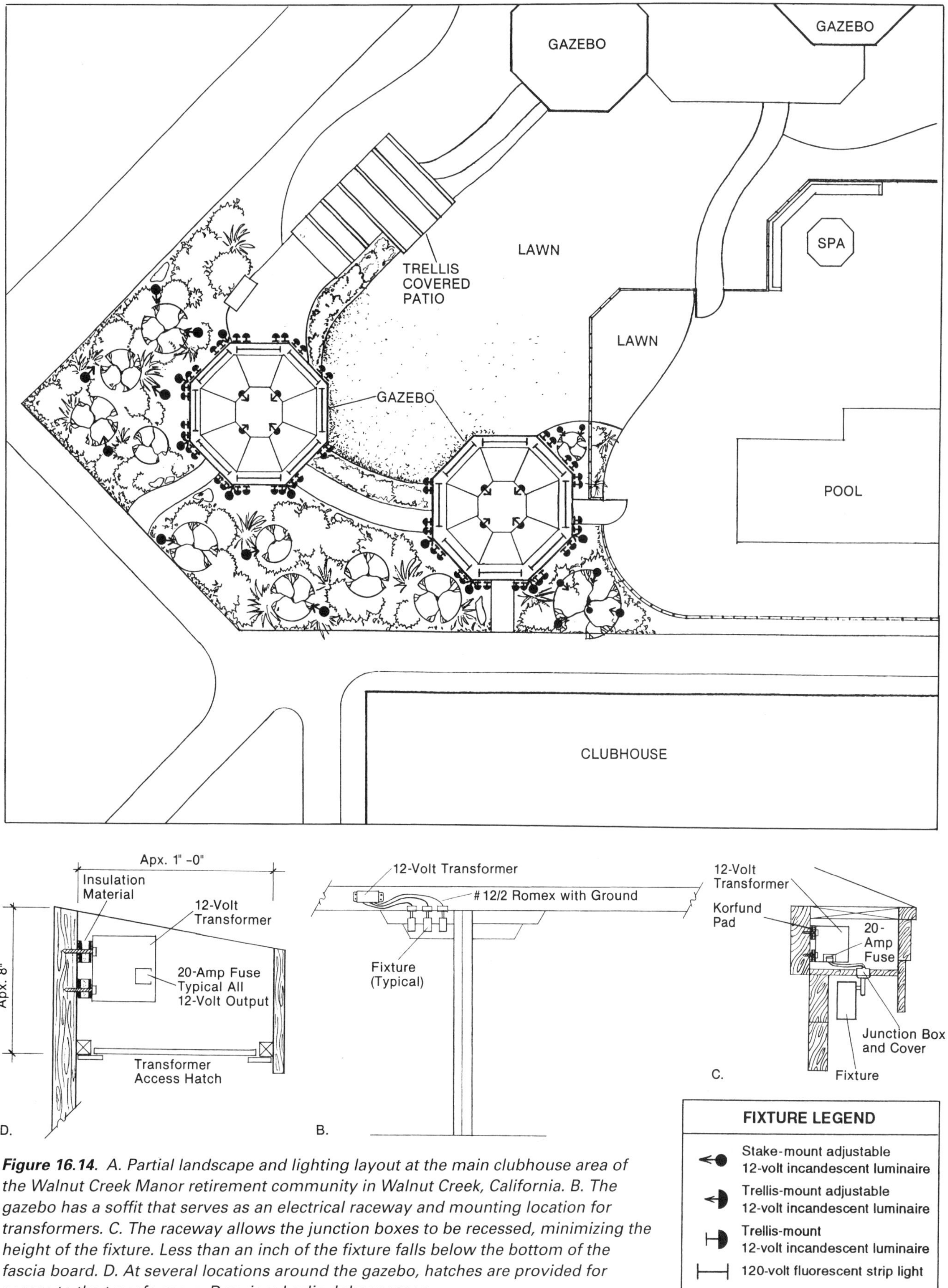

Figure 16.14. *A. Partial landscape and lighting layout at the main clubhouse area of the Walnut Creek Manor retirement community in Walnut Creek, California. B. The gazebo has a soffit that serves as an electrical raceway and mounting location for transformers. C. The raceway allows the junction boxes to be recessed, minimizing the height of the fixture. Less than an inch of the fixture falls below the bottom of the fascia board. D. At several locations around the gazebo, hatches are provided for access to the transformers. Drawing: Lezlie Johannessen.*

Figure 16.15. *This shade trellis over a patio in a Los Altos Hills, California, landscape houses low-voltage fixtures recessed into the steel structure (3-inch by 8-inch beam). The 20-watt R14 flood lamps provide soft downlight for the patio area. Lighting Design: Janet Lennox Moyer; Landscape Design: Emery Rogers and Associates; Photograph: Kenneth Rice Photography, www.kenricephoto.com.*

Figure 16.16. *The owner of this trellis prizes the red roses growing on it. The contrast of the deep red blooms against the white structure makes a strong statement. Located on each side of the path, ground-recessed fixtures using 20-watt MR16 lamps uplight the flowers and accentuate the inside of the structure. Lighting Design: Janet Lennox Moyer; Photograph: © 1990, Douglas A. Salin, www.dougsalin.com.*

Figure 16.17. *MR11 downlights tucked in between pairs of rafter tails at this front porch provide the soft general lighting on the deck. The fixtures are located and aimed to provide spill light over the edge of the deck to make the grade change apparent. Additional downlights are located at the roofline to highlight the native willow shrub at the end of the deck. The sconces are primarily decorative, but graze the stone showing its texture. Lighting Design: Janet Lennox Moyer; Photograph: Kenneth Rice Photography, www.kenricephoto.com.*

the building. Soft washes fill in various roof planes completing the form and strong punches of light accentuate architectural details. Metal halide sources highlight the Tiffany windows to provide a glow from inside the chapel.

People approach both these structures from a number of angles. The lighting of structures needs to take all the approaches and viewing angles into account to present a complete and intriguing view from all possible directions. The designer can use light to direct the viewer's eye or movement through the landscape (see Color Plates 59 & 60).

In large commercial projects with multiple structures, lighting the structures uniformly creates continuity. To draw attention to one structure out of a group of structures or to respond to differences from one structure to another, vary the lighting approach slightly.

Lighting structures does not necessarily mean using accent lighting. One approach concentrates light on areas surrounding the structure (see Figures 16.12 &

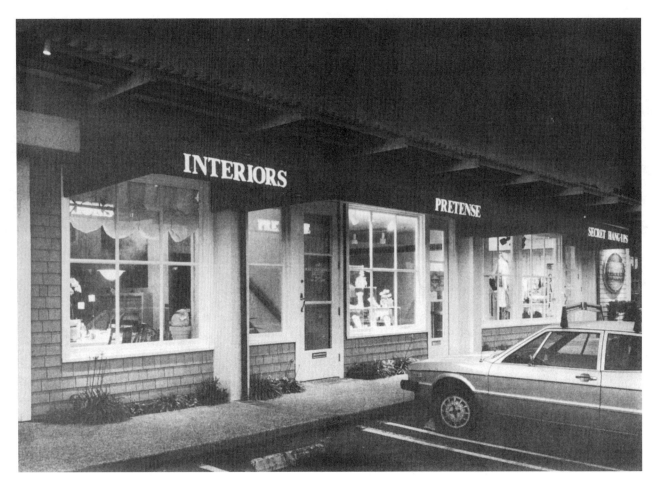

Figure 16.18. Sign lighting at this shopping center backlights the translucent letters with low-voltage miniature lamps in an extruded housing built into the awnings. Low-voltage MR16 adjustable fixtures with linear spread lenses wash the sidewalk. Lighting Design: Janet Lennox Moyer; Photograph: © 1990, Douglas A. Salin, www.dougsalin.com.

Figure 16.19. *Looking up into the awning shows how a custom bracket attaches the fixture extrusion to the awning structure. The 1½-inch size of the extrusion easily integrates into the awning both in style and scale. Lighting Design: Janet Lennox Moyer; Photograph: © 1990, Douglas A. Salin, www.dougsalin.com.*

16.13). At a retirement community in Walnut Creek, California, several gazebos line a main lawn and pool area. In some cases, combining some accent lighting on the surroundings and some on the structures makes sense. The size and scale of the gazebos maintain their presence in the night composition. The lighting focuses on the landscape surrounding the structures.

When lighting glass structures, for example, such as a commercial entry or atrium, lighting the structure internally creates a strong effect (see Figure 18.6). The visual effect treats the structure like a sculpture, while the internal lighting responds to functional needs of the plant or human inhabitants. To create a less dramatic effect and to tie the structure to the environment, light the structure's surroundings (see Figure 14.2).

The structure can also serve as a mounting location for fixtures lighting surrounding paths, plantings, sculptures, or seating areas. Recessing fixtures into an arbor, trellis, or overhang of a pavilion provides light while hiding the equipment (see Figures 16.11, 16.15, & 16.17). In this case, select architectural fixtures with either a damp- or wet-location label, as appropriate (see Chapter 7). More finesse is required to integrate equipment when attaching fixtures to a structure (see Figures 16.18 & 16.19).

Coordinate with the landscape architect during conceptual design to provide room in the structure for wiring raceways, electrical equipment (including junction boxes, ballasts, or transformers, time clock, photocells, motion detectors), and anything that will be required for the proposed lighting design. Removing as much electrical equipment from sight as possible improves the appearance of the structure (see Figures 16.13 & 16.14).

Consider all the technical details of recessing this equipment. Inform the landscape architect of the size of the equipment. The NEC requires specific dimensions surrounding equipment for access. Some equipment (transformers and ballasts) needs a specific amount of surrounding space to dissipate heat. In some cases ventilation holes or fans for cooling may need to be included in structures where equipment will be located. Provide the landscape architect with a clear picture of the appearance of all auxiliary equipment and how it should be laid out as early in the project as possible. This helps in planning the size and location of equipment rooms. Remember that there will be other team members requiring space for equipment (mechanical, irrigation, audio, pool or fountain, etc.). Providing information to the right people regarding equipment needs is as important as gathering information about the project.

Using fixtures as a decorative element on a structure requires balancing scale and style. The fixture should both look appropriate by day and work at night. When selecting fixtures, keep the following in mind:

- Choose the appropriate type of fixture to complement the project style.
- Make sure that the size of the fixture works with the scale of the structure.
- Select a location where the fixture will provide the needed light at night and fit in logically as an element in the daytime composition.
- Determine the mounting location carefully. A few inches in mounting height or width can have a large effect on the daytime appearance of a wall, gate, or fence. The fixture should relate to people, not just to the architecture. Too often, wall-mounted fixtures are located high on the building, relating to an architectural detail rather than to people.
- Consider the pattern of light and shadow the fixture produces on adjacent surfaces.
- Choose the wattage and beamspread of the lamp to integrate with the overall lighting composition.

Refer to Chapter 6 for fixture-type issues. Careful coordination of fixture appearance enhances the overall effect of the landscape.

SIGNAGE

In commercial projects, the lighting of signs may be important to business. Lighted signs attract attention to a store or shopping center. The type of sign lighting provides information about the quality of the shopping center or store. Three sign lighting types are luminous letter, luminous background, and externally lighted signs. Typically, large, bright signs screaming for attention reflect lesser quality. Understated lighting represents higher quality. Moving signs attract attention quickly. To produce predictable results, follow the Illuminating Engineering Society's recommended procedures published in the *IES Lighting Handbook*[1] and see the Bibliography for other sources.

Consider how the signs will be viewed. Some will be seen by motorists as they travel along a street at 25 mph or on a freeway at 55 mph. Others will be seen by pedestrians. The way a sign is meant to be seen influences the required light level. The ambient light level surrounding the sign also affects how much light will be needed. As with all lighting elements, reflectance characteristics of the sign guide wattage selection. Choose light sources compatible with the sign in light output, color, and distribution. Many municipalities limit the type of light source that can be used (for example, no bare neon) or the level of luminance at the sign. Check state and local codes.

A conscious decision needs to be made about the appearance of lighting equipment at the site. Often bare-lamp floodlights are stuck onto a structure or nearby ground. The appearance of these lights in daylight is unsightly. Integrating the lighting fixture equipment into the structure of the sign or into a planned site detail (monument or bollard, for example) presents a more professional, aesthetically pleasing appearance (see Figures 16.18 & 16.19).

Vandalism and maintenance are two other important issues to consider in sign lighting design. The type and quality of materials need to fit the type of installation. Construction techniques need to ensure protection while allowing access for maintenance. Select an efficient light source with long life when the sign will be difficult to maintain due to location (on a roof, above a roadway) or accessibility (when tools are required to disassemble the fixture to relamp).

Each class of objects—sculptures, structures, and signs—plays a specific role in a landscape. The lighting of these elements at night needs to respond to all their visual needs. Make sure that task lighting has been addressed, as well as the appearance of the object in context with the rest of the landscape. Remember that not all elements in a landscape need to be lit at night. Carefully plan which of these elements should be lit and at what level as part of the overall composition.

REFERENCE

1. John E. Kaufman, Ed. *IES Lighting Handbook, Application Volume,* Illuminating Engineering Society of North America, New York, 1987, pp. 17–1 through 17–13.

17

Walkways and Stairs

Walkways and stairs provide a path for movement through a landscape. For the landscape to be usable at night, these paths need to have lighting. This chapter will address issues the lighting designer should consider when planning walkway and stair lighting in order to integrate this element into the overall landscape. The chapter is divided into three main sections: "Walkways," "City Streets and Sidewalks," and "Steps and Staircases." The walkways section covers all the planning issues related to lighting most path types. The portion on city streets and sidewalks discusses specific issues necessary to consider in order to integrate walkways with the street lighting that may be existing or planned by others, and which is often regulated by city ordinances. The section on stairs looks at specific issues relating to lighting walks when there is a change in elevation in a site.

WALKWAYS

Lighting walkways requires understanding the various types of traffic routes that can occur in a landscape. Landscape architects establish a hierarchy of pedestrian walkways during the conceptual design phase of a landscape project based on function and design intent. Walks that have more importance—such as the main route from one destination to another—receive more attention (richer materials and more or higher-quality benches, for example) and a stronger presence in the site (wider surface with a more direct route, for example). Basic walkway types include:

- *Pathway.* A narrow, often meandering walk meant for enjoying the company of friends and the landscape. It is used in both residential projects and large parks.
- *Walkway.* A narrow to medium route from a sidewalk to a building entry. Often, this will be wider than paths but narrower than a sidewalk with richer materials or more interesting paving patterns.
- *Sidewalk.* A medium-width route generally alongside a street with simple pavement materials and details. The materials or paving pattern may change at intersections to provide distinction.
- *Promenade.* A wide public walk meant for leisurely strolls or ceremonial marches. It can flank a street or cross through a landscape. Materials will be of higher quality and paving patterns more intricate.
- *Esplanade.* Similar to a promenade, but typically edging a body of water.

Lighting designers should coordinate light level, fixture type, and lighting pattern with the type of walk. Since pathways have an informal function and layout, the lighting should follow suit. Introduce lower footcandle levels with smaller-scale fixtures (typically, at or below a person's height). While an even light distribution is always preferable, more informal types of walks can tolerate more variation. Sidewalks serve as main traffic routes in neighborhoods and downtown areas. They require higher, more evenly distributed light levels. The fixtures tend to be pole mounted at a height taller than a person with either a utilitarian or a decora-

Figure 17.1. *Downlighting from eaves and trees highlights plant material edging the path to this residence. Spill light from wide-beam lamps (38° to 50°) softly washes the walk itself. The highest light level located at the front door draws the visitor through the garden. To welcome guests, the brick wall just inside the gate entry has the second level of brightness. Lighting Design: Janet Lennox Moyer.*

Figure 17.2. *Comparing the before lighting with the new lighting (see Figure 17.1) illustrates the dramatic effect lighting can have in a landscape. Photograph: Janet Lennox Moyer.*

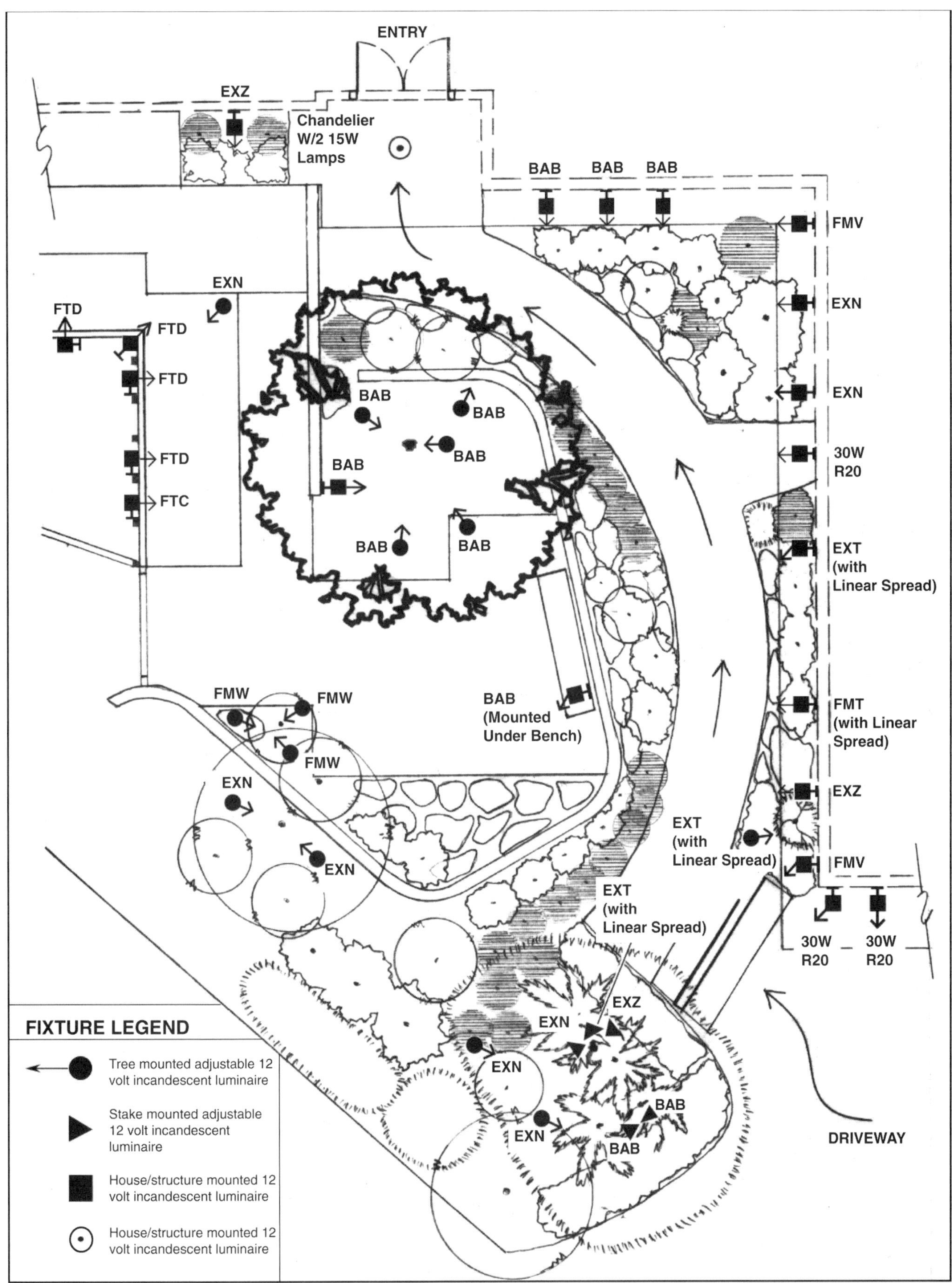

Figure 17.3. *Lighting Plan. Drawing: Lezlie Johannessen*

tive appearance based on location and budget. Promenades and esplanades need higher, more even light levels, with distinctive, often decorative fixtures meant to be a visual element in the overall landscape design.

Lighting for all types of pedestrian routes requires providing good visibility on the path surface, but the lighting on the walk should not draw attention away from more interesting visual aspects of the landscape. In terms of brightness composition, the path or walk seldom has the highest brightness. Reserve accent levels for features such as sculptures, specimen trees, or doors (where a higher light level draws the visitor along the path toward the entry). Instead of a high light level, strive for even distribution on the path surface. Uneven distribution can hide obstacles, distort the walk surface, or confuse pedestrians, causing them to concentrate on the path rather than looking at the beauty around them. People feel comfortable walking along a dimly lit path as long as they are surrounded by or walking toward a higher light level (see Figures 17.1 to 17.3).

Considerations for lighting walkways include the basic issues of safety, security, and aesthetics. Possible lighting approaches include everything from dappled lighting patterns, created as a by-product of lighting through trees or shrubs (see Figure 17.4), to simply meeting minimum footcandle standards established by city regulations. Pedestrian comfort is one goal. Reaching that goal, however, does not dictate that paths or sidewalks must have the brightest light level in a luminous composition. Make sure that the lighting layout unites needs with aesthetics. Walk areas need enough light so that pedestrians do not have to think consciously about the path. Holding the light level down so that the landscape layout, features in the landscape, or buildings and signs draw the viewer's attention presents a more successful composition.

Planning Issues

Some issues to consider in planning walkway lighting include:

- Footcandle level
- Safe movement
- Paving or path materials
- Light patterns
- Fixture selection

Lighting Level

The appropriate footcandle level varies based on location, amount of pedestrian and vehicular traffic, surrounding light levels, and governing laws. Think about the light levels of the general neighborhood. Street lighting varies from rural areas to city areas in both distribution and level. In cities, the street lighting level may vary from one area to another depending on respective activities. High light levels with even distribution are typically used for popular or important business streets, and lower levels for the less important industrial or residential sections. In rural or suburban areas light poles are often placed at street intersections, causing a spotty distribution. When planning walkway lighting in such areas, it is important to inspect the site at night, as one location can have a high ambient level from the street lighting, while another site will be quite dark.

Use the surrounding neighborhood as a cue to determine the appropriate base light level for a given project. In a residential area with a low ambient light level, provide a comparable light level for a project's paths in order to blend into the neighborhood. A front path exposed to street lighting may require a higher light level than a path in a private area. On public paths, as traffic increases, so should the light level.

No hard rules exist for the required footcandle levels (see Figures 2.3 & 2.5) of various walkway types or locations. For commercial sites, check state and local building and energy codes to determine minimum light level requirements. These codes can also include maximum acceptable levels and prescribe acceptable light sources. For residential sites, check the ambient light level from existing or planned street lighting. Footcandle levels for sidewalks vary from ¼ to 5 footcandles. With no street lighting in residential neighborhoods, the natural lighting from a full moon provides less than ¼ footcandle. Remember that brightness impression occurs due to both reflectance of the material and contrast from the lit area to the surround. To increase the *feeling* of safety, introduce light into adjacent areas rather than increasing the footcandle level on the path.

Figure 17.5 illustrates one way to assign light levels based on the importance of elements to the scene. In this diagram the sculpture (1) serves as the prime focal point and should have the brightest light level. Lighting the hedge (2) provides a visual boundary for the scene and adds depth. Fill light on the lawn (3) bridges the large brightness difference between the sculpture and the path. Remember also that people do not see footcandles. Notice how the footcandle levels do not relate directly to the 3:1 to 5:1 brightness ratio guideline. These ratios apply to footlamberts (reflected light). Multiplying the footcandle level by the reflectance of the surface (in percent) provides the footlamberts. In this example, both area 3, the lawn, and area 2, the hedge, can range in light level quite a bit. Both can actually have a higher footcandle level than the sculpture due to their low reflectance. The lawn (3) can be a lower level than the path (4) or a level between the path and the sculpture, depending on the designer's intent for the composition.

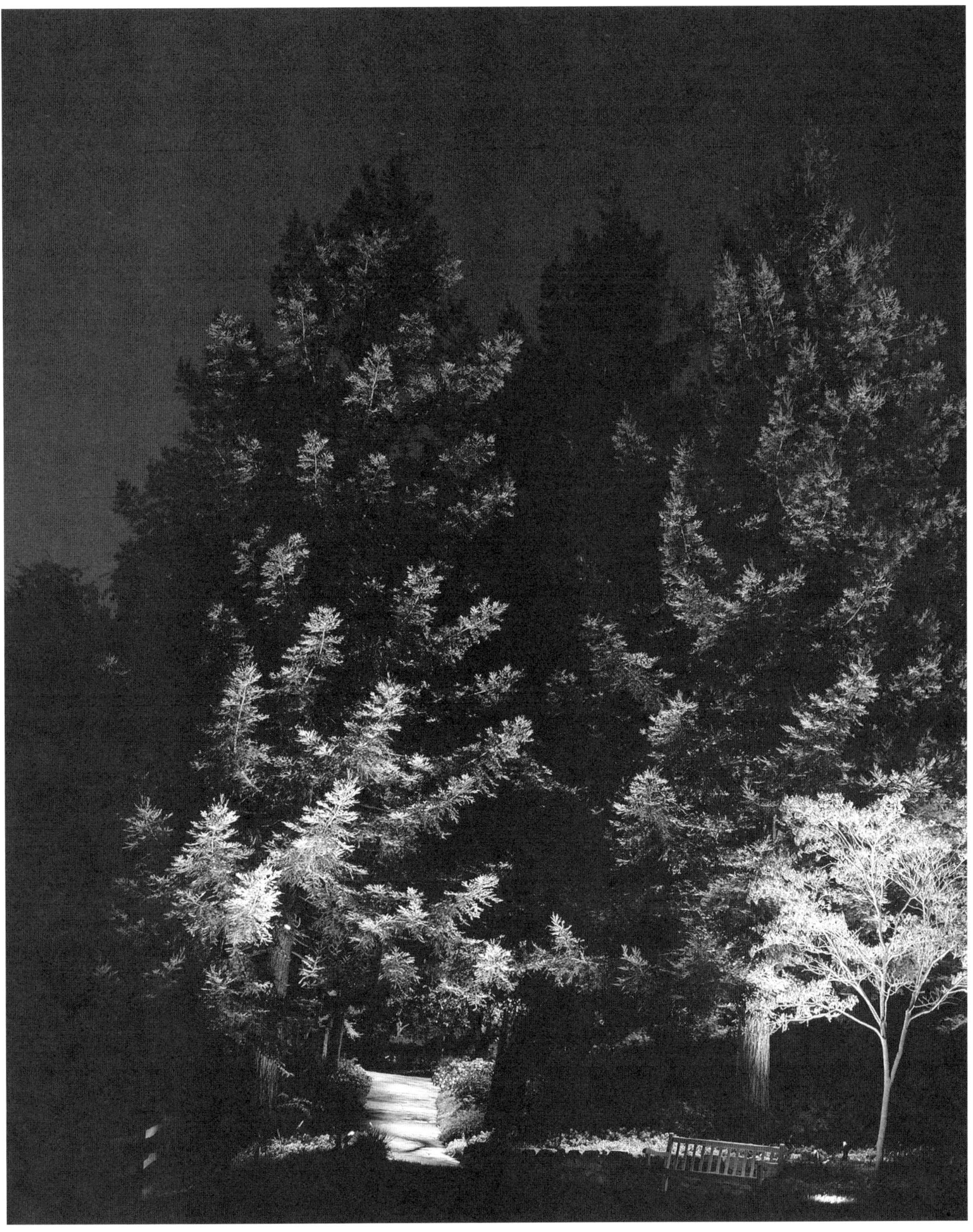

Figure 17.4. *Guests arriving at the Far Niente Vineyards for evening events get dropped off at this Redwood forest walk. Downlighting aimed onto the shrubbery creates filtered light patterns on these plantings and spills over onto the path. Lighting Design: Janet Lennox Moyer, Michael Stewart Hooker, & Paul Schreer; Photograph: Kenneth Rice Photography, www.kenricephoto.com.*

Safe Movement

People feel safe or comfortable when they see the area around them, including boundaries. To provide path lighting that ensures a clear view of the area that a person is about to enter, consider not only footcandle level and even distribution on the path but brightness balance from the path to the other surrounding landscape elements. Primarily a psychological concern, brightness contrast between areas can add either to the feeling of safety or to unease. Comfortable brightness ratios vary from 3:1 to 5:1. For example, if a path level is 1.0 footlambert, a lawn adjacent to it could be three to five times brighter (3.0 to 5.0 fl) or less bright (0.2 to 0.3 fl). A shift in brightness adds interest to a scene. For specific focal points, such as sculptures, provide additional brightness to draw attention—from a 10:1 ratio up to 100:1. Do not, however, use this high a contrast ratio on a focal area without a transition level between it and the walkway to soften the contrast.

Paving or Path Material

Pathway lighting considerations include both the materials used and the layout of the materials. Simple paths using a material with a high reflectance and little or no pattern—poured concrete, for example—can use a low light level. More complicated paths with darker materials—brick paths using multiple pieces in a pattern, for example—require a higher level. The need for a higher level stems partially from the added visual complication of the pattern and also due to the lower reflectance of the brick color.

In informal settings, pads of concrete or large, flat stones placed individually can be used as the pathway (see Figure 17.6). While a simple, effective, and inexpensive path, this type of path requires more attention from people in order to navigate it safely. In lighting such paths, several factors require attention. The shape limits the useful walking area, requiring the pedestrian to make sure that he or she stays in the middle of the pad or stone. The space between stones may be irregular or far enough to require a visual check to make sure that the pedestrian's foot lands on the next stone. If the pad or stone is not flush with the ground, this increases the risk of tripping. This type of path requires a higher light level for psychological comfort.

Two similar issues to consider are how evenly a path is laid and any grade change. When a brick or stone path has been laid unevenly intentionally or has shifted or heaved over time (due to frost, ground settling, or tree roots pushing the paving material), navigating the path safely becomes more difficult. The uneven quality of the walk needs to be identified with light. Additionally, when there is a change of elevation—one or more steps in a path—this requires visual identification. This does not necessarily mean increasing the light level, although that is an option. It does require introducing light in the area of the grade change to ensure that the shift is visible.

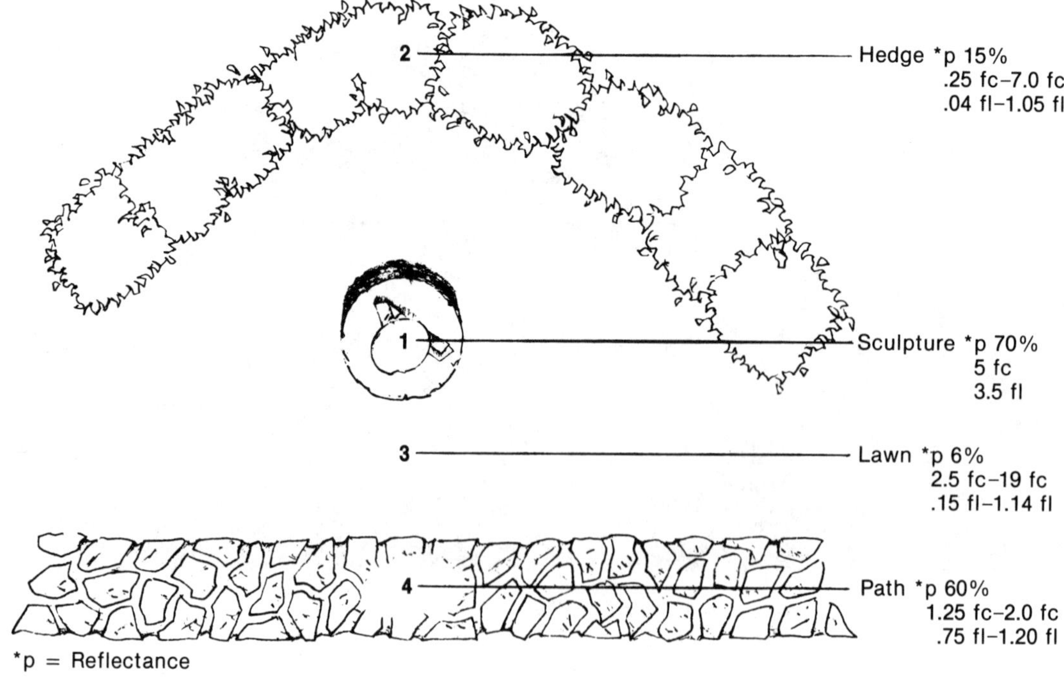

Figure 17.5. *Balancing brightness levels ensures the comfort of people walking on a path while showing important features of the landscape. Drawing: Lezlie Johannessen.*

Width of a path also makes a difference. Wider paths require less concentration on the part of the pedestrian and therefore a lower light level. On narrow paths, when the edge of a pathway is not clearly defined, a higher light level helps provide a view of the boundary.

Light Patterns

The best path lighting possible is an even distribution of light along the walk. Evenly distributed light along a path increases comfort and often presents a better appearance. Patterns of light and dark along a path can confuse visitors or hide potential obstacles along a path. Additionally, an even wash of light calls less attention to itself than does a pattern of light and shadow. Since a path usually does not represent the most interesting or important feature of a landscape, a lighting composition that does not draw attention to the path will be more successful than one that does. Remember that the eye is attracted to light and dark contrast, so circles of light separated by areas of darkness will cause people to concentrate—involuntarily and subconsciously—on the light pattern and therefore the path. An exception to this occurs when the pattern of light is consistently introduced along a path, such as shadow patterns from the moonlighting technique. In this case, the eye tends not to be as attracted to the contrast pattern.

Figure 17.6. This stone path from entry gate to home receives spill light directed onto surrounding plants. The unusual size and shape makes the path difficult to negotiate. Lighting Design & Photograph: Janet Lennox Moyer.

Ambient light level, age of viewers, and path function also influence whether a designer can use a *light pattern* along a walk. Properties that have a fairly high ambient light level surrounding the path can more easily tolerate light patterns on a walk. Remember that as the eye ages, contrast between light and dark becomes exaggerated. This means that paths especially planned for older people (at retirement communities, for example), or where a large portion of the anticipated visitors will be elder citizens, should have less light and less shadow contrast. Walks that are less heavily traveled or more informal (a dirt path through a woodland, for example, that is used mostly during the day) can tolerate a higher level of light and shadow contrast.

To produce even light along the path, the lamp beamspread must be known. Consider whether the fixture modifies the beamspread in any way. For example, does the fixture have a reflector that throws light forward or increases the lamp beamspread in more than one direction? The shape of the fixture can also limit the beam distribution of a lamp (see Figure 17.7).

Plan fixture spacing to overlap the beamspread from adjacent fixtures. This combines the lower light output at the edge of two fixtures' beamspreads to balance with the brighter light directly in front of the fixture (see Figure 17.7A). Generally, the eye detects a 4:1 ratio, so plan fixture placement to produce a light pattern within that range. This means that if there is 1.0 footlambert directly in front of a fixture, at the midpoint between two fixtures the level should not drop below 0.25 fl (of course, getting as close as possible to a 1:1 ratio is best). Calculation of brightness ratio provides a guideline, but best results will occur when fixture spacing is field-tested.

Fixtures placed on the same side of a pathway usually produce a more even spread of light than alternate fixtures on either side of the path. However, alternating sides of the path can work reasonably well when the lamp (or fixture and lamp) beamspread covers three-fourths of the width of the pathway and overlaps the next fixture's beamspread (see Figure 17.7B).

Locate fixtures on both sides of the path for wide paths (approximately 8 feet or more) and paths with heavy traffic or cross traffic. Again, even light provides the most comfortable environment (see Figure 17.7C). Additionally, spacing needs to be realistic. Do not expect a small-scale unobtrusive fixture with no optical control of the lamp to cover more than several feet of a pathway (see Figure 17.7D).

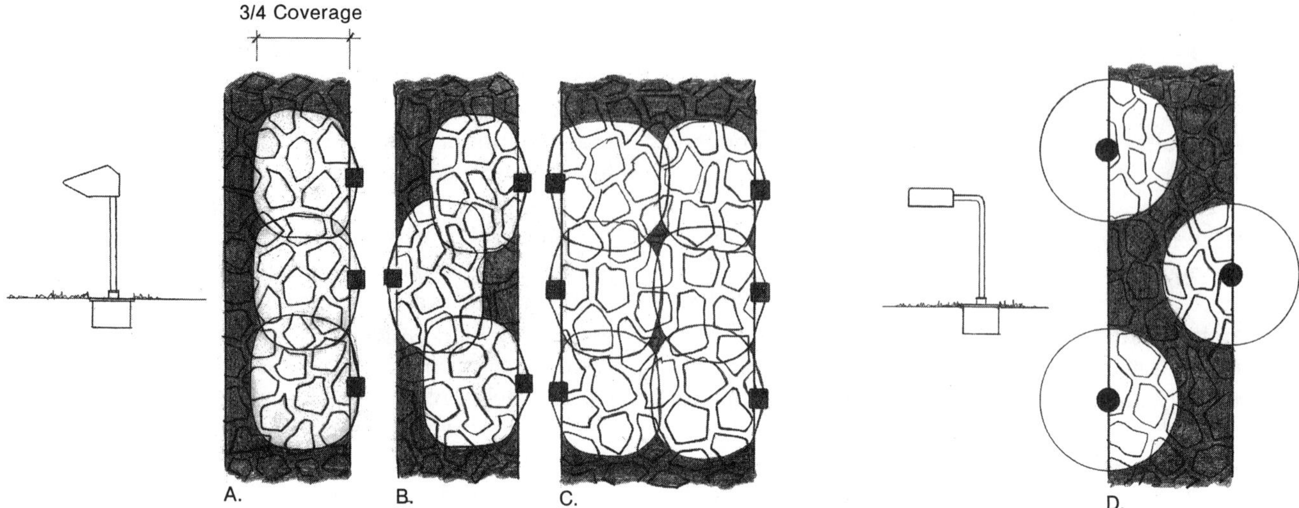

Figure 17.7. Fixture distribution determines spacing. A and C illustrate good coverage. B shows an effective use of alternating fixtures, while D illustrates the brightness imbalance problem normally encountered with alternating fixtures. Drawing: Lezlie Johannessen.

The manufacturer's literature should provide at least a graphic chart of beamspread distribution. Some fixture manufacturers provide candlepower distribution data, which can be used in computer or manual point-by-point calculations.

Fixture Selection

Fixtures can be divided into two basic types: those that serve as part of the decoration of the landscape and those that provide lighting effects from hidden locations. The decision whether to have fixtures flank a path or disappear into the background stems partly from the designer's lighting style or design concept, and partly from the project needs. Sometimes the lighting designer, landscape architect, or owner has strong feelings about whether fixtures should have presence as an element in the landscape or not. Visible fixtures make lighting a more conspicuous component of the landscape design, while hidden fixtures influence the appearance of the landscape without calling attention to the importance of the lighting.

Factors guiding the choice between decorative and hidden fixtures include design intent and the availability of useful fixture location(s). The effect visible fixtures make on the overall composition (both day and night) must be considered. In some residential spaces, having the lighting effect appear from nowhere can add to the charm of the landscape. In other situations, the architectural style requires decorative fixtures. With public spaces, the fixtures often serve as part of the overall space identity and create some of the life or excitement of the space.

When deciding whether to use decorative or hidden fixtures, consider the availability of decorative fixtures with appropriate style for the site. There is not an overabundance of decorative outdoor fixtures available on the market. However, an increasing number of quality fixtures are becoming available. In many commercial projects, the vast size of a site can require fixtures in large quantities, introducing the possibility of designing and manufacturing custom fixtures at a reasonable cost.

Location also influences fixture choice. Sometimes there will not be a good location for either decorative fixtures or hidden fixtures. The spacing of decorative fixtures may need to be so close together (to avoid disturbing patterns of light and dark along a path) that a sea of fixtures stands out in the daytime. Sometimes, in the designer's attempt to minimize the number of fixtures, the height of the fixture becomes too tall to integrate gracefully into the site. When an appropriate location does not exist, the approach must be modified to fit the site. For example, if a hidden fixture is desired but no location exists to mount a fixture without causing glare, choose a simple, unobtrusive path light as a substitute.

The quality of light reaching the path is equally important to whether or not the fixture is seen. Fixtures that create glare detract from the overall landscape lighting and can make navigating the path more difficult or uncomfortable. Careful planning of the aiming angles for downlights (see Figure 14.3) and the brightness of decorative fixtures' lenses avoids glare. A decorative fixture's lens can easily become the brightest element in the visual composition. Typically, a decorative fixture should not become the focal point in a composition, even when its appearance is desirable.

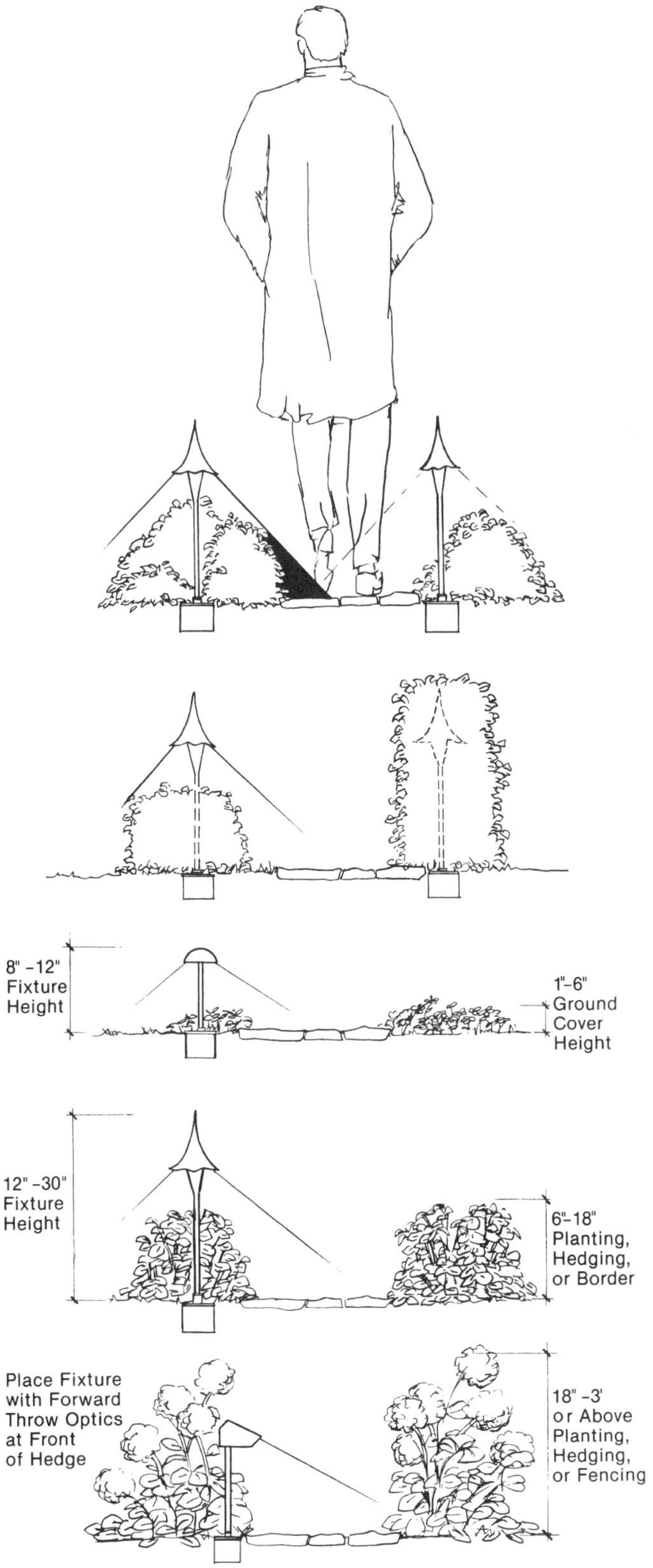

To avoid lensed fixtures from stealing the scene, select a material that will not show the lamp image and specify a lamp that has low enough candlepower to maintain its place in the brightness hierarchy. Avoid using clear glass lenses unless the lamp is not visible in the glass. Select frosted or colored lenses with sufficient thickness to ensure good diffusion of lamp brightness. Lenses can be either glass or plastic. Glass lenses can be formed or ground into patterns to provide sparkle and are available in a variety or mixture of colors. Some plastic lenses offer the advantage of high impact strength (see "Lenses" in Chapter 7).

Decorative walkway fixtures include low path units, bollards, post-top fixtures, hanging, sconces, and pole-mounted fixtures. Manufacturers sometimes offer a family of fixtures to use throughout a site. Hidden fixtures include accent lights that can be mounted in trees or attached to roof overhangs, trellises, or other structures. Keep in mind that the cost of well-

8" -12"
Fixture
Height

1'-6"
Ground
Cover
Height

12" -30"
Fixture
Height

6"-18"
Planting,
Hedging,
or Border

Place Fixture
with Forward
Throw Optics
at Front
of Hedge

18" -3'
or Above
Planting,
Hedging,
or Fencing

Figure 17.8. *Examples of fixture height and placement to coordinate with planting. Drawing: Lezlie Johannessen.*

Figure 17.9. *Along this gradual stair to a backyard, the carefully shielded fixture mounted on a post provides enough light for spacing every five to six steps. Lighting Design: Janet Lennox Moyer; Photograph: ©1990, Douglas A. Salin, www.dougsalin.com.*

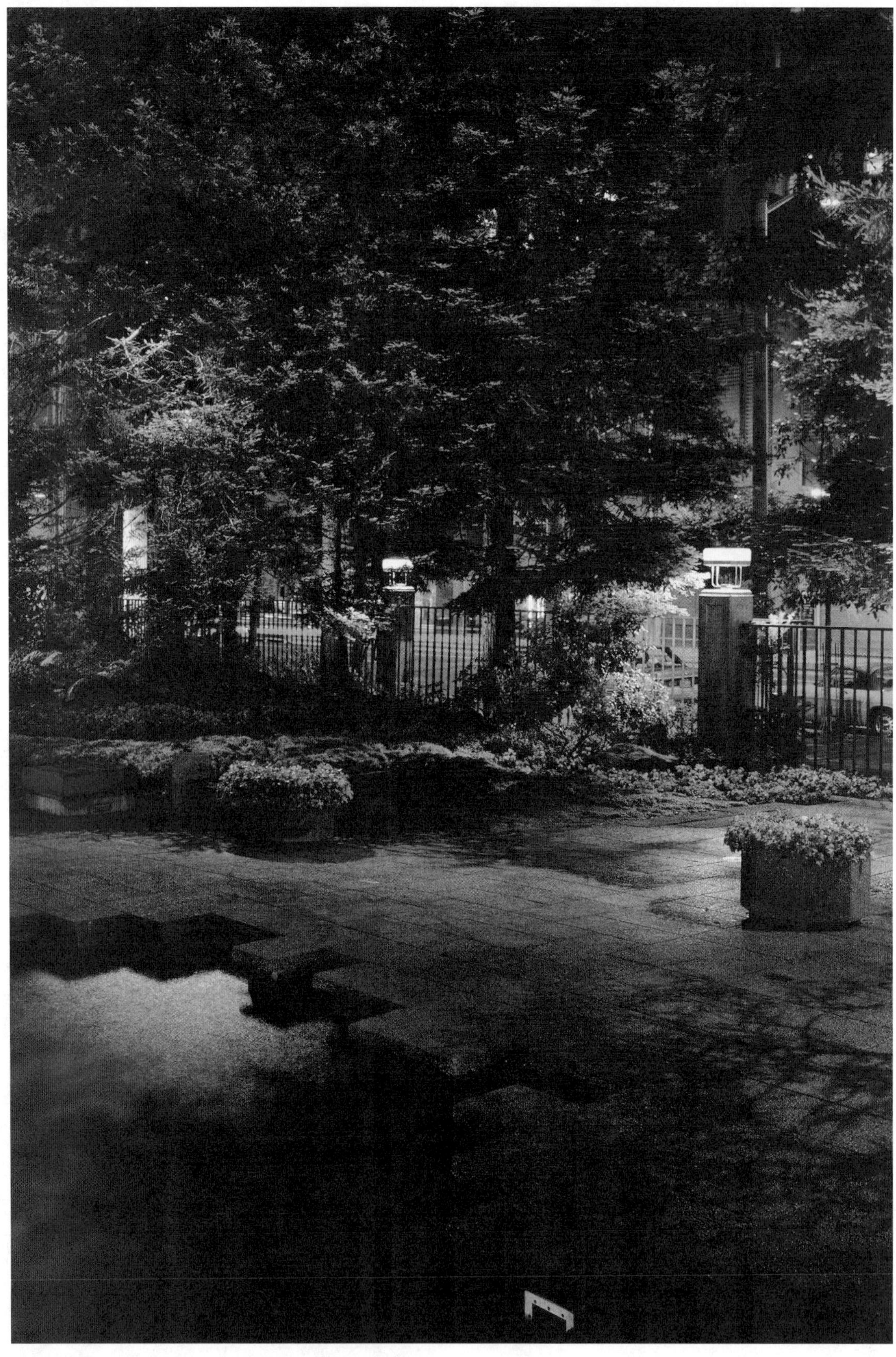

Figure 17.10. *The walkway fixture selected for the edge of Trans America Redwood Park fit onto the existing post. Utilizing careful lamp shielding, the fixture provides general lighting for the sidewalk outside the park, marks the park for visitors to San Francisco, and coordinates in brightness with the plant accent lighting. Lighting Design: Janet Lennox Moyer; Photograph: ©1996, Douglas A. Salin, www.dougsalin.com.*

constructed outdoor fixtures built of high-quality materials will be a significant portion of the lighting budget.

Decorative Fixtures Beyond the aesthetic appearance of a fixture, evaluate size, scale, construction, and light distribution. Large fixtures can overpower the site, while fixtures that are too small can look awkward. In commercial projects, evaluate the need to withstand physical abuse from staff and visitors. At some sites, the possibility of bicycles or motor vehicles knocking into fixtures requires strong construction and secure mounting methods. On some sites, vandalism will be a concern, requiring materials that withstand abuse and tamper-proof locking mechanisms.

Select the appropriate location and spacing of decorative fixtures to ensure that light reaches the path and to enhance the visual appearance along the path. Light from fixtures placed too far back from the path can be blocked, never reaching the path (see Figure 17.8A). Mounting a fixture behind a hedge (see Figure 17.8A, left) causes a shadow on the path. Mounting the fixture in front of a hedge can light both the path and the hedge (see Figure 17.8A, right). Trying to use one fixture to both accent plant material and provide path lighting requires finesse. Patterns of light can break the rhythm of the path and rarely coordinate with the planting. Using a fixture with 360° distribution can produce a circle of light covering both planting and path. Plan the spacing of these fixtures to overlap light distribution from one fixture to the next, creating an even wash of light. Height of the fixture is critical. The fixture head must be a minimum of 6 inches above the mature plant material height to effectively light both planting and path.

The height of decorative fixtures also needs to complement the overall landscape design—too tall a fixture looks gangly and out of place, while too short a fixture is ineffective. Fixtures mounted in a newly planted hedge can become buried over time (see Figure 17.8B, right) unless the hedge is pruned to an appropriate height for the fixture or the fixture is selected for the eventual, mature height of the hedge (see Figure 17.8B, left). The height of decorative fixtures affects the daytime appearance as well as night light distribution. Coordinate the height with the mature height of planting and the fixture's visual appearance in the landscape (see Figure 17.8C).

In period-style homes and estates, decorative fixtures reminiscent of the style add authenticity to the overall appearance of the landscape. In downtown areas of cities, fixtures express or enhance an image. While providing required footcandle levels, they introduce visual interest along the streets in the form of unique shapes and sparkle.

Hidden Fixtures Downlighting paths by mounting fixtures in trees or on structures offers the option to light a walk without evidence of fixtures. This approach requires an appropriate mounting location adjacent to the walk, such as the roof overhang along an office building's walk from the entry to the parking lot. Other possible mounting locations include the trunk or branches of large, mature trees or architectural structures, including fences, trellises, arbors, pergolas, or walls.

Sometimes using a row of decorative fixtures may be undesirable. They can distract from the landscape, create too strong a visual element, cost too much, or require digging up an existing garden to install them. Using downlight locations instead removes the fixture as a visual element in the landscape. It can provide even path lighting using fewer fixtures, since the longer throw distance from the fixture to the ground covers a greater area at the ground. Downlighting can easily combine pathway and planting lighting (see Figures 17.1 to 17.3).

Attaching fixtures to buildings also simplifies the wiring. Circuits do not have to be run out from the building through the landscape. However, this requires planning the lighting during the design of the building or at least including provisions to add lighting at a later date. Fixtures can be attached to buildings after construction when electrical provisions were not originally planned, but the wiring is no longer simple and hiding the wires may require care, adding to the cost.

CITY STREETS AND SIDEWALKS

City sidewalk lighting represents one part of the lighting needs for a downtown area; street lighting represents the other part needed to complete a downtown lighting scheme. The combined lighting for both sidewalks and streets can utilize one or more of three groups of fixtures: tall pole fixtures, medium-height pole fixtures, and bollards. Each fixture type serves a different function and differs based on height. In all cases, the fixtures should be spaced to produce an even flow of light on the sidewalk. Photometric data and spacing guidelines from fixture manufacturers help determine appropriate fixture spacing.

Typically, the street lighting is done by tall pole fixtures. These are functional fixtures spaced evenly along the length of the street, with poles ranging in height from 20 to 30 feet and a profile that blends into the street scene rather than calling attention to themselves. They need good lamp shielding to prevent any glare that could inhibit clear view of pedestrians or other cars by a driver. For many years inexpensive, glaring fixtures, nicknamed cobra heads, were used for this purpose because no inexpensive carefully shielded fixtures

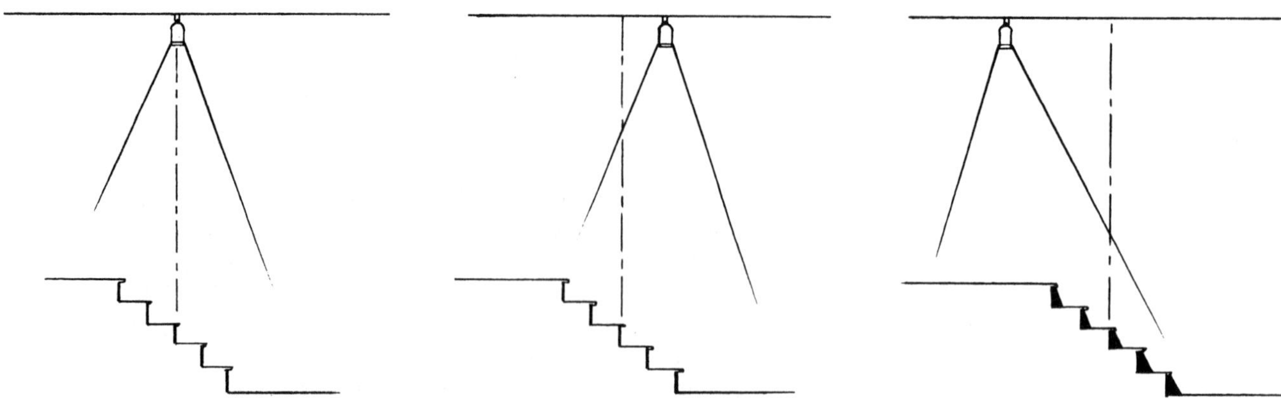

Figure 17.11. *A downlight can often cover a limited set of stairs. Locate the fixture in the middle or toward the bottom of the stairs, not toward the top. Drawing: Lezlie Johannessen.*

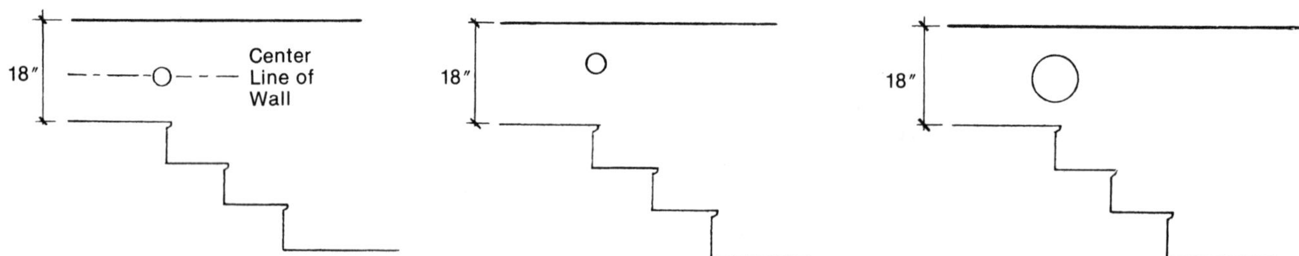

Figure 17.12. *Using one steplight recessed into the side of a stair requires considering a logical location for light distribution. The fixture at the right is too large and too close to the stair tread. While the fixture at the left would work, the location of the middle fixture is preferable. Drawing: Lezlie Johannessen.*

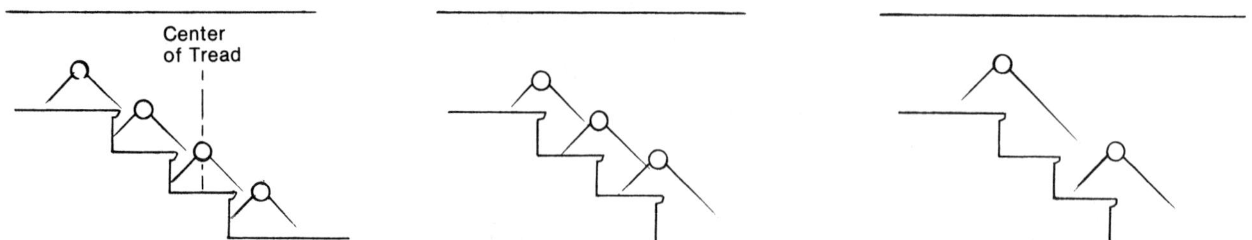

Figure 17.13. *Using more than one side-recessed fixture for a flight of stairs. With limited mounting space, using one fixture per stair creates a nice rhythm. Locating them at the intersection of riser and tread works best. With enough height, a fixture can cover more than one stair. Drawing: Lezlie Johannessen.*

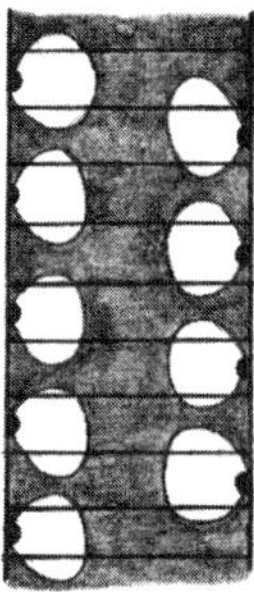
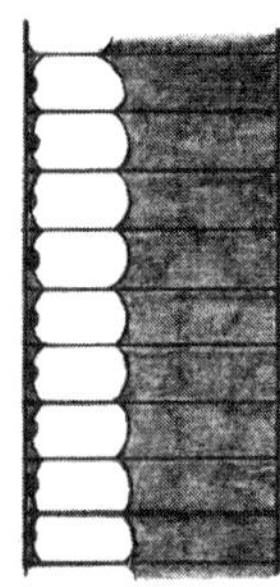
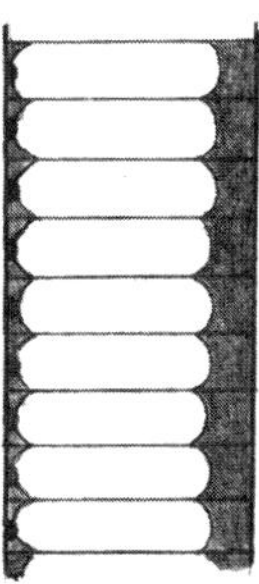

Figure 17.14. *Options for fixture layout on wide stairs. Opposite side placement creates distracting light/dark patterns. Locate fixtures on one side of a staircase and use a forward-throw distribution. Drawing: Lezlie Johannessen.*

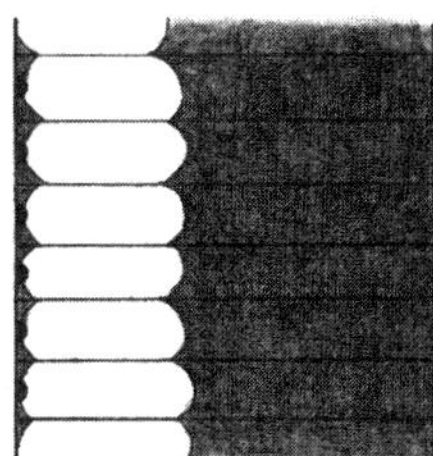
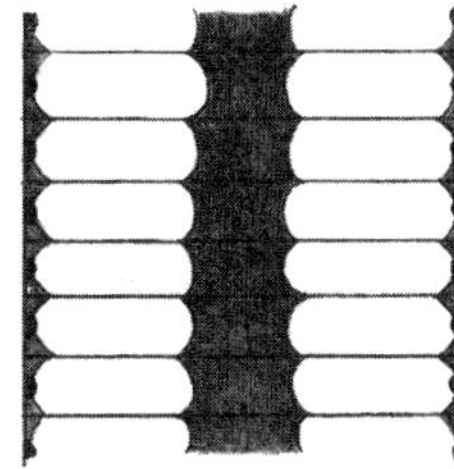
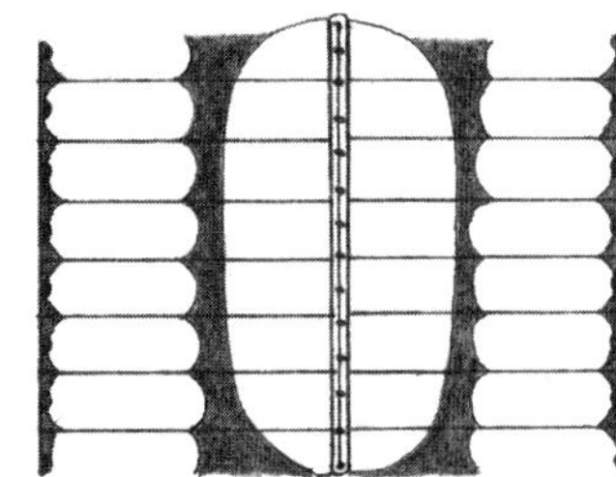

Figure 17.15. *On a wide stair, reasonable coverage with overlapping beamspread may be all that is necessary. Wide stairs with two-way traffic require fixtures on both sides of the stairs. With heavy traffic, adding lighting in the middle of the stairs may be warranted. Drawing: Lezlie Johannessen.*

were available. Now, fixture manufacturers do offer inexpensive, well-shielded, and even handsome-looking street lighting fixtures.

These pole fixtures produce lighting for safe movement of automobiles and may introduce a soft layer of fill light onto the sidewalk. The Illuminating Engineering Society has produced a number of standard practice reports, committee reports, and application guidelines for street, parking lot, tunnel, aviation, and sports lighting (see the "Roadway and Transportation" section of the Bibliography). When a lighting designer works on a downtown improvement project, the street lighting may already exist or be the responsibility of another party. In any case, the sidewalk lighting needs to be coordinated with the street lighting in light level, light source color, and overall effect.

The soft fill light from the tall pole fixtures provides the first layer of light for the sidewalk lighting. However, these typically do not provide enough light for the sidewalk or provide any input to the downtown image.

Pole fixtures in the second group stand from 8 to 15 feet in height. They serve several purposes beyond producing functional light for reading signs and locating businesses. They present a decorative appearance that helps identify or enhance a city's image. To achieve an even light distribution, these fixtures must be located closer together than the tall pole fixtures. The close spacing creates a visual rhythm and unifying effect along the street. They can also add interest to the street scene by creating sparkle or a small area of brightness that calls attention to the luminaire (see Figure 17.10).

An important characteristic of these fixtures is *glow.* The glow can emanate from the lens of the fixture, or from a decorative element added to the fixture: rings of neon, edge-lit acrylic, or fiberoptics. Choose fixtures for this purpose carefully. The brightness level and size of the glow from either the lens or decorative element must be controlled to balance with the ambient light level. Exposed lamps and glowing white globes typically create too high a brightness, distracting the viewer rather than adding interest. At this height, use low-wattage high-intensity discharge (HID) metal halide or high-pressure sodium lamps.

Some fixtures have louver assemblies covering the lamp. These serve two functions. They provide glare shielding by hiding the view of the lamp. At the same time, they direct the distribution out of the fixture. Typically, these louvers catch some of the lamp candlepower at the louver blade edges, creating glow or sparkle.

The third group of city sidewalk fixtures is bollards. These can incorporate signage to direct pedestrians. For example, they may announce bus stops and have schedules incorporated into their body. They provide physical as well as psychological cues to areas of inter-

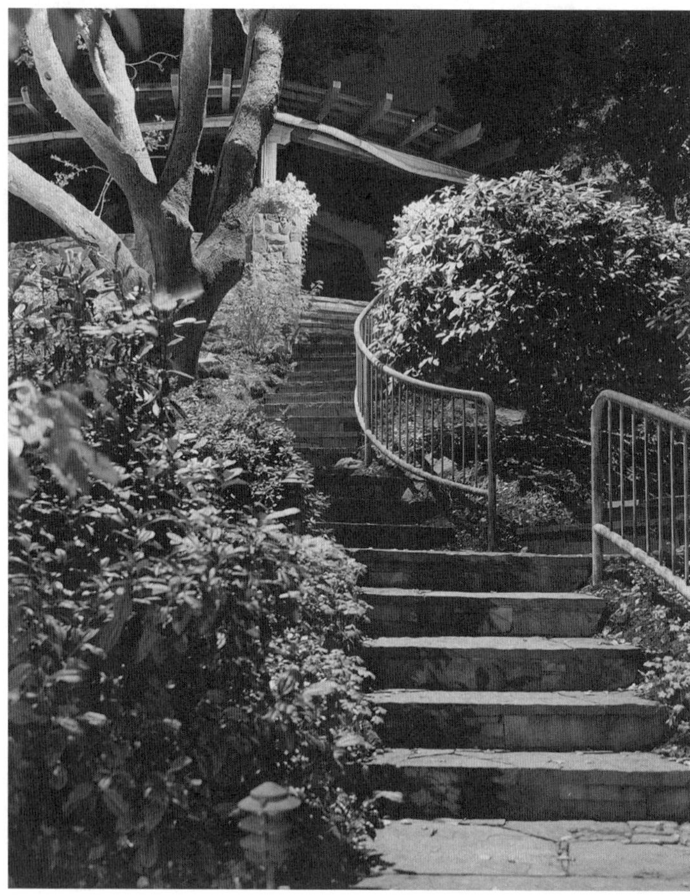

Figure 17.16. *Downlight fixtures mounted in the oak trees on each side of the stairs, at the Far Niente Vineyard, disappear from view. A small number of fixtures create continuous lighting along the stairs, providing safe access to the Cabernet Terrace entertainment area. They also provide views into the surrounding plantings. Lighting Design: Janet Lennox Moyer, Michael Stewart Hooker, and Paul Schreer. Photograph: Kenneth Rice Photography, www.kenricephoto.com.*

est along the street. They can mark areas of caution, such as warning of approaching traffic from underground parking garages or indicating separations between vehicle- and pedestrian-use street areas.

Some bollards are multifunctional. One side of the fixture may have a controlled downlight component for general lighting, while the opposite side may have one or more accent or adjustable light sources for highlighting plantings or buildings. Uplight components integrated into the top can highlight street trees. Using the uplight component requires shielding the light source or using a fixture tall enough to eliminate people's view of the light source. As with all fixtures, lamp brightness needs to be controlled. Many manufacturers make bollards with the lamp located either above or below the lensed portion of the fixture and use optical systems to direct the light distribution. Better-designed fixtures typically cost more, but the value becomes obvious when the fixture is illuminated at night.

STEPS AND STAIRCASES

Step or staircase lighting must provide enough light to identify the presence of the stairs and to differentiate between the risers and treads. The ease of seeing steps depends on the materials selected for the steps, as well as the physical configuration of the stairs. Dark materials require a higher light level. A change in material color from the riser to the tread increases visibility of stairs.

Guidelines exist that architects and landscape architects use for the size and spacing of treads and risers. These guidelines take into account how easily the stairs will be to climb (and how dangerous the steps will be) and defines the character of the stairs—slow or fast-moving, gracious or cramped, awkward or smooth—in relation to the natural movement of human beings. Lighting needs to respond to this physical form of the stairs. Those less easily negotiated require better lighting—calling attention to their configuration to aid in the process of climbing them.

In planning the overall landscape lighting, consider the purpose of the stairs. If they are meant to be used primarily during the day, either do not light them or light them at a low level, to avoid drawing attention to them. However, before deciding not to light a set of steps, evaluate risk to potential users and the liability to all parties from potential injury.

Decide whether to design an even light level across the width of the staircase based on use and client pref-

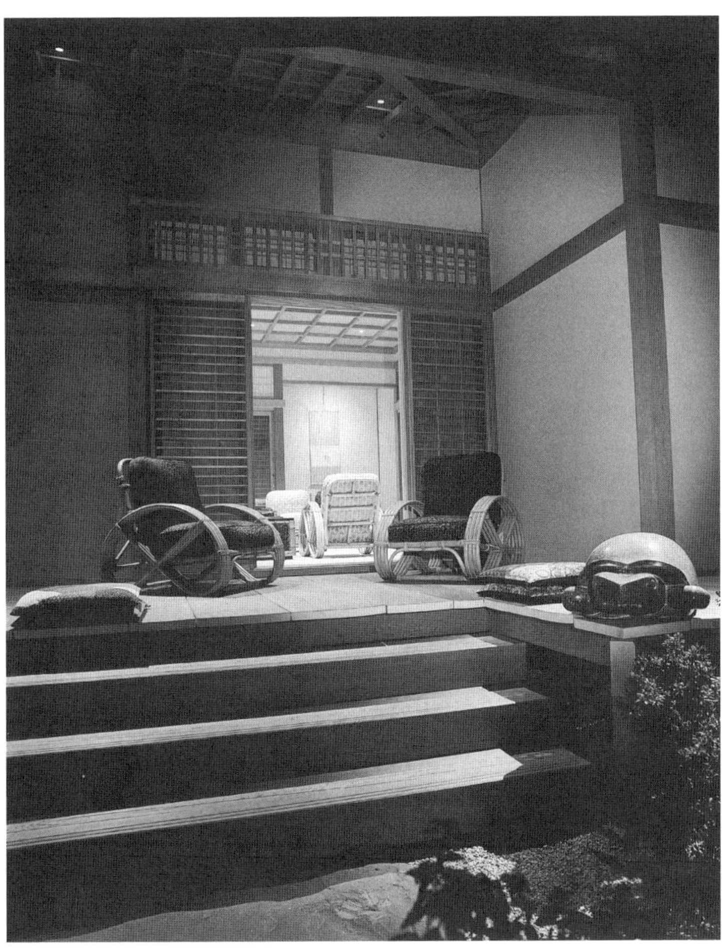

Figure 17.17. Downlighting integrated into an overhanging eave visually connects the arrival path and stair with the living area of this home. The downlight is aimed to focus on the turtle sculpture and light spills over onto the stairs. Lighting Design: Janet Lennox Moyer, Michael Stewart Hooker, and Paul Schreer. Photograph: Kenneth Rice Photography, www.kenricephoto.com.

erence. Consider the way a pattern of light will affect the overall lighting composition. Lighting a portion of the width creates a more intimate effect, while lighting the entire width presents a more public appearance.

Wide stairs do not always require even light across the tread. The purpose of the stair and the amount of traffic help determine whether this is necessary. For wide staircases used primarily during the day or that do not lead to a destination point, light introduced along the side(s) visually identifies the stairs as a precaution to prevent someone from falling (see Figure 3.7).

As with walks, the approach to lighting stairs varies with design intent, type of stair configuration, and function. Light can be introduced from above, from the side of the tread, from the riser, or from a recessed fixture in the overhang of the riser.

Downlight

Mounting an adjustable fixture in a tree or on a roof overhang provides light to the stair without making the fixture visible during the day (see Figures 17.16 & 17.17). Success in this approach requires locating the fixture(s) to minimize shadows (see Figure 17.11). The best results occur when the fixture is centered over the staircase (see Figure 17.11, left). If that location is not possible, move down the staircase, not up (see Figure 17.11, middle). A fixture mounted too far up the staircase creates shadows on the treads (see Figure 17.11, right). Shadows on any or all steps make them difficult to see. When mounting fixtures overhead, control the luminaire aiming angle to avoid creating glare and to shield the lamp (see Figure 14.3).

All downlighting techniques have the ability to integrate stair lighting with other elements of the landscape. The downlight can highlight plantings surrounding the stairs as well as lighting the stairs. This minimizes fixtures while maximizing the lighting effects.

Sidelight

Fixtures recessed into sidewalls provide light only to the stairs. This approach minimizes the visual presence of fixtures during the day. Mounting height above the stair depends on wall height, lamp selected, and fixture optics (if any). To determine the best fixture location in a sidewall, consider:

- Shape of the fixture
- Size of the fixture
- Mounting height
- Location along width of wall in relation to tread nose
- Lamp selection or availability for a specific fixture
- Fixture optics and lamp shielding

Any of these issues or a combination of them can be critical to the selection of a fixture and mounting location (see Figures 17.12 to 17.15). Shape needs to be integrated with the wall and staircase design or the overall project design. Using a palette of compatible fixtures throughout a landscape maintains a unified impression.

The size of a fixture, along with the mounting height above the tread, affects the appearance of fixtures in the wall (see Figure 17.12). Too small a fixture or a mounting height that is visually out of balance for the wall mass can cause fixtures to look awkward. A 2- to 3-inch-diameter fixture looks best located between the centerline of the wall and two-thirds below the top on an 18-inch wall (see Figure 17.12, left). A 4-inch-diameter fixture works when located approximately one-third from the top of the wall (see Figure 17.12, middle). An 8-inch fixture will always be too large for an 18-inch wall regardless of its location vertically on the wall (see Figure 17.12, right). Always consider the size and location above grade when selecting fixtures to be mounted in a side wall.

Consider the mounting height above the tread and the position in relation to the tread in deciding where to place fixtures along a wall (see Figure 17.13). The height of the wall determines how many treads each fixture can light without creating shadows, since it determines how high a fixture can be located above the tread. Fixtures centered on the tread normally provide useful light to that tread only (see Figure 17.13, left). Fixtures located at the intersection of tread and riser, but close to the riser, light two treads (see Figure 17.13, middle). Fixtures located higher on the wall allow light to reach more treads (see Figure 17.13, right).

Lamp wattage and type, along with fixture optics, determine the quantity of light produced. These also determine the spread of light along the rise of the staircase, as well as across its width. Base footcandle level selection on use, reflection characteristics of the stair material(s), and surrounding ambient light level.

As with path lighting, avoid positioning fixtures on alternate sides of the staircase unless the beamspreads overlap. Light patterns created by alternating fixtures can distract or confuse pedestrians (see Figure 17.14, left). Luminaires with little optical control work best when located along the same side of a staircase to produce an even pattern of light showing the relationship of treads to risers (see Figure 17.14, middle). Luminaires with optical control can throw light across the width of the stair, producing even light along the staircase (see Figure 17.14, right).

Whether fixtures will be required on both sides of the staircase depends on the overall width of the staircase, fixture optics, and pedestrian use (see Figure 17.15). For staircases over 4 feet in width consider using fixtures on both sides. However, light traffic flow allows fixture placement on one side (see Figure 17.15, left). People simultaneously moving up and down the staircase or heavy traffic flow in one direction requires positioning fixtures on both sides of the staircase (see Figure 17.15, middle). The addition of a railing along a wide staircase offers an additional fixture location (see Figure 17.15, right). Check national and local barrier-free access codes regarding the type of railings allowed and maximum railing size to determine if light fixtures can be attached to or recessed into the railing.

Tread-Integrated Light

Integrating fixtures into the nose of a tread provides an even wash of light across the width of the tread. The decision to use this approach must be made during the conceptual design phase of the landscape in order to provide appropriate detailing of the stair tread (to hide the fixture from view both during the day and at night). Depending on the depth of the tread, the light may or may not wash the entire surface of the tread. Typically, these fixtures will be low-voltage enclosed strip lights (see "Strip-Light Fixtures" in Chapter 7) with some great advantages—lamp life up to 50,000 hours—and some considerable disadvantages—one lamp failure in a fixture (with lamps wired in series) causes the entire strip to go out.

When using this step lighting approach, plan the wattage and lamp spacing so that the step lighting does not become the prominent feature in the landscape due to its having the highest brightness level. A simple way to ensure that this does not happen is to wire the step lighting on a separate dimming switch.

Decorative Fixtures

Post-mounted fixtures or stem-mounted path lights can also be used for stair lighting. These work best in conjunction with another method to serve as a beginning or ending to the staircase. They can be used alone effectively when the combination of light distribution, stair size, and spacing have been carefully coordinated (see Figure 17.9). The height of the stem and the location of the fixture are critical to the success of this approach. If the fixture is too close to the stair, shadows across the stair may hamper distinguishing the tread from the riser. If the fixture is mounted too far from the edge of the stairs, shadows may again detract from seeing the stair configuration. They function nicely as a marker to denote a change in grade for a pathway with occasional steps.

A series of pathway lights works effectively on staircases with no sidewalls. Select a fixture head with enough recess depth to shield the lamp when seen from below. When using this type of fixture, plan the fixture height to allow lighting several steps at one time.

The lighting of paths, walks, steps, and stairs has special significance in landscape lighting since it specifically addresses the issue of safety. In too many landscapes, however, that is as far as the thinking ever goes. Remember that stairs (just like paths) do not represent the more important visual elements of the landscape. It is entirely possible for paths and stairs to be well lit but for the landscape to look disjointed and displeasing if the rest of the elements fade into oblivion. Always include safety lighting as an integrated portion of the overall lighting for a site. While it is not always possible to do a thorough landscape lighting composition, select some elements to highlight while providing essential lighting to paths or stairs.

18

Building Elevation Lighting

The buildings on a site represent an element in the landscape that should be integrated into the overall landscape lighting scheme (see Figure 18.1). Lighting can be used to interpret the relationship of masses, planes, and building detail. Manipulating the introduction of light onto each of these elements can emphasize or redefine the building's appearance (see Figure 18.4). Successful building lighting not only sculpts an aesthetic appearance, but also integrates the structure into the overall landscape design (allowing a visitor's eye to see it in the appropriate order of importance) and creates a comfortable environment free of light-source glare (see Figures 18.2 & 18.3).

Building lighting can fulfill both utilitarian and decorative functions. Fixtures can be attached to a building, providing safety and security lighting, or mounted in various locations, highlighting the building itself. Most security lighting installed on buildings appears during the day as an ugly afterthought and at night blasts the property and any viewers' eyes. Mounting security

Figure 18.1. *Landscape lighting should include the buildings to complete a composition. Looking back at the house from the pool shows how the lighting ties the pool garden to the house. Here, low voltage incandescent lamps in fixtures mounted under the eaves of the second story highlight architectural detailing such as the lower roof. Lighting Design: Janet Lennox Moyer, Luminae Souter Lighting Design; Photograph: Michael McKinley.*

Figure 18.2. *The Far Niente Winery main winery building from the Chardonnay Garden. Photograph: Janet Lennox Moyer.*

lighting fixtures on a building requires careful selection and placement of fixtures in order to minimally affect the daytime appearance of a building and to control fixture glare at night.

The intent of this chapter is to discuss lighting the building itself as an element in the landscape. Typically, when someone mentions the concept of building lighting, many people automatically think of security lighting. While fixtures for security lighting are often mounted on the building, these fixtures light the grounds, not the building. The concept of building lighting actually refers to highlighting a building's facade. Building lighting serves one or more of these purposes:

- Identifying the location of a building
- Identifying entries, stairs, special functional areas, and service areas
- Attracting attention to a building
- Creating a positive community impression
- Expressing civic pride

This lighting can identify or locate a commercial space (for example, a store, restaurant, or movie theater) for potential customers. Once people know where the building is, the lighting adds the benefit of encouraging people to come to the space at night, as it will be perceived as a safe space. The way lighting renders a building can visually illustrate a business's design philosophy. Flashing, colored signs make one statement, while light that subtly emphasizes the building's shape presents a completely different impression (see Figure 18.5).

When people see that the business owners and city planners have taken the initiative to light buildings after dark, this can help attract other business owners to locate a new facility in the community. The citizens of the community can also express their love for or pride in historical sites, government buildings, monuments, and churches by lighting these structures.

LUMINOUS COMPOSITION

During conceptual design, the lighting designer needs to evaluate the appearance of the building to determine its importance in the luminous composition and to plan how the lighting should render the building. Facade

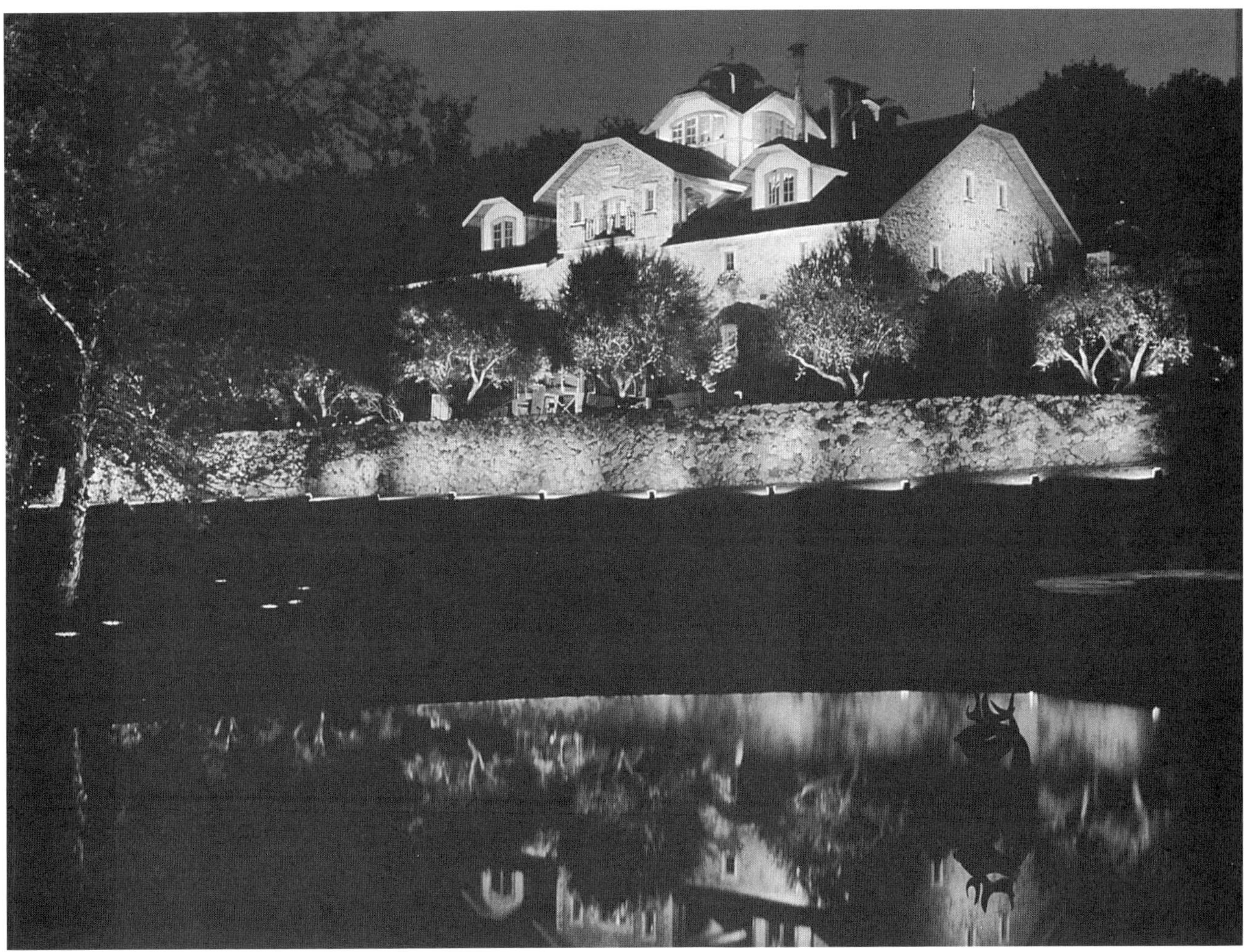

***Figure 18.3.** At night the Far Niente Winery building is visible from Highway 29. Owner Gil Nickel wanted to showcase the beautiful historical design and architecture, which dated from 1885. He preferred the appearance of a clear high-pressure sodium light source for that reason. Lighting Design: Janet Lennox Moyer, Michael Stewart Hooker, & Paul Schreer; Photograph: Kenneth Rice Photography, www.kenricephoto.com.*

lighting requires careful planning to avoid glare from light reflecting off or penetrating windows, to locate fixtures in tight spaces, and to enhance the beauty of the architecture.

Lighting that is not well thought out can destroy the appearance of a building. Too few fixtures leave holes in the effect and often neglect detail. Too many fixtures either create too high a brightness in one or more areas of the building or make the building too bright to integrate with the rest of the site or the neighborhood. The wrong selection of lamp wattage or color can overlight a portion of the facade or clash with surrounding lighting or the building materials. Typically, the buildings that will be lit have a strong presence in the site or neighborhood, which requires extra care to produce a pleasing effect.

Three elements of lighting control the success of facade lighting effects: direction, intensity, and color. Direction of light affects the appearance of texture, shadows, and highlights. It is the tool that can emphasize the three-dimensional aspects of a building or add depth to the view of the building.

A wash of light, with the fixture located away from a building and directly in front, provides an even, flat effect. It shows architectural shape but eliminates texture and shadow, which together show three dimensions (see Figure 18.3). Grazing with an uplight fixture located in front of the facade, but close to the surface, accentuates the underside of architectural detail such as cornices, friezes, window sills, relief sculptures, and architectural frameworking (see Figure 18.5). Downlighting treats the building similarly in accentuating the

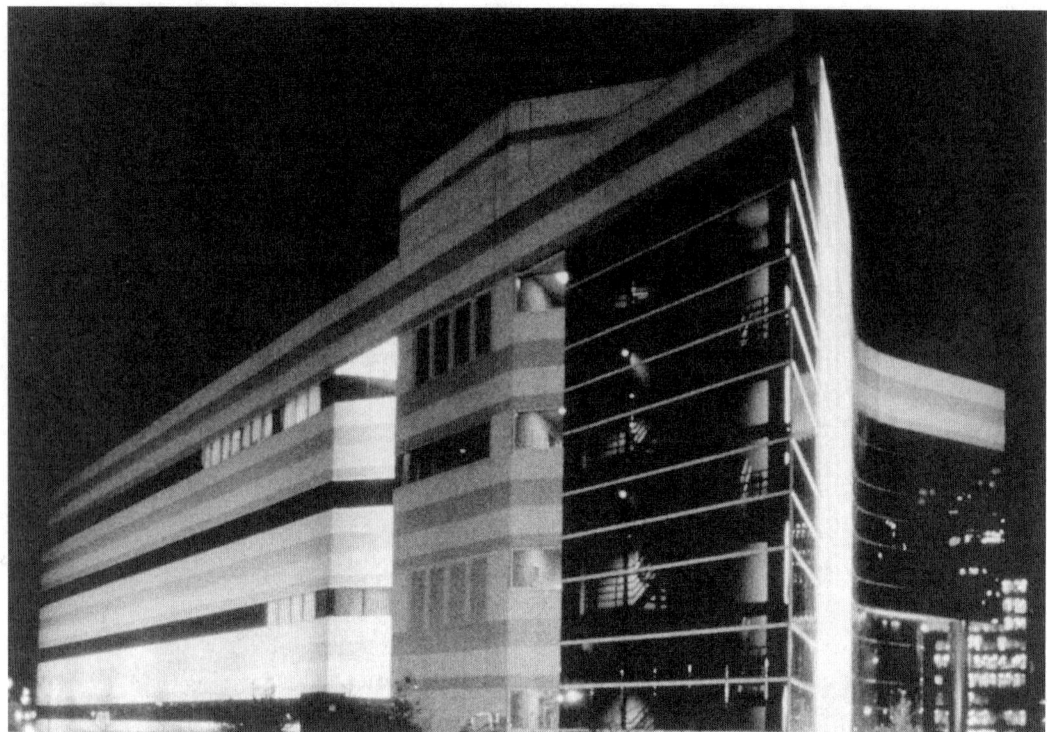

Figure 18.4. *Introducing varying light levels from one plane to another emphasizes the strong lines of this building. The facade lighting uses metal halide lamps with green color filters. Lighting Design: Stefan Graf, Illuminart; Photograph: © 1989, Thomas Weschler.*

texture, but creates the brightest effect at the top side of the details. Additionally, downlighting can provide walkway lighting below. Louvers must be used to control lamp brightness. Locating the fixture to the side of the building creates strong shadows while accentuating texture.

Intensity of light is used to balance the importance of the various parts of a building as well as the rest of the site. The designer needs to evaluate the parts of the building or facade and rank their importance in order to start planning the order of brightness. Quickly sketching possible lighting hierarchies or effects on an elevation, or preferably a perspective drawing of the building, helps to guide the design concept (see "Cohesion" in Chapter 3). Consider the surface reflectance and mounting location in selecting the lamp wattage. As with any luminous composition, the planned pattern of brightness needs to complement the building and create a cohesive image. The lighting treatment can mimic the daytime appearance of the building or create a new appearance.

Color of light can enhance a building's appearance and complement or contrast with other elements of the design. The color can be introduced through a change of lamp type from one fixture to another, or by adding color filters. Filters can be either plastic or glass, depending on the amount of heat created by a specific lamp. Since our eyes have to work hard to perceive color in low light levels, color plays a smaller part in the night environment than in the day environment. Color effects that are too strong or too varied can overpower the building or the overall site lighting.

Floodlighting

Floodlighting produces a flat, shadowless effect. It works well when the building has a strong shape with a lot of detail to hold a viewer's interest. Floodlighting is done by mounting fixtures some distance away from a building's surface to shine at it from the front, producing an even wash, which shows shape. (See Figure 14.55 for the appropriate fixture-spacing ratio.) To produce an even wash, aim the main candlepower of the fixture one-half to one-third the way up the wall. With very tall buildings, multiple fixtures may be required to cover the height.

In floodlighting, a flood distribution lamp is not always used. A spot distribution lamp throws light farther, making it useful for tall walls, but more fixtures will be required since the width spread is limited. Floodlighting minimizes the number of fixtures used and is therefore an economical approach. It does not

Figure 18.5. *A palette of high-pressure sodium light sources accentuates this building's detail—both structural shape and texture—and emphasizes the warm building color. Low-voltage quartz lamps in downlights accentuate the columns and provide a more flattering light color for people. The walkway bollards use metal halide. Lighting Design: Stefan Graf, Illuminart; Photograph: © 1991 Wayne Cable, Cable Studios Inc.*

work well when the building is plain or when the surface to be lit has imperfections that should not be emphasized.

Grazing

Grazing light emphasizes texture and creates strong shadows. To graze a surface, the fixtures must sit close to it. They can aim up, down, or across a surface. To light the width of a wall evenly while highlighting interesting texture or relief detail, the fixture spacing must be closer than when floodlighting. Care must be taken to make sure that the distribution does not introduce an unwanted or disturbing pattern and that the shadows created do not hide other features of the building. Shadows will occur on the opposite side of the detail to be lit from the fixture (see Color Plate 65). Also, when the surface has any defects, including ripples, dents, chips, misalignment, cracks, or patches, grazing will emphasize the imperfection.

A concern to consider in planning a grazing effect is whether light scallops are desirable. Scallops can occur at the top of a wall when downlighting or the bottom of the wall when uplighting. To avoid creating scallops when using any point source lamp, the spacing-to-mounting distance ratio must be less than 1:1. A ratio closer to ½:1 produces a more even pattern. The best way to avoid scallops is to use a linear light source such as fluorescent, neon, or cold cathode. Remember, however, that the vertical throw of fluorescent light is limited (even when the fixture has a good reflector). When scallops are desirable, their spacing should coordinate with the architectural details (within vertical wall demarcations, for example). The introduction of carefully positioned scallops can add interest to a large, plain wall.

Sometimes, due to space constraints, grazing is the only possible technique. Aesthetic restrictions can prohibit mounting floodlights away from the building (on the ground, poles, or other buildings) or when sidewalks or other structures occur close to the wall.

Patterns of Light

Patterns of light can be positive, negative, or projected. Lighting from the side, or grazing, creates patterns of light and shadow emphasizing architectural texture or detail (see Figures 18.10 to 18.13 & Color Plate 66). Negative patterns can be as effective as positive patterns. When a building has a decorative or sun-shading screen, lighting a surface behind it shows the pattern in silhouette. This works best when the lit surface has been washed with light. Shining light onto a sculpture, structure, or plant will produce shadows on adjacent surfaces. This can add interest to a plain surface (see Figure 14.62) or cause visual confusion if the shadows are too strong. Make sure that the number and location of any light patterns relate to the architecture.

Internal Building Lighting

Using all or a portion of the interior lighting system provides another building lighting approach. The interior walls, ceilings, large artwork, or a combination of features can serve as the building lighting. The surface(s) chosen to be lit must have visual interest and occupy a significant portion of the window surface from an outside viewer's perspective (see Figure 18.6). This option also provides an economical way to accentuate buildings with large areas of glass, especially when the architectural framing members are a dark color.

When the designer does not want to provide a view into the building but does want to use the window area to create the lighting effect, an internal floodlighting detail can be planned between the glass and any curtains or shades. Space will be extremely limited, requiring compact equipment and the use of the grazing technique. Fluorescent or another of the linear sources works best due to their ability to produce an even, soft distribution. At the ground floor, a downlight with proper lamp brightness shielding can be used. For upper floors, use an uplight that will hide the fixtures and lamps from most viewers' eyes (unless an adjacent building has windows that would allow someone to look directly at or down into these windows).

Color

Whereas color introduced onto plants changes their natural appearance, people have less instinctive expectations about the appearance of buildings. Color on a building can be used to add interest, increase or decrease psychological depth, or distract from other elements in the composition. Pastel colors or low intensity fit into a composition most easily. Too much or too strong a color becomes theatrical and has limited appeal unless used at an entertainment location such as a fairground, amusement park, or nightclub. Color can be introduced through the use of glass filters or by switching from one light source type to another, such as from incandescent to mercury vapor (see Color Plate 66).

FIXTURE LOCATION

Translating the design concept into a working reality requires selecting the proper fixture location and lamp to produce the intended results. In some cases, the best fixture location required to produce an effect may not exist. There may not be enough space to locate a fixture properly, or the perfect mounting location is in midair. (Although a fixture could be hung from the building, the appearance of such a fixture may not be aesthetically acceptable.) Sometimes it is not possible to provide power to a desired location, especially when lighting is added to an existing building. If a suitable location cannot be found, the designer must rethink the overall design. Another potential problem is limited space (when a standard fixture would be too large to fit), which could either require developing a custom fixture or, again, replanning the concept. Some examples of potential fixture locations are illustrated in Figures 18.7 & 18.8.

The designer must know the characteristics of the surface to be lit—its color, texture, type and quality of construction—to know how to approach the surface and where to locate fixtures. Remember that the surface finish affects the lighting. A highly polished surface (such as glazed tiles, marble, glass, polished metals, or gloss paint) can reflect the image of the light source, which detracts from or destroys the effect. To avoid this problem, the fixture needs to be located and aimed in such a way that the reflected lamp image is not visible from the locations where people will stand to view the structure. Typically, this means aiming at less than a 35° angle off the ground (see Figure 14.3) or careful shielding to block the lamp image.

Fixtures should be hidden whenever possible. Most often, fixtures that highlight facades are functional, not decorative fixtures. Although they might have a clean appearance, seeing these fixtures would detract from the overall site appearance both during the day and at night. One approach is to integrate fixtures into or onto the building. When a lighting designer is involved during the conceptual design of a new building, fixtures can sometimes be located so that they are recessed into the structure (see Figures 16.17 & 18.7). When the lighting is planned after the building has been completed, the fixtures must be placed onto the structure (see Figure 18.7A & Color Plates 63 & 65). When adjustable fixtures are mounted at ground level to uplight a building, locate them behind shrubbery (see Figure 18.8A) or berms (see Figure 18.8C & Color Plates 56 & 57); behind an architectural structure such as a bench, wall, fence, sign, or sculpture; or recess them below grade. Whether the fixture can be hidden at all depends on the property as well as both the hardscape and planting layouts.

Figure 18.6. *At the Apple Computer Research and Development Campus, lighting makes the space feel bright due to uplighting on the high curved ceiling and the walls. A combination of 400-watt (up) and 175-watt (down) 3,000K sconces at the upper floor level sculpts the architecture and 100-watt 3,000K pole-mounted path lights provides even lighting for pedestrians. Lighting Design: Naomi Miller; Photograph: John Sutton Photography © 1993.*

Using multiple fixtures will normally create a more interesting effect than using one fixture to wash the entire building face (see Figure 18.4). The multiple-fixture approach places fixtures closer to the building, limiting the area that each fixture illuminates, and aims the fixture at a steeper angle to minimize or eliminate lamp glare. Steeper aiming angles and closer spacing also avoid unwanted spill light or light pollution imposing on an adjacent property. Using multiple fixtures also provides the opportunity to vary the brightness across a building face, augmenting the architecture or adding interest (see Figure 18.5). Another advantage with multiple fixtures is the ability to control the light level on the wall by choosing lower-wattage lamps.

There are four basic choices for mounting locations and facade lighting will often use more than one. The first option is the adjacent ground (see Figures 18.8A & C and Color Plates 56 & 57). This often provides the best aiming angle and the most even coverage.

The next location would be on the building itself. When the building has a large roof overhang or an intricate crown molding (where a fixture can be integrated during the design of the building), this provides a good way to hide the fixture and a great downlight location (see Figures 16.17 & 18.7). This location can provide highlighting for specific architectural detailing, foundation or pathway lighting, and serve as security floodlighting (see Figure 3.16A). Fixtures mounted under eaves or in architectural details require a careful sensitivity to aesthetic appearance, and all these downlights require louvering to limit lamp glare at ground level. Other options for mounting fixtures on the building itself include placing uplights on or recessed into an architectural ledge or balcony (see Figure 18.7A & B), locating fixtures on a roof to either uplight or downlight another part of the building, placing fixtures inside the cove of a rotunda or pergola, or using decorative fixtures such as sconces or hanging fixtures (see Figure 18.7D & E).

A third mounting location is on a pole or light standard. Often a series of decorative fixtures is designed for the building. In this case, placing fixtures on poles complements sconces or hanging fixtures attached to the building (see Figure 18.7F). Using a pole has the additional benefit of potentially allowing more than one fixture at that location to serve several functions. Additional fixtures can light walkways, plantings, or sculptures. A pole-mounted fixture can sometimes act as a decorative element and provide task lighting, which requires the optics and shielding to be carefully designed and tested. When mounting both a decorative and a utilitarian fixture on the same pole, attention must be paid to the detail and integration of the two elements. Pole-mounted fixtures can also be used simply to provide a wash on a portion of the building (see Figure 18.8B).

Figure 18.7. *Range of potential building-mounted fixture locations for facade lighting. Drawing: Lezlie Johannessen.*

The last option for fixture location is on adjacent buildings. This works well in a city environment, when the site size is limited and the appropriate fixture location is an impractical spot, such as in the middle of the street at grade level. Mounting fixtures on the top of an adjacent building often gets them out of a person's view and provides a steep aiming angle. Use of an adjacent building requires the permission of that building's owner. It helps if the two neighbors have good relations. Often in using another building for fixture loca-

Figure 18.8. Some fixture locations to consider when the fixtures will not be attached to the building. Drawing: Lezlie Johannessen.

tions, power will need to be borrowed from that building as well, with separate controls for the lighting (time switch or photocell) if power cannot be run from one building to the other. Negotiations for the cost of electricity and permission to use the space need to be undertaken immediately and resolved prior to finalizing the design concept and starting working drawings.

EQUIPMENT

The selection of the appropriate lamps and fixtures is based on the desired lighting effects to be created and mounting locations available from which to create them. Planning the hierarchy of brightness and evaluating mounting locations should always be done prior to selecting lamps or fixtures. Additionally, calculations and mock-ups should be done prior to settling on the equipment.

Light Sources

In selecting equipment to produce the desired effects, the lamp is the first consideration. The proper combination of color, beam distribution, and candlepower needs to be found. One lamp will not always be able to satisfy all three requirements. Two lamps (or more) with differing beamspreads will sometimes need to be used together; for example, a spot to illuminate the top of a building and a flood to fill in the lower portion.

Lamp life is also an issue to consider. When the fixture will be difficult to access, a long life is required. The size of the building or portion of a building to be lit should be considered in choosing a lamp. Lighting small areas or specific details of a building often requires the beamspread control of incandescent lamps. For wide expanses of limited height, fluorescent may be the best choice. Larger areas, both in width and height, benefit from the brute strength and expansive beamspread capability of the HID sources.

When a building has an intricate shape, a combination of sources might be necessary. This can mean combining different incandescent sources, using incandescent with fluorescent, or using incandescent, fluorescent, and one or more of the HID sources. When combining sources, pay attention to the variation in color. Sometimes a color filter will need to be added to balance the colors (see Color Plates 63 & 64). In other

Figure 18.9. *New York State's Automated Teller Machine (ATM) Lighting Law makes it difficult to light a bank elevation without offensive glare. This design uses full-cutoff pole-mounted fixtures to achieve the required 2 footcandles of illuminance at a 5′0″ height, within a 60-foot radius of the entry door. The bank appreciates the subtle attractiveness, and the neighbors like the reduced light trespass. Dark-sky enthusiasts approve of the ziggurat uplighting from a single narrow-beam low-wattage metal halide source, as it is virtually captured in the arch, never reaching the sky. Lighting Design: Naomi Miller: Photograph: Randall Perry Photography, 2002.*

cases, a color shift is desired to create interest or affect the appearance of three dimensions.

The pattern of brightness created on a surface depends on the beamspread of the lamps and the spacing between fixtures. In incandescent sources, for example, PAR floods and spots have narrower beamspreads than R lamps. This makes PAR lamps better for vertical throw situations and R lamps better for wide horizontal spreads. When very controlled shapes of light are required, the low-voltage PARs provide the best selection. For fluorescent and HID sources, the fixture often provides a reflector assembly to direct the candlepower into the proper beamspread. Refer to Chapter 6 for more detailed information.

Incandescent

Incandescent sources offer extensive versatility because so many types, wattages, and sizes are available. They are inherently inefficient but more easily controlled than the other sources. Their beam control and range of wattage often make them the only source that can produce a desired effect at the right brightness. For example, uplighting a small turret or other architectural roof detail may be done from the ground with a 50-watt PAR36VNSP (very narrow spot) lamp, which makes the turret stand out as a feature with virtually no spill light from the lamp.

Fluorescent

Fluorescent lamps provide a soft, even distribution when height is not required (for example, washing a one-story building face). High-output lamps can be particularly useful since they produce significantly more light than the standard lamp. Fluorescent lamps require a reflector to direct the light. In the selection of any fluorescent lamp for outdoor use, the combination of lamp and ballast must be carefully coordinated for the environmental conditions because temperature and wind affect their performance (see "Fluorescent Lamps" in Chapter 6).

High-Intensity Discharge

HID lamps offer high output in wide distribution with relatively compact lamp size (compared to fluorescent) and long life (compared to incandescent). The type of HID lamp needs to be chosen carefully for the color appropriate to the situation. The lamps can provide a number of distributions when coupled with the lens and reflector options available from various fixture manufacturers. Coated lamps provide good washes, while clear lamps in combination with a reflector can produce a spike of light for accenting a vertical element. The ballast needs to be selected to work with the expected temperature conditions. Unlike fluorescent sources, HID lamp output is not affected by low temperature since it produces enough heat to maintain operating temperature.

Fixtures

The selection of a specific fixture occurs after the designer has determined which lamp will produce the desired effect. Essentially, the fixture merely holds the lamp. It protects the lamp from the harsh environment, provides the capability to direct the lamp at the needed angle and hold that aiming over time, and for fluorescent and HID lamps it can control the beamspread. The size and shape of the fixture are determined by the lamp size and the reflector (when needed) to control the lamp's beamspread. In incandescent and HID fixtures, the size is also affected by the need to dissipate the lamp heat generated during operation.

For fluorescent and HID fixtures, manufacturers provide photometric information about the beamspread and light output of the combination of fixture and lamp. This is not done as regularly with incandescent fixtures since the lamp filament design, along with the shape and material of the bulb and reflector, determines the beamspread and output. In this case, this information is generated and made available by the lamp manufacturer.

Manufacturers often produce charts that show the beamspread of a fixture and sometimes the initial footcandle levels on a surface based on a given dimension away from the surface and a set aiming angle. These help early in the selection of a fixture to choose a beamspread that provides roughly the required distribution.

The Illuminating Engineering Society and the National Electrical Manufacturers Association together developed a series of beamspread designations that can be used to select the correct beamspread for a specific project situation. The light distribution is listed by beamspread range and projection distance. The beamspread comes from the candlepower distribution pattern of the lamp-fixture combination and is measured to 10 percent of maximum intensity. Asymmetrical floodlights are designated by their horizontal and vertical beamspreads (in that order). A flood with a horizontal spread of 94° (a type 5) and a vertical spread of 34° (a type 3) becomes designated as a beam type 5×3 (see Figure 18.14).

Manufacturers often make one fixture that offers several distributions by changing the optics inserted into the fixture housing. This allows a designer to use one fixture profile as a standard throughout a project where different areas require different distributions.

For the designer to know the light level or actual distribution of a specific fixture for a project, a point calculation needs to be done with the right optical distribution, lamp, mounting height, and tilt. When the designer does not have the computer facilities to do these calculations, the representative or manufacturer will normally provide that information as a service.

Some manufacturers provide vertical footcandle charts for an individual fixture and lamp at a specific mounting height and aiming angle. If the fixture accepts more than one lamp, a multiplying factor will be listed to modify the data to the other lamps (see Figure 18.15).

A third chart type that a manufacturer may provide in their literature is called an iso-candela diagram. This shows the distribution of the fixture graphically, with rings representing candlepower (see Figure 18.16). This plot may be accompanied by a chart of initial footcandles (based on a dimension away from the surface to be lit and a set aiming angle). Once again, the information will be based on one set of criteria, and the designer needs to do the calculations for a specific project.

LIGHTING LEVELS

Several factors contribute to determining the appropriate lighting level. First, evaluate the level of light in the surrounding area. Then, decide the importance of the building in the overall composition. Often, lighting levels will need to vary from one part of the facade to another in order to accentuate the shape of the building. The designer needs to translate the hierarchy of brightnesses determined during conceptual design into actual levels. In determining lighting levels, remember to plan how the building lighting relates to other brightnesses within the site and the surrounding area. (See Figure 18.17 for a guideline for light levels.) Typically, any signage on the building should have the brightest light level.

Calculations must be performed to confirm the correct lamp wattage and beamspread for a desired effect.

Figure 18.10. *As you approach the entrance to the House of Blues Hotel in Chicago at night, the contrast from the blue arrival lighting to the rich, warm colors and vibrant lighting of the interior space draws people. Lighting Design: Michael Stewart Hooker & Paul Schreer, MSH Visual Planners; Photograph: Kenneth Rice Photography, www.kenricephoto.com.*

Figure 18.11. *During the daylight hours all trace of the House of Blues logo and identity simply disappears. Photograph: Janet Lennox Moyer.*

Figure 18.12. *To create the House of Blues logo above the hotel entrance four large-format projectors are located in the adjacent parking deck facility. Lighting Design: Michael Stewart Hooker & Paul Schreer, MSH Visual Planners; Photograph: Janet Lennox Moyer.*

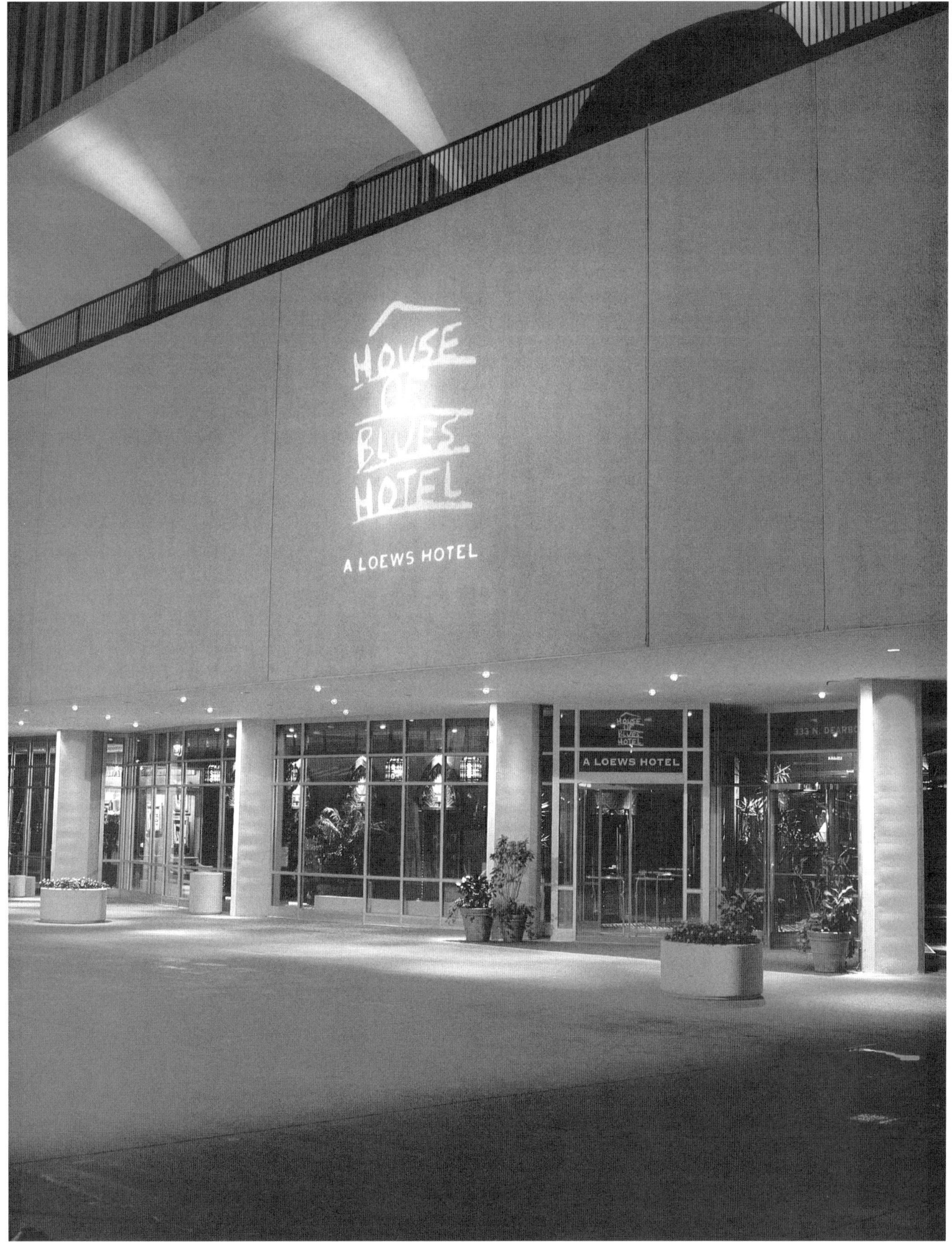

Figure 18.13. *As night deepens, all of the Water Tower Place area becomes a blue environment announcing the House of Blues Hotel and the adjacent club. The lighting utilizes blue metal halide lamps and blue filters on white metal halide and low-voltage halogen sources. Lighting Design: Michael Stewart Hooker and Paul Schreer, MSH Visual Planners; Photograph: Kenneth Rice Photography, www.kenricephoto.com.*

All calculations should be done in footlamberts, not footcandles (as footcandles do not account for surface reflectance). The designer needs to be careful in the selection of which calculation method to use. Various procedures provide differing types of information.

One calculation method, called the beam-lumen method, provides an average brightness level on the surface. This level may not actually occur at any point on the wall and does not provide clear information about actual levels occurring on a wall or the distribution across a surface. A second and preferred method is the point-by-point method, which uses these basic formula:

candlepower × cosine of angle ÷ distance^2 × maintenance factor = maintained footcandles
maintained footcandles at surface × reflectance = maintained footlamberts

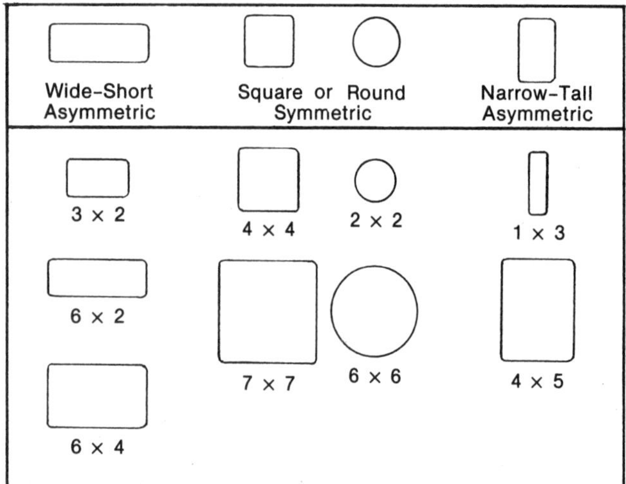

Basic Flood Beamshapes

BEAM TYPE	BEAM SPREAD DEGREE RANGE	PROJECTION DISTANCE
1	10 to 18	240 ft and greater
2	18 to 29	200 to 240 ft
3	29 to 46	175 to 200 ft
4	46 to 70	145 to 175 ft
5	70 to 100	105 to 145 ft
6	100 to 130	80 to 105 ft
7	130 and up	Under 80 ft

Figure 18.14. Sampling of the available floodlight beam distributions with the standard IES-NEMA beamspread classifications. Drawing: Lezlie Johannessen. IES-NEMA beamspreads based on material from RP-6-1988, Recommended Practice for Sports and Recreational Area Lighting, *Illuminating Engineering Society of North America, New York.*

This simple calculation takes into account how far the light will travel to its destination, the reflectance of the surface, and the appropriate maintenance factor for that specific situation. The maintenance factor includes the lumen depreciation of the lamp over time, dirt buildup on the fixture, and the frequency of cleaning the lens and reflector assembly (if used in a fixture).

This calculation can be done for any point on a wall with the output from one fixture or can take into account as many fixtures as contribute to that point. The best way to use this method is on a computer. The computer can calculate the brightness level across the entire surface of a wall both vertically and horizontally. Programs such as Lumen Micro can print out maintained footlamberts as well as a graphic chart showing the pattern of light on the face of a wall. Manufacturers often have the photometrics for all their fixture and lamp combinations on their websites and on disk (though these are typically not available for Macintosh platforms).

Additionally, most manufacturers or manufacturer's representatives can run the calculations for designers who do not have the software programs to do lighting calculations. If not familiar with lighting calculation, designers should request the supplier to advise them of the kind of reports that can be produced and then to demonstrate how to read them. The *IES Lighting Handbook* discusses calculations in more depth, and local IES chapters often hold classes teaching the calculation methods.

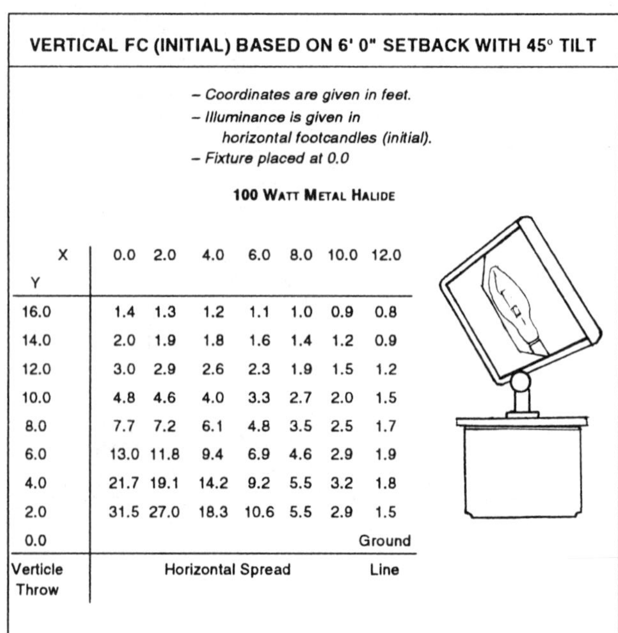

VERTICAL FC (INITIAL) BASED ON 6' 0" SETBACK WITH 45° TILT

- Coordinates are given in feet.
- Illuminance is given in horizontal footcandles (initial).
- Fixture placed at 0.0

100 WATT METAL HALIDE

Y \ X	0.0	2.0	4.0	6.0	8.0	10.0	12.0
16.0	1.4	1.3	1.2	1.1	1.0	0.9	0.8
14.0	2.0	1.9	1.8	1.6	1.4	1.2	0.9
12.0	3.0	2.9	2.6	2.3	1.9	1.5	1.2
10.0	4.8	4.6	4.0	3.3	2.7	2.0	1.5
8.0	7.7	7.2	6.1	4.8	3.5	2.5	1.7
6.0	13.0	11.8	9.4	6.9	4.6	2.9	1.9
4.0	21.7	19.1	14.2	9.2	5.5	3.2	1.8
2.0	31.5	27.0	18.3	10.6	5.5	2.9	1.5
0.0							Ground Line

Verticle Throw — Horizontal Spread

Figure 18.15. Example of a vertical initial footcandle chart. Data courtesy of Hadco Lighting. Drawing: Lezlie Johannessen.

AFL9
Spot

250 Watt
High Pressure Sodium
E-18 clear mogul base "Superior" 30,000 initial lumens
I.T.L. Test No. 34537

See page 15 for I.E.S recommended illuminance for floodlighting and parking lot lighting.

I.E.S Type: **3H x 4V**
Beam Spread: **42.2° H**
50.3° V

Note: All areas of uniformity are based on a lighting system, not individual fixtures. Therefore, areas of uniformity are calculated assuming contributions from adjacent fixtures.

Total area within is 3:1 maximum-to-minimum uniformity of illumination. Use for optimum visual uniformity on facades, walls or signs.

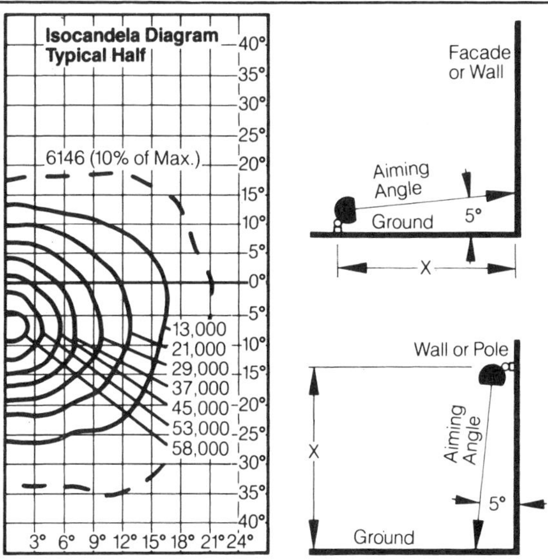

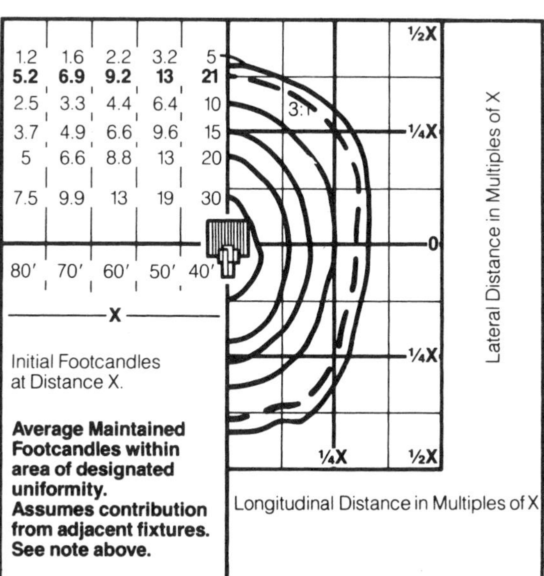

Figure 18.16. *Iso-candela diagram with the accompanying fixture and mounting information. Catalog information courtesy of Kim Lighting.*

While computer calculations can be quite accurate (depending on the accuracy of the input data), the only way to avoid unwanted hot spots, scallop patterns, or any sharp variation in brightness is to do a mock-up. This reassures the owner and designer that the concept works and provides a safety net to evaluate the planned lighting, allowing for any needed revisions prior to the installation.

MAINTENANCE

Keeping the whole facade lighting system functioning is important to the appearance of the building. When portions of the lighting system have burned out or are out of adjustment, it makes the entire building appear, at best, neglected.

For all building lighting systems, the owner or owner's representatives need to be familiarized with all operational and maintenance aspects of the system. They should also receive a complete as-built drawing package showing the location of all fixtures, ballasts, transformers, controls, and any other pertinent equipment. These drawings need to identify the lamp in each fixture for relamping. The owners should keep a stock of spare lamps to ensure that the lighting can be fully operational at all times.

Before completing any project, the lighting designer needs to discuss the maintenance procedures and schedule with the owner. This clarifies not only the importance of the maintenance, but what should be done and how frequently. The designer can train the

RECOMMENDED ILLUMINANCES FOR FLOODLIGHTING

Surface Material	Reflectance in Percent	Surround: Bright	Surround: Dark
		Recommended Footcandle Level	
Light marble, white or cream terra cotta, white plaster	70–85	15	5
Concrete, tinted stucco, light gray and buff limestone, buff face brick	45–70	20	10
Medium gray limestone, common tan brick, sandstone	20–45	30	15
Common red brick, brownstone, stained wood shingles, dark gray brick	10–20*	50	20

* Buildings or areas of materials having a reflectance of less than 20 percent usually cannot be floodlit economically, unless they carry a large amount of high-reflectance trim.

Figure 18.17. *Based on material from the* IES Lighting Handbook, *1987.* Application Volume, *Illuminating Engineering Society of North America, New York, 1987.*

building staff to clean and relamp the equipment. In some cases, the owner may want to retain the designer to review the lighting on an ongoing basis to make sure that the lighting continues to function properly and look its best. The frequency of such reviews depends on the type of equipment installed, the complexity of the system, and whether the lighting needs of the facade change over time.

Beyond all the reasons stated at the beginning of this chapter to consider lighting a building, including it in the landscape lighting helps to ensure that the visual composition will be cohesive. When the building is not included, there will be a large black hole in the composition. Landscape lighting should always include consideration of the building as well as the site.

19

Water Features

Landscape architects frequently use water as an element in their landscape design. It has the ability to introduce excitement or serenity into an environment. Water features can include natural streams or ponds, waterfalls, fountains, and reflecting pools. As an element in a landscape, the lighting designer needs to consider whether the water should be lit, and if so, how. There definitely are times when lighting the water feature is not necessary to the night lighting.

Water features, perhaps more than other landscape architectural elements, require a maintenance commitment from the owner prior to any installation. When one lamp burns out, it leaves a hole in the lighting effect, ruining the beauty of the design. This chapter will look at the types of water features that can occur and their individual lighting issues.

DESIGN CONSIDERATIONS

As with any other element in the landscape, the designer needs to evaluate the water feature's role in the composition. Often, the water feature will be a primary focal point (see Figure 19.12). In other cases, it may be one of several equally important focal elements (such as water sculptures, plants, or architectural structures), and sometimes it should be allowed to blend into the night's darkness. All the viewing locations of the feature need to be identified. For example, when a water feature will be viewed from a car on the highway, rather than by people strolling by, controlling glare for pedestrians will not be an issue. When the water will be viewed from inside a building, its lighting level will have to be equal to or higher than the interior light levels in order to be visible.

The brightness relationship of a focal point water feature to its surroundings should be consistent with the rest of landscape lighting. From one focal point to another the brightness relationship should fall between 3:1 and 5:1. To ensure cohesion in the composition, there should be no more than a 10:1 brightness relationship from the prime focal point to the surroundings (see Figure 2.5). Remember that brightness relationships need to be balanced throughout the entire landscape. Fill light may be needed immediately surrounding a waterfall, fountain, or pool to balance the focal lighting.

Physical Properties of Light

Four effects need to be understood when using light in conjunction with water:

- Refraction of light
- Effect of light on aerated or turbulent water
- Effect of light on flat or smooth water
- Dispersion of light in water

Refraction of Light

As light passes from one medium to another having a different density, the angle at which the light is traveling changes because the velocity of light varies according to the density of the medium through which it is passing. When light passes from water into air, the angle increases as measured from the upward perpendicular. For light passing from air into water, the angle also increases, but this time is measured from the downward perpendicular (see Figure 19.1). At an aiming angle of 49°, all light is reflected back under water and none passes into the air.

Refraction can be used to hide the brightness of the lamps when fixtures are placed in walls of a pool. People will see the lamp brightness of a standard fixture (which has a convex lens) unless the fixture is located in a place where people will not be able to look at it directly. If such a place does not exist, changing the convex lens to a flat lens causes the light rays to bend toward the horizontal, limiting the amount of light shining up toward people's eyes. Adding a fine-mesh louver (such as Cool-Shade material) with approximately 30° shielding ensures that all the lamp brightness will disappear (see Figure 19.2).

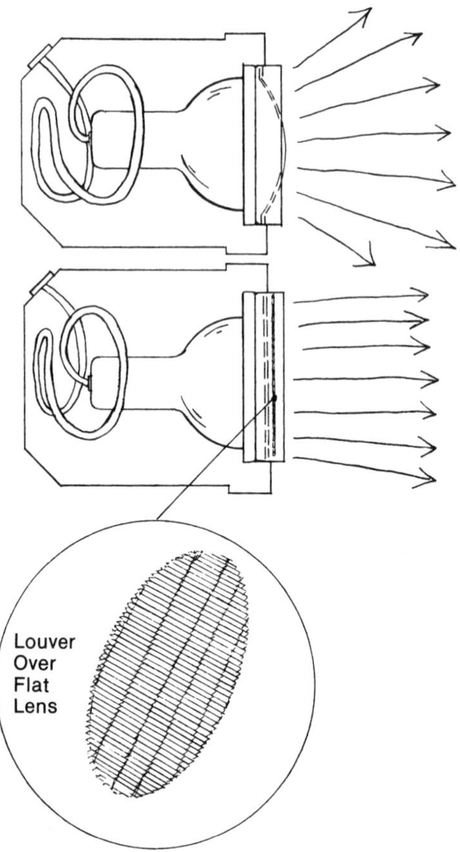

Figure 19.2. Using a flat lens and fine-mesh louver concentrates light rays and shields lamp brightness to eliminate view of the lamp from above water. Drawing: Lezlie Johannessen.

Effect of Light on Aerated or Turbulent Water

Turbulent water has air bubbles intermixed with it. These air bubbles react with light, making the water appear to glow and take on the color of the light shining into them. Because of this, light sources need to be located directly below waterfalls with turbulent water in order to create this glowing effect (see Figure 7.17 & 19.3).

Effect of Light on Flat or Smooth Water

Smooth sheets of water do not have air bubbles mixed in with the water, and light that hits the water either passes through it or reflects off its surface, depending on the angle of the light. Smooth-surfaced waterfalls need to be lit from the front (with the fixtures either in or out of the water), and flat pool or pond surfaces need to be lit from outside the water to create an effect (see Figure 19.4).

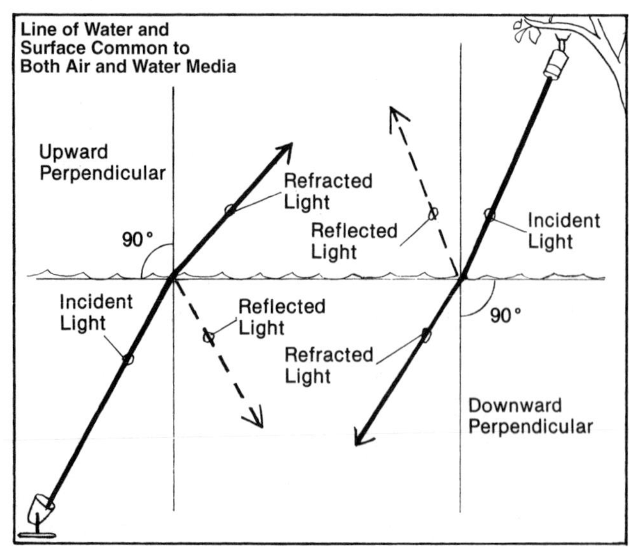

Figure 19.1. Refraction of light from water to air. Drawing: Lezlie Johannessen.

Dispersion of Light in Water

As light travels through water it tends to become scattered by particles in the water. This helps in washing the bottom of a swimming pool with light but reduces the intensity and projection of light when trying to accent a fall, jet, sculpture, or plant material. Perceived brightness drops by 10 percent for each 2 inches of submersion.

Fixture Location

As a starting point, fixtures can be located either below or above water. Lighting effects differ radically from above to below water locations, as do fixture costs, installation costs, and the ease (and therefore cost) of maintenance. All factors—lighting effect, equipment

Figure 19.3. *At Portland Park in Oregon, the lighting fixtures contain 500-watt PAR quartz lamps placed 3 feet apart. The lamps alternate between spot and flood distribution to create an even lighting effect. Lighting Design: Dan Dibble, Beamer Wilkinson; Landscape Architect: Lawrence Halprin & Associates; Fountain Design: Richard Chaix, Beamer Wilkinson; Photograph: E. B. McCulley.*

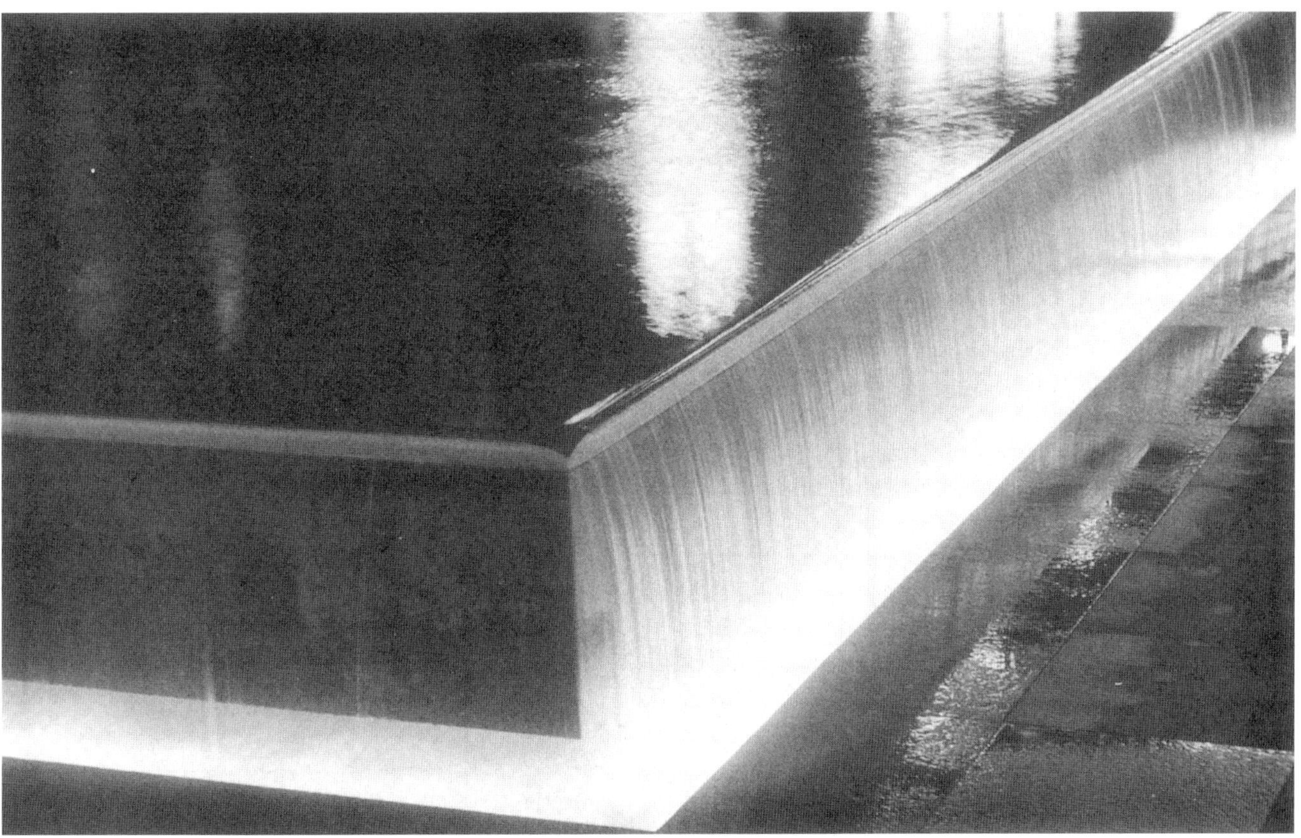

Figure 19.4. *For this smooth sheet of water, fixtures sit just in front of the water, shining at the water's surface. Lighting Design: Dan Dibble, Beamer Wilkinson; Landscape Architect: Lawrence Halprin & Associates; Fountain Design: Richard Chaix, Beamer Wilkinson.*

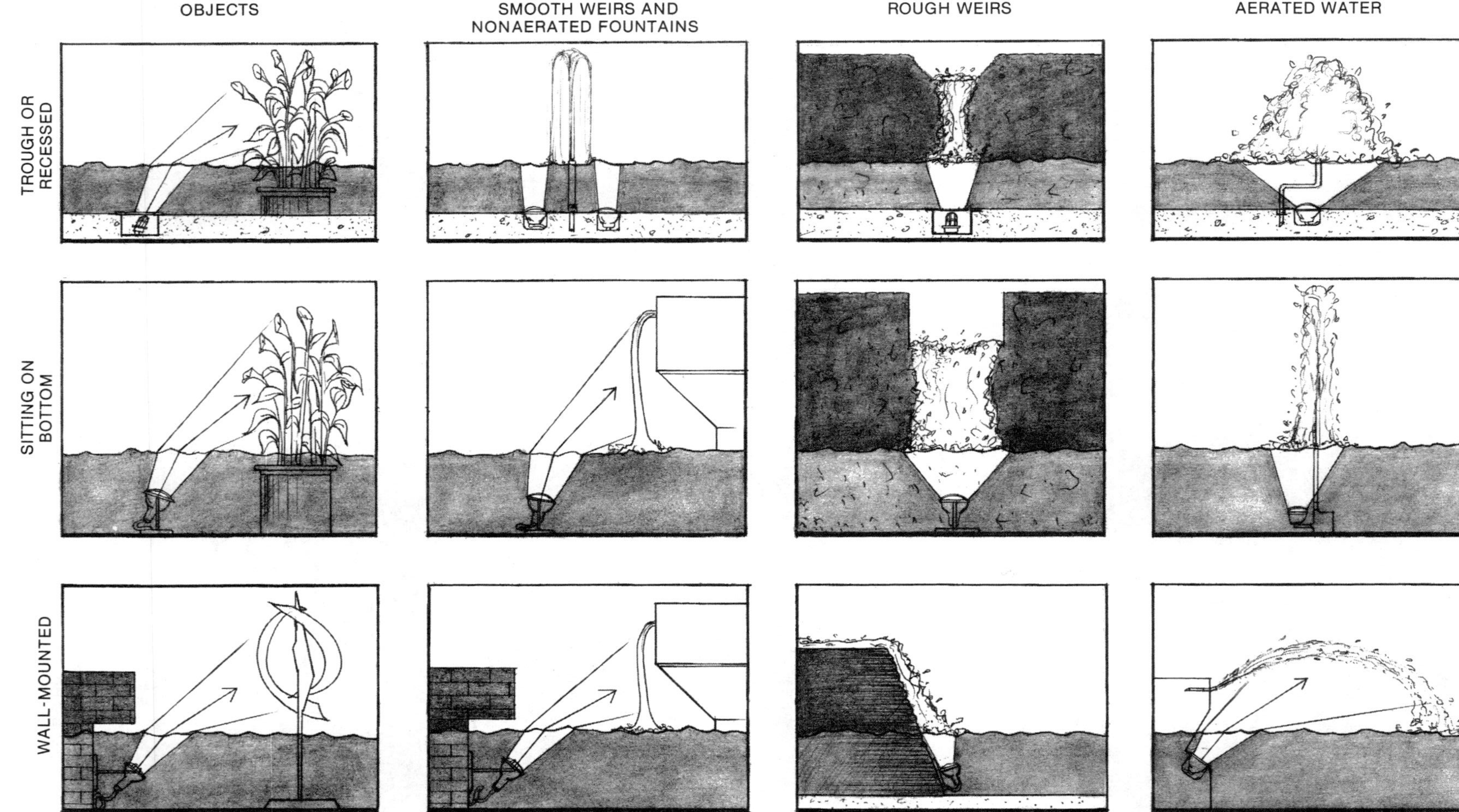

Figure 19.5. *Examples of below-water fixture locations for various types of water features. Drawing: Lezlie Johannessen.*

Figure 19.6. This fountain serves as a view from a central hallway out to a terrace. Two 120-volt incandescent lamps in waterproof fixtures sit on the pool bottom aiming up across the Papyrus and onto the lion's face. Photograph: Kenneth Rice Photography, www.kenricephoto.com.

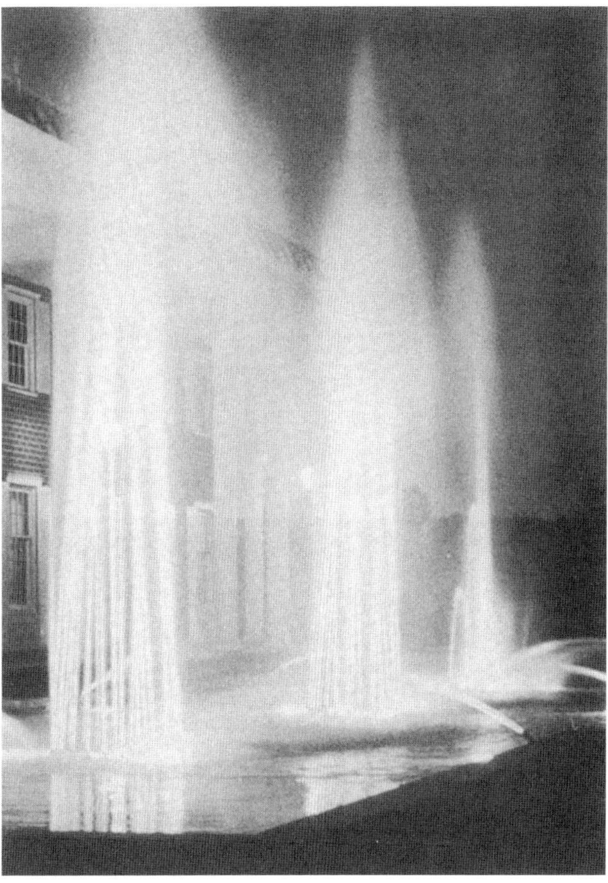

Figure 19.7. This fountain shows a combination of jet effects. The ring of precision jets creates the appearance of a tall, controlled cascade. The uplights for the ring of jets also function to pick up the end of the arch effect, while a fixture located near the nozzle lights the start.

and installation costs, and system maintenance—need to be discussed with the owner prior to deciding fixture locations in a project. For any water lighting to be worth the initial investment, the owner needs to agree to replace burned-out lamps in or on a water feature immediately in order to retain the nighttime beauty of the water feature.

Locating Fixtures Below the Water's Surface

Lighting a water feature from under the water's surface creates dramatic effects. Sprays of water from fountain jets glow against the night sky's darkness. Falls of turbulent water glow, accentuating the water's power. Fixtures for these effects can sit directly on the pool bottom, be recessed into the bottom, or sit in an architectural recess below the bottom (see Figure 19.5). Fixtures located in sidewalls can light the pool walls and floors, accentuating the shape of the body of water or the color and texture of the materials used.

When locating fixtures in water, an important issue to consider is the effect of lighting on fish living in the body of water. The brightness produced from lighting the pool surfaces, including the brightness of the light source(s), may affect the health and happiness of fish. This can be controlled in fixtures shining up to light falls and fountains, but for pool surface lighting, the designer needs to plan some way for the fish to escape the brightness (for example, not lighting one area of the pool that the fish like and always have clear access to), or else the pool should not be lit. Another concern is the effect of the heat produced by lamps on the temperature of the water. Most underwater fixtures use incandescent sources. Incandescent lamps produce more heat than light. Significantly warming or altering the temperature of water can upset or physically harm the fish. If the body of water is large enough or has a mechanical system that can monitor and control temperature, fixtures in the water may not create a problem.

The lighting equipment made to be placed underwater must be constructed to withstand this corrosive environment, be totally watertight (not only when first constructed, but over the life of the fixture in the pool), and meet all the safety requirements of the NEC. This means more involved design and testing, and stronger construction, using more expensive materials than for above-water fixtures. Underwater

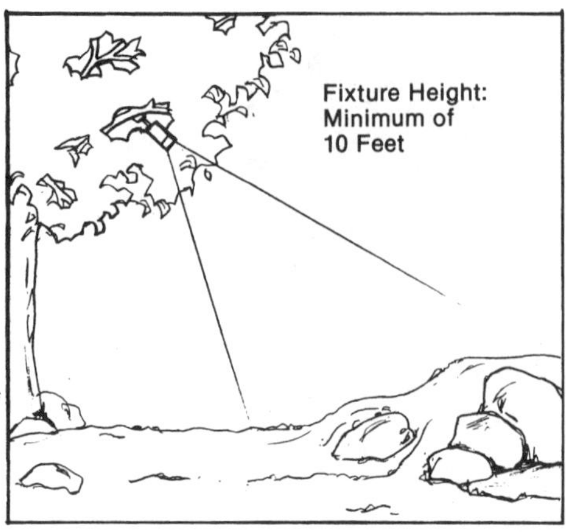

Figure 19.8. *Typical above-water locations for lighting water features. Drawing: Lezlie Johannessen.*

Figure 19.9. *Downlighting highlights the flowering Iris and Water Lily in the pond, while also lighting the stepping-stones across the water's surface. On the right side of the photograph, uplight creates a soft glow in the Japanese Maple and shows off the waterfall. Lighting Design: Janet Lennox Moyer; Photograph: © 1990, Douglas A. Salin—www.dougsalin.com.*

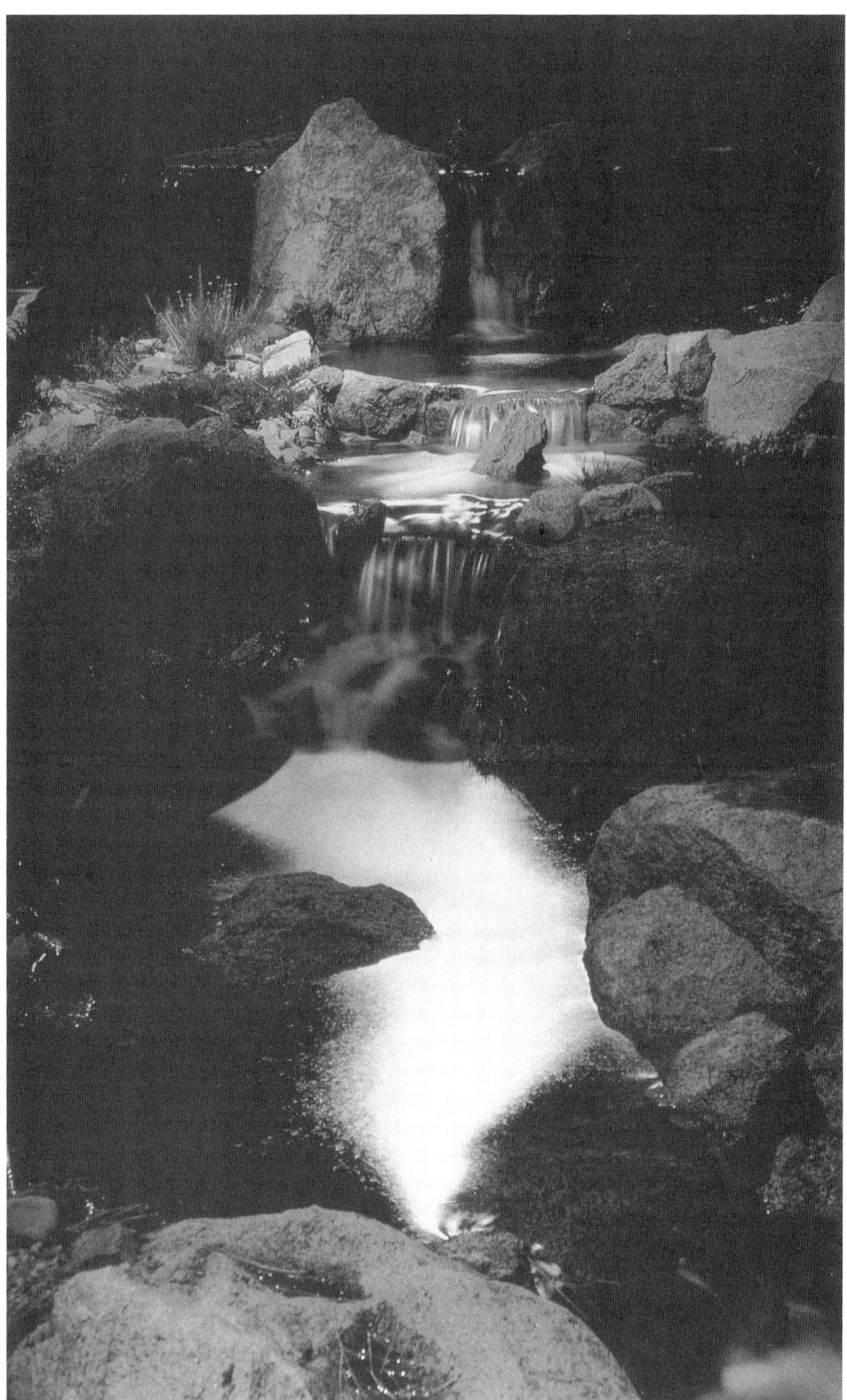

Figure 19.10. *Downlighting softly accents both the water and surrounding landscape at this Lake Tahoe resort. Fixtures mounted in mature Pine trees 40 to 50 feet above the ground remain hidden both during the day and, when activated, at night. This mounting location allowed the use of spot distribution 120-volt lamps between 100 and 300 watts to softly wash large areas of the ground. The introduction of light needed to be carefully controlled in light-level as the surrounding area is totally dark at night. The aiming angles used produce the sparkle on the stream, falls, and pond surfaces. Lighting Design: Janet Lennox Moyer, Luminae Souter Lighting Design; Photograph: Michael McKinley.*

fixtures cost roughly three to five times more than above-water fixtures.

Maintenance is more expensive for underwater equipment due to the need to access the lamp without touching water at the same time. This requires access to the fixture from outside the water, the ability to move the fixture out of the water, or the ability to drain the pool to work on the lighting equipment. In large pools or ponds with fountains, changing the lamps may involve using a boat. Two people row out to the fixtures, and while one person steadies the boat, the other pulls the fixtures into it. The old lamp is then removed and the new one installed. Another option is for someone to wade into the pool and bring the fixtures back to land. Either way, the maintenance of these fixtures requires more intensive labor than do fixtures located above the water's surface.

Locating Fixtures Above the Water's Surface

Lighting a water feature from above the water's surface simplifies the installation and maintenance considerably. The effects tend to be less dramatic than lighting from under water, but they can still be quite effective (see Figure 19.9). Agitated water is more easily lit than still water, but both can produce successful results. Agitated water absorbs and diffuses the light, making the water glow (see Figure 19.10), and also reflects some light, creating sparkle on the water's surface. Still water, such as the surface of a pond, acts like a mirror, reflecting lit objects surrounding the water (see Figure 4.5 & 18.1). Water coming over falls or from fountains sparkles and reflects light shining at it (see Figure 19.4).

Much lighting from above the water's surface will be downlighting (see Figure 19.8). Fixtures can be mounted on adjacent architectural structures or in trees. Sometimes the fixtures will be located on land adjacent to the water feature and aim up or horizontally toward the feature.

Using fixtures located outside the water requires controlling the fixtures' aiming angle to not more than 35° (off the vertical) in order to avoid lamp glare, which not only distracts a viewer but diminishes the effect of lighting the water feature. Providing effective lamp shielding (with louvers or baffles) also helps to minimize lamp brightness. When fixtures are not located underwater, any outdoor fixture can be used. This reduces the initial equipment cost, installation cost, and maintenance costs significantly.

The effect of light on fish is again a concern, but to a lesser extent. Obviously, heat will not be a concern, but the brightness from the light source can potentially bother the fish. Plant material growing in the water or along the water's edge may provide some shelter from the light. Keeping light from covering all areas of the body of water also aids the fish in finding some relief from it.

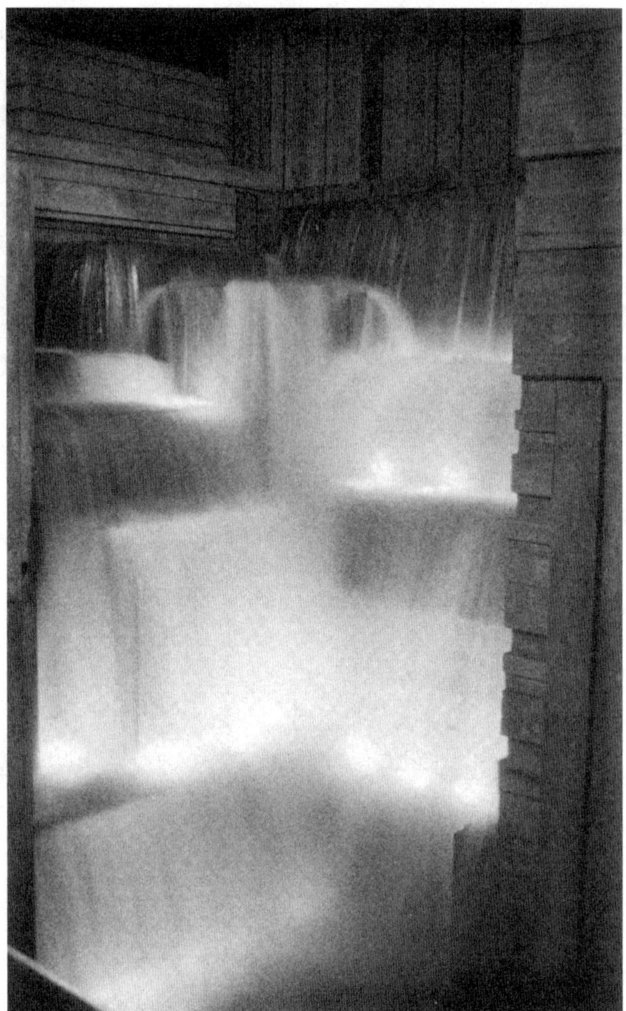

Figure 19.11. At the Seattle Freeway Park in Washington, the water feature incorporates many short falls with rough weirs. The lamps range in wattage from 250 to 1,000 watts, depending on the fall height. Lighting Design: Dan Dibble, Beamer Wilkinson; Landscape Architect: Lawrence Halprin & Associates; Fountain Design: Richard Chaix, Beamer Wilkinson.

TYPES OF WATER FEATURES

The water features utilized in a landscape can include one or more of the following: waterfalls, fountains, pools or ponds (both man-made and naturally occurring), and streams or rivers. Each type of water feature can differ in size and characteristics. Therefore, there are no rote instructions as to the lighting of each type, but guidelines and issues to consider in planning the lighting for each.

Waterfalls

This refers to a fall of water from one horizontal body of water over a vertical drop into another horizontal body of water. Waterfalls can vary both in height and width from a few inches to tens of feet. In one water feature there may be several man-made waterfalls of varying heights and widths (see Figure 19.3) or there may be

***Figure 19.12.** Outside the Museum of Science and History in Fort Worth, Texas, the walkways are softly lit by 100-watt clear mercury lamps mounted in fixtures up in the trees. The accent lighting on the fountain, which varies in height up to 20 feet (depending on the intensity of the wind) utilizes three 300-watt PAR56 narrow spot incandescent sources. This lamp choice responds to the height of water and creates a color contrast to add to the focal point attraction. Courtesy of Greenlee Landscape Lighting. Lighting Design: Doug Greenlee; Photograph: Lloyd R. Reeder.*

one spectacular natural fall. When more than one waterfall occurs, the designer needs to consider if all should be lit and, if not, which ones should be lit in order to create a cohesive appearance at night.

A key characteristic to know about a fall is the type of *weir* used. This term refers to the edge that the water falls over when making a vertical drop. The weir can be smooth or it can be rough. When water falls over a smooth weir, it falls as a sheet—with no air bubbles. In this case, the location of a fixture must be in front of the water, shining at it (see Figures 19.4 & 19.5). This creates a sparkle of light on the water's surface. The selection of lamp and layout of fixtures is similar to wallwashing any surface (see Figure 14.55). The fixtures need to be located far enough in front of the fall that the lamp's beamspread covers the height of the fall, and close enough together that the beamspreads overlap.

When the weir is rough, the water moving over it contains air bubbles. This means that the water will be agitated and should be lit internally using an uplight to create a glow as light interacts with the air bubbles in the water. The location of the fixture in the body of water below becomes critical, and there is little room for error. The fixture must be situated at the point where the falling water hits the surface of the lower body of water in order for the light to travel from this lower body of water up into the falling water (see Figures 19.5 & 19.11). If the fixture is too far in front or behind the falling water, the light does not become absorbed by it. The location where the falling water hits the horizontal water can vary due to the amount of water flow. More water moving faster will tend to land farther out than will a small amount of water moving slowly. When a pool consultant is involved in the project, they can often calculate this landing point. Using fixtures that sit on the pool bottom rather than ones that are recessed into the pool bottom offer the opportunity to delay the decision of the exact location of fixtures for waterfalls until after the fall has been tested. If the fall will not flow continually, however, these fixtures would be visible, which may not be desirable.

Lamp selection is based on the height of the fall. Typically, flood lamps are used to provide width, but as the height of the fall increases, narrower beam spreads may be required. A general rule is not to space fixtures more than 3 feet apart on center. For shorter falls, a closer spacing may be needed to produce an even effect.

Fountains

In fountains, the configuration of the water display must be identified, including the number of jets; the type of water effect(s) (column or stream, cascade, mound, dome) and patterns (see Figure 19.13) they create; the height of each effect; and the overall width of the display. Aerated effects should be lit from below, while smooth water effects need to be lit from the front (see Figure 19.5).

When a single jet or group of individual streams is used to create a pattern shining straight up, each stream should have a minimum of two fixtures. This ensures that the lighting effect will be visible from all sides of the stream (see Figure 19.14 & 19.15). When one or more jets produce streams that project water across the body of water, each jet needs at least one fixture at the point where the stream hits the water's surface. When the stream is long, more than one fixture may be required to cover the water effect adequately (see Figure 19.7). When a pattern of streams is created by one

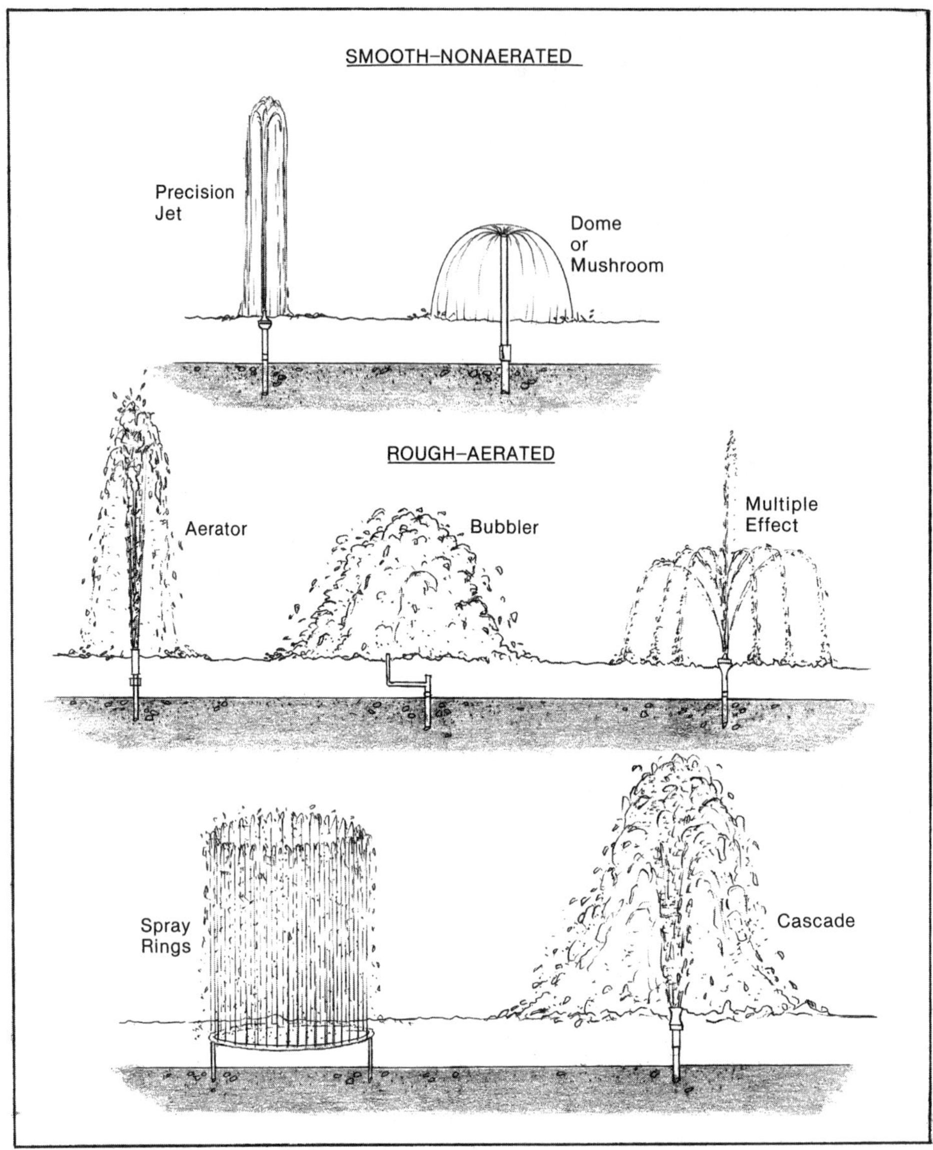

Figure 19.13. *Examples of fountain types. Drawing: Lezlie Johannessen.*

nozzle, both the minimum and maximum width and height of the pattern needs to be known in order to select the proper lamp and to place the fixtures. Sometimes multiple water streams are created using one pipe in a ring or other shape. In this case, the lighting needs to address all the nozzle sprays in width and height. This does not necessarily require one fixture per nozzle; sometimes a group of fixtures covering the entire display is effective.

Pool and Pond Surfaces

This category of water feature includes both natural and man-made bodies of water. It can be a natural pond, a man-made pool or series of pools at grade or at varying levels, or an area where water collects in a stream. Pools and ponds can be either internally or externally lit. Internal lighting accentuates the shape, walls, bottom, finish materials, and textures. External light creates a sparkle or glow on the surface of agitated water or on objects in the water (see Figure 19.6).

Pools and ponds can be quite large, and they rarely represent the most important element(s) in a landscape. Internally lighting them may draw too much attention to them, disrupting the desired brightness for the composition. Pools with a natural bottom often have soil particles floating in the water, which makes them a less desirable feature to light than a body of water with a man-made bottom and clear water. Additionally, man-made pool bottoms with a light reflectance show dirt

Figure 19.14. Downlighting highlights the flowering Iris and Water Lily in the pond, while also lighting the stepping-stones across the water's surface. On the right side of the photograph, uplight creates a soft glow in the Japanese Maple and shows off the waterfall. Lighting Design: Janet Lennox Moyer; Photograph: ©1990, Douglas A. Salin—www.dougsalin.com

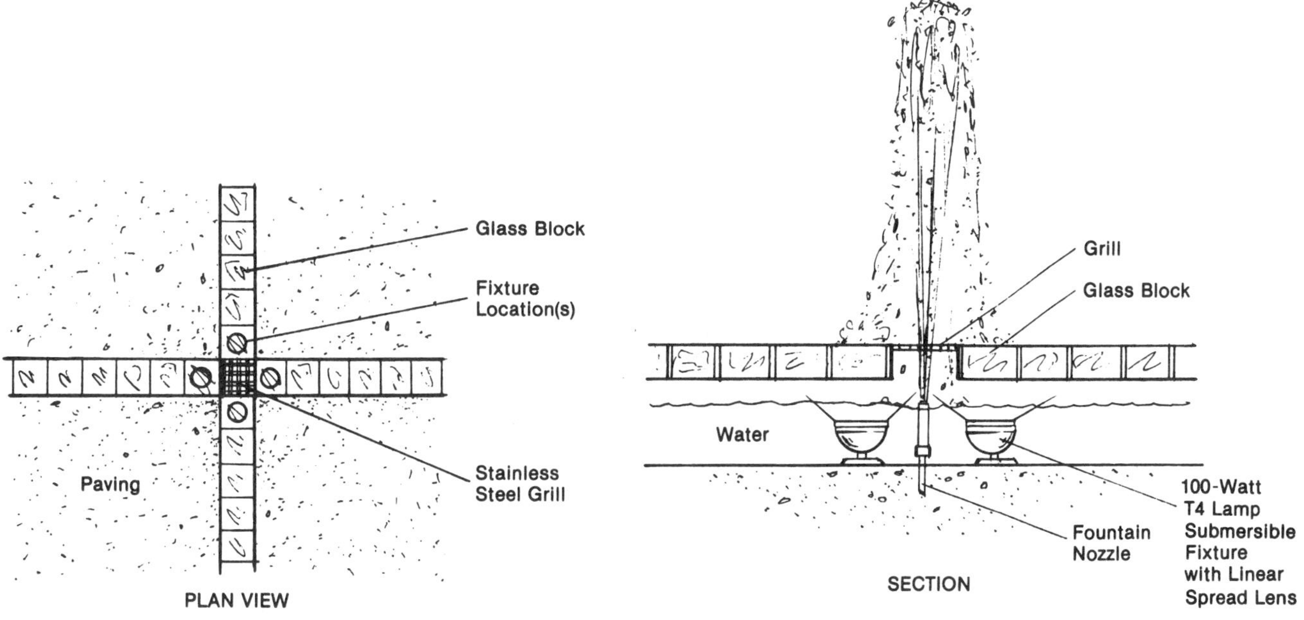

Figure 19.15. Plan and elevation of the lighting for a fountain. Drawing: Lezlie Johannessen.

and equipment (if it hasn't been well hidden). Lighting from outside the water works better for this type of body of water.

Sometimes man-made pools have an interesting shape or wall and bottom materials that could be emphasized. In order to light them effectively, the walls and bottom need to have a relatively high reflectance. Multiple fixtures may also be needed to avoid distracting hot spots in the pool. However, with a high reflectance, the pool(s) often appear(s) too important in the lighting composition, due to size. Using a low-wattage lamp helps keep the visual effect of the pool(s) in balance. Connecting the fixtures on a separate dimmer can help maintain visual balance.

Lighting the water surface of a natural or man-made pool from an external downlight creates a glow on moving water. This could be a natural pool at the bottom of a waterfall in a stream, or a man-made pool that has water movement due to a fall or fountain (see Figure 19.10).

SAFETY

NEC Article 680 covers the construction and installation of equipment and wiring for underwater lighting. As discussed earlier in Chapter 10, the *NEC®* is updated continually and should be referred to for the most recent regulations when starting a project. This section of the code differentiates between swimming pools or hot tubs and decorative pools. Both types of pools are required to have all metal parts and equipment within their boundaries bonded together and grounded to eliminate the potential for electrical shock. Both are also required to have all lighting equipment connected to a ground-fault circuit interrupting device. Both must have a setback of at least 4 feet from the inside wall of the structure for junction boxes and transformers, 5 feet for all switches and fixtures outside the water, and 10 feet for receptacles.

All fixtures installed below the water must be labeled by an accepted testing laboratory (such as UL or ETL) for *submersible use.* Some differences occur between swimming pools and decorative pools in the installation requirements for lighting fixtures. For example, in swimming pools the fixtures must be a minimum of 18 inches below the normal surface of the water, except for fixtures specifically labeled for use at a minimum depth of 4 inches below the water surface. In decorative pools, the fixture lens must be below the water level, but no specific dimension is required. A reasonable minimum to use is 2 inches below the low water level.

In decorative pools, the code requires that exposed cords be limited in length to 10 feet. All fixtures installed in the pool must be installed so that they can be serviced without reducing the water level of the pool. This means that all fixtures recessed into the structure of the pool must be a niche type. All fixtures must have stabilizing bases or must be securely mounted. This means that all fixtures located where water is moving should be attached to the pool bottom. The fixture lens should be covered with an exterior metal grid, called a rock guard, that prevents people from touching the lens (which could burn the person or break the lens, potentially causing an electrical shock). Additionally, the cord should have a strain-relief fitting to eliminate pulling the fixture's electrical connection apart (see Figure 19.16).

EQUIPMENT FOR UNDERWATER USE

A primary objective in underwater lighting is to hide the fixtures from view, not just to eliminate the lamp brightness, but also to avoid seeing all the electrical cords, connections, and boxes, which will detract from the water feature. Due to the incompatibility of water and electricity and potential harm to people, the construction and installation of underwater equipment is strictly governed by the NEC and the laboratories that test equipment for safety.

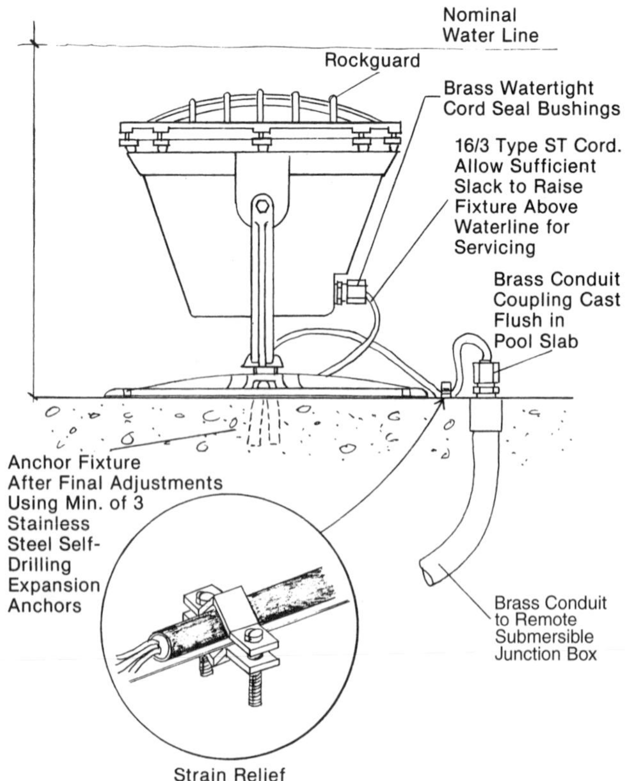

Figure 19.16. *Installation details for a submersible accent-type fixture. Drawing: Lezlie Johannessen.*

Lamps

As with any lighting, the lamps create the effects. In this area of landscape lighting, incandescent lamps are the main source used. They offer the controllability and wide range of wattage needed to fulfill widely differing situations. Many types of lamps are used, including 120-volt long-life A-lamps, the 120-volt PAR family (38, 46, 56, & 64 sizes), various types of 120-volt quartz, and 12-volt MR16 and PAR36 types. The wattage can vary from 75 to 1,000 watts, depending on the specific situation. Quartz lamps are becoming widely used because of their smaller size and considerable candlepower output. In the future, fixtures utilizing compact fluorescent and HID lamps may be available.

The height and width of a water feature determines the wattage and beamspread of the lamp required. Tall falls and fountains require spot distributions. Floods and wide floods are used for shorter distances and wide areas. Flood beamspreads work well for large single jet effects or small multiple effects, using a 1:1 height-to-width ratio for coverage. Wide-flood beamspreads work for large multiple jets and other configurations using a 2:1 height-to-width ratio for coverage. See candlepower recommendations for fountains in Figure 19.17. These can also be used as a guide for the wattages required for waterfalls.

The addition of a color filter over a lamp adds fantasy to the water feature, since the light transfers the color to the water. This effect is dramatic and should be used carefully. As with color used elsewhere in landscape lighting, exhibitions and amusement parks can use this strong effect. Most properties should limit the use of color.

The addition of a color filter also decreases light output. Designers can request the transmittance information of specific filters from the fixture or the filter manufacturer, but generally, yellow filters transmit only 50 percent, and blue can decrease the output by as much as 88 percent. The use of colored filters requires increasing the lamp wattage or adding more fixtures to create the desired effect.

Fixtures

The fixtures for use underwater are very different from those used in the rest of landscape lighting. The materials used to make the fixtures are typically copper, brass, or stainless steel. The fixtures must be entirely sealed to prevent water from entering the lamp housing. Underwater fixtures rely on the surrounding water to dissipate the heat generated by the lamp. The fixtures need to have a low-water cutoff device so that the fixture will not continue to operate when it is not entirely submerged. If the fixture is allowed to operate in this condition, it can cause the lens to explode and the lamp to fail prematurely.

The location of the fixture underwater is critical. It needs to be far enough underwater always to be submerged, but for uplighting situations, it should be as close to the surface as possible. The recommended minimum is between 2 and 4 inches below the water surface. Additionally, the deeper the fixture in the water, the more the color of light shifts toward yellow (as the blue light gets filtered out).

Fixtures need to have strong locking mechanisms, such as yoke locks, to maintain the desired aiming angle

UNDERWATER LIGHTING WATTAGE TABLE

	HEIGHT OF FOUNTAIN EFFECT									
Light Distribution	5'	10'	15'	20'	25'	30'	35'	40'	45'	50'
Wide Flood	250	500	1000	2000	3000					
Flood	150	300	500	900	1000	1500	2000			
Spot	150	150	250	300	500	600	1000	1200	2000	2000

MINIMUM BEAM CANDLEPOWER REQUIREMENTS*

Water Effect Height (ft.)	5	10	15	20	25	30	35	40	45	50
Candlepower Required (x1000)	4	11	21	24	50	69	91	115	144	170

* Candlepower shown is initial average in central 5° cone for Spots; central 10° for Floods.

Figure 19.17. *Data courtesy of Hydrel.*

due to the force of water—not just under falls, but wherever there is a current or steady movement of water. Securely attaching fixtures to the pool structure (as required by code) ensures that the lighting effect will not be lost due to movement of the fixture by the force of water, by the maintenance staff, or by vandals.

Fiber Optics

Underwater lighting can benefit from the use of fiberoptic technology (see "Fiber Optics" in Chapter 7). All of the restrictions that accompany putting electrical devices such as lighting fixtures underwater favor fiber optics, since none of the electrical components needs to be in the water. This allows easy access to the lamp for maintenance, minimizes the number of lamps and sometimes the overall wattage, and can create incredible effects (see Figure 19.18). Individual fiber-optic ends can be attached or embedded into the steps of a water fall to create individual pinpoints of light. With fiber optics, the light source is located in a mechanical room, which makes maintenance simple. Also, filters and templates can be attached to the housing to change the color of light gradually over time or to control which fibers receive light, creating perceived movement of the light. Fiber optics in swimming pools can outline the pool shape and in hot tubs can provide practical internal lighting (see Figure 19.19).

Lamps and fixtures must be chosen and placed carefully to create desired effects on still or moving bodies of water. Despite the technical challenges, lighting water features can provide some of the most stunning effects in landscape lighting.

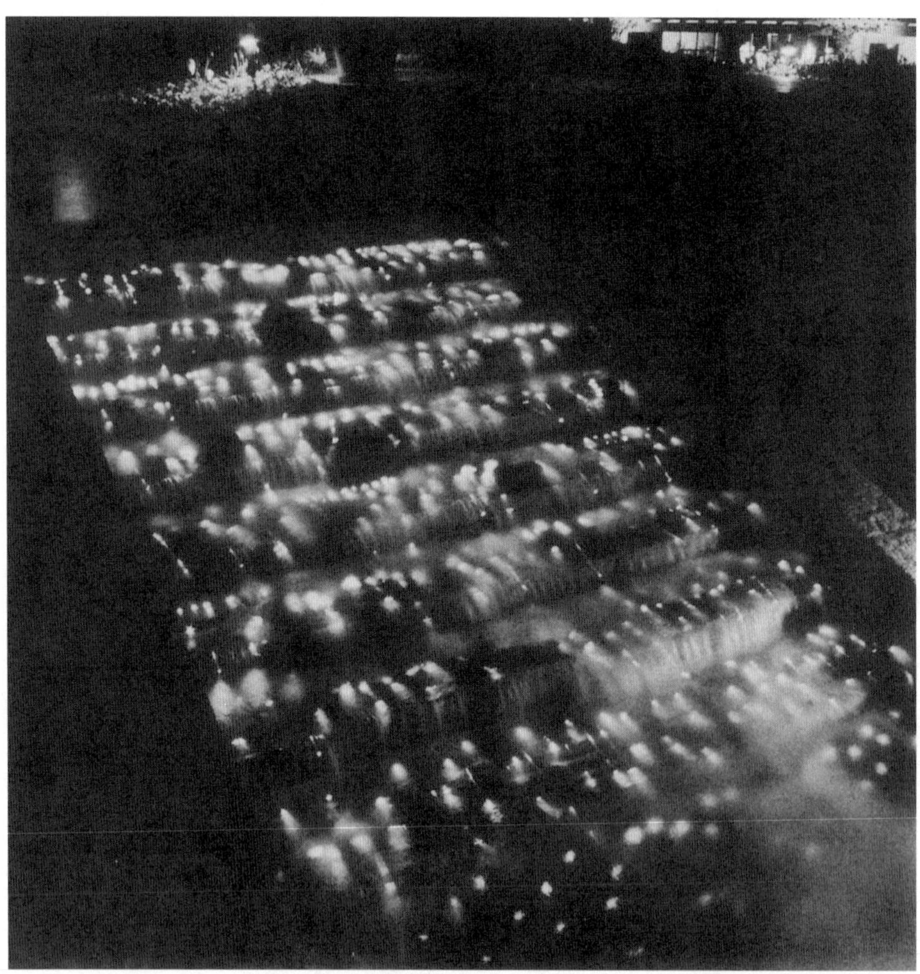

Figure 19.18. *Multiple fiber-optic filaments embedded into the walls of this cascade create the effect of lit water droplets moving down the fall. An illuminator (light fixture) with a 150-watt MR16 lamp uses an art wheel (template) with a pattern of holes to provide light randomly to the individual bundles, creating the movement effect. Lighting Design: Ross DeAlessi, Luminae Souter Lighting Design; Landscape Architect: Ray Lopez, Landmark Land; Photograph: Ross DeAlessi.*

Figure 19.19. *A permanently mounted lens contains multiple fiber-optic bundles that run back to the fixture in the equipment room. In addition to simple maintenance, no lamp heat exists in the pool. Lighting Design: Janet Lennox Moyer, Luminae Souter Lighting Design; Photograph: Janet Lennox Moyer.*

Appendix

PROJECT:____________________

INDEX OF INTERIOR LIGHTING SYSTEM DRAWINGS

Drawing Sheet Number	Drawing Sheet Name	ID / ISSUE DATE 1 / DATE
L-0.0	Index of Drawings and Drawing Symbols	
L-0.1	Lighting General Notes and Numbered Notes	
L-1.1.1	Lighting Zone Plan	
L-1.2.1	Lighting Control Zone Plan	
L-2.1.1.1	Floor Level Lighting Plan - Area 1	
L-2.1.1.2	Floor Level Dimensioned Lighting Plan - Area 1	
L-2.1.1.3	Floor Level Lighting Lamp Plan - Area 1	
L-2.1.2.1	Ceiling Level Lighting Plan - Area 1	
L-2.1.2.2	Ceiling Level Dimensioned Lighting Plan - Area 1	
L-2.1.2.3	Ceiling Level Lighting Lamp Plan - Area 1	
L-3.1.1	Transformer Schedule(s) and Load Schedule(s)	
L-3.2.1	Control Device Schedule(s) and Control Station Schedule(s)	
L-4.1.1	Lighting Control Diagrams	
L-4.2.1	Lighting Control Panel Layouts	
L-5.1.1	Lighting Wiring Diagrams	
L-5.1.2	Lighting Wiring Diagrams	
L-6.1.1	Lighting Fixture Details	
L-7.1.1	Lighting Installation Details	
L-7.1.2	Lighting Installation Details	
L-7.2.1	Equipment Installation Details	
L-8.1.1	Fiber Optics Installation Details	
L-8.2.1	Fiber Optics Schedules	

5/4/2004 MSH VISUAL PLANNERS, LLC © 2004 1 of 1

Figure A.1a.

FIBER OPTIC CONTROL SYMBOLS	
FOC-1A, FOC-2A, etc.	Letter refers to Fiber-Optic Cable Type Designation
FOI-1, FOI-2, etc.	Letter refers to Fiber-Optic Illuminator Type Designation
	End Light Fiber Optic with Lensed Adjustable Fitting
	Side Light Fiber-Optic Cable
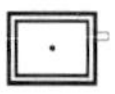	Fiber-Optic Illuminator
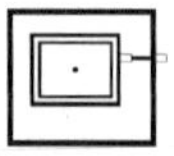	Below-Grade Fiber-Optic Illuminator
	Fiber-Optic Cable Feed Line in Conduit Sleeve

Figure A.1b.

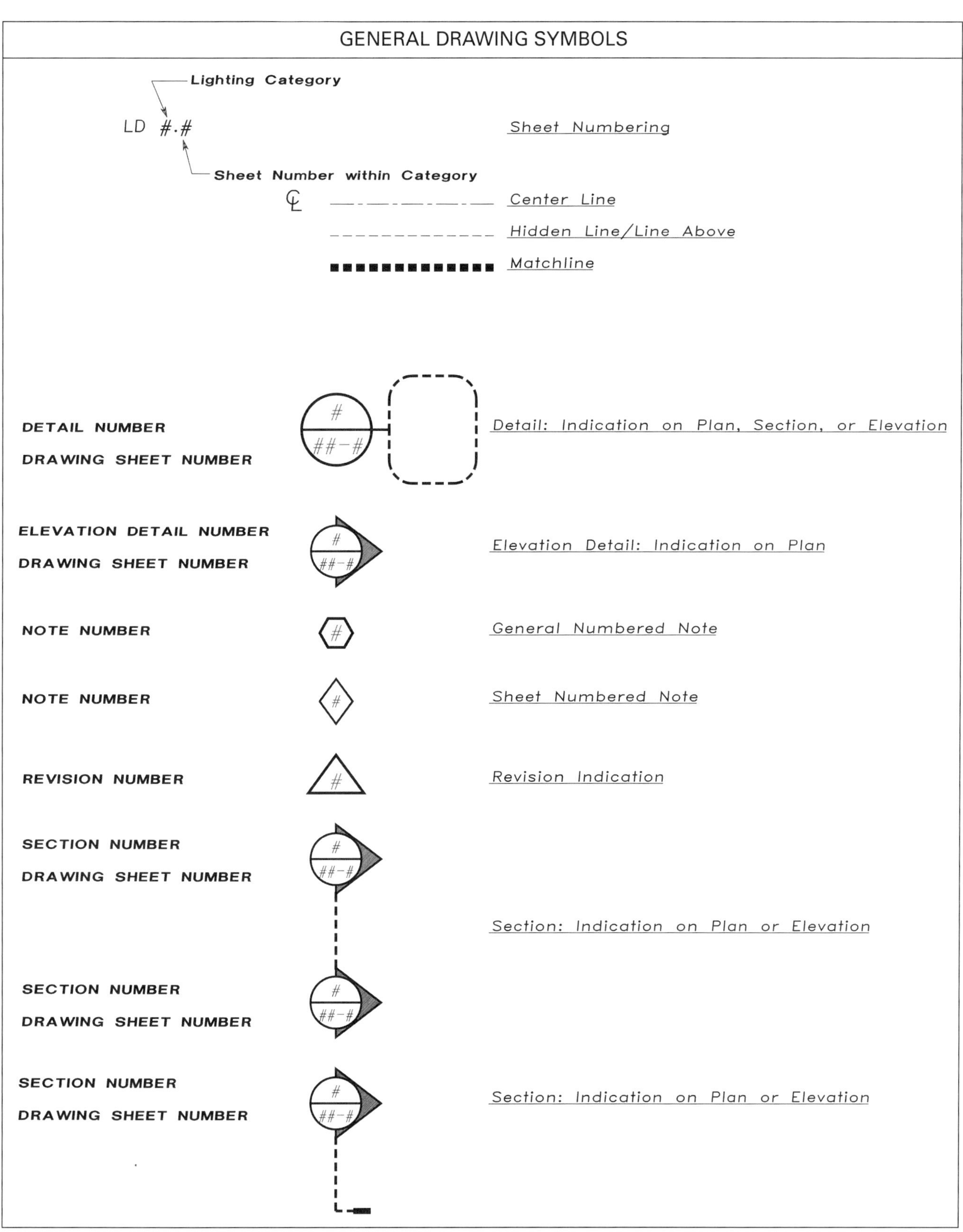

GENERAL DRAWING SYMBOLS
Lighting Category
LD #.#
Sheet Numbering
Sheet Number within Category
Center Line
Hidden Line/Line Above
Matchline
DETAIL NUMBER
DRAWING SHEET NUMBER
#
##-#
Detail: Indication on Plan, Section, or Elevation
ELEVATION DETAIL NUMBER
DRAWING SHEET NUMBER
Elevation Detail: Indication on Plan
NOTE NUMBER
General Numbered Note
NOTE NUMBER
Sheet Numbered Note
REVISION NUMBER
Revision Indication
SECTION NUMBER
DRAWING SHEET NUMBER
Section: Indication on Plan or Elevation
SECTION NUMBER
DRAWING SHEET NUMBER
SECTION NUMBER
DRAWING SHEET NUMBER
Section: Indication on Plan or Elevation

Figure A.2.

LANDSCAPE FIXTURE SYMBOLS

Symbol	Description
SA, SB, SC, SC1, etc.	Letter refers to Site Lighting Fixture Type Designation

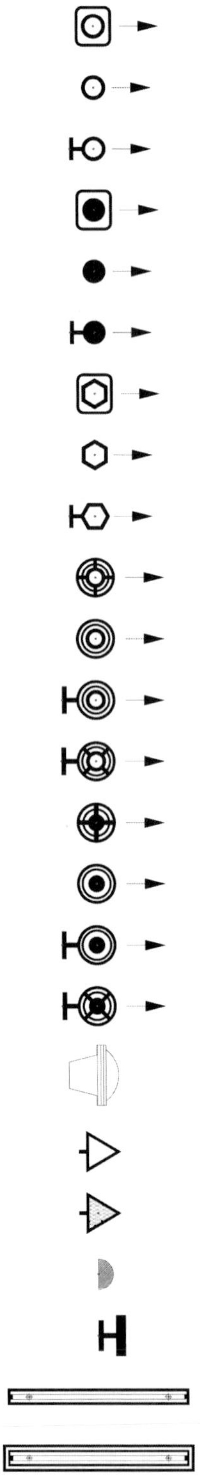

Description
12-Volt Incandescent Direct-Burial Accent Lighting Fixture
12-Volt Ground-Mount Accent Lighting Fixture
12-Volt Tree/Structure-Mounted Accent Lighting Fixture
120-Volt Incandescent Direct-Burial Accent Lighting Fixture
120-Volt Incandescent Ground-Mount Accent Lighting Fixture
120-Volt Incandescent Tree/Structure-Mounted Accent Lighting Fixture
120-Volt HID Direct-Burial Accent Lighting Fixture
120-Volt HID Ground-Mount Accent Lighting Fixture
120-Volt HID Tree/Structure-Mounted Accent Lighting Fixture
12-Volt Submersible Niche-Style Bottom-Mount Accent Lighting Fixture
12-Volt Submersible Base-Style Bottom-Mount Accent Lighting Fixture
12-Volt Submersible Base-Style Wall-Mount Accent Lighting Fixture
12-Volt Submersible Niche-Style Wall-Mount Accent Lighting Fixture
120-Volt Submersible Niche-Style Bottom-Mount Accent Lighting Fixture
120-Volt Submersible Base-Style Bottom-Mount Accent Lighting Fixture
120-Volt Submersible Base-Style Wall-Mount Accent Lighting Fixture
120-Volt Submersible Niche-Style Wall-Mount Accent Lighting Fixture
12-Volt Submersible Niche-Style Wall-Mount Swimming Pool Lighting Fixture
12-Volt Path Lighting Fixture
120-Volt Path Lighting Fixture
12-Volt Recessed Step Lighting Fixture
120-Volt Recessed Step Lighting Fixture
120-Volt Fluorescent Above-Grade Lighting Fixture
120-Volt Fluorescent Direct-Burial Lighting Fixture

Figure A.3.

CONTROL SYSTEM SYMBOLS

S	Single-Pole Switch
S_3	Three-Way Switch
S_4	Four-Way Switch
S_K	Single-Pole Keyed Switch (Additional Subscripts indicate Keys)
S_{K3}	Three-Way Keyed Switch (Additional Subscripts indicate Keys)
S_{K4}	Four-Way Keyed Switch (Additional Subscripts indicate Keys)
S_P	Single-Pole Switch with Pilot Light
S_{P3}	Three-Way Switch with Pilot Light
S_{P4}	Four-Way Switch with Pilot Light
S_{WP}	Single-Pole Switch in Waterproof Enclosure
S_{WP3}	Three-Way Switch in Waterproof Enclosure
S_{WP4}	Four-Way Switch in Waterproof Enclosure
S_F ID	Fan Switch/Controller (Subscript indicates Type)
S_T ID	Timer Switch (Subscript indicates Type)
DS	Door Switch
D ID	Single-Pole Line Voltage Dimmer Switch
D ID	Single-Pole Low Voltage Load-Rated Dimmer Switch
D_3 ID	Three-Way Line Voltage Dimmer Switch
D_3 ID	Three-Way Low Voltage Load-Rated Dimmer Switch
D ID	Single-Pole Dimmer Switch (Subscript indicates Type)
D_3 ID	Three-Way Dimmer Switch (Subscript Indicates Type)
[S] ID	Single-Pole Switch with Digital Network Interface (Subscript indicates ID)
[S] 3 ID	Three-Way Switch with Digital Network Interface (Subscript indicates ID)
[D] ID	Single-Pole Dimmer Switch with Digital Network Interface (Subscript indicates ID)
[D] 3 ID	Three-Way Dimmer Switch with Digital Network Interface (Subscript indicates ID)
NCPU-#	Digital Network Interface Central Processing Cabinet (# indicates ID)
SCS ID	Remote Scene Control Station (Subscript indicates ID)
RPJ ID	Remote Programming Jack (Subscript indicates ID)
RCJ ID	Remote Control Jack (Subscript indicates ID)
RSJ ID	Remote Scene Control Jack (Subscript indicates ID)
PSC ID	Preset Scene Control Station (Subscript indicates ID)
LCC ID	Lighting Control Console (Subscript indicates ID)
RCS ID	Remote Control Station (Subscript indicates ID)
IR	Remote Lighting Control Infrared Signal Receiver
Ⓡ	Remote Lighting Control Relay

Figure A.4.

ABBREVIATIONS

A or AMP	Ampere
ADJ	Adjustable
AC	Alternating Current
AFF	Above Finished Floor
AFG	Above Finished Grade
AG	Above Grade
APPROX	Approximately
ASYM	Asymmetric, Asymmetrical, Asymmetrically
ATC	Astronomic Time Controller
AWG	American Wire Gauge
BG	Below Grade
BMS	Building Management System
BS	British Standard
BSI	British Standards Institute
BSG	British Standard Gauge, Wire Gauge
BTY	Battery
CDA	Control Device Assembly
CIE	Commission Internationale de L'Eclairage
CKT	Circuit
CL	Center Line
CLG	Ceiling
CPU	Central Processing Unit
D	Dimmer
DB	Direct Burial
DC	Direct Current
DIA	Diameter
DJ	Distribution Junction Box
DWG	Drawing
EA	Each
EC	Electrical Sub Contractor
ELC	Exterior Lighting Consultant
ELP	Emergency Lighting Panel
EM	Emergency
EMB	Emergency Battery (Remote)
ELPP	Emergency Lighting and Power Panel
ELV	Electronic Low–Voltage (Load Type)
EQ	Equal
ES	Essential
ES	Essential Lighting Panel
ESLPP	Essential Lighting and Power Panel
FDI	Fluorescent Dimming Interface
FL	Flood
FLU	Fluorescent (Load Type)
GC	General Contractor
GFI	Ground Fault Interrupter
GRND	Ground
HID	High Intensity Discharge (Load Type)
HOR	Horizontal
HPS	High Pressure Sodium
ID	Inside Diameter
IEC	International Electrotechnical Commission
II	Irrelevant Information
INC	Incandescent (Load Type)
INCL	Included
IP	IEC International Protection
IR	Infrared Receiver
K	Kelvin
KVA	Kilo Volt Ampere
KW	Kilowatt
L	Load
LC	Lighting Consultant
LCC	Lighting Control Console
LP	Lighting Panel
LPP	Lighting and Power Panel
LRP	Lighting Relay Panel
LSP	Linear Spread
LT	Lighting Track
LV	Low–Voltage (Load Type)
LVT	Low–Voltage Transformer
MAX	Maximum
MFL	Medium Flood
MH	Metal Halide
MIN	Minimum
MLV	Magnetic Low–Voltage (Load Type)
MTR	Motor (Load Type)
N	Network Interface Remote Control Station
NA	Not Applicable
NCPU	Network Central Processing Unit
NEC	National Electric Code (USA)
NO	Number
NOM	Nominal
NORM	Normal
NIC	Not in Contract
NSP	Narrow Spot
NTS	Not To Scale
OC	On Center
OD	Outside Diameter
PROJ	Projection
PS	Porcelain Socket
PSC	Preset Scene Control Station
R	Relay
RAD	Radius
RCJ	Remote Control Jack
RCS	Remote Control Station
RD	Remote Dimmer
RDA	Remote Dimmer Assembly
REF	Reference
REV	Revision
RFI	Radio Frequency Interference
RLT	Recessed Lighting Track
RND	Round
RP	Relay Panel
RSJ	Remote Scene Control Jack
S	Switch
SCHED	Schedule
SCS	Remote Scene Control Station
SIM	Similar
SLP	Site Lighting Panel
SP	Spot
SPEC	Specification
SPR	Spread
SQ	Square
STD	Standard
SUSP	Suspended
SYM	Symmetric, Symmetrical, Symmetrically
T	Transformer
TBD	To Be Determined
TC	Time Clock
TP	Top of Pavement
TYP	Typical
UL	Underwriter's Laboratories, Inc. (USA)
UON	Unless Otherwise Noted
V	Volts
VA	Volt Ampere
VAC	Volts AC
VDC	Volts DC
VDT	Visual Display Terminal
VERT	Vertical
VNSP	Very Narrow Spot
VWFL	Very Wide Flood
W	Watts
W/	With
W/O	Without
WFL	Wide Flood
WP	Waterproof
WR	Water Resistant
WSLT	Wire System Lighting Track
XFMR	Transformer

Figure A.5.

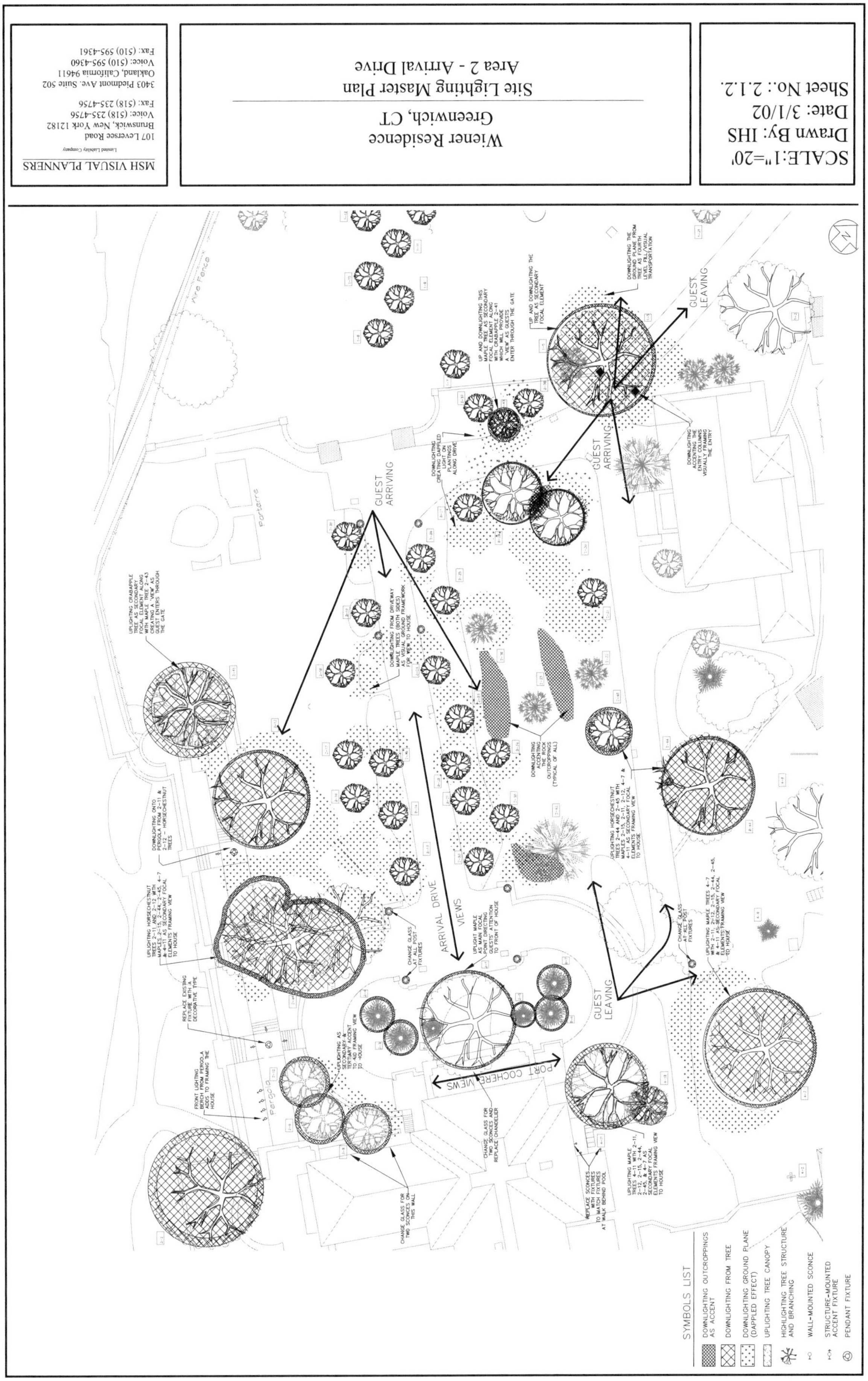

SCALE:1"=20'
Drawn By: IHS
Date: 3/1/02
Sheet No.: 2.1.2.
Wiener Residence
Greenwich, CT
Site Lighting Master Plan
Area 2 - Arrival Drive
MSH VISUAL PLANNERS
Limited Liability Company
107 Leversee Road
Brunswick, New York 12182
Voice: (518) 235-4756
Fax: (518) 235-4756
3403 Piedmont Ave. Suite 502
Oakland, California 94611
Voice: (510) 595-4360
Fax: (510) 595-4361
GUEST ARRIVING
GUEST LEAVING
ARRIVAL DRIVE
VIEWS
PORT COCHERE VIEWS
Parterre
Pergola
SYMBOLS LIST
DOWNLIGHTING OUTCROPPINGS AS ACCENT
DOWNLIGHTING FROM TREE
DOWNLIGHTING GROUND PLANE (DAPPLED EFFECT)
UPLIGHTING TREE CANOPY
HIGHLIGHTING TREE STRUCTURE AND BRANCHING
WALL-MOUNTED SCONCE
STRUCTURE-MOUNTED ACCENT FIXTURE
PENDANT FIXTURE

Figure A.6.

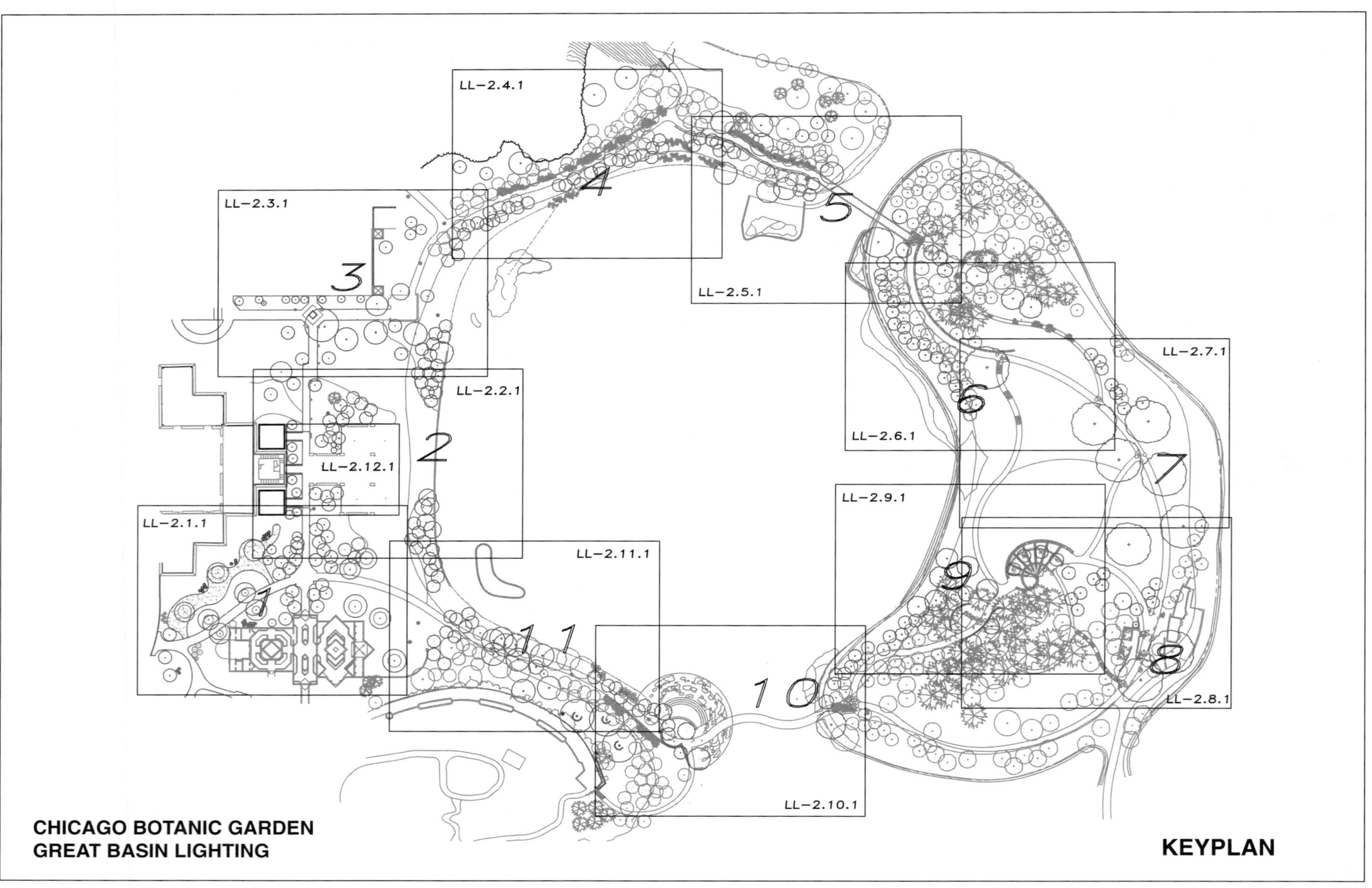
LL−2.4.1
LL−2.3.1
LL−2.5.1
LL−2.2.1
LL−2.7.1
LL−2.12.1
LL−2.6.1
LL−2.9.1
LL−2.1.1
LL−2.11.1
LL−2.8.1
LL−2.10.1
CHICAGO BOTANIC GARDEN
GREAT BASIN LIGHTING
KEYPLAN

Figure A.7.

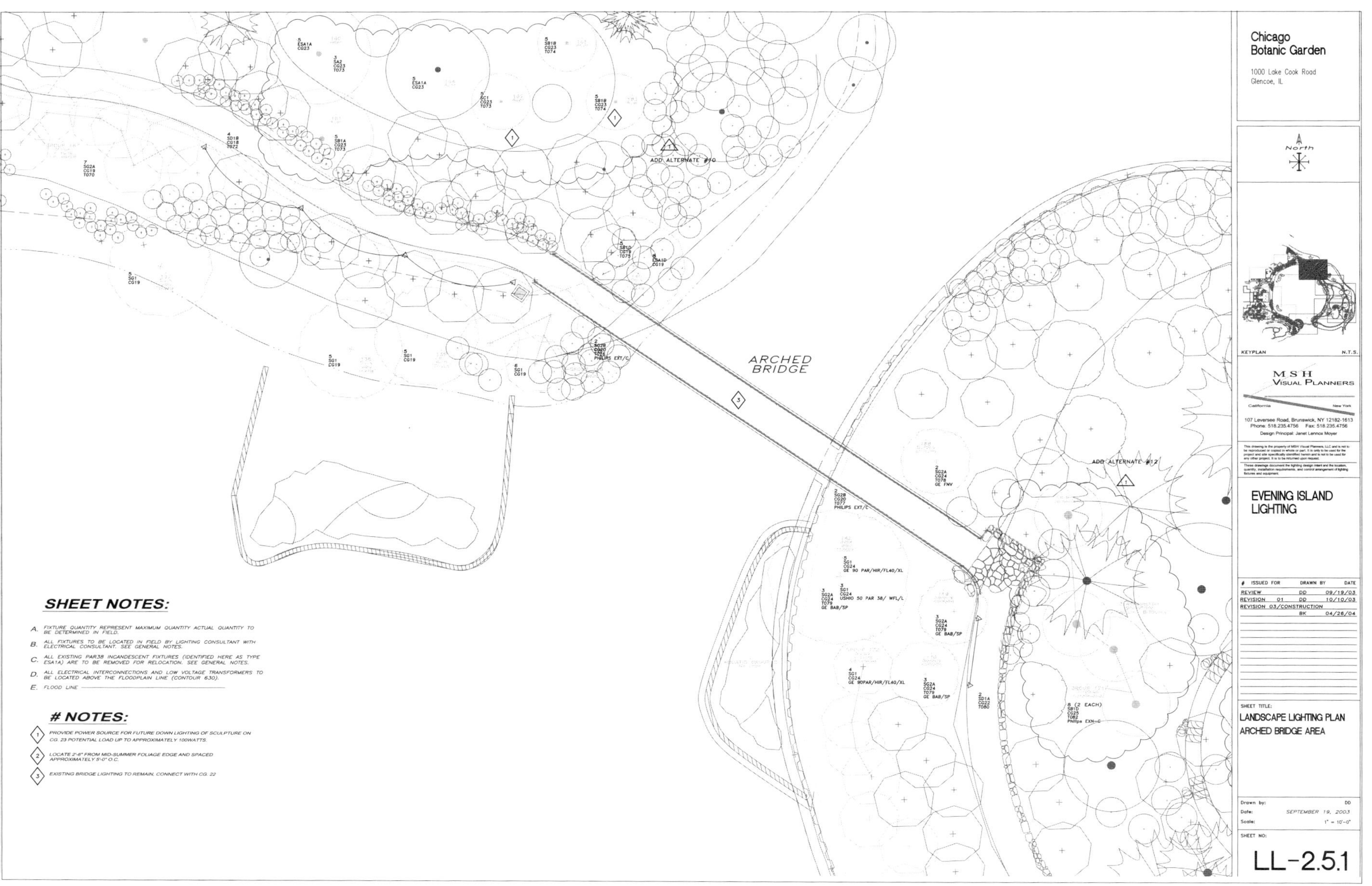
Chicago Botanic Garden
1000 Lake Cook Road
Glencoe, IL
North
KEYPLAN
N.T.S.
M S H
VISUAL PLANNERS
California
New York
107 Leversee Road, Brunswick, NY 12182-1613
Phone: 518.235.4756 Fax: 518.235.4756
Design Principal: Janet Lennox Moyer
EVENING ISLAND LIGHTING
ISSUED FOR DRAWN BY DATE
REVIEW DD 09/19/03
REVISION 01 DD 10/10/03
REVISION 03/CONSTRUCTION BK 04/26/04
SHEET TITLE:
LANDSCAPE LIGHTING PLAN
ARCHED BRIDGE AREA
Drawn by: DD
Date: SEPTEMBER 19, 2003
Scale: 1" = 10'-0"
SHEET NO:
LL-2.5.1
ARCHED BRIDGE
ADD ALTERNATE #10
ADD ALTERNATE #12
SHEET NOTES:
A. FIXTURE QUANTITY REPRESENT MAXIMUM QUANTITY ACTUAL QUANTITY TO BE DETERMINED IN FIELD.
B. ALL FIXTURES TO BE LOCATED IN FIELD BY LIGHTING CONSULTANT WITH ELECTRICAL CONSULTANT. SEE GENERAL NOTES.
C. ALL EXISTING PAR38 INCANDESCENT FIXTURES (IDENTIFIED HERE AS TYPE ESA1A) ARE TO BE REMOVED FOR RELOCATION. SEE GENERAL NOTES.
D. ALL ELECTRICAL INTERCONNECTIONS AND LOW VOLTAGE TRANSFORMERS TO BE LOCATED ABOVE THE FLOODPLAIN LINE (CONTOUR 630).
E. FLOOD LINE
NOTES:
1 PROVIDE POWER SOURCE FOR FUTURE DOWN LIGHTING OF SCULPTURE ON CG. 23 POTENTIAL LOAD UP TO APPROXIMATELY 100WATTS.
2 LOCATE 2'-6" FROM MID-SUMMER FOLIAGE EDGE AND SPACED APPROXIMATELY 5'-0" O.C.
3 EXISTING BRIDGE LIGHTING TO REMAIN. CONNECT WITH CG. 22

Figure A.8.

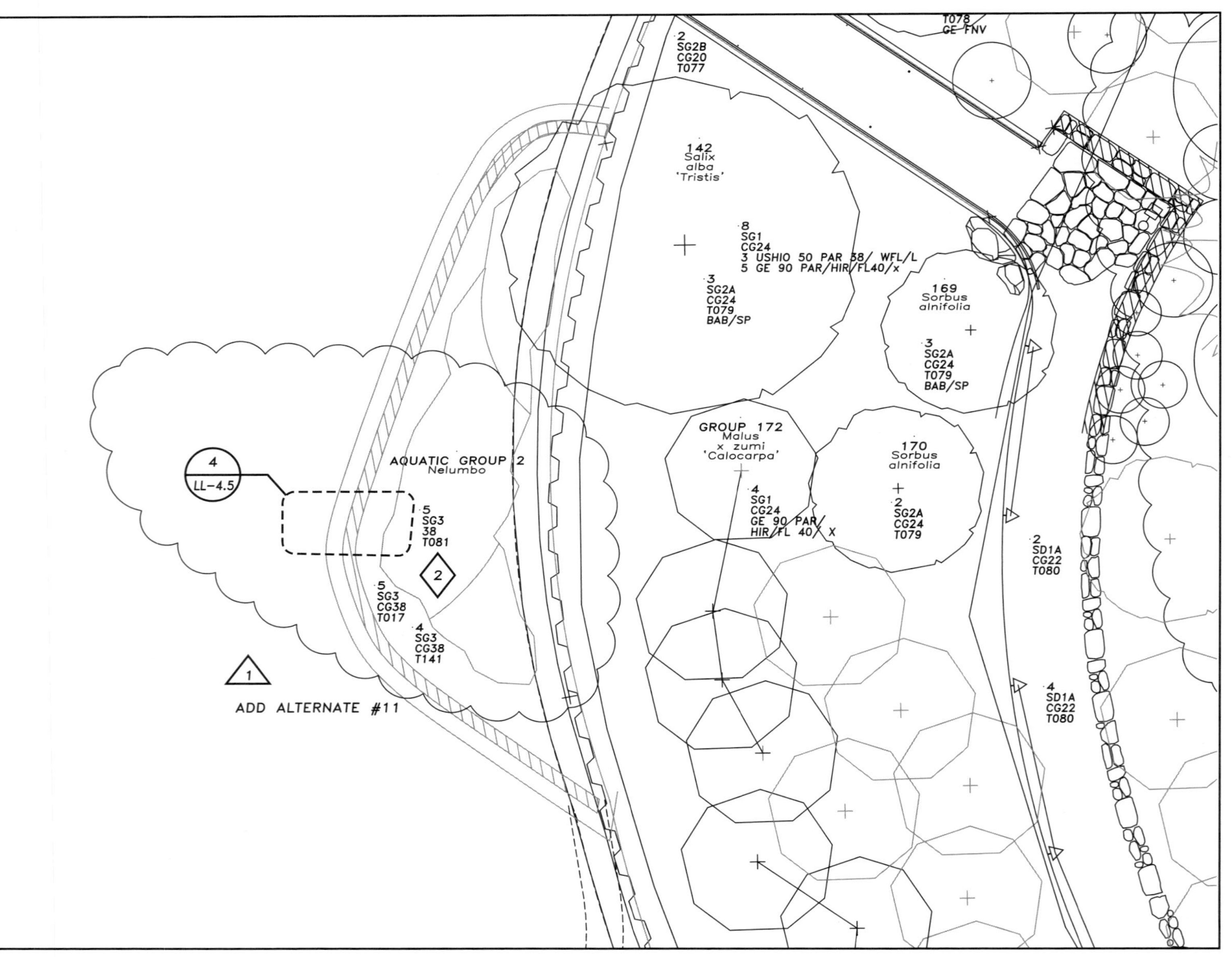

T078
GE FNV
2
SG2B
CG20
T077
142
Salix
alba
'Tristis'
8
SG1
CG24
3 USHIO 50 PAR 38/ WFL/L
5 GE 90 PAR/HIR/FL40/x
3
SG2A
CG24
T079
BAB/SP
169
Sorbus
alnifolia
3
SG2A
CG24
T079
BAB/SP
GROUP 172
Malus
x zumi
'Calocarpa'
4
SG1
CG24
GE 90 PAR/
HIR/FL 40/ X
170
Sorbus
alnifolia
2
SG2A
CG24
T079
2
SD1A
CG22
T080
4
SD1A
CG22
T080
AQUATIC GROUP 2
Nelumbo
4
LL-4.5
5
SG3
38
T081
2
5
SG3
CG38
T017
4
SG3
CG38
T141
1
ADD ALTERNATE #11

Figure A.9.

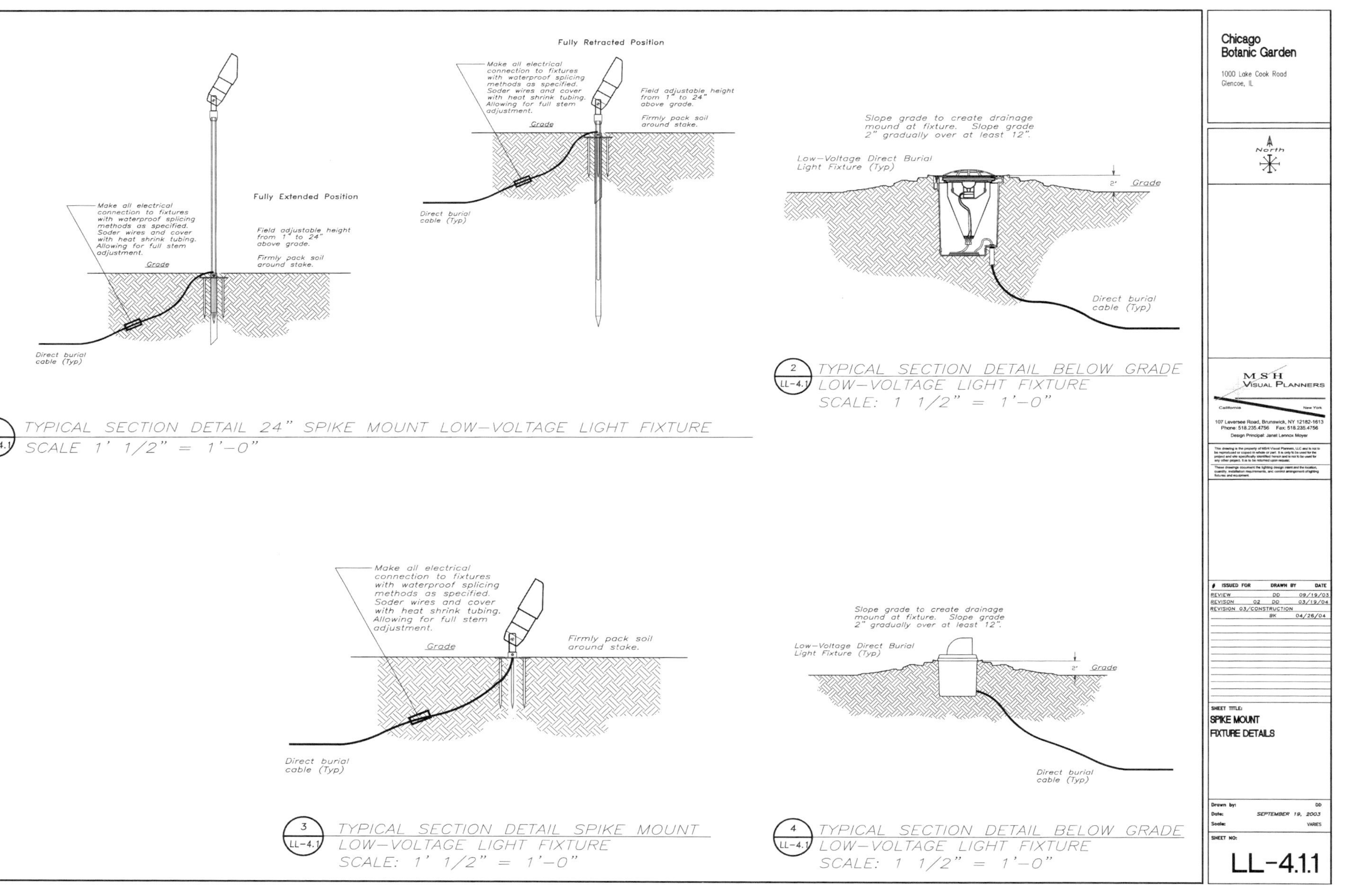
Fully Extended Position
Make all electrical connection to fixtures with waterproof splicing methods as specified. Soder wires and cover with heat shrink tubing. Allowing for full stem adjustment.
Grade
Field adjustable height from 1" to 24" above grade.
Firmly pack soil around stake.
Direct burial cable (Typ)
Fully Retracted Position
Make all electrical connection to fixtures with waterproof splicing methods as specified. Soder wires and cover with heat shrink tubing. Allowing for full stem adjustment.
Grade
Field adjustable height from 1" to 24" above grade.
Firmly pack soil around stake.
Direct burial cable (Typ)
1
LL-4.1
TYPICAL SECTION DETAIL 24" SPIKE MOUNT LOW–VOLTAGE LIGHT FIXTURE
SCALE 1' 1/2" = 1'–0"
Slope grade to create drainage mound at fixture. Slope grade 2" gradually over at least 12".
Low–Voltage Direct Burial Light Fixture (Typ)
2"
Grade
Direct burial cable (Typ)
2
LL-4.1
TYPICAL SECTION DETAIL BELOW GRADE
LOW–VOLTAGE LIGHT FIXTURE
SCALE: 1 1/2" = 1'–0"
Make all electrical connection to fixtures with waterproof splicing methods as specified. Soder wires and cover with heat shrink tubing. Allowing for full stem adjustment.
Grade
Firmly pack soil around stake.
Direct burial cable (Typ)
3
LL-4.1
TYPICAL SECTION DETAIL SPIKE MOUNT
LOW–VOLTAGE LIGHT FIXTURE
SCALE: 1' 1/2" = 1'–0"
Slope grade to create drainage mound at fixture. Slope grade 2" gradually over at least 12".
Low–Voltage Direct Burial Light Fixture (Typ)
2"
Grade
Direct burial cable (Typ)
4
LL-4.1
TYPICAL SECTION DETAIL BELOW GRADE
LOW–VOLTAGE LIGHT FIXTURE
SCALE: 1 1/2" = 1'–0"
Chicago Botanic Garden
1000 Lake Cook Road
Glencoe, IL
North
MSH VISUAL PLANNERS
California
New York
107 Leversee Road, Brunswick, NY 12182-1613
Phone: 518.235.4756 Fax: 518.235.4756
Design Principal: Janet Lennox Moyer
ISSUED FOR DRAWN BY DATE
REVIEW DD 09/19/03
REVISON 02 DD 03/19/04
REVISION 03/CONSTRUCTION BK 04/26/04
SHEET TITLE:
SPIKE MOUNT
FIXTURE DETAILS
Drawn by: DD
Date: SEPTEMBER 19, 2003
Scale: VARIES
SHEET NO:
LL-4.1.1

Figure A.10.

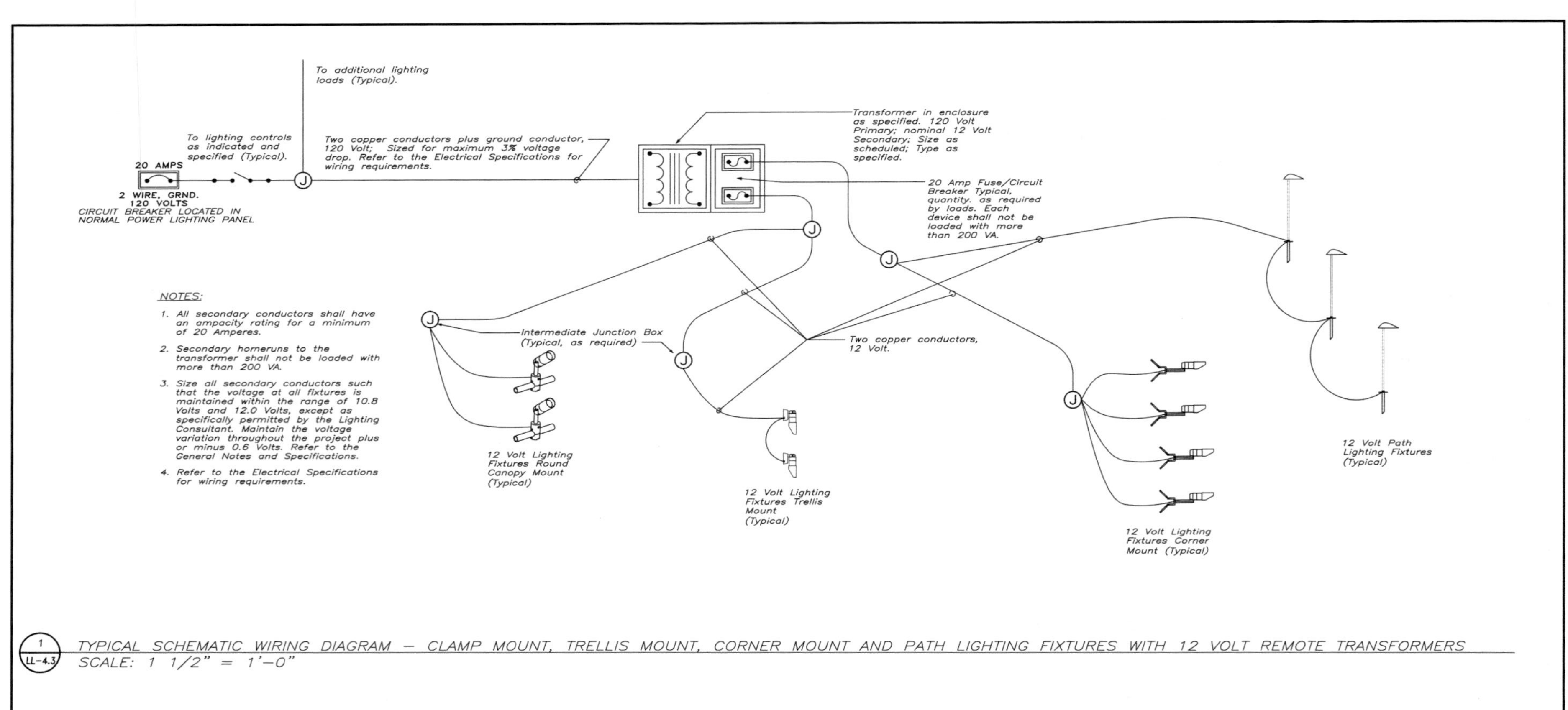

To additional lighting loads (Typical).
To lighting controls as indicated and specified (Typical).
20 AMPS
2 WIRE, GRND. 120 VOLTS
CIRCUIT BREAKER LOCATED IN NORMAL POWER LIGHTING PANEL
Two copper conductors plus ground conductor, 120 Volt; Sized for maximum 3% voltage drop. Refer to the Electrical Specifications for wiring requirements.
Transformer in enclosure as specified. 120 Volt Primary; nominal 12 Volt Secondary; Size as scheduled; Type as specified.
20 Amp Fuse/Circuit Breaker Typical, quantity. as required by loads. Each device shall not be loaded with more than 200 VA.
NOTES:
1. All secondary conductors shall have an ampacity rating for a minimum of 20 Amperes.
2. Secondary homeruns to the transformer shall not be loaded with more than 200 VA.
3. Size all secondary conductors such that the voltage at all fixtures is maintained within the range of 10.8 Volts and 12.0 Volts, except as specifically permitted by the Lighting Consultant. Maintain the voltage variation throughout the project plus or minus 0.6 Volts. Refer to the General Notes and Specifications.
4. Refer to the Electrical Specifications for wiring requirements.
Intermediate Junction Box (Typical, as required)
Two copper conductors, 12 Volt.
12 Volt Lighting Fixtures Round Canopy Mount (Typical)
12 Volt Lighting Fixtures Trellis Mount (Typical)
12 Volt Lighting Fixtures Corner Mount (Typical)
12 Volt Path Lighting Fixtures (Typical)
TYPICAL SCHEMATIC WIRING DIAGRAM — CLAMP MOUNT, TRELLIS MOUNT, CORNER MOUNT AND PATH LIGHTING FIXTURES WITH 12 VOLT REMOTE TRANSFORMERS
SCALE: 1 1/2" = 1'-0"
1
LL-4.3

Figure A.11.

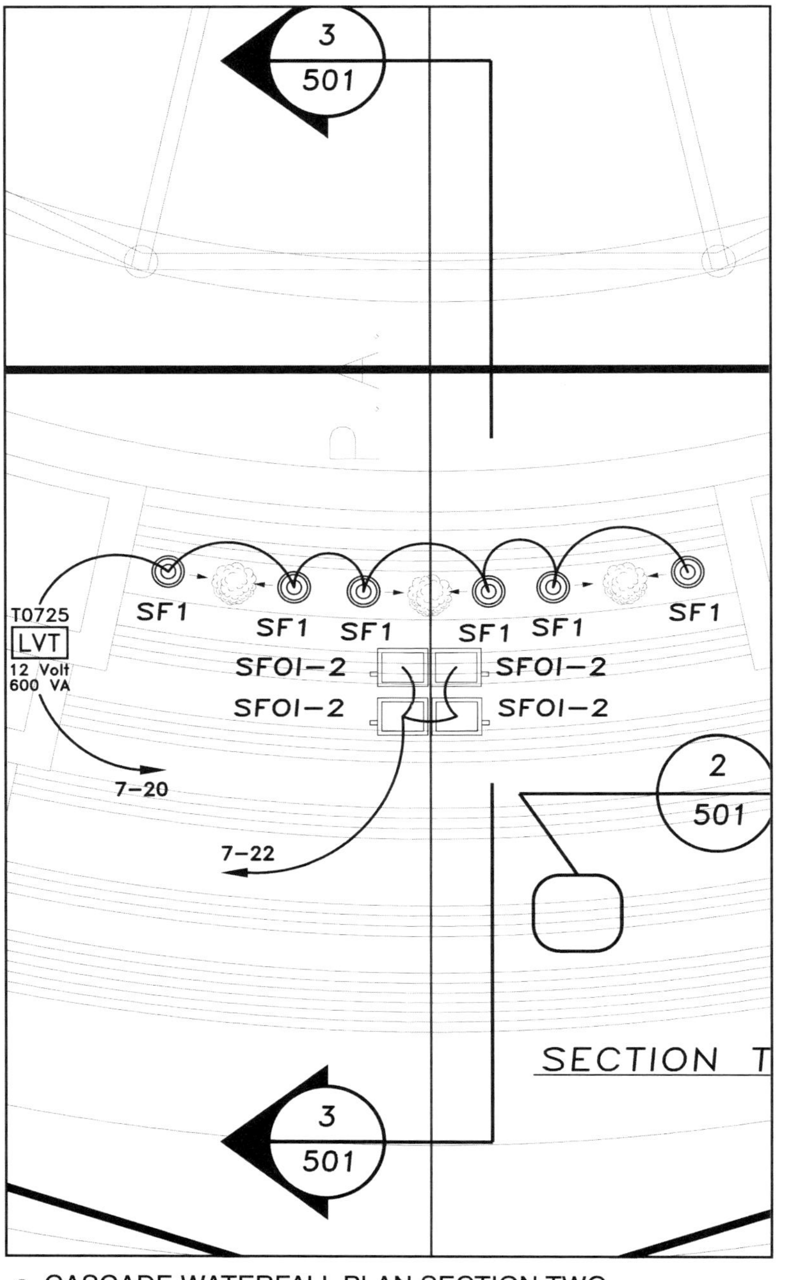

a. CASCADE WATERFALL PLAN SECTION TWO

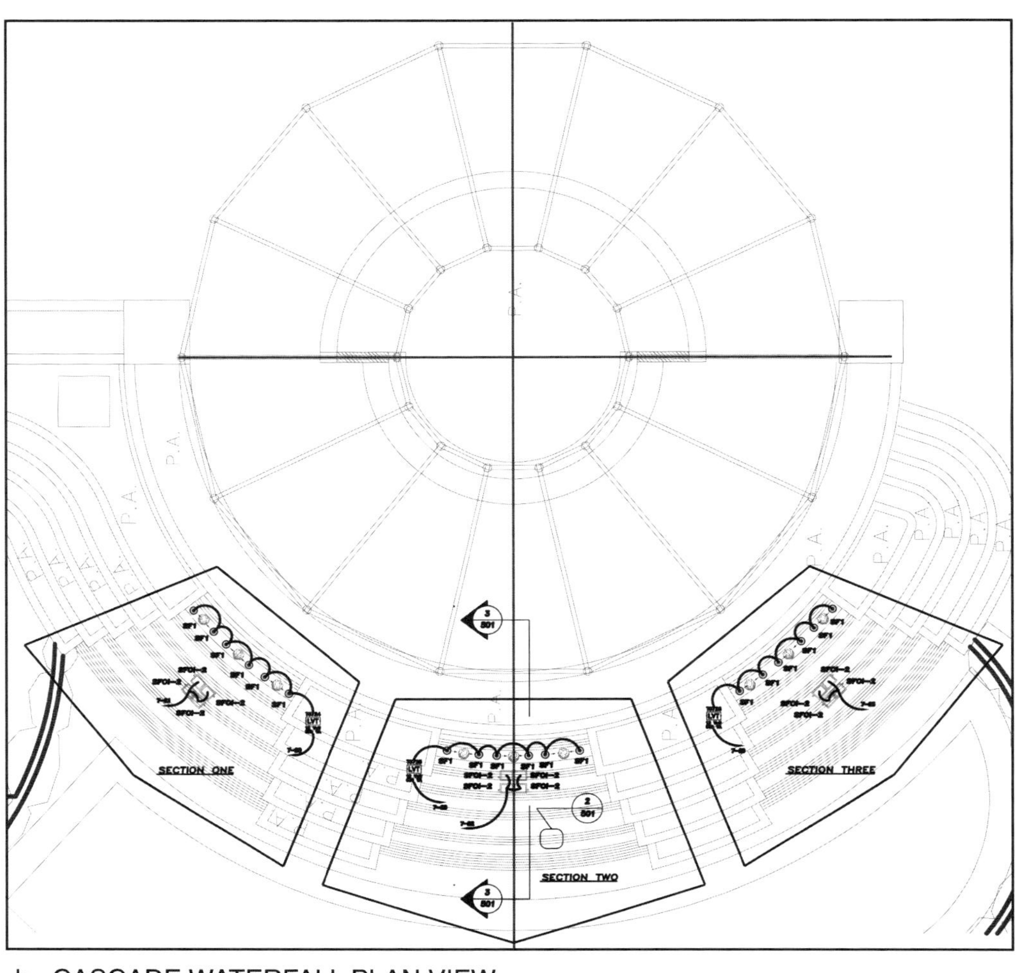

b. CASCADE WATERFALL PLAN VIEW

Figure A.12.

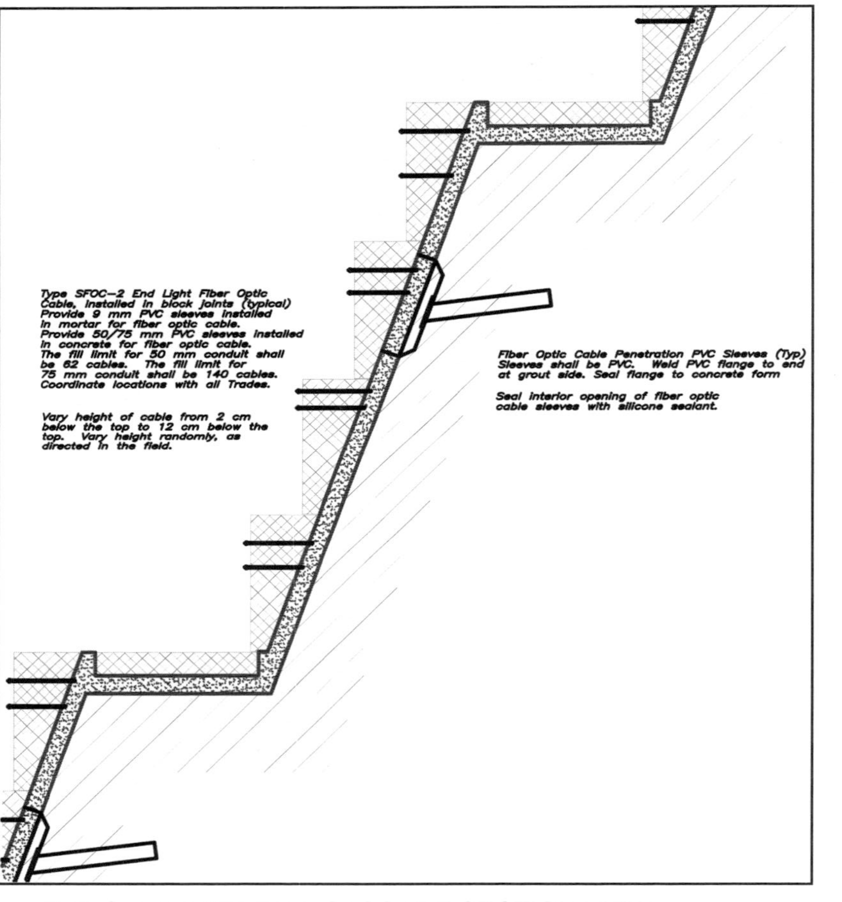
Type SFOC-2 End Light Fiber Optic Cable, installed in block joints (typical)
Provide 9 mm PVC sleeves installed in mortar for fiber optic cable.
Provide 50/75 mm PVC sleeves installed in concrete for fiber optic cable.
The fill limit for 50 mm conduit shall be 62 cables. The fill limit for 75 mm conduit shall be 140 cables.
Coordinate locations with all Trades.
Vary height of cable from 2 cm below the top to 12 cm below the top. Vary height randomly, as directed in the field.
Fiber Optic Cable Penetration PVC Sleeves (Typ)
Sleeves shall be PVC. Weld PVC flange to end at grout side. Seal flange to concrete form
Seal interior opening of fiber optic cable sleeves with silicone sealant.

a. TYPICAL WATERFALL CASCADE SECTION VIEW

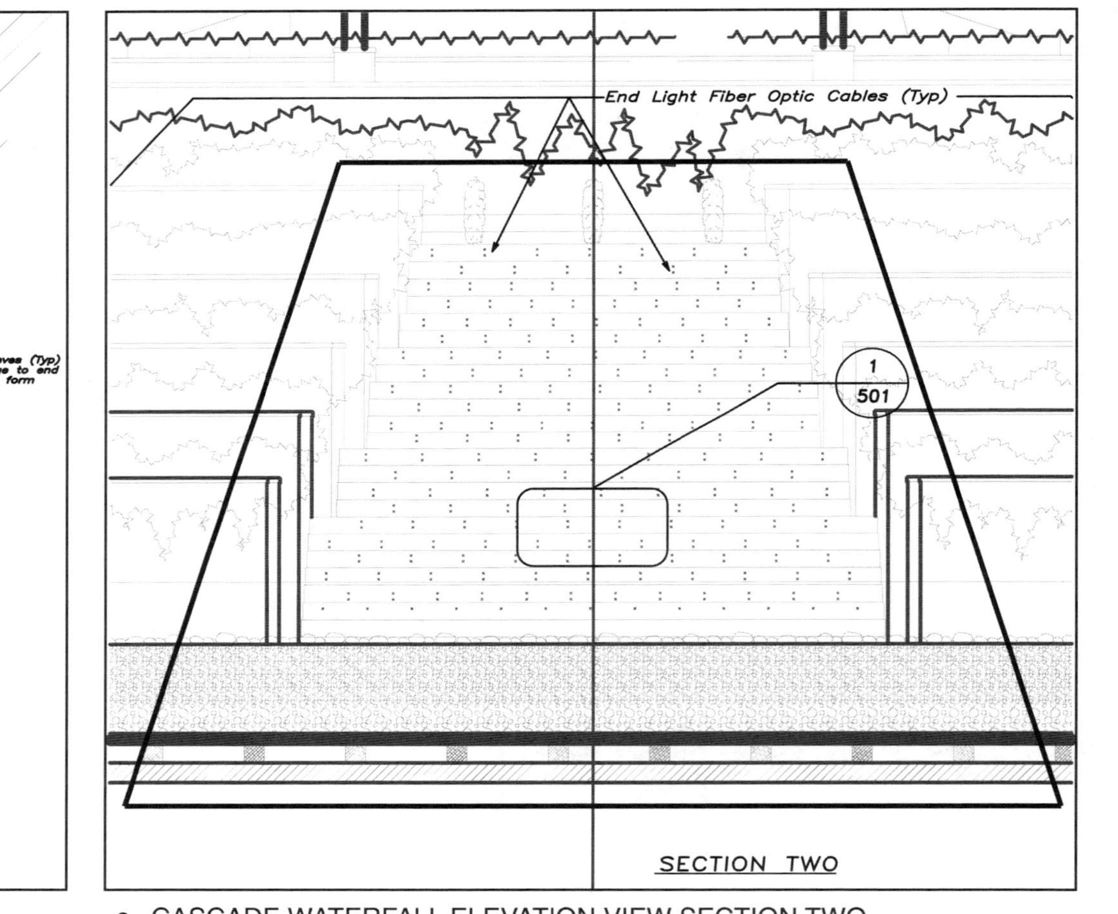
End Light Fiber Optic Cables (Typ)
1
501
SECTION TWO

c. CASCADE WATERFALL ELEVATION VIEW SECTION TWO

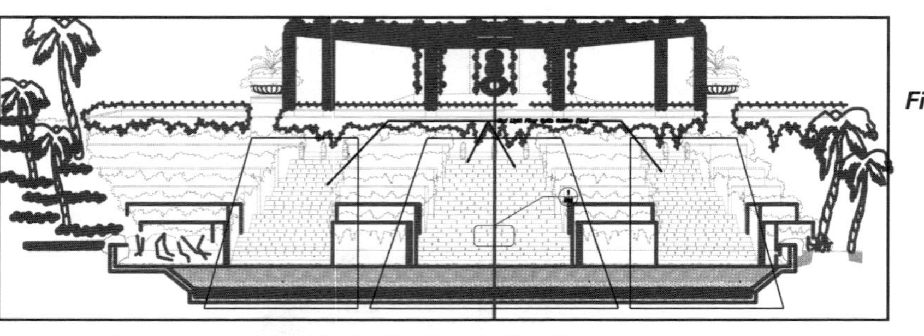

b. CASCADE WATERFALL ELEVATION VIEW

Figure A.13.

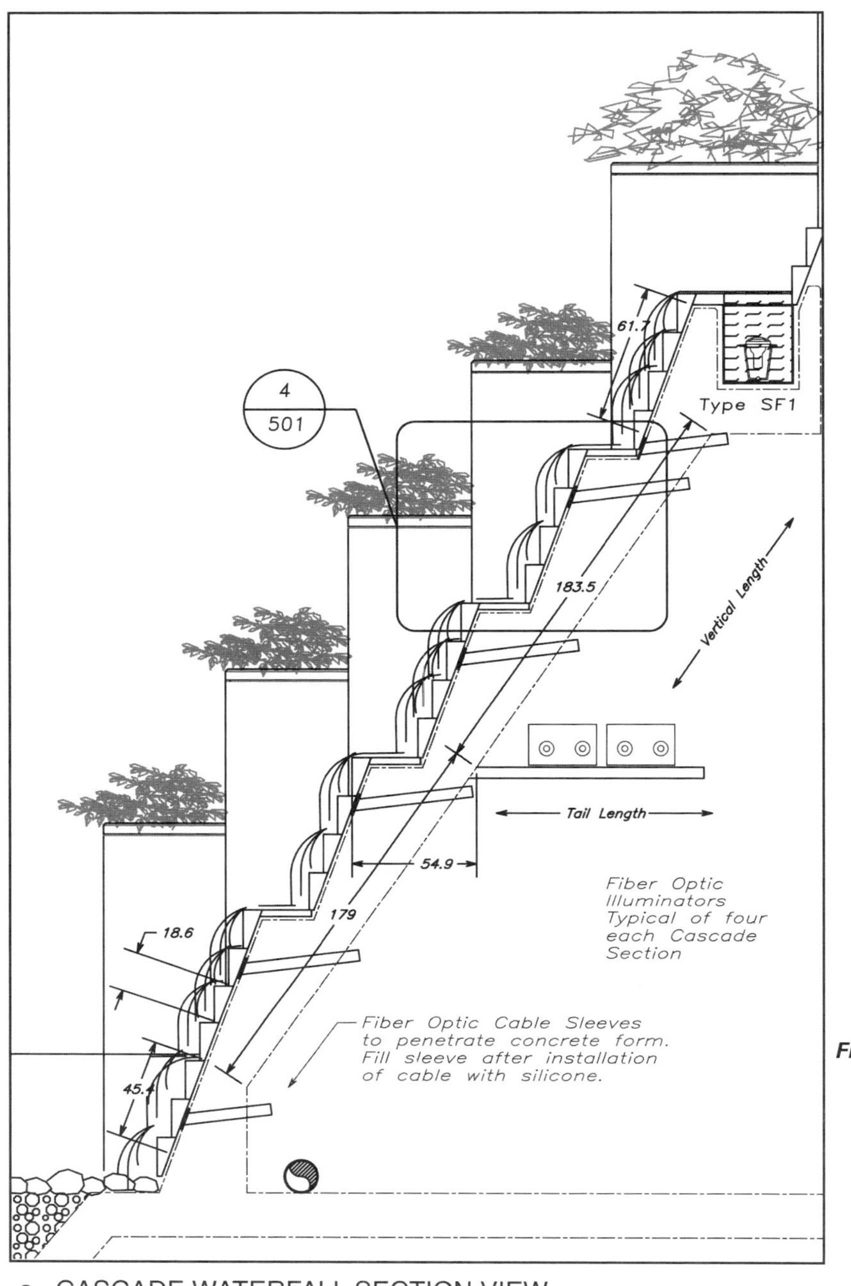

a. CASCADE WATERFALL SECTION VIEW

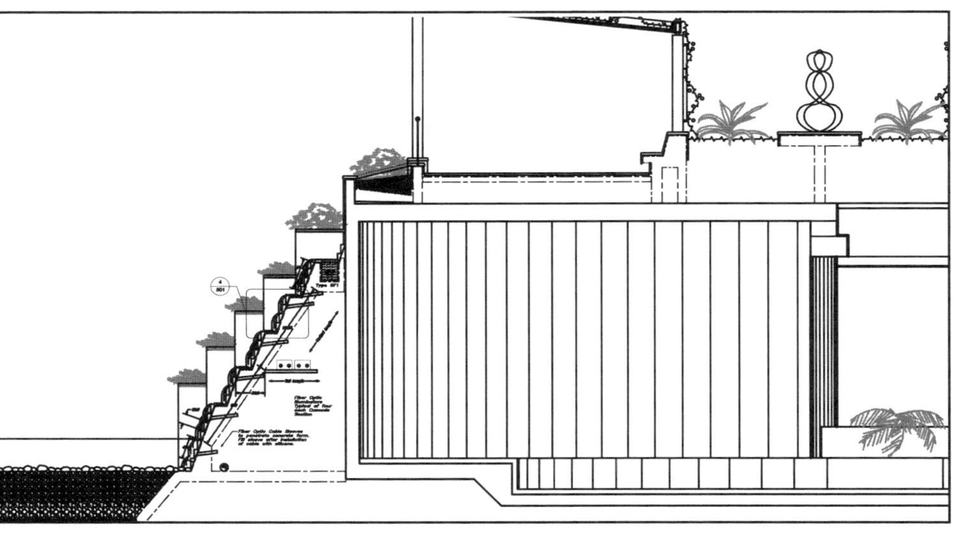

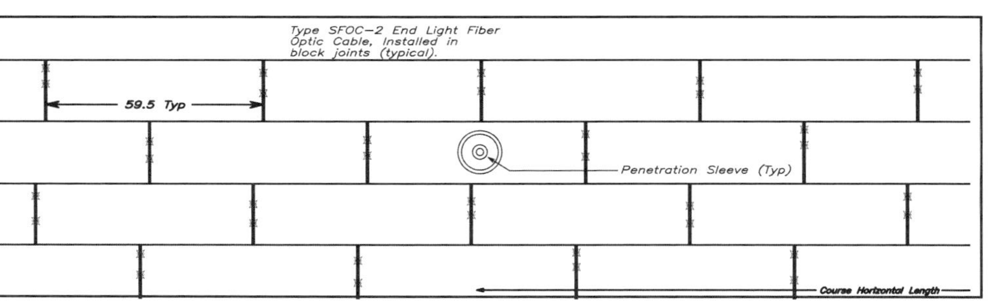

Figure A.14.

PROJECT: ROYAL GARDEN SUITES

Cascade Section Two

Course Layer Number	Estimated Course Layer Length (cm)	Estimated Mortar Joint Quantity	Estimated Fiber Optic Cable Quantity	Estimated Course Horizontal Length (cm)	Single Course Vertical Length (cm)	Single Cable Tail Length (cm)	Estimated Total Vertical Tail Length (cm)	Estimated Fiber Optic Cable Length (cm)
1	376.346	7	14	1,540	220	100	4,480	6,020
2	378.999	7	14	1,540	200	100	4,200	5,740
3	381.652	7	14	1,540	180	100	3,920	5,460
4	384.305	7	14	1,540	160	100	3,640	5,180
5	436.455	8	16	2,508	140	100	3,840	6,348
6	439.108	8	16	2,508	120	100	3,520	6,028
7	441.761	8	16	2,508	100	100	3,200	5,708
8	444.414	8	16	2,508	80	100	2,880	5,388
9	456.322	9	18	2,524	60	100	2,880	5,404
10	498.977	9	18	2,524	40	100	2,520	5,044
11	501.63	9	18	2,524	20	100	2,160	4,684
12	504.283	9	18	2,524	0	100	1,800	4,324
13	561.75	10	20	3,730	20	100	2,400	6,130
14	564.403	10	20	3,730	40	100	2,800	6,530
15	567.055	11	22	3,746	60	100	3,520	7,266
16	569.711	11	22	3,746	80	100	3,960	7,706
17	579.202	11	22	3,746	100	100	4,400	8,146
18	581.855	11	22	3,746	120	100	4,840	8,586
19	584.508	11	22	3,746	140	100	5,280	9,026
20	627.195	12	24	5,190	160	100	6,240	11,430
21	629.847	12	24	5,190	180	100	6,720	11,910
22	632.5	12	12	2,595	200	100	3,600	6,195
Total	**11,142**	**207**	**402**					**148,253**

Figure A.15.

EXTERIOR FIBER OPTIC SYSTEM SCHEDULE

System	Effect/Function	Cable Type	Cable Quantity	Fitting Type	Fitting Quantity	Illuminator(s) Type	Illuminator Quantity	System Nominal Maintained Light Output (No Color)	System Supplier	Remarks
Water Temple Pool	Edge Light Water Temple Pool Perimeter	SFOC-1A	1	NA	NA	SFOI-1A	2		Drama Lighting	
	Edge Light Water Temple Perimeter	SFOC-1B	2	NA	NA	SFOI-1B	2			
		System Total:	***3***		***0***		***4***			
Water Temple Step	Step 1 Perimeter	SFOC-1E1	1	NA	NA	SFOI-1A	1		Drama Lighting	
	Step 2 Perimeter	SFOC-1E2	1	NA	NA	SFOI-1B	1			
	Step 3 Perimeter	SFOC-1E3	1	NA	NA	SFOI-1B	0			
	Step 4 Perimeter	SFOC-1E4	1	NA	NA	SFOI-1A	1			
	Step 5 Perimeter	SFOC-1E5	1	NA	NA	SFOI-1B	1			
	Step 6 Perimeter	SFOC-1E6	1	NA	NA	SFOI-1B	0			
		System Total:	***6***		***0***		***2***			
Water Temple Structure	Ceiling Indirect Uplight	SFOC-1C	2	NA	NA	SFOI-1C	2		Drama Lighting	
	Roof Accent Light	SFOC-1D	2	NA	NA	SFOI-1C	2			
		System Total:	***4***		***0***		***4***			
Water Temple Fountain	Fountain 1 Uplight	SFOC-3A	3	SFOF-2	3	SFOI-3	1	600 FC @ 30 cm	Drama Lighting	
	Fountain 2 Uplight	SFOC-3B	3	SFOF-2	3	SFOI-3	0	600 FC @ 30 cm		
	Fountain 3 Uplight	SFOC-3C	3	SFOF-2	3	SFOI-3	0	600 FC @ 30 cm		
		System Total:	***9***		***9***		***1***			
Cascade Waterfall	Waterfall Section 1	SFOC-2	387	SFOF-1	387	SFOI-2	4	30 FC @ 30 cm	Drama Lighting	
	Waterfall Section 2	SFOC-2	402	SFOF-1	402	SFOI-2	4	30 FC @ 30 cm		
	Waterfall Section 3	SFOC-2	387	SFOF-1	387	SFOI-2	4	30 FC @ 30 cm		
		System Total:	***1176***		***1176***		***12***			

EXTERIOR FIBER OPTIC FITTING SCHEDULE

Fitting Type	Fitting Description	Effect	Fitting Nominal Size	Fitting Photometric Distribution	Cable Type	Cable Quantity (each fitting)	Fitting Quantity	Remarks
SFOF-1	Fixed lens end light	Cascade Waterfall	6 mm Optic	120 degree	SFOC-2	1	1176	
						Fitting Subtotal:	***1176***	
SFOF-2	Adjustable lens end light	Water Temple Fountain Uplight		40 degree	SFOC-3	1	9	
						Fitting Subtotal:	***9***	

Figure A.16.

EXTERIOR FIBER OPTIC CABLE SCHEDULE

Cable Type	Cable Description	Cable Size	Cable Material	Cable Quantity	Estimated Total Illuminated Length Each (m)	Estimated Total Feed Length Each (m)	Fitting Type	Illuminator(s) Type	Remarks
SFOC-1A	60 degree side emitting solid core	13.7 mm core dia.	Acrylic	1	22.67	2.00	NA	SFOI-1A	Lumenyte LEF Cable
SFOC-1B	60 degree side emitting solid core	13.7 mm core dia.	Acrylic	2	23.59	8.00	NA	SFOI-1B	Lumenyte LEF Cable
			Cable Subtotal:	***3***	***69.85***	***18.00***			
SFOC-1E1	60 degree side emitting solid core	13.7 mm core dia.	Acrylic	1	5.40	3.00	N/A	SFOI-1A	Lumenyte LEF Cable
SFOC-1E2	60 degree side emitting solid core	13.7 mm core dia.	Acrylic	1	5.40	4.50	N/A	SFOI-1B	Lumenyte LEF Cable
SFOC-1E3	60 degree side emitting solid core	13.7 mm core dia.	Acrylic	1	5.40	4.00	N/A	SFOI-1B	Lumenyte LEF Cable
SFOC-1E4	60 degree side emitting solid core	13.7 mm core dia.	Acrylic	1	5.40	3.00	N/A	SFOI-1A	Lumenyte LEF Cable
SFOC-1E5	60 degree side emitting solid core	13.7 mm core dia.	Acrylic	1	5.40	4.00	N/A	SFOI-1B	Lumenyte LEF Cable
SFOC-1E6	60 degree side emitting solid core	13.7 mm core dia.	Acrylic	1	5.40	4.50	N/A	SFOI-1B	Lumenyte LEF Cable
			Cable Subtotal:	***6***	***64.80***	***4.50***			
SFOC-1C	60 degree side emitting solid core	13.7 mm core dia.	Acrylic	2	5.80	5.00	N/A	SFOI-1C	Lumenyte LEF Cable
SFOC-1D	60 degree side emitting solid core	13.7 mm core dia.	Acrylic	2	6.90	5.00	N/A	SFOI-1C	Lumenyte LEF Cable
			Cable Subtotal:	***4***	***32.40***	***23.00***			
SFOC-2	Stranded clad end light	3.3 mm OD 64 strand (.25 mm)	Acrylic	1176	0.00	4819.20	SFOF-1	SFOI-2	See Sheet FED-501 for more schedules
			Cable Subtotal:	***1176***	***0.00***	***4,819.20***			
SFOC-3A	Solid core clad end light	18 mm core dia.	Acrylic	3	0.00	24.00	SFOF-2	SFOI-3	Lumenyte End Light Cable
SFOC-3B	Solid core clad end light	18 mm core dia.	Acrylic	3	0.00	27.00	SFOF-2	SFOI-3	Lumenyte End Light Cable
SFOC-3C	Solid core clad end light	18 mm core dia.	Acrylic	3	0.00	28.50	SFOF-2	SFOI-3	Lumenyte End Light Cable
			Cable Subtotal:	***9***	***0.00***	***238.50***			

EXTERIOR FIBER OPTIC ILLUMINATOR SCHEDULE

Illuminator Type	Illuminator Description	Illuminator Color Capability	Lamp Type	Cable Type	Illuminator Cable Capacity	Illuminator Quantity	Remarks
SFOI-1A	100 Watt Xenon - Horizontal Mount	Random DMX Programmable, 4 Colors	100 W Xenon	SFOC-1	1	4	
SFOI-1B	100 Watt Xenon - Horizontal Mount	Random DMX Programmable, 4 Colors	100 W Xenon	SFOC-1	2	4	
SFOI-1C	100 Watt Xenon - Horizontal Mount	Random DMX Programmable, 4 Colors	100 W Xenon	SFOC-1	1	4	
					Illuminator Subtotal:	***12***	
SFOI-2	100 Watt Xenon - Horizontal Mount	Random DMX Programmable, 8 Colors	100 W Xenon	SFOC-2	96	12	
					Illuminator Subtotal:	***12***	
SFOI-3	100 Watt Xenon - Horizontal Mount	Random DMX Programmable, 8 Colors	100 W Xenon	SFOC-3	9	1	
					Illuminator Subtotal:	***1***	

Figure A.17.

PROJECT: CHICAGO BOTANICAL GARDEN

Remote Low Voltage Transformer Schedule

Transformer Number	Rated Size (VA)	Maximum Load	Rated Secondary Voltage(s)	Transformer Electrical Type	Transformer Mounting Type	Fixture Type ID	Fixture Quantity	Fixture Lamp Quantity	Maximum Lamp Load (ea)	Fixture Load (Watts)	Total Load (Watts)	Remaining Capacity (Watts)	Number of Secondary Circuits	Transformer Location	Load Number	Sheet Number
T 001	840	670	12, 13, 14, 15, 16, 18, 20	Mag.		SB1D	10	1	50	50	500	170	3		CG1	LL-2.1.1
T 002	360	285	12, 13, 14, 15	Mag.		SD1A	7	1	20	20	140	145	1		CG2	LL-2.1.1
T 003	360	285	12, 13, 14, 15	Mag.		SD1A	8	1	20	20	160	125	1		CG2	LL-2.1.1
T 004	1120	895	12, 13, 14, 15, 16, 18, 20, 22	Mag.		SC1	11	1	75	75	825	70	4		CG1	LL-2.1.1
T 005	840	670	12, 13, 14, 15, 16, 18, 20	Mag		SB1A	6	1	50	50	600	70	3		CG1	LL-2.1.1
						SB1C	6	1	50	50						
T 006	1120	895	12, 13, 14, 15, 16, 18, 20, 22	Mag.		SB1A	10	1	50	50	900	(5)	4		CG1	LL-2.1.1
						SB1D	8	1	50	50						
T 007	1120	895	12, 13, 14, 15, 16, 18, 20, 22	Mag.		SC1	10	1	75	75	750	145	4		CG1	LL-2.1.1
T 008	840	670	12, 13, 14, 15, 16, 18, 20	Mag.		SB1C	4	1	50	50	200	470	3		CG1	LL-2.1.1
T 021	840	670	12, 13, 14, 15, 16, 18, 20	Mag.		SB1B	7	1	50	50	650	20	3		CG5	LL-2.1.1
						SC1	4	1	75	75						
T 022	1120	895	12, 13, 14, 15, 16, 18, 20, 22	Mag.		SB1A	15	1	50	50	750	145	4		CG3	LL-2.1.1
T 023	1120	895	12, 13, 14, 15, 16, 18, 20, 22	Mag.		SB1C	15	1	50	50	750	145	4		CG3	LL-2.1.1
T 032	840	670	12, 13, 14, 15, 16, 18, 20	Mag.		SB1D	10	1	50	50	500	170	3		CG7	LL-2.2.1
T 046	1120	895	12, 13, 14, 15, 16, 18, 20, 22	Mag.		SC1	5	1	75	75	750	145	2		CG13	LL-2.3.1
						SC2	5	1	75	75						
T 047	600	480	12, 13, 14, 15, 16, 17	Mag.		SA4A	12	1	35	35	480	0	2		CG14	LL-2.3.1
				Mag.		SD1A	3	1	20	20						
T 048	1120	895	12, 13, 14, 15, 16, 18, 20, 22	Mag.		SA4A	6	1	35	35	810	85	4		CG17	LL-2.3.1
						SB1C	12	1	50	50						
T 049	600	480	12, 13, 14, 15, 16, 17	Mag.		SB1A	5	1	50	50	400	80	2		CG17	LL-2.3.1
						SCB1C	3	1	50	50						
T 066	500	400	12, 13, 14, 15			SG2A	6	1	50	50	300	100	2		CG19	LL-2.4.1
T 067	600	480	12, 13, 14, 15, 16, 17	Mag.		SG2A	9	1	50	50	450	30	2		CG19	LL-2.4.1
T 068	500	400	12, 13, 14, 15	Mag.		SG2A	7	1	50	50	350	50	2		CG19	LL-2.4.1
T 069	360	285	12, 13, 14, 15	Mag.		SB1A	5	1	50	50	250	35	1		CG23	LL-2.4.1
T 080	360	285	12, 13, 14, 15	Mag.		SD1A	6	1	20	20	120	165	1		CG22	LL-2.5.1
T 081	840	670	12, 13, 14, 15, 16, 18, 20	Mag.		SG3	7	1	75	75	525	145	3		CG23	LL-2.5.1
T 082	1100	880		Mag.		SB2D	8	1	50	50	400	480			CG25	LL-2.5.1
T 098	360	285	12, 13, 14, 15	Mag.		SB1D	3	1	50	50	150	135	1		CG27	LL-2.8.1
T 099	840	670	12, 13, 14, 15, 16, 18, 20	Mag.		SA4A	6	1	35	35	610	60	3		CG27	LL-2.8.1
						SB1D	8	1	50	50						
T 100	1120	895	12, 13, 14, 15, 16, 18, 20, 22	Mag.		SA3	4	1	35	35	740	155	4		CG29	LL-2.9.1
						SB3	12	1	50	50						
T 101	840	670	12, 13, 14, 15, 16, 18, 20	Mag.		SB3	12	1	50	50	600	70	3		CG29	LL-2.9.1
T 121	1120	895	12, 13, 14, 15, 16, 18, 20, 22	Mag.		SB1A	15	1	50	50	750	145	4		CG33	LL-2.11.1
T 135	840	670	12, 13, 14, 15, 16, 18, 20	Mag.		SC2	9	1	75	75	675	(5)	3		CG15	LL-2.3.1
T 136	840	670	12, 13, 14, 15, 16, 18, 20	Mag.		SC2	7	1	75	75	525	145	3		CG13	LL-2.3.1

Figure A.18.

PROJECT: OLBRICH ROSE GARDEN

Remote Low Voltage Transformer Schedule

Trans. Number	Rated Size (W)	Rated Secondary Voltage(s)	Trans. Electrical Type	Trans. Mounting Type	Fixture Type ID	Fixture Quantity	Fixture Lamp Quantity	Maximum Lamp Load (ea)	Fixture Load (Watts)	Load (Watts)	Total Load (Watts)	Remaining Capacity (Watts)	Preliminary Transformer Location	Control Group Number	Sheet Number	Load Description	Remarks
T 0101	600	12, 13, 14, 15, 16, 17	Mag.	Exterior	SB-2	8	1	50	50	400	400	200	Tower Mechanical Room	CG1	LL-2.1	Tower Interior Lighting-1st Floor	Provide 2 Feeds (see Sheet LL-2.1)
T 0102	600	12, 13, 14, 15, 16, 17	Mag.	Exterior	SB-2	6	1	50	50	400	500	200	Tower Mechanical Room	CG1	LL-2.1	Tower Upper Level	Provide 2 Feeds (see Sheet LL-2.1)
					SB-3	2	1	50	50	100							
T 0103	600	12, 13, 14, 15, 16, 17	Mag.	Exterior	SB-2	8	1	50	50	400	400	200	Tower Mechanical Room	CG1	LL-2.1	Viewing Platform	Provide 2 Feeds (see Sheet LL-2.1)
T 0006	840	12, 13, 14, 15, 16, 18, 20	Mag.	Exterior	SE-1	8	1	20	20	160	560	280	Tower Mechanical Room	CG1	LL-2.1	Bridge Lighting & Trellis Fixtures	Provide 6 Feeds (see Sheet LL-2.1)
					SA-1	20	1	35	35	400							
T 0007	840	12, 13, 14, 15, 16, 18, 20	Mag.	TBD	SC-1	2	1	35	35	70	770	70	In Planting	CG2	LL-1.1.2	Tree 23 (7 SB-1) & Tree 25 (2 SB-1)	
					SB-1	9	1	50	50	450			Area- TBD			Both get 1 SC-1	
					SB-1	*5*	*1*	*50*	50	250			ON SITE			***FUTURE Lighting for Tree 25***	Fixtures not to be provided as part of current project
T 0422	840	12, 13, 14, 15, 16, 18, 20	Mag.	TBD	SA-1	10	1	35	35	350	750	90	In Planting	CG3	LL-1.1.1	Trees #19 & 20	
					SB-1	8	1	50	50	400			Area TBD ON Site			Future Lighting for Trees #19 & 20	Fixtures not to be provided as part of current project
T 0423	500	12, 13, 14, 15, 16, 17	Mag.	TBD	SA-1	5	1	35	35	175	375	125	In Planting	CG3	LL-1.1.1	Tree #17	
					SB-1	4	1	50	50	200			Area TBD ON Site			Future Lighting for Tree #17	Fixtures not to be provided as part of current project
T 0545	840	12, 13, 14, 15, 16, 18, 20	Mag.	TBD	SB-1	9	1	50	50	450	705	135	In Planting Areas TBD ON SITE	CG3	LL-1.1.1	Tree Group 50a (3 Trees- 1 SC-1 ea & 3 SB-1 ea)	
					SC-1	3	1	35	35	105							
					SB-1	3	1	50	50	150						Future Lighting for Tree Group 50a (1 ea)	Fixtures not to be provided as part of current project
T 0546	600	12, 13, 14, 15, 16, 17	Mag.	TBD	SC-1	2	1	35	35	70	470	130	In Planting Areas TBD ON SITE	CG3	LL-1.1.1	Future Lighting for Tree Group 50b (2 Trees1 SC-1ea and 4 SB-1 ea)	Provide power allocation to Transformer & Fixture area(s)
					SB-1	8	1	50	50	400						Future Lighting for Tree Group 50b (1 ea)	Transformer & Fixtures not to be provided as part of current project
T 0547	1120	12, 13, 14, 15, 16, 18, 20, 22	Mag.	TBD	SB-1	9	1	50	50	450	1005	115	In Planting Areas TBD ON SITE	CG3	LL-1.1.1	Tree Group 49 (3 Trees- 1 SC-1 ea & 3 SB-1 ea)	
					SC-1	3	1	35	35	105							
					SB-1	9	1	50	50	450						Future Lighting for Tree Group 49 (3 ea)	Fixtures not to be provided as part of current project
									0								

Figure A.19.

APPROVED MR-16 AND MRC-16 LAMP PALETTES									
Bi-Pin Base (GX5.3/GU5.3)									
Lamp Type	Designation Code	Rated Voltage	Rated Wattage	Beam Distribution	Beam Candlepower	Rated Avg. Life (hrs)	Remarks	Approved Mfgs.	Manufacturer Ordering Code
MR-16	EZX	12	20	7 degree	7,400	3,000	Constant Color	GE	Q20MR16/C/VNSP7
MRC-16	ESX/C	12	20	10 degree	7,000	4,000	Closed Lamp - Continuum Color	Philips	20MRC16/CC/SP10
MR-16	ESX	12	20	15 degree	3,750	5,000	Constant Color	GE	Q20MR16/C/NSP15
MRC-16	BBF/C	12	20	24 degree	1,700	4,000	Closed Lamp - Continuum Color	Philips	20MRC16/CC/NFL24
MR-16	BBF	12	20	24 degree	1,200	4,000		Ushio	1000028-BBF
MRC-16	BAB/C	12	20	38 degree	800	4,000	Closed Lamp - Continuum Color	Philips	20MRC16/CC/FL38
MR-16	BAB	12	20	40 degree	525	5,000	Constant Color	GE	Q20MR16/C/FL40
MR-16	BAB/60	12	20	60 degree	270	4,000		BLV	BLV187819

APPROVED MR-11 AND ALR-12 LAMP PALETTES									
Double Contact Bayonet Base (BA15d)									
Lamp Type	Designation Code	Rated Voltage	Rated Wattage	Beam Distribution	Beam Candlepower	Rated Avg. Life (hrs)	Remarks	Approved Mfgs.	Manufacturer Ordering Code
ALR-12	GBD	12	20	6 degree	7,000	2,000	Closed Lamp - Clear	Philips	20ALR12/NSP6
MR-11	FSS	12	20	10 degree	3,800	2,000		Ushio	1000607-FSS
ALR-12	GBE	12	20	18 degree	1,400	2,000	Closed Lamp - Frosted	Philips	20ALR12/SP18
MR-11	FST	12	20	20 degree	750	2,000		Ushio	1000609-FST
MR-11	FSV	12	20	30 degree	600	2,000		Ushio	1000611-FSV
ALR-12	GBF	12	20	32 degree	350	2,000	Closed Lamp - Frosted	Philips	20ALR12/FL32
MR-11	GDX	12	35	10 degree	6,000	2,000		Ushio	1000655-GDX
MR-11	GDY	12	35	20 degree	2,400	2,000		Ushio	1000657-GDY
MR-11	GDZ	12	35	30 degree	1,300	2,000		Ushio	1000659-GDZ

APPROVED HALOGEN INCANDESCENT PAR 38 LAMP PALETTES							
Beam Type	Designation Code	Rated Voltage	Lamp Wattage	Beam Distribution	Beam Candlepower	Rated Avg. Life (hrs)	Approved Mfgs.
Wide Flood	45PAR38/WFL50/120Volt	120	45	45 degree	600	2,500	Ushio
IR Flood	90PAR/HIR/FL40/XL	120	90	40 degree	2,800	5,000	GE
Flood	100PAR/H/FL25	130	100	25 degree	4,000	4,000	GE
IR Flood	100 PAR/HIR/FL40		100	40 degree	3,400	3,000	GE

APPROVED CERAMIC PAR-20, METAL HALIDE LAMP PALETTES									
PAR 20 - Medium Screw Base (E26)									
Beam Type	Designation Code	Rated Voltage	Lamp Wattage	Beam Distribution	Beam Candlepower	Rated Avg. Life (hrs)	Remarks	Approved Mfgs.	Manufacturer Ordering Code
SP	35PAR20/SP	120	39	10 degree	23,000	9,000	3,000 K; 81 CRI	Philips	CDM35/PAR20/SP
SP	35PAR20/SP	120	39	10 degree	22,000	10,000	3,000 K; 85 CRI	GE	CMH39/UPAR20/SP10
FL	35PAR20/FL	120	39	30 degree	5,000	9,000	3,000 K; 81 CRI	Philips	CDM35/PAR20/FL
FL	35PAR20/FL	120	39	30 degree	7,500	10,000	3,000 K; 85 CRI	GE	CMH39/UPAR20/FL30

Figure A.20.

PROJECT: SAPERSTEIN, LOHANTON										
Load Schedule										
Zone:	Main House—First Floor									
Load Number	Load Location	Load Description	Fixture Type	Load Rating Type	Transformer Number(s)	Load Quantity	Maximum Load - Each (Watts)	Maximum Total Load (Watts)	Control Device Number	Drawing Sheet Number
MH 101	Game Room Building Exterior	Sconces	F	INC	NA	25	50	1250	1.1.1	A6.1
MH 102	Jeanine's Office Terrace	Downlights	A-1	MLV	T12	8	50	400	1.8.2	A6.1
MH 103	Covered Terrace Stair and FirePit Patio	Downlights	A-1	MLV	T13	6	50	300	1.7.3	A6.1
MH 104	Great Room Covered Terrace	Downlights	A-1	MLV	T14	8	50	400	2.2.3	A6.1
MH 114	Walk to Garage	Downlights	H	INC	NA	3	50	150	1.5.3	A6.1
MH 116	Back Door Area and Walk To Guest House	Downlights	H A-1	INC MLV	NA T25	1 17	50 50	900	1.4.1	A6.1
MH 138	Glazed Porch 126-Pendant	Pendant	N	INC	NA	1	200	200	2.7.2	A6.1
MH 139	Glazed Porch 126-Table Lighting	Downlights	B	MLV	NA	4	50	200	2.4.4	A6.1
MH 140	Dining 132-Accent	Downlights	B	MLV	NA	7	50	350	2.6.2	A6.1
MH 154	Hall 122-Pendant	Pendant	O	INC	NA	2	200	400	2.2.1	A6.1
MH 155	Hall 122 Accent	Downlights	A3b A3d A	MLV MLV MLV	T81 T81 T81	2 2 2	50 50 50	300	1.3.4	A6.1
ZONE TOTAL MAXIMUM LOAD (WATTS)								4,850		

PROJECT: FRIEDKIN at LUPINE RIDGE										
Load Schedule — Revised 12/12/03										
Zone:	Second Residence and Local Landscape									
Load Number	Load Location	Load Description	Fixture Type or Xfmr#	Load Rating Type	Load Quantity	Maximum Load - Each (Watts)	Maximum Total Load (Watts)	Power Source	Control Device Number	Drawing Sheet Number
SR1-01	Outdoor Dining	Landscape Accent	T0104	MLV	1	240	240		PSC-1	L2.2.1
SR1-02	Outdoor Dining	Bar Accent	T0105	MLV	1	240	240		PSC-1	L2.2.1
SR1-03	Outdoor Dining	Fireplace Accent	T0103	MLV	1	240	240		PSC-1	L2.2.1
SR1-04	Outdoor Dining	Chandeliers	SA-2	INC	2	600	1200		PSC-1	L2.2.1
SR1-05	Outdoor Dining	Table Accent	T0106	MLV	1	240	240		PSC-1	L2.2.1
SR1-06	Outdoor Dining	Cabinet Accent	T0102	MLV	1	240	240		PSC-1	L2.2.1
SR3-01	Loggia	Sconces	SA-3	INC	4	180	720			L2.2.1
SR3-02	Patio	Downlights	T0101	MLV	1	240	240			L2.2.1
SR3-03	Loggia	Trellis Downlights	T0117	MLV	1	600	600			L2.2.1
SR3-04	North Exterior Walk	Sconces	SA-3	INC	2	180	360			L2.2.1
							4,320			

Figure A.21.

PROJECT: FRIEDKIN at LUPINE RIDGE									
Preset Scene Control Station Schedule — Revised 12/12/03									
PSC-1	***Outdoor Dining***								
Control Channel Number	***Load Description***	***Fixture type or Xfmr Number (s)***	***Load Quantity***	***Load Rating Type***	***Maximum Load Each***	***Load Number(s)***	***Total Load Watts***	***PSC Load Watts***	***Remarks***
1	Landscape Accent	T0104	1	MLV	240	SR1-01	240	240	
2	Bar Accent	T0105	1	MLV	240	SR1-02	240	240	
3	Fireplace Accent	T0103	1	MLV	240	SR1-03	240	240	
4	Chandaliers	SA-2	2	INC	600	SR1-04	1200	50	***Note 2***
5	Table Accent	T0106	1	MLV	240	SR1-05	240	240	
6	Cabinet Accent	T0102	1	MLV	240	SR1-06	240	240	
						TOTAL LOAD (WATTS)	***2,400***		
				PRESET SCENE CONTROL STATION TOTAL LOAD (WATTS)				***1,250***	
Preset Scene Control Station Location:Laundry Closet									

PSC NOTES:

NOTE 1 - *This channel requires a 20-Amp capacity Lutron HP-2 Power Booster Remote Dimming Module.*
NOTE 2 - *This channel requires a 20-Amp capacity Lutron NGRX-PB Power Booster Remote Dimming Module.*
NOTE 3 - *This channel requires a 1000-Watt capacity Lutron GRX-ELVI Remote Dimming Interface Module for electronic low-voltage loads.*
NOTE 4 - *This channel requires a 16-Amp capacity Lutron GRX-FDBI Remote Dimming Interface Module for fluorescent dimming loads.*
NOTE 5 - *This channel requires a 30-Amp capacity Tomstar Contactor, normally open, SL20-1DDP, for switched HID loads.*
NOTE 6 - *This channel requires a 100–200 Watt (1.7 Amp) capacity Lutron LDC-1.7-TCP Lamp Debuzzing Coil. Locate in line to loads.*
NOTE 7 - *This channel requires a 200–400 Watt (3.3 Amp) capacity Lutron LDC-3.3-TCP Lamp Debuzzing Coil. Locate in line to loads.*
NOTE 8 - *This channel requires a 400–800 Watt (6.7 Amp) capacity Lutron LDC-6.7-TCP Lamp Debuzzing Coil. Locate in line to loads.*

PROJECT: FRIEDKIN at LUPINE RIDGE						
Homeworks Station Schedule						
Station Number	Station Location	Size: 1,5, 10,15	Button Number	Engraving per button	Loads per button	Notes
RCS-1	2nd Residence	**10**	1	TERRACE	SR1-01 through SR1-06	Scene
Outdoor Dining	Dining Terrace door to Dining Room		2	SITE	SR1-01, SR3-01 through SR3-04, SR4-01 through SR4-03, & EXT-01 through EXT-13	Scene—**more loads in future**
			3	GARDEN	SR1-01	Dim—**more loads in future**
			4	BAR	SR1-02	Dim
			5	SITE PATH	SR1-01, SR4-03, EXT-01, EXT-06, & SR3-01 through SR3-04	Scene—**more loads in future**
			6	LIVING ROOM	SR2-01 through SR2-10	Scene
			7	TABLE	SR1-05	Dim
			8	CHANDELIER	SR1-04	Dim
			9	ACCENT	SR1-03 & SR1-06	Dim
			10	INTERIOR PATH	SR2-03 &SR2-08	Scene
			Left	ON	All Loads this device	Loads/Function may
			Right	OFF	All Loads this device	change in future

Figure A.22.

PROJECT: SAPERSTEIN, LOHANTON								
Control Device Schedule								
		Device Assembly ID:	***CDA-MH1***		Device Assembly Type:	***Lutron HWI-PNL-8***		
		Device Assembly Locat	***Storage area under Covered Terrace***					
		Device Assembly Power Source:			Device Assembly Power T	***Feed Thru***		
		Device Voltage:	***120 VAC***					
Control Module Number	*Control Dimmer Number*	*Control Device Type*	*Control Device Rating*	*Load Description*	*Load Rating Type*	*Maximum Load (Watts)*	*Total Module Load*	*Load Number(s)*
1.1	***1***	Dimmer	20 Amps	Game Room Building Exterior: Sconces	INC	1,250	1,600	MH101
	2	Dimmer	20 Amps	Great Room 124—Under Balcony: Downlights	MLV	150		MH153
	3	Dimmer	20 Amps	Master Bedroom 211—Art over bed: Downlights	MLV	150		MH213
	4	Dimmer	20 Amps	Library 153—Piano Keys: Downlights	MLV	50		MH150
1.2	***1***	Dimmer	20 Amps	Bedroom 115 Pendants: Pendants	INC	1,200	1,600	MH118
	2	Dimmer	20 Amps	Dining 132—Accent Table Lighting: Downlights	MLV	100		MH142
	3	Dimmer	20 Amps	Library 153—Art: Downlights	MLV	100		MH151
	4	Dimmer	20 Amps	Great Room 124—Fireplace : Downlights	MLV	200		MH126
				ASSEMBLY TOTAL MAXIMUM LOAD (WATTS):		***3,200***		

PROJECT: SAPERSTEIN, LOHANTON							
Preset Scene Settings							
Scene: Game Room Main Path				**Fade in:** 5 seconds **Fade out:** 5 seconds			
Planned by:	JKL						
Comments:							
Load Number	***Load Level***	***Remarks***		***Load Number***	***Load Level***	***Remarks***	
GR102	60	ON/OFF		GH106	15		
GR106	40						
MH102	15						
MH103	40						
MH104	60						
GH101	40						

PROJECT: SAPERSTEIN, LOHANTON					
Control Stations Schedule					
Station Number	Station Location	Size: 1,2,3, 4,5,6,7 or 8	Button Number	Engraving per button	Loads per button
RCS-1	Game Room 112 by	6	1	Stage 1	GR103, GR104, GR110, GR111, GR112
	Terrace Door		2	Stage 2	GR103, GR104, GR110, GR111, GR112
			3	Stage 3	GR103, GR104, GR110, GR111, GR112
			4	Main Path	GR102, GR106, MH102, MH103, MH104
			5	Guest Path	GR102, GR106, GH102, GH104
			6	Terrace	GR101, GR102

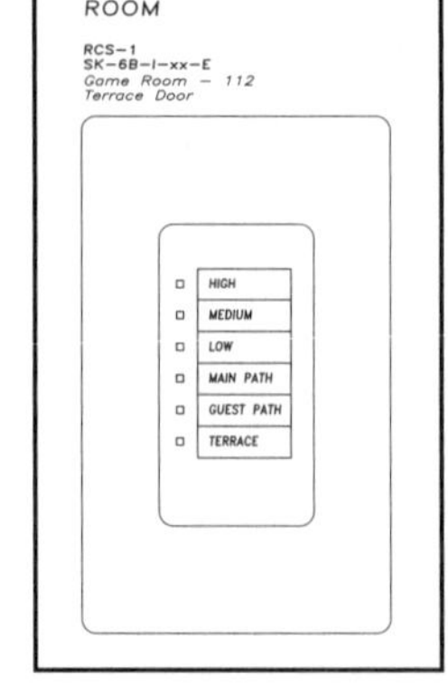

Figure A.23.

Sun and Moon Data for One Day Page 1 of 1

U.S. Naval Observatory
Astronomical Applications Department

Sun and Moon Data for One Day

The following information is provided for Garden City Park, Nassau County, New York (longitude W73.7, latitude N40.8):

```
Tuesday
4 May 2004                Eastern Daylight Time

                 SUN
Begin civil twilight       5:19 a.m.
Sunrise                    5:49 a.m.
Sun transit               12:51 p.m.
Sunset                     7:54 p.m.
End civil twilight         8:25 p.m.

                 MOON
Moonrise                   6:43 p.m. on preceding day
Moon transit              12:15 a.m.
Moonset                    5:37 a.m.
Moonrise                   8:02 p.m.
Moonset                    6:09 a.m. on following day
```

Full Moon on 4 May 2004 at 4:34 p.m. Eastern Daylight Time.

Census Bureau map of Garden City Park area

http://aa.usno.navy.mil/cgi-bin/aa_pap.p 5/4/2004

Figure A.24.

Location: W073° 40′, N40° 45′

GARDEN CITY PARK, NEW YORK
Rise and Set for the Sun for 2004

Astronomical Applications
U. S. Naval Observatory
Washington, DC 20392-542

Eastern Standard Time

	Jan.		Feb.		Mar.		Apr.		May		June		July		Aug.		Sept.		Oct.		Nov.		
Day	Rise	Set	Rise	Set	Rise	Set	Rise	Set	Rise	Set	Rise	Set	Rise	Set	Rise	Set	Rise	Set	Rise	Set	Rise	Set	Ris
	h m	h m	h m	h m	h m	h m	h m	h m	h m	h m	h m	h m	h m	h m	h m	h m	h m	h m	h m	h m	h m	h m	h
01	0719	1637	0705	1712	0628	1746	0538	1820	0453	1851	0425	1920	0427	1930	0452	1910	0522	1826	0552	1736	0626	1650	070
02	0719	1638	0704	1713	0626	1748	0536	1821	0451	1852	0425	1921	0428	1930	0453	1909	0523	1825	0553	1734	0627	1649	070
03	0719	1639	0703	1714	0625	1749	0534	1822	0450	1853	0425	1921	0428	1929	0454	1907	0524	1823	0554	1733	0628	1648	070
04	0719	1640	0702	1715	0623	1750	0533	1823	0449	1854	0424	1922	0429	1929	0454	1906	0525	1821	0555	1731	0629	1647	070
05	0719	1641	0701	1716	0622	1751	0531	1824	0448	1855	0424	1923	0429	1929	0455	1905	0526	1820	0556	1729	0630	1646	070
06	0719	1642	0700	1718	0620	1752	0529	1825	0447	1856	0424	1923	0430	1929	0456	1904	0527	1818	0557	1728	0631	1645	070
07	0719	1643	0659	1719	0619	1753	0528	1826	0445	1857	0423	1924	0431	1928	0457	1903	0528	1816	0558	1726	0633	1644	070
08	0719	1644	0658	1720	0617	1754	0526	1827	0444	1858	0423	1925	0431	1928	0458	1901	0529	1815	0559	1725	0634	1643	070
09	0719	1645	0657	1721	0615	1755	0525	1828	0443	1859	0423	1925	0432	1927	0459	1900	0530	1813	0600	1723	0635	1642	070
10	0718	1646	0656	1723	0614	1756	0523	1829	0442	1900	0423	1926	0433	1927	0500	1859	0531	1811	0601	1721	0636	1641	070
11	0718	1647	0654	1724	0612	1758	0521	1830	0441	1901	0423	1926	0433	1927	0501	1857	0532	1810	0602	1720	0637	1640	070
12	0718	1648	0653	1725	0611	1759	0520	1831	0440	1902	0423	1927	0434	1926	0502	1856	0533	1808	0603	1718	0639	1639	071
13	0718	1649	0652	1726	0609	1800	0518	1832	0439	1903	0423	1927	0435	1926	0503	1855	0534	1806	0604	1717	0640	1638	071
14	0717	1650	0651	1728	0607	1801	0517	1833	0438	1904	0423	1927	0436	1925	0504	1853	0535	1805	0605	1715	0641	1637	071
15	0717	1651	0649	1729	0606	1802	0515	1835	0437	1905	0423	1928	0437	1924	0505	1852	0536	1803	0606	1714	0642	1636	071
16	0716	1652	0648	1730	0604	1803	0514	1836	0436	1906	0423	1928	0437	1924	0506	1851	0537	1801	0607	1712	0643	1635	071
17	0716	1654	0647	1731	0602	1804	0512	1837	0435	1907	0423	1928	0438	1923	0507	1849	0538	1800	0608	1711	0644	1635	071
18	0716	1655	0645	1732	0601	1805	0511	1838	0434	1908	0423	1929	0439	1922	0508	1848	0539	1758	0610	1709	0646	1634	071
19	0715	1656	0644	1734	0559	1806	0509	1839	0434	1909	0423	1929	0440	1922	0509	1846	0540	1756	0611	1708	0647	1633	071
20	0714	1657	0643	1735	0557	1807	0508	1840	0433	1910	0423	1929	0441	1921	0510	1845	0541	1754	0612	1706	0648	1633	071
21	0714	1658	0641	1736	0556	1808	0506	1841	0432	1911	0424	1929	0442	1920	0511	1843	0542	1753	0613	1705	0649	1632	071
22	0713	1659	0640	1737	0554	1809	0505	1842	0431	1912	0424	1930	0442	1919	0512	1842	0543	1751	0614	1703	0650	1631	071
23	0713	1701	0638	1738	0552	1810	0503	1843	0431	1913	0424	1930	0443	1918	0513	1840	0544	1749	0615	1702	0651	1631	071
24	0712	1702	0637	1739	0551	1811	0502	1844	0430	1914	0424	1930	0444	1918	0514	1839	0545	1748	0616	1701	0652	1630	071
25	0711	1703	0636	1741	0549	1812	0501	1845	0429	1915	0425	1930	0445	1917	0515	1837	0546	1746	0617	1659	0654	1630	071
26	0710	1704	0634	1742	0547	1814	0459	1846	0429	1915	0425	1930	0446	1916	0516	1836	0547	1744	0619	1658	0655	1629	071
27	0710	1705	0633	1743	0546	1815	0458	1847	0428	1916	0425	1930	0447	1915	0517	1834	0548	1743	0620	1657	0656	1629	071
28	0709	1707	0631	1744	0544	1816	0457	1848	0427	1917	0426	1930	0448	1914	0518	1833	0549	1741	0621	1655	0657	1629	071
29	0708	1708	0630	1745	0543	1817	0455	1849	0427	1918	0426	1930	0449	1913	0519	1831	0550	1739	0622	1654	0658	1628	071
30	0707	1709			0541	1818	0454	1850	0426	1919	0427	1930	0450	1912	0520	1829	0551	1738	0623	1653	0659	1628	071
31	0706	1710			0539	1819			0426	1919			0451	1911	0521	1828			0624	1652			071

Add one hour for daylight time, if and when in use.

Figure A.25.

SPECIFICATIONS CHECKLIST

Fixture

Operation Voltage
Mounting Method & Accessories- Stake, Canopy etc.
Housing — Materials, Assembly, Gasketing
Dimensions
Vertical Tilt and Horizontal Aiming Adjustments
Aiming Adjustment Locking Mechanism
Fixture Wiring
Anti-Wicking Method & Materials
Reflector Material and Finish
Sealed Lens Material
Sealing and Gasketing Methods & Materials
Distribution Accessories: Louvers, Lenses, Filters
Lamp Access Method & Tools Requirement
Shielding Accessories: Shroud, Rock Guard, etc.
Light Distribution Characteristics/Photometry
Mounting Location & Height or Suspension Length
Label—Damp, Wet, Wet/Dry, Submersible, Salt Spray, etc.
Finish Color, Material, & Method

Lamp

Quantity
Wattage
Shape/Size
Voltage
Beam Distribution
Center Beam Candlepower / Lumen Output
Base Type
Coatings
Color Temperature (Correlated)
Color Coordinates
Color Rendering Index
Color Stability
Average Life
Lumen Depreciation
Starting Temperature

Transformer

Type:Torodal, Magnetic, Electronic, etc.
Primary Voltage
Secondary Voltage(s)
Load Capacity (VA or Wattage)
Power Factor
Operating Temperature Range
Electrical Characteristics
Loss Factor
Electrical Harmonics
Noise Level
Enclosure
Mounting Type
Fusing/Breaker(s)
Integral Photocell, Time Switch, and/or Dimmer

Ballast

Type
ANSI Designation
Primary Voltage
Lamp Type and Quantity
Circuit Type
Power Factor
Operating Temperature Range
Starting Temperature
Starting Current
Operating Current (Load)
Electrical Characteristics
Noise Level
Enclosure
Mounting Type
Fusing/Breaker(s)

Louvers

Material
Cell Shape
Size
Thickness
Finish
Shielding Angle
Heat Resistance
Framing

Lenses & Filters

Material
Size
Heat Resistance
Thickness
Framing
Photometric Distribution
Coatings
Transmission
Color Transmission
Color Coordinates (Illuminant C)
Correlated Color Temperature
Color Shift (Mired)

Mounting Hardware

Stake

Material
Fixed or Adjustable
Adjustment Dimensions
Locking Mechansim
Finish
Wiring Compartment

Junction Box Mount

Material
Above or Below Grade
Mounting Collar
Concrete Pour
Gasketing
Access and Enclosure Type

Tree Mount

Size and Shape
Material
Finish
Wiring Compartment
Canopy or Hanging Mechanism
Strap
Fasteners

Structure Mount

Size and Shape
Material
Finish
Wiring Compartment
Fasteners
Type: Canopy, Plate, Channel, Corner, Clamp

Electrical Wire/Cable

Material
Maximum Voltage
Ampacity
Gauge
Size (Circular Mils)
Resistance (X/R)
Insultation Type
Maximum Operating Temperature
Cladding and Coating
Label
Weather Resistance
Chemical Resistance
UV Resistance

Figure A.26.

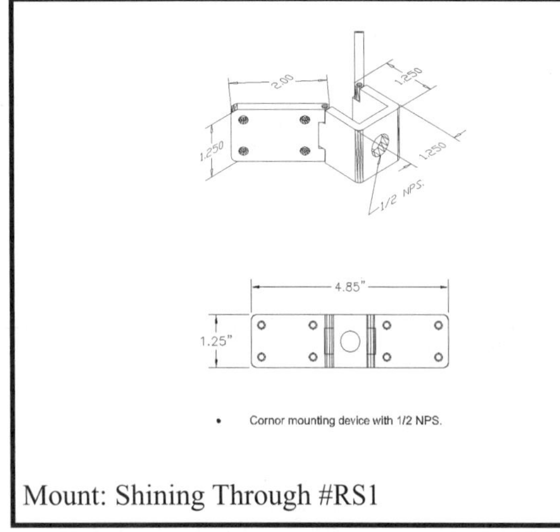

Mount: Shining Through #RS1

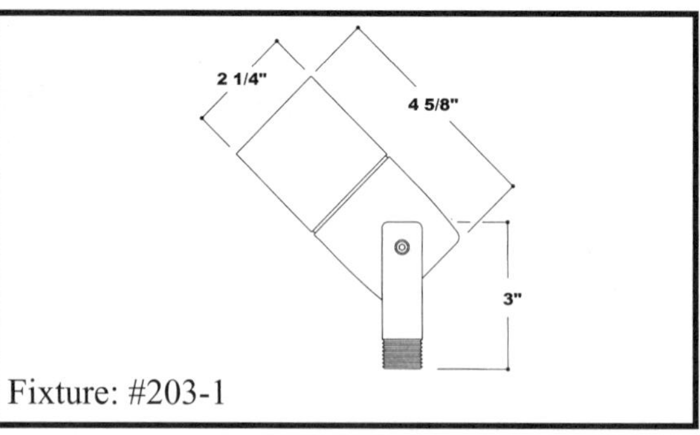

Fixture: #203-1

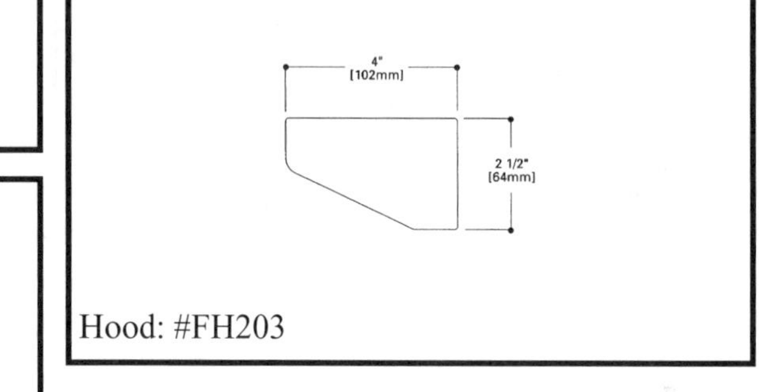

Hood: #FH203

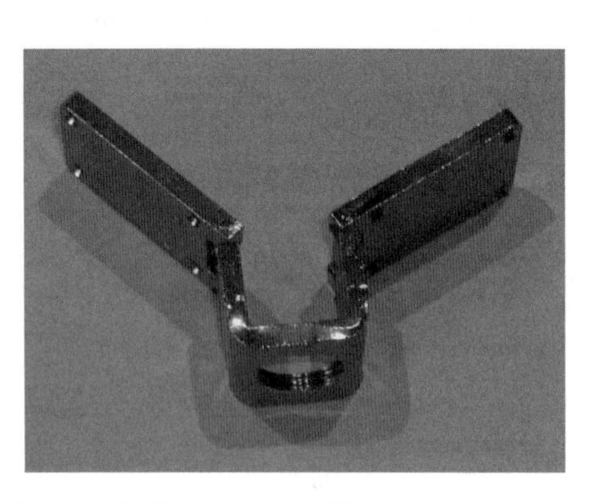

Mount: Shining Through #RS1

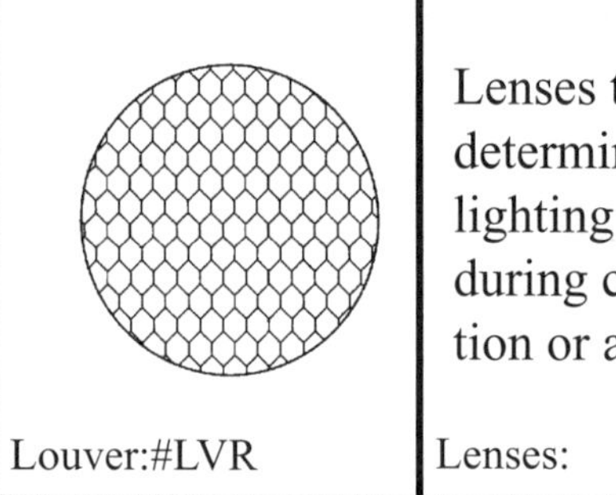

Louver:#LVR

Lenses to be determined by lighting consultant during construction or aiming.

Lenses:

DESCRIPTION: Corner-mounted low-voltage adjustable accent light with threaded flush-lens type bezel, angled glare shield, articulated threaded stainless steel corner mount, louver and remote transformer.
Refer to fixture schedule for description

FINISH: City Silver powder coat finish

VOLTAGE: 12V

LAMP: MR 16 lamp—GE, Ushio or Philips—provide lamps as indicated on lighting plan or as directed by lighting consultant.

FIXTURE WATTAGE: 50W Max

CATALOG #: Fixture: Lumiere #203-1CS/FH203CS/LVR
Mount: Shining Through #RSI—City Silver

TYPE: **SB4**

MANUFACTURER: Fixture: Lumiere
Mount: Shining Through 818-707-0154

PROJECT NAME:
Chicago Botanic Garden
Glencoe, IL

MSH Visual Planners
Limited Liability Company

Brunswick, New York
518.235.4756

Oakland, California
510.595.4360

Figure A.27.

MSH Visual Planners

Limited Liability Company
107 Leversee Road, Brunswick, New York 12182-1613
Phone and FAX — 518-235-4756 Email — moyerj@nycap.rr.com

Lighting Fixture Submittal Review Project:______________________________

Review Date:________________________Reviewer:______________________________

Fixture Type:___________Manufacturer:_______________Model#:________________

Specified/Substituted Product:____

Review Code:____

Physical Data
- Construction:_______________________________________
- Finish:____
- Accessories:____
- Louvers:____
- Lens:____
- Reflectors:____
- Assembly Detail:____________________________________

Ballast Data
- Type:____
- Manufacturer:_______________________________________
- Rating/Circuit:_____________________________________
- Breaker/Fuse:_______________________________________
- Location/Physical:__________________________________

Transformer Data
- Type:____
- Manufacturer:_______________________________________
- Rating/Circuit:_____________________________________
- Breaker/Fuse:_______________________________________
- Location/Physical:__________________________________

Lamp Data
- Type:____
- Manufacturer:_______________________________________
- Performance:____

Installation Data
- Details:____

Photometric Data
- Photometric Performance:____________________________

Sample Data
- Sample Submission:__________________________________

Remarks:____

- ____
- ____
- ____

Review Codes

1 Approved
2 Approved as Noted
3 Approved as Noted—Revise and resubmit for RECORD
4 Revise and Resubmit
5 Not Approved
6 Incomplete Submittal—Resubmit with ALL DATA in accordance with specified requirements for Lighting Fixtures Submittals

Review is only for conformance with the design concept of the Work and compliance with the information given in the Contract Documents.

The Contractor is responible for Dimensions to be confirmed and correlated at the site; for information that pertains solely to the fabrication processes or to the means, methods, techniques, sequences, and procedures of construction; and for coordination of the Work of all Trades.

Figure A.28.

Project:________________
Area:________________
Location:________________

Lighting System
Focus Record

Focused By:________________
Recorded By:________________
Date:________________

Fixture ID	Type	Mounting Location	Lamp Type	Lens Type	Louver Type	Filter Type(s)	Shielding Remarks	Aiming

MSH Visual Planners, LLC

Page ___ of ___

Figure A.29.

LIGHTING MANUFACTURERS DIRECTORY

ABS Ltg. Corp.
83 Water St., New Haven, Conn. 06511 (203) 865-5343 ph. (203) 773-1019 fax
www.abslighting.com

Accent Lights
354 Idaho Maryland Rd., Grass Valley, Calif. 95945 (530) 477-5483 or (866) 372-LITE ph. (530) 477-6125 fax
www.accentlights.com

Airey-Thompson Co.
5310 N. Irwindale Ave., Irwindale, Calif. 91706 (800) 421-6196 ph. (626) 960-3525 fax

Alesco, a Div. of Sylvan Designs, Inc.
8955 Quartz Ave., Northridge, CA 91324 (818) 998-6868 ph. (818) 998-7241 fax
www.sylvandesign.com

American Glass Light
979 3rd Ave., New York, N.Y. 10022 (212) 371-4800 ph. (212) 371-4874 fax
www.americanglasslight.com

Ameron International
1020 B St., Fillmore, Calif. 93015 (800) 552-6376 ph. (805) 524-1537 fax
www.ameronpoles.com

Antique Street Lamps, Inc.
2011-B W. Rundberg Lane, Austin, Tex. 78758 (512) 977-8444 ph. (512) 977-9622 fax
www.antiquestreetlamps.com

Architectural Area Lighting, Inc.
14249 Artesia Blvd., La Mirada, Calif. 90638 (714) 994-2700 ph. (714) 994-0522 fax
www.aal.net

Arroyo Craftsman
4509 Little John St., Baldwin Park, Calif. 91706 (626) 960-9411 ph. (626) 960-9521 fax
www.arroyo-craftsman.com

Artemide
1980 New Hwy., Farmingdale, N.Y. 11735 (631) 694-9292 ph. (631) 694-9275 fax
www.artemide.com

B-K Lighting
40429 Brickyard Dr., Madera, Calif. 93638 (559) 438-5800 ph. (559) 438-5900 fax
www.bklighting.com

Beachside
145 Hekili St., Kailua, Hawaii 96734 (800) 405-6732 or (808) 263-5717 (OAHU) (808) 263-7961 fax
www.beachsidelighting.com

Belfer Ltg.
1703 Valley Rd., P.O. Box 2079, Ocean, N.J. 07712 (732) 493-2666 ph. (732) 493-2941 fax
www.belferlighting.com

Bega, A Forms and Surfaces Company
1000 BEGA Way, Carpinteria, Calif. 93013 (805) 684-0533 ph. (805) 566-9474 fax
www.bega-us.com

Beta-Calco
88 St. Regis Crescent South, Toronto, ON, M3J 1Y8 Canada (416) 531-9942 ph. (416) 531-6199 fax
www.betacalco.com

Boyd Ltg. Co.
944 Folsom St., San Francisco, Calif. 94107-1007 (415) 778-4300 ph. (415) 778-4319 fax
www.boydlighting.com

Bronzelite Commercial Landscape Lighting
100 Craftway, Littlestown, Pa. 17340 (800) 273-1569 ph. 717-359-9545 fax
www.bronzelite.com

D.M. Braun & Co.
411 West Lambert, Suite 404, Brea, Calif. 92821 (714) 674-0855 ph. (714) 674-0860 fax
www.dmbraunco.com

CS Lighting
5614 Eastport Blvd., Richmond, Va. 23231 (800) 277-2852 or (804) 795-1476 ph. (804) 226-4951 fax
www.cslighting.com

Coe Studios
1214-4th St., Berkeley, Calif. 94710 (510) 527-2950 ph. (510) 527-0103 fax
www.coestudios.com

Cooper Lighting
1121 Highway 74 South, Peachtree City, Ga. 30269 (770) 486-4800 ph.
www.cooperlighting.com

Cooper Crouse-Hinds
P.O. Box 4999, Syracuse, N.Y. 13221 (315) 477-5531 ph. (315) 477-5179 fax
www.crouse-hinds.com

Corbett
2816 Commodore Dr., Carollton, Tex. 75007 (800) 267-2388 or (972) 512-8800 ph. (800) 351-6628 fax
www.corbettlighting.com

Creative Light Source Inc.
985 Trade Dr., Suite E, North Las Vegas, Nev. 89030 (800) 833-8188 or (702) 897-1400 ph. (702) 897-1414 fax
www.creativelightsourceinc.com

D.M. Lighting
417 W. Foothill Blvd. Ste. B-514, Glendora, Calif. 91741 (mailing); 3192 Factory Dr., Pomona, CA 91768 (factory) (909) 595-7075 ph. (909) 595-0670 fax
www.dmlightingonline.com

Devine Lighting
2000 Electric Way, Christiansburg, Va. 24073 (540) 382-6111
www.hubbell-ltg.com

Dreamscape Ltg. Mfg., Inc.
5521 Washington Blvd., Culver City, Calif. 90016 (323) 933-5760 ph. (323) 933-3607 fax
www.dreamscapelighting.com

Edison Price Ltg.
41-50 22nd St., Long Island City, N.Y. 11101 (718) 685-0700 ph. (718) 786-8530 fax
www.epl.com

ELA
17891 Arenth Ave., City of Industry, Calif. 91748 (800) 423-6561 or (626) 965-0821 ph. 626-965-9494 fax
www.ela-lighting.com

Elliptipar, Inc.
114 Boston Post Rd., West Haven, Conn. 06516 (203) 931-4455 ph. (203) 931-4464 fax
www.ellipitpar.com

Elsco Lighting Products Ltd.
7440 Tranmere Dr., Mississauga, ON 15S 1K4 Canada (905) 673-2535 ph. (905) 673-0792 fax
www.elscolighting.com

Escort
51 North Elm St., Wernersville, Pa. 19565 (800) 856-7948 or (610) 670-2517 ph. (610) 670-5170 fax
www.escortlighting.com

Exterieur Vert Lighting, LLC (part of Targetti Group)
1513 E. S. Gertrude Place, Santa Ana, Calif. 92705 (714) 957-6101 ph. (714) 957-1501 fax
www.exterieurvert.com

Fiberstars
44259 Nobel Drive, Fremont, Calif. 94538 (800) 327-7877 or (510) 490-0719 ph. (510) 490-3247 fax
www.fiberstars.com

Forecast Ltg. Co.
1600 Fleetwood Dr., Elgin, Ill. 60123 (847) 622-0416 (ext. 340) ph. (847) 622-2542 fax
www.forecastltg.com

Forum, Inc.
908 Old Freeport Rd, Pittsburgh, Pa. 15238 (412) 781-5970 ph. (412) 781-5971 fax
www.forumlighting.com

Gardco
2661 Alvarado St., San Leandro, Calif. 94577 (800) 227-0758 or (510) 357-6900 ph. (510) 357-3088 fax
www.gardcolighting.com

Greenlee Ltg. Inc., Subsidiary of LSI Lighting Systems, Inc.
1300 Hutton Dr., #110, Carrollton, Tex. 75006 (972) 466-1133 ph. (972) 446-2202 fax
www.lsi-industries.com/index.php/greenlee.html

Gross Chandelier Co.
9777 Reavis Park Dr., St. Louis, Mo. 63123 (800) 331-2425 or (314) 631-6000 ph. (314) 631-7800 fax
www.glighting.com

Hadco
P.O. Box 128, 100 Craftway, Littlestown, Pa. 17340 (717) 359-7131 ph. (717) 359-9289 fax
www.hadcolighting.com

Hammerworks
6 Fremont St., Worcester, Mass. 01603 (508) 755-3434 ph. 118 Main St., Meredith, NH 03253 (603) 279-7352 ph.
www.hammerworks.com

Hanover Lantern, A Div. of Hoffman Products, Inc.
350 Kindig Ln., Hanover, Pa. 17331 (717) 632-6464 ph. (717) 632-5039 fax
www.hanoverlantern.com

W. F. Harris Ltg., Inc.
4015 Airport Extension Rd., Monroe, N.C. 28111 (800) 842-9345 or (704) 283-7477 ph. (704) 283-6880 fax.
www.wfharris.com

Herwig Lighting
Box 768, Russellville, Ariz. 72811 (800) 643-9523 or (479) 968-2621 ph. (479) 968-6422 fax
www.herwig.com

Hess Form + Licht
Schlachthausstrasse 19-19/3 D-78050 Villingen-Schwenningen, Germany, 49 7721 920-0 ph. 49 7721 920-250 fax
www.hess-form-licht.de

HessAmerica
427 Hyatt St., P,O, Box 28, Gaffney, S.C. 29342-0028 (864) 487-3535 ph. (864) 487-3175 fax
www.hessamerica.com

Hevi Lite, INC.
7524 Deering Ave., Canoga Park, Calif. 91303 (818) 710-0728 ph. (818) 710-0756 fax.
www.hevilite.com

Hinkley Lighting
12600 Berea Rd., Cleveland, Ohio 44111 (800) 446-5539 or (216) 671-3300 ph. (216) 671-4537 fax

Hubbell, Inc./Ltg. Div.
2000 Electric Way, Christiansburg, Va. 24073-2500 (540) 382-6111 ph. (540) 382-1526 fax
www.hubbell-ltg.com

Hydrel
12881 Bradley Ave., Sylmar, Calif. 91342 (800) 750-9773 or (818) 362-9465 ph. (818) 362-6548 fax
www.hydrel.com

Johnson Art Studio
3120 Capitola Rd., Santa Cruz, Calif. 95062 (800) 203-1663 or (831) 464-0567 ph. (831) 464-1325 fax
www.johnsonartstudio.com

Kichler
7711 E. Pleasant Valley Rd, P.O. Box 318010, Cleveland, Ohio 44131-8010 (800) 659-9000 ph. or (216) 573-1001 fax
www.kichler.com

Kim Lighting
16555 E. Gale Ave., City of Industry, Calif. 91745 (626) 968-5666 ph. (626) 369-2695 fax mailing: P.O. Box 60080, City of Industry, Calif. 91716-0080
www.kimlighting.com

H. Kira Design and Manufacturing
3525 Old Conejo Rd. #107, Newbury Park, Calif. 91320 (805) 480-4881 ph./fax

Lightolier
631 Airport Rd, Fall River, Mass. 02720 (508) 679-8131 ph. (508) 674-4710 fax
www.lightolier.com

Lightron
500 Hudson Valley Avenue, New Windsor, N.Y. 12553 (845) 562-5500 ph. (845) 562-3082 fax
www.lsilightron.com

Lithonia Lighting
P.O. Box A, Conyers, Ga. 30012 (770) 922-9000 ph. (770) 860-9403 fax
www.lithonia.com

Lucifer Ltg. Co.
414 Live Oak St., San Antonio, Tex. 78202 (800) 879-9797 or (512) 227-7329 ph. (210) 227-4967 fax
www.luciferlighting.com

Lumark, a Div. of Cooper Lighting
1121 Highway 74 South, Peachtree City, Ga. 30269 (770) 486-4800 ph.
www.cooperlighting.com/brands/lumark

Lumec, Inc.
640 Curé-Boivin Blvd., Boisbriand, Que., J7G 2A7 Canada (450) 430-7040 ph. (450) 430-1453 fax
www.lumec.com

Lumenyte Intl. Corp.
74 Icon, Foothill Ranch, Calif. 92610 (949) 829-5200 ph. (949) 829-5201 fax
www.lumenyte.com

Lumiere, a Div. of Cooper Lighting
1121 Highway 74 South, Peachtree City, Ga. 30269 (770) 486-4800 ph.
www.cooperlighting.com/brands/lumiere

Lutrex
3555 NW 53 Court, Fort Lauderdale, Fla. 33309 (954) 717-4155 ph. (954) 717-4157 fax
www.lutrex.com

McGraw-Edison, a Div. of Cooper Lighting
1121 Highway 74 South, Peachtree City, Ga. 30269 (770) 486-4800 ph.
www.cooperlighting.com/brands/mcgraw-edison

Megabay Lighting Enterprises Pty. Ltd.
14 Industrial Ave. PO Box 3517, Caloundra, Qld., Australia 4551 61 7 5491 7433 ph. 61 7 5491 7338 fax
www.megabay.com

Moldcast
14249 Artesia Blvd., LaMirada, Calif. 90638 (714) 562-8434 ph. (714) 994-0522 fax
www.moldcast.com

Domenico Neri, S.P.A.
S.S. Emilia 1622 (Ponte Ospedaletto), 47020 Longiano (FC) Italy 39 (0547) 65-21-11 ph. 39 (0547) 54-074 fax
www.neri.biz

Nightscaping
1705 E. Colton Ave., Redlands, Calif. 92374 (800) 544-4840 or (714) 794-2121 ph. (909) 794-7292 fax
www.nightscaping.com

Niland Company
320 N. Clark, El Paso, Tex. 79905 (800) 648-9013 ph. or (888) 779-3065 fax
www.nilandco.com

Noral ASA
P.O. Box 159, Ørje, N-1871 Norway 47 69 81 02 00 ph. 47 69 81 02 51 fax
www.noral.net

North Star Ltg., Inc.
2150 Parkes Dr., Broadview, Ill. 60155 (800) 229-4330 or (708) 681-4330 ph. (708) 681-4006 fax
www.nslights.com

Nowell's, Inc.
Box 295, Sausalito, Calif. 94966 (415) 332-4933 ph. (415) 332-4936 fax
www.nowells-inc.com

Nulco Lighting
30 Beecher St., Pawtucket, R.I. 02860 (401) 728-5200 ph. (401) 728-8210 fax
www.nulcolighting.com

Nulite
850 Edwards Ave., Harahan, La. 70123 (800) 256-1603 or (504) 733-3300 ph. (504) 736-1617 fax
www.nulite.com

Old California Lantern Company
975 N. Enterprise St. Orange, Calif. 92867 (800) 577-6679 ph. (714) 771-5714 fax
www.oldcalifornia.com

Peerless Ltg. Corp.
2246 Fifth St., Berkeley, Calif. 94710 (510) 845-2760 ph. (510) 845-2776 fax
www.peerless-lighting.com

Phoenix Day
1355 Donner Ave., San Francisco, Calif. 94124 (415) 822-4414 ph. (415) 822-3987 fax
www.phoenixday.com

Louis Poulsen Ltg., Inc.
3260 Meridian Pkwy., Fort Lauderdale, Fla. 33331 (954) 349-2525 ph. (954) 349-2550 fax
www.louispoulsen.com

Prescolite, a Div. of Hubbell Lighting
101 Corporate Dr., Spartanburg, S.C. 29303 (864) 599-6000 ph. (864) 626-380 fax
www.prescolite.com

Prudential Lighting
1774 East 21st. St., Los Angeles, Calif. 90058 (213) 746-0360 ph. (213) 746-8838 fax
www.prulite.com

Rainbow Lighting
3545 Commercial Ave, Northbrook, Ill. 60062 (847) 480-1136 ph. (847) 480-7315 fax
www.rainbowlightinginc.com

Roberts Step Light
8413 Mantle Ave., Oklahoma City, Okla. 73132 (800) 654-8268 or (405) 728-4595 ph. (405) 728-4878 fax
www.robertssteplite.com

Rockscapes
9185 Kelvin Ave., Chatsworth, Calif. 91311 (800) 677-6811 or (818) 882-2955 ph. (818) 882-7136 fax
www.rockscapes.net

Roman Fountains
P.O. Box Drawer 10190, Albuquerque, N.M. 87184 (800) 794-1801 ph. (505) 343-8086 fax
www.romanfountains.com

Sentry Electric Company
185 Buffalo Avenue, Freeport, N.Y. 11520 (516) 379-4660 ph. (516) 378-0624 fax
www.sentrylighting.com

Shaper Lighting
1141 Marina Way S., Richmond, Calif. 94804-3742 (510) 234-2370 ph. (510) 234-2371 fax
www.shaperlighting.com

Site-Lite
10829 Michael Hunt Dr., S. El Monte, Calif. 91733 (818) 443-2655 ph.

Spaulding
1736 Dreman Ave., Cincinnati, Ohio 45223 (513) 541-3486 ph. (513) 541-1454 fax
www.spauldinglighting.com

Spring City Elect. Mfg. Co.
Hall and Main St., Spring City, Pa. 19475 (610) 948-4000 ph. (610) 948-5577 fax
www.springcity.com

SPJ
2107 Chico Ave., South El Monte, Calif. 91733 (800) 469-3637 or (626) 433-4800 ph. (626) 433-4839 fax
www.spjlighting.com

Starfire Ltg., Inc.
7 Donna Dr., Wood-Ridge, N.J. 07075 (800) 443-8823 ph. (201) 438-9541 fax
www.starfirelighting.com

Stella Industries, Inc.
1286 S. Lyon St., Santa Ana, Calif. 92706 (714) 836-7868 ph. (714) 863-1610 fax

Sternberg Lighting
7401 Oak Park Ave., Niles, Ill. 60714 (800) 621-3376 ph. (847) 588-3440 fax
www.sternberg.com

Sterner Ltg. Systems, Inc., (including Infranor), a Div. of Hubbell Lighting, Inc.
351 Lewis Ave. W., Winsted, Minn. 55395 (800) 328-7480 ph. (320) 485-2881 fax
www.sternerlighting.com

Stonco
2345 Vauxhall Rd., Union, N.J. 07083 (908) 964-7000 ph. (908) 964-1404 fax
www.stoncolighting.com

Sylvan Designs, Inc.
8921 Quartz Ave., Northridge, Calif. 91324 (818) 998-6868 ph. (818) 998-7241 fax
www.sylvandesigns.com

Targetti North America
1513 E. St. Gertrude Place, Santa Ana, Calif. 92705, (714) 957-6101 ph. (714) 957-1501 fax
www.targetti.com

Teka Illumination
86 Gibson Rd. #3, Templeton, Calif. 93465 (805) 434-3511 ph. (805) 434-3512 fax
www.teka-illumination.com

Timberwork
P.O. Box 1169, Gresham, Ore. 97030 (503) 492-3089 ph. (503) 492-0998 fax
www.timberwork.com

Times Square Lighting
5 Kay Fries Dr., Stony Point, N.Y. 10980 (845) 947-3034 ph. (845) 947-3047 fax
www.tslight.com

Tokistar Ltg., Inc.
1561 Gemini Pl, Anaheim, Calif. 92801 (714) 772-7005 ph. (714) 772-7014 fax
www.tokistar.com

Trend Lighting
2700 Sidney St., St. Louis, Mo. 63104 (800) 325-9532 or (314) 773-1340 ph. (314) 773-5741 fax
www.trendlighting.com

Visco (Valley Iron & Steel)
29579 Awbrey Ln., Eugene, Ore. 97402 (541) 688-7741 or (800) 341-1444 ph. (541) 461-0951 fax
www.visco-light.com

Wendelighting (A Div. of Jacksen Intl., Ltd.)
611 W. Huntington Dr., Suite A, Monrovia Calif. 91016 (800) 528-0101 ph. (626) 303-0046 fax
www.wendelighting.com

Wide-Lite (manufacturers of imperial bronzelights)
P.O. Box 606, San Marcos, Tex. 78667 (512) 392-5821 ph. (512) 753-1122 fax
www.wide-lite.com

Winona Lighting
3760 West 4th St., Winona, Minn. 55987 (800) 328-5291 ph. (507) 454-4808 fax
www.winonalighting.com

Zumtobel Staff Ltg.
330 Route 9W, Highland, N.Y. 12528 (800) 448-4131 ph. (845) 691-6289 fax
www.zumtobelstaff.us

CONTROLS

Honeywell, Inc.
101 Columbia Rd., Morristown, N.J. 07962 (973) 455-2000 ph. (973) 455-4807 fax
www.honeywell.com

ILC
5229 Edina Industrial Blvd., Edina, N.J. 55439 (952) 829-1900 ph. (800) 922-8004 fax
www.ilc-usa.com

Intermatic, Inc.
Intermatic Plaza, Spring Grove, Ill 60081 (815) 675-2321 ph.
www.intermatic.com

Leviton Mfg. Co., Inc.
59-25 Little Neck Pky., Little Neck, N.Y. 11362-2591 (718) 229-4040 ph. (800) 832-9538 fax
www.leviton.com

RAB Electric (manufacturers of Light Alert)
170 Ludlow Ave., Northvale, N.J. 07647 (201) 784-8600 ph. (201) 784-0077 fax
www.RABweb.com

LiteTouch
3400 South West Temple, Salt Lake City, Utah 84115 (888) litetch or (801) 486-8500 ph. (801) 486-8569 fax
www.litetouch

Lightolier
631 Airport Rd, Fall River, Mass. 02720 (508) 679-8131 ph. (508) 674-4710 fax
www.lightolier.com

Lutron Electronics Co., Inc.
7200 Suter Rd., Coopersburg, Pa. 18036-1299 (888) 588-7661 ph. (610) 282-3090 fax
www.lutron.com

Sterner Ltg. Systems, Inc. (including Infranor and Simes)
351 Lewis Ave. W., PO Box 805, Winsted, Minn. 55395-0805 (800) 328-7480 ph. (320) 485-2881 fax
www.sternerlighting.com

Strand Lighting Inc.
6603 Darin Way, Cypress, Calif. 90630 (714) 230-8200 ph. (714) 899-0042 fax
www.strandlighting.com

Times Square Lighting
5 Kay Fries Dr., Stony Point, N.Y. 10980 (845) 947-3034 ph. (845) 947-3047 fax
www.tslight.com

Tork
One Grove St., Mt. Vernon, N.Y. 10550 (914) 664-3542 ph. (914) 664-5052 fax
www.tork.com

Vantage Controls, Inc.
1061 South 800 East, Orem, Utah 84097 (800) 555-9891 or (801) 229-2800 ph. (801) 224-0355 fax
www.vantagecontrols.com

Voigt Ltg. Industries, Inc.
135 Fort Lee Rd., Leonia, N.J. 07605 (201) 461-2493 ph. (201) 461-7827 fax

Wide-Lite
P.O. Box 606, San Marcos, Tex. 78667 (512) 392-5821 ph. (512) 753-1122 fax
www.wide-lite.com

ACCESSORIES

A.L.P. Ltg. & Clg. Products, Inc.
6333 Gross Point Rd., Niles, Ill. 60714 (773) 774-9550 ph. (773) 594-3874 fax

Abrisa Industrial Glass, Inc.
200 South Hallock Dr., Santa Paula, Calif. 93060 (800) 350-5000 ph. (805) 525-8604 fax.
www.abrisa.com

Advance Transformer Co.
10275 W. Higgins Rd., Rosemont, Ill. 60018 (800) 322-2086 or (847) 390-5000 ph. (847) 768-7768 fax
www.advancetransformer.com

American Louver Co.
7700 N. Austin Ave., Skokie, Ill. 60077 (800) 323-4250 or (847) 470-3300 ph. (847) 470-0420 fax
www.americanlouver.com

Ameron International/Concrete Ltg. Poles
1020 B Street, Fillmore, Calif. 93015 (800) 55AMERON ph. (805) 524-1537 fax
www.ameronpoles.com

California Landscape Ltg., A Div. of Kina Enterprises, Inc.
31260 Cedar Valley Dr., Westlake Village, Calif. 91362 (800) 457-0710 ph. (sales) (818) 889-6300 ph. (headquarters) (800) 457-0730 fax
www.callite.com

Computer Power Systems Inc.
3421 State Rd. 419, Winter Springs, Fla. 32708 (877) 327-7373 or (407) 327-7373 ph. (407) 327-7333 fax
www.cpsfl.com

Formed Plastics, Inc.
207 Stonehinge Ln., Carle Place, N.Y. 11514 (516) 334-2300 ph. (516) 334-2679 fax
www.formedplastics.com

Jefferson Electric, A Division of MagneTek, Inc.
9650 South Franklin Dr., Franklin, Wis. 53132-8847 (414) 209-1620 or (800) 892-3755 ph. (414) 209-1621 or (800) 942-5169 fax
www.jeffersonelectric.com

Lee Filters, A Division of Colortran, Inc.
2237 North Hollywood Way, Burbank, Calif. 91505 (800) 576-5055 or (818) 238-1220 ph.
www.leefiltersusa.com

Louvers Intl.
849 Church Court, Elmhurst, Ill. 60126 (800) 543-3765 or (630) 782-9977 ph. (630) 782-9991 fax
www.louversintl.com

Universal Lighting Technologies
26 Century Blvd. Suite 500, Nashville, Tenn. 37214-3683 (800) 206-0075 or (615) 316-5100 ph. (800) 225-5278 fax
www.universalballast.com

Nova Industries, Inc.
999 Montague Ave., San Leandro, Calif. 94577 (510) 357-0171 ph. (510) 357-3832 fax

Robertson Worldwide
13611 Thornton Rd., Blue Island, Ill. 60406 (800) 323-5633 ph. (877) 388-2420 fax
www.robertsonww.com

3M Electrical Products Div.
6801 Riverplace Blvd., Austin, Tex. 78726 (800) 545-3573 ph. (800) 245-0329 fax
www.3m.com

The Wiremold Co.
60 Woodlawn St., West Hartford, Conn. 06110-0639 (800) 621-0049 or (860) 233-6251 ph. (860) 232-2062 fax
www.wiremold.com

LAMP MANUFACTURERS

Duro-Test Lighting
12401 McNulty Rd. Suite 101, Philadelphia, Pa. 19154 (800) BUY-DURO ph. (888) 959-7250 fax
www.duro-test.com

General Electric
1975 Noble Rd. Nela Park, Cleveland, Ohio 44112 (216) 266-2121 ph.
www.gelighting.com

Litetronics Intl., An RCS Industries Co.
4104 West 123rd St., St Alsip, Ill. 60803 (800) 860-3392 or (708) 389-8000 ph. (708) 371-0627 fax
www.litetronics.com

OSRAM Sylvania Inc.
100 Endicott St., Danvers, Mass. 01923 (978) 777-1900 ph. (978) 750-2152 fax
www.sylvania.com

Philips Ltg. Co.
P.O. Box 6800, 200 Franklin Square Dr., Somerset, N.J. 08875-6800 (732) 563-3000 or (800) 555-0050 ph.
www.lighting.philips.com/nam

Microlamp Inc
2942 North West 60th St., Fort Lauderdale, Fla. 33309 (800) 431-4956 or (957) 970-7171 ph. (954) 970-7196 fax
www.microlamp.com

Ushio America, Inc.
5440 Cerritos Ave., Cypress, Calif. 90630 (714) 236-8600 or (800) 838-7446 ph. (714 229-3180 or (800) 776-3641 fax
www.ushio.com

Venture Ltg. Intl.
32000 Aurora Rd., Solon, Ohio 44139 (800) 451-2606 or (440) 248-3510 ph. (440) 349-7771 fax
www.venturelighting.com

Bibliography

CODES AND STANDARDS

Donald J. Fink and H. Wayne Beet, Eds., *Standard Handbook for Electrical Engineers,* 12th Edition, McGraw-Hill, New York, 1987.

George V. Hart and Sammie Hart, *Ugly's Electrical References,* United Printing Arts, Houston, Tex., 1987.

National Fire Protection Association, Eds., *National Electrical Code, 1990,* National Fire Protection Association, Quincy, Mass., 1989.

Underwriters' Laboratories, Eds., *Junction Boxes for Swimming Pool Lighting Fixtures, UL 1241,* 4th Edition, Underwriters' Laboratories Inc., Triangle Park, N.C., 1989.

Underwriters' Laboratories, Eds., *Standard for Incandescent Lighting Fixtures, UL 1571,* 2nd Edition, Underwriters' Laboratories Inc., Triangle Park, N.C., 1989.

Underwriters' Laboratories, Eds., *Standard for Swimming Pool Lighting Fixtures, UL 676,* 5th Edition, Underwriters' Laboratories Inc., Triangle Park, N.C., 1986.

CORROSION, FINISHES, AND MATERIALS

J. T. N. Atkinson and H. Van Droffelaar, *Corrosion and Its Control, An Introduction to the Subject,* National Association of Corrosion Engineers, Houston, Tex., 1982.

Kenneth G. Budinski, *Engineering Materials Properties and Selection,* 3rd Edition, Prentice Hall, Englewood, Cliffs, N.J., 1989.

Ana Diaz, "Metal Corrosion: Understanding How It Works Can Help You Build More Life into Your Structures," *Fine Homebuilding,* Sept. 1990.

Einar Mattson, *Basic Corrosion Technology for Scientists and Engineers,* Ellis Horwood, Chichester, West Sussex, England, 1989.

V. R. Pludeck, *Design and Corrosion Control,* Wiley, New York, 1977.

Terry C. Richardson, *Industrial Plastics, Theory and Application,* Delmar Publishers, New York, 1989.

Herbert H. Uhlig and R. Winston Revie, *Corrosion and Corrosion Control, An Introduction to Corrosion Science and Engineering,* 3rd Edition, Wiley, New York, 1985.

DESIGN

Carolyn M. Bloomer, *Principles of Visual Perception,* Van Nostrand Reinhold, New York, 1976.

Peter H. Lindsay and Donald A. Norman, *Human Information Processing, An Introduction to Psychology,* 2nd Edition, Academic Press, New York, 1977.

Freeman Patterson, *Photography & the Art of Seeing,* Van Nostrand Reinhold, Toronto, 1979.

Clarence Rainwater, *Light and Color,* Western Publishing, Racine, Wis., 1971.

GENERAL LIGHTING

Committee on Light Control and Equipment Design of the IES, *IES Guide to Design of Light Control (LM-17),* Illuminating Engineering Society of North America, New York, 1959.

John E. Kaufman, Ed., *IES Lighting Handbook, Application Volume,* Illuminating Engineering Society of North America, New York, 1987.

John E. Kaufman, Ed., *IES Lighting Handbook, Reference Volume,* Illuminating Engineering Society of North America, New York, 1987.

North American Philips Lighting, Eds., *Lighting Handbook,* North American Philips Lighting Corp., Somerset, N.J., 1984.

James L. Nuckolls, *Interior Lighting for Environmental Designers,* Wiley, New York, 1976.

Fran Kellogg Smith and Fred. J. Bertolone, *Bringing Interiors to Light,* Whitney Library of Design, New York, 1986.

Lee Watson, *Lighting Design Handbook,* McGraw-Hill, New York, 1990.

LIGHT AND PLANT GROWTH

M. Black and J. Chapman, Eds., *Light and Plant Growth,* Topics in Plant Physiology: I, Unwin Hyman, London, 1988.

H. A. Borthwick, *Some Principles of Growing Plants with Artificial Light,* United States Department of Agriculture, Agricultural Research Service, Crops Research Division, Beltsville, Md.

James A. Buck, "High Intensity Discharge Lamps for Plant Growth Application," *TRANSACTIONS of the ASAE,* Vol. 16, No. 1, 1973.

A. E. Canham, Ed., "Recent Developments in the Use of Electricity in Horticulture in the U.S.A.," *Symposium on Electricity and Artificial Light in Horticulture,* U.S. Department of Agriculture, Beltsville, Md., 1969.

C. A. Conover, R. T. Poole, and R. W. Henley, "Growing Acclimatized Foliage Plants," *Florida Foliage Grower,* Vol. 12, No. 9, Sept. 1975.

GTE Products Corporation, Commercial Engineering Department, "Applied Lighting," *GTE Sylvania Engineering,* Bulletins 0-294, 0-286, 0-278, and 0-339, Sylvania Lighting Center, Salem, Mass.

GTE Products Corporation, Commercial Engineering Department, "Fluorescent Lamps," *GTE Sylvania Engineering,* Bulletins 0-262 and 0-285, Sylvania Lighting Center, Salem, Mass.

Christos C. Mpelkas, "Indoor Landscaping for Healthy, Beautiful Workplaces," *Architectural Lighting,* New York, Feb. 1987.

R. van der Veen and G. Meijer, *Light and Plant Growth,* Macmillan, New York, 1959.

PLANT MATERIALS

Nancy M. Adams, *New Zealand Nature Series: New Zealand Native Trees (Parts 1 & 2),* Reed Publishing Group, Auckland, 1983.

Liberty Hyde Bailey, Ethel Zoe Bailey, and the Staff of the Liberty Hyde Bailey Hortorium, *Hortus Third, A Concise Dictionary of Plants Cultivated in the United States and Canada,* Macmillan, New York, 1976.

Peter Barber, and C. E. Lucas Phillips, *The Trees Around Us,* Weindenfeld and Nicolson and the Royal Horticultural Society, London, 1975.

Andreas Bartels, *Gardening with Dwarf Trees and Shrubs,* Timber Press, Portland, Oreg., 1986.

Peter Beales, *Roses,* Henry Holt and Company, New York, 1992.

Kenneth A. Beckett, *The Concise Encyclopedia of Garden Plants,* Orbis Publishing, London, 1983.

Fred Berry and John Kress, *Heliconia: An Identification Guide,* Smithsonian Institution Press, Washington, DC, 1991.

Susan Chamberlin, *Hedges, Screens and Espaliers,* HP Books, Tucson, Ariz., 1983.

Claude Chidamian, *The Book of Cacti and Other Succulents,* Timber Press, Portland, Oreg., 1984.

Coombes, Allen J. *Dictionary of Plant Names,* Timber Press, Portland, Oreg., 1985.

Gordon Courtwright, *Trees and Shrubs for Temperate Climates,* Revised Edition, Timber Press, Portland, Oreg., 1979.

Gordon Courtwright, *Tropicals,* Timber Press, Portland, Oreg., 1988.

James Underwood Crockett, *Bulbs,* Joan D. Manley, New York, 1971.

Willy Cullmann, Erich Gotz, and Gerhard Groner. *The Encyclopedia of Cacti,* Alphabooks, Dorset, 1986.

Rick Darke, *The Color Encyclopedia of Ornamental Grasses,* Timber Press, Portland, Oreg., 1999.

Brian Davis, *The Gardener's Illustrated Encyclopedia of Trees and Shrubs,* Rodale, Emmaus, Penn., 1987.

Lys de Bray, *Lys de Bray's Manual of Old-Fashioned Flowers,* Oxford Illustrated Press, Oxford, 1984.

Gordon P. DeWolf, Jr., Ed., *Taylor's Guide to Trees,* Houghton Mifflin, Boston, 1988.

Don Dimond and Michael MacCaskey, *All About Ground Covers,* Ortho, San Francisco, 1982.

Michael A. Dirr, *Dirr's Hardy Trees and Shrubs,* Timber Press, Portland, Oreg., 1997.

Christine Eslick, *A Field Guide to Native Plants of Australia,* Murdoch Books, North Sydney, 1997.

Ronald L. Evans, *Handbook of Cultivated Sedums,* Science Reviews Ltd., Middlesex, 1983.

Raymond J. Evison, *Making the Most of Clematis,* Burall & Floraprint Ltd., Wisbech, 1979.

Barbara Ferguson, Ed., *All About Trees,* Ortho, San Francisco, 1982.

Nicola Ferguson and Fred McGourtyed, *Right Plant, Right Place,* Summit Books, New York, 1984.

Harrison L. Flint, *Landscape Plants for Eastern North America,* John Wiley & Sons, New York, 1997.

Garden Club of America, *Plants That Merit Attention,* Vol. 1: *Trees,* Timber Press, Portland, Oreg., 1984.

James Gardiner and Vincent Page, Eds., *Magnolias,* Globe Pequot Press, Chester, Conn., 1989.

S. Millar Gault, *The Dictionary of Shrubs,* Rainbird Publishing Group Ltd., London, 1984.

Alfred Byrd Graf, *Tropica: Color Cyclopedia of Exotic Plants and Trees,* Roehrs Co., East Rutherford, N.J., 1986.

Victor Graham, *Growing Succulent Plants Including Cacti,* Timber Press, Portland, Oreg., 1987.

William Carey Grimm, *The Illustrated Book of Trees,* Stackpole Books, Mechanicsburg, Penn., 1983.

Christopher, Grey-Wilson, Ed., *A Manual of Alpine and Rock Garden Plants,* Timber Press, Portland, Oreg., 1989.

Winton Harding and Christopher Grey-Wilson, Eds., *Saxifrages: A Gardener's Guide to the Genus,* Friary Press, Dorset, 1992.

Erik Haustein, *The Cactus Handbook,* Chartwell Books Inc., Secaucus, N.J., 1988.

Royton E. Heath, *Collectors' Alpines,* Timber Press, Portland, Oreg., 1981.

Hillier Arboretum, *The Hillier Color Dictionary of Trees and Shrubs,* Van Nostrand Reinhold, New York, 1982.

Sandra Holmes, *Handbook of Plant Types,* Hodder and Stoghton, Suffolk, 1987.

Herman Jacobsen, *A Handbook of Succulent Plants,* 3 vols., Blandford Press, Dorset, 1960.

David J. Jones, *Encyclopedia of Ferns,* Lothian Publishing Co., Melbourne, 1987.

John Karmali, *The Beautiful Plants of Kenya,* Westlant Sundries Ltd., Nairobia, 1988.

Angela Kay Kepler, *Proteas in Hawai'i,* Mutual Publishing Company, Honolulu, 1988.

Jack Krempin, *Palms & Cycads Around the World,* Herron Book Distributors, Kangaroo Point, Queensland, 1995.

Arthur R. Kruckeberg, *Gardening with Native Plants of the Pacific Northwest: an Illustrated Guide.* University of Washington Press, Seattle, 1982.

Toni Lawson-Hall and Rothera Brian, *Hydrangeas A Gardener's Guide,* Timber Press, Portland, Oreg., 1996.

Janet Meakin Poor and Nancy Peterson Brewster, *Plants That Merit Attention,* Vol. 2: *Shrubs,* Timber Press, Portland, Oreg., 1996.

Judy Mielke, *Native Plants for Southwestern Landscapes,* University of Texas Press, Austin, 1993.

Bob Perry, *Landscape Plants for Western Regions,* Land Design Publishing, Claremont, Calif., 1992.

Brian Proudley and Valerie Proudley, *Heathers in Colour,* Blandford Press, Dorset, 1983.

Reader's Digest Association, Ed., *Encyclopedia of Garden Plants and Flowers,* The Reader's Digest Association Ltd., London, 1985.

Lee Reich, *The Pruning Book,* Taunton Press, Newtown, Conn., 1997.

Murdoch Riley, *New Zealand Shrubs and Small Trees,* Viking Sevenseas Ltd., Wellington, 1985.

Murdoch Riley, *New Zealand Trees and Ferns,* Viking Sevenseas Ltd., Wellington, 1983.

Tony Rodd, *The Ultimate Book of Trees and Shrubs for Australian Gardens,* Random House (Australia), Milsons Point, 1996.

S. H. Sohmer and R. Gustafson, *Plants and Flowers of Hawai'i,* University of Hawaii Press, Honolulu, 1987.

William T. Stearn, *Botanical Latin,* New Edition, David & Charles, North Pomfret, Ver., 1983.

Frederic B. Stresau, *Florida My Eden,* Florida Classics Library, Port Salerno, Fla., 1986.

John Street, *Rhododendrons,* Globe Pequot Press, Guilford, Conn., 1987.

Sunset Books, *National Garden Book,* Sunset Books Inc., Menlo Park, Calif., 1997.

Sunset Books, *Western Garden Book,* Sunset Books Inc., Menlo Park, Calif., 1986.

Philip Swindells, *Ward Lock Book of the Water Garden,* Ward Lock Ltd., London, 1985.

Graham Stuart Thomas, *Perennial Garden Plants or The Modern Florilegium,* J. M. Dent and Sons Ltd., London, 1976.

Graham Stuart Thomas, *Plants for Ground-Cover,* J. M. Dent and Sons Ltd., London, 1989.

Graham Stuart Thomas, *The Rock Garden and Its Plants,* J. M. Dent and Sons Ltd., London, 1970.

John Hunter Thomas and Denis R. Parnell, *Native Shrubs of the Sierra Nevada,* University of California Press, Berkeley, 1974.

Alan Titchmarsh, *Climbers and Wall Plants,* Ward Lock Ltd., London, 1987.

Elizabeth Tootill, Ed., *The Facts on File Dictionary of Botany,* Facts on File, Inc., Aylesbury, 1984.

D. M. van Gelderen and J. R. P. van Hoey Smith, *Conifers: The Illustrated Encyclopedia,* 2 vols., Timber Press, Portland, Oreg., 1996.

J. D. Vertrees, *Japanese Maples,* Timber Press, Portland, Oreg., 1978.

Vaclav Vetvicka, *The Illustrated Book of Trees and Shrubs,* Octopus Books, London, 1985.

Fred Walden, *A Dictionary of Trees,* Great Outdoors Publishing Company, St. Petersburg, Fla., 1963.

Christopher Warner, *Climbing Roses,* Globe Pequot Press, Guilford, Conn., 1988.

D. A. Webb and R. J. Gornall, *Saxifrages of Europe,* Christopher Helm Ltd., London, 1989.

Del Weniger, *Cacti of Texas and Neighboring States,* University of Texas Press, Austin, 1984.

John W. Wrigley and Fagg Murray, *Australian Native Plants* 4th Edition, Reed Books, Melbourne, 1996.

Geoffrey Yates, *The Gardener's Book of Heathers,* Frederick Warne Publishers, London, 1985.

Peter F. Yeo, *Hardy Geraniums,* Timber Press, Portland, Oreg., 1985.

Mark R. Zilis, *The Hosta Handbook,* Q&Z Nursery Inc., Rochelle, Ill., 2000.

Robert L. Zion, *Trees for Architecture and the Landscape,* Reinhold, New York, 1968.

ROADWAY AND TRANSPORTATION

Illuminating Engineering Society of North America, Eds., *American National Standard, Practice for Tunnel Lighting, RP-22,* Illuminating Engineering Society of North America, New York, 1987.

Illuminating Engineering Society of North America, Eds., *American National Standard, Roadway Lighting, RP-8,* Illuminating Engineering Society of North America, New York, 1983.

John E. Kaufman, Ed., *IES Lighting Handbook, Application Volume,* Illuminating Engineering Society of North America, New York, 1987, Chapters 13, to 16.

Recommended Practices Subcommittee of the IES Aviation Lighting Committee, *IES Recommended Practice for Airport Road Automobile Parking Area Lighting, RP-17,* Illuminating Engineering Society of North America, New York, 1987.

Subcommittee on Off-Roadway Facilities of the IES Roadway Lighting Committee, *Lighting for Parking Facilities, RP-20,* Illuminating Engineering Society of North America, New York, 1985.

Task Force on Value of Public Lighting of the IES Committee on Roadway Lighting, *Value of Public Roadway Lighting, CP-31,* Illuminating Engineering Society of North America, New York, 1989.

SOILS

Kermit C. Berger, *Introductory Soils,* MacMillan, New York, 1968.

S. W. Buol, F. S. Hole, and R. J. McCracken, *Soil Genesis and Classification,* Iowa State University Press, Ames, Iowa, 1973.

SPORTS AND FLOODLIGHTING

General Electric Company, Eds., *Floodlighting, 205-71322,* General Electric Company, Cleveland, Ohio, 1989.

General Electric Company, Lamp Business Division, *Sign Lighting, TP-124,* General Electric Co., Cleveland, Ohio, 1972.

General Electric Company, Large Lamp Department, *Building Floodlighting, TP-115,* General Electric Company, Cleveland, Ohio, 1968.

IES Committee on Sports and Recreational Areas Lighting, *Current Recommended Practice for Sports Lighting, RP-6-88,* Illuminating Engineering Society of North America, New York, 1989.

IES Highway Signs Subcommittee of the Roadway Lighting Committee, *Recommended Practice for Roadway Sign Lighting, RP-19,* Illuminating Engineering Society of North America, New York, 1976.

Index